Distributed AI Systems

A practical guide to building scalable training, inference, and serving systems for production AI

Fuheng Wu

<packt>

Distributed AI Systems

玄心

Distributed AI Systems

Portfolio Director: Kunal Chaudhari
Relationship Lead: Rithika Shetty
Project Manager: Ankit Maroli
Content Engineer: Deepayan Bhattacharjee
Technical Editor: Aditya Bharadwaj
Copy Editor: Deepayan Bhattacharjee
Indexer: Tejal Soni
Production Designer: Ganesh Bhadwalkar
Growth Lead: Vinishka Kalra

First published: June 2026

Production reference: 1290626

Published by Packt Publishing Ltd.
Grosvenor House
11 St Paul's Square
Birmingham
B3 1RB, UK.

ISBN 978-1-80730-171-2
www.packtpub.com

To my parents, Chuntao He and Zongyuan Wu.

– Fuheng Wu

Foreword

I have known Fuheng Wu for many years. We have both worked at Bloomberg and Uber, and we have stayed in the same field ever since—as I went on to Meta, Anyscale, and NVIDIA, we kept trading notes on distributed AI. At Uber, we exchanged technical ideas constantly: I was working on OpenSearch while he was building distributed AI systems with Petastorm and training models with Horovod on Michelangelo. I have seen that production-first instinct up close—the debugging sessions, the cluster failures, the pressure to ship under real constraints. When he told me he was writing this book, I had no doubt it would be grounded in that experience, not textbook abstraction. That distinction has never mattered more, because AI has entered an era where progress increasingly depends not only on better models, but on the systems capable of training and serving them.

That shift is happening in one of the most transformative epochs in the history of technology. The rapid evolution of artificial intelligence—moving from niche statistical models to gargantuan large language models and multimodal systems spanning billions or even trillions of parameters—has fundamentally shifted our relationship with computing. Yet, as the mathematical formulation of these models remains elegantly bound to deep learning fundamentals, the engineering reality of executing them has exploded in complexity. Today, the bottleneck to AI progress is no longer just algorithmic creativity; it is fundamentally a system engineering challenge.

Building a neural network on a single GPU has become a commoditized task, abstracted away by modern software libraries. However, taking that same network and distributing its training across thousands of specialized chips, or orchestrating low-latency, high-throughput inference for millions of concurrent users, is an entirely different beast. It requires a profound, multidisciplinary mastery over physical hardware, high-speed networking topologies, memory management tricks, complex software orchestration, and algorithmic nuances. It is a domain where a single misplaced communication bottleneck can degrade hardware utilization from pristine efficiency to a crawl, rendering millions of dollars of compute infrastructure idle.

For too long, knowledge in the distributed AI space has been siloed. Engineers looking to master this domain have had to piece together disparate academic papers, fragmented blog posts, tribal knowledge from elite tech companies, and chaotic open-source repository documentation. There has been a glaring gap between theoretical high-level explanations of parallelism and the actual code required to run stable, fault-tolerant workloads—from launching multi-node training on HPC clusters to serving models reliably in production.

Distributed AI Systems: A practical guide to building scalable training, inference, and serving systems for production AI is the comprehensive blueprint the industry has desperately needed—and a book I wish Fuheng had written years ago.

Fuheng Wu has done something remarkable with this text. He has demystified the black box of infrastructure engineering for AI. Rather than treating training, inference, and cluster management as isolated domains, this book treats them as an integrated lifecycle. It systematically walks the reader through the complete operational pipeline—from understanding the silicon and high-speed interconnects that form the physical bedrock, to mastering PyTorch DDP, FSDP, DeepSpeed ZeRO optimization, and Megatron-style tensor, pipeline, and expert parallelism for multi-node scaling.

Crucially, this book recognizes that training is only half the battle. In real-world AI deployments, serving these models efficiently is where the economic and engineering viability of AI is won or lost. By diving deep into distributed inference fundamentals, vLLM, and SGLang, Fuheng equips engineers with the tools to tame memory fragmentation and unlock massive throughput. The book also covers running multi-node training on HPC clusters with SLURM and assembling a production serving stack with Kubernetes, GPU scheduling, and observability—so your systems don't just work in theory, they remain resilient and maintainable under real workloads.

Whether you are a machine learning engineer seeking to scale your models beyond the limits of a single accelerator, a platform engineer tasked with building a modern AI cluster, or an architect designing the next generation of enterprise AI infrastructure, this book will serve as your definitive guide. Fuheng's hands-on, code-first approach translates intimidating infrastructure challenges into predictable, repeatable engineering methodologies.

As you read these chapters, I encourage you to not just absorb the code, but to deeply study the underlying patterns of resource estimation, memory management, and network communication. The frameworks of today will inevitably evolve, but the distributed systems principles meticulously laid out in this book will remain the foundation of AI infrastructure for years to come.

Gang Zhao

Staff Engineer at NVIDIA, Anyscale, Meta, Uber

June 2026

Contributors

About the author

Fuheng Wu is a Principal ML Tech Lead at Oracle Generative AI, specializing in distributed training, inference, and GPU systems for enterprise AI workloads. He has delivered core components of Oracle's large-scale vision and document-AI models and Oracle Code Assist (Oracle's AI coding copilot), and co-authored a Microsoft–Oracle blog on high-performance deep learning with ONNX Runtime. A graduate of the Singapore–MIT Alliance, where he studied linear algebra with Gilbert Strang of MIT, he began his career in applied machine learning at NetEase, then worked on Wall Street in quantitative finance—pricing convertible bonds at Bloomberg and developing algorithmic trading strategies at WorldQuant—before joining Uber, where he built distributed training systems on Michelangelo with Petastorm and Horovod.

Fuheng has hands-on experience across PyTorch Distributed, DeepSpeed, Megatron-style parallelism, Kubernetes GPU clusters, and production LLM serving. He has contributed to open-source projects including SGLang, vLLM, genai-bench, pyLLaMA, chatLLaMA, and HiQ, and is the author of *Mathematics for AI and Machine Learning*. He teaches Generative AI foundations at the McCombs School of Business, University of Texas at Austin, and mentors students preparing for AI Olympiads. Writing as Xuan Xin, he is also the author of the poetic memoir *Above the Clouds: From Mountain Springs to the Edge of AI in Silicon Valley* and the music album *Let's Train the Model* (2024), which renders deep learning and AI concepts as music. Beyond technology, he is a Zen calligrapher and volunteer math tutor.

I am grateful to receive detailed feedback on early drafts of this book from:

Liu Yong — Ph.D, NUS, Huaizheng Zhang — Staff Research Scientist, ByteDance, Junwei Zhang — GenAI | Engineer | Moderator | 18K+ followers | x{Uber, DoorDash}, Junnan Li — Research Director @Salesforce; Time-Series, CUA, and Multimodal AI (BLIP), Jerry Liu — Co-founder/CEO @ LlamaIndex, Henry Mao — Co-founder @ smithery.ai | Prev. co-founder of Jenni.ai (exited), Doris Xin — CEO & Co-Founder @ Disarray | UC Berkeley CS PhD | Ex-LinkedIn, Google, Databricks, You Yang — NUS Professor, Juncong Jack Wu — USA AI Olympiad Nationals Bronze, 2026; Canada AI Olympiad National Qualifier Distinguished Honor Roll, National Team Selection Top 18; USACO Silver

About the reviewer

Xuanyu Zhang is a machine learning engineer specializing in distributed AI infrastructure, large language model serving, and inference performance optimization. His work focuses on the systems layer behind modern generative AI, including model-serving runtimes, speculative decoding, quantization, continuous batching, GPU performance engineering, and multi-GPU and multi-node deployment of large-scale models.

Xuanyu has worked on production machine learning and AI infrastructure at leading technology and AI companies, including Apple, Together AI, and Mistral AI. Across these roles, he has contributed to the design, optimization, and deployment of high-performance systems for large-scale model inference, bridging cutting-edge AI research with reliable production engineering. His experience spans both practical system implementation and deep technical evaluation of distributed training and inference architectures.

As a reviewer of *Distributed AI Systems*, Xuanyu brought an industry practitioner's perspective to the book, with particular attention to the accuracy, clarity, and practical usefulness of its explanations and exercises on large language model training and inference systems. His review focused on ensuring that the material would be technically rigorous, accessible to engineers and researchers, and grounded in real-world AI infrastructure challenges.

Table of Contents

Preface xxxi

Free benefits with your book xxxv

Chapter 1: Introduction to Modern Distributed AI 1

Overview 1

Why modern AI requires distribution 2

The scale challenge • 4

Estimating model resource requirements • 5

Training memory requirements • 6

Inference memory requirements • 16

GPU requirements estimation • 17

Real-World considerations • 17

The evolution from classic ML to foundation models • 18

The modern AI model lifecycle 19

Training: the learning phase • 20

Inference: the prediction/generation phase • 20

Serving: the production system • 21

Decision framework: when do you need distributed systems? 21

Decision tree: quick reference • 22

Understanding the decision tree • 22

Hands-On: running distributed training 23

Environment setup • 24

Single-GPU baseline • 25

Multi-GPU distributed training • 26

Extended training: CIFAR-10 with 20 epochs • 28

Distributed inference: throughput scaling • 30

Distributed AI fundamentals with PyTorch 31

The distributed AI stack • 31
Process Groups and Ranks • 34
Initializing the process group • 34
Collective operations • 36
AllReduce • 36
AllGather • 37
Broadcast • 39
Reduce • 40
Gather • 42
Scatter • 43
ReduceScatter • 45
AlltoAll • 46
Choosing the right operation • 48
DistributedDataParallel (DDP) • 48
DistributedSampler • 49
Launching distributed jobs • 50
Code summary 50
References 51
Exercises 51
Process group initialization • 51
Manual AllReduce implementation • 52
Broadcast with verification • 53
DistributedSampler wrapper • 54
Gradient synchronization timing • 55
Expected learning outcomes • 56

Chapter 2: GPU Hardware, Networking, and Parallelism Strategies 57

Computational power: AI clusters and metrics 57
What is computational power? • 57
Why clusters? • 59
AI clusters: built for training and inference • 60
Key metrics for AI clusters • 61

Central Processing Unit (CPU) 64

CPU Architecture Basics • 64

CPU-GPU Interaction • 65

NUMA and CPU affinity • 65

CPU requirements for distributed training • 66

Graphics Processing Unit (GPU) 66

Understanding GPU memory and compute architecture • 66

Key architecture milestones • 69

What these numbers mean for training • 69

Graphics Processing Unit (GPU) product families • 70

Choosing the right GPU • 71

Architecture features that matter • 71

Tensor Processing Unit (TPU) 72

Why TPUs exist • 72

TPU architecture: systolic arrays • 73

TPU generations • 73

TPU pod architecture • 73

TPU vs GPU: when to use which • 74

TPU programming model • 75

Sparse core (since v4) • 75

Neural Processing Unit (NPU) 76

What makes NPUs different • 76

NPU architecture: AI cores and memory • 77

Training vs inference NPUs • 77

NPU software stack • 78

NPU vs. GPU: when to choose which • 78

NPU interconnects and scaling • 78

The NPU landscape • 79

High-Speed interconnects: the network backbone 79

Chip programming systems: SPMD and CUDA 81

Programming models vs. execution models • 81

SPMD: single program, multiple data • 81

CUDA's execution model: SIMT • 82
Why SIMT over SIMD? • 83
CUDA thread indexing • 83
Memory hierarchy in CUDA • 84
How frameworks use CUDA • 84
SPMD in distributed training • 85
AMD and other alternatives • 85
Distributed communication: patterns and primitives 85
Parallelism: core strategies 86
Parallelism taxonomy table • 87
The three questions for parallelism determination • 88
Data parallelism: replicated and sharded • 89
Model parallelism: compute sharding • 89
Combining Strategies • 90
Composition patterns (hybrid parallelism) • 90
Strategy selection: choosing the right approach 91
Training strategy decision tree • 91
Key considerations for training • 94
Inference strategy decision tree • 94
Key considerations for inference • 96
Practical tips • 97
Hands-On: hardware inspection and bandwidth testing 97
Environment Setup • 97
Step 1: inspect GPU hardware • 97
Step 2: inspect hardware topology • 98
Step 3: measure Single-GPU memory bandwidth • 99
Step 4: benchmark Inter-GPU communication • 100
Step 5: analyze results • 102
Code summary 103
Notes and references 104
Exercises 104
GPU hardware inspector • 104

Memory requirement calculator • 105
Topology detection and analysis • 106
Parallelism strategy selector • 107
Expected learning outcomes • 109

Chapter 3: Distributed Training with PyTorch DDP 111

How DDP works internally 111
The basic flow • 112
Data Parallel (DP) vs. Distributed Data Parallel (DDP) • 113
Gradient bucketing: why it matters • 114
Communication–Computation overlap • 114
The AllReduce operation • 115
Mixed precision and gradient scaling • 116
Buffer Synchronization • 117
DDP forward pass implementation details • 117
DDP Computation–Communication overlap implementation • 118

Setting up Single-Node DDP 118
Using torchrun (recommended) • 118
Understanding the environment variables • 121
Using DistributedSampler • 121
DataLoader internals for distributed training • 124
Device selection best practices • 125
A complete single node example • 126

Setting up Multi-Node DDP 128
Multi-Node rchitecture • 129
Launching Multi-Node training • 129
Using SLURM for Multi-Node launch • 130
Network configuration • 131
Environment variables for Multi-Node • 132
A complete Multi-Node example • 132

Debugging and troubleshooting........ 133
Hangs: the most common problem • 134

Wrong results or inconsistent gradients • 136

CUDA out of memory • 137

Performance issues • 139

Network debugging • 141

Profiling DDP performance 141

Using torch.profiler.profile for DDP analysis • 141

Analyzing Computation–Communication overlap • 145

Profiling Multi-Node DDP • 146

Optimizing DDP performance 148

Mixed precision training • 148

Gradient accumulation • 149

Communication overlap optimization • 150

Tuning bucket sizes • 151

Finding unused parameters • 151

Static graph optimization • 152

Checkpointing and resuming distributed jobs 152

Saving checkpoints • 153

Loading checkpoints • 153

Saving RNG state for reproducibility • 154

Atomic checkpointing • 155

Checkpointing best practices • 155

Advanced DDP features 156

Gradient hooks • 156

Communication hooks • 156

Handling uneven inputs with join() • 157

Best practices and common patterns 158

Elastic data parallelism 160

How elastic training works • 160

Launching elastic training • 161

When to use elastic training • 162

Complete example: DDP with a transformer 162

Summary 162

Code summary 163

References 164

Exercises 164

Implement manual gradient synchronization • 164

Compare DP vs DDP performance • 165

Implement gradient bucketing • 166

Implement Fault-Tolerant DDP training • 167

Analyze communication patterns with NCCL • 168

Expected learning outcomes • 170

Chapter 4: Scaling with Fully Sharded Data Parallel (FSDP) 171

From DDP to FSDP 171

Why FSDP enables Larger-Than-Memory models 172

How FSDP works • 173

FSDP1 vs FSDP2: the evolution • 174

Original FSDP (FSDP1) • 175

FSDP2: the per-parameter sharding API 177

Device mesh: the foundation • 178

Key parameters • 179

Hierarchical sharding • 181

A complete working example: T5 summarization with FSDP 182

Checkpointing with FSDP2 187

Using the DCP API (recommended) • 187

Manual sharded checkpointing • 188

Full state dict for evaluation • 190

Prefetching: optimizing communication 191

Forward prefetching • 191

Backward prefetching • 192

When to use prefetching • 192

Activation checkpointing and offloading 192

Why activation checkpointing matters with FSDP • 193

Using activation checkpointing • 193

CPU offloading • 194
When to use offloading • 195
Performance optimization 195
Profiling FSDP training • 195
Optimizing communication • 196
Optimizing activation memory • 197
Memory profiling • 197
Multi-node FSDP training 197
Setting up multi-node FSDP • 198
Network configuration for multi-node • 198
Checkpointing on multi-node • 199
SLURM integration • 199
Scaling considerations • 200
Debugging FSDP issues 201
Out of Memory (OOM) • 201
Hanging or deadlocked • 201
Slow training • 201
Incorrect results • 202
Debugging tools • 202
Comparing FSDP2 with ZeRO and DDP 202
Memory and performance • 203
When to use what • 203
Practical tips 203
Initialization best practices • 204
Data loading and gradient clipping • 204
Mixed precision • 204
Progressive Optimization • 204
Advanced topics 205
Hybrid sharding (HSDP) • 205
Compiler integration • 205
Other integrations • 205
FSDP via SPMD for TPU/XLA • 205

Summary 207

Code Summary 208

Useful links 208

Notes and references 209

Exercises 210

Implement manual parameter sharding • 210

Compare FSDP sharding strategies • 211

Implement custom FSDP wrapping policy • 212

Implement mixed precision with FSDP • 213

Implement FSDP checkpointing • 214

Expected learning outcomes • 215

Chapter 5: Beyond State Sharding with DeepSpeed and Megatron 217

Beyond state sharding 217

ZeRO stage 1: optimizer state partitioning 218

ZeRO stage 2: optimizer state and gradient partitioning 220

ZeRO stage 3: full sharding (like FSDP) 221

ZeRO-Offload: CPU memory extension 222

ZeRO-Infinity: NVMe offload for massive models 223

ZeRO++: Communication-Optimized ZeRO 226

Megatron: computation parallelism as a second axis 228

State sharding vs. computation sharding • 228

Tensor Parallelism: sharding the layer • 229

Pipeline Parallelism: sharding the depth • 231

Sequence parallelism and context parallelism: long contexts • 233

DeepSpeed-Ulysses: an alternative to ring attention • 236

Expert Parallelism: scaling MoE models • 238

Why FSDP2 cannot replace Megatron • 240

Hybrid Parallelism: combining state and computation sharding • 241

Megatron core: Production-Ready library • 242

Megatron-FSDP: optimized state sharding • 242

Distributed optimizer: Memory-Efficient optimization • 243

FP8 training: Next-Generation precision • 244
When do you need Megatron? • 245
Real-World training configurations • 245
Complete training example with Megatron • 248
Hybrid Parallelism in practice 249
The Two-Axis view • 249
Building a hybrid configuration • 250
Why this works • 250
Choosing your configuration • 250
Operational realities • 251
Performance optimization best practices • 251
Configuration patterns • 252
Choosing the right strategy 252
A decision framework • 253
Understanding the Trade-Offs • 254
Concrete memory example • 254
Summary 254
Code summary 255
Useful links 256
References 257
Exercises 258
Compare ZeRO stages • 258
Implement CPU offloading • 259
Implement Tensor Parallelism • 261
Implement Pipeline Parallelism • 262
Configure Hybrid Parallelism • 263
Expected learning outcomes • 264

Chapter 6: Distributed Inference and vLLM 267

From training to inference 267
Introduction to vLLM 268
Prerequisites • 268

Installation • 268

Docker Setup • 268

Install and run from package manager (uv, conda, pip) • 272

Compile, install, and run from local source • 274

Offline inference • 274

Online inference • 275

KV cache 276

Decoder-Only transformer architecture • 277

Text generation process: prefill and decode • 279

The decode phase and its inefficiencies • 281

KV cache solution • 283

PagedAttention: solving KV cache fragmentation 286

The KV cache fragmentation problem • 287

How PagedAttention works • 288

Eliminating padding FLOPs • 289

Connection to distributed inference • 291

Motivation: the "out of memory" problem 291

Overview of the vLLM architecture 292

Overview of parallelism strategies in vLLM 293

Tensor Parallelism (TP) 294

The linear algebra foundations • 294

Benefits of Tensor Parallelism • 294

When to use Tensor Parallelism • 295

Data Parallelism (DP) for throughput scaling 295

Combining Data Parallelism with other strategies • 296

Deployment modes • 296

Benefits and Trade-Offs • 297

Pipeline Parallelism (PP) 298

The pipeline bubble problem • 298

Chunked prefill for smoother pipelines • 299

Expert Parallelism (EP): A modifier flag for MoE models 299

Understanding MoE architecture • 300

Decoder layer structure • 301

Expert structure • 302

Routing mechanism • 302

How Expert Parallelism modifies behavior • 303

Combining parallelism strategies 304

TP + PP: the standard Multi-Node configuration • 304

Expert Parallelism combinations • 305

TP + DP: scaling both ways • 305

The EP activation constraint • 306

Hands-On examples 306

Basic vLLM setup with Tensor Parallelism • 306

Multi-Node with TP and PP • 306

Custom chunked prefill configuration • 307

Profiling with Nsight Systems • 308

Best practices • 308

Summary 308

Code summary 309

Useful links 310

References 311

Exercises 311

Implement KV cache management • 311

Implement continuous batching • 312

Benchmark vLLM throughput • 313

Implement speculative decoding • 315

Deploy vLLM with OpenAI-Compatible API • 316

Expected learning outcomes • 318

Subscribe to Deep Engineering 318

Chapter 7: Cross-Request Optimization with SGLang 319

A different philosophy for distributed inference 319

Prerequisites • 320

Installation • 320

Docker Setup • 320

Overview of the SGLang architecture 324

SGLang core theory 326

RadixAttention: prefix cache reuse • 326

Structured output decoding with XGrammar • 329

Operator fusion • 331

Zero-overhead scheduler • 331

Router-based distributed architecture 332

SGLang model gateway architecture • 333

When Router-based architecture excels • 333

Prefill/Decode disaggregation 334

PD disaggregation architecture • 335

Transfer engines • 336

PD disaggregation setup • 336

Distributed inference architecture and parallelism strategies 337

Tensor Parallelism: weight sharding • 338

Pipeline Parallelism: layer sharding • 339

Data Parallelism: Request-level replication • 339

Hybrid Parallelism: combining strategies • 341

Communication patterns • 341

Multi-node SGLang deployment 342

Multi-node with Tensor Parallelism • 342

Router-based multi-node deployment • 343

Router policies and load balancing • 344

Session affinity and cache locality • 345

Fault tolerance • 345

Expert for MoE models 346

Speculative Decoding 347

Data-Parallel attention 348

Production deployment patterns 348

Hands-on examples 349

Basic multi-node deployment • 349

PD disaggregation with Mooncake • 350
Testing session affinity • 351
MoE model with EP+TP • 352
Summary 353
Code summary 354
Useful links 355
Reference 356
Exercises 356
Implement RadixAttention cache • 356
Benchmark prefix caching • 357
Implementing constrained decoding • 359
Implement Multi-turn conversation with state • 360
Implement parallel generation with fork • 361
Expected learning outcomes • 363

Chapter 8: Running Distributed Training with SLURM 365

Introduction to clusters for HPC and AI training 365
Why SLURM for AI training? • 366
SLURM architecture: A brief overview • 367
Setting up SLURM for Multi-GPU training 368
Simulating a Multi-Node cluster • 369
Quick setup and verification • 370
Submitting distributed training jobs 371
Interactive execution with srun 371
Batch submission with sbatch • 372
Understanding SLURM environment variables • 373
Launching distributed training frameworks with SLURM 376
DDP with SLURM • 377
FSDP with SLURM {#sec:slurm-fsdp-example} • 379
DeepSpeed with SLURM • 380
Megatron-LM with SLURM • 383
Advanced SLURM features for training 387

Job arrays for hyperparameter tuning • 387
Interactive jobs with salloc • 388
Job dependencies • 388
Checkpointing and job resumption • 389
Monitoring and debugging **389**
Job monitoring • 390
Logging and output • 391
Profiling distributed training • 392
Best practices **393**
Resource allocation • 393
Checkpointing strategy • 393
Handling failures • 394
Troubleshooting common issues **394**
Nodes not available • 394
GPU allocation issues • 395
Communication Errors • 395
Job hanging • 395
Code summary **396**
Useful links **396**
References **397**
Exercises **398**
Write a basic SLURM job script • 398
Implement automatic checkpointing with SLURM • 398
Configure Multi-Node NCCL communication • 400
Implement job array for hyperparameter search • 402
Monitor and profile SLURM jobs • 404
Expected learning outcomes • 406

Chapter 9: Production LLM Serving Stack 407

Anatomy of a production LLM serving system **407**
Request routing and traffic management **411**
Routing strategies • 412

Load balancing • 412
Canary deployments and A/B testing • 413
Operations: observability, reliability, and cost 414
Observability • 415
Reliability and fault tolerance • 415
Cost optimization • 416
Deploying LLM serving on kubernetes 416
Local development with k3d • 419
Deploying vLLM on k3d • 421
Cleanup • 424
Multi-Model and Multi-Engine serving • 424
Multi-Model routing • 424
Multi-Engine routing • 427
Kubernetes deployment with llm-d 430
What is llm-d? • 431
Key features • 431
Deployment architecture • 433
Getting started with llm-d • 434
Well-Lit paths • 435
Monitoring and observability • 436
Choosing Your Path • 436
Multi-Model serving • 436
Comparing k3d and llm-d approaches • 440
Summary 441
Code summary 441
Useful links 442
References 442
Exercises 443
Build an API gateway with model routing • 443
Implement rate limiting middleware • 444
Implement canary deployment with automated rollback • 446
Add distributed tracing with OpenTelemetry • 447

Deploy multi-model serving on k3d • 449

Expected learning outcomes • 450

Chapter 10: Distributed Benchmarking and Performance Optimization 451

The performance gap in distributed systems 451

Why benchmarking matters 452

Benchmarking fundamentals 453

Understanding percentile latencies • 453

Efficiency metrics • 453

Benchmarking methodology • 454

Training benchmarking 454

Key training metrics • 455

PyTorch profiler • 456

NVIDIA Nsight Systems • 456

Custom training benchmark • 457

Measuring scaling efficiency • 458

Validating distributed training accuracy • 458

Network and communication profiling • 459

Scaling bottleneck analysis • 460

Inference benchmarking 461

Key inference metrics • 461

Benchmarking tools: genai-bench • 464

Custom inference benchmarks • 465

Cold start vs warm performance • 465

Reasoning and multi-step models • 466

Validating inference accuracy • 466

Summary 467

Code summary 468

Useful links 468

Reference 469

Exercises 469

Multiple choice questions • 469
Short answer questions • 471
Answer Key • 471
Expected learning outcomes • 472

Chapter 11: The Evolving Landscape of Distributed AI 473

The evolution of distributed AI ... 473
Where we stand today • 473
The new bottlenecks • 474
Emerging trends at a glance • 474
Mixture of experts: the dominant architecture ... 475
The Edge-cloud continuum ... 475
Why edge AI matters now • 476
Practical On-device models • 476
Edge-cloud coordination • 477
Parallelism at scale ... 478
The communication revolution • 478
Hierarchical parallelism • 478
Sequence parallelism for long contexts • 479
Ring attention • 479
When things go wrong: fault tolerance ... 479
The checkpointing challenge • 480
Detecting and handling failures • 480
Elastic training • 480
Beyond text: multimodal distributed training ... 481
The Cross-modal challenge • 481
Handling multiple modalities • 482
Federated learning: an alternative paradigm ... 482
The federated paradigm • 482
Where federated learning thrives • 483
The challenges of heterogeneity • 484
Modern federated techniques • 484

Federated learning for LLMs • 485
The flower framework • 485
When to consider federated learning • 486
Agentic AI: the next frontier **486**
Why agents need distribution • 486
Multi-agent patterns • 487
Distributed tool execution • 487
Reasoning agents • 488
The economics of scale **488**
Workload distribution • 489
Resource management • 489
Multi-tenant GPU sharing • 489
Gradient compression • 490
Preparing for the future **490**
Skills to develop • 490
Staying current • 491
Summary **491**
Code summary **492**
Useful links **493**
References **495**
Exercises **496**
Multiple choice questions • 496
Short answer questions • 496
Hands-on exercise • 497
Implement basic MoE routing • 497

Chapter 12: Unlock Your Exclusive Benefits **499**

Unlock this Book's Free Benefits in 3 Easy Steps **500**
Appendix **502**
OpenAI-Compatible API Endpoints **502**

Other Books You May Enjoy 506

Subscribe to Deep Engineering 510

Index 511

Preface

Large AI models now reach billions or even trillions of parameters. Training and serving them is no longer a single-GPU exercise—it is a distributed systems problem. You need to reason about GPU memory, high-speed interconnects, collective communication, job schedulers, inference batching, and production observability, often in the same week. Many resources explain one layer well: a training framework here, an inference engine there, a Kubernetes guide somewhere else. What has been missing is a single path from distributed training through inference to production serving, with runnable code you can execute on your own hardware.

This book is that path. Complete with hands-on code examples, it guides you to build distributed AI systems from the ground up—covering everything from distributed training and inference to production serving. The goal is not to memorize APIs, but to build intuition: why gradient synchronization hangs, when FSDP beats DDP, how PagedAttention changes serving economics, what to profile before you tune. If you work through the examples chapter by chapter, you will be able to scale workloads from a single GPU to a multi-node cluster and deploy inference systems that are faster, more memory-efficient, and easier to operate. The frameworks will keep evolving; the systems patterns in this book are what endure.

Who this book is for

This book is for ML engineers, AI researchers, and DevOps engineers who need to train or serve large AI models at scale. Platform engineers, HPC cluster administrators, and cloud architects will be able to advance their skill set with this guide. A basic understanding of Python and PyTorch fundamentals is necessary to get started. Prior knowledge of distributed systems, cluster schedulers, or container orchestration is helpful but not required—the book covers these concepts from the ground up, starting with resource estimation, data preparation, and hardware fundamentals.

What this book covers

Chapter 1, Introduction to Modern Distributed AI, introduces resource estimation, data preparation, and your first distributed training example with PyTorch.

Chapter 2, GPU Hardware, Networking, and Parallelism Strategies, covers GPU architecture, high-speed interconnects, and the parallelism strategies used throughout the rest of the book.

Chapter 3, Distributed Training with PyTorch DDP, walks through data parallelism on single-node and multi-node clusters, including debugging and performance tuning.

Chapter 4, Scaling with Fully Sharded Data Parallel (FSDP), explains parameter sharding, hybrid sharding, and checkpointing for memory-efficient training.

Chapter 5, Beyond State Sharding with DeepSpeed and Megatron, covers DeepSpeed ZeRO optimization and Megatron-style tensor, pipeline, and expert parallelism, and when to choose each framework.

Chapter 6, Distributed Inference and vLLM, introduces inference fundamentals, PagedAttention, continuous batching, and tensor/expert parallelism for serving.

Chapter 7, Cross-Request Optimization with SGLang, explores structured generation, radix attention, and router-based serving optimizations.

Chapter 8, Running Distributed Training with SLURM, shows how to launch and manage multi-node training jobs on HPC clusters.

Chapter 9, Production LLM Serving Stack, builds a complete serving stack with Kubernetes, GPU scheduling, routing, and observability.

Chapter 10, Distributed Benchmarking and Performance Optimization, covers benchmarking methodologies, profiling tools, and systematic performance tuning.

Chapter 11, The Evolving Landscape of Distributed AI, surveys emerging trends including MoE architectures, edge–cloud coordination, and future directions.

To get the most out of this book

You will need a machine with at least one NVIDIA GPU to run most examples; multi-GPU and multi-node setups are used in later chapters on distributed training and inference. Linux is the primary environment throughout, and all code examples use Python with PyTorch. Familiarity with the command line, virtual environments, and basic deep learning concepts (models, optimizers, loss functions) will help you move faster.

We recommend cloning the example code repository and working through each chapter's exercises in order—the early chapters establish hardware and parallelism concepts that later chapters build on. When you do not have local GPU access, cloud notebooks (such as Kaggle) with multiple GPUs can substitute for some exercises, as described in Chapter 1. For cluster-focused chapters, a SLURM environment or a local Kubernetes cluster with GPU nodes is ideal but not strictly required to understand the launch patterns and configuration.

Download the example code files

You can download the example code files for this book from GitHub at `https://github.com/PacktPublishing/Distributed-AI-Systems`. If code has been updated since publication, you will find the latest version on GitHub. You can also download the code files by visiting the book's page on Packt's website and entering the name of the book in the search box. Follow the link to the book's product page and check the Support section.

We also have other code bundles from our rich catalog of books and videos available at `https://github.com/PacktPublishing/`. Check them out!

Download the color images

We also provide a PDF file that has color images of the screenshots/diagrams used in this book. You can download it here: `https://packt.link/gbp/9781807301712`.

Conventions used

There are a number of text conventions used throughout this book.

`CodeInText`: Indicates code words in text, database table names, folder names, filenames, file extensions, pathnames, dummy URLs, user input, and Twitter handles. For example: Mount the downloaded `WebStorm-10*.dmg` disk image file as another disk in your system.

A block of code is set as follows:

```
import json
from sglang import Engine

llm = Engine(model_path="Qwen/Qwen2.5-0.5B-Instruct")
schema = {
    "type": "object",
    "properties": {"name": {"type": "string"}, "age": {"type": "number"}},
    "required": ["name", "age"],
}
```

Any command-line input or output is written as follows:

```
docker pull lmsysorg/sglang:latest-runtime
```

Bold: Indicates a new term, an important word, or important information. For instance, words in menus or dialog boxes appear in the text like this. For example: The `wordByWord()` function uses *regular expressions to separate the words* found in each line of the input file.

> **Note**
>
> Warnings or important notes appear like this.

Get in touch

Feedback from our readers is always welcome.

General feedback: If you have questions about any aspect of this book or have any general feedback, please email us at `customercare@packt.com` and mention the book's title in the subject of your message.

Errata: Although we have taken every care to ensure the accuracy of our content, mistakes do happen. If you have found a mistake in this book, we would be grateful if you reported this to us. Please visit `http://www.packt.com/submit-errata`, click **Submit Errata**, and fill in the form.

Piracy: If you come across any illegal copies of our works in any form on the internet, we would be grateful if you would provide us with the location address or website name. Please contact us at `copyright@packt.com` with a link to the material.

If you are interested in becoming an author: If there is a topic that you have expertise in and you are interested in either writing or contributing to a book, please visit .

Free benefits with your book

This book comes with free benefits to support your learning. Activate them now for instant access (see the "*How to Unlock*" section for instructions).

Here's a quick overview of what you can instantly unlock with your purchase:

EPUB PDF

DRM-Free PDF Version

Download DRM-free PDF and ePub copies of this book.

7-Day Packt Library Access

Get 7-day unlimited access to 8,000+ books and videos. No credit card required.

Available for first-time Packt+ trial users only.

Next-Gen Reader Access

Read this book on Packt Reader with progress sync, dark mode and note-taking.

How to unlock

Scan the QR code (or go to `packtpub.com/unlock`). Search for this book by name, confirm the edition, and then follow the steps on the page.

UNLOCK NOW

Note: Keep your invoice handy. Purchases made directly from Packt don't require one

Share your thoughts

Once you've read *Distributed AI Systems,* we'd love to hear your thoughts! Scan the QR code below to go straight to the Amazon review page for this book and share your feedback.

`https://packt.link/r/1807301710`

Your review is important to us and the tech community and will help us make sure we're delivering excellent quality content.

1

Introduction to Modern Distributed AI

Building scalable AI systems from a single GPU to distributed clusters

> *A distributed system is one in which the failure of a computer you didn't even know existed can render your own computer unusable.*
>
> *Leslie Lamport, 1987*

Overview

Modern AI models have grown beyond what single GPUs can handle. Large language models now range from several billion to over a trillion parameters. Training models with tens of billions of parameters on a single GPU would take months, if they even fit in memory. Serving these models at scale requires distributed architectures.

This chapter walks through resource estimation, decision frameworks for choosing between distributed training, fine-tuning, or inference, and practical examples to get you started.

Why modern AI requires distribution

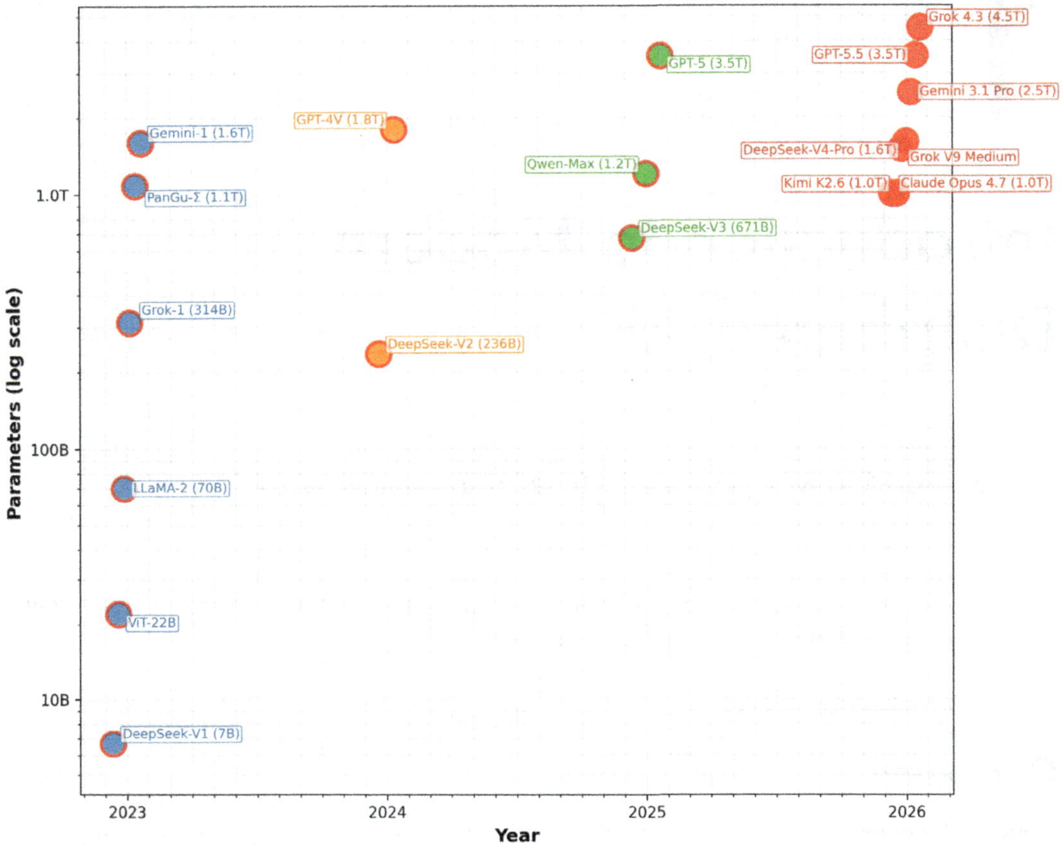

Figure 1.1: Model Parameters vs. Year

A few years ago, you could train most models on a single GPU. ResNet-50 on ImageNet took a couple of days. Today, training a 70B parameter language model on a single GPU would take months, if it even fits in memory. The models got bigger, the datasets got bigger, and single-GPU training became impractical.

As shown in *Figure 1.1*, the exponential growth in model parameters over recent years is evident. Looking at recent models detailed in *Table 1.1*, the scale is clear[1]. GPT-4 has over 1 trillion parameters, and frontier models continue to push well beyond that scale[2]. Training them requires thousands of GPUs working together[3]. Even smaller models like Llama 2 (70B parameters) need multiple GPUs just to fit in memory, let alone train efficiently.

This isn't just a training problem—serving these models at scale for production workloads demands distributed inference architectures that can handle thousands of concurrent requests.

The era of single-machine AI is over; modern AI systems are inherently distributed by design. According to PyTorch's distributed training documentation, distributed training involves spreading the training workload across multiple worker nodes, which is particularly beneficial for large models and compute-intensive tasks in deep learning. Additionally, industry reports indicate that training trillion-parameter models requires infrastructure investments of tens of millions of dollars[4], making distributed computing not just a technical necessity but an economic imperative for modern AI development.

Model	Parameters	Company	Year
ViT-22B	22B	Google	2023
Grok-1	314B	xAI	2023
Gemini-1	1.6T	Google	2023
LLaMA-2	70B	Meta	2023
PanGu-Σ	1.085T	Huawei	2023
DeepSeek-V1	6.7B	DeepSeek	2023
GPT-4V	~1.8T	OpenAI	2024
DeepSeek-V2	236B	DeepSeek	2024
Qwen-Max	~1.2T	Alibaba	2025
GPT-5	~2–5T	OpenAI	2025
DeepSeek-V3	671B	DeepSeek	2025
Gemini 3.1 Pro	~2–3T	Google	2026
Grok 4.3	~3–6T	xAI	2026
Claude Opus 4.7	~1T+	Anthropic	2026
GPT-5.5	~2–5T	OpenAI	2026

Model	Parameters	Company	Year
Kimi K2.6	1T	Moonshot AI	2026
DeepSeek-V4-Pro	1.6T	DeepSeek	2026
Grok V9 Medium	1.5T	xAI	2026
Claude Mythos 5	~10T	Anthropic	2026

Table 1.1: Comparison of Large AI Models

The scale challenge

Take a 70B parameter model as an example. In full precision (FP32), the model weights alone need 280GB of memory. No mainstream datacenter GPU holds that much today—even H200 (141 GB) and B200 (192 GB) fall short (*Chapter 2* discusses GPU generations and memory trends). You need multiple GPUs just to load the model, let alone train it.

Training these models takes thousands of GPU-hours. A single GPU training run would take months. The datasets are massive too—trillions of tokens. Loading and preprocessing this data efficiently requires *distributed pipelines*.

The mismatch is clear: model size and compute requirements have grown *exponentially*, while single-GPU memory and compute have grown *linearly* at best.

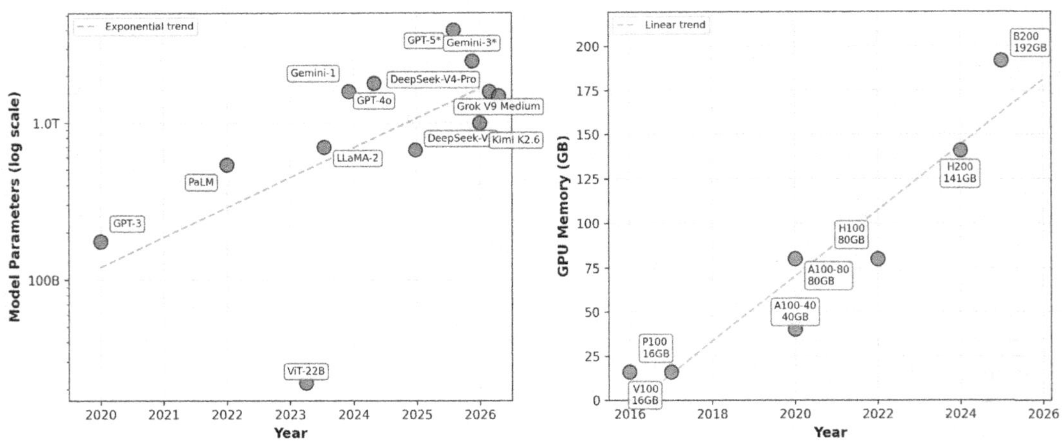

Figure 1.2: Growth Mismatch: Exponential Model Growth vs. Linear GPU Growth

Estimating model resource requirements

Before you start training or deploying, you need to know how much memory and compute you'll need. Get this wrong, and you'll hit out-of-memory errors or waste money on over-provisioned infrastructure.

The memory footprint depends on what you're storing. For model weights alone, the calculation is straightforward. Each parameter in FP32 takes 4 bytes, FP16/BF16 takes 2 bytes, Int8 takes 1 byte, and Int4 takes 0.5 bytes. For a 7B parameter model, that's 28GB in FP32, 14GB in BF16 (or FP16), 7GB in Int8, and 3.5GB in Int4.

Here's a quick reference for common precision formats:

Format	Bytes	Format Details	Primary Usage
FP32	4	32-bit floating point (1 sign, 8 exponent, 23 mantissa)	Training, high-precision inference
BF16	2	16-bit bfloat (1 sign, 8 exponent, 7 mantissa)	Training (preferred), inference
FP16	2	16-bit float (1 sign, 5 exponent, 10 mantissa)	Inference
FP8 E4M3	1	8-bit float (1 sign, 4 exponent, 3 mantissa)	Inference (activations, weights)
FP8 E5M2	1	8-bit float (1 sign, 5 exponent, 2 mantissa)	Training (gradient storage)
MXFP8	~1	E4M3 + 32-value block scale	Blackwell training
NVFP4	~0.5	E2M1 + 16-value block scale	Blackwell inference
Int8	1	8-bit integer	Quantized inference
Int4	0.5	4-bit integer	Quantized inference (extreme compression)

Note that FP8 has two formats: E4M3 (higher precision, used for inference activations and weights) and E5M2 (wider dynamic range, used for storage). Both use 1 byte per parameter but serve different purposes. On NVIDIA Blackwell, **MXFP8** refines Hopper-style per-tensor FP8 with finer block scaling; **NVFP4** pushes below 8-bit for inference (and some training stacks).

Both use microscaling—effective memory is slightly above the nominal bits per value. See *Chapter 2* for hardware context and *Chapter 5* for FP8 training.

For training, BF16 (bfloat16) is preferred over FP16 (float16). BF16 has the same exponent range as FP32 (8 bits) but reduced mantissa (7 bits), giving it the same dynamic range as FP32. This makes training more stable—less likely to overflow or underflow. FP16 has a smaller exponent range (5 bits), which can cause numerical issues during training. Modern GPUs (A100, H100) have Tensor Cores optimized for BF16. For inference, both FP16 and BF16 work, but BF16 is still preferred for consistency with training.

But model weights are just the start. During training, you also need space for gradients, optimizer states, and activations. For inference, you need KV cache for attention mechanisms. The KV cache is crucial for LLM inference—it stores the key-value pairs from previous tokens in the sequence, allowing the model to avoid recomputing attention over the entire sequence for each new token. This dramatically speeds up autoregressive generation, but it requires significant memory that scales with batch size and sequence length. The total memory requirement can be several times larger than just the model weights.

Training memory requirements

Training needs way more memory than inference. You need to store model weights, gradients (one per parameter), optimizer states, and activations from the forward pass.

Optimizer State

The optimizer state size depends on which optimizer you use. Take Stochastic Gradient Descent (SGD) as an example: the model weights are updated according to this formula:

$$w_{t+1} = \boxed{w_t} - \eta \boxed{g_t}$$

where:

- w_t: model parameters at iteration t
- w_{t+1}: updated parameters
- g_t: gradient of loss w.r.t. parameters at iteration t ($g_t = \nabla_w L(w_t)$)
- η: learning rate (used for both SGD and Adaptive Moment Estimation (Adam))

The boxed variables are what we need to keep in memory. SGD only needs the learning rate η (a scalar) to update parameters. Looking at the formula, you compute g_t during backprop, then subtract η g_t from w_t. The optimizer state is justη —negligible memory. You need to store w_t (model weights) and g_t (gradients), but no additional optimizer tensors.

Adaptive Moment Estimation (Adam)'s formula is more complex:

$$w_{t+1} = w_t - \eta \frac{\beta_1 m_{t-1} + (1-\beta_1) g_t}{\sqrt{\beta_2 v_{t-1} + (1-\beta_2) {g_t}^2} + \epsilon} \cdot \frac{\sqrt{1-\beta_2^t}}{1-\beta_1^t}$$

Variable definitions are as follows:

- β_1: decay rate for the first moment (mean)
- β_2: decay rate for the second moment (uncentered variance)
- m_{t-1}: first-moment estimate from the previous step
- v_{t-1}: second-moment estimate from the previous step
- ϵ : small constant for numerical stability
- t: iteration index used for bias correction

Adam needs more. The formula shows it maintains two per-parameter tensors: m_{t-1} (first-moment estimate) and v_{t-1} (second-moment estimate). Both m_{t-1} and v_{t-1} have the same shape as w_t—one value per parameter. So Adam stores m_{t-1} (1× model size) and v_{t-1} (1× model size), totaling 2× model size for optimizer states.

β_1 and β_2 are hyperparameters - scalar constants (typically β_1=0.9, β_2=0.999). You store them once as configuration, not per parameter. Same with η (learning rate) and ϵ - they're scalars, negligible memory. Only tensors with the same shape as w_t (one value per parameter) need significant memory: w_t, g_t, m_{t-1}, and v_{t-1}.

That's why Adam needs 2× the model size for optimizer states compared to SGD's near-zero overhead. AdamW (Adam with decoupled weight decay) has the same memory requirements as Adam—both maintain m_{t-1} and v_{t-1}, totaling 2× model size. The only difference is how weight decay is applied (AdamW applies it directly to parameters, while Adam adds it to gradients).

Here's a summary of optimizer state memory requirements for common optimizers:

Optimizer	Optimizer States	Memory
SGD	Learning rate η (scalar)	~0×
SGD+Momentum	v_{t-1} (velocity/momentum)	1×
Nesterov	v_{t-1} (velocity/momentum)	1×

Optimizer	Optimizer States	Memory
Adagrad	Accumulated gradient squares	1×
RMSProp	v_{t-1} (second moment)	1×
Adam	m_{t-1} (first moment) + v_{t-1} (second moment)	2×
AdamW	m_{t-1} (first moment) + v_{t-1} (second moment)	2×
Adafactor	Row and column statistics (factorized)	~0.5×
LAMB	m_{t-1} (first moment) + v_{t-1} (second moment)	2×
Lion	m_{t-1} (first moment only)	1×
Nadam	m_{t-1} (first moment) + v_{t-1} (second moment)	2×
AMSGrad	m_{t-1} (first moment) + v_{t-1} (second moment) + v_{max}	3×
SparseAdam	m_{t-1} (first moment) + v_{t-1} (second moment, sparse)	2×
Shampoo	Left and right preconditioner matrices per parameter	>2× (varies)
AdaBelief	m_{t-1} (first moment) + s_{t-1} (belief term)	2×

The table shows optimizer states only. You still need to store model weights (1×) and gradients (1×) regardless of which optimizer you use.

Activation Output

Activation layers (like ReLU, GELU, sigmoid) don't have parameters—they're just functions applied element-wise. But their outputs (activation outputs, often shortened to "activations") need to be stored in memory during training.

Consider a simple 3-layer DNN `SimpleDNN` as below:

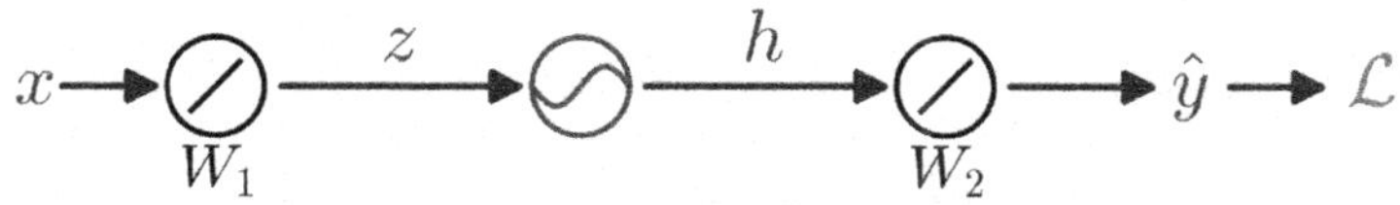

Figure 1.3: SimpleDNN

The data flow is $x \to z \to h \to \hat{y}$ with Linear $\longrightarrow$ Sigmoid $\longrightarrow$ Linear layers, where input x passes through the first linear layer to produce z, then through the sigmoid activation to produce h, and finally through the second linear layer to produce the prediction ŷ. The code in PyTorch would be as follows:

```
class SimpleDNN(nn.Module):
    def __init__(self, input_dim, output_dim, hidden_dim=1, bias=False):
        super(SimpleDNN, self).__init__()
        self.linear1 = nn.Linear(input_dim, hidden_dim, bias=bias)  # x -> z
        self.activation = nn.Sigmoid()                              # z -> h
        self.linear2 = nn.Linear(hidden_dim, output_dim, bias=bias) # h -> y_hat

    def forward(self, x):
        z = self.linear1(x)      # z = W_1 * x
        h = self.activation(z)   # h = sigmoid(z)
        y_hat = self.linear2(h)  # y_hat = W_2 * h
        return y_hat
```

The forward pass is:

$$z = W_1 x, h = \sigma(z), \hat{y} = W_2 h, L = \frac{1}{2}(y - \hat{y})^2$$

To compute gradients using backpropagation, we apply the chain rule.

For $\frac{\partial L}{\partial W_2}$:

$$\frac{\partial L}{\partial W_2} = \frac{\partial L}{\partial \hat{y}} \cdot \frac{\partial \hat{y}}{\partial W_2} = (\hat{y} - y) \cdot h$$

The gradient depends on h—the activation output from the sigmoid layer. You need h stored in memory to compute this gradient.

For $\frac{\partial L}{\partial W_1}$, the chain is longer:

$$\frac{\partial L}{\partial W_1} = \frac{\partial L}{\partial \hat{y}} \cdot \frac{\partial \hat{y}}{\partial h} \cdot \frac{\partial h}{\partial z} \cdot \frac{\partial z}{\partial W_1}$$

Expanding each term: $\frac{\partial L}{\partial \hat{y}} = \hat{y} - y$ (needs ŷ), $\frac{\partial \hat{y}}{\partial h} = W_2$ (needs W_2), $\frac{\partial h}{\partial z} = \sigma'(z) = \sigma(z)(1 - \sigma(z)) = h(1 - h)$ (needs h), and $\frac{\partial z}{\partial W_1} = x$ (needs input x).

So:

$$\frac{\partial L}{\partial W_1} = (\hat{y} - y) \cdot W_2 \cdot h(1 - h) \cdot x$$

This gradient requires both h (the activation output from the sigmoid layer) and x (the input data). That's why activation outputs and input data must be kept in memory during the forward pass until their gradients are computed during backpropagation.

An interesting observation is that z is not needed. Looking at the gradient computation, we need $\frac{\partial h}{\partial z} = \sigma'(z)$ to compute $\frac{\partial L}{\partial W_1}$. For sigmoid, the derivative is $\sigma'(z) = \sigma(z)(1-\sigma(z)) = h(1-h)$. Since we already have h stored from the forward pass, we can compute the derivative directly from h without needing the original z value. This is a property of sigmoid and some other activation functions—their derivatives can be expressed in terms of their outputs, so you don't need to store the pre-activation values.

However, this isn't true for all activation functions. Some activation functions have derivatives that explicitly depend on the input value z, not just the output h. This means you cannot compute the derivative from h alone—you need to store the original z value.

To understand which activation functions require storing the pre-activation value z versus those that can compute derivatives from the post-activation value h alone, let's examine the derivatives of common activation functions:

Activation	Formula	Derivative
Sigmoid	$\sigma(z) = \frac{1}{1+e^{-z}}$	$\sigma'(z) = \sigma(z)(1-\sigma(z))$
Tanh	$\tanh(z) = \frac{e^z - e^{-z}}{e^z + e^{-z}} = 2\sigma(2 \cdot z) - 1$	$\tanh'(z) = 1 - \tanh^2(z) = \text{sech}^2(z)$
ReLU	$\text{ReLU}(z) = \max(0, z)$	$\text{ReLU}'(z) = 1 \text{ if } z > 0,\ 0 \text{ if } z \le 0$
Leaky ReLU	$\text{LeakyReLU}(z) = \max(\alpha z, z)$	$\text{LeakyReLU}'(z) = 1 \text{ if } z > 0,\ \alpha \text{ if } z \le 0$
ELU	$\text{ELU}(z) = \begin{cases} z & \text{if } z > 0 \\ \alpha(e^z - 1) & \text{if } z \le 0 \end{cases}$	$\text{ELU}'(z) = \begin{cases} 1 & \text{if } z > 0 \\ \alpha e^z & \text{if } z \le 0 \end{cases}$
GELU	$\text{GELU}(z) = z \cdot \Phi(z)$	$\text{GELU}'(z) = \Phi(z) + z \cdot \phi(z)$
Swish	$\text{Swish}(z) = z \cdot \sigma(z)$	$\text{Swish}'(z) = \sigma(z) + z \cdot \sigma(z)(1-\sigma(z))$
Mish	$\text{Mish}(z) = z \cdot \tanh(\text{Softplus}(z)) = z \cdot \tanh(\ln(1+e^z))$	$\text{Mish}'(z) = \frac{e^z(4(z+1) + 4e^{2z} + e^{3z} + e^z(4z+6))}{(1+e^z)^2(1+e^{2z})}$
GEGLU	$\text{GEGLU}(z) = z \odot \text{GELU}(z)$	$\text{GEGLU}'(z) = \text{GELU}(z) + z \cdot \text{GELU}'(z) = \text{GELU}(z) + z(\Phi(z) + z \cdot \phi(z))$
ReGLU	$\text{ReGLU}(z) = z \odot \text{ReLU}(z)$	$\text{ReGLU}'(z) = \begin{cases} 2z & \text{if } z > 0 \\ 0 & \text{if } z \le 0 \end{cases}$
SwiGLU	$\text{SwiGLU}(z) = z \odot \text{Swish}(z) = z^2 \cdot \sigma(z)$	$\text{SwiGLU}'(z) = 2z \cdot \sigma(z) + z^2 \cdot \sigma(z)(1-\sigma(z))$
Softplus	$\text{Softplus}(z) = \ln(1 + e^z)$	$\text{Softplus}'(z) = \sigma(z) = \frac{1}{1+e^{-z}}$
Softmax	$\text{Softmax}(\mathbf{z})_i = \frac{e^{z_i}}{\sum_{j=1}^{n} e^{z_j}}$	$\nabla_z \text{Softmax}(\mathbf{z})_{ij} = \begin{cases} \text{Softmax}(\mathbf{z})_i(1 - \text{Softmax}(\mathbf{z})_i) & \text{if } i = j \\ -\text{Softmax}(\mathbf{z})_i \cdot \text{Softmax}(\mathbf{z})_j & \text{if } i \ne j \end{cases}$

Note

Activation table conventions

All activations above are element-wise (each output depends only on its corresponding input), except Softmax which is vector-valued (takes a vector input and produces a probability distribution that sums to 1). The derivative of Softmax is a Jacobian matrix, denoted by ∇_z. The parameter α in Leaky ReLU and ELU is a constant hyperparameter (typically $\alpha = 0.01$ for Leaky ReLU and $\alpha = 1.0$ for ELU). The GLU (Gated Linear Unit) family (GEGLU, ReGLU, SwiGLU) are gated activations that use element-wise multiplication $\odot$) to combine two branches: one branch passes through unchanged (z) and the other branch applies an activation function. In practice, GLU variants are often implemented with separate linear projections for the two branches, but the simplified form shown here uses the same input z for both branches.

Looking at the derivatives, we can categorize activation functions based on whether their derivatives can be expressed purely in terms of the output h:

- **Derivatives expressible in terms of output only**: Sigmoid, Tanh, and Softplus fall into this category. As we saw with sigmoid, $\sigma'(z) = h(1-h)$ depends only on h. Similarly, $\tanh'(z) = 1 - h^2$ and $\text{Softplus}'(z) = \sigma(z)$ can be computed from the output. For these functions, you only need to store h during the forward pass.
- **Derivatives requiring the input** z: ReLU, Leaky ReLU, ELU, GELU, Swish, Mish, and the GLU family (GEGLU, ReGLU, SwiGLU) require storing z because their derivatives explicitly contain z or depend on the sign of z. For ReLU, you need to know whether $z > 0$ or $z \leq 0$ to compute the derivative. For GELU, Swish, Mish, and GLU variants, the derivative formulas contain z explicitly, making it impossible to recover z from h alone.

Let's examine GELU and Swish in detail to illustrate why they require storing z. For GELU (Gaussian Error Linear Unit), the exact form uses the cumulative distribution function:

$$h = z \cdot \phi(z)$$

where Φ is the cumulative distribution function of the standard normal distribution. The derivative is:

$$\frac{\partial h}{\partial z} = \Phi(z) + z \cdot \phi(z)$$

where ϕ is the probability density function (PDF) of the standard normal. This derivative explicitly contains z in the term $z \cdot \phi(z)$.

In practice, GELU is often approximated using tanh for computational efficiency.

$$h = 0.5 \cdot z \cdot (1 + tanh(\sqrt{\frac{2}{\pi}} \cdot (z + c \cdot z^3)))$$

where $c \approx 0.044715$ is a constant. The derivative of this approximation is:

$$\frac{\partial h}{\partial z} = 0.5 \cdot \left(1 + \tanh\left(\sqrt{\frac{2}{\pi}} \cdot (z + c \cdot z^3)\right)\right)$$

$$+0.5 \cdot z \cdot \left(1 - \tanh^2\left(\sqrt{\frac{2}{\pi}} \cdot (z + c \cdot z^3)\right)\right) \cdot \sqrt{\frac{2}{\pi}} \cdot (1 + 3c \cdot z^2)$$

Even with the tanh approximation, the derivative still explicitly contains z in multiple terms, including z itself and z^2 and z^3 inside the tanh arguments. Since tanh is not easily invertible and the expression involves z in multiple places, you cannot recover z from h alone. Therefore, you need to store the original z value to compute the derivative during backpropagation, regardless of whether you use the exact GELU form or the tanh approximation.

Similarly, Swish (also known as SiLU, Sigmoid Linear Unit) has:

$$h = z \cdot \sigma(z)$$

with derivative:

$$\frac{\partial h}{\partial z} = \sigma(z) + z \cdot \sigma(z)(1 - \sigma(z))$$

Again, the derivative contains z explicitly, and you cannot express it purely in terms of h. To compute $\frac{\partial h}{\partial z}$, you need both z and $\sigma(z)$, which means storing the original z value.

In practice, frameworks like PyTorch store whatever intermediate values are needed to compute gradients during backpropagation. For activation functions whose derivatives can be expressed in terms of their outputs (like sigmoid), the framework may only store the post-activation values. For functions whose derivatives require the input (like GELU or Swish), the framework stores the pre-activation values. The autograd system automatically determines what needs to be saved based on the operations in the computation graph, ensuring gradients can be computed correctly while minimizing memory usage where possible.

During the forward pass, you compute and store all layer activation outputs (we call these "activations" for short). During backpropagation, you compute gradients layer by layer from the last layer backward. For each layer, you need its activation outputs to compute gradients. Once you've computed a layer's gradient and updated its parameters, you can free that layer's activation outputs—they're no longer needed. However, during the backward pass, there's overlap: while computing gradients for one layer, you still have activation outputs from earlier layers in memory. The peak memory occurs when you have both activations (from forward pass) and gradients (from backward pass) simultaneously.

The activation memory scales with batch size and sequence length—larger batches or longer sequences mean more activation outputs to store. Techniques like gradient checkpointing trade compute for memory by recomputing activations instead of storing them all.

Training Stage

During training, memory usage varies across different stages of the training loop. Understanding when each component is needed helps you estimate peak memory requirements and identify optimization opportunities.

```
for epoch in range(num_epochs):
    model.train()                           # set to training mode
    for x_batch, y_batch in dataloader:     # iterate over batches
        optimizer.zero_grad()               # 1. clear gradients
        y_hat = model(x_batch)              # 2. forward pass
        loss = criterion(y_hat, y_batch)    # 3. compute loss
        loss.backward()                     # 4. backward pass
        optimizer.step()                    # 5. update parameters
```

Let's break down what happens in each step and what's stored in memory:

Step 2 (Forward pass): The model computes predictions `y_hat` from inputs `x_batch`. During this process, it stores intermediate activations (like h in our earlier example) that will be needed for backpropagation. At this point, memory contains: model weights w_t, activations, and optimizer states (like m_{t-1} and v_{t-1} for Adam) from previous iterations.

Step 4 (Backward pass): `loss.backward()` computes gradients $g_t = \nabla_w L(w_t)$ for all parameters. This requires the activations stored during the forward pass. Memory now contains: w_t, activations (still needed), gradients g_t, and optimizer states.

Step 5 (Optimizer step): `optimizer.step()` updates parameters from w_t to w_{t+1} using the gradients g_t and the optimizer's internal state. For Adam, this means using m_{t-1} and v_{t-1} along with g_t to compute the update. After this step, the optimizer states are updated (e.g., m_{t-1} becomes m_t, v_{t-1} becomes v_t) and stored for the next iteration. Activations can now be freed since they're no longer needed.

Activations, gradients, and optimizer states don't all exist in memory at the same time. During the forward pass, only activations are actively used—gradients don't exist yet, and optimizer states persist from previous iterations but aren't accessed. During the backward pass, activations, and gradients overlap because you need activations to compute gradients. During the optimizer step, gradients, and optimizer states overlap as the optimizer uses both to update parameters. Activations are typically freed after the backward pass completes, so they don't overlap with optimizer states.

The peak memory usage occurs during the backward pass when both activations and gradients are in memory simultaneously. After the backward pass, activations can be freed, so the optimizer step only needs gradients and optimizer states.

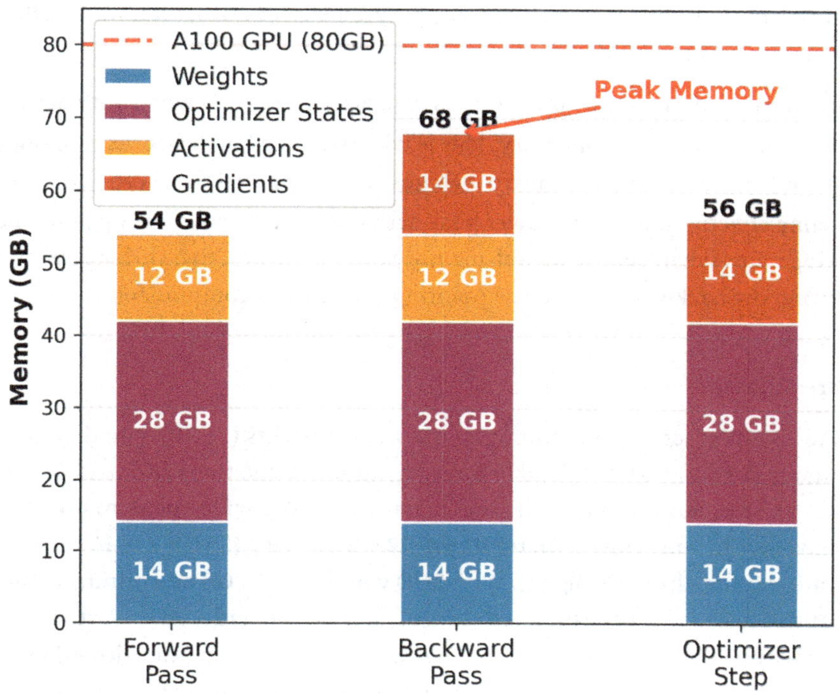

Figure 1.4: Training Memory Timeline

As illustrated in *Figure 1.4*, the timeline shows memory usage across the training loop for a 7B model with Adam, assuming **BF16 throughout**—weights, gradients, and optimizer states (m, v) all stored at 2 bytes per parameter. This is a clean teaching example. Many production setups use **mixed precision** differently: forward and backward in BF16 (via `torch.autocast`), but optimizer states—and sometimes a master copy of weights—in FP32, which pushes optimizer memory toward 56 GB (4 bytes × 2 states × 7B parameters) rather than 28 GB.

Here's how each stage maps to the code. On line 2 (`y_hat = model(x_batch)`), the forward pass computes and stores activations. Memory usage is weights (14 GB) plus optimizer states (28 GB) plus activations (12 GB), totaling 54 GB. Gradients don't exist yet.

On line 4 (`loss.backward()`), the backward pass is where peak memory occurs. During backpropagation, you need both activations to compute gradients and the gradients being computed. Memory usage is weights (14 GB) plus optimizer states (28 GB) plus activations (12 GB) plus gradients (14 GB), totaling 68 GB. This is the peak because activations and gradients overlap in memory.

On line 5 (`optimizer.step()`), after the backward pass completes, activations can be freed. The optimizer uses gradients and its internal states to update parameters. Memory usage is weights (14 GB) plus optimizer states (28 GB) plus gradients (14 GB), totaling 56 GB. Activations are no longer needed.

The peak memory of 68 GB occurs during `loss.backward()` (line 4) when both activations and gradients are simultaneously in memory. This is why reducing batch size, using **gradient accumulation** (run several smaller micro-batches and call `optimizer.step()` only after the last one—same effective batch size, lower peak activation memory), or using gradient checkpointing helps when you hit out-of-memory errors: the first two shrink activation memory during the backward pass; checkpointing trades extra compute for less activation storage.

Memory breakdown:

For the same 7B Adam setup (BF16 throughout): model weights (14 GB) + gradients (14 GB) + optimizer states (28 GB) = **56 GB fixed** before activations. Activations add 8–16 GB depending on batch size and sequence length—the timeline uses 12 GB, giving a **peak of 68 GB** (56 + 12) during backward. The full range is therefore **64–72 GB** per GPU (56 GB + 8–16 GB activations), not a separate estimate from the figure. With SGD you'd save 28 GB on optimizer states, but Adam's adaptive learning rates usually converge faster, so the trade-off is worth it in most cases. That's why a 7B model needs at least an A100 (80 GB) for training with Adam under this footprint; FP32 optimizer states or master weights push requirements higher. Smaller GPUs won't cut it without sharding (FSDP, DeepSpeed) or other techniques covered later in the book.

Inference memory requirements

Inference memory requirements differ from training in that they primarily consist of model weights and the key-value (KV) cache used for attention computation. The KV cache stores precomputed key-value pairs from previous tokens in the sequence, enabling efficient autoregressive generation by avoiding redundant attention computations over the entire sequence history. While this optimization significantly accelerates inference, the KV cache introduces a memory overhead that scales linearly with batch size, sequence length, and model depth—*Chapter 6* covers sizing it in detail.

The memory footprint of inference scales with three primary factors: model size, batch size, and sequence length. For a 70B parameter model using BF16 precision, the model weights consume approximately 140 GB. With a batch size of 32 and sequence length of 2048, the KV cache adds an additional 20-40 GB, resulting in a total memory requirement of 160-180 GB. This exceeds the capacity of a single A100 GPU (80 GB), necessitating multi-GPU configurations or model parallelism strategies for inference workloads.

The memory requirements become substantially more demanding for models with ultra-long context windows. The `meta-llama/Llama-4-Scout-17B-16E-Instruct` model, for instance, supports a 10 million token context window. Despite being a 17B parameter Mixture of Experts (MoE) model with 16 experts—where only a subset of experts are activated per token—the KV cache alone can exceed 1 TB of memory for a single sequence at full context length[5]. This scale of memory requirement renders single-node inference architectures infeasible, making distributed inference systems with dozens of GPUs not merely beneficial but fundamentally necessary. The computational and memory demands of ultra-long context models establish distributed systems as the only viable deployment architecture.

GPU requirements estimation

Estimating GPU requirements requires accounting for both model memory and operational overhead. For training workloads, the calculation begins with the model's memory footprint, to which a 10-20% safety margin must be added to accommodate communication buffers and framework overhead. Consider a 13B parameter model using BF16 precision: the base memory requirement is approximately 72 GB per GPU. With the safety margin applied, this increases to 85 GB. Since an A100 GPU provides 80 GB of memory, this configuration necessitates 2 GPUs using model parallelism or Fully Sharded Data Parallel (FSDP) strategies.

Inference requirements follow a similar calculation methodology, combining model weights with KV cache memory. A 70B parameter model in BF16 requires 140 GB for weights alone. When accounting for KV cache overhead, the total memory requirement reaches 160-180 GB. This necessitates a minimum of 2 A100 GPUs, or alternatively, Int8 quantization can reduce weight memory to approximately 70 GB, potentially enabling single-GPU deployment with careful KV cache management.

Real-World considerations

Practical deployment introduces additional memory overhead beyond the base model requirements. The PyTorch framework typically consumes 1-2 GB, while the operating system requires 5-10 GB. Distributed training architectures allocate an additional 2-5 GB per GPU for communication buffers. Checkpointing operations create temporary memory spikes that must be accounted for in capacity planning. A conservative approach adds a 20-30% buffer to base estimates to accommodate these overheads and operational variations.

Memory optimization strategies play a critical role in practical deployments. Mixed precision training using BF16 (or FP16/BF16 for inference) reduces memory consumption by approximately 50% compared to FP32, with minimal impact on model accuracy. For inference workloads, Int8 quantization can further halve memory requirements while maintaining acceptable accuracy degradation. Monitoring actual memory usage through tools such as `nvidia-smi` provides empirical validation of theoretical estimates. It is important to recognize that activation memory scales linearly with batch size; when encountering out-of-memory (OOM) errors, reducing batch size represents the most immediate mitigation strategy.

Quick Reference Table[6]:

Model Size	FP32 Weights	BF16 Weights	Training (BF16+Adam)	Inference (BF16)
1B	4 GB	2 GB	~8 GB	2–4 GB
7B	28 GB	14 GB	~60–70 GB	14–20 GB
13B	52 GB	26 GB	~110–130 GB	26–35 GB
70B	280 GB	140 GB	~600–700 GB	140–180 GB

The evolution from classic ML to foundation models

The progression from classic machine learning to modern foundation models represents a fundamental shift in computational requirements and architectural paradigms. Classic machine learning models were designed to operate on single machines, with traditional algorithms—including linear regression, logistic regression, decision trees, random forests, support vector machines (SVM), and gradient boosting methods (XGBoost, LightGBM)—typically comprising thousands to millions of parameters and training on datasets that fit entirely in system memory.

The deep learning era introduced models with hundreds of millions of parameters, exemplified by architectures such as ResNet and BERT. While these models necessitated GPU acceleration, they remained manageable on single-device configurations. The contemporary foundation model era has fundamentally altered this landscape: models now span billions to trillions of parameters (e.g., GPT-4, Gemini, LLaMA), requiring distributed systems as an architectural prerequisite rather than an optimization.

This transition to distributed AI has enabled breakthrough capabilities, including models capable of understanding and generating human-like text, code, and multimodal content. The shift has also catalyzed enterprise adoption, with organizations deploying AI systems at scale for production workloads. Furthermore, distributed architectures have accelerated research progress through faster iteration cycles enabled by parallel experimentation across multiple compute nodes.

The modern AI model lifecycle

Building AI models isn't a one-shot process. It's a cycle: you collect data, train a model, deploy it, see how it performs, then go back and improve the data or model. Each stage feeds into the next.

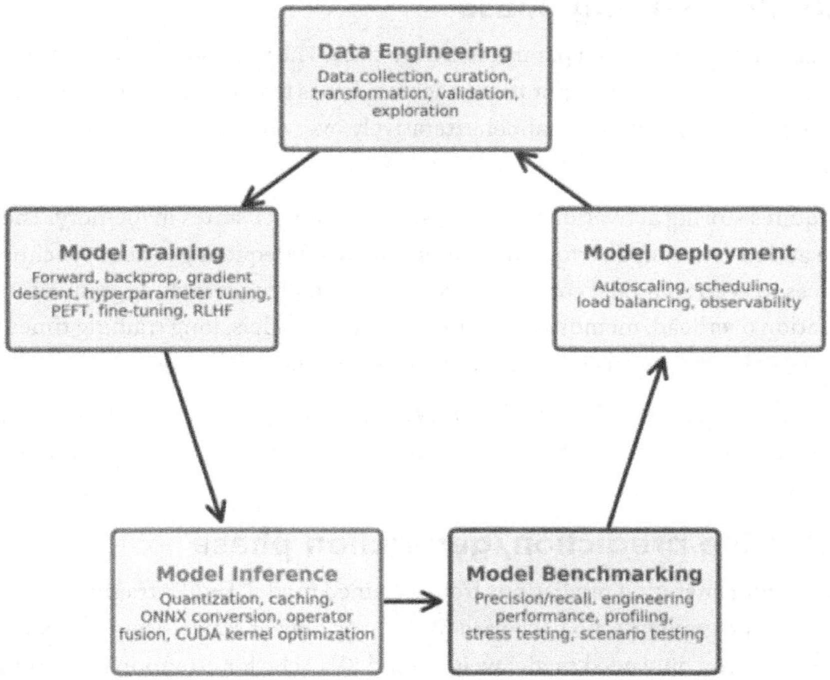

Figure 1.5: Modern AI Model Lifecycle

As shown in *Figure 1.5*, the lifecycle begins with data engineering, where terabytes of data are collected, curated, transformed, validated, cleaned, and prepared for training. Training follows, involving forward passes, backpropagation, gradient descent, hyperparameter tuning, and even fine-tuning. Once trained, models undergo inference optimization through quantization, ONNX conversion, operator fusion, and CUDA kernel optimization. Before deployment, comprehensive benchmarking evaluates model performance through precision and recall metrics, engineering performance profiling, bottleneck analysis, and stress testing, with distributed evaluation accelerating testing on large datasets. Production deployment requires autoscaling, scheduling, load balancing, observability, API gateways, and monitoring infrastructure to handle thousands of requests per second. Production feedback identifies data collection priorities and model failure modes, completing the cycle by informing subsequent data engineering efforts and model improvements.

This book focuses on the distributed technologies you need for training, inference, benchmarking, and deployment. Data engineering gets a brief overview but isn't the main focus. Distributed data processing is important, but it's a well-established topic. Spark, Dask, and Ray have been around for years. This book's main focus is on AI-specific distributed challenges: training large models, optimizing inference, and serving them at scale.

Training: the learning phase

Training is about learning model parameters from data. The process follows a pattern: forward pass through the model, loss computation, backward pass to compute gradients, and gradient update to adjust parameters. This happens iteratively over multiple epochs until the model converges.

Training requires storing activations, gradients, and optimizer states in memory. The compute is intensive and iterative. In distributed training, you need frequent gradient synchronization across devices to keep all model copies consistent. The challenges include gradient synchronization overhead, memory constraints for large models, long training times that can span days to weeks, and the need for fault tolerance and checkpointing.

Training a 7B parameter model on 1 trillion tokens typically requires 8 A100 GPUs (80GB each) and about 2 weeks of continuous training. You need careful gradient synchronization to maintain training stability across all GPUs.

Inference: the prediction/generation phase

Inference is about generating predictions from a trained model. Unlike training, you only need a forward pass—no gradients, no backward pass, no optimizer states. Memory requirements are lower because you only need model weights and KV cache for attention mechanisms. The compute per request is lower, but you need high throughput to serve many requests at once. Communication is minimal, mostly only for distributed inference.

The challenges include latency (sub-second for interactive apps), throughput (thousands of requests per second), efficient memory usage through KV cache management, and effective batching and scheduling. Serving a 70B parameter model for chat requires optimized inference engines like vLLM or SGLang, continuous batching to maximize GPU utilization, and careful KV cache management for variable-length sequences.

Serving: the production system

Serving is about providing reliable, scalable access to models. It's not just running inference—it's building a production system with a model runner, API gateway, load balancer, and monitoring. The requirements include high availability, fault tolerance, and observability. At scale, you're dealing with multi-model, multi-tenant systems.

The challenges include system reliability and uptime, multi-model routing and load balancing, cost optimization through GPU utilization and autoscaling, and observability for debugging. A production LLM serving platform might include multiple model variants (different sizes, fine-tuned versions), A/B testing infrastructure, canary deployment pipelines, and distributed tracing and monitoring.

Here is a table of *Training vs Inference vs Serving*:

Aspect	Training	Inference	Serving
Goal	Learn parameters	Generate predictions	Provide access
Memory	High (activations + gradients)	Medium (weights + KV cache)	Variable
Computation	Iterative, intensive	Single forward pass	Request-driven
Communication	Frequent (gradients)	Medium	API-level
Latency	Hours to days	Milliseconds to seconds	Milliseconds
Throughput	Samples per second	Tokens per second	Requests per second

Decision framework: when do you need distributed systems?

Distributed systems add complexity, communication overhead, and cost. Use them when you have to, not when you want to.

Decision tree: quick reference

As shown in *Figure 1.6*, the decision framework is summarized in the decision tree below. Start by identifying your use case: training (or fine-tuning) versus inference and serving.

Understanding the decision tree

When training or fine-tuning, start by checking whether your model fits in memory. Calculate model size in BF16 (parameters × 2 bytes). If it exceeds single GPU capacity, you'll need model or parameter parallelism like FSDP or tensor parallelism. A 13B model needs 26GB for weights alone. Add Adam optimizer states and you're looking at 78GB total, which is cutting it close to an 80GB A100.

If the model fits but training drags on for weeks or months, data parallelism can speed things up. Training a 7B model on 1T tokens takes about two weeks on 8 GPUs, compared to months on a single GPU.

When both model size and training time are manageable, your fine-tuning approach matters. Parameter-efficient methods like LoRA and QLoRA change the equation. QLoRA on a 70B model fits in a 48GB GPU because it only trains adapter weights, while full fine-tuning of the same model needs multiple GPUs. But if the base model doesn't fit, you still need model parallelism regardless of which training method you choose.

Large datasets where data loading becomes the bottleneck benefit from distributed data loading. Multi-terabyte datasets are good candidates for data parallelism.

For inference or serving, the logic is similar. If the model exceeds single GPU memory, use model parallelism. A 70B model in BF16 needs 140GB for weights. With KV cache, you're looking at 160-180GB, which requires at least 2 A100 GPUs. If memory is fine but you need high throughput—thousands of requests per second—use multiple GPUs for distributed inference. Real-time services that need sub-second latency at high throughput often require tensor parallelism or multiple inference instances. When both memory and throughput fit within single GPU limits, stick with one GPU and use optimized engines like vLLM or SGLang to maximize efficiency.

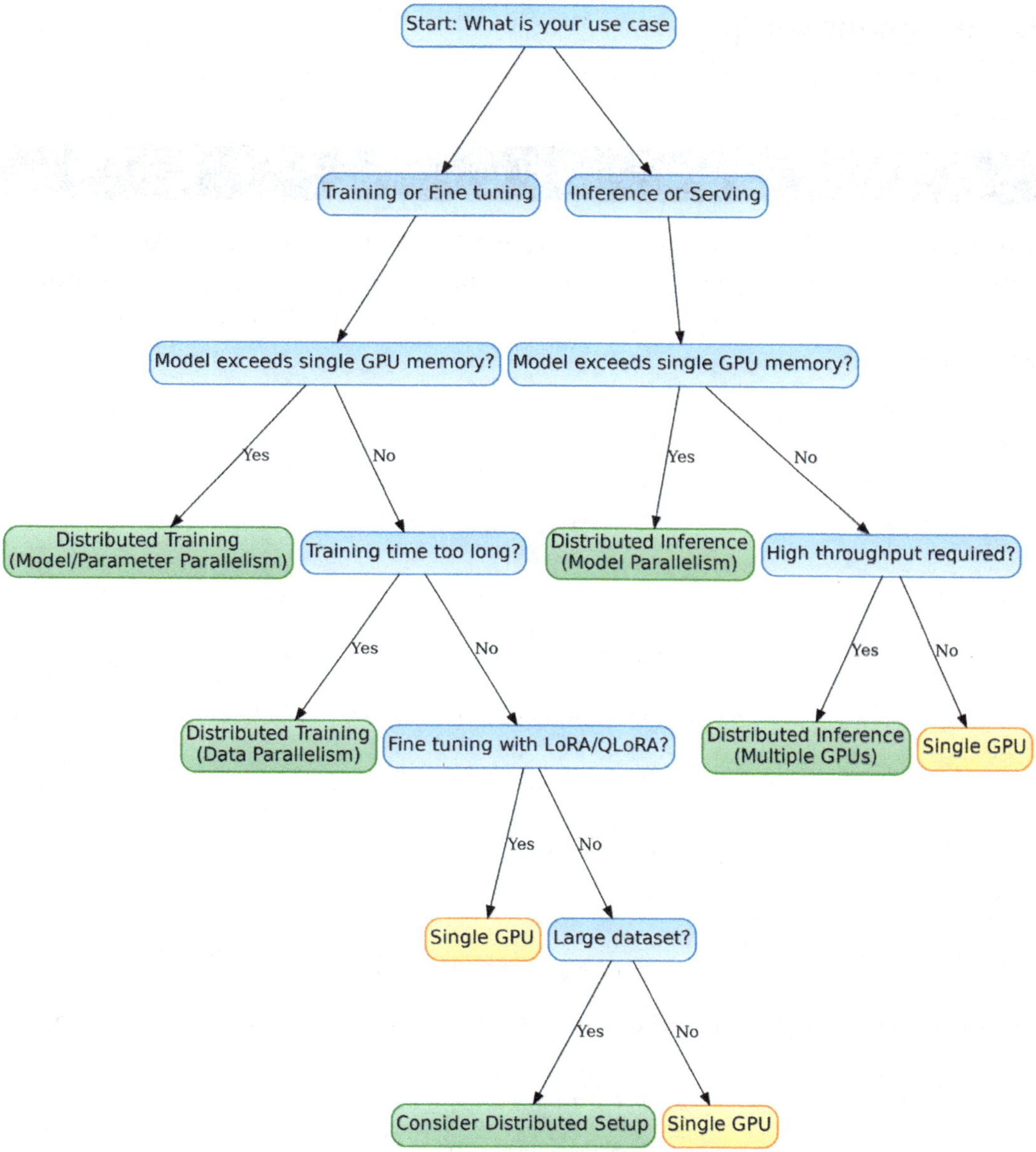

Figure 1.6: Decision Framework: When Do You Need Distributed Systems?

Hands-On: running distributed training

We'll begin with a simple baseline to establish a performance reference point, then move to distributed training to see the speedup in action.

Environment setup

In this book, we will use PyTorch as our main framework, and the code can be cloned from this book's git repo.

```
git clone https://github.com/PacktPublishing/Distributed-AI-Systems
```

To run the code, it is best if you have access to a multiple-GPU machine, such as A10, A100 or H100/200 or even B200. If you don't have access to multiple GPUs locally, Kaggle offers free multi-GPU environments. Log in to `https://www.kaggle.com`, click Create, and select Notebook.

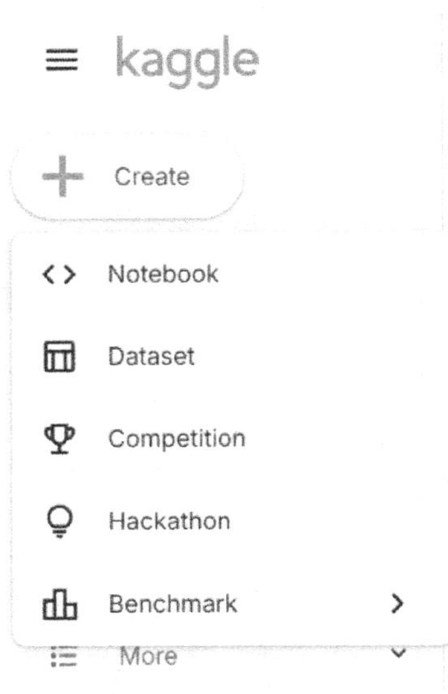

Figure 1.7: Kaggle Notebook Creation

Once you've created a Jupyter notebook, go to Settings → Accelerator and select GPU T4x2.

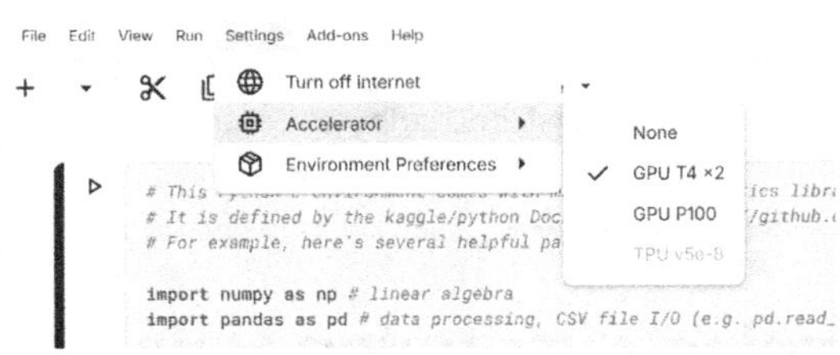

Figure 1.8: Kaggle GPU Settings

You should now have 2 T4 GPUs available. To verify your GPU setup, run the code in `code/check_cuda.py`:

```
1 |import torch
2 |print(f"CUDA available: {torch.cuda.is_available()}")
3 |print(f"Number of GPUs: {torch.cuda.device_count()}")
4 |for i in range(torch.cuda.device_count()):
5 |    props = torch.cuda.get_device_properties(i)
6 |    vram_gb = props.total_memory / (1024**3)
7 |    print(f"GPU {i}: {props.name} ({vram_gb:.1f} GB)")
```

Code explanation:

- 2: Checks if CUDA is available on the system
- 3: Gets the total number of GPUs
- 5: Retrieves properties for the current GPU
- 6: Converts memory from bytes to GB

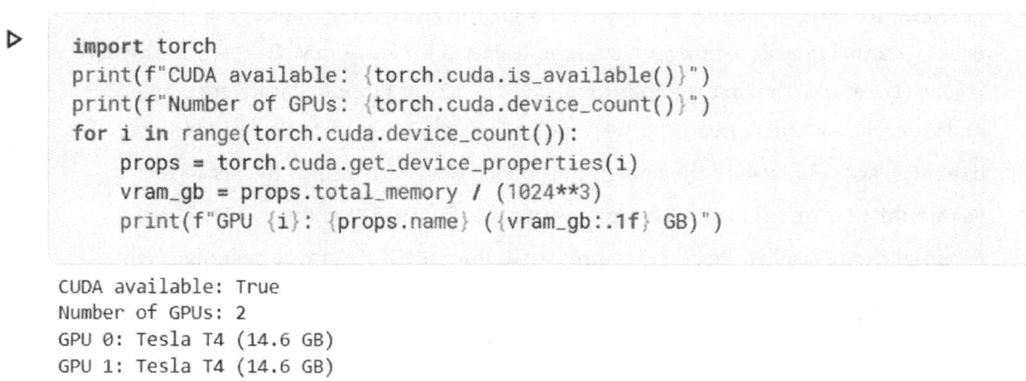

Figure 1.9: GPU setup - 2 Tesla T4 GPUs

As shown in *Figure 1.9*, running this should show your available GPUs.

Single-GPU baseline

We'll use ResNet18, a lightweight 18-layer convolutional neural network designed for image classification. It's small enough to train quickly while still demonstrating distributed training concepts effectively. For the dataset, we'll use FashionMNIST—70,000 grayscale images (28×28 pixels) across 10 clothing categories. It's a drop-in replacement for MNIST that's slightly more challenging, making it ideal for quick experiments.

Run the baseline training script:

```
python code/single_gpu_baseline.py
```

After 3 epochs, you should see output similar to this:

```
Epoch 1/3, Loss: 0.4164, Accuracy: 84.94%
Epoch 2/3, Loss: 0.2936, Accuracy: 89.17%
Epoch 3/3, Loss: 0.2531, Accuracy: 90.58%

Total training time: 8.78s
```

Your exact results will vary depending on your hardware, but the loss and accuracy values should be similar. This baseline gives us a reference point—we'll use the same model architecture in the distributed version for a fair comparison.

> Note
>
> **ResNet18** and **FashionMNIST**
>
> ResNet18 from torchvision is designed for 3-channel RGB images, but FashionMNIST uses 1-channel grayscale images. To adapt ResNet18 for FashionMNIST, we modify two layers: (1) Replace the first convolutional layer to accept 1 input channel instead of 3: `model.conv1 = nn.Conv2d(1, 64, kernel_size=7, stride=2, padding=3, bias=False)`. (2) Replace the final fully connected layer to output 10 classes for FashionMNIST: `model.fc = nn.Linear(model.fc.in_features, 10)`. These minimal changes allow ResNet18 to process FashionMNIST's grayscale images while preserving the rest of the architecture's proven design.

Multi-GPU distributed training

Now let's run the distributed version. The script uses the same ResNet18 model on FashionMNIST, but splits the work across multiple GPUs.

```
torchrun --nproc_per_node=2 code/multi_gpu_ddp.py
```

Or use the launch script:

```
bash code/launch_torchrun.sh
```

With 2 GPUs, you'll see similar loss and accuracy values, but the training completes in 5.91 seconds instead of 8.78 seconds—a **1.48× speedup**.

We tested scaling from 1 to 8 GPUs to see how performance improves:

GPUs	Training Time	Speedup
1	8.78s	1.00×
2	5.91s	1.48×
4	3.69s	2.38×
6	2.92s	3.01×
8	2.44s	3.60×

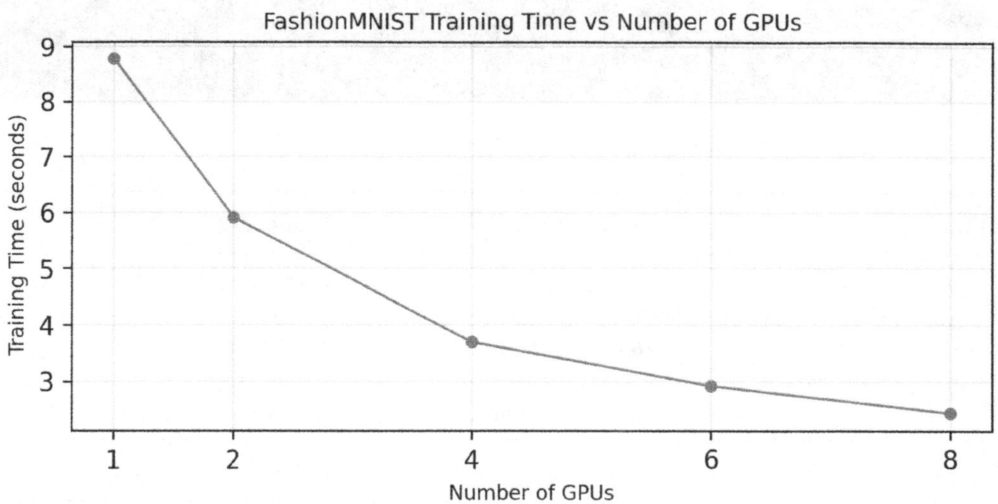

Figure 1.10: FashionMNIST Scaling Performance

Training time drops from 8.78 seconds to 2.44 seconds with 8 GPUs, achieving a **3.6× speedup**. Adding more GPUs significantly reduces training time and accelerates development cycles. The speedup becomes even more pronounced with larger workloads, as we'll see next.

Extended training: CIFAR-10 with 20 epochs

For a more realistic workload, we tested ResNet18 on CIFAR-10 with 20 epochs. CIFAR-10 is larger and more complex than FashionMNIST, with 50,000 training images using 3-channel RGB images of 32×32 pixels. This better showcases the benefits of distributed training.

Run the single-GPU baseline:

```
python code/single_gpu_extended.py --epochs 20
```

Then test distributed training:

```
torchrun --nproc_per_node=2 code/multi_gpu_ddp_extended.py --epochs 20
torchrun --nproc_per_node=4 code/multi_gpu_ddp_extended.py --epochs 20
torchrun --nproc_per_node=6 code/multi_gpu_ddp_extended.py --epochs 20
torchrun --nproc_per_node=8 code/multi_gpu_ddp_extended.py --epochs 20
```

The results show even better scaling:

GPUs	Training Time	Speedup
1	73.00s (1.22 min)	1.00×
2	46.47s (0.77 min)	1.57×
4	27.72s (0.46 min)	2.63×
6	21.24s (0.35 min)	3.44×
8	18.20s (0.30 min)	4.01×

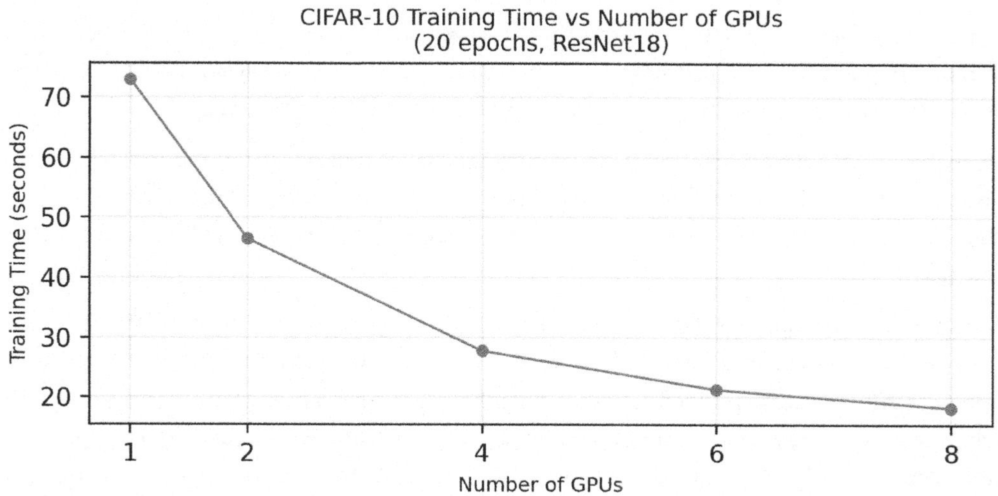

Figure 1.11: CIFAR-10 Scaling Performance

Training time drops from 73 seconds to 18.2 seconds with 8 GPUs, achieving a **4.01× speedup** —better than the FashionMNIST results. The larger computation workload per epoch means gradient synchronization takes a smaller fraction of total time. With 20 epochs, communication overhead is amortized across more training steps. Each GPU has enough computation work between communication steps to maximize parallel efficiency.

This demonstrates why distributed training is essential for large-scale model training. As computation per step increases, the relative cost of communication decreases, leading to better scaling efficiency. For models with billions of parameters, distributed training scales even more effectively, with speedups approaching linear scaling as computation dominates the training time. The DDP approach shown here uses data parallelism, where each GPU holds a complete copy of the model and processes different data. This is the simplest form of distributed training, suitable for models that fit on a single GPU. For larger models that exceed single-GPU memory, later chapters will explore advanced parallelism strategies such as tensor parallelism (splitting model layers across GPUs), pipeline parallelism (splitting model stages across GPUs), and hybrid approaches that combine multiple parallelism techniques.

Distributed inference: throughput scaling

While training focuses on reducing time-to-convergence, inference focuses on throughput—how many requests you can process per second. Distributed inference allows multiple GPUs to process different requests simultaneously, dramatically increasing throughput.

We benchmarked ResNet18 inference on FashionMNIST to measure throughput scaling. Unlike training, inference has no gradient synchronization overhead—each GPU simply processes its assigned requests independently. This makes distributed inference highly efficient for serving scenarios.

There are two common approaches to distributing inference requests. The data-split pattern (`multi_gpu_inference.py`) pre-divides requests among GPUs using `DistributedSampler`, where each GPU processes a fixed subset of data. This approach is simple and efficient for batch processing. The request-split pattern (`multi_gpu_inference_queue.py`) assigns requests dynamically in round-robin fashion, where each GPU processes requests as they are assigned, simulating a real queue system. This pattern is better for production serving where requests arrive asynchronously.

Run the benchmarks. Start with the single-GPU baseline:

```
python code/single_gpu_inference.py --requests 1000
```

Then test distributed inference with the data-split pattern:

```
torchrun --nproc_per_node=2 code/multi_gpu_inference.py --requests 1000
torchrun --nproc_per_node=4 code/multi_gpu_inference.py --requests 1000
torchrun --nproc_per_node=8 code/multi_gpu_inference.py --requests 1000
```

And the request-split pattern:

```
torchrun --nproc_per_node=2 code/multi_gpu_inference_queue.py \
  --requests 1000
```

Example results from benchmarking:

GPUs	Pattern	Time	Throughput	Speedup
1	Baseline	1.85s	541.00 req/s	1.00×
2	Data-split	0.98s	1025.45 req/s	1.89×
2	Request-split	1.22s	819.09 req/s	1.51×

With 2 GPUs using the data-split pattern, we achieve **1.89× speedup**, nearly doubling the throughput. The data-split pattern achieves near-linear scaling because each GPU processes independent requests with minimal coordination overhead. The request-split pattern shows slightly lower throughput (1.51×) due to the overhead of round-robin assignment and all GPUs needing to iterate through the dataset, but it's more flexible for dynamic request handling in production environments where requests arrive asynchronously.

Both patterns demonstrate the power of distributed inference: throughput scales almost linearly with the number of GPUs, making it ideal for production serving workloads that require high request rates. The inference patterns shown here use data parallelism, suitable for models that fit on a single GPU. For large language models that exceed single-GPU memory, later chapters will explore advanced techniques such as expert parallelism, sequence parallelism, tensor parallelism, and serving frameworks like vLLM and SGLang.

Distributed AI fundamentals with PyTorch

Now that you've seen distributed training and inference in action, let's understand the fundamental concepts and APIs that make them work.

The distributed AI stack

Distributed AI systems are built in layers, from high-level frameworks down to physical hardware. Understanding this stack helps you debug issues, optimize performance, and make informed decisions about which tools to use.

While the stack applies to all distributed frameworks (PyTorch, JAX, TensorFlow), this book uses PyTorch as the primary example. The concepts translate to other frameworks, but the APIs and implementation details differ. We'll focus on PyTorch's distributed APIs throughout.

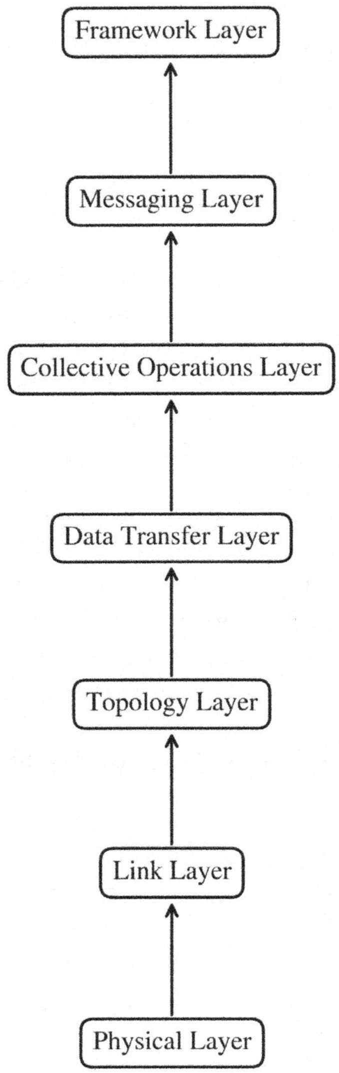

Figure 1.12: The Distributed AI Stack: From Framework to Physical Layer

At the top sits the framework layer. This is where you write your code—PyTorch's `torch.distributed` module, `DDP`, `FSDP`, and the rest. When you define a model and call `loss.backward()`, PyTorch handles the gradient computation and decides when communication needs to happen. You don't think about network packets or hardware links at this level. You just write training loops and let PyTorch orchestrate the distributed operations.

Below the framework, PyTorch organizes your tensors into buckets. Instead of sending each gradient tensor separately, DDP groups multiple tensors together. This reduces communication overhead. If you have thousands of small gradient tensors, sending them one by one would be inefficient. Bucketing batches them together, so you make fewer network calls. This happens automatically—you don't control it directly, but understanding it helps when you're debugging why communication takes longer than expected.

The collective operations layer defines what communication pattern to use. AllReduce sums gradients across all ranks and distributes the result back. AllGather collects data from all ranks. Broadcast sends data from one rank to all others. These are the primitives that higher-level APIs like DDP use. When DDP synchronizes gradients, it's calling AllReduce under the hood. This layer defines what needs to happen, not how it's implemented.

The data transfer layer is where the actual implementation lives. NCCL (NVIDIA Collective Communications Library) is the most common backend for GPU training. It implements AllReduce and other collectives in ways optimized for NVIDIA GPUs. GLOO is a CPU-based backend, useful for testing when you don't have GPUs. PyTorch defaults to NCCL for GPU backends and GLOO for CPU backends, which covers most use cases. MPI is another option, mainly for CPU clusters. When you initialize a process group with `backend="nccl"`, you're choosing which library will handle the actual data movement.

The network topology determines how devices are connected. In a ring topology, GPUs form a ring—each GPU sends data to the next one in the ring. This is simple but can create bottlenecks. Fat-Tree topologies provide multiple paths between devices, reducing congestion. Mesh and Torus topologies offer different trade-offs between complexity and bandwidth. The topology affects how NCCL routes data, which impacts both bandwidth and latency.

Physical links carry the data. NVLink connects GPUs within a single node at high bandwidth—roughly 600 GB/s–1.8 TB/s per GPU depending on generation (see *Chapter 2*). When you have multiple GPUs in one machine, they communicate over NVLink. InfiniBand with RDMA (Remote Direct Memory Access) enables direct memory access across nodes without involving the CPU. This is crucial for multi-node training. PCIe connects GPUs to CPUs, and Ethernet is slower but more common. The link layer determines the raw bandwidth available.

At the bottom sits the physical hardware—GPUs for parallel compute, TPUs for tensor operations (see *Chapter 2*), CPUs for coordination. This layer determines your raw compute capacity and memory limits. No amount of optimization in the layers above can overcome hardware limitations here.

When you call `dist.all_reduce()` in your code, the request flows down this entire stack. PyTorch organizes your tensors into buckets, calls the AllReduce collective operation, NCCL implements it using the network topology it discovers, data moves over NVLink links intra-node or InfiniBand links inter-node, and the results end up back in GPU memory. Understanding this flow helps when you're debugging why communication is slow or why a distributed job hangs. Is it a topology issue? A link bandwidth problem? Or something in the collective operation itself? Knowing the stack helps you narrow it down.

Now that we've seen how the layers fit together, let's look at the fundamental concepts you'll work with in PyTorch. The essential building blocks are process groups, ranks, and communication primitives. These form the foundation for all distributed operations, whether you're using DDP or FSDP for data-parallel training, implementing custom parallelism strategies, or building distributed inference systems.

Process Groups and Ranks

In distributed training, multiple processes work together. Each process runs on a different GPU or node. PyTorch organizes these processes into a process group. Within a process group, each process has a unique rank—an integer identifier starting from 0. The total number of processes is called the world size.

The term "world" refers to the entire distributed job—all processes participating in the training or inference task. The world size is the total number of processes across all nodes and GPUs. For example, if you're training on 2 nodes with 4 GPUs each, your world size is 8.

If you have 4 GPUs, you'll have 4 processes. Process 0 runs on GPU 0, process 1 on GPU 1, and so on. The rank tells each process which GPU it should use and which part of the data it should process.

There are two types of ranks: global rank and local rank. The global rank is unique across all processes in the entire distributed job (the world), ranging from 0 to world_size - 1. The local rank is unique only within a single node, starting from 0 on each node. For example, in a 2-node setup with 4 GPUs per node, node 0 has local ranks 0-3 (global ranks 0-3), and node 1 has local ranks 0-3 (global ranks 4-7). The local rank typically corresponds to the GPU index on that node, which is why you often see `torch.cuda.set_device(local_rank)` in distributed code.

Initializing the process group

Before any distributed operations, you need to initialize the process group. This tells PyTorch how processes should communicate. The most common backend for GPU training is NCCL (NVIDIA Collective Communications Library).

The basic initialization pattern looks like this:

```
import torch.distributed as dist

def setup(rank, world_size):
    dist.init_process_group(
        backend="nccl",  # Use NCCL for GPU communication
        rank=rank,       # This process's rank
        world_size=world_size  # Total number of processes
    )
    torch.cuda.set_device(rank)  # Set which GPU this process uses
```

The simplest test to verify your distributed setup works is in `code/distributed_basic_test.py`. It's a basic distributed test that verifies process group initialization and communication. It doesn't use DDP—it just tests that multiple processes can communicate.

Test with multiple GPUs:

```
torchrun --nproc_per_node=2 code/distributed_basic_test.py
```

If you only have one GPU but want to test the distributed logic, simulate multiple processes on a single GPU:

```
CUDA_VISIBLE_DEVICES=0 torchrun --nproc_per_node=2 code/multi_gpu_simulation.py
```

Either way, you'll see "Rank 0 says hello" and "Rank 1 says hello" printed from different processes, confirming that your distributed setup works.

When you start running distributed training or inference with `torchrun`, you might notice a warning about `OMP_NUM_THREADS`. This happens because PyTorch wants to control CPU thread usage to avoid overloading your system. You can silence the warning by setting `OMP_NUM_THREADS=4` (or whatever value fits your system) right before the `torchrun` command:

```
OMP_NUM_THREADS=4 torchrun --nproc_per_node=2 code/distributed_basic_test.py
```

Set it in your shell before `torchrun` starts—setting it inside your Python script won't work because `torchrun` checks the environment before launching your processes.

Collective operations

Collective operations are the building blocks of distributed communication. They define how data moves between processes. Each operation has a specific use case. Understanding them helps you choose the right one for your task and debug communication issues.

PyTorch provides eight main collective operations. Let's walk through each one with code examples.

AllReduce

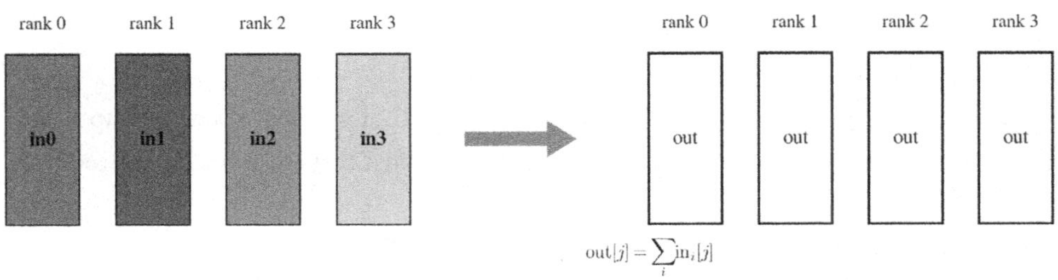

Figure 1.13: AllReduce Operation: Reduction Across All Ranks

As shown in *Figure 1.13*, AllReduce is the most common operation in distributed training. It performs a reduction (sum, max, min) across all ranks and stores the result in every rank's buffer. This is an all-to-all communication pattern where every rank contributes data and every rank receives the aggregated result.

AllReduce is the fundamental building block of data-parallel training. In DistributedDataParallel (DDP), each rank computes gradients on its local data shard during the backward pass. These local gradients must be synchronized across all ranks to ensure model consistency. DDP uses AllReduce to sum gradients from all ranks and distributes the averaged result back to every rank[7]. After AllReduce, all ranks have identical gradient values, allowing them to update their model parameters in lockstep. Without AllReduce, each rank would update parameters using only its local gradients, causing model divergence and training instability.

The reduction operation can be SUM (most common for gradients), MAX (for finding maximum values), MIN (for finding minimum values), or PRODUCT (rarely used). For gradient synchronization, SUM is used, and the result is typically divided by world_size to compute the average. This averaging ensures that the effective batch size scales with the number of ranks—training with 8 GPUs processes 8× more data per step than single-GPU training.

AllReduce is more efficient than the equivalent sequence of Reduce followed by Broadcast. While both achieve the same result, NCCL optimizes AllReduce as a single operation using algorithms like ring AllReduce or tree AllReduce, which minimize communication steps and bandwidth usage. The ring algorithm, for example, requires only (world_size - 1) communication steps, compared to 2 × (world_size - 1) steps for the Reduce+Broadcast sequence.

```
# Each rank has different input
tensor = torch.tensor([rank + 1, rank + 2, rank + 3], device=device)
# After all_reduce with SUM, all ranks have the same result
dist.all_reduce(tensor, op=dist.ReduceOp.SUM)
# Result: [sum(1..world_size), sum(2..world_size+1), sum(3..world_size+2)]
```

Run the demo:

```
OMP_NUM_THREADS=1 torchrun --nproc_per_node=2 code/collective-operation/
demo_allreduce.py
```

The communication cost of AllReduce scales with both data size and world size, but optimized implementations like NCCL's ring AllReduce achieve near-linear scaling efficiency. For large models with millions of parameters, AllReduce can become a bottleneck, which is why techniques like gradient compression, bucketing, and overlapping communication with computation are crucial for performance.

AllGather

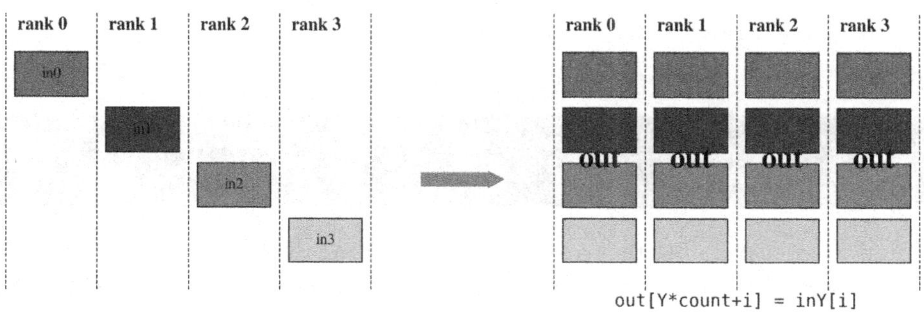

Figure 1.14: AllGather Operation: Gathering Data from All Ranks

As illustrated in *Figure 1.14*, AllGather collects data from all ranks and distributes the concatenated result to every rank. Each rank contributes N values, and every rank receives world_size × N values. The output is ordered by rank index, with rank 0's data first, followed by rank 1's data, and so on. This is an all-to-all communication pattern where every rank both sends and receives data from all other ranks.

AllGather is essential when you need every rank to have a complete view of data distributed across all ranks. Unlike AllReduce, which aggregates data (sum, max, min), AllGather preserves all individual contributions and concatenates them. This makes AllGather ideal for collecting embeddings, feature representations, or intermediate activations from all GPUs for global operations like attention mechanisms, batch normalization across ranks, or distributed evaluation metrics.

In Fully Sharded Data Parallel (FSDP) training, AllGather is used to reconstruct full parameter shards before forward and backward passes. Each rank holds a shard of the model parameters, and AllGather collects all shards so each rank can compute on the complete model. After computation, the shards are redistributed using ReduceScatter. This pattern allows training models larger than single-GPU memory while maintaining parameter consistency.

Other common use cases include collecting predictions from all ranks for ensemble evaluation, gathering feature maps for cross-rank attention in transformer models, collecting statistics for distributed batch normalization, and synchronizing embeddings or token representations in language model training. AllGather is also used in pipeline parallelism to collect outputs from different pipeline stages.

```
# Each rank has different input
input_tensor = torch.tensor([rank * 10 + 1, rank * 10 + 2], device=device)
# Prepare output list
output_list = [torch.zeros_like(input_tensor) for _ in range(world_size)]
dist.all_gather(output_list, input_tensor)
# All ranks now have: [rank0_data, rank1_data, ..., rankN_data]
```

Run the demo:

```
OMP_NUM_THREADS=1 torchrun --nproc_per_node=2 code/collective-operation/
demo_allgather.py
```

The communication cost of AllGather scales with data size and world size. Each rank sends N values and receives world_size × N values, so the total data movement is $\text{world\_size}^2 \times N$. This quadratic scaling makes AllGather expensive for large world sizes, which is why FSDP and other sharding strategies use AllGather selectively and combine it with ReduceScatter to minimize communication overhead.

> **Note**
>
> **AllReduce Decomposition** ReduceScatter followed by AllGather is equivalent to AllReduce. Some systems use this decomposition for optimization, particularly in FSDP, where the ReduceScatter and AllGather operations can be overlapped with computation to hide communication latency.

Broadcast

As shown in *Figure 1.15*, Broadcast copies data from a root rank to all other ranks. Only the root rank needs to have the data initially. After the operation, all ranks have identical data. This is a one-to-all communication pattern—the simplest form of data distribution in distributed systems.

Broadcast is fundamental to distributed training initialization. When you start training, rank 0 typically loads the model weights, optimizer state, or checkpoint data. These must be distributed to all ranks so every process starts with identical model parameters. Without Broadcast, each rank would need to independently load the same data, which wastes I/O bandwidth and storage access. Broadcast ensures all ranks begin training with synchronized state.

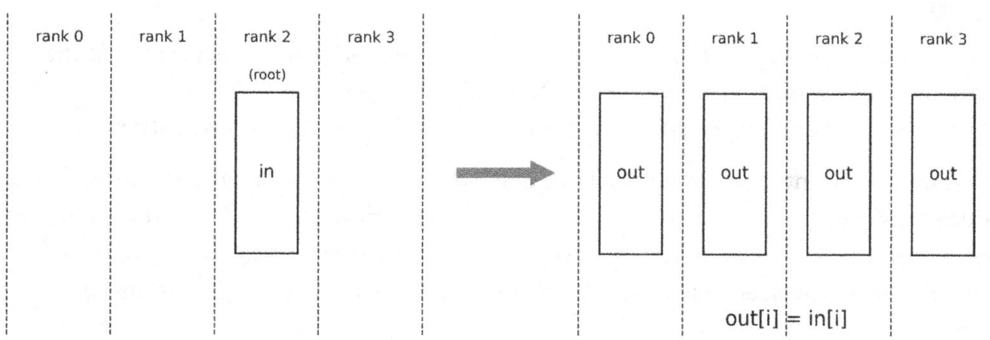

Figure 1.15: Broadcast Operation: Sending Data from Root to All Ranks

Use Broadcast for distributing model weights after loading from disk, sharing hyperparameters (learning rate, batch size, training configuration), synchronizing random seeds for reproducibility, and sending control signals or flags to coordinate distributed execution. In custom parallelism strategies, Broadcast is used to replicate model shards or synchronize state across pipeline stages.

Broadcast is also a building block for other collective operations. As mentioned in the AllReduce section, AllReduce can be decomposed into Reduce (collect data to root) followed by

Broadcast (distribute result back to all ranks). However, NCCL optimizes AllReduce as a single operation, making it more efficient than the two-step decomposition.

```
root = 0
if rank == root:
    tensor = torch.tensor([10.0, 20.0, 30.0], device=device)
else:
    tensor = torch.zeros(3, device=device)
# After broadcast, all ranks have [10.0, 20.0, 30.0]
dist.broadcast(tensor, src=root)
```

Run the demo:

```
OMP_NUM_THREADS=1 torchrun --nproc_per_node=2 code/collective-operation/
demo_broadcast.py
```

The communication cost of Broadcast scales with the data size but is independent of the number of ranks—the root sends the same amount of data regardless of world size. This makes Broadcast efficient for distributing large tensors (like model weights) across many GPUs, as the bandwidth is amortized across all receiving ranks.

Reduce

As illustrated in *Figure 1.16*, Reduce performs the same reduction as AllReduce, but only the root rank receives the result. Other ranks' buffers are unchanged. This is an all-to-one communication pattern, where data flows from all ranks toward a single destination.

Reduce is more efficient than AllReduce when only one rank needs the aggregated result. Since AllReduce distributes the result to all ranks, it requires an additional Broadcast step that Reduce avoids. This saves bandwidth and reduces communication overhead when the aggregated data is only needed for centralized operations like logging, checkpointing, or decision-making.

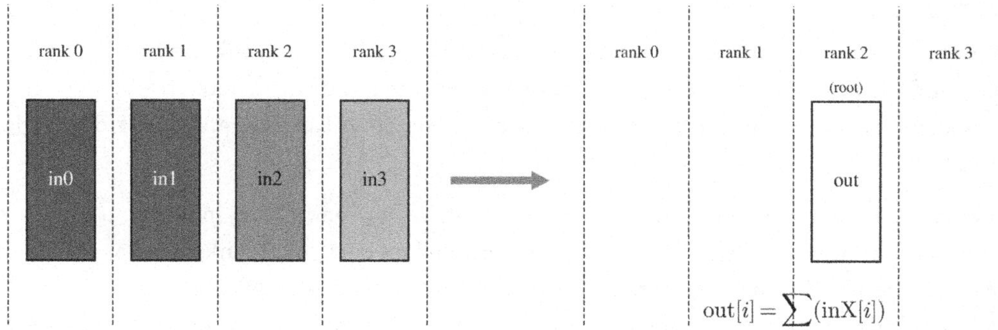

Figure 1.16: Reduce Operation: Reduction to Root Rank Only

The primary use case for Reduce is collecting metrics and statistics from all ranks to rank 0. During training, each rank computes local metrics (loss, accuracy, gradient norms) on its data shard. Reduce aggregates these metrics so rank 0 can log the global statistics, save checkpoints with aggregated values, or make training decisions (early stopping, learning rate scheduling) based on global state. Other common use cases include collecting validation results from all ranks, aggregating profiling data for performance analysis, and gathering error counts or convergence indicators for distributed monitoring.

Unlike AllReduce, which ensures all ranks have synchronized state, Reduce leaves other ranks' buffers unchanged. This means after Reduce, only the root rank has the aggregated result—other ranks still have their original local values. If you need all ranks to have the result, use AllReduce instead or follow Reduce with a Broadcast operation.

```
root = 0
tensor = torch.tensor([rank + 1, rank + 2, rank + 3], device=device)
dist.reduce(tensor, dst=root, op=dist.ReduceOp.SUM)
# Only root has the sum; other ranks unchanged
```

Run the demo:

```
OMP_NUM_THREADS=1 torchrun --nproc_per_node=2 code/collective-operation/
demo_reduce.py
```

Reduce followed by Broadcast is equivalent to AllReduce. However, NCCL optimizes AllReduce as a single operation, making it more efficient than the explicit two-step sequence. Use Reduce only when you specifically need the aggregated result on a single rank and don't need to distribute it back to others.

Gather

As shown in *Figure 1.17*, Gather collects data from all ranks to the root rank. Each rank sends N values, and the root receives world_size × N values concatenated and ordered by rank index. This is an all-to-one communication pattern, where data flows from all ranks toward a single destination.

Gather is the inverse of Scatter and is essential for centralized operations in distributed training. Unlike AllGather, which distributes collected data back to all ranks, Gather only sends data to the root rank, making it more efficient when only one rank needs the complete dataset. This is particularly useful for I/O operations, logging, checkpointing, and centralized decision-making.

The primary use case for Gather is collecting results from all ranks to rank 0 for processing or saving. During training, each rank computes predictions, metrics, or intermediate results on its local data shard. Gather collects these results so rank 0 can aggregate them, save checkpoints, log global statistics, or perform centralized evaluation. Other common use cases include collecting validation predictions for ensemble evaluation, gathering feature representations for centralized analysis, collecting debugging information from all ranks, and aggregating model outputs for final inference or serving.

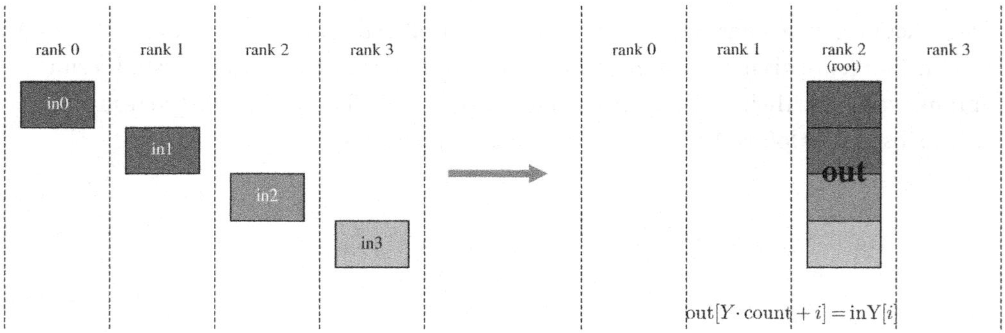

Figure 1.17: Gather Operation: Collecting Data from All Ranks to Root

The output ordering is deterministic—rank 0's data comes first, followed by rank 1's data, and so on. This ordering is crucial when reconstructing distributed data structures or when rank order matters for downstream processing. The root rank must pre-allocate the output list with space for all ranks' contributions, while non-root ranks pass `None` for the output list parameter.

```
root = 0
input_tensor = torch.tensor([rank * 10 + 1, rank * 10 + 2], device=device)
if rank == root:
    output_list = [torch.zeros_like(input_tensor) for _ in range(world_size)]
    dist.gather(input_tensor, output_list, dst=root)
    # Root has all data concatenated
else:
    dist.gather(input_tensor, None, dst=root)
```

Run the demo:

```
OMP_NUM_THREADS=1 torchrun --nproc_per_node=2 code/collective-operation/
demo_gather.py
```

The communication cost of Gather scales with data size and world size. The root rank receives world_size × N values, so bandwidth requirements increase linearly with the number of ranks. For large datasets, this can create a bottleneck at rank 0, which is why AllGather is preferred when all ranks need the collected data, as it distributes the bandwidth load across all ranks.

Scatter

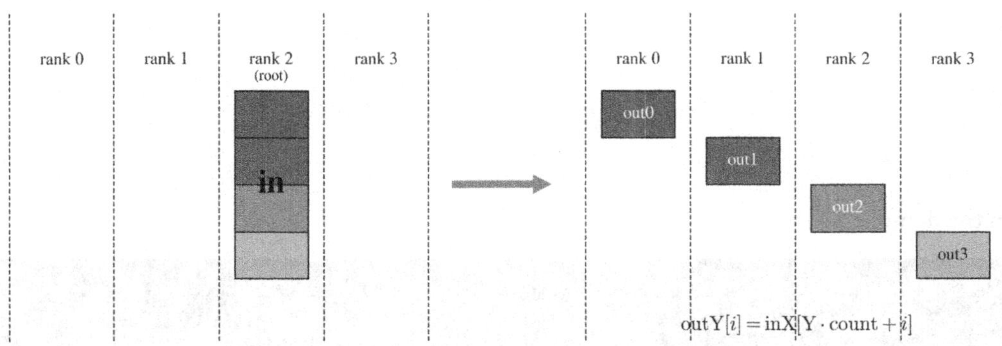

Figure 1.18: Scatter Operation: Distributing Data from Root to All Ranks

As illustrated in *Figure 1.18*, Scatter is the inverse of Gather. The root rank distributes data to all ranks, with each rank receiving a different chunk. This is a one-to-all communication pattern where a single source distributes different data to multiple destinations.

Scatter is essential for initializing distributed training when data needs to be partitioned across ranks. Unlike Broadcast, which sends identical data to all ranks, Scatter sends different chunks to each rank, enabling data parallelism where each rank processes a unique subset of the dataset. This is particularly useful for distributing large datasets that are too big to fit on a single rank, or when you want to pre-partition data for efficient distributed processing.

The primary use case for Scatter is distributing different data chunks from one rank to all ranks, such as splitting a large dataset across GPUs. The root rank prepares a list of tensors, one for each rank, and Scatter distributes them so rank 0 receives the first chunk, rank 1 receives the second chunk, and so on. Other common use cases include distributing model shards in custom parallelism strategies, splitting input batches across ranks for data-parallel processing, distributing configuration parameters that differ per rank, and initializing distributed state with rank-specific data.

The root rank must prepare a scatter_list containing world_size tensors, each of the same shape. Each rank receives the tensor corresponding to its rank index. Non-root ranks pass `None` for the scatter_list parameter, as they don't need to provide input data. All ranks must pre-allocate the output_tensor with the correct shape to receive their chunk.

```
root = 0
if rank == root:
    scatter_list = [torch.tensor([r * 10 + 1, r * 10 + 2], device=device)
                    for r in range(world_size)]
output_tensor = torch.zeros(2, device=device)
if rank == root:
    dist.scatter(output_tensor, scatter_list=scatter_list, src=root)
else:
    dist.scatter(output_tensor, scatter_list=None, src=root)
# Each rank receives its chunk
```

Run the demo:

```
OMP_NUM_THREADS=1 torchrun --nproc_per_node=2 code/collective-operation/
demo_scatter.py
```

The communication cost of Scatter scales with data size but is independent of world size from the root's perspective—the root sends the same total amount of data regardless of the number of ranks. However, in practice, Scatter is often less efficient than using DistributedSampler for data partitioning, as DistributedSampler avoids the need to load all data on rank 0 before distribution.

ReduceScatter

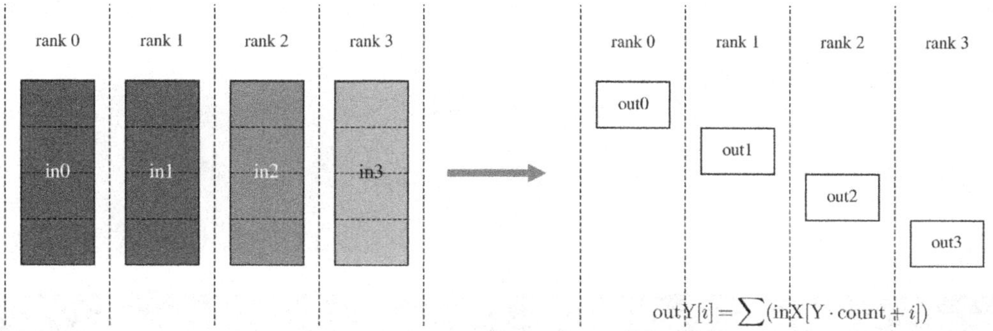

Figure 1.19: ReduceScatter Operation: Reduce Then Scatter

As shown in *Figure 1.19*, ReduceScatter combines Reduce and Scatter. It performs a reduction across all ranks, then scatters the result in equal-sized chunks. Each rank receives a different chunk based on its rank index. This is a key operation in sharded parallelism strategies, enabling efficient gradient synchronization and parameter update distribution.

ReduceScatter is fundamental to Fully Sharded Data Parallel (FSDP) training. In FSDP, model parameters are sharded across ranks, with each rank holding a fraction of the total parameters. During the backward pass, each rank computes gradients for its local parameter shard. However, since parameters are sharded, gradients from all ranks must be reduced and then redistributed so each rank updates its shard with the corresponding gradient chunk. ReduceScatter performs this operation efficiently in a single step, avoiding the overhead of separate Reduce and Scatter operations.

The input to ReduceScatter is structured as a list of tensors on each rank, where each tensor corresponds to a shard that will be reduced with corresponding shards from other ranks. After reduction, each rank receives the reduced chunk corresponding to its rank index. This pattern ensures that rank 0 gets the first chunk of the reduced result, rank 1 gets the second chunk, and so on, maintaining shard alignment with the parameter distribution.

Use ReduceScatter in FSDP and other sharded parallelism strategies where each rank needs a shard of the reduced result. This includes gradient synchronization in FSDP (reducing gradients and distributing shards), parameter update distribution after optimization, gradient accumulation across micro-batches in large model training, and custom sharding strategies that require per-shard reductions.

```
# Each rank has input of size world_size * N
input_list = [torch.tensor([rank * 10 + i, rank * 10 + i + 1], device=device)
              for i in range(world_size)]
input_tensor = torch.cat(input_list)
# Each rank receives a chunk of the reduced result
output_tensor = torch.zeros(2, device=device)
dist.reduce_scatter(output_tensor, input_list, op=dist.ReduceOp.SUM)
```

Run the demo:

```
OMP_NUM_THREADS=1 torchrun --nproc_per_node=2 code/collective-operation/
demo_reducescatter.py
```

The communication cost of ReduceScatter is similar to AllReduce, but the output is distributed rather than replicated. Each rank sends world_size × N values (for reduction) and receives N values (its shard), resulting in more efficient memory usage than AllReduce when only shards are needed. ReduceScatter followed by AllGather is equivalent to AllReduce, and some systems use this decomposition for optimization, particularly in FSDP where the operations can be overlapped with computation.

AlltoAll

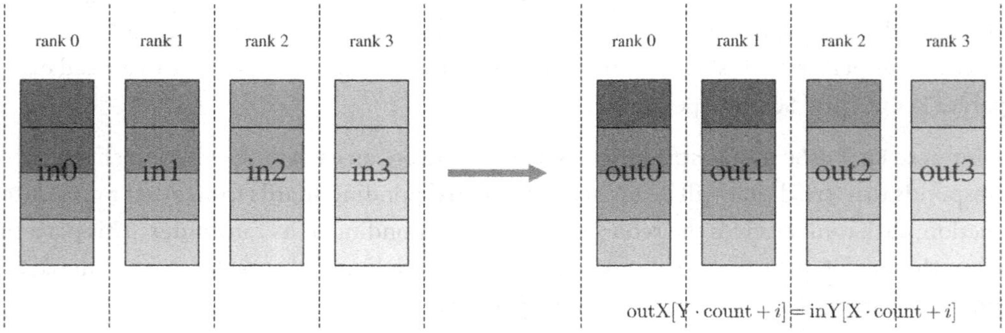

Figure 1.20: AlltoAll Operation: All-to-All Communication

As illustrated in *Figure 1.20*, AlltoAll is the most general operation. Each rank sends different data to every other rank. Each rank provides world_size chunks and receives world_size chunks —one from each rank. This creates a complete all-to-all communication pattern where every rank exchanges data with every other rank simultaneously.

AlltoAll is the most complex and general collective operation, enabling sophisticated communication patterns that other collectives cannot express. Unlike AllGather, which concatenates data from all ranks, AlltoAll allows each rank to send different data to each destination rank, creating a personalized communication pattern. This flexibility makes AlltoAll essential for tensor parallelism, where different parts of tensors need to be exchanged between ranks in specific patterns.

The primary use case for AlltoAll is tensor parallelism, where model layers are split across ranks and different tensor slices need to be exchanged. For example, in column-parallel linear layers, each rank holds a different column slice of the weight matrix. During the forward pass, input activations must be distributed across ranks (one slice per rank), and during the backward pass, output gradients must be collected and redistributed. AlltoAll handles these complex exchange patterns efficiently. Other common use cases include sequence parallelism in transformer models (exchanging sequence chunks), expert parallelism in Mixture-of-Experts models (routing tokens to different experts), and custom parallelism strategies requiring arbitrary data exchanges.

Each rank prepares an input_list containing world_size chunks, where chunk[i] is sent to rank i. After AlltoAll, each rank receives an output_list where output_list[i] contains data received from rank i. This creates a complete permutation of data across all ranks, enabling complex communication topologies that cannot be achieved with simpler collectives.

```
# Each rank prepares data to send to each other rank
input_list = []
for dst_rank in range(world_size):
    chunk = torch.tensor([rank * 100 + dst_rank * 10 + 1,
                          rank * 100 + dst_rank * 10 + 2], device=device)
    input_list.append(chunk)
# Each rank receives data from all ranks
output_list = [torch.zeros(2, device=device) for _ in range(world_size)]
dist.all_to_all(output_list, input_list)
```

Run the demo:

```
OMP_NUM_THREADS=1 torchrun --nproc_per_node=2 code/collective-operation/
demo_alltoall.py
```

The communication cost of AlltoAll is the highest among all collectives, as it requires every rank to send data to every other rank. The total data movement is $world\_size^2 \times chunk\_size$, creating quadratic scaling with world size. This makes AlltoAll expensive for large world sizes, which is why it's used selectively in tensor parallelism and other advanced parallelism strategies where the communication pattern cannot be expressed with simpler collectives.

Note

AlltoAll Requires NCCL

AlltoAll requires the NCCL backend. GLOO (CPU backend) doesn't support it. If you see an error with `--use_cpu`, switch to GPU mode. This limitation exists because AlltoAll's complex communication pattern benefits significantly from GPU-optimized communication libraries like NCCL.

Choosing the right operation

So when do you use which operation? For gradient synchronization, AllReduce (see *Figure 1.13*) is the standard choice. DDP uses it automatically when you wrap your model—you don't need to call it yourself. If you need to collect embeddings or metrics from all ranks, AllGather (see *Figure 1.14*) is what you want. It gives every rank a copy of data from all other ranks.

When you have data on one rank that needs to go to everyone else, Broadcast (see *Figure 1.15*) is the simplest option. Think of it as one-to-all communication. The inverse is Gather (see *Figure 1.17*)—when all ranks have data and you need to collect it on one rank, usually rank 0 for logging or saving. Scatter (see *Figure 1.18*) does the opposite, distributing different chunks from one rank to all others.

For sharded parallelism strategies like FSDP, you'll see ReduceScatter (see *Figure 1.19*) and AlltoAll (see *Figure 1.20*). ReduceScatter combines reduction with scattering, which is efficient when each rank only needs a shard of the result. AlltoAll is the most general case, where every rank sends different data to every other rank. This shows up in tensor parallelism.

Most of the time, you won't call these operations directly. DDP handles AllReduce (see *Figure 1.13*) for you during gradient synchronization. FSDP uses ReduceScatter (see *Figure 1.19*) and AllGather (see *Figure 1.14*) under the hood. But understanding what each operation does helps when you're debugging why communication is slow or when you need to implement custom parallelism strategies that the standard APIs don't cover.

DistributedDataParallel (DDP)

Among the various distributed training strategies, DDP is the simplest to understand and use. It requires minimal changes to your single-GPU training code, and it's the most common starting point for distributed training. This section provides a brief overview of DDP. *Chapter 3* covers DDP in depth with detailed implementation, optimization techniques, and best practices.

DDP wraps a model for data-parallel distributed training. When you wrap a model with DDP, PyTorch automatically synchronizes gradients across all processes. Each process computes gradients on its local data, then DDP averages these gradients before updating the model.

DDP assumes each process has a complete copy of the model. Only the data is partitioned—each process trains on a different subset, but all processes maintain identical model parameters after each training step. DDP works well when your model fits on a single GPU. For larger models, FSDP (Fully Sharded Data Parallel) shards the model across GPUs while still using data parallelism. Later chapters will cover FSDP and other parallelism strategies like tensor parallelism and pipeline parallelism.

Wrap a model with DDP:

```
from torch.nn.parallel import DistributedDataParallel as DDP

model = YourModel().cuda(rank)
model = DDP(model, device_ids=[rank])
```

After wrapping, use the model exactly as you would in single-GPU training. DDP handles synchronization during `loss.backward()`.

DistributedSampler

Each process should train on different data, so you need a DistributedSampler. It splits the dataset so each process gets a unique subset. Without it, all processes see the same data, defeating the purpose of distributed training.

```
from torch.utils.data import DataLoader, DistributedSampler

sampler = DistributedSampler(
    dataset,
    num_replicas=world_size,  # Total number of processes
    rank=rank  # This process's rank
)
dataloader = DataLoader(dataset, batch_size=32, sampler=sampler)
```

Call `sampler.set_epoch(epoch)` at the start of each epoch to ensure data shuffling works correctly across epochs.

Launching distributed jobs

The modern approach uses `torchrun`, which handles process spawning automatically:

```
torchrun --nproc_per_node=2 code/multi_gpu_ddp.py
```

This launches 2 processes on the current machine. For multi-node training, specify `--nnodes`, `--node_rank`, and `--master_addr` as well.

This command uses several distributed primitives we've covered: `init_process_group()` to set up communication, `barrier()` to synchronize dataset downloading, `DistributedSampler` to partition data, and `DDP`, which internally uses `allreduce()` to synchronize gradients during `loss.backward()`.

This chapter walked through resource estimation, decision frameworks, and practical examples for distributed AI systems. The core idea is simple: estimate your requirements first, then decide whether you actually need distributed systems. Don't assume you need them—calculate memory and compute needs, check if your model fits, and only then consider distribution.

Now that we understand when and why to use distributed systems, we need to understand the hardware they run on. The next chapter explores GPU hardware, networking topologies, and the fundamental parallelism strategies that make distributed AI possible. Understanding these foundations is crucial for making informed decisions about which distributed approach to use.

Code summary

- `torch.distributed`: Core module for distributed computing in PyTorch (training and inference)
- `dist.init_process_group()`: Initialize the process group for distributed communication with backends (NCCL, Gloo)
- `dist.all_reduce()`: Apply reduction (sum, max, min, etc.) to tensors across all ranks and stores result in all ranks
- `dist.all_gather()`: Collective operation that gathers tensors from all ranks and concatenates them on all ranks
- `dist.broadcast()`: Broadcasts a tensor from the source rank to all other ranks
- `dist.reduce()`: Reduces tensors from all ranks to a single destination rank (typically rank 0)
- `dist.gather()`: Gathers tensors from all ranks to a single destination rank

- `dist.scatter()`: Scatters a list of tensors from the source rank to all other ranks
- `dist.reduce_scatter()`: Reduces tensors across all ranks and scatters the result to all ranks
- `dist.all_to_all()`: Sends different data chunks from each rank to every other rank

References

1. The tilde (~) indicates approximate parameter counts. Many large models are closed-source, so exact parameter counts are not publicly disclosed. These approximations are based on inference from model architecture, training costs, and industry estimates.
2. Wu, "The LLM Parameter Lie," *Summer in Charlotte* (diary), June 7, 2026. `https://wu-99.com/diary/20260607.html#the-llm-parameter-lie`. Discusses MoE total vs. active parameters, unreliable regression-based probes, industry estimates for frontier closed models (GPT-4 ~1.76T total, Claude Opus 4.x ~5T MoE, GPT-5/Gemini 3.1 in a ~2T–5T band), and Claude Mythos 5 as the first publicly discussed ~10T-class model (~800B–1.2T active per token).
3. SemiAnalysis, "GPT-4 Architecture, Infrastructure, Training Dataset, Costs, Vision, MoE," 2023; Epoch AI, "Compute Trends Across Three eras of Machine Learning," 2023
4. Epoch AI, "Trends in GPU price-performance," 2024; SemiAnalysis, "The Cost of Training Large Language Models," 2023; OpenAI, "GPT-4 Technical Report," 2023
5. Llama 4 in vLLM - `https://blog.vllm.ai/2025/04/05/llama4.html`
6. Training estimates assume Adam optimizer and moderate batch size. Actual values vary based on architecture, sequence length, and batch size.
7. AllReduce is the most common collective operation in distributed training

Exercises

Process group initialization

Implement a function to initialize a distributed process group with proper error handling.

Requirements:

- Function signature: `setup_distributed(rank, world_size, backend='nccl')`
- Initialize the process group using `torch.distributed.init_process_group()`
- Set the CUDA device for the current rank: `torch.cuda.set_device(rank)`
- Add error handling for cases where CUDA is not available

- Return True if successful, False otherwise
- Print a message indicating successful initialization with rank and world_size

Test your function:

```
import torch.distributed as dist
import os

# Simulate rank and world_size from environment
rank = int(os.environ.get('RANK', 0))
world_size = int(os.environ.get('WORLD_SIZE', 1))

if setup_distributed(rank, world_size):
    print(f"Rank {rank}/{world_size} initialized successfully")
    dist.destroy_process_group()
```

Manual AllReduce implementation

Implement a manual gradient averaging function using AllReduce, simulating what DDP does internally.

Requirements:

- Function signature: `average_gradients(model, world_size)`
- Iterate through all parameters in the model
- For each parameter with `requires_grad=True`:
    - Use `dist.all_reduce()` with `op=dist.ReduceOp.SUM` to sum gradients across all ranks
    - Divide the gradient by `world_size` to get the average
- Handle the case where gradients might be `None` (skip those parameters)

Test your function:

```
import torch
import torch.nn as nn
import torch.distributed as dist

# Create a simple model
model = nn.Linear(10, 1).cuda()
loss_fn = nn.MSELoss()
```

```
# Forward and backward pass
x = torch.randn(32, 10).cuda()
y = torch.randn(32, 1).cuda()
output = model(x)
loss = loss_fn(output, y)
loss.backward()

# Average gradients across ranks
average_gradients(model, world_size=2)

# Verify gradients are averaged (should be same on all ranks after all_reduce)
print(f"Gradient on rank {rank}: {model.weight.grad}")
```

Broadcast with verification

Implement a function that broadcasts a tensor from rank 0 to all other ranks and verifies the result.

Requirements:

- Function signature: `broadcast_and_verify(tensor, root=0)`
- If current rank is root: create or use the provided tensor
- If current rank is not root: create a zero tensor of the same shape
- Use `dist.broadcast()` to send data from root to all ranks
- After broadcast, verify that all ranks have identical data
- Return the broadcasted tensor and a boolean indicating if verification passed

Test your function:

```
import torch
import torch.distributed as dist

rank = dist.get_rank()
world_size = dist.get_world_size()

if rank == 0:
    # Root rank creates data
    data = torch.tensor([1.0, 2.0, 3.0, 4.0, 5.0], device='cuda')
else:
    data = None
```

```
result, verified = broadcast_and_verify(data, root=0)
print(f"Rank {rank}: {result}, Verified: {verified}")
```

DistributedSampler wrapper

Create a wrapper class for `DistributedSampler` that automatically handles epoch setting.

Requirements:

- Class name: `AutoEpochDistributedSampler`
- Inherit from `torch.utils.data.distributed.DistributedSampler`
- Override `__iter__()` to automatically call `set_epoch()` with an internal epoch counter
- Add a method `reset()` to reset the epoch counter
- Add a method `get_epoch()` to return the current epoch number
- The sampler should increment the epoch counter each time `__iter__()` is called

Test your function:

```
from torch.utils.data import Dataset, DataLoader
import torch.distributed as dist

# Dummy dataset
class DummyDataset(Dataset):
    def __init__(self, size=100):
        self.data = list(range(size))

    def __len__(self):
        return len(self.data)

    def __getitem__(self, idx):
        return self.data[idx]

dataset = DummyDataset(100)
sampler = AutoEpochDistributedSampler(
    dataset,
    num_replicas=world_size,
    rank=rank
)
dataloader = DataLoader(dataset, batch_size=10, sampler=sampler)

# Iterate through epochs - epoch should auto-increment
```

```
for epoch in range(3):
    for batch in dataloader:
        pass  # Process batch
    print(f"Epoch {sampler.get_epoch()} completed")
```

Gradient synchronization timing

Write a script that measures the time taken for gradient synchronization using AllReduce.

Requirements:

- Function signature: `measure_sync_time(model, num_iterations=10)`
- Create a model with configurable size (number of parameters)
- Run forward and backward pass
- Time the `dist.all_reduce()` operation for all gradients
- Return average synchronization time in milliseconds
- Test with different model sizes (1M, 10M, 100M parameters) and different world sizes
- Print results showing how sync time scales with model size and world size

Test your function:

```
import torch
import torch.nn as nn
import time
import torch.distributed as dist

def create_model(num_params):
    """Create a simple model with approximately num_params parameters"""
    # Simple linear layers to approximate parameter count
    layers = []
    # Rough calculation: for Linear(in, out), params = in * out + out
    # This is simplified - adjust as needed
    return nn.Sequential(
        nn.Linear(1000, num_params // 2000),
        nn.ReLU(),
        nn.Linear(num_params // 2000, 10)
    ).cuda()

model_sizes = [1e6, 10e6, 100e6]  # 1M, 10M, 100M parameters

for size in model_sizes:
```

```
    model = create_model(int(size))
    sync_time = measure_sync_time(model, num_iterations=10)
    print(f"Model size: {size/1e6:.1f}M params, "
          f"Avg sync time: {sync_time:.2f} ms, "
          f"World size: {dist.get_world_size()}")
```

Expected learning outcomes

After completing these exercises, you should be able to:

- Calculate memory requirements for different model sizes and precisions
- Initialize distributed process groups correctly
- Understand how gradient synchronization works in DDP
- Use collective operations (AllReduce, Broadcast) effectively
- Work with DistributedSampler for data partitioning
- Measure and analyze communication overhead in distributed training

Get this book's PDF version and more

Scan the QR code (or go to `packtpub.com/unlock`). Search for this book by name, confirm the edition, and then follow the steps on the page.

UNLOCK NOW

Note: Keep your invoice handy. Purchases made directly from Packt don't require an invoice.

2

GPU Hardware, Networking, and Parallelism Strategies

Understanding hardware topology and parallelism strategies for distributed AI

> *The innovation isn't just about chips, it's about the entire stack.*
>
> *Jensen Huang*

Computational power: AI clusters and metrics

In *Chapter 1*, we established why distributed AI is essential—models have grown beyond single-GPU capacity, and the computational gap between model requirements and hardware capabilities continues to widen. Now we need to understand the hardware foundation that makes distributed training possible. Before diving into GPU specifics, let's step back and understand what we're really building: AI clusters that deliver massive computational power. The numbers matter here—when you're training a 70B parameter model, you're not just using a few GPUs. You're orchestrating hundreds or thousands of them, and the way they're connected determines whether your training job finishes in days or weeks.

What is computational power?

Computational power, or compute capacity, measures how many operations a system can perform per second. For AI workloads, we care about **floating-point operations per second (FLOPS)**. The scale is exponential: a single modern GPU like the H200 delivers around 1,000 TFLOPS (teraFLOPS, or 10^{12} operations per second) for FP16 operations. A cluster with 1000 such GPUs gives you roughly 1,000 PFLOPS (petaFLOPS, 10^{15} operations per second), or 1

EFLOPS (exaFLOPS, 10^{18} operations per second): 1000 GPUs × 1000 TFLOPS = 10^6 TFLOPS = 1000 PFLOPS = 1 EFLOPS.

But here's the thing: raw FLOPS numbers don't tell the whole story. Peak throughput depends on precision—FP64 for traditional HPC, FP32 as a training baseline, FP16/BF16 for modern AI training, FP8 and lower for inference and quantization (see the precision-format table in *Chapter 1*). When someone says "this cluster delivers 500 PFLOPS," ask at what precision: an HPC cluster might quote FP64, while an AI cluster quotes FP16 or BF16. The same hardware can show very different numbers depending on which format you measure.

The growth in computational demand for AI has been staggering. Large language models require computational resources that grow by orders of magnitude over a few years, depending on workload and model scaling, while hardware capabilities grow only about 3x in the same period. This gap is why distributed training isn't optional—it's **the only way** to train modern models in reasonable time.

As shown in *Figure 2.1*, model memory requirements have grown exponentially while single-GPU memory capacity has increased more gradually. This widening gap makes distributed training not just beneficial, but essential for training modern large-scale models within reasonable timeframes [1].

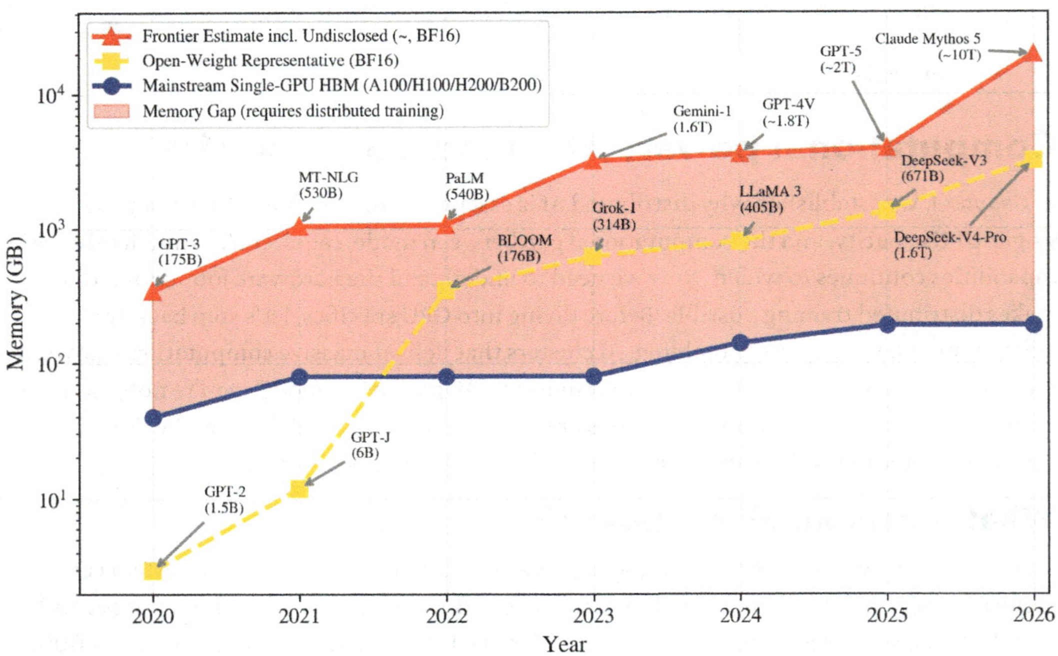

Figure 2.1: GPU Memory Capacity vs. Model Memory Requirements

Why clusters?

A single GPU, even a high-end one, isn't enough for modern AI workloads. A 70B parameter model with FP16 weights takes about 140 GB just to store the model. Add gradients, optimizer states, and activations, and you're looking at 500+ GB per training step. That's beyond what any single GPU can hold.

A **cluster** is a group of computers (nodes) connected by high-speed networks, working together as a single system. Each node typically has multiple GPUs, CPUs, memory, and storage. The key insight is that by coordinating work across many nodes, you can:

- **Scale memory**: Distribute model parameters, gradients, and optimizer states across GPUs
- **Scale compute**: Process larger batches or train faster by parallelizing work
- **Scale storage**: Handle datasets that don't fit on a single machine

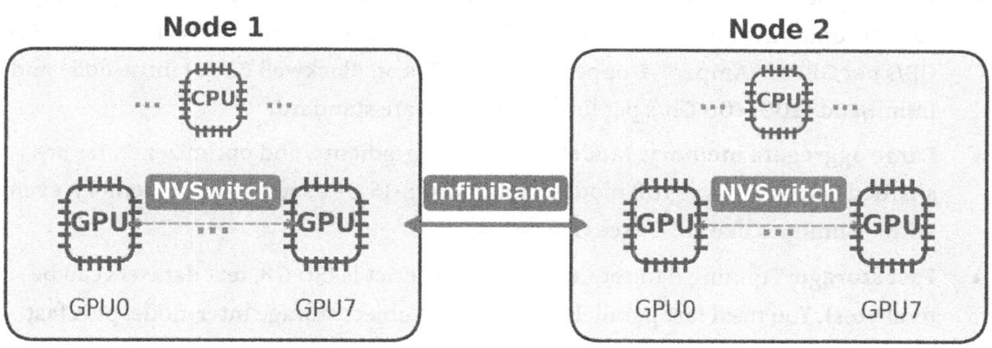

Figure 2.2: AI Cluster

As illustrated in *Figure 2.2*, an AI cluster consists of multiple nodes, each containing multiple CPUs and GPUs (typically 8 GPUs per node in modern systems). Intra-node, GPUs are connected via NVSwitch, providing all-to-all connectivity at NVLink speeds (300–900 GB/s per GPU on Ampere–Hopper systems, up to 1.8 TB/s on Blackwell B200; all figures aggregate bidirectional per GPU). Inter-node, GPUs communicate via high-speed networks such as InfiniBand (200-400 Gb/s per link), enabling distributed training and inference across the entire cluster. This architecture allows work to be coordinated across all available resources. The cluster shown demonstrates how memory can be scaled by distributing model parameters, gradients, and optimizer states across GPUs, while compute can be scaled by parallelizing workloads across nodes. Each node operates as an independent server with its own CPUs, memory, and storage, but the high-speed network connections (NVSwitch intra-node,

InfiniBand inter-node) allow them to work together as a unified system for large-scale AI workloads.

Clusters aren't new—they've been used in high-performance computing (HPC) for decades. What's different for AI is the communication patterns. HPC workloads often do large, infrequent data exchanges. AI training does frequent, smaller exchanges (gradient synchronization every step), which makes network bandwidth and latency critical. We will discuss how to run distributed training jobs on SLURM-managed clusters in *Chapter 8*.

AI clusters: built for training and inference

An **AI cluster** is a cluster specifically designed for AI workloads. Unlike general-purpose cloud data centers that handle diverse workloads, AI clusters are optimized for the unique characteristics of deep learning:

For training, AI clusters need:

- **High-bandwidth interconnects**: Gradient synchronization happens every training step. If communication is slow, GPUs sit idle waiting for gradients. NVLink (300-900 GB/s per GPU on Ampere–Hopper, up to 1.8 TB/s on Blackwell B200) intra-node and InfiniBand (200-400 Gb/s per link) inter-node are standard.
- **Large aggregate memory**: Model parameters, gradients, and optimizer states are sharded across GPUs. A 70B model might need 8-16 GPUs just to fit in memory, even with techniques like FSDP (see *Chapter 4*).
- **Fast storage**: Training datasets are large (ImageNet is 150 GB, text datasets can be terabytes). You need fast parallel filesystems or object storage inter-node, plus fast local NVMe per node (see CPU pairing below).

For inference, the requirements shift (see *Chapter 6* and *Chapter 9*):

- **Lower latency networking**: While training cares about bandwidth, inference cares about latency. Users expect responses in milliseconds, not seconds.
- **Efficient memory usage**: KV caches for attention mechanisms can consume significant memory. You need to balance cache size (for longer context) against memory limits.
- **Load balancing**: Inference workloads are bursty. You need to route requests efficiently across GPUs and handle traffic spikes.

The hardware topology—how GPUs connect intra-node and how nodes connect inter-node—directly impacts what parallelism strategies work. A cluster where all GPUs are connected via NVSwitch (all-to-all connectivity) can use tensor parallelism effectively. A cluster where GPUs are only connected via PCIe will struggle with communication-heavy strategies.

Key metrics for AI clusters

When you're evaluating or optimizing an AI cluster, you need concrete metrics. Raw FLOPS numbers are marketing—what matters is how efficiently you use the hardware. Here are the metrics that actually matter:

Model FLOPS Utilization (MFU) is the most important metric for training efficiency. It measures what percentage of peak hardware FLOPS you're actually using:

```
MFU = (Model FLOPs per iteration / Iteration time) / Peak FLOPS
```

MFU tells you if you're compute-bound or limited by something else. A well-optimized cluster might achieve 40-60% MFU for large models. If MFU is low (say, 20%), you're likely hitting memory bandwidth limits, communication bottlenecks, or inefficient kernel launches.

For a 70B parameter transformer model training on H100 GPUs, you might see:

- **Theoretical FLOPs per iteration**: ~860 TFLOP (depends on batch size, sequence length)
- **Iteration time**: ~2.0 seconds
- **Actual FLOPS per second**: ~860 TFLOP / 2.0 s ≈ 430 TFLOPS
- **Peak H100 FLOPS**: ~989 TFLOPS (BF16)
- **MFU**: 430/989 ≈ 43%

That puts you in the 40-60% range many teams aim for on large models. If MFU is much lower (say, 20%), you're likely hitting memory bandwidth limits, communication overhead, or small batch sizes that don't keep GPUs busy.

You can run the same check on your own training jobs. Start with how many tokens each step touches—on one GPU that's usually microbatch size times sequence length; multiply by data-parallel width if you want the whole cluster. For a dense transformer, a workable FLOP estimate is about six times the parameter count per token (forward and backward combined) [2]. Your trainer logs give you step time; divide those FLOPs by wall-clock seconds and by the peak matmul rate from the datasheet at the precision you train in—BF16 or FP16 on an H100, not the FP8 number on the marketing slide. The 70B walk-through above is just those pieces plugged into one line.

Linear scaling measures how well performance scales with cluster size. The formula is:

```
Linear scaling = (Multi-GPU throughput) / (Single-GPU throughput × GPU count)
```

Perfect scaling gives you 1.0 (100%). In practice, you'll see 0.7-0.9 for well-optimized clusters. If scaling drops below 0.5, you have a communication bottleneck.

GPU utilization is simpler—it's the percentage of time GPUs spend computing vs. waiting. You can check it with:

```
nvidia-smi --query-gpu=utilization.gpu --format=csv,noheader
```

High utilization (90%+) is good, but it doesn't tell you if you're using the right kernels or if communication is blocking computation. MFU is more informative.

Communication efficiency measures how well you're using network bandwidth:

```
Communication efficiency = Actual bandwidth / Theoretical bandwidth
```

For InfiniBand HDR (200 Gb/s), you might achieve 180 Gb/s actual bandwidth, giving 90% efficiency. If efficiency is low, you might have topology issues, packet loss, or suboptimal communication patterns.

Throughput (samples per second or tokens per second) is what you care about for training speed. There are two ways to measure it:

Cluster throughput (total tokens processed per second across all GPUs):

```
Throughput_cluster = (Global batch size × Sequence length) / Total training time
```

Per-GPU throughput (tokens per second per GPU):

```
Throughput_per_GPU = (Global batch size × Sequence length) / (Total training time
× GPU count)
```

Higher throughput is better, but you need to balance it with convergence—larger batches might train faster per iteration but need more iterations to converge.

Resource utilization breaks down where time is spent:

- **GPU compute time**: Actual matrix multiplications
- **Memory transfer time**: Moving data between CPU and GPU, or between GPUs
- **Communication time**: Gradient synchronization, AllReduce operations
- **Idle time**: Waiting for data, synchronization, or other bottlenecks

A well-optimized cluster spends 70-80% of time in compute, 10-20% in communication, and minimal time idle.

Energy efficiency matters for large clusters. **FLOPS per Watt** measures compute efficiency:

```
FLOPS/Watt = Total FLOPS / Total power consumption
```

An H100 delivers about 1.4 TFLOPS/Watt at FP16. Higher is better—it means you're getting more compute for the same power bill.

PUE (Power Usage Effectiveness) measures datacenter efficiency:

```
PUE = Total facility power / IT equipment power
```

A PUE of 1.0 means all power goes to IT equipment (impossible in practice). Real datacenters achieve 1.2-1.5. Lower is better—it means less power is wasted on cooling and overhead.

Reliability metrics matter when you're running week-long training jobs:

- **MTBF (Mean Time Between Failures)**: Average time between system failures. For a 10,000 GPU cluster, you might see failures every few hours.
- **Availability**: Percentage of time the system is operational. Target: 99%+ for production clusters.
- **MTTR (Mean Time To Recovery)**: Average time to recover from a failure. Good clusters recover in minutes, not hours.

Communication latency is critical for distributed training. AllReduce latency should be:

- **Intra-node (NVLink)**: < 1 ms for typical gradient sizes
- **Inter-node (InfiniBand)**: < 5 ms for inter-node communication
- **P99 latency**: The 99th percentile latency matters more than average—one slow node can stall the entire training job

When you're benchmarking a cluster, measure these metrics at different scales: 8 GPUs, 64 GPUs, 512 GPUs, 2048 GPUs. The metrics that degrade with scale (like linear scaling or communication efficiency) tell you where your bottlenecks are.

With this foundation in place, let's examine the hardware components that make clusters work. We'll start with CPUs, which orchestrate the entire system, then move to GPUs where the actual computation happens, followed by alternative accelerators, interconnect technologies, and finally how to choose parallelism strategies based on your cluster's topology.

Central Processing Unit (CPU)

While GPUs do the heavy lifting in distributed training, CPUs play a crucial supporting role. Understanding CPU architecture helps you optimize data loading, manage GPU coordination, and debug performance bottlenecks.

CPU Architecture Basics

CPUs are built around the **von Neumann architecture**: a central processing unit with arithmetic logic unit (ALU), control unit (CU), and memory unit (registers). Unlike GPUs optimized for throughput, CPUs optimize for latency—fast single-threaded execution with complex control logic.

The key difference: CPUs spend most of their silicon on control logic and cache, not compute units. A modern CPU might have 8-64 cores, each with complex out-of-order execution, branch prediction, and multi-level caches. GPUs have thousands of simple cores optimized for parallel workloads.

For distributed training, CPUs handle:

- **Data loading and preprocessing**: Reading from disk, decoding images, tokenizing text
- **Orchestration**: Launching GPU kernels, managing process groups, handling communication
- **System management**: Memory allocation, process scheduling, network stack

If your CPU is the bottleneck, GPUs sit idle waiting for data. This is why data loading pipelines matter—you need enough CPU cores and fast storage to keep GPUs fed.

CPU-GPU Interaction

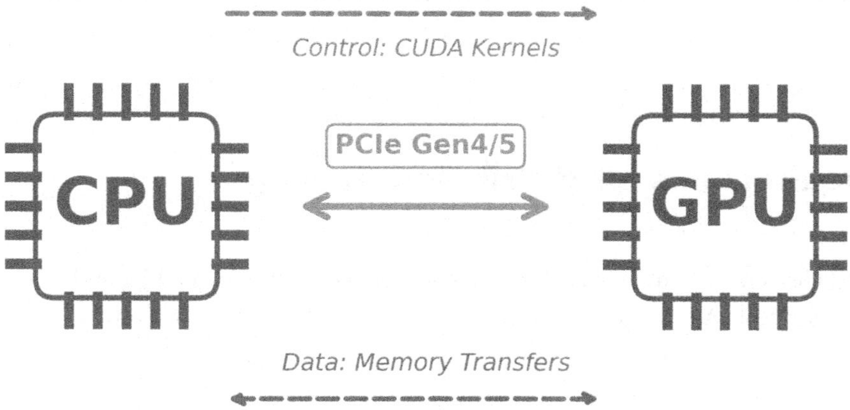

Figure 2.3: CPU-GPU Interaction

When you run distributed training, here's what happens:

1. **CPU launches GPU kernels**: Your Python code (running on CPU) calls PyTorch, which generates CUDA kernels. The CPU sends these to the GPU via PCIe.
2. **CPU manages memory**: CPU allocates GPU memory, transfers data from CPU RAM to GPU memory, and coordinates multi-GPU communication
3. **CPU handles communication**: For multi-node training, CPU processes handle network communication (InfiniBand, Ethernet) and coordinate with NCCL for GPU collectives

As shown in *Figure 2.3*, the PCIe connection between CPU and GPU is often a bottleneck. PCIe Gen 4 x16 gives you about 31.5 GB/s per direction (~63 GB/s bidirectional), while NVLink between GPUs gives 300-900 GB/s per GPU on Ampere–Hopper (up to 1.8 TB/s on Blackwell B200), aggregate bidirectional. This is why you want GPUs to communicate directly via NVLink, not through the CPU.

NUMA and CPU affinity

Modern servers have multiple CPU sockets (NUMA nodes). Each socket has its own memory controllers and PCIe lanes. GPUs connected to different sockets have different memory access patterns.

You can check NUMA topology:

```
numactl --hardware
```

For distributed training, try to keep processes on the same NUMA node as their GPUs. This reduces memory access latency. PyTorch doesn't do this automatically—you may need to set CPU affinity manually or use `numactl` when launching jobs.

CPU requirements for distributed training

For a typical 8-GPU server:

- **CPU cores**: You want at least 2-4 CPU cores per GPU for data loading and orchestration. An 8-GPU system should have 16-32 CPU cores minimum.
- **Memory**: CPU RAM should be 1.5-2x GPU memory for data staging. With 8×80GB GPUs, you want at least 1 TB CPU RAM.
- **PCIe lanes**: Each GPU needs PCIe x16. An 8-GPU system needs 128 PCIe lanes, which typically means dual-socket CPUs (AMD EPYC or Intel Xeon).
- **NVMe storage**: For an 8-GPU training node, target **~10–20 GB/s aggregate sequential read** from local NVMe (e.g., two to four PCIe Gen4/Gen5 drives, often RAID-0) so dataloaders and checkpoint I/O do not stall the GPUs. Terabyte-scale datasets usually live on a cluster parallel filesystem; local NVMe still matters for per-node cache and scratch space.

The CPU doesn't need to be the latest generation—it's not doing the compute. But it needs enough cores and PCIe bandwidth to keep GPUs busy. Now let's turn to the component that does the heavy lifting: GPUs.

Graphics Processing Unit (GPU)

When you're building distributed training systems, the GPU architecture matters. NVIDIA has been iterating on GPU designs since 2010, and each generation brings changes that affect how you design your training pipeline. Here's what you need to know about the GPUs you're likely to encounter.

Understanding GPU memory and compute architecture

GPUs are built for throughput, not latency. Unlike CPUs that optimize for fast single-threaded execution, GPUs pack thousands of simple cores and prioritize high-bandwidth memory access. When you're training large models, this design pays off—but it also means you need to think differently about memory and compute.

The memory hierarchy matters. Registers are fastest but tiny. Shared memory (L1 cache) is fast but limited. L2 cache sits between shared memory and device DRAM, which is your main GPU memory. When you see "out of memory" errors, it's usually the device DRAM that's full, not the caches.

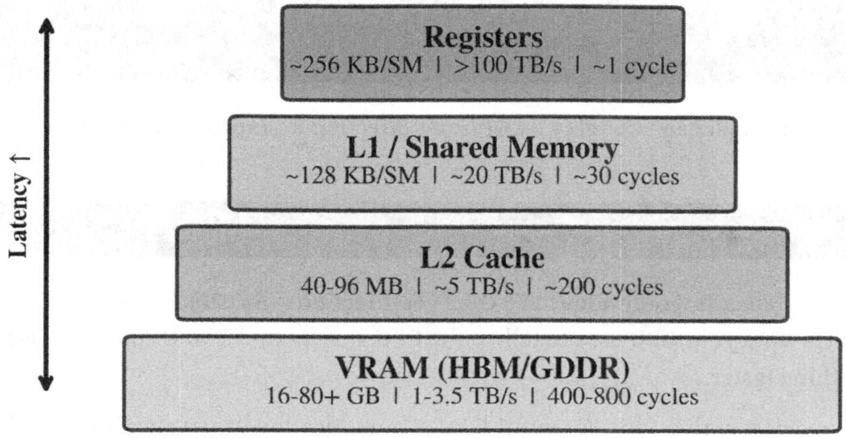

Figure 2.4: GPU Memory Hierarchy Architecture

As illustrated in *Figure 2.4*, the GPU memory hierarchy consists of multiple levels, each with different characteristics: registers provide the highest bandwidth and lowest latency but have minimal capacity; L1/shared memory offers fast access with limited capacity per streaming multiprocessor (SM); L2 cache provides a larger shared cache with moderate bandwidth; and VRAM (HBM/GDDR) offers the largest capacity but with higher latency and lower bandwidth relative to the smaller memory levels. This hierarchy reflects the fundamental tradeoff in memory design: higher bandwidth and lower latency come at the cost of reduced capacity, while larger capacity requires accepting higher latency and lower bandwidth.

One thing that trips people up: memory bandwidth often becomes the bottleneck before compute does. If your kernels are memory-bound, adding more compute won't help. You can spot this by profiling—if your GPU utilization is low but memory bandwidth is maxed out, you're memory-bound.

To see what you're working with, check your GPU specs:

```
nvidia-smi \
  --query-gpu=name,memory.total,pcie.link.gen.max,pcie.link.width.max \
  --format=csv
```

Here's what you might see on different systems. An H200 system with 8 GPUs:

```
$ nvidia-smi --query-gpu=name,memory.total,pcie.link.gen.max,pcie.link.width.max
--format=csv
name, memory.total [MiB], pcie.link.gen.max, pcie.link.width.max
NVIDIA H200, 143771 MiB, 5, 16
NVIDIA H200, 143771 MiB, 5, 16
...
```

That's PCIe Gen 5 with 16 lanes—roughly 64 GB/s per direction. Compare that to a consumer RTX 4090:

```
NVIDIA GeForce RTX 4090, 24564 MiB, 4, 16
```

PCIe Gen 4, same 16 lanes, but only about 31.5 GB/s per direction (~63 GB/s bidirectional). The PCIe connection is what your GPU uses to talk to the CPU, but for multi-GPU communication, you want something faster.

But PCIe is just one part of the story. For multi-GPU communication, you want NVLink—direct GPU-to-GPU links that bypass the CPU entirely. To see what your system actually has, run:

```
nvidia-smi topo -m
```

This shows the topology matrix. The output can be dense, but here's what to look for:

If you see `NV18`, `NV12`, or `NV4` between GPUs, you have NVLink. That's good—those links give you 300-900 GB/s per GPU on Ampere–Hopper (up to 1.8 TB/s on Blackwell B200), aggregate bidirectional, way faster than PCIe. In a well-configured system like a DGX or HGX box, you'll see all GPUs connected via NVLink through an NVSwitch, meaning every GPU can talk to every other GPU at full speed.

If you see `PIX` or `PXB` between GPUs, they're only connected via PCIe. That works, but you'll hit bandwidth limits faster. You might also see `NODE` or `SYS`, which means the connection crosses NUMA boundaries—another thing that can slow things down.

Here's a real example from an H200 system with NVSwitch. All 8 GPUs show `NV18` connections to each other:

```
GPU0    GPU1    GPU2    GPU3    GPU4    GPU5    GPU6    GPU7
GPU0     X      NV18    NV18    NV18    NV18    NV18    NV18    NV18
GPU1    NV18     X      NV18    NV18    NV18    NV18    NV18    NV18
```

That's the ideal setup. Every GPU can communicate with every other GPU at NVLink speeds. In a standard server, you might see some GPUs only connected via `PIX` or `PXB`, which means they're going through PCIe. That still works, but you'll want to be more careful about which GPUs you pair together for communication-heavy operations.

One more thing: notice the CPU affinity column. GPUs 0-3 might be on NUMA node 0, while GPUs 4-7 are on NUMA node 1. If you're doing multi-node training, try to keep processes on the same NUMA node when possible—cross-NUMA communication adds latency.

Key architecture milestones

Through Pascal (2016): Fermi and Pascal established CUDA and early NVLink for multi-GPU systems—you are unlikely to see them in production AI clusters today.

Volta and Ampere (2017–2020): Volta introduced Tensor Cores; the A100 (Ampere) added TF32/BF16, NVLink 3.0 (600 GB/s per GPU), and NVSwitch. A100s remain common for inference and older training fleets, but new large-scale training builds have moved on.

Hopper (2022) is the current workhorse for distributed training. The H100 brought FP8, Transformer Engine for dynamic precision switching, and NVLink 4.0 (900 GB/s per GPU, aggregate bidirectional). The H200 keeps the same compute but adds HBM3e capacity (141 GB vs 80 GB on H100)—important when model state and activations dominate memory.

Blackwell (2024) is the high-end NVIDIA training generation if you're building a new cluster today. Roadmaps already name successors such as Vera Rubin, so check SKU lists and lead times with your vendor or cloud provider before you commit. The B200 doubles NVLink bandwidth to 1.8 TB/s per GPU (aggregate bidirectional), uses a dual-die package (two dies per module), and raises HBM bandwidth to 8 TB/s per GPU—roughly 2× the transformer training throughput of an H100 at scale. Within the same generation, higher-memory Blackwell variants (e.g., B300-class GPUs) add HBM capacity for very large models; they often trade higher power and stricter cooling requirements for the extra headroom.

What these numbers mean for training

When you're choosing GPUs for distributed training, you care about three things:

Memory capacity and bandwidth: A 70B parameter model with FP16 weights needs about 140 GB just for the model. Add gradients, optimizer states (Adam uses 2x model size), and activations, and you're looking at 500+ GB per training step. The H100 has 80 GB HBM3, the H200 has 141 GB, and the B200 has 192 GB (288 GB on higher-memory Blackwell variants such as B300-class GPUs). More memory means larger batch sizes or fewer GPUs needed.

HBM bandwidth matters too. The A100 has 2 TB/s, H100 has 3 TB/s, and B200 has 8 TB/s (all per GPU). However, interconnect bandwidth (NVLink/InfiniBand) is typically the main bottleneck for gradient synchronization across GPUs. HBM bandwidth primarily affects local operations like reduce kernels and fused operators—higher HBM bandwidth means faster local reductions and memory-bound operations.

Compute throughput: This is where Tensor Cores shine. The H100 delivers about 1 PFLOP for FP16, while the B200 hits 2.25 PFLOP. But raw FLOPS don't tell the whole story—you need to look at what precision you're actually using. FP8 training can be 2x faster than FP16, but not all models train well at FP8. Hopper's Transformer Engine (carried forward on Blackwell) automatically switches between FP8 and FP16 during training; NVIDIA's H100 architecture whitepaper reports **up to 6× higher training throughput on transformer workloads vs A100** when FP8 and Transformer Engine are enabled[3]—not a guarantee for every model or stack.

Interconnect bandwidth: NVLink bandwidth (per GPU, aggregate bidirectional) determines how fast GPUs can synchronize gradients. A100 has 600 GB/s, H100 has 900 GB/s, and B200 has 1.8 TB/s (all per GPU, aggregate bidirectional). When you're doing data parallelism, you're doing AllReduce operations every step. Faster NVLink means less communication overhead.

Graphics Processing Unit (GPU) product families

NVIDIA ships GPUs in different form factors depending on your needs:

HGX (Hyperscale GPU eXchange) is a baseboard module that OEMs integrate into servers. An HGX H100 has 8 H100 GPUs connected via NVSwitch, giving you 640 GB total HBM, 900 GB/s NVLink per GPU, and about 3.6 TB/s NVSwitch bisection bandwidth across the baseboard. You buy this from server vendors like Dell, Supermicro, or Inspur, who add CPUs, storage, and networking.

DGX (Deep GPU Xceleration) is NVIDIA's complete system. A DGX H100 is a pre-integrated server with 8 H100s, AMD EPYC CPUs, NVMe storage, and InfiniBand networking. It's more expensive but comes with optimized software stack and support. DGX systems are what most AI companies use for training—they're tested, documented, and just work.

SuperPOD scales beyond a single server. A DGX SuperPOD connects multiple DGX systems (typically 32-64 nodes) via InfiniBand, creating a cluster with thousands of GPUs. The GB200 SuperPOD connects 8 GB200 NVL72 units (each with 72 GPUs, on the order of 130 TB/s NVLink capacity per rack per NVIDIA specifications) for a total of 576 GPUs, with additional NVLink switching between racks.

The GB200 NVL72 is interesting—it's a liquid-cooled rack unit with 36 GB200 superchips (72 GPUs total) connected via NVLink. NVIDIA markets it as a "single massive GPU" because NVLink ties the rack together with very high bandwidth—but that is marketing, not a programming model. You still run 72 GPUs with explicit parallelism (TP/PP/DP, collectives, and deliberate tensor placement); frameworks shard the model for you. Do not expect transparent unified memory like CPU NUMA. The benefit is fast intra-rack communication for trillion-parameter training, not one logical device with no distributed code.

Choosing the right GPU

For most distributed training, you'll be choosing between H100, H200, or B200. Here's the decision tree:

- **H100**: Still the workhorse. 80 GB memory, 3 TB/s bandwidth, 900 GB/s NVLink. Good balance of performance and availability. Use this if you're building a cluster now and need proven hardware.
- **H200**: Same compute as H100 but 141 GB memory. Use this if you're memory-bound—larger models, longer sequences, or when you want bigger batch sizes. The extra memory costs more but can reduce the number of GPUs you need.
- **B200**: Flagship Blackwell for training—192 GB HBM, 8 TB/s memory bandwidth, 1.8 TB/s NVLink per GPU. Use it when you need maximum throughput and can get capacity; the dual-die design gives you roughly 2× the H100's compute, at a premium, and availability varies by quarter and region.

One thing to watch: **availability** matters as much as the spec sheet. Demand spikes and product transitions often leave older GPUs in production while newer SKUs ramp, so lead times, cloud quotas, and which generation is easiest to buy can flip quarter to quarter. Confirm any backlog rumor with your vendor or cloud provider before you freeze a design—high-demand parts have seen multi-month waits in past cycles, and that eases or returns as new silicon ships. Roadmap announcements beyond Blackwell can reshuffle what you can actually source, so check again when you're ready to buy.

For inference, the calculus changes. B200's FP4 performance (20 PFLOP) makes it attractive for high-throughput inference, but the cost per request matters more than peak FLOPS. Many inference deployments still use A100 or even consumer GPUs because they're cheaper and good enough.

Architecture features that matter

Tensor Cores are the secret sauce. They're specialized units that do matrix multiplication 10-100x faster than CUDA cores. Every modern training framework (PyTorch, TensorFlow, JAX) uses them automatically through cuBLAS and cuDNN. You don't need to write special code—just make sure you're using FP16/BF16/FP8 precision.

Transformer Engine (Hopper and Blackwell) automatically switches between FP8 and FP16 during training. It monitors activation statistics and uses FP8 when safe, FP16 when needed for accuracy—the source of the up-to-6× transformer training claims cited above[3].

MIG (Multi-Instance GPU) on A100 and H100 lets you partition a single GPU into multiple virtual GPUs. Each partition gets dedicated memory and compute. This is useful for cloud providers who want to rent GPU time to multiple customers, but for training large models, you'll want the full GPU.

NVLink-C2C in Grace Hopper systems connects the CPU and GPU with 900 GB/s bandwidth (aggregate bidirectional). This lets the GPU access CPU memory directly, useful for models that don't fit in GPU memory. The Grace CPU has 512 GB LPDDR5X, so a GH200 system gives you 608 GB total addressable memory (96 GB GPU + 512 GB CPU).

When you're designing distributed systems, these architectural details determine your parallelism strategy. High NVLink bandwidth means tensor parallelism is viable. Large memory means you can fit bigger models or use fewer GPUs. Fast HBM means you can process larger batches without hitting memory bandwidth limits.

While NVIDIA GPUs dominate the distributed training landscape, it's worth understanding alternative accelerators. Google's Tensor Processing Units (TPUs) offer a different architectural approach optimized specifically for neural networks, and Neural Processing Units (NPUs) represent another domain-specific option. Understanding these alternatives helps when choosing hardware or porting code between platforms.

Tensor Processing Unit (TPU)

Google's Tensor Processing Unit (TPU) offers a different architectural approach from GPUs. TPUs are application-specific integrated circuits (ASICs) designed from the ground up for neural network workloads. If you're working at Google or using Google Cloud, you'll encounter TPUs. Understanding how they differ from GPUs helps when choosing hardware or porting code between platforms.

Why TPUs exist

Google started designing TPUs in 2013 when they realized that running neural networks on CPUs was too expensive. Their prediction: if people used 3 minutes of voice search per day with neural network-based speech recognition, they'd need to double their datacenter capacity. CPUs couldn't scale cost-effectively, and GPUs at the time (2013) weren't optimized for neural networks.

TPU v1 shipped in 2016—just 15 months from design to deployment. That's fast for a chip. The first silicon worked without any mask changes, which is rare. The key insight: neural networks don't need the flexibility of CPUs or GPUs. They're mostly matrix multiplication, so you can build a chip that does one thing extremely well.

TPU architecture: systolic arrays

The core of a TPU is the **Matrix Multiply Unit (MXU)**, which uses a **systolic array** architecture. Unlike GPUs that use thousands of CUDA cores with registers and caches, a systolic array is a grid of processing elements (PEs) where data flows through the array like a heartbeat—hence "systolic."

Here's how it works: instead of storing intermediate results in registers and fetching them later, data flows directly from one PE to the next. Each PE multiplies two values and passes results to neighbors. This eliminates most memory accesses because data is reused as it flows through the array. For matrix multiplication, this is incredibly efficient—you read each input value once and reuse it many times.

TPU v1 had a 256×256 systolic array (65,536 PEs) running at 700 MHz, giving about 92 TOPS for INT8 operations. TPU v2 and later use 128×128 arrays but have multiple MXUs per chip. The systolic design means TPUs excel at dense matrix multiplication but aren't as flexible as GPUs for other operations.

TPU generations

Google's line evolved in a few jumps that still show up in papers and pod design: **v1 (2016)** was inference-only (INT8 over PCIe); **v2** added BF16 training, HBM, and chip-to-chip links; **v4** added **Sparse Core** for embeddings, **3D torus** pods at thousands of chips, and **optical circuit switching (OCS)**. Early generations are no longer offered on GCP, but those milestones explain the vocabulary in older write-ups.

On Google Cloud, the currently relevant public TPU families include **v5e/v5p**, **Trillium**, **TPU7x/Ironwood**, and the newer eighth-generation **TPU 8t/8i** line, though availability depends on region, quota, and deployment mode. Peak FLOPS, memory per chip, pod size, and regional availability change every generation, but the stack stays the same: **JAX or TensorFlow through XLA**, with `jax.jit` and pod sharding as in the section below. Check Google Cloud TPU documentation `https://cloud.google.com/tpu/docs` for which SKUs you can bind.

TPU pod architecture

A **TPU Pod** is Google's term for a TPU cluster. Unlike GPU clusters that use InfiniBand switches, TPU Pods use custom interconnects. Newer generations scale pod size and fabric details; the ideas below come from v2–v4 designs but still describe how traffic tends to flow on a torus:

- **2D torus** (early pods): Chips on a grid, each with four neighbors (edges wrap). Good local bandwidth; distant pairs take more hops.

- **3D torus** (from v4 onward): Six neighbors per chip (a 3D mesh with wraparound). Shorter diameter than 2D for the same chip count—important at pod scale.
- **Optical circuit switching (OCS)**: Introduced at v4 scale—MEMS optical switches route light between chips with less conversion loss. Routes can be reconfigured for fault tolerance.

The torus topology is different from GPU clusters' Clos/fat-tree networks. Torus is cheaper (fewer switches, simpler wiring) and has lower latency for local communication, but it's less flexible for scaling and load balancing. Clos networks are non-blocking (any input can talk to any output at full bandwidth simultaneously), while torus networks can have congestion.

TPU vs GPU: when to use which

Use TPUs if:

- You're at Google or using Google Cloud Platform
- Your workload is mostly dense matrix multiplication (transformers, CNNs)
- You want maximum performance for specific models (Google optimizes the TPU software stack for their models)
- You're training at Google scale (thousands of chips)

Use GPUs if:

- You need flexibility (different model architectures, research)
- You're using PyTorch (TPU support exists but GPU is first-class)
- You need to run on-premises or multi-cloud
- Your workload has sparse operations or irregular patterns
- You need practical debugging—opaque XLA errors, weaker profilers than NVIDIA Nsight, and little public community support unless you are a large Google/GCP customer

Performance characteristics:

- TPUs excel at dense matrix ops. Per-chip peak FLOPS varies by generation (v4 was about 275 TFLOPS BF16; Trillium, Ironwood, and 8th-gen SKUs are higher—see GCP specs)—roughly Ampere-class per chip at the v4 era, not H100-class (~990 TFLOPS BF16/FP16 dense). End-to-end transformer training can still be competitive at pod scale when XLA and the workload match the stack.

- GPUs are more general-purpose. They handle sparse operations, custom kernels, and mixed workloads better.
- TPU software stack (XLA compiler) is highly optimized but less flexible. You compile your model to XLA, and the compiler generates optimized code. This can be faster than GPU for supported operations but harder to debug.

Debugging and tooling: On GPUs you get mature tools (`nvidia-smi`, Nsight, PyTorch profiler) and a large community. On TPUs, failures often show up as **opaque XLA compilation errors** (long compiler logs, little line-level context), profiling is less mature, and help is mostly **GCP/ Google channels**—not Stack Overflow depth. For teams learning distributed training, that friction is a real cost next to FLOPS and price per hour.

Cost and availability:

- TPUs are only available on Google Cloud. You can't buy them.
- GPU pricing varies by cloud provider and availability. H100s are expensive but available from multiple vendors.
- TPU pricing is per-hour on GCP. For large-scale training, TPUs can be cost-effective if your workload fits.

TPU programming model

TPUs run through **XLA (Accelerated Linear Algebra)**. You write TensorFlow or JAX code; XLA lowers it to TPU instructions. That is a different workflow from GPUs, where you typically rely on CUDA kernels and libraries such as cuDNN rather than a whole-program compile step.

The trade-off is startup time. The first run compiles the full graph and can take minutes; later runs reuse the compiled binary and are much faster. GPUs usually start quicker but may carry more per-step runtime overhead.

For multi-chip training, TensorFlow distribution strategies remain common. In JAX, use `jax.jit` **with sharding annotations**—`PartitionSpec` and `NamedSharding` on a device mesh —to describe how tensors map across the pod; use `jax.shard_map` when you need explicit per-chip logic. Placement still matters on a torus: shard tensors so most traffic stays between neighbors, and let XLA optimize the rest. Poor layouts still show up as slow steps or confusing errors at debug time.

Sparse core (since v4)

Sparse Core debuted on TPU v4 and remains part of later training-oriented generations (including embedding-heavy **TPU 8t** workloads). Embedding layers map discrete IDs to dense vectors; access is irregular and does not fit pure systolic matmuls. Sparse Core tiles fetch and process those lookups with dedicated HBM paths—algorithm-hardware co-design that GPUs usually handle in software.

If you train recommendation models or models with large embedding tables, check whether your GCP SKU includes Sparse Core. For transformer-only workloads it matters less.

Beyond GPUs and TPUs, another class of accelerators has emerged: Neural Processing Units (NPUs), which represent a broader category of domain-specific AI chips. While less common in large-scale training, NPUs are worth understanding as they represent a different trade-off between flexibility and efficiency.

Neural Processing Unit (NPU)

Neural Processing Units (NPUs) represent another approach: domain-specific architecture (DSA) chips optimized for AI workloads. NPUs are ASICs (Application-Specific Integrated Circuits) designed from the ground up for neural network operations, trading general-purpose flexibility for efficiency.

What makes NPUs different

NPUs are built around **AI Cores**—specialized units optimized for matrix multiplication, convolution, and other neural network primitives. Early GPUs grew out of graphics; today's training GPUs lean on similar specialized blocks (Tensor Cores, matrix units), so the historical "GPU vs NPU" story is as much about **software and go-to-market** as about a fundamentally different die.

The architecture tradeoff is a useful mental model, not a hard boundary:

- **CPUs** — general-purpose control and orchestration
- **GPUs** — throughput-oriented parallel processors with a large software stack
- **NPUs** — AI-first designs that trade flexibility for efficiency

Convergence: Those lines are blurring. Modern datacenter GPUs are less "graphics chips" every generation—NVIDIA **Tensor Cores** are domain-specific matrix engines for training and inference, and AMD **MI300X** (CDNA3) dedicates much of the die to matrix units and HBM in ways that look very NPU-like. Pure NPUs still differ in software (proprietary stacks, edge focus), but when you're choosing hardware you're usually comparing **degrees of specialization**, not three separate species. Ecosystem (CUDA/ROCm, PyTorch, NCCL) still matters more than the label on the slide.

You'll still run into a mixed deployment landscape. **Huawei Ascend** (910C and later) pairs datacenter NPUs with rack-scale **SuperPoD** systems on custom interconnects—common in China and some export markets. **AWS Trainium** is Amazon's training ASIC on EC2, from **Trainium2** instances up to multi-rack clusters. **Google's Edge TPU** is a separate, low-power line for edge inference, not the cloud TPU pods in the previous section. Regional vendors such as **Cambricon MLU** matter where their stacks and supply chains fit your workload. Specs and SKUs change fast—check vendor docs before you lock in hardware.

NPU architecture: AI cores and memory

NPU architecture centers on **AI Cores**—dedicated compute units for neural network operations. Each AI Core typically includes:

- **Matrix multiplication units**: Optimized for GEMM (General Matrix Multiply) operations
- **Vector processing units**: For element-wise operations, activations, normalization
- **Specialized units**: For operations like pooling, convolution, attention

Memory hierarchy is critical. NPUs use high-bandwidth memory (HBM) similar to GPUs, but the memory subsystem is often simpler—fewer cache levels, more direct paths to compute units. This reduces latency but requires careful memory management.

Training-focused datacenter NPUs today often ship **64–128+ GB HBM** per chip with **hundreds of TFLOPS** of BF16/FP16 peak (vendor-dependent—well above the early 200–300 TFLOPS class). The architecture still centers on many AI Cores per die and matrix-heavy execution.

Training vs inference NPUs

Like GPUs, NPUs come in training and inference variants:

Training NPUs need:

- High precision support (FP32, BF16, FP16) for stable gradient computation
- Large memory capacity for model parameters, gradients, and optimizer states
- High-bandwidth interconnects for multi-chip training
- Flexibility to support various model architectures

Inference NPUs (like Edge TPU) prioritize:

- Lower precision (INT8, INT4) for efficiency
- Lower power consumption for edge deployment
- Lower latency for real-time applications
- Cost efficiency for mass deployment

The same chip rarely excels at both. Training requires flexibility and precision; inference requires efficiency and low cost.

NPU software stack

NPU software stacks are typically more proprietary than GPU ecosystems. Each vendor provides their own framework and runtime (e.g., MindSpore, CANN). Unlike CUDA which works across NVIDIA GPUs, NPU software is often vendor-specific.

This creates a lock-in risk: code written for one vendor's NPUs won't run on other NPUs without significant porting. The ecosystem is fragmented compared to CUDA's dominance in the GPU space.

However, some frameworks are trying to abstract this. PyTorch has experimental support for some NPU backends, and ONNX Runtime can target multiple NPU vendors. But the experience isn't as seamless as GPU development.

NPU vs. GPU: when to choose which

Choose NPUs if:

- You have specific workloads that NPUs optimize for (certain model types or operations)
- You're building edge devices where power efficiency matters more than flexibility
- You're working with vendors who provide NPU-optimized solutions
- You need alternatives to NVIDIA GPUs for specific use cases

Choose GPUs if:

- You need flexibility (research, different model architectures)
- You want the largest ecosystem (PyTorch, TensorFlow, JAX all have first-class GPU support)
- You need to run on multiple clouds or on-premises
- You're doing general-purpose ML work, not just specific NPU-optimized workloads

Performance comparison: NPUs can match or exceed GPUs for specific workloads they're optimized for. Training performance can be comparable to A100 for certain models. But GPUs have broader model support and better software ecosystem.

Cost: NPU pricing varies by vendor and region. GPU ecosystem maturity often makes GPUs the better choice for most use cases, but NPUs can be cost-effective for specific workloads or regions.

NPU interconnects and scaling

Like GPUs, NPUs need high-bandwidth interconnects for distributed training. NPU vendors use custom collective communication services and interconnects. NPU clusters can scale to thousands of chips, similar to GPU clusters.

The interconnect topology matters. NPU systems typically use a hierarchical architecture with chip-to-chip, node-to-node, and cluster-level interconnects. Understanding this topology helps when designing distributed training strategies.

One challenge: NPU interconnects are often proprietary. Unlike InfiniBand which is an open standard, NPU interconnects are vendor-specific. This can make multi-vendor clusters difficult.

The NPU landscape

NPUs don't look like GPUs. NVIDIA still dominates global GPU training; NPUs split across hyperscalers, regions, and short product cycles. Tesla has wound down Dojo; Graphcore was acquired by SoftBank and is no longer a standalone comparison point. What you'll actually encounter are **hyperscaler stacks—Trainium** on AWS, **Ascend SuperPoD** on Huawei Cloud—and edge parts like **Google's Edge TPU**, each with its own collectives and compilers.

For distributed training, NPUs are viable where the vendor stack matches your framework and region, but expect **more porting work than CUDA/NCCL**. GPUs remain the default for multi-cloud and research flexibility; NPUs can win on **cost, locality, or tuned workloads** in specific deployments.

Now that we've covered the compute hardware (CPUs, GPUs, TPUs, and NPUs), we need to understand how these components communicate. The interconnect technology—how chips talk to each other—is often the bottleneck in distributed training. Fast interconnects enable efficient gradient synchronization and data movement, while slow interconnects can cripple performance regardless of how powerful your compute hardware is.

High-Speed interconnects: the network backbone

There are several ways GPUs connect, and which one matters depends on whether you're talking about intra-node or inter-node communication.

Within a single server:

PCIe is what you get by default. Every GPU connects to the CPU via PCIe, and if there's no NVLink, GPUs talk to each other through the CPU too. It works, but it's the slowest option—typically 16-64 GB/s depending on PCIe generation. The latency is also higher since everything goes through the CPU.

NVLink is NVIDIA's direct GPU-to-GPU interconnect. When two GPUs have NVLink between them, they can talk directly without involving the CPU. Bandwidth is much higher—300-900 GB/s per GPU on Ampere–Hopper (up to 1.8 TB/s on Blackwell B200), aggregate bidirectional. The catch is that not all systems have it, and even when they do, not all GPU pairs might be connected.

NVSwitch is what you see in high-end systems like DGX or HGX boxes. It's essentially a switch that connects all GPUs via NVLink, giving you all-to-all connectivity. Every GPU can talk to every other GPU at full NVLink speed simultaneously. This is what you want for large-scale distributed training intra-node.

Across multiple servers:

InfiniBand is the standard for multi-node GPU clusters. When you're running distributed training across multiple servers, GPUs on different nodes need to communicate, and that's where InfiniBand comes in. It provides high-bandwidth, low-latency networking—typically 200-400 Gb/s (25-50 GB/s) per port, with sub-microsecond latency. Modern systems use InfiniBand HDR (200 Gb/s) or NDR (400 Gb/s).

The key feature that makes InfiniBand fast is **RDMA (Remote Direct Memory Access)**. RDMA allows network adapters to read and write memory directly without involving the CPU or kernel. InfiniBand was designed from the ground up to support RDMA natively—it's built into the protocol. When you use InfiniBand, you get RDMA by default.

You'll see InfiniBand NICs in the `nvidia-smi topo -m` output—those are the network interface cards that connect your server to the cluster network. When NCCL does multi-node communication, it uses **GPUDirect RDMA**, which is NVIDIA's implementation that extends RDMA to GPU memory. This allows data to transfer directly from GPU memory on one node to GPU memory on another node, completely bypassing the CPU and system RAM. That's why it's so fast.

Ethernet is the other option for multi-node networking. There are two flavors:

Standard Ethernet (TCP/IP) works, but it's slower. You're looking at 10-100 Gb/s per port, and latency is higher because everything goes through the kernel network stack. For small clusters or when cost is a concern, it can work, but you'll see performance degradation as you scale up.

RoCE (RDMA over Converged Ethernet) is the interesting one. As the name suggests, it's RDMA over Ethernet instead of InfiniBand. So RDMA isn't exclusive to InfiniBand—it's a capability that can be implemented over different network technologies. RoCE v2 gives you the same RDMA benefits (GPU-to-GPU direct memory access, bypassing the CPU) but over standard Ethernet infrastructure. Bandwidth is comparable—100-400 Gb/s depending on the NIC—but latency is typically higher than InfiniBand, and you need proper switch configuration (DCB/PFC) to avoid packet loss under load.

The practical difference: InfiniBand is purpose-built for HPC workloads and tends to be more reliable at scale. RoCE works when you're already on Ethernet infrastructure, but you need to tune it carefully (DCB/PFC, lossless fabrics).

For most on-prem clusters, InfiniBand is still the default choice. If you have existing Ethernet infrastructure instead, RoCE is a viable alternative. Bandwidth and latency still dominate gradient sync at scale, so benchmark what your environment actually provides.

If you're buying hardware, DGX systems are pre-integrated—NVIDIA ships you a complete system with GPUs, CPUs, networking (including InfiniBand), and software stack. HGX is more modular—it's a baseboard design that OEMs use to build custom servers. Both can include NVSwitch for intra-node communication and InfiniBand for inter-node.

To actually measure your interconnect bandwidth, you can use NCCL tests or write a simple benchmark. The `code/bandwidth_test.py` script gives you a basic single-GPU test. For multi-GPU intra-node, you'll want to use `nccl-tests`. For inter-node clusters, NCCL tests will show you InfiniBand bandwidth.

Understanding hardware is only half the story. To write efficient distributed training code, you also need to understand how chips are programmed. The programming model (how you write code) and execution model (how hardware runs it) are different layers, and knowing both helps when debugging performance or porting code between platforms.

Chip programming systems: SPMD and CUDA

Understanding how chips are programmed helps you write efficient distributed training code. The programming model (how you write code) and execution model (how hardware runs it) are different layers, and knowing both helps when debugging performance or porting code between platforms.

Programming models vs. execution models

Programming models are abstractions for developers. They define how you structure code, what concepts you use (threads, blocks, kernels), and how you express parallelism. You write code using the programming model.

Execution models describe how hardware actually runs your code. The hardware might execute SIMD instructions, but you program it using threads. The compiler bridges this gap.

For distributed training, you're usually working at the programming model level (PyTorch, TensorFlow, JAX), but understanding the execution model helps when things go wrong or when you need to optimize.

SPMD: single program, multiple data

SPMD (Single Program, Multiple Data) is the programming model that CUDA uses. The idea: you write one program (kernel), and it runs on multiple threads, each processing different data.

Here's a simple CUDA kernel that adds two vectors:

```
__global__ void vectorAdd(float *A, float *B, float *C, int N) {
    int i = blockIdx.x * blockDim.x + threadIdx.x;
    if (i < N) {
        C[i] = A[i] + B[i];
    }
}
```

You launch this with:

```
vectorAdd<<<numBlocks, threadsPerBlock>>>(A, B, C, N);
```

Each thread executes the same code (`vectorAdd`), but `threadIdx.x` gives each thread a unique ID, so they process different array elements. This is SPMD: one program, multiple data elements.

SPMD is different from SIMD (Single Instruction, Multiple Data). SIMD is an execution model —hardware executes one instruction on multiple data elements simultaneously. SPMD is a programming model—you write code as if each thread is independent, even though hardware might execute them in SIMD fashion.

CUDA's execution model: SIMT

NVIDIA GPUs execute SPMD programs using **SIMT (Single Instruction, Multiple Thread)**. Here's how it works:

Thread hierarchy: CUDA organizes threads into a hierarchy:

- **Thread**: The smallest unit. Each thread has its own registers and can execute independently.
- **Warp**: A group of 32 threads that execute together. This is the hardware scheduling unit.
- **Block**: A group of threads (typically 128-1024) that can share memory and synchronize.
- **Grid**: A collection of blocks that execute the same kernel.

Warp execution: When you launch a kernel, the GPU groups threads into warps. All 32 threads in a warp execute the same instruction simultaneously (SIMD-style), but each thread operates on different data. If threads in a warp take different branches (divergence), the warp executes both paths sequentially, which hurts performance.

Fine-grained multithreading (FGMT): GPUs use FGMT to hide memory latency. When one warp is waiting for memory, the scheduler switches to another warp that's ready to execute. This keeps the execution units busy even when individual warps are stalled.

This is why GPU utilization matters. If you have enough warps, the GPU can hide latency by switching between them. If you don't have enough parallelism, warps sit idle waiting for memory and utilization drops.

Why SIMT over SIMD?

SIMT (what GPUs use) is more flexible than traditional SIMD (what CPUs use for vectorization):

Data alignment: SIMD requires data to be aligned and contiguous. SIMT doesn't—each thread can access different memory locations independently. This makes irregular memory patterns easier to handle.

Branch divergence: In SIMD, if one element takes a different branch, you execute both paths and mask results. SIMT handles this more gracefully—threads can diverge, though it still costs performance.

Programming model: SIMT lets you write scalar code (one thread, one element) that gets compiled to SIMD execution. You don't need to manually vectorize or think about vector widths.

Dynamic grouping: SIMT hardware dynamically groups threads into warps. You don't need to know the warp size when writing code—the hardware handles it.

CUDA thread indexing

Understanding thread indexing is crucial for writing correct CUDA kernels. Each thread has identifiers:

- `threadIdx.x/y/z`: Thread's position within its block (0 to blockDim.x-1)
- `blockIdx.x/y/z`: Block's position within the grid
- `blockDim.x/y/z`: Number of threads per block (set at launch)
- `gridDim.x/y/z`: Number of blocks in the grid

To compute a global thread ID for a 1D grid:

```
int i = blockIdx.x * blockDim.x + threadIdx.x;
```

For a 2D grid (common for image processing):

```
int row = blockIdx.y * blockDim.y + threadIdx.y;
int col = blockIdx.x * blockDim.x + threadIdx.x;
```

The key insight: you use these indices to determine which data each thread processes. If you have N elements and launch M threads, thread i processes element i (with bounds checking).

Memory hierarchy in CUDA

CUDA exposes a memory hierarchy that maps to hardware:

- **Registers**: Fastest, private to each thread. Limited quantity (typically 64KB per SM).
- **Shared memory**: Fast, shared within a block. Used for communication and caching. Typically 48KB or 96KB per SM.
- **Global memory**: Slow but large. All threads can access it. This is GPU DRAM (HBM).
- **Constant memory**: Read-only, cached. Good for values that don't change.
- **Texture memory**: Cached, optimized for 2D access patterns.

For distributed training, you're mostly using global memory (model weights, activations, gradients). But understanding shared memory helps when writing custom kernels or optimizing data loading.

How frameworks use CUDA

When you write PyTorch code like:

```
output = torch.matmul(input, weight)
```

PyTorch doesn't generate CUDA kernels on the fly. Instead, it calls pre-compiled kernels from libraries like cuBLAS (for matrix multiplication) or cuDNN (for convolutions). These libraries are highly optimized and use techniques like:

- **Kernel fusion**: Combining multiple operations into one kernel to reduce memory traffic
- **Tile-based algorithms**: Breaking large matrices into tiles that fit in shared memory
- **Tensor Core usage**: Automatically using Tensor Cores when available

You rarely write CUDA kernels directly for distributed training. But understanding how CUDA works helps when:

- Debugging performance issues (why is my GPU utilization low?)

- Writing custom operations (maybe you need a fused kernel)
- Understanding framework limitations (why can't PyTorch do X?)

SPMD in distributed training

SPMD extends naturally to distributed training. Each GPU runs the same program (your training script), but processes different data:

- **Data parallelism**: Each GPU gets a different batch. Same model, different data.
- **Model parallelism**: Each GPU gets different model layers. Same data, different model parts.

The communication primitives (AllReduce, AllGather, etc.) coordinate between GPUs, but each GPU still executes the same program structure.

This is why distributed training frameworks (DDP, see *Chapter 3*; FSDP, see *Chapter 4*) feel similar to single-GPU training—you're still writing SPMD code, just with communication added.

AMD and other alternatives

AMD GPUs use a different execution model. AMD's CDNA architecture (MI300X) uses **SIMD execution units** rather than SIMT. Each Compute Unit (CU) has 4 SIMD units, and the scheduler picks which SIMD unit to use.

ROCm (AMD's CUDA alternative) provides a CUDA-like programming interface, but the hardware execution is different. This can lead to performance differences—code optimized for NVIDIA GPUs might not run as well on AMD GPUs.

For distributed training, stick with NVIDIA if possible. The ecosystem (CUDA, cuDNN, NCCL) is mature and well-optimized. AMD is catching up, but NVIDIA still has the advantage in software support.

Now that we understand how individual chips work and how they're programmed, we need to understand how multiple chips communicate during distributed training. The communication patterns and primitives determine how efficiently gradients and data flow between GPUs.

Distributed communication: patterns and primitives

Chapter 1 defines Broadcast, AllReduce, AllGather, ReduceScatter, and the rest, with diagrams and runnable demos. Those calls describe *what* must happen between ranks; in production, **NCCL** (PyTorch's default GPU backend, `backend="nccl"`) implements them over the interconnects above. CPU-only or debugging jobs may use Gloo instead. The training mappings you will see again in later chapters: **AllReduce** for DDP gradient sync (*Chapter 3*);

ReduceScatter and **AllGather** for FSDP-style sharding (*Chapter 4*); **AllGather** every layer in tensor parallelism (below).

A 900 GB/s NVLink or 400 Gb/s InfiniBand port is an upper bound, not your AllReduce throughput. Collectives add startup latency, and NCCL may choose ring- or tree-style algorithms depending on message size and topology. Frameworks also hide some of the cost: DDP buckets gradients so AllReduce can overlap with backward compute (*Chapter 3*). That is why the interconnect section ended with NCCL benchmarks—effective collective bandwidth is what limits training, not the peak number on a slide.

NCCL discovers the same topology you inspect with `nvidia-smi topo -m` (hands-on below): NVLink versus PCIe between GPUs, NICs for inter-node traffic. When communication is slow or hangs, try these before you change your parallelism strategy:

- `NCCL_DEBUG=INFO` — prints which paths and algorithms NCCL picked (NVLink, PCIe, InfiniBand). Run a short job; turn off for long production runs.
- `NCCL_IB_DISABLE=1` — disables InfiniBand/RoCE so traffic falls back to TCP sockets. Helps isolate a bad IB setup; use `NCCL_IB_DISABLE=0` (or unset) on clusters that should train over IB.
- `NCCL_TOPO_FILE=/path/to/topo.xml` — overrides auto-discovered topology when visibility is wrong (containers, odd PCIe trees, partial GPU sets). Rare; see NCCL documentation for the XML format.

On multi-node clusters, set `NCCL_SOCKET_IFNAME` (e.g. `ib0`) so NCCL uses the high-speed NIC from the interconnect section, not a management Ethernet port. Additional flags are covered with DDP troubleshooting in *Chapter 3*.

The hands-on at the end of this chapter closes the loop: after `topo -m`, run `code/allreduce_microbench.py` with `torchrun` (same launch pattern as `distributed_basic_test.py` in *Chapter 1*) to measure AllReduce on your real links. Compare the printed bus bandwidth to the NVLink and InfiniBand ranges above—that gap tells you how much headroom parallelism strategy can buy.

With links, collectives, and NCCL behavior on the table, the next question is how to split model and batch across GPUs: the parallelism strategies that follow.

Parallelism: core strategies

There are several ways to split work across GPUs. Each has tradeoffs, and you'll often combine them. But first, let's get the terminology right—there's a lot of confusion about what counts as "model parallelism" versus "data parallelism."

The key distinction is simple: **are you sharding computation or state?** If a single sample's forward pass requires multiple GPUs to complete, that's model parallelism. If each GPU processes samples independently and you just synchronize gradients or shard optimizer states, that's data parallelism.

Parallelism taxonomy table

The following table provides a canonical taxonomy of all parallelization and scaling techniques used in large-model training and inference. The classification is based on **what is being sharded**: computation, model state, or data.

Parallelism	Category	Sub-Category	Phase	Implementation
Data Parallel (DP)	Data	Replicated model, data sharded	Training	PyTorch DDP (*Chapter 3*) / Horovod
Fully Sharded Data Parallel (FSDP)	State	Full state sharding	Training	PyTorch FSDP (*Chapter 4*)
ZeRO-1	State	Optimizer state sharding	Training	DeepSpeed (*Chapter 5*)
ZeRO-2	State	Optimizer + gradient sharding	Training	DeepSpeed (*Chapter 5*)
ZeRO-3	State	Parameter + grad + opt sharding	Training	DeepSpeed (*Chapter 5*)
Tensor Parallelism (TP)	Computation	Intra-layer (hidden/head) split	Training/Inference	Megatron-LM (*Chapter 5*)

Parallelism	Category	Sub-Category	Phase	Implementation
Sequence Parallelism	Computation	Sequence-length dimension split	Training	Megatron-LM (*Chapter 5*)
Context Parallelism	Computation	Long-context attention/KV split	Inference	vLLM (*Chapter 6*) / SGLang (*Chapter 7*)
Pipeline Parallelism (PP)	Computation	Inter-layer/ stage split	Training/ Inference	GPipe / DeepSpeed PP (*Chapter 5*)
Expert Parallelism (MoE EP)	Computation	Sparse conditional compute	Training/ Inference	DeepSpeed-MoE (*Chapter 5*)
Operator/ Intra-op Parallelism	Computation	Generic op-level sharding (SPMD)	Training/ Inference	XLA SPMD / JAX `jit` +sharding / PyTorch DTensor

The three questions for parallelism determination

To classify any parallelism technique, ask three questions:

1. **Does it split computation?** Is the forward/backward pass itself divided across devices, or only model state (parameters, gradients, optimizer states)?
2. **Must a single sample cross devices?** Does processing one sample require multiple devices, or can each device handle samples independently?
3. **Does it introduce new device-to-device collaboration?** Does it need new communication patterns, or use existing primitives like AllReduce?

What the answers tell you:

- **Model parallelism** (Computation category): Answers "Yes" to questions 1 and 2. Examples: TP, PP, EP, Sequence, Context Parallelism.

- **State sharding** (State category): Answers "No" to questions 1 and 2, "Yes" to question 3. Examples: FSDP (*Chapter 4*), ZeRO (*Chapter 5*). These are NOT model parallelism—they shard state but don't split computation.
- **Data parallelism** (Data category): Answers "No" to questions 1 and 2, "Yes" to question 3. Example: DDP (*Chapter 3*). Each GPU processes different samples independently.

Data parallelism: replicated and sharded

Replicated Data Parallelism (DDP) (see *Chapter 3*) is the simplest. You replicate the entire model on each GPU and split the batch across GPUs. Each GPU processes different data samples independently, then you synchronize gradients using AllReduce. It's easy to implement and works great when your model fits on a single GPU. The downside is that you're storing the full model on every GPU, so memory usage scales with the number of GPUs.

Sharded Data Parallelism (FSDP/ZeRO) doesn't replicate the model. Instead, you shard parameters, gradients, and optimizer states across GPUs. FSDP (see *Chapter 4*) shards all three. ZeRO (see *Chapter 5*) has stages—Stage 1 shards optimizer states, Stage 2 adds gradients, Stage 3 adds parameters. Both let you train much larger models with the same number of GPUs.

FSDP and ZeRO are **not model parallelism**—they shard state, not computation. Each GPU still processes samples independently. You're just not storing the full model state on each GPU.

Model parallelism: compute sharding

Model parallelism means the computation of a single sample is split across multiple GPUs. There are several ways to do this:

Tensor Parallelism (TP) splits individual layers across GPUs. Instead of replicating a layer, you split the weight matrix. For example, if you have a linear layer with a 4096×4096 weight matrix, you might split it into two 4096×2048 matrices on two GPUs. During the forward pass, each GPU computes part of the output, then you AllGather to combine results. This lets you fit larger layers, but communication happens every layer, which can be expensive.

Sequence Parallelism splits computation along the sequence length dimension. Different GPUs handle different token positions in the same sequence. This is often combined with tensor parallelism in systems like Megatron-LM (see *Chapter 5*). It's useful for very long sequences where attention computation becomes the bottleneck.

Context Parallelism is similar to sequence parallelism but specifically for long-context scenarios. It splits attention computation and KV cache management across GPUs, allowing you to handle context windows that don't fit on a single GPU. This is particularly important for inference with long prompts (see *Chapter 6*).

Pipeline Parallelism (PP) splits the model depth-wise. GPU 0 handles layers 0-10, GPU 1 handles layers 11-20, and so on. You pipeline microbatches through the stages to keep all GPUs busy. The challenge is pipeline bubbles—when one stage finishes before the next is ready, GPUs sit idle. Getting the scheduling right matters.

Expert Parallelism (EP) is for MoE (Mixture of Experts) models. You distribute different experts across GPUs, and tokens get routed to the right expert. If you have 64 experts and 8 GPUs, each GPU might hold 8 experts. The tricky part is load balancing—some experts get more traffic than others, so you need good routing. This is still model parallelism because a single sample's forward pass may require multiple GPUs (different experts for different tokens).

Combining Strategies

In practice, you'll combine these. A common setup for a 70B model might be: FSDP (*Chapter 4*) for memory efficiency, plus some tensor parallelism (*Chapter 5*) for the largest layers, plus pipeline parallelism if you have enough GPUs. For MoE models, you might do expert parallelism plus data parallelism across expert groups.

Composition patterns (hybrid parallelism)

The following table shows common composition patterns. These are combinations of primitive strategies, not new primitives themselves:

Composition Pattern	Constituent Primitives	Typical Use Case	Representative Systems
DP + TP	Data + Computation	Large dense LLM training	Megatron-LM (*Chapter 5*)
DP + PP	Data + Computation	Deep models with limited memory	GPipe + DDP (*Chapter 3*)
DP + TP + PP	Data + Computation	Multi-thousand-GPU training	Megatron-DeepSpeed (*Chapter 5*)
DP + EP	Data + Computation	Sparse MoE models	DeepSpeed-MoE (*Chapter 5*)
FSDP + TP	State + Computation	Memory-efficient large LLMs	PyTorch FSDP (*Chapter 4*) + Megatron (*Chapter 5*)

Composition Pattern	Constituent Primitives	Typical Use Case	Representative Systems
ZeRO-3 + PP	State + Computation	Extreme-scale models	DeepSpeed (*Chapter 5*)
TP + Context Parallelism	Computation + Computation	Long-context inference	vLLM (*Chapter 6*) / SGLang (*Chapter 7*)

Most people don't implement these from scratch—you'll use PyTorch's DDP (*Chapter 3*)/FSDP (*Chapter 4*), DeepSpeed's ZeRO (*Chapter 5*), or libraries like Megatron-LM (*Chapter 5*) that handle the tensor parallelism details. But understanding what's happening under the hood helps when things go wrong.

Strategy selection: choosing the right approach

Below is a systematic way to think about it.

Training strategy decision tree

Figure 2.5 provides a systematic decision tree to guide your training strategy selection.

Step 1: Does a full model replica fit on one device?

If yes, use **replicated data parallelism (DDP)** (see *Chapter 3*). It's simple, and you'll get good speedup as long as communication doesn't dominate. This is the starting point for most models.

If not, move to sharded data parallelism.

Step 2: Use sharded data parallelism (FSDP/ZeRO)

FSDP (see *Chapter 4*) or ZeRO-3 (see *Chapter 5*) shard parameters, gradients, and optimizer states. This alone might be enough—try it first before adding model parallelism.

Step 3: Is computation of one sample split across devices?

If you're still memory-limited or want better throughput, you might need to split computation. This is where true model parallelism comes in.

Step 4: How is computation split?

- **Tensor/Head/Hidden dimension**: Use **tensor parallelism** (see *Chapter 5*). Good for large layers that don't fit on one GPU. Requires fast interconnects (NVLink or high-bandwidth InfiniBand) since communication happens every layer.
- **Sequence length**: Use **sequence parallelism** (see *Chapter 5*). Often combined with tensor parallelism for very long sequences.
- **Layer/Stage**: Use **pipeline parallelism** (see *Chapter 5*). Good for deep models where you have enough GPUs to split layers. Watch out for pipeline bubbles.
- **Experts/Sparse routing**: Use **expert parallelism** (see *Chapter 5*). Only for MoE models. Requires good load balancing.

Step 5: Hybrid combinations

Most large models use combinations:

- **DP + TP**: Data parallelism inter-node, tensor parallelism intra-node
- **DP + PP**: Data parallelism with pipeline stages
- **DP + TP + PP**: All three combined for very large models
- **DP + EP**: Data parallelism with expert parallelism for MoE

Step 6: System-level optimizations

If memory is still insufficient:

- **Activation checkpointing**: Recompute activations during backward (almost always used with FSDP, see *Chapter 4*)
- **CPU/NVMe offloading**: Move optimizer states or parameters off GPU (slower but enables larger models)

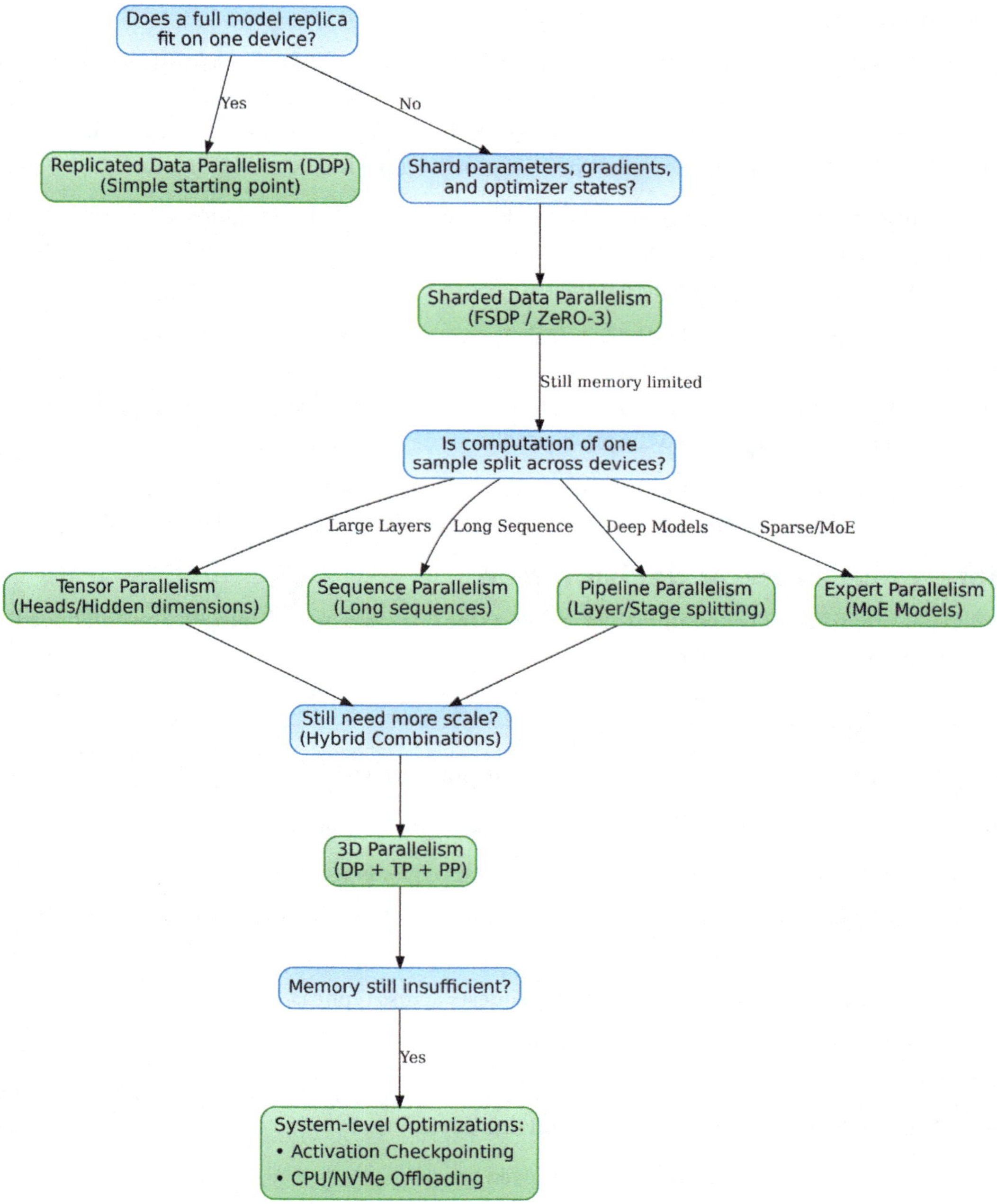

Figure 2.5: Training Strategy Decision Tree

Key considerations for training

Network topology matters. If you're on a system where some GPU pairs are connected via NVLink and others via PCIe, try to keep communication-heavy operations (like tensor parallelism) on the NVLink-connected pairs. PyTorch and most frameworks don't do this automatically, so you might need to set process groups or device placement manually.

Interconnect speed determines what's feasible. Tensor parallelism requires communication every layer, so you need fast interconnects (NVLink for intra-node, InfiniBand for inter-node). If you only have PCIe, avoid tensor parallelism—stick with FSDP/ZeRO or pipeline parallelism.

Memory vs. throughput tradeoff. FSDP/ZeRO maximize memory efficiency but don't necessarily improve throughput. Tensor parallelism can improve throughput (by splitting large layers) but uses more memory per GPU. Pipeline parallelism can improve throughput if you have enough GPUs and can keep the pipeline full.

Start simple, add complexity only if needed. Most models can be trained with just DDP or FSDP. Each additional parallelism strategy adds complexity and potential failure modes.

Inference strategy decision tree

Inference has different constraints than training (see *Chapter 6* and *Chapter 9*). You don't need to store gradients or optimizer states, but you do need to handle KV cache for attention, and latency matters more than throughput in many cases. *Figure 2.6* provides a systematic decision tree to guide your inference strategy selection.

Step 1: Are you scaling a single request or multiple requests?

If you're serving multiple requests, start with **request-level parallelism** (see *Chapter 7*):

- **Batching**: Group multiple requests into batches for better GPU utilization
- **Multiple model replicas**: Run multiple copies of the model to serve more concurrent requests
- **Load-balanced serving**: Distribute requests across replicas

If you're scaling a single request (e.g., very large model or long context), move to model parallelism.

Step 2: Does the model computation fit on one device?

If yes, use **single-GPU inference** with optimized kernels:

- **FlashAttention**: Optimized attention kernels that reduce memory and improve speed
- **Quantization**: INT8/INT4 quantization to reduce memory and increase throughput
- **Kernel fusion**: Combine operations to reduce kernel launch overhead

If not, you need model parallel inference.

Step 3: How is computation split?

- **Tensor/Head/Hidden dimension**: Use **tensor parallelism**. Common in inference systems like vLLM (see *Chapter 6*) and TensorRT-LLM. Requires fast interconnects.
- **Long Context/KV**: Use **context parallelism** (see *Chapter 6*). Essential for long-context inference where the context window doesn't fit on one GPU. Splits attention computation and KV cache across GPUs.
- **Layer/Stage**: Use **pipeline parallelism**. Less common in inference than training, but useful for very large models where you want to keep latency low.
- **Experts**: Use **expert parallelism**. Only for MoE models. Routes tokens to experts on different GPUs.

Step 4: Is memory or KV cache the bottleneck?

For inference, KV cache can be a major memory bottleneck, especially with long contexts and many concurrent requests. Use system-level serving techniques:

- **KV Cache Paging / PagedAttention**: Virtualize KV cache memory, allowing you to serve more concurrent requests than would fit in GPU memory. Used in vLLM (see *Chapter 6*).
- **KV Cache Disaggregation**: Store KV cache on separate devices or in CPU memory, fetching as needed. Useful for very long contexts (see *Chapter 6*).
- **CPU/NVMe Offloading**: Move model parameters or KV cache off GPU. Slower but enables serving larger models or more concurrent requests (see Chapter 9).

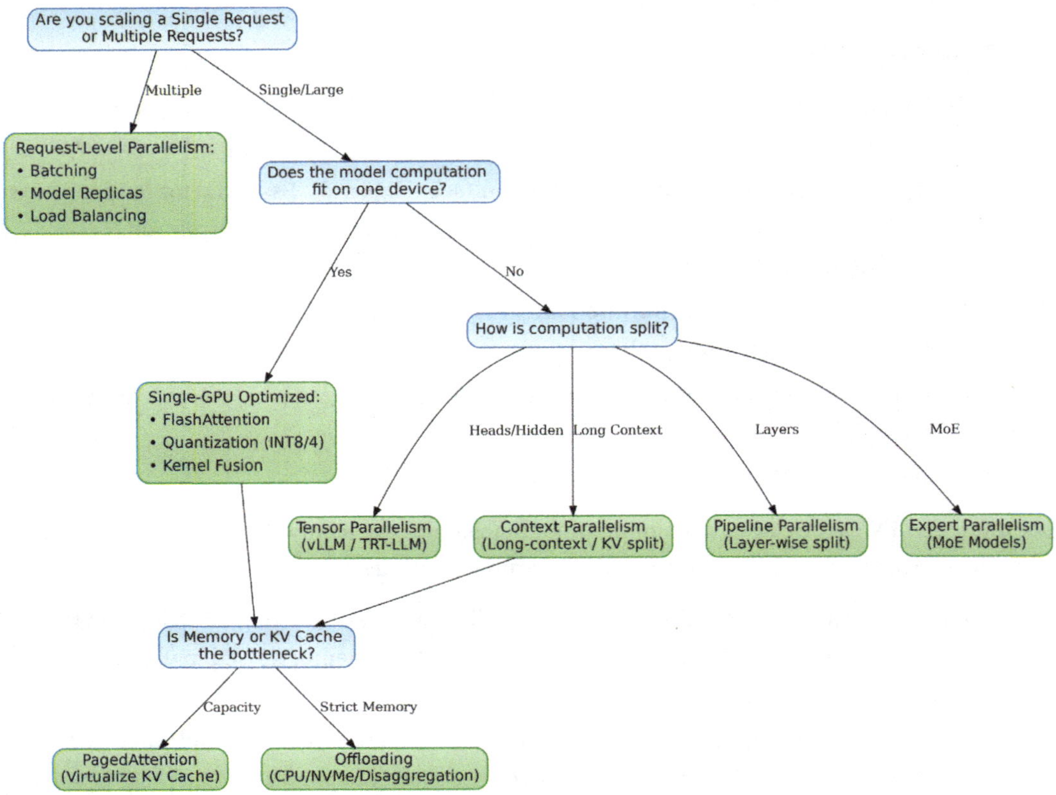

Figure 2.6: Inference Strategy Decision Tree

Key considerations for inference

- **Latency vs. throughput.** Serving cares about TTFT and per-token latency; model parallelism adds communication every layer—use only when needed (*Chapter 6*, *Chapter 9*).
- **KV cache.** Unlike training, memory is dominated by KV cache at long context and high concurrency; PagedAttention and related techniques are essential (*Chapter 6*).
- **Batching and replicas.** Replicate and batch requests before reaching for TP (*Chapter 6*, *Chapter 7*, *Chapter 9*).
- **Quantization.** INT8/INT4 often fits a model on one GPU without retraining (*Chapter 6*).
- **Start simple.** Single GPU with quantization and fused kernels before TP/PP (*Chapter 6*).

Practical tips

- **Profile before you optimize.** Use `nvidia-smi` to watch memory usage, and PyTorch's profiler to see where time is spent. You might think communication is the bottleneck, but it could be data loading or something else.
- **Use NCCL for GPU collectives.** It's optimized and handles NVLink automatically. The alternative backends (GLOO, MPI) are slower.
- **Mixed precision helps.** FP16 or BF16 cuts memory and bandwidth in half. Most models train fine with it, and the speedup is significant.
- **Watch out for NUMA.** If you're on a multi-socket system, try to keep processes on the same NUMA node. Cross-NUMA communication adds latency.
- **Test on small scale first.** Get your parallelism strategy working on 2-4 GPUs before scaling to many nodes. Debugging is much easier at small scale.

Hands-On: hardware inspection and bandwidth testing

Understanding your hardware topology and bandwidth characteristics is crucial before designing distributed training strategies. This hands-on section walks through inspecting GPU hardware, measuring memory bandwidth, and benchmarking inter-GPU communication.

Environment Setup

The code examples are available in the `code/` directory. If you haven't already, clone the repository:

```
git clone https://github.com/PacktPublishing/Distributed-AI-Systems
cd Distributed-AI-Systems/chapter2-gpu-hardware-networking-and-parallelism-strategies
```

You'll need a machine with at least one GPU (preferably multiple GPUs) to run these examples. For multi-GPU tests, you'll need 2 or more GPUs connected via NVLink or PCIe.

Step 1: inspect GPU hardware

Start by verifying your GPU setup and gathering basic hardware information. Run the `check_cuda.py` script (expect **well under a second**):

```
python code/check_cuda.py
```

This script displays essential GPU information:

```
1  |import torch
2  |print(f"CUDA available: {torch.cuda.is_available()}")
3  |print(f"Number of GPUs: {torch.cuda.device_count()}")
4  |for i in range(torch.cuda.device_count()):
5  |    props = torch.cuda.get_device_properties(i)
6  |    vram_gb = props.total_memory / (1024**3)
7  |    print(f"GPU {i}: {props.name}")
8  |    print(f"  Total memory: {vram_gb:.1f} GB")
9  |    print(f"  Compute capability: {props.major}.{props.minor}")
10 |    print(f"  Multiprocessors: {props.multi_processor_count}")
```

Code explanation:

- 2: Checks if CUDA is available on the system
- 3: Gets the total number of GPUs
- 5: Retrieves properties for each GPU
- 6: Converts memory from bytes to GB

Example output on an H100 system:

```
CUDA available: True
CUDA version: 12.1
Number of GPUs: 8

GPU 0: NVIDIA H100
  Total memory: 80.0 GB
  Compute capability: 9.0
  Multiprocessors: 132
...
```

This confirms your GPUs are detected and shows memory capacity, compute capability, and multiprocessor count. The compute capability (9.0 for H100) indicates which CUDA features are supported.

Step 2: inspect hardware topology

To understand how your GPUs are connected, use `nvidia-smi` to inspect the topology (runs **instantly**—no training job):

```
nvidia-smi topo -m
```

This displays a connection matrix showing how GPUs connect to each other. Look for:

- `NV18`, `NV12`, `NV4`: NVLink connections (good—high bandwidth)
- `PIX` **or** `PXB`: PCIe connections (slower, but still functional)
- `NODE` **or** `SYS`: Crosses NUMA boundaries (adds latency)

Example output showing NVLink connectivity:

```
        GPU0    GPU1    GPU2    GPU3    GPU4    GPU5    GPU6    GPU7
GPU0     X      NV18    NV18    NV18    NV18    NV18    NV18    NV18
GPU1    NV18     X      NV18    NV18    NV18    NV18    NV18    NV18
```

All GPUs showing `NV18` connections means every GPU can communicate with every other GPU at NVLink speeds—ideal for tensor parallelism and other communication-heavy strategies.

You can also check PCIe generation and width:

```
nvidia-smi --query-gpu=name,memory.total,pcie.link.gen.max,pcie.link.width.max --
format=csv
```

This shows PCIe Gen 4/5 and x16 width, which determine CPU-GPU bandwidth (~31-64 GB/s per direction).

Step 3: measure Single-GPU memory bandwidth

Before testing inter-GPU communication, establish a baseline by measuring single-GPU memory bandwidth. This tells you the maximum memory throughput of each GPU:

```
python code/bandwidth_test.py
```

Expect **a few seconds** on a modern GPU (200 warmup-style iterations over 64 MB tensors).

The script measures bandwidth by copying data within GPU memory. Each `copy_` reads `a` and writes `b`, so we count **2×** the tensor size per iteration (combined read+write traffic):

```
import torch
import time
size_mb = 64
iterations = 200
nbytes = size_mb * 1024 * 1024
a = torch.randn(nbytes // 4, device='cuda')
b = torch.empty_like(a)
# Warmup
```

```
9  for _ in range(10):
10     b.copy_(a)
11 torch.cuda.synchronize()
12 # Benchmark
13 t0 = time.time()
14 for _ in range(iterations):
15     b.copy_(a)
16 torch.cuda.synchronize()
17 t1 = time.time()
18 bytes_moved = 2 * nbytes * iterations  # read a + write b per iteration
19 bandwidth_gb_per_s = bytes_moved / (1024**3) / (t1 - t0)
20 print(f"Effective bandwidth (read+write): {bandwidth_gb_per_s:.2f} GB/s")
```

Code explanation:

- 6: Creates a tensor on GPU (float32 = 4 bytes per element)
- 7: Creates an empty tensor of the same size
- 10: Copies data within GPU memory
- 18: Each copy moves 2× nbytes (read from `a`, write to `b`)

Example results (hardware-dependent):

```
GPU Memory Bandwidth Test
Data size: 64 MB
Iterations: 200
Effective bandwidth (read+write): 1980.45 GB/s
```

Typical effective copy bandwidth (read+write combined):

- **H100**: 2-3 TB/s (2000-3000 GB/s)
- **A100**: 1.5-2 TB/s (1500-2000 GB/s)
- **H200**: 2-3 TB/s (2000-3000 GB/s)

If your measured bandwidth is significantly lower, you might have memory bandwidth saturation or other bottlenecks. This baseline helps you understand whether memory bandwidth is limiting your training performance.

Step 4: benchmark Inter-GPU communication

For distributed training, inter-GPU communication bandwidth is often more critical than single-GPU memory bandwidth. The `allreduce_microbench.py` script measures AllReduce performance across multiple GPUs—launch with `torchrun` the same way you ran `distributed_basic_test.py` in *Chapter 1*. With the defaults below (100 MB tensors, 50 iterations), expect **roughly a few seconds to tens of seconds** on 2–4 GPUs—not minutes.

```
torchrun --nproc_per_node=2 code/allreduce_microbench.py
```

For 4 GPUs:

```
torchrun --nproc_per_node=4 code/allreduce_microbench.py
```

The script times `dist.all_reduce` and reports two bandwidth numbers. **Algorithm bandwidth** is what NCCL benchmarks use: each rank holds `size_mb`, and all `n` ranks participate, so useful throughput is `n × size / time`. **Bus bandwidth** adjusts for how much data actually crosses the interconnect in a ring AllReduce—about `2×(n-1)/n` of the per-rank tensor size on each of the `n` ranks, or `2×(n-1)×size` **total** per iteration:

```
1  |import torch.distributed as dist
2  |size = size_mb * 1024 * 1024 // 4  # float32 elements per GPU
3  |tensor = torch.ones(size, device=f'cuda:{local_rank}')
4  |for _ in range(warmup):
5  |    dist.all_reduce(tensor, op=dist.ReduceOp.SUM)
6  |torch.cuda.synchronize()
7  |start = time.time()
8  |for _ in range(iterations):
9  |    dist.all_reduce(tensor, op=dist.ReduceOp.SUM)
10 |torch.cuda.synchronize()
11 |elapsed = time.time() - start
12 |size_bytes = size_mb * 1024 * 1024
13 |n = world_size
14 |alg_bytes = size_bytes * n * iterations
15 |bus_bytes = size_bytes * 2 * (n - 1) * iterations  # ring: 2*(n-1)/n per rank
× n
16 |ranks
17 |alg_bw_gb_s = alg_bytes / (1024**3) / elapsed
18 |bus_bw_gb_s = bus_bytes / (1024**3) / elapsed  # equals alg_bw * 2*(n-1)/n
```

Code explanation:

- 3: Tensor size in float32 elements on each GPU

- 5: AllReduce sums tensors across all ranks
- 15: Ring AllReduce moves ~2×(n–1)×size bytes on the network per iteration (NCCL may pick tree instead)

Example output for 2 GPUs with NVLink (numbers vary by hardware and driver):

```
AllReduce Benchmark Results
World size: 2 GPUs
Tensor size: 100 MB per GPU
Iterations: 50
Total time: 0.248 seconds
Algorithm bandwidth: 40322.58 MB/s (39.38 GB/s)
Bus bandwidth (ring estimate): 40322.58 MB/s (39.38 GB/s)
```

For `n = 2`, the ring factor `2×(n-1)/n` is 1, so algorithm and bus bandwidth coincide. For 4 GPUs, bus bandwidth is `1.5×` algorithm bandwidth under the ring model.

Expected **AllReduce bus bandwidth** (message-size dependent; 100 MB is in a reasonable range):

- **NVLink-connected GPUs**: often tens of GB/s up to low hundreds of GB/s
- **PCIe-only GPU pairs**: often ~10–50 GB/s

These are effective collective throughput numbers, not the **peak NVLink link** specs quoted in datasheets (300–900 GB/s per GPU on Ampere–Hopper, up to 1.8 TB/s on Blackwell B200). If you see much lower AllReduce bandwidth than the ranges above, check topology with `nvidia-smi topo -m`. GPUs connected only via PCIe will show significantly lower bandwidth, which affects what parallelism strategies are feasible.

Step 5: analyze results

Compare your measured bandwidths to theoretical values:

Metric	Your System	Expected Range	Notes
Single-GPU HBM	? GB/s	H100: 2-3 TB/s A100: 1.5-2 TB/s	Lower values indicate memory bottlenecks
Inter-GPU AllReduce (NVLink)	? GB/s	tens–low hundreds of GB/s (bus)	From Step 4: message-size dependent

Metric	Your System	Expected Range	Notes
Inter-GPU AllReduce (PCIe)	? GB/s	~10–50 GB/s (bus)	Much slower than NVLink

What these numbers mean:

- **High HBM bandwidth but low inter-GPU bandwidth**: Your system is good for single-GPU workloads but will struggle with communication-heavy parallelism (tensor parallelism, frequent AllReduce). Prefer FSDP/ZeRO or pipeline parallelism.
- **High inter-GPU bandwidth (NVLink)**: Your system can efficiently use tensor parallelism and other communication-heavy strategies. All GPUs connected via NVSwitch is ideal.
- **Low inter-GPU bandwidth (PCIe-only)**: Avoid tensor parallelism—communication overhead will dominate. Stick with FSDP/ZeRO or pipeline parallelism where communication is less frequent.

These measurements help you choose the right parallelism strategy for your hardware. In later chapters, we'll see how DDP, FSDP, and other frameworks use these communication primitives, but understanding the underlying bandwidth characteristics helps when debugging performance issues.

For real workloads, you'll use the higher-level APIs in PyTorch or DeepSpeed, but understanding what's happening underneath helps when things don't work as expected.

With this hardware foundation in place, we're ready to start building distributed training systems. In *Chapter 3*, we'll dive into PyTorch DDP (DistributedDataParallel), which is the most common way to do replicated data parallelism. DDP is the workhorse of distributed training—it's what most production training pipelines use, and understanding how it works is essential for building scalable AI systems. We'll cover the setup, common pitfalls, debugging techniques, and how to optimize it for your workloads.

Code summary

- `nvidia-smi`: Command-line utility to monitor GPU status and utilization
- `torch.cuda.device_count()`: Get the number of available CUDA devices
- `torch.cuda.get_device_name()`: Get the name of a CUDA device
- `torch.cuda.is_available()`: Check if CUDA is available
- `torch.distributed.get_world_size()`: Get the total number of processes in the distributed group

- `torch.distributed.get_rank()`: Get the rank of the current process
- `torch.distributed.get_backend()`: Get the backend name (e.g., 'nccl', 'gloo')
- `nvidia-ml-py`: Python library for querying NVIDIA GPU information
- `ibstat`: Command to check InfiniBand adapter status

Notes and references

1. GPU memory capacity data from NVIDIA specifications: A100 (2020, 80GB), H100 (2022, 80GB HBM3), H200 (2023, 141GB HBM3e), B200 (2024, 192GB); each new generation typically adds HBM capacity and NVLink bandwidth, so later flagship GPUs follow the same trend even though the figure shows representative deployed SKUs. Model memory requirements calculated from published parameter counts (see @tbl:model-comparison) using BF16 precision (2 bytes per parameter): GPT-3 175B (2020, ~350GB), LLaMA-2 70B (2023, ~140GB), DeepSeek-V2 236B (2024, ~472GB), DeepSeek-V3 671B (2025, ~1342GB), DeepSeek-V4-Pro 1.6T (2026, ~3200GB). The figure uses these disclosed milestones; larger approximate counts (marked ~ in the table) are omitted. Values shown represent single-GPU memory requirements for model weights only; actual training requires additional memory for gradients, optimizer states, and activations, further necessitating distributed training.
2. Chowdhery et al., "PaLM: Scaling Language Modeling with Pathways," *Journal of Machine Learning Research* 24 (2023): 1–113, Appendix B (6N matmul FLOPs per token and model FLOPs utilization). Kaplan et al., "Scaling Laws for Neural Language Models," arXiv:2001.08361, 2020.
3. NVIDIA, "NVIDIA H100 Tensor Core GPU Architecture," whitepaper, 2022, `https://resources.nvidia.com/en-us-hopper-architecture` (Transformer Engine with FP8; up to 6× training throughput on transformer models vs A100). For independently audited results on large language-model training, see NVIDIA, "Breaking MLPerf Training Records with NVIDIA H100 GPUs," Technical Blog, 2023, `https://developer.nvidia.com/blog/breaking-mlperf-training-records-with-nvidia-h100-gpus/` (MLPerf Training 3.0; GPT-3 175B and BERT with Transformer Engine and FP8).

Exercises

GPU hardware inspector

Implement a comprehensive GPU hardware inspection function that gathers detailed information about available GPUs.

Requirements:

- Function signature:

```
inspect_gpu_hardware()
```

- Return a dictionary with the following keys for each GPU:
    - `name`: GPU name
    - `memory_total_gb`: Total memory in GB
    - `memory_free_gb`: Free memory in GB
    - `compute_capability`: Compute capability as a string (e.g., "9.0")
    - `multiprocessor_count`: Number of streaming multiprocessors
    - `cuda_version`: CUDA version
- Handle the case where CUDA is not available (return empty list)
- Print a formatted summary table showing all GPU information

Test your function:

```
import torch

gpu_info = inspect_gpu_hardware()
print(f"Found {len(gpu_info)} GPU(s)")

for i, info in enumerate(gpu_info):
    print(f"\nGPU {i}:")
    print(f"  Name: {info['name']}")
    print(f"  Memory: {info['memory_total_gb']:.1f} GB total, "
          f"{info['memory_free_gb']:.1f} GB free")
    print(f"  Compute Capability: {info['compute_capability']}")
    print(f"  Multiprocessors: {info['multiprocessor_count']}")
```

Memory requirement calculator

Implement a function to calculate memory requirements for training models with different precisions and optimizer configurations.

Requirements:

- Function signature:

```
calculate_training_memory(num_params, precision='bf16', optimizer='adam',
batch_size=1, seq_length=2048)
```

- Calculate memory for:
    - Model parameters (weights)
    - Gradients (same size as parameters)
    - Optimizer states:
        - Adam: 2× parameter size (momentum + variance)
        - SGD: 1× parameter size (momentum only)
    - Activations: approximate as `batch_size × seq_length × hidden_size × num_layers × bytes_per_element`
- Precision options: 'fp32' (4 bytes), 'bf16'/'fp16' (2 bytes), 'int8' (1 byte)
- Return a dictionary with breakdown: `{'parameters': ..., 'gradients': ..., 'optimizer': ..., 'activations': ..., 'total': ...}`
- All values in GB

Test your function:

```
# 70B parameter model with BF16, Adam optimizer
memory = calculate_training_memory(
    num_params=70e9,
    precision='bf16',
    optimizer='adam',
    batch_size=4,
    seq_length=2048
)

print("Memory Requirements (GB):")
for key, value in memory.items():
    print(f"  {key}: {value:.2f} GB")
```

Topology detection and analysis

Implement a function that parses `nvidia-smi topo -m` output to detect GPU interconnect topology.

Requirements:

- Function signature:

  ```
  analyze_gpu_topology()
  ```

- Use `subprocess` to run `nvidia-smi topo -m` and capture output
- Parse the topology matrix to identify:
  - GPUs connected via NVLink (look for NV18, NV12, NV4)
  - GPUs connected only via PCIe (look for PIX, PXB)
  - All-to-all connectivity (all GPUs can reach all other GPUs via NVLink)
- Return a dictionary with:
  - `num_gpus`: Number of GPUs
  - `nvlink_pairs`: List of GPU pairs connected via NVLink
  - `pcie_only_pairs`: List of GPU pairs connected only via PCIe
  - `has_all_to_all_nvlink`: Boolean indicating if all GPUs have NVLink to all others
  - `recommended_parallelism`: Suggested parallelism strategy based on topology

Test your function:

```
import subprocess

topology = analyze_gpu_topology()
print(f"Number of GPUs: {topology['num_gpus']}")
print(f"NVLink pairs: {topology['nvlink_pairs']}")
print(f"PCIe-only pairs: {topology['pcie_only_pairs']}")
print(f"All-to-all NVLink: {topology['has_all_to_all_nvlink']}")
print(f"Recommended strategy: {topology['recommended_parallelism']}")
```

Parallelism strategy selector

Implement a function that recommends parallelism strategies based on model size, hardware topology, and training requirements.

Requirements:

- Function signature:

  ```
  recommend_parallelism_strategy(model_size_gb, num_gpus, topology_info,
  has_nvlink_all_to_all, training_type='training')
  ```

- Consider:
    - Model size vs. single GPU memory
    - Topology (NVLink all-to-all vs. PCIe-only)
    - Training vs. inference requirements
- Return a dictionary with:
    - `primary_strategy`: Main parallelism approach (DDP, FSDP, TP, PP, or hybrid)
    - `reasoning`: Explanation of why this strategy was chosen
    - `alternative_strategies`: List of other viable options
    - `estimated_gpu_count`: Minimum GPUs needed
    - `memory_per_gpu_gb`: Estimated memory per GPU

Test your function:

```
# 70B model (140 GB in BF16) on 8 GPUs with NVLink all-to-all
strategy = recommend_parallelism_strategy(
    model_size_gb=140,
    num_gpus=8,
    topology_info={'has_all_to_all_nvlink': True},
    has_nvlink_all_to_all=True,
    training_type='training'
)

print(f"Recommended: {strategy['primary_strategy']}")
print(f"Reasoning: {strategy['reasoning']}")
print(f"Estimated GPUs needed: {strategy['estimated_gpu_count']}")
print(f"Memory per GPU: {strategy['memory_per_gpu_gb']:.1f} GB")
```

Expected learning outcomes

After completing these exercises, you should be able to:

- Query GPU hardware properties programmatically using PyTorch and CUDA APIs
- Calculate memory requirements for training large models with different precisions and optimizers
- Parse and interpret GPU topology information from `nvidia-smi`
- Identify NVLink vs PCIe connectivity between GPUs
- Recommend appropriate parallelism strategies based on model size and hardware topology
- Understand the relationship between GPU interconnects and parallelism efficiency

3

Distributed Training with PyTorch DDP

Scaling training across multiple GPUs with DistributedDataParallel

> *The search for the ultimate algorithm is a search for scale.*
>
> *Richard Sutton*

How DDP works internally

In *Chapter 2*, we explored the hardware foundation and parallelism strategies that make distributed training possible. Now we turn to the practical implementation: **DistributedDataParallel (DDP)**, PyTorch's standard approach for data-parallel distributed training. DDP is how you actually scale training across multiple GPUs—whether they're in a single machine or spread across a cluster.

The core idea is elegant: replicate your model on every GPU, shard your data across GPUs, and synchronize gradients after each backward pass. Each GPU processes a different batch of data, computes gradients independently, then all GPUs average their gradients together. This ensures every model replica stays in sync while leveraging parallel computation.

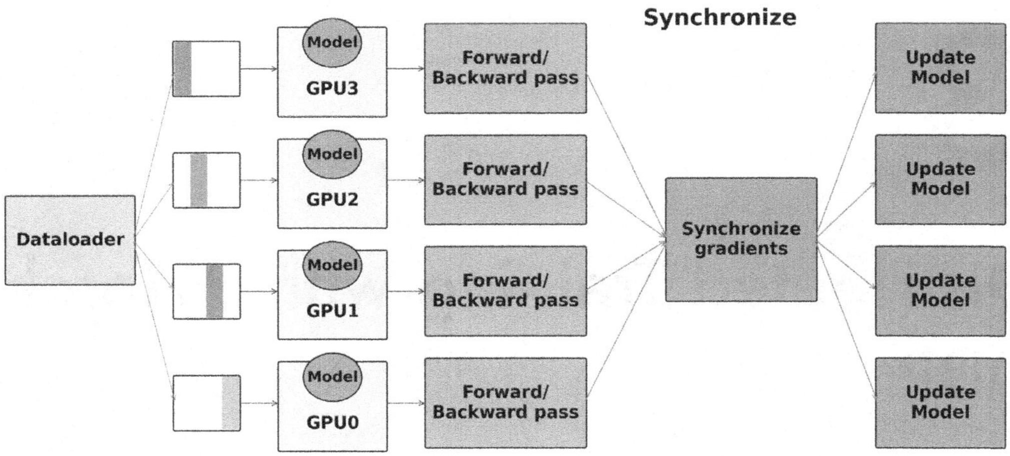

Figure 3.1: DDP Workflow

Figure 3.1 illustrates the complete DDP training workflow. Data flows from the dataloader to each GPU's data shard, through forward and backward passes, then gradients are synchronized across all GPUs before model parameters are updated. The magic happens during the backward pass—DDP automatically aggregates gradients from all processes using efficient collective communication primitives (like AllReduce) and ensures every process has the same updated parameters.

The basic flow

Following the workflow shown in *Figure 3.1*, here's what happens during a single training step with DDP:

1. **Forward pass**: Each process runs forward on its own data shard. The model is identical on all processes, but each process sees different data thanks to `DistributedSampler`. As illustrated in the figure, data flows from the dataloader to each GPU's data shard, then through the model for forward computation.
2. **Backward pass**: Each process computes gradients locally. This is where DDP kicks in—instead of each process updating its model independently, DDP collects all gradients. The backward pass computes gradients for each parameter in parallel across all GPUs.
3. **Gradient synchronization**: DDP uses AllReduce (via NCCL on GPUs) to sum gradients across all processes, then divides by `world_size` so every rank holds the mean gradient —the same update you would get from one GPU with the global batch. This is the

critical synchronization step shown in the center of Figure 3.1, where gradients from all GPUs are aggregated.

4. **Parameter update**: Each process applies the optimizer step using the synchronized gradients. Since all processes started with the same parameters and applied the same gradients, they end up with identical parameters. The final step updates each model replica with the synchronized gradients, maintaining consistency across all processes.

This is **data parallelism**: the model is replicated, but data is sharded. Each GPU processes a different batch, and gradients are averaged. Compare this to **model parallelism** (covered in later chapters), where the model itself is split across GPUs.

Data Parallel (DP) vs. Distributed Data Parallel (DDP)

Before DDP, PyTorch had `DataParallel` (DP), which is still available but discouraged in favor of DDP—the official docs recommend `DistributedDataParallel` even for single-node multi-GPU training. DP uses a single-process, multi-threaded approach that runs on a single machine. It has several limitations: Python's GIL prevents true parallelism, all gradient synchronization happens on GPU 0, creating a bottleneck, and it can't scale across multiple machines.

Distributed Data Parallel (DDP) addresses these limitations.

DDP uses a multi-process architecture instead of multi-threading. Each GPU runs in its own process, which avoids Python's GIL limitations and enables true parallelism. Unlike DP, DDP can scale across multiple machines connected via network. You're not limited to GPUs in a single machine—you can train on hundreds or thousands of GPUs across a cluster.

Communication is more efficient too. DDP uses optimized collective communication primitives like Ring AllReduce and tree algorithms. These distribute the work across all GPUs, not just GPU 0. Instead of one GPU doing all the work, every GPU participates in the gradient synchronization. This eliminates the single-GPU bottleneck that plagues DP.

DDP also overlaps gradient synchronization with computation. While one bucket of gradients is being synchronized, the next bucket can start computing. This hides communication latency, making the overall training faster. All GPUs participate equally in gradient synchronization, creating a balanced workload across the entire system.

For these reasons, DDP is the standard for distributed training—use it even on a single machine.

Gradient bucketing: why it matters

If DDP synchronized every gradient tensor individually, you'd have thousands of small AllReduce operations. Each AllReduce has overhead—network latency, kernel launch overhead, synchronization costs. The solution is **gradient bucketing**: DDP groups small gradient tensors into buckets and performs AllReduce on entire buckets.

Here's how it works: DDP analyzes your model's parameter order (the order they appear in `model.parameters()`). It groups consecutive parameters into buckets based on size. When the backward pass reaches a bucket boundary, DDP triggers an AllReduce for that bucket. The default bucket size is 25 MB, but you can tune it with `bucket_cap_mb`.

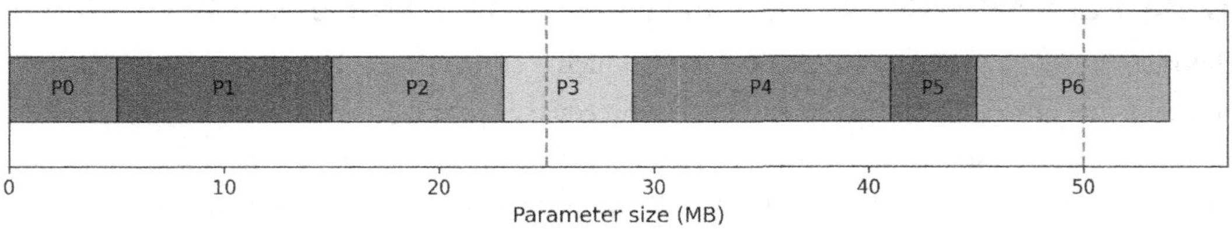

Figure 3.2: Gradient bucketing: parameters in buckets by size

Figure 3.2 shows parameter segments and bucket boundaries. Bucketing reduces communication overhead, but there's a tradeoff: larger buckets mean fewer AllReduce calls (less overhead) but later synchronization (gradients aren't available until the bucket is ready). Smaller buckets mean earlier synchronization but more overhead. For most models, the default 25 MB works well, but you might tune it for very large or very small models.

Communication–Computation overlap

The real performance win comes from **overlapping communication and computation**. While DDP is doing AllReduce for one bucket, your backward pass can continue computing gradients for the next bucket. This hides communication latency behind computation.

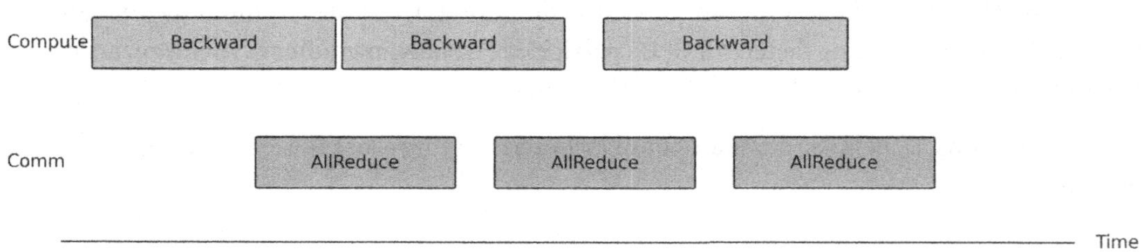

Figure 3.3: Overlap of backward compute and AllReduce

Figure 3.3 illustrates the overlap. DDP achieves overlap by:

- Launching AllReduce operations asynchronously
- Using CUDA streams to overlap communication kernels with compute kernels
- Processing buckets in the order they're ready (not necessarily parameter order)

For overlap to work, you need enough computation between bucket boundaries. If your model has very few parameters or very small layers, there might not be enough work to overlap. In that case, you'll see communication time dominate, and overlap won't help much.

You can check if overlap is working by profiling. If you see AllReduce operations happening concurrently with backward compute, overlap is working. If AllReduce happens sequentially after all gradients are computed, overlap isn't happening (maybe your model is too small or there's a synchronization point blocking it).

The AllReduce operation

AllReduce is the core collective operation that makes DDP work. As detailed in *Chapter 1* (see the "Collective Operations" section), AllReduce takes gradients from all processes, sums them, and distributes the result back to all processes. On GPUs, DDP uses NCCL (NVIDIA Collective Communications Library) to implement AllReduce efficiently using algorithms like **ring AllReduce** and **tree AllReduce**, which NCCL selects automatically based on your hardware topology.

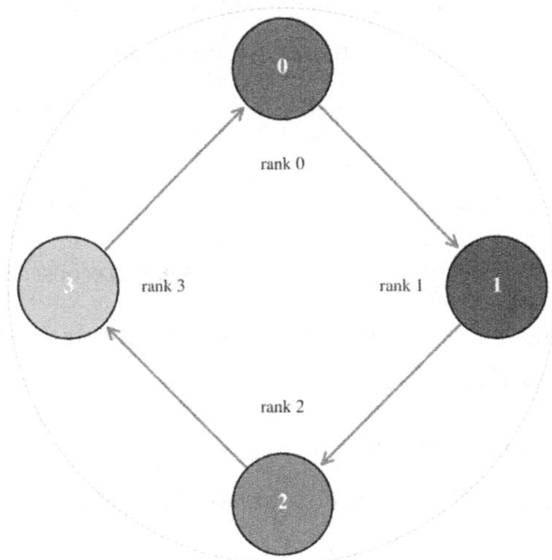

Figure 3.4: Ring AllReduce: four ranks with clockwise data flow

Figure 3.4 shows the **ring topology**: ranks are arranged in a logical ring, and data flows in one direction (e.g., clockwise). In ring AllReduce, each rank holds a chunk of the full tensor. In the first phase (reduce-scatter), each rank sends its chunk to the next rank and receives from the previous, accumulating partial sums so that after N-1 steps (for N ranks) each rank has the full sum for one chunk. In the second phase (all-gather), ranks exchange these reduced chunks until every rank has the complete reduced result. The ring algorithm is **bandwidth-optimal**: it moves only 2 · (N-1)/N times the tensor size, regardless of N, and uses each link in the ring efficiently. NCCL may instead choose **tree AllReduce** (or other variants) when it detects a topology where a tree layout has lower latency or better fits the physical interconnect (e.g., NVLink vs PCIe vs network).

Understanding which algorithm is in use helps when debugging performance. If gradient synchronization is slow, possible causes include: (1) NCCL picked an algorithm that does not match your topology (e.g., a ring over a network that is not a physical ring); (2) network or interconnect bandwidth is saturated; (3) small message sizes that don't amortize the fixed cost of the collective. You can inspect NCCL's choices and timings via `NCCL_DEBUG=INFO` or PyTorch profiler; comparing AllReduce time to the theoretical ring cost (tensor size divided by per-link bandwidth) can tell you whether you are bandwidth-bound or latency-bound.

Mixed precision and gradient scaling

When using **FP16** mixed precision, gradients can underflow (become zero) because FP16 has a narrow exponent range. The solution is **gradient scaling**: multiply loss by a scale factor before backward, then unscale gradients before the optimizer step. **BF16** shares FP32's exponent range, so underflow is rare and `GradScaler` is usually unnecessary—`autocast(dtype=torch.bfloat16)` is often enough on supported hardware.

Figure 3.5: AMP + DDP: scale, backward, AllReduce, unscale, step

Figure 3.5 shows the pipeline. DDP works with PyTorch's Automatic Mixed Precision (AMP). The flow below is for **FP16 with** `GradScaler`:

1. Scale loss: `loss = loss * scale`
2. Backward: `loss.backward()` (gradients are also scaled)
3. DDP AllReduce: Synchronizes scaled gradients
4. Unscale: Divide gradients by scale before optimizer step
5. Update scale: Adjust scale factor based on gradient overflow detection

The key point is DDP synchronizes gradients **after** they're scaled. Each process scales its own gradients, then DDP sums the scaled gradients. After AllReduce, all processes have the same scaled gradients, which are then unscaled before the optimizer step.

If you're using FP16 AMP with DDP, use `GradScaler`: create it before wrapping the model with DDP, and call `scaler.step()` and `scaler.update()` on every process (not just rank 0). For BF16 training you typically omit the scaler.

Buffer Synchronization

DDP doesn't just synchronize gradients—it also synchronizes **buffers**. Buffers are model parameters that don't require gradients, like BatchNorm running mean and variance. During the forward pass, DDP broadcasts buffers from rank 0 to all other ranks to ensure consistency.

This happens automatically, but there's a performance consideration: buffer synchronization adds communication overhead. If your model has many buffers or large buffers, this can slow down training. You can disable it with `broadcast_buffers=False`, but only if you're sure buffers don't need synchronization (e.g., you're not using BatchNorm, or you're manually synchronizing buffers).

For most models, keeping `broadcast_buffers=True` (the default) is the right choice. BatchNorm and similar layers need synchronized statistics to work correctly in distributed training.

DDP forward pass implementation details

Understanding how DDP maintains model consistency during the forward pass helps when debugging. In PyTorch, all models inherit from `torch.nn.Module`, which maintains two key dictionaries:

- `_parameters`: Network parameters that require gradients
- `_buffers`: Non-parameter data that persists (e.g., BatchNorm's running mean and variance)

DDP ensures model consistency through `_sync_module_states`, which synchronizes both `_parameters` and `_buffers` across all processes. This happens in two places:

1. **During DDP initialization**: When you create a DDP model, it synchronizes initial parameters and buffers from rank 0 to all other ranks
2. **Before each forward pass**: If `broadcast_buffers=True` (the default), DDP synchronizes buffers before forward pass to ensure all processes have the same buffer values

This synchronization ensures that all processes start with identical model states, which is crucial for maintaining consistency during training.

DDP Computation–Communication overlap implementation

The overlap mechanism in DDP is implemented using autograd hooks, parameter bucketing, and a reducer component. Here's how it works:

Autograd Hooks: DDP registers hooks on model parameters. These hooks are triggered when gradients are computed during backward pass. The hook function marks the parameter gradient as "ready" for reduction.

Parameter Bucketing: The reducer organizes parameter gradients into buckets based on the `bucket_cap_mb` setting. Parameters are assigned to buckets in roughly reverse order of `model.parameters()` (reverse order because gradients are computed in reverse during backward pass). This ensures gradients in the same bucket become ready around the same time.

Reducer: When all gradients in a bucket are ready, the reducer launches an asynchronous AllReduce operation for that bucket. While AllReduce is in progress, backward pass continues computing gradients for the next bucket, achieving overlap.

Unused Parameters: If a parameter isn't used in forward pass (e.g., in conditional models), its gradient never becomes ready, causing the bucket to wait forever. Setting `find_unused_parameters=True` tells DDP to analyze the computation graph to identify unused parameters and mark them as ready without waiting for their gradients. This adds overhead but prevents hangs.

The key insight: DDP doesn't wait for all gradients before starting communication. Instead, it communicates gradients as soon as buckets are ready, overlapping communication with ongoing computation.

Setting up Single-Node DDP

The simplest DDP setup is single-node multi-GPU: one machine with multiple GPUs. This is where most people start, and it's what you'll use for development and smaller-scale training.

Using torchrun (recommended)

The modern way to launch DDP training is with `torchrun` (or `torch.distributed.run` in older PyTorch versions). `torchrun` handles process creation, environment variable setup, and error handling. It's the recommended launcher for most cases.

Here's a minimal example. Save it as a script, or use the provided `code/train_ddp_single_mini.py` in this chapter's directory.

```
import os
import torch
import torch.distributed as dist
import torch.nn as nn
from torch.nn.parallel import DistributedDataParallel as DDP
from torch.utils.data.distributed import DistributedSampler

def setup():
    """Initialize process group and set device."""
    # torchrun sets these environment variables automatically
    rank = int(os.environ['RANK'])
    local_rank = int(os.environ['LOCAL_RANK'])
    world_size = int(os.environ['WORLD_SIZE'])
    # Set device for this process
    torch.cuda.set_device(local_rank)
    device = torch.device(f'cuda:{local_rank}')
    # Initialize process group
    dist.init_process_group(backend='nccl')
    return rank, local_rank, world_size, device

def cleanup():
    """Clean up process group."""
    dist.destroy_process_group()

def main():
    rank, local_rank, world_size, device = setup()
    # Create model and move to device
    model = nn.Linear(10, 1).to(device)
    model = DDP(model, device_ids=[local_rank])
    # Create dummy data
    data = torch.randn(64, 10).to(device)
    target = torch.randn(64, 1).to(device)
    # Training step
    optimizer = torch.optim.SGD(model.parameters(), lr=0.01)
    loss_fn = nn.MSELoss()
    for epoch in range(10):
        # DistributedSampler would go here for real data
        optimizer.zero_grad()
```

```
            output = model(data)
            loss = loss_fn(output, target)
            loss.backward()
            optimizer.step()
            if rank == 0:
                print(f'Epoch {epoch}, Loss: {loss.item():.4f}')
    cleanup()

if __name__ == '__main__':
    main()
```

Launch it with (from the chapter directory or pass the path to the script):

```
torchrun --nproc_per_node=4 code/train_ddp_single_mini.py
```

This launches 4 processes, one per GPU (assuming you have 4 GPUs). `torchrun` automatically sets `RANK`, `LOCAL_RANK`, `WORLD_SIZE`, `MASTER_ADDR`, and `MASTER_PORT` environment variables. The sample output is like:

```
Epoch 0, Loss: 1.3706
Epoch 1, Loss: 1.3595
Epoch 2, Loss: 1.3488
Epoch 3, Loss: 1.3386
Epoch 4, Loss: 1.3287
Epoch 5, Loss: 1.3193
Epoch 6, Loss: 1.3103
Epoch 7, Loss: 1.3016
Epoch 8, Loss: 1.2932
Epoch 9, Loss: 1.2852
```

Understanding the environment variables

When using `torchrun`, these environment variables are set **automatically**:

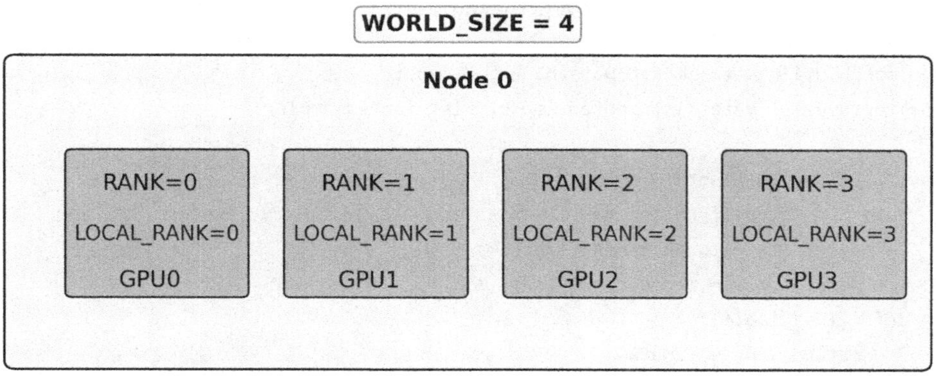

Figure 3.6: RANK, LOCAL_RANK, WORLD_SIZE for a single node with 4 GPUs

Figure 3.6 shows RANK and LOCAL_RANK for a single node with four GPUs (as in the `torchrun --nproc_per_node=4` example above). Variables:

- **RANK**: Global rank of this process (0 to WORLD_SIZE-1)
- **LOCAL_RANK**: Local rank within this node (0 to number of GPUs per node - 1)
- **WORLD_SIZE**: Total number of processes
- **MASTER_ADDR**: IP address of the master node (for single-node, this is localhost)
- **MASTER_PORT**: Port for process group initialization (torchrun picks a free port)

For single-node training, you typically only care about `LOCAL_RANK` (to set which GPU this process uses) and `RANK` (to identify the main process for logging/checkpointing).

Using DistributedSampler

The key to data parallelism is ensuring each process sees different data. `DistributedSampler` does this by sharding the dataset across processes.

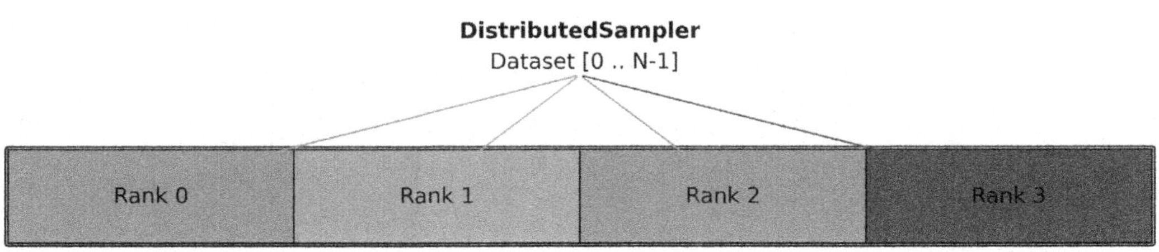

Figure 3.7: DistributedSampler shards dataset across ranks

Figure 3.7 illustrates how the full dataset is split into contiguous, non-overlapping shards: each rank receives a distinct segment of indices (e.g., with four ranks and N samples, rank 0 gets indices (0 ... $\lceil N/4 \rceil$ - 1), rank 1 the next quarter, and so on), so no sample is seen by more than one process and the union of all shards covers the dataset.

```
from torch.utils.data import DataLoader, Dataset
from torch.utils.data.distributed import DistributedSampler

class MyDataset(Dataset):
    def __init__(self, size=1000):
        self.data = torch.randn(size, 10)
        self.labels = torch.randn(size, 1)
    def __len__(self):
        return len(self.data)
    def __getitem__(self, idx):
        return self.data[idx], self.labels[idx]

def get_dataloader(rank, world_size, batch_size=32):
    dataset = MyDataset(size=1000)
    # Create DistributedSampler
    sampler = DistributedSampler(
        dataset,
        num_replicas=world_size,
        rank=rank,
        shuffle=True,  # Shuffle data each epoch
        drop_last=True # avoids DDP sync issues
    )
    # Create DataLoader with sampler
    dataloader = DataLoader(
        dataset,
        batch_size=batch_size,
        sampler=sampler,
        num_workers=4,
        pin_memory=True  # Faster CPU->GPU transfer
    )
    return dataloader, sampler

def train():
    rank, local_rank, world_size, device = setup()
    dataloader, sampler = get_dataloader(rank, world_size)
    model = create_model().to(device)
```

```
    model = DDP(model, device_ids=[local_rank])
    for epoch in range(10):
        # CRITICAL: Set epoch for DistributedSampler
        # This ensures different shuffling each epoch
        sampler.set_epoch(epoch)
        for batch_idx, (data, target) in enumerate(dataloader):
            data = data.to(device)
            target = target.to(device)
            # Training step...
            pass
    cleanup()
```

A runnable version of this pattern is in `code/train_ddp_sampler.py`. From the chapter directory, run:

```
$ export CUDA_VISIBLE_DEVICES=0,1,2,3
$ torchrun --nproc_per_node=4 code/train_ddp_sampler.py
```

Example output:

```
Epoch 0 avg loss: 1.2798
Epoch 1 avg loss: 1.2930
Epoch 2 avg loss: 1.2105
Epoch 3 avg loss: 1.2596
Epoch 4 avg loss: 1.0808
Epoch 5 avg loss: 1.0864
Epoch 6 avg loss: 1.0570
Epoch 7 avg loss: 1.0612
Epoch 8 avg loss: 1.0212
Epoch 9 avg loss: 0.9214
Done.
```

`DistributedSampler` assigns each process a disjoint subset of the dataset. For example, with 4 processes and 1000 samples, each process receives 250 samples. Shuffling is controlled by the sampler: set `shuffle=True` on the sampler, and leave the DataLoader's `shuffle` at its default (or omit it), since the sampler already determines the order of indices.

At the start of each epoch you must call `sampler.set_epoch(epoch)`. This seeds the sampler's shuffle with the epoch index so that each epoch sees a different ordering. If you omit this call, every epoch will iterate over the data in the same order.

The `drop_last` argument matters for synchronization. When it is `True`, the sampler drops the last incomplete batch so that every rank performs the same number of steps; that avoids one rank running ahead and blocking in collective calls. If you set `drop_last=False` (for instance to use every sample in a small dataset), some ranks may have one extra batch. In that case the training loop should use DDP's `join()` context so that ranks that finish early wait for the others; otherwise the process can deadlock.

DataLoader internals for distributed training

Understanding how `DataLoader` works internally helps optimize data loading performance. When you create a `DataLoader` with `num_workers > 0`, PyTorch uses multi-process data loading.

Single-process vs Multi-process:

The `DataLoader` chooses between `_SingleProcessDataLoaderIter` (for `num_workers=0`) and `_MultiProcessDataLoaderIter` (for `num_workers > 0`) based on the `num_workers` parameter.

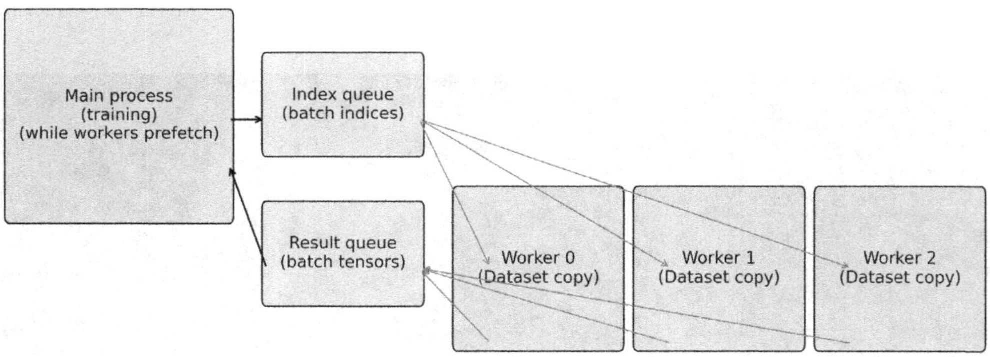

Figure 3.8: DataLoader with workers, index and result queues

Figure 3.8 illustrates the execution flow when `num_workers > 0`. The main process enqueues batch indices into the index queue. Each worker process maintains its own copy of the dataset, dequeues batch indices, loads, and preprocesses the corresponding data, and enqueues the resulting batch tensors into the result queue. The main process then consumes batches from the result queue for training. The annotation "while workers prefetch" highlights that training on the current batch overlaps with workers preparing subsequent batches, enabling pipeline parallelism between data loading and computation. This design decouples data loading from model computation through inter-process queues, reducing input pipeline bottlenecks.

Multi-process data loading works as follows:

1. **Main process**: Creates an index queue and a result queue. It also spawns worker processes.
2. **Worker processes**: Each worker process:
    - Reads indices from the index queue
    - Fetches corresponding data from the dataset
    - Applies transforms/preprocessing
    - Puts processed data into the result queue
3. **Prefetching**: While the main process is using the current batch for training, workers are already loading the next batch. This overlaps data loading with computation.
4. **Pin memory**: If `pin_memory=True`, a separate thread copies data from CPU to GPU memory asynchronously, further overlapping data transfer with computation

DistributedSampler integration: When using `DistributedSampler`, each process's `DataLoader` only sees the indices assigned to that process. The sampler ensures no data overlap between processes.

Performance tips:

- Set `num_workers` per rank (each process spawns its own workers, so the node runs `num_workers × world_size` workers in total). A practical start is `min(8, cpu_cores_per_node / gpus_per_node / 2)` on each rank
- Use `pin_memory=True` for faster CPU-to-GPU transfer
- Set `prefetch_factor=2` (default) to prefetch batches ahead
- Use `persistent_workers=True` to keep workers alive between epochs (reduces startup overhead)

Device selection best practices

When setting up DDP, you need to assign each process to a GPU. The standard approach:

```
local_rank = int(os.environ['LOCAL_RANK'])
torch.cuda.set_device(local_rank)
device = torch.device(f'cuda:{local_rank}')
```

This ensures process 0 uses GPU 0, process 1 uses GPU 1, etc. Always use `LOCAL_RANK` for device selection—don't use `RANK` (which is global across all nodes).

You can also set `CUDA_VISIBLE_DEVICES` before launching to restrict which GPUs are visible:

```
CUDA_VISIBLE_DEVICES=0,1,2,3 torchrun --nproc_per_node=4 code/
train_ddp_multi_mini.py
```

This makes only GPUs 0-3 visible, and `LOCAL_RANK` will map to these GPUs (LOCAL_RANK 0 → GPU 0, LOCAL_RANK 1 → GPU 1, etc.).

A complete single node example

Here's a complete example that trains a small CNN on CIFAR-10 with DDP. It uses **torchrun** (as earlier), so rank and world size come from the environment:

```
import torch
import torch.nn as nn
import torch.distributed as dist
import torch.optim as optim
from torch.nn.parallel import DistributedDataParallel as DDP
from torch.utils.data.distributed import DistributedSampler
import torchvision
import torchvision.transforms as transforms
import os

def setup():
    rank = int(os.environ['RANK'])
    local_rank = int(os.environ['LOCAL_RANK'])
    world_size = int(os.environ['WORLD_SIZE'])
    dist.init_process_group(backend='nccl')
    torch.cuda.set_device(local_rank)
    return rank, local_rank, world_size

def cleanup():
    dist.destroy_process_group()

class Net(nn.Module):
    def __init__(self):
        super().__init__()
        self.conv1 = nn.Conv2d(3, 6, 5)
        self.pool = nn.MaxPool2d(2, 2)
        self.conv2 = nn.Conv2d(6, 16, 5)
        self.fc1 = nn.Linear(16 * 5 * 5, 120)
        self.fc2 = nn.Linear(120, 84)
```

```
        self.fc3 = nn.Linear(84, 10)

    def forward(self, x):
        x = self.pool(torch.relu(self.conv1(x)))
        x = self.pool(torch.relu(self.conv2(x)))
        x = x.view(-1, 16 * 5 * 5)
        x = torch.relu(self.fc1(x))
        x = torch.relu(self.fc2(x))
        x = self.fc3(x)
        return x

def get_dataloader(rank, world_size, batch_size=128):
    transform = transforms.Compose([
        transforms.ToTensor(),
        transforms.Normalize((0.5, 0.5, 0.5), (0.5, 0.5, 0.5))
    ])
    trainset = torchvision.datasets.CIFAR10(
        root='./data', train=True, download=True, transform=transform
    )
    sampler = DistributedSampler(
        trainset, num_replicas=world_size, rank=rank, shuffle=True
    )
    trainloader = torch.utils.data.DataLoader(
        trainset, batch_size=batch_size, sampler=sampler,
        num_workers=4, pin_memory=True
    )
    return trainloader, sampler

def main():
    rank, local_rank, world_size = setup()
    device = torch.device(f'cuda:{local_rank}')
    model = Net().to(device)
    model = DDP(model, device_ids=[local_rank])
    criterion = nn.CrossEntropyLoss()
    optimizer = optim.SGD(model.parameters(), lr=0.001, momentum=0.9)
    trainloader, sampler = get_dataloader(rank, world_size)
    for epoch in range(10):
        sampler.set_epoch(epoch)
        model.train()
        for batch_idx, (data, target) in enumerate(trainloader):
            data, target = data.to(device), target.to(device)
```

```
            optimizer.zero_grad()
            output = model(data)
            loss = criterion(output, target)
            loss.backward()
            optimizer.step()
            if rank == 0 and batch_idx % 100 == 0:
                print(f'Epoch {epoch}, Batch {batch_idx}, Loss: {loss.item():.
4f}')
    if rank == 0:
        print('Training finished')
    cleanup()

if __name__ == '__main__':
    main()
```

A runnable version is in `code/train_ddp_cifar10.py`. From the chapter directory, run:

```
torchrun --nproc_per_node=4 code/train_ddp_cifar10.py
```

Use your number of GPUs in place of 4; to limit which devices are used, set `CUDA_VISIBLE_DEVICES` before the command. On first run, CIFAR-10 is downloaded into `./data` (relative to the current working directory). Only rank 0 prints loss and the final message; the other ranks run silently. The example uses a fixed 10 epochs; for production, make the number of epochs (and other hyperparameters) configurable via config or the command line. Same pattern as the minimal example: one entry point, environment variables set by torchrun.

Setting up Multi-Node DDP

Multi-node DDP runs one process per GPU across multiple machines. You get both scale (models that don't fit on one node, or faster training with many GPUs) and a clear layout: each machine is a *node*, and the total number of processes is the *world size*.

Multi-Node rchitecture

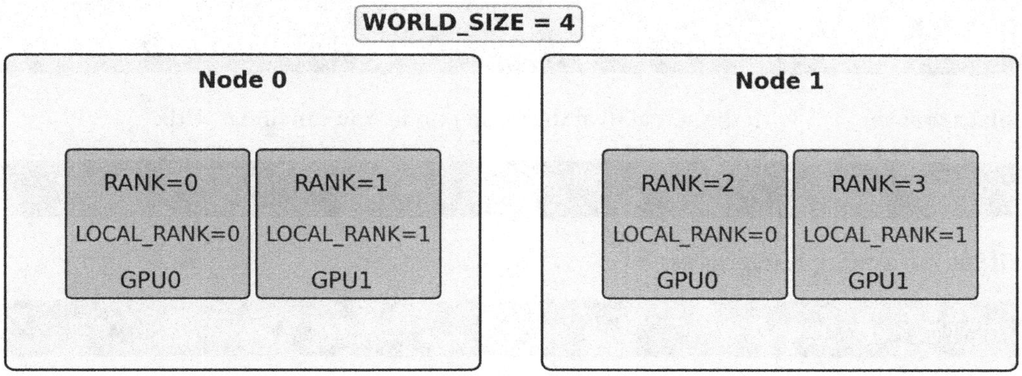

Figure 3.9: RANK and LOCAL_RANK for 2 nodes × 2 GPUs (multi-node)

Figure 3.9 shows the layout for two nodes with two GPUs each: WORLD_SIZE 4, with RANKs 0–3. Node 0 runs the processes with RANK 0 and 1 (each with LOCAL_RANK 0 and 1); node 1 runs RANK 2 and 3 (again LOCAL_RANK 0 and 1 on that node). The same pattern scales—e.g. 4 nodes × 8 GPUs per node gives world size 32, with 8 processes per node.

Communication cost follows that layout. GPUs on the same node use NVLink (hundreds of GB/s); GPUs on different nodes use InfiniBand or Ethernet, which is slower per link (tens of GB/s) but can still yield high aggregate bandwidth. NCCL exploits this by reducing inside each node first, then across nodes, then broadcasting the result back—keeping cross-node traffic down.

Launching Multi-Node training

Multi-node training requires every process to agree on where to rendezvous and how many processes there are. That means specifying: the master node's address and port, total number of nodes, and each node's rank. One way to do that is to run `torchrun` on each node and pass these as flags; torchrun then sets `MASTER_ADDR`, `MASTER_PORT`, `WORLD_SIZE`, `NODE_RANK`, and `NNODES` (and per-process `RANK`, `LOCAL_RANK`) for you. Job schedulers like SLURM (see below) are another common way—they set the same variables from the job layout.

For the 2 nodes × 2 GPUs layout above, run the following on each node. On the master node (node 0):

```
torchrun --nnodes=2 --nproc_per_node=2 --node_rank=0 \
  --master_addr=<master_ip> --master_port=29500 code/train_ddp_multi_mini.py
```

On the worker node (node 1):

```
torchrun --nnodes=2 --nproc_per_node=2 --node_rank=1 \
  --master_addr=<master_ip> --master_port=29500 code/train_ddp_multi_mini.py
```

Replace `<master_ip>` with the actual IP of the master node. You can find it with:

```
hostname -I
```

Or if you have multiple interfaces:

```
ip addr show | grep inet
```

For larger runs (e.g. 4 nodes × 8 GPUs), use the same pattern and set `--nnodes=4`, `--nproc_per_node=8`, and `--node_rank=0,1,2,3` on the respective nodes.

Using SLURM for Multi-Node launch

Most HPC clusters use SLURM for job scheduling. We cover SLURM and multi-node launch in detail in *Chapter 8*; below is a minimal example for the same 2 nodes × 2 GPUs layout used above:

```
#!/bin/bash
#SBATCH --job-name=ddp_train
#SBATCH --nodes=2
#SBATCH --ntasks-per-node=2
#SBATCH --gres=gpu:2
#SBATCH --time=24:00:00
#SBATCH --partition=gpu
# Get node list
export MASTER_ADDR=$(scontrol show hostnames $SLURM_JOB_NODELIST | head -n 1)
export MASTER_PORT=29500
export WORLD_SIZE=$SLURM_NTASKS
export RANK=$SLURM_PROCID
export LOCAL_RANK=$SLURM_LOCALID
# Launch training
srun python code/train_ddp_multi_mini.py
```

Or using torchrun with SLURM:

```
#!/bin/bash
#SBATCH --job-name=ddp_train
#SBATCH --nodes=2
#SBATCH --ntasks-per-node=2
#SBATCH --gres=gpu:2
#SBATCH --time=24:00:00
export MASTER_ADDR=$(scontrol show hostnames $SLURM_JOB_NODELIST | head -n 1)
export MASTER_PORT=29500
srun torchrun --nnodes=$SLURM_NNODES --nproc_per_node=2 \
  --node_rank=$SLURM_NODEID --master_addr=$MASTER_ADDR --master_port=$MASTER_PORT
code/train_ddp_multi_mini.py
```

For larger jobs (e.g. 4 nodes × 8 GPUs), set `--nodes=4`, `--ntasks-per-node=8`, `--gres=gpu:8`, and `--nproc_per_node=8` in the torchrun variant.

Network configuration

For multi-node training, network bandwidth and latency matter. InfiniBand is preferred over Ethernet because:

- Higher bandwidth: 200-400 Gb/s per link vs. 10-100 Gb/s for Ethernet
- Lower latency: Sub-microsecond vs. microseconds
- RDMA support: Direct GPU-to-GPU memory access

If you're using InfiniBand, make sure:

- All nodes are on the same InfiniBand subnet
- NCCL can detect InfiniBand interfaces (set `NCCL_IB_DISABLE=0` if needed)
- Firewall allows the master port (or disables firewall for cluster network)

You can test connectivity as follows. Raw InfiniBand bandwidth (`ib_write_bw`) is optional; nccl-tests https://github.com/NVIDIA/nccl-tests (e.g. `all_reduce_perf`) is closer to what DDP uses because it runs NCCL collectives on your fabric:

```
# Optional: raw IB bandwidth
ib_write_bw          # on node 0
ib_write_bw <node0_ip>  # on node 1
# Recommended: NCCL collective benchmark (after building nccl-tests)
# ./build/all_reduce_perf -b 8 -e 128M -f 2 -g <gpus_per_node>
```

Environment variables for Multi-Node

Multi-node uses the same variables as single-node—`RANK`, `LOCAL_RANK`, `WORLD_SIZE`, `MASTER_ADDR`, and `MASTER_PORT`—all set by torchrun or your job launcher (see "Understanding the Environment Variables"). On multiple nodes, `MASTER_ADDR` must be the master node's real IP address, not localhost, and every node must use the same `MASTER_PORT` (pick a free port on the master—reusing `29500` across back-to-back jobs can hit "address already in use" while the socket is in `TIME_WAIT`). Torchrun also sets `NODE_RANK` (this node's index from 0 to num_nodes−1) and `NNODES`. When you launch with SLURM, you usually pass the node index and node count into torchrun from `$SLURM_NODEID` and `$SLURM_NNODES`.

Before your first multi-node run, verify a few cluster basics that might otherwise produce hangs or mysteriously slow jobs:

- **Matching software stack**: CUDA driver, NCCL, and PyTorch builds should match on every node. A rank on an older driver—or a different PyTorch build—is a common source of `init_process_group` hangs and cryptic NCCL errors.
- `MASTER_ADDR` **is an IP, not a hostname**: Every node must reach the same address on the cluster network. Hostnames that resolve differently per node (or only on the master) break rendezvous even when the launch command looks correct.
- **Pick the right network interface**: On machines with multiple NICs (management Ethernet plus InfiniBand), NCCL may bind to the wrong one. Set `NCCL_SOCKET_IFNAME` to the cluster fabric interface (e.g. `ib0`; check with `ip addr`). See the Performance Issues section for an example when debugging slow cross-node AllReduce.

A complete Multi-Node example

The same training script can be used for both single-node and multi-node; only the launch command changes. A runnable version is in `code/train_ddp_multi_mini.py`. Its structure looks like this:

```
import os
import torch
import torch.distributed as dist
import torch.nn as nn
from torch.nn.parallel import DistributedDataParallel as DDP

def setup():
    """Initialize process group. Works for both single-node and multi-node
(torchrun sets env vars)."""
```

```
    rank = int(os.environ['RANK'])
    local_rank = int(os.environ['LOCAL_RANK'])
    world_size = int(os.environ['WORLD_SIZE'])
    torch.cuda.set_device(local_rank)
    dist.init_process_group(backend='nccl')
    return rank, local_rank, world_size

def main():
    rank, local_rank, world_size = setup()
    if rank == 0:
        print(f'Initialized process group: world_size={world_size}')
        print(f'Master: {os.environ.get("MASTER_ADDR")}:
{os.environ.get("MASTER_PORT")}')
    # Create model
    model = nn.Linear(10, 1).to(local_rank)
    model = DDP(model, device_ids=[local_rank])
    # Training loop...
    # (same as single-node example)
    dist.destroy_process_group()

if __name__ == '__main__':
    main()
```

Launch for multi-node (2×2 layout). On each node, set the env vars then run torchrun (on node 0 use `NODE_RANK=0`, on node 1 use `NODE_RANK=1`):

```
export MASTER_ADDR=<master_ip>    # IP of node 0
export MASTER_PORT=29500
export NODE_RANK=0                # 0 on master, 1 on worker node
torchrun --nnodes=2 --nproc_per_node=2 --node_rank=$NODE_RANK \
  --master_addr=$MASTER_ADDR --master_port=$MASTER_PORT code/
train_ddp_multi_mini.py
```

Debugging and troubleshooting

DDP training can fail in many ways. Most failures fall into a few categories: hangs, wrong results, out-of-memory errors, or performance issues. Let's go through each category with common causes and fixes.

Hangs: the most common problem

DDP hangs are usually caused by mismatched collective operations. Every process must call the same collectives in the same order. If one process calls `all_reduce` while another is waiting for something else, everything hangs.

Symptom: Training starts but hangs at a specific point, often during `init_process_group` or during the first backward pass.

Common causes:

1. **Mismatched WORLD_SIZE**: If processes have different `WORLD_SIZE` values, initialization hangs

```
# WRONG: Different processes see different world_size
world_size = torch.cuda.device_count()  # Might differ per node
# RIGHT: Use environment variable set by launcher
world_size = int(os.environ['WORLD_SIZE'])
```

2. **Conditional collectives**: If some processes skip a collective call, others hang waiting

```
# WRONG: Only rank 0 calls all_reduce
if rank == 0:
    dist.all_reduce(tensor)
# RIGHT: All processes call all_reduce
dist.all_reduce(tensor)
```

3. **Firewall blocking ports**: If `MASTER_PORT` is blocked, processes can't communicate

```
# Test if port is accessible
telnet <master_ip> <master_port>
# Or use a different port
export MASTER_PORT=29501
```

4. **Process group / NCCL timeout**: PyTorch's process-group watchdog timeout is set in Python, not via an `NCCL_TIMEOUT` environment variable (that name is not read by PyTorch). The default is 30 minutes. For slow clusters or large jobs, pass a larger `timeout` to `init_process_group`:

```
from datetime import timedelta
```

```
dist.init_process_group(
    backend='nccl',
    timeout=timedelta(minutes=60),  # default is 30 minutes
)
```

For the NCCL backend, that timeout is enforced on collectives only when blocking wait is enabled. Set these before `init_process_group` (PyTorch 2.2+ names; older releases use `NCCL_ASYNC_ERROR_HANDLING` and `NCCL_BLOCKING_WAIT` without the `TORCH_` prefix):

```
export TORCH_NCCL_ASYNC_ERROR_HANDLING=1
export TORCH_NCCL_BLOCKING_WAIT=1
```

For hang debugging, add targeted NCCL logging (verbose but readable):

```
export NCCL_DEBUG=INFO
export NCCL_DEBUG_SUBSYS=INIT,COLL
```

Debugging hangs:

Add logging to see where each process gets stuck:

```
import logging
logging.basicConfig(level=logging.INFO)

def setup():
    rank = int(os.environ['RANK'])
    local_rank = int(os.environ['LOCAL_RANK'])
    logging.info(f'Rank {rank}: Starting setup')
    torch.cuda.set_device(local_rank)
    logging.info(f'Rank {rank}: Set device')
    dist.init_process_group(backend='nccl')
    logging.info(f'Rank {rank}: Initialized process group')
    return rank
```

Run with one process first to test basic correctness:

```
# Test single-process first
CUDA_VISIBLE_DEVICES=0 python code/train_ddp_multi_mini.py  # Should work without
DDP
# Then test with torchrun
torchrun --nproc_per_node=1 code/train_ddp_multi_mini.py  # Single process with
```

```
DDP
# Then scale up
torchrun --nproc_per_node=2 code/train_ddp_multi_mini.py
```

Wrong results or inconsistent gradients

Two problems are often confused. **Loss that does not decrease or diverges** usually indicates a real bug (data sharding, learning rate after global batch scaling, missing `set_epoch()`, etc.). **Different loss values across separate runs** with the same command is often normal—CUDA and NCCL are not fully deterministic unless you enable slow deterministic mode.

Symptoms:

- Loss doesn't decrease or diverges → treat as a bug (see **When loss stalls or diverges** below)
- Different curves on separate runs with the same seed → often expected; only chase bit-level reproducibility for regression tests

When loss stalls or diverges, check the following:

1. **Missing DistributedSampler.set_epoch()**: Without this, all epochs see data in the same order

```
# WRONG: Same data order every epoch
for epoch in range(10):
    for data, target in dataloader:
        # Training...
# RIGHT: Shuffle data each epoch
for epoch in range(10):
    sampler.set_epoch(epoch)  # CRITICAL
    for data, target in dataloader:
        # Training...
```

2. **Different random seeds across ranks**: If each process seeds RNGs differently, ranks will disagree and training can look wrong. Use the same seed setup on every rank:

```
# Set seeds on all processes
def set_seed(seed):
    torch.manual_seed(seed)
    torch.cuda.manual_seed_all(seed)
    np.random.seed(seed)
    random.seed(seed)
```

```
# Call this after setup(), before creating model
set_seed(42)
```

3. **Data leakage**: If `DistributedSampler` isn't used correctly, processes might see overlapping data

```
# WRONG: Using shuffle=True in DataLoader with DistributedSampler
dataloader = DataLoader(dataset, shuffle=True, sampler=sampler)  #
Conflict!
# RIGHT: Shuffle in sampler, not DataLoader
sampler = DistributedSampler(dataset, shuffle=True)
dataloader = DataLoader(dataset, sampler=sampler)  # No shuffle=True here
```

When separate runs differ but loss still looks healthy, that is usually CUDA/NCCL non-determinism, not a DDP bug. To tighten reproducibility for regression tests (slower training):

```
torch.backends.cudnn.deterministic = True
torch.backends.cudnn.benchmark = False
torch.use_deterministic_algorithms(True)
```

Verifying correctness:

Compare single-GPU vs multi-GPU **loss trends** with the same global batch size and learning rate. They need not match step-by-step; a large systematic gap (e.g. 4× worse loss with 4 GPUs) suggests a setup bug such as wrong per-GPU batch size or gradients summed instead of averaged.

CUDA out of memory

OOM errors are common when scaling to multiple GPUs. The issue is that DDP replicates the model on each GPU, so memory usage scales with the number of GPUs.

Symptom: `RuntimeError: CUDA out of memory` during training.

Common causes:

1. **Batch size too large**: Even with DDP, per-GPU batch size matters

```
# If global batch size is 128 and you have 4 GPUs
# Per-GPU batch size should be 32, not 128
global_batch_size = 128
per_gpu_batch_size = global_batch_size // world_size
```

2. **Gradients accumulating**: If you're doing gradient accumulation, make sure to zero gradients

```
# WRONG: Gradients accumulate across accumulation steps
for i, (data, target) in enumerate(dataloader):
    loss = model(data, target)
    loss.backward()  # Gradients accumulate!
    if (i + 1) % accumulation_steps == 0:
        optimizer.step()
# RIGHT: Zero gradients at the start of accumulation
optimizer.zero_grad()
for i, (data, target) in enumerate(dataloader):
    loss = model(data, target)
    loss = loss / accumulation_steps  # Scale loss
    loss.backward()
    if (i + 1) % accumulation_steps == 0:
        optimizer.step()
        optimizer.zero_grad()
```

3. **Large activations**: Some models (e.g., transformers with long sequences) have large activation memory
   Solutions:
   - **Reduce batch size**: Lower per-GPU batch size
   - **Gradient checkpointing**: Trade compute for memory by recomputing activations

   ```
   from torch.utils.checkpoint import checkpoint
   # Replace
   output = model(x)
   # With
   output = checkpoint(model, x)
   ```

   - **Mixed precision**: Use FP16/BF16 to halve memory usage

   ```
   from torch.cuda.amp import autocast, GradScaler
   scaler = GradScaler()
   for data, target in dataloader:
       optimizer.zero_grad()
       with autocast():
           output = model(data)
   ```

```
        loss = criterion(output, target)
    scaler.scale(loss).backward()
    scaler.step(optimizer)
    scaler.update()
```

- **Clear cache (between jobs only)**: `torch.cuda.empty_cache()` returns reserved-but-unused memory to the driver; it does **not** lower peak memory during an active training step. Calling it inside the training loop forces synchronization and slows training—use it between separate jobs or processes, not every iteration.

Performance issues

If training runs but is slow, the bottleneck is usually communication, data loading, or inefficient kernels.

Symptom: GPU utilization is low or training is slower than expected.

Common causes:

1. **Data loading bottleneck**: If CPU can't keep up with GPU, GPUs sit idle

```
# Increase num_workers
dataloader = DataLoader(dataset, num_workers=8, pin_memory=True)
# Or use prefetching
from torch.utils.data import DataLoader
dataloader = DataLoader(dataset, num_workers=8, prefetch_factor=2)
```

2. **Small batch size**: If batch size is too small, GPUs aren't fully utilized

```
# Increase batch size (if memory allows)
batch_size = 128  # Instead of 32
```

3. **Communication overhead**: If model is small or communication is slow, AllReduce dominates

```
# Profile to see where time is spent
with torch.profiler.profile(
    activities=[torch.profiler.ProfilerActivity.CPU,
torch.profiler.ProfilerActivity.CUDA],
    record_shapes=True,
) as prof:
    # Training step
    pass
```

```
print(prof.key_averages().table(sort_by="cuda_time_total"))
```

4. **Inefficient NCCL topology**: NCCL might pick a suboptimal algorithm or the wrong network interface (see the multi-node checklist under Setting Up Multi-Node DDP)

```
# Set NCCL debug to see what algorithm is used
export NCCL_DEBUG=INFO
# Force specific algorithm (advanced, usually not needed)
export NCCL_IB_DISABLE=0
export NCCL_SOCKET_IFNAME=ib0  # cluster fabric NIC, not management
Ethernet
```

Debugging performance:

Use PyTorch profiler to identify bottlenecks:

```
from torch.profiler import profile, record_function, ProfilerActivity
with profile(
    activities=[ProfilerActivity.CPU, ProfilerActivity.CUDA],
    record_shapes=True,
    profile_memory=True,
) as prof:
    with record_function("training_step"):
        # Your training step
        output = model(data)
        loss = criterion(output, target)
        loss.backward()
        optimizer.step()
# Print results
print(prof.key_averages().table(sort_by="cuda_time_total", row_limit=20))
```

Check GPU utilization:

```
# Monitor GPU utilization
watch -n 1 nvidia-smi
# Or use dstat
dstat -cdngy
```

Network debugging

For multi-node training, network issues are common. Use NCCL debugging:

```
# Enable NCCL debug logging
export NCCL_DEBUG=INFO
export NCCL_DEBUG_SUBSYS=INIT,COLL
# Test NCCL connectivity
python -c "import torch; torch.distributed.init_process_group('nccl');
print('OK')"
```

Check InfiniBand connectivity:

```
# List InfiniBand devices
ibdev2netdev
# Optional: raw IB bandwidth
ib_write_bw  # On one node
ib_write_bw <other_node_ip>  # On another node
# Recommended for DDP: NCCL collective tests (nccl-tests)
```

See the Network Configuration section above for when to prefer nccl-tests https://github.com/NVIDIA/nccl-tests over raw `ib_write_bw`.

Profiling DDP performance

Before optimizing DDP, you need to understand where time is spent. PyTorch's profiler provides detailed insights into DDP's computation-communication overlap, gradient synchronization overhead, and data loading bottlenecks.

Using torch.profiler.profile for DDP analysis

The `torch.profiler.profile` context manager captures detailed timing information for CPU and CUDA operations. For DDP, you want to profile:

- Forward pass time
- Backward pass time (gradient computation)
- AllReduce communication time
- Overlap between computation and communication
- Data loading time

Here's a complete example of profiling DDP training:

```
import torch
import torch.nn as nn
from torch.nn.parallel import DistributedDataParallel as DDP
from torch.profiler import profile, record_function, ProfilerActivity
import torch.distributed as dist

def train_with_profiling(model, dataloader, optimizer, criterion,
num_iterations=10):
    """Train with profiling to analyze DDP performance."""
    rank = dist.get_rank()
    # Create profiler
    with profile(
        activities=[ProfilerActivity.CPU, ProfilerActivity.CUDA],
        record_shapes=True,
        profile_memory=True,
        with_stack=True,  # Enable stack traces for deeper analysis
    ) as prof:
        with record_function("training_loop"):
            for i, (data, target) in enumerate(dataloader):
                if i >= num_iterations:
                    break
                data = data.cuda(rank, non_blocking=True)
                target = target.cuda(rank, non_blocking=True)
                # Forward pass
                with record_function("forward_pass"):
                    output = model(data)
                    loss = criterion(output, target)
                # Backward pass (where DDP communication happens)
                with record_function("backward_pass"):
                    loss.backward()
                # Optimizer step
                with record_function("optimizer_step"):
                    optimizer.step()
                    optimizer.zero_grad()
    # Print profiling results (only on rank 0 to avoid duplicate output)
    if rank == 0:
        # Print key averages sorted by CUDA time
        print("=" * 20)
        print("DDP Performance Profile - Key Averages")
```

```
        print("=" * 20)
        print(prof.key_averages().table(
            sort_by="cuda_time_total",
            row_limit=30
        ))
        # Print events sorted by self CUDA time (excludes child operations)
        print("\n" + "=" * 80)
        print("Top Operations by Self CUDA Time")
        print("=" * 20)
        print(prof.key_averages().table(
            sort_by="cuda_time_total",
            row_limit=20
        ))
        # Export to Chrome trace format for visualization
        prof.export_chrome_trace("ddp_trace.json")
        print("\nChrome trace exported to ddp_trace.json")
        print("Open chrome://tracing or https://ui.perfetto.dev/ to visualize")
    return prof
```

A runnable script is in `code/profile_ddp.py`. From the chapter directory run (use 2 or more GPUs, or omit `CUDA_VISIBLE_DEVICES` if you have multiple GPUs):

```
CUDA_VISIBLE_DEVICES=0,1 torchrun --nproc_per_node=2 code/profile_ddp.py
```

Rank 0 prints key profile tables and writes `ddp_trace.json` to the current working directory.

PyTorch's `export_chrome_trace()` produces a Chrome trace JSON file—a timeline of CPU and CUDA events. Figure 3.10 shows a representative DDP run. These viewers are enough for spotting AllReduce overlap and data-loader gaps; for kernel-level NCCL analysis or cross-rank visibility on multi-GPU and multi-node runs, use NVIDIA Nsight Systems (`nsys`) instead (see Chapter 10).

To inspect the timeline:

1. Open Chrome at `chrome://tracing`, or open ui.perfetto.dev https://ui.perfetto.dev/ in any browser
2. Load the exported `.json` file (in Perfetto, drag the file onto the page)

Chrome and Perfetto organize CUDA events by **stream**. DDP runs backward compute on the default stream and launches NCCL AllReduce on separate communication streams (see the overlap mechanism earlier in this chapter). Bars that overlap in time but sit on different stream rows indicate overlap; events on the same stream are sequential regardless of horizontal alignment.

- **AllReduce operations:** `nccl:all_reduce` or similar gradient synchronization across ranks.
- **Overlap indicators:** Backward compute kernels (e.g., `ConvolutionBackward0`, `LinearBackward`) running concurrently with AllReduce on a different stream.
- **Communication overhead:** AllReduce time as a share of total step time—under 20% is good, 20–40% is acceptable, over 40% suggests a bottleneck. These bands depend on model size and cluster topology (a small model on NVLink might sit near 5%; a large model over Ethernet can land near 50% and still be expected).
- **Bucket boundaries:** Multiple AllReduce operations during backward pass—one per gradient bucket.

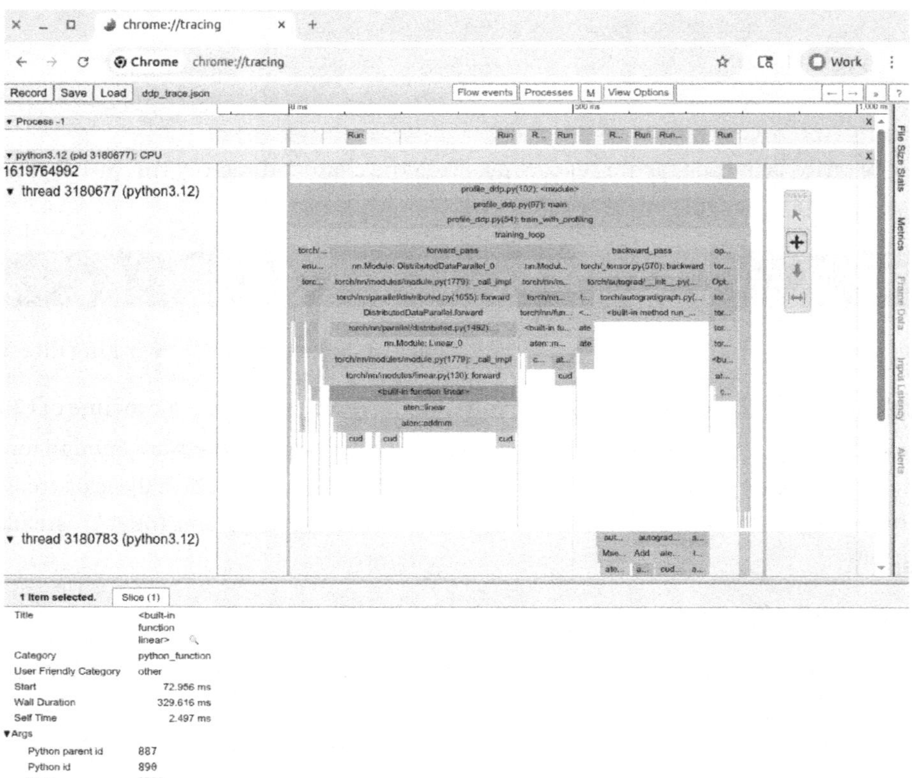

Figure 3.10: Chrome Tracing View of a DDP Run

Analyzing Computation–Communication overlap

The key metric for DDP performance is whether communication overlaps with computation. In the trace, look for AllReduce on a communication stream running concurrently with backward kernels on the compute stream—not merely adjacent boxes on the same row.

Here's a focused example that profiles just the backward pass to analyze overlap:

```
def analyze_ddp_overlap(model, loss):
    """Analyze computation-communication overlap in DDP backward pass."""
    rank = dist.get_rank()
    with profile(
        activities=[ProfilerActivity.CUDA],
        record_shapes=True,
        with_stack=True,
    ) as prof:
        with record_function("backward_with_ddp"):
            loss.backward()
    if rank == 0:
        # Look for AllReduce operations
        events = prof.key_averages()
        # Filter for NCCL AllReduce operations
        allreduce_ops = [e for e in events if 'nccl' in e.key.lower() and
'allreduce' in e.key.lower()]
        backward_ops = [e for e in events if 'backward' in e.key.lower() or
'gradient' in e.key.lower()]
        print("=" * 20)
        print("DDP Overlap Analysis")
        print("=" * 20)
        print(f"AllReduce operations found: {len(allreduce_ops)}")
        print(f"Backward operations found: {len(backward_ops)}")
        # Check if AllReduce overlaps with backward compute
        total_allreduce_time = sum(e.cuda_time_total for e in allreduce_ops)
        total_backward_time = sum(e.cuda_time_total for e in backward_ops)
        print(f"\nTotal AllReduce time: {total_allreduce_time / 1000:.2f} ms")
        print(f"Total backward compute time: {total_backward_time / 1000:.2f} ms")
        # If backward time >> AllReduce time, overlap is working
        if total_backward_time > total_allreduce_time * 1.5:
            print("✓ Good overlap: Computation time exceeds communication time")
            print("  This indicates AllReduce is happening concurrently with
gradient computation")
```

```
        else:
            print("⚠ Limited overlap: Communication time is significant")
            print("
Consider: larger bucket size, faster interconnects, or larger models")
        # Export trace for detailed visualization
        prof.export_chrome_trace("ddp_overlap_trace.json")
```

A runnable script that does only this overlap analysis is in `code/profile_ddp_overlap.py`. From the chapter directory run:

```
torchrun --nproc_per_node=2 code/profile_ddp_overlap.py
```

Rank 0 prints the AllReduce vs backward times and writes `ddp_overlap_trace.json`. With the script's minimal model (a single linear layer), backward compute is negligible, so you will typically see "Total backward compute time: 0.00 ms" and "Limited overlap"—that is expected; with larger models, backward time dominates, and overlap becomes visible.

Example output:

```
DDP Overlap Analysis
=====================
AllReduce operations found: 1
Backward operations found: 1
Total AllReduce time: 1.06 ms
Total backward compute time: 0.00 ms
⚠ Limited overlap: Communication time is significant
  Consider: larger bucket size, faster interconnects, or larger models
...
```

Profiling Multi-Node DDP

For multi-node training, you want to profile communication between nodes separately from intra-node communication:

```
def profile_multi_node_ddp(model, dataloader, optimizer, criterion):
    """Profile DDP with focus on inter-node vs intra-node communication."""
    rank = dist.get_rank()
    local_rank = rank % torch.cuda.device_count()
    with profile(
        activities=[ProfilerActivity.CPU, ProfilerActivity.CUDA],
        record_shapes=True,
```

```
    ) as prof:
        # Training step
        for data, target in dataloader:
            data = data.cuda(local_rank)
            target = target.cuda(local_rank)
            output = model(data)
            loss = criterion(output, target)
            loss.backward()
            optimizer.step()
            optimizer.zero_grad()
            break  # Profile just one iteration
    if rank == 0:
        events = prof.key_averages()
        # Analyze NCCL operations
        nccl_ops = [e for e in events if 'nccl' in e.key.lower()]
        print("=" * 20)
        print("Multi-Node DDP Communication Analysis")
        print("=" * 20)
        for op in nccl_ops[:10]:  # Top 10 NCCL operations
            print(f"{op.key}: {op.cuda_time_total / 1000:.2f} ms")
        # Export for detailed analysis
        prof.export_chrome_trace(f"ddp_multinode_rank{rank}.json")
```

A runnable script is in `code/profile_ddp_multinode.py`. From the chapter directory run:

```
torchrun --nproc_per_node=2 code/profile_ddp_multinode.py
```

Rank 0 prints the top 10 NCCL operations and writes `ddp_multinode_rank0.json`.

Example output:

```
Multi-Node DDP Communication Analysis
====================================
nccl:all_reduce: 0.18 ms
ncclKernel_AllReduce_Sum_f32_RING_LL: 0.18 ms
Example: Profiling ResNet50 on CIFAR-10
```

To practice profiling a larger model, use the script in `code/profile_ddp_resnet50.py`. It runs ResNet50 on CIFAR-10 with DDP for 5 iterations under the profiler. Rank 0 prints a table of the top operations (by CUDA time) and exports `resnet50_ddp_trace.json` in the current working directory. CIFAR-10 is downloaded to `./data` on first run. From the chapter directory run:

```
torchrun --nproc_per_node=2 code/profile_ddp_resnet50.py
```

Open `resnet50_ddp_trace.json` at chrome://tracing or in Perfetto UI https://ui.perfetto.dev/ and use the same checklist as before: look for AllReduce operations, whether they overlap with backward compute, and how communication time compares to total step time. With ResNet50 you should see more backward compute and a clearer picture of overlap than with the minimal linear model in the earlier scripts.

Optimizing DDP performance

Once you've profiled and identified bottlenecks, optimize in this order: mixed precision and gradient accumulation when memory or effective batch size is the limit; data-loader tuning and overlap hygiene (`no_sync()`, avoiding blocking syncs in backward); `bucket_cap_mb` last, when profiling shows a communication-bound backward pass.

Mixed precision training

Mixed precision (FP16 or BF16) reduces memory use and can improve throughput. PyTorch's Automatic Mixed Precision (AMP) provides a straightforward way to use it:

```
from torch.cuda.amp import autocast, GradScaler
scaler = GradScaler()
for epoch in range(10):
    for data, target in dataloader:
        optimizer.zero_grad()
        # Forward pass in mixed precision
        with autocast():
            output = model(data)
            loss = criterion(output, target)
        # Backward pass with scaling
        scaler.scale(loss).backward()
        # Optimizer step with unscaling
        scaler.step(optimizer)
        scaler.update()
```

`GradScaler` scales the loss before backward so that small gradients do not underflow; it also detects overflow (inf or NaN), skips the optimizer step when overflow is detected, and adjusts the scale factor over time. FP16 uses a 5-bit exponent and 10-bit mantissa and can underflow easily. BF16 uses an 8-bit exponent (as in FP32) and a 7-bit mantissa, so it is more stable with less precision loss. For training, BF16 is often preferred; for inference, FP16 is commonly used and can be faster. To use BF16 when the hardware supports it:

```
# Use BF16 (if supported)
with autocast(dtype=torch.bfloat16):
    output = model(data)
```

With DDP, the scaler should be created before wrapping the model in DDP, and `scaler.step()` and `scaler.update()` must be called on every process. The scaler skips the optimizer step when it detects overflow.

Gradient accumulation

Gradient accumulation simulates a larger batch size without increasing memory use: parameters are updated only every few steps, while gradients are accumulated over those steps. The pattern looks like this:

```
accumulation_steps = 4
optimizer.zero_grad()
for i, (data, target) in enumerate(dataloader):
    output = model(data)
    loss = criterion(output, target) / accumulation_steps
    # AllReduce only on the last micro-batch in each window
    if (i + 1) % accumulation_steps != 0:
        with model.no_sync():
            loss.backward()
    else:
        loss.backward()
        optimizer.step()
        optimizer.zero_grad()
# If the epoch ends mid-window, step the remaining gradients once
if (i + 1) % accumulation_steps != 0:
    optimizer.step()
    optimizer.zero_grad()
```

It is useful when the desired batch size does not fit in memory, when a larger effective batch size is needed for training stability, or when the dataset size is not divisible by the per-step batch size. With DDP, `backward()` triggers AllReduce by default, so wrap intermediate micro-batches in `model.no_sync()` and run AllReduce only on the last backward in each accumulation window—otherwise, you pay for `accumulation_steps` collectives per optimizer step instead of one.

Communication overlap optimization

DDP is designed to overlap communication (AllReduce) with backward computation so that gradient synchronization does not add its full cost to the step time. How much overlap is achieved depends on how the training loop and data pipeline are set up. The following three aspects are worth attention.

1. **Avoid blocking operations in backward**: Don't call `synchronize()` or blocking operations during backward pass

```
# WRONG: Blocks and prevents overlap
loss.backward()
torch.cuda.synchronize()  # Blocks!
optimizer.step()
# RIGHT: Let DDP handle synchronization
loss.backward()
optimizer.step()  # DDP synchronizes automatically
```

2. **Use asynchronous data loading**: Keep data loading pipeline busy:

```
dataloader = DataLoader(
    dataset,
    batch_size=batch_size,
    num_workers=8,  # Parallel data loading
    pin_memory=True,  # Faster CPU->GPU transfer
    prefetch_factor=2  # Prefetch batches
)
```

3. **Profile to verify overlap**: Use profiler to see if AllReduce overlaps with compute:

```
with torch.profiler.profile(
    activities=[ProfilerActivity.CUDA],
    record_shapes=True,
) as prof:
    loss.backward()
# Check if AllReduce overlaps with backward compute
print(prof.key_averages().table())
```

Tuning bucket sizes

DDP groups gradients into buckets for AllReduce. The default bucket size is 25 MB, but you can tune it:

```
model = DDP(
    model,
    device_ids=[local_rank],
    bucket_cap_mb=50  # Increase from default 25 MB
)
```

Larger buckets mean fewer AllReduce calls and lower communication overhead, but gradients are synchronized later in the backward pass. Smaller buckets synchronize earlier and can improve overlap on slow interconnects, at the cost of more AllReduce invocations. Larger buckets tend to work well for large models, for fast interconnects such as NVLink, or when profiling shows that communication dominates. Smaller buckets are more appropriate for small models, for slow or cross-node links, or when memory for communication buffers is limited.

A suitable value can be found by profiling a few choices (e.g. 10, 25, 50, and 100 MB), running a short training segment for each, and comparing throughput. The default 25 MB is a reasonable starting point for most setups.

```
bucket_sizes = [10, 25, 50, 100]  # MB
for bucket_size in bucket_sizes:
    model = DDP(model, device_ids=[local_rank], bucket_cap_mb=bucket_size)
    # Run training for a few iterations
    # Measure throughput
    # Record results
```

Finding unused parameters

By default, DDP assumes all parameters receive gradients. If some parameters don't (e.g., in conditional models), DDP will hang waiting for gradients that never come.

Enable `find_unused_parameters=True`:

```
model = DDP(
    model,
    device_ids=[local_rank],
    find_unused_parameters=True  # Slower but handles unused params
)
```

Setting `find_unused_parameters=True` adds overhead, since DDP must traverse the computation graph to determine which parameters receive gradients; it is best enabled only when the model actually has unused parameters. When possible, structuring the model so that every parameter receives a gradient avoids this cost; for conditional models, that may require some restructuring.

Static graph optimization

When the computation graph does not change between iterations, enabling `static_graph` as `True` allows DDP to optimize communication:

```
model = DDP(
    model,
    device_ids=[local_rank],
    static_graph=True  # Graph structure is static
)
```

With `static_graph=True`, DDP assumes that the set of used and unused parameters is fixed and that the graph structure is identical every iteration; it can then optimize communication patterns accordingly. This applies naturally to models without conditional logic, or to any model whose graph has been verified to be static. Whether a given model can use a static graph can be inspected after a few training iterations via DDP's internal logging:

```
# After training for a few iterations
ddp_logging_data = model._get_ddp_logging_data()
can_set_static_graph = ddp_logging_data.get("can_set_static_graph", False)
if can_set_static_graph:
    print("Can enable static_graph=True")
```

Checkpointing and resuming distributed jobs

After optimizing your DDP training, you'll want to save progress regularly. Long training jobs need checkpointing, and with DDP, you need to save and restore model state, optimizer state, and random number generator state correctly. The patterns below use rank-0-only `torch.save`, which fits replicated DDP weights; at larger scale, gathering full state to one rank becomes a write bottleneck. For parallel sharded saves, PyTorch provides `torch.distributed.checkpoint` (DCP)—each rank writes its shard—covered in *Chapter 4*.

Saving checkpoints

Only rank 0 should write checkpoints to avoid race conditions:

```
def save_checkpoint(model, optimizer, epoch, loss, filepath):
    rank = dist.get_rank()
    if rank == 0:
        checkpoint = {
            'epoch': epoch,
            'model_state_dict': model.module.state_dict(),  # Note: .module
            'optimizer_state_dict': optimizer.state_dict(),
            'loss': loss,
        }
        # Save scaler state if using AMP
        if scaler is not None:
            checkpoint['scaler_state_dict'] = scaler.state_dict()
        torch.save(checkpoint, filepath)
        print(f'Checkpoint saved: {filepath}')
    # All processes wait for rank 0 to finish
    dist.barrier()
```

When saving DDP model state, the state dict must be taken from the underlying module via `model.module.state_dict()`, not from the DDP wrapper itself (`model.state_dict()`), because the DDP wrapper exposes the real model as its `.module` attribute.

Loading checkpoints

Each process loads the same checkpoint file so that all replicas resume from an identical state:

```
def load_checkpoint(model, optimizer, filepath, scaler=None):
    rank = dist.get_rank()
    # All processes load from the same file
    checkpoint = torch.load(filepath, map_location=f'cuda:{rank}')
    # Load model state
    model.module.load_state_dict(checkpoint['model_state_dict'])
    # Load optimizer state
    optimizer.load_state_dict(checkpoint['optimizer_state_dict'])
    # Load scaler state if using AMP
    if scaler is not None and 'scaler_state_dict' in checkpoint:
        scaler.load_state_dict(checkpoint['scaler_state_dict'])
    start_epoch = checkpoint['epoch'] + 1
    best_loss = checkpoint['loss']
```

```
    if rank == 0:
        print(f'Checkpoint loaded: {filepath}')
        print(f'Resuming from epoch {start_epoch}')
    return start_epoch, best_loss
```

Saving RNG state for reproducibility

Fully reproducible resumes require saving and restoring random number generator state (PyTorch, CUDA, and optionally Python and NumPy). The following stores RNG state in the checkpoint:

```
def save_checkpoint_with_rng(model, optimizer, epoch, filepath):
    rank = dist.get_rank()
    if rank == 0:
        checkpoint = {
            'epoch': epoch,
            'model_state_dict': model.module.state_dict(),
            'optimizer_state_dict': optimizer.state_dict(),
            'rng_state': torch.get_rng_state(),
            'cuda_rng_state': torch.cuda.get_rng_state_all(),
        }
        # Also save Python and NumPy RNG if used
        import random
        import numpy as np
        checkpoint['python_rng_state'] = random.getstate()
        checkpoint['numpy_rng_state'] = np.random.get_state()
        torch.save(checkpoint, filepath)

def load_checkpoint_with_rng(model, optimizer, filepath):
    rank = dist.get_rank()
    checkpoint = torch.load(filepath, map_location=f'cuda:{rank}')
    model.module.load_state_dict(checkpoint['model_state_dict'])
    optimizer.load_state_dict(checkpoint['optimizer_state_dict'])
    # Restore RNG states
    torch.set_rng_state(checkpoint['rng_state'])
    torch.cuda.set_rng_state_all(checkpoint['cuda_rng_state'])
    import random
    import numpy as np
    random.setstate(checkpoint['python_rng_state'])
    np.random.set_state(checkpoint['numpy_rng_state'])
    return checkpoint['epoch']
```

Atomic checkpointing

If the process crashes while writing, a partially written file can corrupt the checkpoint. Atomic writes—writing to a temporary file then renaming it to the final path—ensure the on-disk checkpoint is either complete or absent:

```
import os
import tempfile

def save_checkpoint_atomic(model, optimizer, epoch, filepath):
    rank = dist.get_rank()
    if rank == 0:
        # Write to temporary file first
        temp_file = filepath + '.tmp'
        checkpoint = {
            'epoch': epoch,
            'model_state_dict': model.module.state_dict(),
            'optimizer_state_dict': optimizer.state_dict(),
        }
        torch.save(checkpoint, temp_file)
        # Atomic rename
        os.rename(temp_file, filepath)
        print(f'Checkpoint saved: {filepath}')
    dist.barrier()
```

Checkpointing best practices

Checkpoints should be written on a regular schedule (e.g. every N epochs or every N iterations), and multiple checkpoints should be retained rather than overwriting a single file. Only rank 0 should write to storage to avoid race conditions; after it finishes, a `dist.barrier()` ensures all processes see the checkpoint before training continues. Periodically verifying that saved checkpoints load correctly avoids surprises when resuming or recovering from failure.

The same checkpoint patterns (rank-0-only writes, barriers, atomic saves, load at startup) are reused for fault-tolerant and elastic training, where workers may be restarted after failures; see *Elastic data parallelism*.

Now that we've covered the essentials of DDP setup, debugging, profiling, optimization, and checkpointing, let's explore some advanced features that DDP provides for specialized use cases.

Advanced DDP features

DDP has several advanced features for specialized use cases: gradient hooks, communication hooks, and join() for uneven inputs. These features give you fine-grained control over DDP's behavior when you need to customize gradient synchronization or handle edge cases.

Gradient hooks

Hooks can be registered on parameters to inspect or modify gradients during the backward pass. The hook receives the gradient tensor and must return a gradient (the same or a modified one). Because the model is wrapped in DDP, the parameter is accessed via `model.module.*`:

```
def gradient_hook(grad):
    # Inspect or modify gradient
    print(f'Gradient norm: {grad.norm().item()}')
    return grad  # Must return gradient
# Register hook on a parameter
model.module.fc.weight.register_hook(gradient_hook)
```

Running a small example with:

```
torchrun --nproc_per_node=2 code/ddp_gradient_hook.py
```

produces output such as:

```
  [rank 0] gradient norm: 5.7640
Gradient hook ran during backward.
```

Such hooks are often used to clip gradients, to log or monitor gradient norms during training, or to apply other per-parameter modifications before the optimizer updates the weights.

Communication hooks

Communication hooks replace DDP's default gradient synchronization with custom logic. The hook is invoked once per bucket; it receives the bucket's buffer, performs whatever reduction or transformation is desired, and must return a future that completes with the (possibly modified) tensor so that DDP can continue. Registering a hook that performs a plain AllReduce looks like this:

```
def allreduce_hook(state, bucket):
    """Custom hook that does AllReduce on gradient bucket."""
    tensor = bucket.buffer()
```

```
    # Custom AllReduce (e.g., with compression)
    dist.all_reduce(tensor, async_op=False)
    # Return future (DDP expects this)
    fut = torch.futures.Future()
    fut.set_result(tensor)
    return fut
# Register hook
model.register_comm_hook(state=None, hook=allreduce_hook)
```

A runnable example is in `code/ddp_comm_hook.py`. From the chapter directory, run:

```
$ torchrun --nproc_per_node=2 code/ddp_comm_hook.py
```

Output is printed from inside the hook as each bucket is reduced; for example:

```
[rank 0] comm hook: AllReduce on bucket (numel=2048)
[rank 0] comm hook: AllReduce on bucket (numel=1024)
[rank 0] comm hook: AllReduce on bucket (numel=64)
```

Typical applications include gradient compression (e.g. quantization or sparsification), custom reduction operations, and gradient filtering. Communication hooks are advanced: an incorrect implementation can break DDP or cause incorrect training, so they are best used only when the synchronization semantics are well understood.

Handling uneven inputs with join()

When different processes have different amounts of data (uneven inputs), some ranks finish their iteration before others; DDP then hangs because the remaining processes are still waiting in collective communication. The `join()` context manager avoids this by letting early-finished processes participate in dummy AllReduce operations so they stay in sync with ranks that are still training. The training loop is wrapped with `model.join()`:

```
from torch.nn.parallel import DistributedDataParallel as DDP

model = DDP(model, device_ids=[local_rank])
# Wrap training loop with join()
with model.join():
    for data, target in dataloader:
        # Training step
        output = model(data)
        loss = criterion(output, target)
```

```
        loss.backward()
        optimizer.step()
```

A runnable example is in `code/ddp_join_demo.py`: rank 0 has two batches and rank 1 has three, so without `join()` the run would hang when rank 0 finishes early. From the chapter directory:

```
$ torchrun --nproc_per_node=2 code/ddp_join_demo.py
```

Example output:

```
Running with join(): rank 0 has 2 batches, rank 1 has 3 batches.
  [rank 0] step 1 done.
  [rank 0] step 2 done.
join() demo finished (no hang).
```

Rank 0 completes its two steps and then participates in dummy AllReduces for rank 1's third step before both exit.

`join()` is appropriate when the dataset size is not divisible by batch size × world_size, when different processes have different dataset sizes, or when using dynamic batching.

Best practices and common patterns

The following practices keep DDP training reliable and efficient: validation order, launch choice, reproducibility, data loading, profiling, and checkpointing.

Always validate single-process first. Before scaling to multiple GPUs, single-GPU training should be verified:

```
# Test without DDP first
CUDA_VISIBLE_DEVICES=0 python code/train_ddp_multi_mini.py
# Then test with DDP (single process)
torchrun --nproc_per_node=1 code/train_ddp_multi_mini.py
# Then scale up
torchrun --nproc_per_node=4 code/train_ddp_multi_mini.py
```

Use torchrun for launching. `torchrun` is the recommended launcher: it handles process creation and cleanup, sets the required environment variables (e.g. `RANK`, `LOCAL_RANK`, `WORLD_SIZE`), produces clearer error messages than manual spawning, and supports elastic training when restarts are needed. Manual process spawning is only necessary when the launcher cannot meet a specific deployment or scheduling requirement.

Set seeds for reproducibility. Random seeds should be set on all processes:

```
def set_seed(seed):
    torch.manual_seed(seed)
    torch.cuda.manual_seed_all(seed)
    np.random.seed(seed)
    random.seed(seed)
    torch.backends.cudnn.deterministic = True
set_seed(42)  # After setup(), before creating model
```

Profile before optimizing. Guessing what is slow is unreliable; profiling identifies bottlenecks:

```
with torch.profiler.profile(
    activities=[ProfilerActivity.CPU, ProfilerActivity.CUDA],
    record_shapes=True,
) as prof:
    # Training step
    pass
print(prof.key_averages().table(sort_by="cuda_time_total"))
```

Monitor GPU utilization. GPU utilization can be watched in real time with `watch -n 1 nvidia-smi` or tools like `dstat`:

```
# Real-time monitoring
watch -n 1 nvidia-smi
# Or use dstat
dstat -cdngy
```

Low utilization often indicates a data-loading or communication bottleneck.

Use mixed precision. For most training, mixed precision (FP16/BF16) reduces memory use and often doubles throughput with minimal code change; it is worth enabling unless there is a specific reason not to.

Keep checkpoints. Long training jobs often fail; checkpoints should be saved regularly and loading should be tested.

Test multi-node early. Multi-node training has different failure modes than single-node (network issues, differing hardware); if multi-node is planned, it should be tested early.

Elastic data parallelism

Elastic data parallelism extends data-parallel training with fault tolerance and optional elasticity. In standard DDP, a single node or process failure brings down the entire job. Long-running or multi-day training on shared or preemptible clusters often cannot afford that: you want the run to recover from failures and, in some environments, to scale the number of workers up or down as nodes join or leave. Elastic data parallelism addresses that by adding a *process and fault-tolerance* layer around the same gradient-synchronization logic that DDP already provides.

In PyTorch this process layer is built into `torchrun`. It starts and monitors worker processes, detects crashes, and re-runs a coordination step called **rendezvous** so that a new worker group can form—with the same or a different number of nodes. Gradient synchronization is still performed by DDP inside each worker; the elastic layer does not implement AllReduce or any training logic. It only manages process lifecycle and recovery. So in practice, elastic data parallelism is DDP (gradient sync) plus the fault-tolerant process management that torchrun provides when you enable it.

You launch with the same tool you have been using: `torchrun`. Without any elastic or rendezvous options, it behaves as a static launcher and your job is ordinary DDP. When you add `--max-restarts`, `--rdzv-id`, `--rdzv-backend`, and `--rdzv-endpoint`—and optionally a node range such as `--nnodes=MIN:MAX`—you enable fault tolerance or elasticity. If a rank crashes, the launcher stops all workers, runs rendezvous again, respawns the worker group, and invokes your training script once more. If your script loads and saves checkpoints, training can resume from the last saved state; DDP itself is unaware of the restart. Two modes are available: **fault-tolerant** (fixed number of nodes; workers are restarted up to `--max-restarts`, world size unchanged) and **elastic** (`--nnodes=MIN:MAX`, so nodes can leave or join and world size can change between runs). For the full API, launch options, and implementation details, see the official **Torch Distributed Elastic** (TDE) documentation.[1]

How elastic training works

Workers are formed through **rendezvous**. Nodes contact a rendezvous endpoint (for example, a host, and port where the c10d backend is running) and wait until the required number of participants is reached—for elastic jobs, any number between MIN and MAX. The rendezvous then completes and each process receives a global `RANK` and `WORLD_SIZE`. These values can change after a restart or a membership change, so the training script must not hard-code assumptions about them; when world size changes, effective global batch size changes too (per-rank batch × world size), which shifts gradient noise and step-based learning-rate schedules—loss spikes right after a resize are often this dynamics, not a DDP bug. Each node runs an **elastic agent** that starts and monitors local workers, participates in rendezvous, and restarts the worker group when a node fails or leaves: the agent stops all workers, runs a new rendezvous, and restarts. Agents coordinate via a **rendezvous backend**. The **c10d** backend uses a TCP store and needs no extra services; you pass `--rdzv-backend=c10d` and `--rdzv-endpoint=host:port` (port defaults to 29400). The **etcd** and **etcd-v2** backends use an etcd server (v2 API must be enabled); prefer etcd-v2, as the etcd backend is legacy and may be removed.

Launching elastic training

Run the same `torchrun` command on every node (or let your job scheduler do it). On a **single node**, fault-tolerant training is runnable as-is with the rendezvous endpoint on localhost:

```
torchrun --nnodes=1 --nproc_per_node=2 --max_restarts=2 \
    --rdzv_id=elastic_one_node --rdzv_backend=c10d \
    --rdzv_endpoint=127.0.0.1:29400 \
    code/train_elastic_checkpoint.py
```

One process is started per GPU; if one fails, the launcher restarts the group up to `--max_restarts` times. The script `train_elastic_checkpoint.py` loads and saves checkpoints so that after a restart, training resumes from the last epoch.

Multi-node elastic (2–4 nodes, 2 GPUs per node, up to 3 restarts): run the same command on every node, replacing the endpoint with the master's hostname or IP:

```
torchrun --nnodes=2:4 --nproc_per_node=2 --max_restarts=3 \
    --rdzv_id=my_job --rdzv_backend=c10d \
    --rdzv_endpoint=MASTER_HOST:29400 \
    code/train_elastic_checkpoint.py
```

`--rdzv_id` must be the same on all nodes; `--rdzv_endpoint` is the host and port where the c10d store runs (the master node). For **fault-tolerant** mode with a fixed number of nodes (no elasticity), use `--nnodes=2` instead of `--nnodes=2:4`.

Progress across restarts is only preserved when the training script checkpoints: load the latest checkpoint at startup (if present), train, and save periodically (e.g. every epoch). Only rank 0 should write; use a temporary file then rename for atomic writes (see the Checkpointing section earlier in this chapter). The script `code/train_elastic_checkpoint.py` used in the commands above follows this pattern. For clearer error summaries (including tracebacks) when a worker fails, the entrypoint can be decorated with `@record` from `torch.distributed.elastic.multiprocessing.errors`.[2]

When to use elastic training

Elastic or fault-tolerant training is appropriate for long-running jobs (days or weeks) that cannot afford to lose all progress on a single node failure, for unreliable or shared clusters where node failures or preemptions are frequent, or when the number of nodes must be scaled up or down during the run (elastic mode only). For short jobs or stable, dedicated clusters, standard DDP with plain `torchrun` is simpler and usually sufficient.

Complete example: DDP with a transformer

The script `code/train_transformer_ddp.py` ties together DDP setup, `DistributedSampler` with `set_epoch()`, mixed precision (autocast and GradScaler), and per-epoch checkpointing on rank 0, using a small GPT-style transformer (embedding, positional encoding, transformer blocks, next-token prediction). It uses a **dummy dataset** (random token IDs) so you can run it without downloading real data; the same wiring applies when you swap in a real dataset. To try real data, you can plug in a tokenized corpus (e.g. the data pipeline from NanoGPT[3], a small slice of a public dataset like C4 or OpenWebText, or any `Dataset` that returns integer token sequences).

From the chapter directory, the script can be launched with:

```
$ torchrun --nproc_per_node=8 code/train_transformer_ddp.py
```

In the script, the dummy dataset or model can be replaced with real data or a larger architecture. The DDP, AMP, and checkpointing logic remains unchanged. That pattern—a single entrypoint, `torchrun` for launch, and a training loop that loads and saves checkpoints—is what scales to many GPUs and allows recovery from failures, and it carries over directly to production workloads.

Summary

DDP is the foundation of distributed training in PyTorch. Throughout this chapter, we've covered how DDP works internally, how to set it up for single-node and multi-node training, how to debug common issues, how to profile and optimize performance, and how to handle advanced scenarios like checkpointing, asynchronous training, and elastic scaling.

Understanding how DDP works—gradient synchronization, bucketing, overlap—helps you write efficient training code and debug issues when they arise. The key concepts we've explored include:

- **Gradient synchronization**: DDP uses AllReduce to aggregate gradients across all processes, ensuring model consistency
- **Computation-communication overlap**: DDP overlaps gradient synchronization with computation to hide communication latency
- **Process management**: Using `torchrun` for launching and managing DDP processes
- **Data sharding**: Using `DistributedSampler` to ensure each process sees different data
- **Performance optimization**: Profiling, mixed precision, gradient accumulation, overlap hygiene, and bucket tuning
- **Fault tolerance**: Checkpointing and elastic training for long-running jobs

DDP is mature, well-optimized, and suitable for most distributed training scenarios. However, for very large models that don't fit on a single GPU, you'll need to move beyond DDP to techniques like FSDP (Fully Sharded Data Parallel), which we'll cover in the next chapter. FSDP extends DDP by sharding model parameters across GPUs, enabling training of models that are too large for any single GPU's memory.

Code summary

- `torch.distributed.init_process_group()`: Initialize the process group for distributed communication
- `DistributedDataParallel`: PyTorch wrapper for data-parallel distributed training
- `DistributedSampler`: Sampler that partitions dataset across multiple processes
- `torch.distributed.all_reduce()`: Collective operation that sums tensors across all ranks
- `torch.distributed.barrier()`: Synchronize all processes in the group
- `torch.distributed.get_rank()`: Get the rank of the current process
- `torch.distributed.get_world_size()`: Get the total number of processes
- `torchrun`: PyTorch launcher for distributed training
- `torch.nn.parallel.DistributedDataParallel`: DDP wrapper class
- `torch.distributed.destroy_process_group()`: Clean up the process group

References

1. https://docs.pytorch.org/docs/stable/distributed.elastic.html
2. PyTorch Elastic errors documentation:https://pytorch.org/docs/stable/elastic/errors.html
3. https://github.com/karpathy/nanoGPT

Exercises

Implement manual gradient synchronization

Implement gradient synchronization manually using `torch.distributed` primitives to understand what DDP does internally.

Requirements:

- Function signature:

```
def sync_gradients(model: nn.Module, world_size: int) -> None:
    """Synchronize gradients across all ranks using AllReduce."""
    pass
```

- Iterate through all model parameters with `requires_grad=True`
- Use `dist.all_reduce()` with `ReduceOp.SUM` to sum gradients
- Divide by `world_size` to compute the average
- Handle parameters with `None` gradients (skip them)

Test your implementation:

```
import torch
import torch.nn as nn
import torch.distributed as dist

# Simple model
model = nn.Linear(100, 10).cuda()

# Forward and backward
x = torch.randn(32, 100).cuda()
y = torch.randn(32, 10).cuda()
loss = nn.MSELoss()(model(x), y)
```

```
loss.backward()

# Sync gradients manually
sync_gradients(model, world_size=dist.get_world_size())

# Verify: gradients should be identical across all ranks
print(f"Rank {dist.get_rank()}: weight grad sum =
{model.weight.grad.sum().item():.4f}")
```

Compare DP vs DDP performance

Write a benchmark script that compares DataParallel (DP) and DistributedDataParallel (DDP) performance.

Requirements:

- Create a ResNet-50 model for benchmarking
- Implement training loop for both DP and DDP
- Measure:
    - Throughput (samples/second)
    - GPU memory usage per device
    - GPU utilization percentage
- Run with 2, 4, and 8 GPUs (if available)
- Plot scaling efficiency: `efficiency = (N_gpu * throughput_N) / (1 * throughput_1)`

Test your implementation:

```
import torch
import torch.nn as nn
from torchvision.models import resnet50
import time

def benchmark_dp(model, batch_size, num_iterations):
    """Benchmark DataParallel."""
    model = nn.DataParallel(model)
    # ... training loop
    return throughput

def benchmark_ddp(model, batch_size, num_iterations, rank, world_size):
    """Benchmark DistributedDataParallel."""
```

```
    model = DDP(model, device_ids=[rank])
    # ... training loop
    return throughput

# Compare results
dp_throughput = benchmark_dp(resnet50().cuda(), batch_size=64, num_iterations=100)
ddp_throughput = benchmark_ddp(resnet50().cuda(), batch_size=64,
num_iterations=100, rank, world_size)

print(f"DP throughput: {dp_throughput:.1f} samples/sec")
print(f"DDP throughput: {ddp_throughput:.1f} samples/sec")
print(f"DDP speedup: {ddp_throughput/dp_throughput:.2f}x")
```

Implement gradient bucketing

Implement a simplified version of DDP's gradient bucketing to understand communication optimization.

Requirements:

- Class signature:

```
class GradientBucketer:
    def __init__(self, model: nn.Module, bucket_size_mb: float = 25.0):
        """Initialize bucketer with model and bucket size."""
        pass

    def create_buckets(self) -> list[list[nn.Parameter]]:
        """Group parameters into buckets based on size."""
        pass

    def sync_bucket(self, bucket: list[nn.Parameter]) -> None:
        """Synchronize gradients for a single bucket."""
        pass

    def sync_all(self) -> None:
        """Synchronize all buckets in reverse order."""
        pass
```

- Group parameters into buckets of approximately `bucket_size_mb` megabytes
- Flatten gradients within each bucket for efficient AllReduce

- Sync buckets in reverse order (last layer first, like DDP)
- Measure and report communication time per bucket

Test your implementation:

```
from torchvision.models import resnet50

model = resnet50().cuda()
bucketer = GradientBucketer(model, bucket_size_mb=25.0)

# Show bucket structure
buckets = bucketer.create_buckets()
for i, bucket in enumerate(buckets):
    size_mb = sum(p.numel() * 4 / 1e6 for p in bucket)
    print(f"Bucket {i}: {len(bucket)} params, {size_mb:.1f} MB")

# Forward/backward
x = torch.randn(32, 3, 224, 224).cuda()
loss = model(x).sum()
loss.backward()

# Sync with timing
import time
start = time.time()
bucketer.sync_all()
print(f"Total sync time: {(time.time() - start) * 1000:.1f} ms")
```

Implement Fault-Tolerant DDP training

Create a training script with checkpointing and automatic recovery from failures.

Requirements:

- Save checkpoints periodically (every N steps)
- Checkpoint should include:
    - Model state dict
    - Optimizer state dict
    - Learning rate scheduler state
    - Current epoch and step
    - Random states (torch, numpy, python)
- Implement automatic resume from latest checkpoint

- Handle rank 0 saving with barrier synchronization
- Test recovery by killing and restarting training

Test your implementation:

```
import torch
import torch.distributed as dist
from torch.nn.parallel import DistributedDataParallel as DDP

class FaultTolerantTrainer:
    def __init__(self, model, optimizer, checkpoint_dir, save_every=100):
        self.model = model
        self.optimizer = optimizer
        self.checkpoint_dir = checkpoint_dir
        self.save_every = save_every
        self.step = 0
        self.epoch = 0

    def save_checkpoint(self):
        """Save checkpoint (rank 0 only)."""
        pass

    def load_checkpoint(self) -> bool:
        """Load latest checkpoint if exists. Return True if loaded."""
        pass

    def train_step(self, batch):
        """Single training step with periodic checkpointing."""
        pass

# Usage
trainer = FaultTolerantTrainer(model, optimizer, "./checkpoints")
if trainer.load_checkpoint():
    print(f"Resumed from step {trainer.step}")

for epoch in range(trainer.epoch, num_epochs):
    for batch in dataloader:
        trainer.train_step(batch)
```

Analyze communication patterns with NCCL

Write a script that profiles NCCL communication patterns during DDP training.

Requirements:

- Use `torch.cuda.Event` to measure communication time
- Profile different collective operations:
    - AllReduce (gradient sync)
    - Broadcast (parameter sync)
    - AllGather (if used)
- Measure bandwidth utilization: `bandwidth = data_size / time`
- Compare with theoretical peak bandwidth
- Generate a report showing communication bottlenecks

Test your implementation:

```
import torch
import torch.distributed as dist


def profile_allreduce(tensor_size_mb: float, num_iterations: int = 10):
    """Profile AllReduce performance."""
    tensor = torch.randn(int(tensor_size_mb * 1e6 / 4)).cuda()

    # Warmup
    for _ in range(3):
        dist.all_reduce(tensor)
    torch.cuda.synchronize()

    # Profile
    start = torch.cuda.Event(enable_timing=True)
    end = torch.cuda.Event(enable_timing=True)

    start.record()
    for _ in range(num_iterations):
        dist.all_reduce(tensor)
    end.record()
    torch.cuda.synchronize()

    time_ms = start.elapsed_time(end) / num_iterations
    bandwidth_gbps = (tensor_size_mb * 2 / 1000) / (time_ms / 1000)  # Ring
AllReduce: 2x data

    return time_ms, bandwidth_gbps
```

```
# Test different sizes
for size_mb in [1, 10, 100, 500]:
    time_ms, bw = profile_allreduce(size_mb)
    print(f"Size: {size_mb:4d} MB, Time: {time_ms:6.2f} ms, Bandwidth: {bw:.1f}
GB/s")
```

Expected learning outcomes

After completing these exercises, you should be able to:

- Understand how gradient synchronization works at a low level
- Compare and contrast DP vs DDP performance characteristics
- Implement gradient bucketing for communication optimization
- Build fault-tolerant distributed training systems
- Profile and analyze NCCL communication patterns
- Identify and resolve communication bottlenecks in DDP training

Get this book's PDF version and more

4

Scaling with Fully Sharded Data Parallel (FSDP)

Training models larger than single GPU memory with parameter sharding

> *The data center is the new unit of computing.*
>
> *Jensen Huang, CEO of NVIDIA*

From DDP to FSDP

Fully Sharded Data Parallel (FSDP) is a training strategy that shards model parameters, gradients, and optimizer state across multiple devices so that each device holds only a fraction of the full model. In *Chapter 3*, we used DDP, which replicates the entire model on every GPU—effective when the model fits in a single GPU's memory. When the model (plus gradients and optimizer state) exceeds that memory, DDP is no longer viable. FSDP addresses this by distributing the model and its training state across GPUs, so you can train models that are larger than the memory of any one device.

PyTorch provides two main FSDP APIs for GPU training, plus a separate implementation for TPU:

- **FSDP1** (`FullyShardedDataParallel`): The original wrapper class using a flat-parameter approach.

- **FSDP2** (`fully_shard()`): The newer per-parameter-sharding design, accessed via `fully_shard()`. Simpler, more flexible, and the direction PyTorch is moving.
- **FSDP via SPMD** (`SpmdFullyShardedDataParallel`): For XLA/TPU devices, using GSPMD for automatic parallelization.

Throughout this chapter, we use **FSDP** (without a number) when discussing the general technique—sharding parameters, all-gather, reduce-scatter—that applies to both APIs. When the distinction matters, we say **FSDP1** or **FSDP2** explicitly.

This chapter focuses on FSDP2 for GPU training—it's the recommended approach for new projects on CUDA devices. FSDP1 still works and remains in use in production codebases; for example, Wan2.2 uses PyTorch FSDP together with DeepSpeed Ulysses for multi-GPU inference.[1] We summarize FSDP1 below and then concentrate on FSDP2. For TPU training, see *FSDP via SPMD for TPU/XLA*.

Why FSDP enables Larger-Than-Memory models

The basic idea is straightforward: instead of keeping the full model on every GPU, you split it up. Each GPU holds a shard of the parameters. During forward pass, you **all-gather** the parameters you need. During backward, you compute gradients on the local shard, then **reduce-scatter** to aggregate across GPUs.

But let's dig deeper into why this matters. When training a large model with DDP, each GPU needs to store:

1. **Model parameters**: The weights themselves. For a 7B parameter model in BF16, that's 7B × 2 bytes = 14 GB.
2. **Gradients**: Same size as parameters. Another 14 GB for BF16.
3. **Optimizer states**: For Adam, momentum and variance are 2× the parameter size in FP32. That's 7B × 4 bytes × 2 = 56 GB.
4. **Activations**: Depends on batch size and sequence length, but can easily be tens of GB for large models

So for a 7B model with Adam, parameters, gradients, and optimizer states alone are 14 + 14 + 56 = 84 GB per GPU—more than an 80 GB H100 can hold, and activations are not yet counted. Mixed-precision Adam also keeps an FP32 master copy of the weights (~28 GB more for 7B), so the realistic DDP footprint is closer to 112 GB. With FSDP, those components are sharded across GPUs: each device holds 1/N of each (N = number of GPUs). With 8 GPUs, that is 84 / 8 = 10.5 GB per GPU for the three items above, leaving headroom for activations. In practice, that is the difference between fitting the same 7B model on 8 GPUs with FSDP versus not fitting on a single 80 GB GPU with DDP.

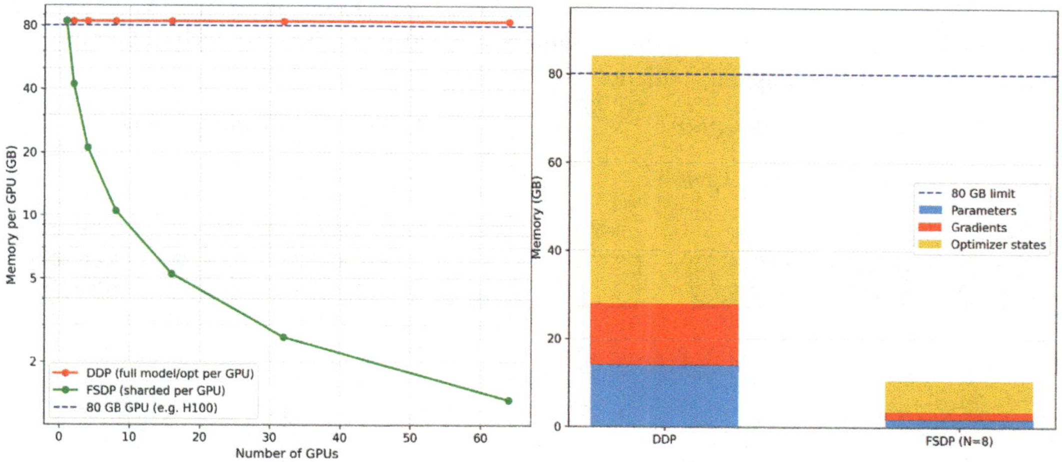

Figure 4.1: Per-GPU memory: DDP vs. FSDP for a 7B model

Figure 4.1 illustrates the comparison: with DDP, each GPU holds the full 84 GB (parameters, gradients, and optimizer state) and exceeds an 80 GB device; with FSDP, memory per GPU falls as 84/N, and at 8 GPUs the 10.5 GB per GPU leaves room for activations.

> Note
>
> **Activations are not sharded**
>
> FSDP shards only parameters, gradients, and optimizer state—not activations. Each GPU still stores activations for its share of the batch during forward and backward, so activation memory remains a per-GPU cost. Techniques like activation checkpointing (recomputing activations in backward instead of storing them) are often used with FSDP to free headroom for the temporarily all-gathered parameters.

How FSDP works

The core idea behind FSDP comes from the ZeRO (Zero Redundancy Optimizer) paper from Microsoft Research (2019).[2] ZeRO observed that in data-parallel training, each GPU holds a full copy of the model, gradients, and optimizer state—most of which is redundant. By partitioning these across GPUs and gathering them only when needed, you can train much larger models without changing the underlying data-parallel algorithm. We cover ZeRO in detail in *Chapter 5*; here we focus on PyTorch's native implementation of these ideas.

PyTorch's FSDP implements this idea using two collective operations. During forward pass, when a layer needs its parameters, FSDP **all-gathers** them from all GPUs—temporarily reconstructing the full parameter tensor (see *Chapter 1*). After the layer finishes, the gathered parameters are freed. During backward pass, gradients are computed locally on the full (temporarily gathered) parameters, then **reduce-scattered** across GPUs so each GPU ends up with its shard of the aggregated gradients (see *Chapter 1*).

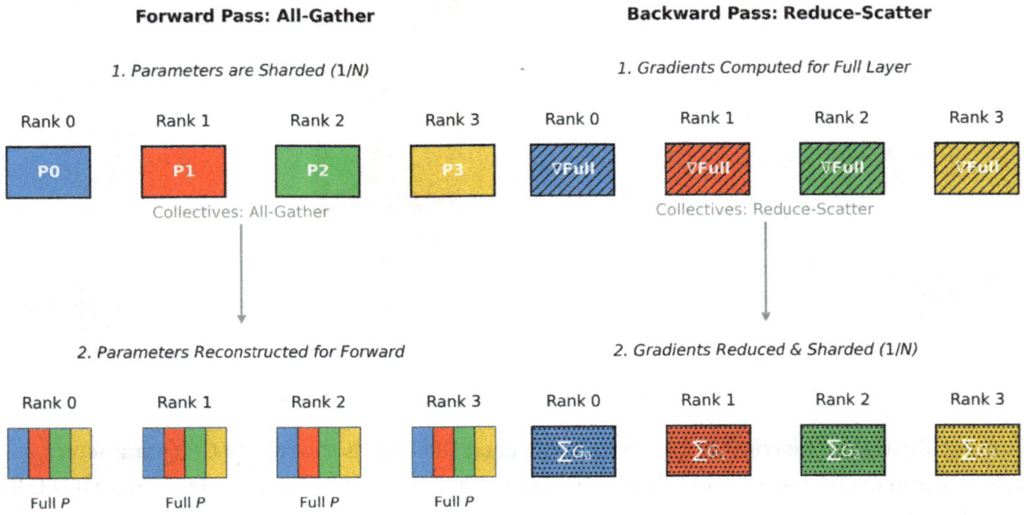

Figure 4.2: FSDP: All-Gather in forward, Reduce-Scatter in backward

Figure 4.2 illustrates these two steps. In the left panel (forward), each rank holds one parameter shard (1/N); after All-Gather, every rank has the full parameters temporarily. In the right panel (backward), each rank has full gradients; after Reduce-Scatter, each rank keeps only its shard of the reduced gradients (1/N).

The key insight is that you don't need all parameters at once. Neural networks process layers sequentially—forward through layer 1, then layer 2, and so on. FSDP exploits this by all-gathering parameters for the current layer, using them, then freeing them before moving to the next layer. This is why activation checkpointing pairs well with FSDP: it reduces activation memory, leaving room for the temporarily all-gathered parameters.

FSDP1 vs FSDP2: the evolution

PyTorch's original FSDP (released in 2021, often called FSDP1) used a **flat-parameter** design borrowed from FairScale's implementation. It flattens all parameters in a wrapped module into a single contiguous `FlatParameter` tensor, then shards that tensor across GPUs. This worked, but had limitations: all parameters in a group had to share the same dtype, frozen parameters needed separate groups, and the flattening made it harder for compilers to optimize communication patterns.

FSDP2 (introduced in 2024 via PyTorch RFC #114299[3]) takes a different approach: **per-parameter sharding** using DTensor with `Shard(0)`. Instead of flattening, it shards each parameter tensor individually on dimension 0. A linear layer weight of shape (4096, 1024) with 4 GPUs becomes four shards of shape (1024, 1024)—each rank holds one quarter of the rows. No flattening, no `FlatParameter` class. When dimension 0 isn't evenly divisible by the world size, FSDP2 pads the tensor; very small parameters may be replicated instead of sharded.

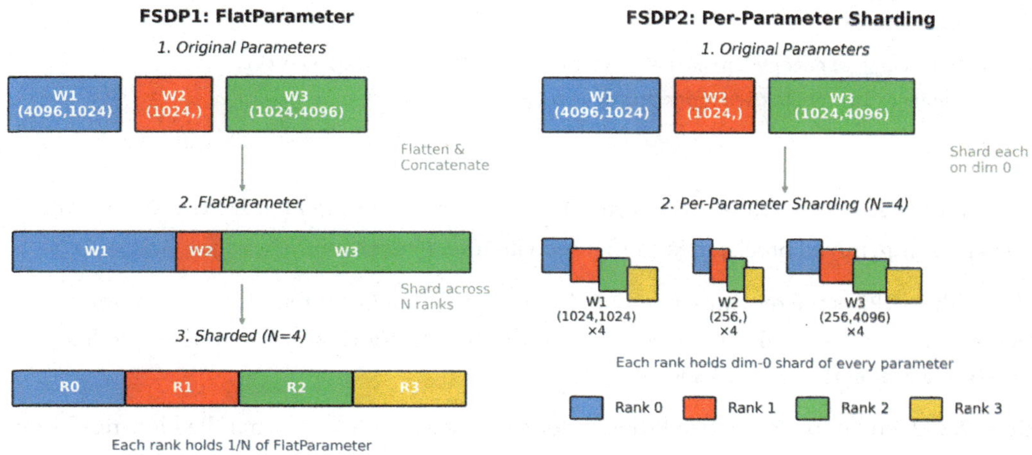

Figure 4.3: FSDP1 vs FSDP2 parameter layout

Figure 4.3 illustrates the difference. FSDP1 (left) concatenates parameters W1, W2, W3 into a single flat tensor before sharding across ranks. FSDP2 (right) shards each parameter independently on dimension 0—each rank holds a slice of every parameter.

The per-parameter design is simpler (~3k lines of code vs ~14k for FSDP1) and more flexible. You can mix dtypes (some parameters in fp8, others in bf16), keep frozen and trainable parameters in the same group, save sharded checkpoints without gathering, and give compilers visibility into individual parameters for better optimization. The collectives are the same—All-Gather and Reduce-Scatter—but the parameter layout is fundamentally different.

Original FSDP (FSDP1)

The **original FSDP** (often called FSDP1) is the wrapper class `FullyShardedDataParallel` in `torch.distributed.fsdp`. It flattens the parameters of each wrapped module into a single `FlatParameter` object (one instance of the class) and shards that across ranks; the same all-gather and reduce-scatter ideas apply. Usage is similar to DDP: you wrap the model (or submodules via `wrap()`), then train as usual.

```
from torch.distributed.fsdp import FullyShardedDataParallel as FSDP
from torch.distributed.fsdp import ShardingStrategy

model = FSDP(
    model,
    sharding_strategy=ShardingStrategy.FULL_SHARD,  # ZeRO-3 style
    device_id=torch.cuda.current_device(),
)
```

You can use `FSDP.set_state_dict_type()` and `StateDictConfig` / `OptimStateDictConfig` for checkpointing; mixed precision is configured via `MixedPrecision`.

Although FSDP2 is the recommended API for new projects, FSDP1 remains relevant for technical reasons beyond simple legacy inertia. Consider **Wan2.2**, an open-source video generative model that still uses FSDP1.[1]

First, Wan2.2 relies on DeepSpeed Ulysses for sequence parallelism to handle high-resolution video frames. Ulysses uses specific all-to-all patterns for attention head distribution that were hardened against FSDP1's interface. While FSDP2's `DeviceMesh` is designed for multi-dimensional parallelism, hybrid FSDP + Ulysses setups often find FSDP1's hooks into `distributed_c10d` group calls more stable and predictable.

Second, the Mixture-of-Experts architecture (27B total / 14B active parameters) requires precise control over non-uniform sharding. FSDP1's manual wrapping strategy via `ModuleWrapPolicy` gives developers granular control when experts are swapped or offloaded dynamically across timesteps—often easier to debug than FSDP2's `fully_shard` annotations for this use case.

Third, the model uses UMT5-XXL for text encoding, a massive frozen parameter block. Many optimized T5 wrappers in the Hugging Face ecosystem are built for FSDP1's `ShardedGradScaler` and auto-wrap policies. Moving the entire pipeline (encoder + DiT + VAE) to FSDP2 would require rewriting the T5 integration to avoid mixed-version distributed errors.

When you encounter or extend such projects, understanding the wrapper-class style and flat-parameter behavior of FSDP1 becomes essential.

FSDP2: the per-parameter sharding API

For new projects, FSDP2 offers a cleaner design. Instead of wrapping modules in a class, FSDP2 uses `fully_shard()` as a function that modifies modules in place—more functional and composable. This is a significant departure from the original FSDP, which used a wrapper class similar to DDP.

Here's what the API looks like. A complete runnable example is in `code/train_fsdp2.py`:

```
torchrun --nproc_per_node=2 code/train_fsdp2.py
```

The core pattern:

```
from torch.distributed.fsdp import fully_shard, MixedPrecisionPolicy
from torch.distributed.device_mesh import init_device_mesh

# Initialize device mesh
mesh = init_device_mesh("cuda", (world_size,))

# Apply FSDP to your model
fully_shard(
    model,
    mesh=mesh,
    mp_policy=MixedPrecisionPolicy(param_dtype=torch.bfloat16),
)
```

The key difference from the original FSDP is that `fully_shard()` modifies the model in place. It doesn't return a wrapped model—your model becomes an FSDP model. This makes it easier to compose with other transformations and works better with `torch.compile`.

For a minimal transformer example with hierarchical sharding (each block wrapped separately), see `code/fsdp2_basic.py`:

```
torchrun --nproc_per_node=2 code/fsdp2_basic.py
```

Device mesh: the foundation

The `DeviceMesh` is a new abstraction in PyTorch that represents a logical arrangement of devices. For FSDP, you typically use a 1D mesh (all GPUs in a single dimension):

```
from torch.distributed.device_mesh import init_device_mesh

# 1D mesh for standard FSDP (4 GPUs)
mesh = init_device_mesh("cuda", (4,))
```

This creates a mesh where all GPUs are arranged in a single dimension. For 4 GPUs, this is `[0, 1, 2, 3]`.

For very large clusters, full sharding across all GPUs can create excessive cross-node communication. Hybrid Sharded Data Parallel (HSDP) addresses this by sharding parameters only within each node while replicating across nodes—trading some memory for reduced inter-node traffic. We cover HSDP in detail in *Hybrid sharding*; for now, here's how to set up a 2D mesh:

```
# 2D mesh for hybrid sharding
# 2 nodes × 4 GPUs per node = 8 GPUs total
mesh = init_device_mesh("cuda", (2, 4))
```

This arranges GPUs in a 2D grid, which is useful for very large-scale training where you want to shard within a node but replicate across nodes.

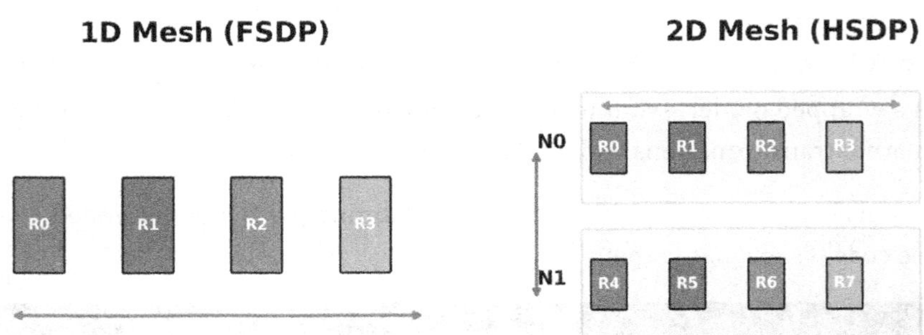

Figure 4.4: Device Mesh: 1D (FSDP) vs 2D (HSDP)

Figure 4.4 shows the two mesh configurations. In the 1D mesh (left panel), four GPUs labeled R0–R3 form a single sharding group—each GPU holds a different shard of every parameter. In the 2D mesh (right panel), N0 and N1 represent two physical nodes (e.g., two servers connected via InfiniBand). Within each node, GPUs are sharded along dim 1 (the green arrow), so R0–R3 in N0 each hold different parameter shards. Across nodes, GPUs at the same position share identical shards along dim 0 (the red arrow)—R0 in N0 and R4 in N1 hold the same data. This hybrid approach keeps the heavy all-gather traffic within the fast intra-node interconnect (NVLink) while only exchanging gradients across the slower inter-node network.

Key parameters

The `fully_shard()` function accepts several parameters that control sharding behavior. The `mesh` parameter specifies the `DeviceMesh` over which to shard—typically a 1D mesh for standard FSDP or a 2D mesh for hybrid sharding (HSDP).

The most important parameter is `reshard_after_forward`, which controls the memory-communication tradeoff. When set to `True` (the default), parameters are resharded immediately after each layer's forward pass, freeing memory but requiring an additional all-gather during backward. This corresponds to ZeRO-3 behavior. Setting it to `False` keeps parameters in memory after forward, which uses more memory but eliminates the backward all-gather—similar to ZeRO-2. You can also pass an integer to reshard to an intermediate size; for example, `reshard_after_forward=2` shards across only 2 GPUs instead of all GPUs, mimicking ZeRO++'s hybrid parameter zero (hpZ).

For most memory-constrained scenarios, the default `True` is the right choice. If you have memory headroom and communication is your bottleneck, try `False`.

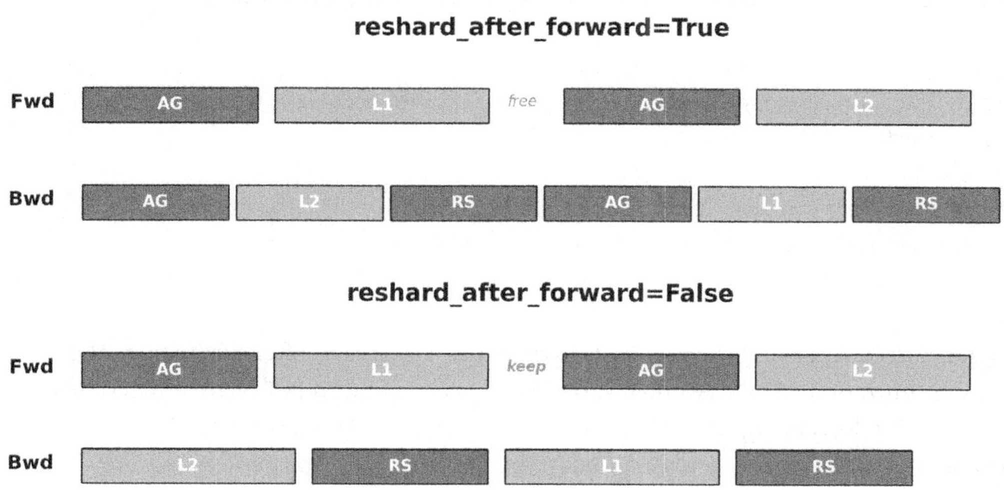

Figure 4.5: reshard_after_forward: True vs. False

Figure 4.5 compares the two modes. Each row shows the forward (Fwd) and backward (Bwd) passes for a two-layer model. The colored blocks represent: AG (All-Gather, purple) for collecting sharded parameters, L1/L2 (Compute, yellow) for layer computation, and RS (Reduce-Scatter, red) for distributing gradients. With `reshard_after_forward=True` (top), parameters are freed after each layer's forward pass (marked "free") and must be all-gathered again in backward—this keeps memory low but doubles the all-gather communication. With `False` (bottom), parameters stay in memory after forward (marked "keep"), so the backward pass skips all-gather entirely—higher peak memory but less communication.

Mixed precision is configured through `mp_policy`. You specify `param_dtype` for parameter storage (e.g., `torch.bfloat16`), `reduce_dtype` for gradient reduction (often `torch.float32` for numerical stability), and optionally `output_dtype` for layer outputs:

```
mp_policy = MixedPrecisionPolicy(
    param_dtype=torch.bfloat16,
    reduce_dtype=torch.float32,
)
```

Because FSDP2 shards per-parameter rather than flattening into a single buffer, you can mix dtypes freely—some layers in fp8, others in bf16. The original FSDP required all parameters in a group to share the same dtype.

Finally, `offload_policy` enables CPU offloading when GPU memory is exhausted:

```
from torch.distributed.fsdp import CPUOffloadPolicy

fully_shard(
    model,
    mesh=mesh,
    offload_policy=CPUOffloadPolicy(pin_memory=True),
)
```

Offloading introduces a performance cost, so treat it as a last resort after exhausting other memory optimizations. The slowdown varies widely depending on PCIe generation, CPU memory bandwidth, and optimizer state size—rough empirical ranges are 20–50% for CPU offloading.

Hierarchical sharding

Beyond these per-call parameters, FSDP2 gives you control over *where* in the model hierarchy sharding boundaries are placed. You can apply `fully_shard()` at different levels—for example, wrapping individual transformer blocks while leaving the embedding layer unsharded:

```
# Shard each transformer layer individually
for layer in model.transformer.layers:
    fully_shard(layer, mesh=mesh)

# Don't shard the embedding layer (it's small)
# fully_shard(model.embedding, mesh=mesh)  # Skip this
```

This gives you fine-grained control over what gets sharded. Small layers (like embeddings) might not benefit from sharding and can add communication overhead, so you can leave them unsharded.

Figure 4.6 contrasts the two approaches. Both panels show a transformer model with an embedding layer (Embed), four transformer blocks (Block 0–3), and an output head (Head). The red dashed boxes indicate FSDP unit boundaries. With hierarchical sharding (left), each transformer block is wrapped as a separate FSDP unit by calling `fully_shard(block)` in a loop, while the embedding and head remain unsharded. This means all-gather and reduce-scatter happen at block boundaries, enabling prefetching (the next block's parameters can be gathered while the current block computes) and fine-grained memory management (only one block's full parameters need to be in memory at a time). With flat sharding (right), a single `fully_shard(model)` call wraps the entire model as one FSDP unit. This is simpler but requires gathering all parameters at once, leading to higher peak memory.

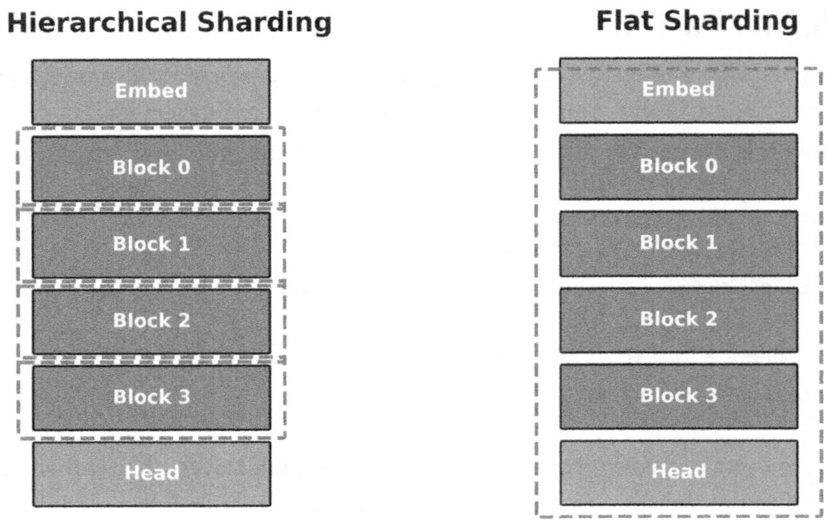

Figure 4.6: Hierarchical vs flat sharding

A complete working example: T5 summarization with FSDP

A complete runnable example in `code/FSDP/` trains **T5 (FLAN-T5)**[4] for text summarization with both FSDP1 and FSDP2, including checkpointing, mixed precision, and example training logs.

The example provides three entry points so you can compare single-GPU training, FSDP1, and FSDP2 on the same task and model:

- **FSDP1**: `T5_training_FSDP1.py` wraps FLAN-T5 with `FullyShardedDataParallel`, `ShardingStrategy.FULL_SHARD`, mixed precision, and FSDP1-style state dict handling. Use it when working with codebases that still rely on the original FSDP API.
- **FSDP2**: `T5_training_FSDP2.py` uses `fully_shard()` and the Distributed Checkpoint (DCP) API; this is the recommended script for new projects.
- **Single-GPU baseline**: `T5_training_Single.py` trains the same model on one GPU (no FSDP), useful for checking correctness and for comparing memory and throughput.

All scripts live in `code/FSDP/`. Before running the training scripts, download the WikiHow dataset from the `code/FSDP/` directory by running:

```
bash download_dataset.sh
```

to fetch the CSV files into `data/`. The README there describes model choices (flan-t5-small through flan-t5-xxl), VRAM requirements, and command-line options.

Running the example. Single-GPU baseline:

```
python code/FSDP/T5_training_Single.py
```

FSDP1 on 2 GPUs:

```
torchrun --nnodes 1 --nproc_per_node 2 code/FSDP/T5_training_FSDP1.py
```

FSDP2 on 2 GPUs:

```
torchrun --nnodes 1 --nproc_per_node 2 code/FSDP/T5_training_FSDP2.py
```

Larger models (e.g., `--model-name google/flan-t5-xl` or `google/flan-t5-xxl`) may require a smaller batch size.

Comparison. The numbers below are from example runs on H200 GPUs. Single-GPU training keeps the full model on one device; when the model fits, it can have the highest iteration throughput (it/s) per GPU, but with 2 GPUs the epoch completes in less wall-clock time because the batch is distributed (e.g. XL: 49 s vs 91 s). Single-GPU does not scale to models that exceed one GPU's memory such as FLAN-T5-XXL. FSDP1 and FSDP2 shard parameters, gradients, and optimizer state across GPUs, so memory per GPU drops and larger models can be trained.

For the smaller FLAN-T5-XL (3B) model, single-GPU training fits on one H200; with 2 GPUs, FSDP1 cuts memory per GPU roughly in half and finishes each epoch in less wall-clock time (49 s vs 91 s). That speedup comes mainly from spreading the batch across two GPUs—the per-GPU iteration rate (it/s) is nearly unchanged—not from FSDP making each step faster. Table 4.1 gives the numbers.

Mode	GPUs	Mem/GPU	Peak mem/ GPU	Throughput	Time/epoch
Single	1	~43 GB	~58 GB	~4.36 it/s	~91 s
FSDP1	2	~22 GB	~33 GB	~4.09 it/s	~49 s

Table 4.1: FLAN-T5-XL (3B): single-GPU vs FSDP1 (2 GPUs). Example runs on H200 GPUs

For FLAN-T5-XXL (11B parameters), single-GPU training runs out of memory (OOM) even on an H200 (140 GB). Table 4.2 compares FSDP1 and FSDP2 on 2 GPUs.

Mode	GPUs	Mem/GPU	Peak mem/ GPU	Throughput	Time/epoch
Single	1	OOM	OOM	—	—
FSDP1	2	~84 GB	~105 GB	~1.96 it/s	~101 s
FSDP2	2	~84 GB	~105 GB	~1.86 it/s	~106 s

Table 4.2: Comparison of single-GPU, FSDP1, and FSDP2 on FLAN-T5-XXL (11B). Example runs on H200 GPUs

The table shows near-identical memory and throughput for FSDP1 and FSDP2 on this setup. The case for FSDP2 here is not raw speed—it is the simpler API, tighter `torch.compile` integration, and sharded checkpoints through DCP, which matter more as jobs and codebases grow.

Code Analysis: The following snippets show how the T5 example implements loading, hierarchical sharding, and mixed precision.

FSDP1: policies and wrapper. In FSDP1, a **policy** is a configuration object you pass into the wrapper: the **mixed-precision policy** specifies dtypes for parameters and gradients (e.g. bfloat16) to save memory and speed up compute; the **wrap policy** is a callable that tells FSDP which submodules to wrap as separate FSDP units (here, each `T5Block`), so sharding is hierarchical and all-gather/reduce-scatter happen at block boundaries. The script obtains both from `get_policies`, then wraps the already-loaded model with the `FSDP` wrapper class. The code snippet below is from `T5_training_FSDP1.py` and `policies/wrapping.py`.

```
# get_policies (T5_training_FSDP1.py): mixed precision + wrap policy
def get_policies(cfg, rank):
    mixed_precision_policy = None
    if cfg.mixed_precision:
        # e.g. policies.bfSixteen for bfloat16
        mixed_precision_policy = policies.bfSixteen
    wrapping_policy = policies.get_t5_wrapper()  # targets T5Block
    return mixed_precision_policy, wrapping_policy

# Wrap policy (policies/wrapping.py): wrap each T5Block as an FSDP unit
def get_t5_wrapper():
    from torch.distributed.fsdp.wrap import transformer_auto_wrap_policy
```

```
    return functools.partial(
        transformer_auto_wrap_policy,
        transformer_layer_cls={T5Block},
    )

# Apply FSDP (T5_training_FSDP1.py): model already from setup_model()
mixed_precision_policy, t5_auto_wrap_policy = get_policies(train_config, rank)
model = FSDP(model,
    auto_wrap_policy=t5_auto_wrap_policy,
    mixed_precision=mixed_precision_policy,
    sharding_strategy=fsdp_config.sharding_strategy,
    device_id=torch.cuda.current_device(),
    limit_all_gathers=fsdp_config.limit_all_gathers)
```

FSDP2: mixed precision policy. FSDP2 uses `MixedPrecisionPolicy` (not the FSDP1 `MixedPrecision` object). The script calls `get_policies(train_config, rank)` to build the policy from config; that policy is then passed into every `fully_shard(...)` call via `fsdp_kwargs["mp_policy"]`. The code snippet below is from `T5_training_FSDP2.py`.

```
from torch.distributed.fsdp import fully_shard, MixedPrecisionPolicy

def get_policies(cfg, rank):
    """Establish mixed precision policy for FSDP2 (no wrap policy; sharding is
explicit)."""
    mp_policy = None
    if cfg.mixed_precision:
        bfloat_available = bfloat_support()
        if bfloat_available and not cfg.use_fp16:
            mp_policy = MixedPrecisionPolicy(
                param_dtype=torch.bfloat16,
                reduce_dtype=torch.bfloat16,
            )
            if rank == 0:
                print("bFloat16 enabled for mixed precision - using
MixedPrecisionPolicy")
        elif cfg.use_fp16:
            mp_policy = MixedPrecisionPolicy(
                param_dtype=torch.float16,
                reduce_dtype=torch.float16,
            )
```

```
    return mp_policy

# In fsdp_main: get policy once, then pass into every fully_shard call
mp_policy = get_policies(train_config, rank)
fsdp_kwargs = {}
if mp_policy is not None:
    fsdp_kwargs["mp_policy"] = mp_policy
# ... later: fully_shard(block, **fsdp_kwargs) and fully_shard(model,
**fsdp_kwargs)
```

FSDP2: load model, then shard each block and the root. The model is loaded with `from_pretrained` and moved to the device. There is no auto wrap policy: the script explicitly loops over `model.encoder.block` and `model.decoder.block` (each element is a `T5Block`) and calls `fully_shard(block, **fsdp_kwargs)` so each block becomes a separate sharded unit, then calls `fully_shard(model, **fsdp_kwargs)` to wrap the root. Order matters—children are sharded before the root.

Note that this example omits the `mesh` parameter. When running with a single process group (the common case), `fully_shard()` infers the default mesh from the world size. For multi-dimensional parallelism (e.g., HSDP), you would explicitly pass `mesh` as shown in earlier sections. The code snippet below is from `T5_training_FSDP2.py`.

```
from torch.distributed.fsdp import fully_shard

model = T5ForConditionalGeneration.from_pretrained(model_name)
model = model.to(device)

# fsdp_kwargs already holds mp_policy from get_policies()

# Shard encoder blocks (each T5Block becomes one FSDP unit)
if hasattr(model, 'encoder') and hasattr(model.encoder, 'block'):
    for block in model.encoder.block:
        fully_shard(block, **fsdp_kwargs)
# Shard decoder blocks
if hasattr(model, 'decoder') and hasattr(model.decoder, 'block'):
    for block in model.decoder.block:
        fully_shard(block, **fsdp_kwargs)
# Shard the entire model (root); children must already be sharded
fully_shard(model, **fsdp_kwargs)
```

For models that do not fit in memory even for loading, see *Initialization best practices* (meta device, `to_empty`, and `reset_parameters`).

Checkpointing with FSDP2

Once your model is sharded and training, you'll want to save checkpoints. Long runs can fail—hardware errors, preemptions, bugs—and losing days of progress is painful. With FSDP2, checkpointing is simpler than before: because sharded state dicts match the training representation, each rank just saves its shard directly. No gathering to rank 0, no resharding on load. Saving and loading happen locally, which is faster and uses less memory.

There are two approaches: using the Distributed Checkpoint (DCP) API or manually handling sharded state dicts.

Using the DCP API (recommended)

The DCP API is the recommended way to save and load FSDP2 checkpoints. It handles all the complexity of sharded state dicts. A complete runnable example is in `code/fsdp2_checkpoint_dcp.py`:

```
torchrun --nproc_per_node=2 code/fsdp2_checkpoint_dcp.py
```

The key functions are `save_checkpoint_dcp` and `load_checkpoint_dcp`:

```
from torch.distributed.checkpoint.state_dict import (
    get_model_state_dict, get_optimizer_state_dict,
    set_model_state_dict, set_optimizer_state_dict, StateDictOptions,
)
import torch.distributed.checkpoint as dcp

def save_checkpoint_dcp(model, optimizer, epoch, checkpoint_dir):
    """Save checkpoint using DCP API."""
    model_state_dict = get_model_state_dict(
        model=model,
        options=StateDictOptions(full_state_dict=False, cpu_offload=True),
    )
    optim_state_dict = get_optimizer_state_dict(
        model=model, optimizers=optimizer,
        options=StateDictOptions(full_state_dict=False, cpu_offload=True),
    )
    checkpoint_path = os.path.join(checkpoint_dir, f"epoch_{epoch}")
    dcp.save({"model": model_state_dict, "optimizer": optim_state_dict, "epoch":
```

```
epoch},
             checkpoint_id=checkpoint_path)

def load_checkpoint_dcp(model, optimizer, checkpoint_dir, epoch):
    """Load checkpoint using DCP API."""
    checkpoint_path = os.path.join(checkpoint_dir, f"epoch_{epoch}")
    opt = get_optimizer_state_dict(model, optimizers=optimizer,
options=StateDictOptions(full_state_dict=False))
    state_dict = {"model": get_model_state_dict(model,
options=StateDictOptions(full_state_dict=False)),
                  "optimizer": opt,
                  "epoch": 0}
    dcp.load(state_dict, checkpoint_id=checkpoint_path)
    set_model_state_dict(model, state_dict["model"],
options=StateDictOptions(full_state_dict=False))
    set_optimizer_state_dict(model, optimizers=optimizer,
optim_state_dict=state_dict["optimizer"],
                              options=StateDictOptions(full_state_dict=False))
    return state_dict["epoch"]
```

The save path is straightforward: each rank writes its shard with `dcp.save`. Loading is less obvious—`dcp.load` does **not** return a new state dict. Instead, you build a **template** by calling `get_model_state_dict` and `get_optimizer_state_dict` on the already-initialized, sharded model, and optimizer on this rank. Pass that dict to `dcp.load`; DCP fills each entry **in place** from the checkpoint shards. The template tells DCP what keys, shapes, and shard layouts to expect; skipping it—loading before the model is constructed and sharded on each rank—is a common source of shape mismatches or uninitialized-parameter errors. The final `set_model_state_dict` and `set_optimizer_state_dict` calls finish PyTorch's documented load path; they are especially needed for optimizer state, even when model parameters were already updated in place through the template references. No gathering to rank 0 and no broadcast—each rank reads only its shards.

Manual sharded checkpointing

If you need more control, you can manually handle sharded state dicts. Here's how:

```
def save_checkpoint_manual(model, optimizer, epoch, checkpoint_dir):
    """Manually save sharded checkpoint."""
    rank = torch.distributed.get_rank()
    # Get sharded state dict
    model_sd = model.state_dict()  # Already sharded
```

```
    # Get optimizer state dict (also sharded)
    optim_sd = optimizer.state_dict()
    checkpoint_path = os.path.join(checkpoint_dir, f"epoch_{epoch}")
    os.makedirs(checkpoint_path, exist_ok=True)
    # Each rank saves its shard
    model_path = os.path.join(checkpoint_path, f"model_rank_{rank}.pt")
    optim_path = os.path.join(checkpoint_path, f"optim_rank_{rank}.pt")
    torch.save(model_sd, model_path)
    torch.save(optim_sd, optim_path)
    # Save metadata on rank 0
    if rank == 0:
        metadata = {"epoch": epoch, "world_size":
torch.distributed.get_world_size()}
        torch.save(metadata, os.path.join(checkpoint_path, "metadata.pt"))
        print(f"Checkpoint saved to {checkpoint_path}")

def load_checkpoint_manual(model, optimizer, checkpoint_dir, epoch):
    """Manually load sharded checkpoint."""
    rank = torch.distributed.get_rank()
    checkpoint_path = os.path.join(checkpoint_dir, f"epoch_{epoch}")
    # Each rank loads its shard
    model_path = os.path.join(checkpoint_path, f"model_rank_{rank}.pt")
    optim_path = os.path.join(checkpoint_path, f"optim_rank_{rank}.pt")
    model_sd = torch.load(model_path, map_location="cpu")
    optim_sd = torch.load(optim_path, map_location="cpu")
    model.load_state_dict(model_sd)
    optimizer.load_state_dict(optim_sd)
    if rank == 0:
        metadata = torch.load(os.path.join(checkpoint_path, "metadata.pt"))
        print(f"Checkpoint loaded from {checkpoint_path}, epoch
{metadata['epoch']}")
    return epoch
```

The manual approach gives you more control but requires careful handling of sharded state dicts. The DCP API is recommended for most use cases.

Full state dict for evaluation

Sometimes you need a full (unsharded) state dict, for example to save a final model for inference or to share with others. You can gather all shards to rank 0:

```
def save_full_checkpoint(model, optimizer, epoch, checkpoint_path):
    """Save full (unsharded) checkpoint on rank 0."""
    rank = torch.distributed.get_rank()
    # Get full state dict (gathers all shards to rank 0)
    model_state_dict = get_model_state_dict(
        model=model,
        options=StateDictOptions(
            full_state_dict=True,  # Gather all shards
            cpu_offload=True,
        ),
    )
    optim_state_dict = get_optimizer_state_dict(
        model=model,
        optimizers=optimizer,
        options=StateDictOptions(
            full_state_dict=True,
            cpu_offload=True,
        ),
    )
    # Only rank 0 saves
    if rank == 0:
        checkpoint = {
            "model": model_state_dict,
            "optimizer": optim_state_dict,
            "epoch": epoch,
        }
        torch.save(checkpoint, checkpoint_path)
        print(f"Full checkpoint saved to {checkpoint_path}")
    torch.distributed.barrier()
```

This gathers all shards to rank 0, which uses more memory but gives you a single checkpoint file that can be loaded on any number of GPUs.

Prefetching: optimizing communication

With checkpointing sorted out, the next concern is performance. FSDP adds communication overhead—every forward pass needs an all-gather to reconstruct parameters, and every backward pass needs a reduce-scatter for gradients. Fast interconnects like NVLink reduce this overhead, but they don't eliminate it.

One way to hide this latency is prefetching: start fetching parameters for the next layer while the current layer is still computing. The key insight is that modern GPUs can execute computation and communication concurrently on different hardware units (CUDA streams for compute, NVLink/PCIe for transfers). If computation takes longer than communication, the all-gather finishes before it's needed and you pay no latency penalty.

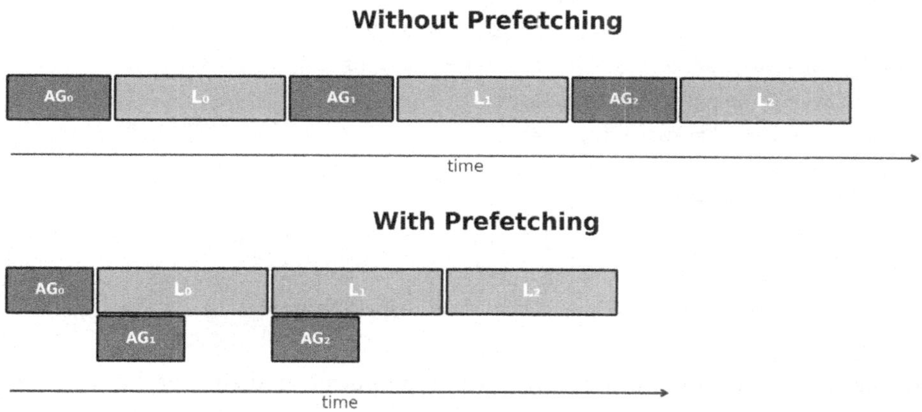

Figure 4.7: Prefetching timeline: without vs. with

Figure 4.7 illustrates the difference. Without prefetching (top), each layer must wait for its all-gather (AG) to complete before computing—the operations are sequential. With prefetching (bottom), while layer L0 computes, the all-gather for L1 runs in parallel on a separate stream. By the time L0 finishes, L1's parameters are already available. The total time shrinks because communication is hidden behind computation.

Forward prefetching

Forward prefetching all-gathers parameters for upcoming layers while processing the current layer:

```
def set_modules_to_forward_prefetch(model, num_to_forward_prefetch):
    """Set forward prefetching for transformer layers."""
    for i, layer in enumerate(model.layers):
        if i >= len(model.layers) - num_to_forward_prefetch:
```

```
            break
        layers_to_prefetch = [
            model.layers[i + j] for j in range(1, num_to_forward_prefetch + 1)
        ]
        layer.set_modules_to_forward_prefetch(layers_to_prefetch)
```

This tells each layer to prefetch parameters for the next `num_to_forward_prefetch` layers. While layer `i` is computing, it's already all-gathering parameters for layers `i+1`, `i+2`, etc.

Backward prefetching

Backward prefetching is similar but for the backward pass. It prefetches parameters needed for gradient computation:

```
def set_modules_to_backward_prefetch(model, num_to_backward_prefetch):
    """Set backward prefetching for transformer layers."""
    for i, layer in enumerate(model.layers):
        if i < num_to_backward_prefetch:
            continue
        layers_to_prefetch = [
            model.layers[i - j] for j in range(1, num_to_backward_prefetch + 1)
        ]
        layer.set_modules_to_backward_prefetch(layers_to_prefetch)
```

This prefetches parameters for previous layers while computing gradients for the current layer.

When to use prefetching

Prefetching works best when your model has many layers (10+) and each layer does enough computation to hide the communication latency. If layers are small or your interconnect is already fast (NVLink, high-bandwidth InfiniBand), the benefit shrinks—you might even add overhead from the extra scheduling logic.

The practical advice: start without prefetching. Profile your training loop, and if communication shows up as a bottleneck, try adding prefetching with `num_to_forward_prefetch=2` and `num_to_backward_prefetch=2`. Adjust from there based on what the profiler tells you.

Activation checkpointing and offloading

Activation checkpointing is almost always used with FSDP. Instead of storing all activations during forward, you recompute them during backward. This can cut activation memory by 50-80%, which is crucial when you're already memory-constrained.

Why activation checkpointing matters with FSDP

With FSDP, you're already sharding parameters, gradients, and optimizer states. Activations can still be a memory bottleneck, especially for large batch sizes or long sequences. Activation checkpointing trades computation for memory: you recompute activations during backward instead of storing them.

Activation memory scales with model architecture and batch size. A back-of-the-envelope estimate for a transformer is:

$$\text{Activation Memory} \approx L \times B \times S \times H \times \text{bytes per element} \times k$$

where L is the number of layers, B is batch size, S is sequence length, H is hidden dimension, and k is a factor (typically 10–20) accounting for intermediate tensors in attention and MLP blocks. This is not a precise formula—actual memory depends on implementation details like whether attention scores are materialized, MLP expansion ratio, and framework overhead. But it gives you the right order of magnitude. For a 7B model (L=32, H=4096) with sequence length 2048 and batch size 8 in fp16:

$$32 \times 8 \times 2048 \times 4096 \times 2 \times 12 \approx 52 \text{ GB}$$

With activation checkpointing, you store only the inputs to each checkpointed block rather than all intermediate tensors, reducing memory by 50–80%. The tradeoff is recomputing activations during backward (roughly 30% slower forward pass, but backward is similar since you'd compute gradients anyway).

Using activation checkpointing

The simplest approach is to checkpoint the entire model:

```
from torch.utils.checkpoint import checkpoint

# After applying FSDP
fully_shard(model, mesh=mesh)

# Wrap forward pass with checkpointing
def forward_with_checkpoint(x):
    return checkpoint(model, x)
```

But you can be more selective. For transformers, you typically checkpoint individual layers:

```
class TransformerBlockWithCheckpoint(nn.Module):
    def __init__(self, args: ModelArgs, use_checkpoint=False):
```

```
        super().__init__()
        self.use_checkpoint = use_checkpoint
        self.attention_norm = nn.LayerNorm(args.dim)
        self.attention = Attention(args)
        self.ffn_norm = nn.LayerNorm(args.dim)
        self.feed_forward = FeedForward(
            args.dim, hidden_dim=4 * args.dim, dropout_p=args.dropout_p
        )

    def forward(self, x):
        if self.use_checkpoint:
            # Checkpoint the entire block
            return checkpoint(self._forward_impl, x)
        else:
            return self._forward_impl(x)

    def _forward_impl(self, x):
        h = x + self.attention(self.attention_norm(x))
        out = h + self.feed_forward(self.ffn_norm(h))
        return out
```

Then enable checkpointing for some layers:

```
# Checkpoint every other layer to balance memory and speed
for i, layer in enumerate(model.layers):
    layer.use_checkpoint = (i % 2 == 0)
```

CPU offloading

CPU offloading moves parameters, gradients, and optimizer states to CPU memory, freeing GPU memory at the cost of slower training. The FSDP2 API supports this:

```
from torch.distributed.fsdp import CPUOffloadPolicy

fully_shard(
    model,
    mesh=mesh,
    offload_policy=CPUOffloadPolicy(pin_memory=True),
)
```

Sharded parameters are copied to the GPU before each all-gather; gradients and the optimizer step run on the CPU. This adds significant overhead but can be necessary for very large models. The actual slowdown depends on PCIe generation (3.0 vs 4.0 vs 5.0), CPU memory bandwidth, NUMA topology, and optimizer state size—empirically 20-50% is common, but your mileage will vary. If CPU RAM is also exhausted, NVMe offload is a DeepSpeed ZeRO-Infinity feature (*Chapter 5*), not something FSDP2 provides natively.

When to use offloading

CPU offloading should come late in your optimization sequence. If you've already enabled full-shard and activation checkpointing, reduced batch size and sequence length as much as you can, and you're still hitting OOM, then offloading makes sense. For most models, full-shard plus activation checkpointing is enough without touching offloading.

Performance optimization

Once you have FSDP working, you'll want to optimize performance. The main bottlenecks are communication (all-gather/reduce-scatter) and activation memory. Let's look at how to profile and optimize.

Profiling FSDP training

Use PyTorch's profiler to understand where time is spent. A complete runnable example is in `code/fsdp2_profile.py`:

```
torchrun --nproc_per_node=2 code/fsdp2_profile.py
```

The key pattern is wrapping your training loop with `profile()` and using `record_function()` to label different phases:

```
from torch.profiler import profile, record_function, ProfilerActivity
rank = dist.get_rank()
with profile(
    activities=[ProfilerActivity.CPU, ProfilerActivity.CUDA],
    record_shapes=True,
    profile_memory=True,
) as prof:
    for i in range(num_iterations):
        with record_function("forward"):
            output = model(data)
            loss = criterion(output, target)
        with record_function("backward"):
```

```
            loss.backward()
        with record_function("optimizer"):
            optimizer.step()
            optimizer.zero_grad()
if rank == 0:
    print(prof.key_averages().table(sort_by="cuda_time_total", row_limit=30))
    prof.export_chrome_trace(f"fsdp_trace_rank{rank}.json")
```

Only rank 0 prints and exports the trace. Since FSDP runs the same operations across all ranks synchronously, the timing patterns are nearly identical---examining one rank's trace is usually sufficient. If you suspect load imbalance or stragglers, you can remove the `if rank == 0` guard to export traces from all ranks and compare them.

The trace file `fsdp_trace_rank0.json` is in Chrome trace format. See *Chapter 3* for how to open and interpret these traces. The short version: open `chrome://tracing` in Chrome, click "Load", and select the `.json` file. In the timeline, look for all-gather and reduce-scatter operations—ideally they overlap with computation. If you see them blocking, prefetching might help. Also check peak memory usage (`profile_memory=True` enables this) to see if activations are eating more than expected.

Optimizing communication

If the profiler shows communication as a bottleneck, you have a few options. Prefetching (covered earlier) can overlap communication with computation. If you have memory headroom, setting `reshard_after_forward=False` avoids the all-gather in backward—parameters stay unsharded after forward, so backward doesn't need to fetch them again:

```
fully_shard(model, mesh=mesh, reshard_after_forward=False)
```

This trades memory for speed. Only use it if you have headroom after profiling.

Hardware matters too. NVLink for intra-node and InfiniBand for inter-node make a big difference. Check that NCCL is actually using them:

```
export NCCL_IB_DISABLE=0 && export NCCL_DEBUG=INFO
```

The debug output will show which interconnects NCCL detected.

Optimizing activation memory

If activation memory is the bottleneck, the simplest fix is reducing batch size or sequence length—smaller inputs mean fewer activations to store. But if you need a large effective batch size for convergence, gradient accumulation lets you get there without the memory cost:

```
accumulation_steps = 4
optimizer.zero_grad()
for i, (data, target) in enumerate(dataloader):
    loss = criterion(model(data), target) / accumulation_steps
    loss.backward()
    if (i + 1) % accumulation_steps == 0:
        optimizer.step()
        optimizer.zero_grad()
```

This gives you the effective batch size of `batch_size * accumulation_steps` but with the memory footprint of a single `batch_size`. You can also try selective checkpointing—checkpoint only some layers instead of all, and experiment to find the right balance between memory and recomputation overhead.

Memory profiling

To understand where memory goes, sprinkle some print statements through your code:

```
def print_memory_usage(step_name):
    allocated = torch.cuda.memory_allocated() / 1e9
    reserved = torch.cuda.memory_reserved() / 1e9
    print(f"{step_name}: allocated={allocated:.2f}GB, reserved={reserved:.2f}GB")
print_memory_usage("Before model")
print_memory_usage("After FSDP")
print_memory_usage("After forward")
print_memory_usage("After backward")
```

This tells you how much memory is used at each stage. If "After forward" is much higher than "After FSDP", activations are the culprit. If "After backward" stays high, gradients or optimizer state might be the issue. For a more detailed breakdown, `nvidia-smi` shows total GPU memory usage, and PyTorch's `torch.cuda.memory_summary()` gives a full allocation report.

Multi-node FSDP training

Multi-node FSDP works the same way as multi-node DDP—you need process group initialization and proper networking. The main difference is checkpointing: with FSDP2, sharded state dicts are straightforward—each rank writes its shard, and you can load them back without all-gather.

Setting up multi-node FSDP

The setup is similar to multi-node DDP. On each node, you need to:

1. Set environment variables for process group initialization
2. Launch training with `torchrun`
3. Ensure network connectivity between nodes

On the master node (node 0):

```
torchrun --nnodes=2 --nproc_per_node=8 --node_rank=0
--master_addr=<master_ip> --master_port=29500 code/train_fsdp2.py
```

On worker node (node 1):

```
torchrun --nnodes=2 --nproc_per_node=8 --node_rank=1
--master_addr=<master_ip> --master_port=29500 code/train_fsdp2.py
```

Replace `<master_ip>` with the actual IP address of the master node. You can find it with:

```
hostname -I
```

Network configuration for multi-node

For multi-node FSDP, network bandwidth and latency are critical. FSDP does more communication than DDP (all-gather and reduce-scatter), so fast interconnects are even more important.

InfiniBand is preferred over Ethernet because:

- Higher bandwidth: 200-400 Gb/s per link vs. 10-100 Gb/s for Ethernet
- Lower latency: Sub-microsecond vs. microseconds
- RDMA support: Direct GPU-to-GPU memory access

Make sure NCCL is using InfiniBand:

```
export NCCL_IB_DISABLE=0 && export NCCL_DEBUG=INFO
```

Check the NCCL logs to verify it's using InfiniBand. You should see messages like:

```
NCCL INFO NET/IB: Using [device] for node [rank]
```

Checkpointing on multi-node

With FSDP2, checkpointing is straightforward even on multi-node. Each rank saves its shard, so you need shared storage accessible from all nodes.

Option 1: Shared filesystem (NFS, Lustre, etc.)

If all nodes mount the same filesystem, each rank can write directly:

```
checkpoint_dir = "/shared/checkpoints"  # Mounted on all nodes
save_checkpoint_dcp(model, optimizer, epoch, checkpoint_dir)
```

Option 2: Parallel writes to local storage

Each node writes locally, then you sync later:

```
# Each node writes to local storage
local_checkpoint_dir = f"/local/checkpoints/node_{node_rank}"
save_checkpoint_dcp(model, optimizer, epoch, local_checkpoint_dir)
```

Then sync to shared storage after training (or use a distributed filesystem).

Option 3: Object storage (S3, etc.)

Use a library like `s3fs` to write directly to S3:

```
import s3fs

fs = s3fs.S3FileSystem()
checkpoint_path = f"s3://bucket/checkpoints/epoch_{epoch}"
# Save using DCP with S3 backend
```

The sharded approach helps since each rank only writes its shard (smaller files, less bandwidth).

SLURM integration

Most HPC clusters use SLURM for job scheduling. Below is a minimal example for multi-node FSDP:

```
#!/bin/bash
#SBATCH --job-name=fsdp_train
#SBATCH --nodes=4
#SBATCH --ntasks-per-node=8
#SBATCH --gres=gpu:8
```

```
#SBATCH --time=24:00:00
#SBATCH --partition=gpu

# Get node list
export MASTER_ADDR=$(scontrol show hostnames $SLURM_JOB_NODELIST | head -n 1)
export MASTER_PORT=29500

srun torchrun --nnodes=$SLURM_NNODES --nproc_per_node=8 --node_rank=$SLURM_NODEID
--master_addr=$MASTER_ADDR --master_port=$MASTER_PORT train_fsdp2.py
```

Or using `torchrun` directly with SLURM:

```
#!/bin/bash
#SBATCH --job-name=fsdp_train
#SBATCH --nodes=4
#SBATCH --ntasks-per-node=8
#SBATCH --gres=gpu:8

export MASTER_ADDR=$(scontrol show hostnames $SLURM_JOB_NODELIST | head -n 1)
export MASTER_PORT=29500

srun torchrun --nnodes=$SLURM_NNODES --nproc_per_node=8 --node_rank=$SLURM_NODEID
--master_addr=$MASTER_ADDR --master_port=$MASTER_PORT train_fsdp2.py
```

We cover SLURM in detail in *Chapter 8*.

Scaling considerations

As you scale to more nodes, communication overhead grows. Make sure your model is large enough that computation still dominates—otherwise you're paying for GPUs that spend most of their time waiting on the network.

Checkpointing also gets trickier. With many nodes, you end up with many shard files. A distributed filesystem or object storage that handles small files well (like Lustre or S3) helps here. And with more hardware comes more failures—save checkpoints frequently, and consider elastic training if your cluster supports it.

Network topology matters too. Nodes on the same network segment with InfiniBand will outperform nodes scattered across racks connected by slower links.

Debugging FSDP issues

FSDP adds complexity, and when things go wrong, the error messages aren't always helpful. Here's how to approach common problems.

Out of Memory (OOM)

OOM errors are common when first setting up FSDP. A quick sanity check is whether parameters are actually sharded. Under FSDP2 they are DTensors—`param.shape` is the global shape, so use the local tensor to see your shard:

```
for name, param in model.named_parameters():
    local = param.to_local() if hasattr(param, "to_local") else param
    print(f"{name}: local_shape={local.shape}, device={param.device}")
```

If parameters look right but you're still OOM, activations are likely the culprit. Use the memory profiling approach from earlier to confirm, then reduce batch size, sequence length, or enable activation checkpointing. Also watch for memory leaks—tensors accumulating across iterations because you forgot to detach or delete them.

Hanging or deadlocked

FSDP hangs when processes get out of sync. The most common cause is conditional logic that only some ranks execute:

```
# BAD: only rank 0 runs this collective-triggering code
if rank == 0:
    model.some_operation()

# GOOD: all ranks execute the same code
model.some_operation()
```

Other causes: unbalanced data (one rank runs out of batches before others), checkpoint loading failures on some ranks, or NCCL issues. For NCCL problems, enable debug logging with `export NCCL_DEBUG=INFO` and look for errors in the output.

Slow training

If training is slower than expected, profile first—guessing wastes time. Check whether communication overlaps with computation; if not, try prefetching. For multi-node, verify InfiniBand is being used (`NCCL_DEBUG=INFO` shows this). Activation checkpointing adds ~30%

overhead, so make sure the memory savings justify it. And confirm mixed precision is actually enabled if your hardware supports it.

Incorrect results

Incorrect results usually come from one of a few places. First, check that all ranks use the same random seed:

```
torch.manual_seed(42)
torch.cuda.manual_seed_all(42)
```

Second, verify `DistributedSampler` is set up correctly and you're calling `sampler.set_epoch(epoch)` each epoch—forgetting this means all epochs see the same shuffle. Third, check that gradients are being synchronized by printing gradient norms across ranks. If all else fails, run the same model on a single GPU to establish a baseline, then scale up and compare.

Debugging tools

A few tools help with FSDP debugging. For NCCL issues, `export NCCL_DEBUG=INFO` (or `NCCL_DEBUG_SUBSYS=ALL` for more detail) shows what's happening at the communication layer. The PyTorch profiler (covered earlier) reveals communication patterns and bottlenecks. For memory issues, `torch.cuda.memory_summary()` gives a detailed breakdown. And for distributed-specific problems, `torch.distributed.set_debug_level(torch.distributed.DebugLevel.DETAIL)` enables verbose logging from the distributed runtime.

Comparing FSDP2 with ZeRO and DDP

Choosing between DDP, ZeRO (DeepSpeed), and FSDP2 depends on your model size and ecosystem preferences.

DDP is the simplest option. Every GPU holds a full copy of the model, gradients, and optimizer state. Communication is just gradient synchronization (AllReduce), which is well-optimized. Use DDP when your model fits on a single GPU—this covers most models up to ~7B parameters on modern GPUs with mixed precision.

ZeRO (from DeepSpeed) does staged sharding: ZeRO-1 shards optimizer states, ZeRO-2 adds gradients, and ZeRO-3 shards everything including parameters. It's production-tested and integrates with DeepSpeed's other features like ZeRO-Offload (CPU) and ZeRO-Infinity (NVMe). The trade-off is adding DeepSpeed as a dependency and learning its APIs.

FSDP2 is PyTorch-native and does full sharding like ZeRO-3. The per-parameter design is simpler (~3k lines vs ~14k for FSDP1), integrates well with `torch.compile`, and doesn't require external dependencies. It's newer than ZeRO, so there are fewer battle-tested examples, but it's the direction PyTorch is moving.

Memory and performance

To make this concrete: a 7B parameter model with Adam optimizer needs ~84 GB per GPU with DDP (parameters + gradients + optimizer states, all replicated). With FSDP2 or ZeRO-3 on 8 GPUs, that drops to ~10.5 GB per GPU—everything is sharded 8 ways.

Performance-wise, DDP is fastest when the model fits (less communication). For models that don't fit, FSDP2 and ZeRO-3 perform similarly—both do all-gather and reduce-scatter, and the difference comes down to implementation details and network topology rather than fundamental design. Choose based on ecosystem fit, not performance.

When to use what

If your model fits on a single GPU, use DDP—it's simpler and faster. If it doesn't fit, try optimization first (mixed precision, activation checkpointing, gradient accumulation). Still OOM? Switch to FSDP2; the migration is straightforward since the API is similar. If you need DeepSpeed-specific features like ZeRO-Offload or ZeRO-Infinity, or you're already in the DeepSpeed ecosystem, use ZeRO instead.

Practical tips

A few lessons from real-world FSDP usage are worth highlighting.

When saving checkpoints with FSDP2, the sharded state dict matches the training representation—each rank saves only its shard. The DCP API (covered earlier) handles this efficiently. Avoid gathering all shards to rank 0 for a full checkpoint unless you specifically need it for inference; the gather is slow and can OOM on large models.

Shared parameters require some care. If the same tensor appears in multiple places in your model (e.g., tied embeddings), those uses must live in the same FSDP group. FSDP's parameter swapping doesn't preserve sharedness across groups, so structure your model to keep shared parameters in the same module hierarchy or avoid sharing altogether.

Memory profiling often reveals surprises. The bottleneck isn't always where you expect. Use `torch.profiler` or `nvidia-smi` to investigate. Common culprits include activations (address with checkpointing), temporary tensors that accumulate across iterations (detach or explicitly delete them), and DataLoader with `pin_memory=True` on memory-constrained systems.

Finally, remember that reshard_after_forward defaults to True, which saves memory by resharding after forward but requires an additional all-gather in backward. If you have memory headroom and communication is your bottleneck, try setting it to False to keep parameters unsharded between passes.

Initialization best practices

For very large models, create on the meta device first, apply FSDP, then move to the actual device and initialize:

```
with torch.device("meta"):
    model = Transformer(args)
fully_shard(model, mesh=mesh)
model.to_empty(device=device)
model.reset_parameters()
```

This avoids ever materializing the full model on a single device. Make sure all ranks use the same seed so parameters initialize identically.

Data loading and gradient clipping

Use DistributedSampler and call sampler.set_epoch(epoch) each epoch—forgetting this means all epochs see the same shuffle. Gradient clipping works with FSDP; just call torch.nn.utils.clip_grad_norm_ as usual and FSDP handles the unsharding/resharding automatically.

Mixed precision

BF16 is generally better than FP16 for parameters (wider dynamic range, less overflow risk). Keep gradient reduction in FP32 (reduce_dtype=torch.float32) for numerical stability. Get FSDP working without mixed precision first, then add it.

Progressive Optimization

Start simple: FSDP2 with mixed precision. If you hit OOM, add activation checkpointing. Still OOM? Reduce batch size or sequence length. CPU offloading is the last resort—it works, but the slowdown is significant. Don't optimize prematurely; get it working first.

Advanced topics

Hybrid sharding (HSDP)

At very large scale, you might want to shard within a node but replicate across nodes—this reduces inter-node communication, which is typically slower than intra-node (NVLink vs InfiniBand). Use a 2D mesh:

```
mesh = init_device_mesh("cuda", (4, 8))  # 4 nodes × 8 GPUs per node
fully_shard(model, mesh=mesh)  # 2D mesh: replicate dim 0, shard dim 1 (HSDP)
```

This shards parameters across 8 GPUs within each node, but replicates them across 4 nodes. The tradeoff: more memory usage (4× replication) but less cross-node traffic.

Compiler integration

FSDP2 works well with `torch.compile`—apply FSDP first, then compile:

```
fully_shard(model, mesh=mesh)
model = torch.compile(model)
```

The per-parameter design helps here. The compiler can see individual parameters rather than a flattened buffer, so it can optimize all-gather and reduce-scatter patterns more effectively.

Other integrations

FSDP2 works naturally with gradient accumulation and learning rate scheduling—no special handling needed. For mixed precision, use `MixedPrecisionPolicy` instead of the standard AMP context manager. Custom communication hooks are available for fine-grained control, but most users won't need them.

FSDP via SPMD for TPU/XLA

This chapter has focused on FSDP2 for GPU training using CUDA devices. However, PyTorch also provides FSDP via SPMD for TPU/XLA devices, which uses a different approach based on GSPMD (Generalized Single-Program Multiple-Data) for automatic parallelization.

Key differences from GPU FSDP2:

- **Uses SPMD mode**: The XLA compiler automatically partitions computation based on sharding annotations, rather than explicit all-gather/reduce-scatter operations

- **Mesh-based sharding**: Uses PyTorch/XLA's `Mesh` abstraction with named dimensions (e.g., `('fsdp', 'model')`)
- **Compiler-driven**: The XLA compiler handles communication optimization, similar to how JAX's `pmap` works

A complete example is in `code/fsdp_spmd_tpu.py`. Note that this requires TPU hardware—it will not run on GPU:

```
# On a TPU VM:
python code/fsdp_spmd_tpu.py
```

The core pattern:

```
import torch_xla.runtime as xr
import torch_xla.distributed.spmd as xs
from torch_xla.experimental.spmd_fully_sharded_data_parallel import (
    SpmdFullyShardedDataParallel as FSDPv2
)

xr.use_spmd()  # Enable SPMD mode

# Create mesh with 'fsdp' axis
num_devices = xr.global_runtime_device_count()
mesh = xs.Mesh(np.array(range(num_devices)), (num_devices, 1), ('fsdp', 'model'))

# Shard inputs and wrap model
x = xs.mark_sharding(x, mesh, ('fsdp', None))
model = FSDPv2(model, mesh)
```

Use FSDP via SPMD when training on TPU devices or when you want compiler-optimized communication patterns. The XLA compiler handles communication optimization automatically, similar to JAX's `pmap`. For GPU training, use the `fully_shard()` API covered in this chapter—it gives you explicit control over communication patterns and doesn't require XLA.

For more details, see the PyTorch/XLA SPMD documentation.[5]

Summary

FSDP2 is PyTorch's answer to training models that don't fit on a single GPU. By sharding parameters, gradients, and optimizer states across GPUs, it lets you train models 8×, 16×, or larger than what a single GPU can hold.

It's worth stepping back to understand what FSDP changes—and what it doesn't. FSDP transforms the memory ceiling from a single-GPU constraint to a cluster-wide constraint. A model that requires 160 GB of memory (parameters + gradients + optimizer states) can run on 8 GPUs with 24 GB each, because each GPU holds only 1/8 of the total. This is a fundamental shift: you're no longer limited by the largest GPU you can buy, but by how many GPUs you can connect.

However, FSDP is still **data parallelism** at its core. Each GPU processes different data batches, and the model computation itself isn't split across devices—every GPU executes the same operations, just on different shards that get all-gathered when needed. This distinguishes FSDP from model parallelism (tensor parallelism, pipeline parallelism), where different GPUs compute different parts of the model simultaneously. FSDP scales memory, not compute per sample. For compute scaling, you still rely on larger batch sizes across more GPUs, just like DDP.

This architectural distinction matters when choosing your parallelism strategy. FSDP alone can take you surprisingly far—models up to hundreds of billions of parameters on large clusters. But for the largest models (trillion+ parameters) or when you need to reduce per-sample latency, you'll combine FSDP with tensor or pipeline parallelism. We cover these combinations in later chapters.

The practical advice is simple: if DDP works, use DDP—it's faster and simpler. When your model outgrows a single GPU, try optimization first (mixed precision, activation checkpointing, gradient accumulation). If you're still OOM, switch to FSDP2. Start with full sharding and the DCP API for checkpointing, profile to find bottlenecks, and test on 2-4 GPUs before scaling to many nodes. Don't optimize blindly—let the profiler guide you.

The code examples in this chapter are complete and runnable. Try them on your hardware to see sharding in action: each rank holds only its portion of the model, and the all-gather/reduce-scatter operations happen automatically.

FSDP2 handles most large model training scenarios well. But what if even full sharding isn't enough? What if you need CPU or NVMe offloading to push memory limits further, or optimized communication patterns for training across many nodes? That's where DeepSpeed's ZeRO comes in. In the next chapter, we'll explore ZeRO-Offload, ZeRO-Infinity, and ZeRO++—

features that extend beyond what FSDP2 currently offers—and when to choose DeepSpeed over PyTorch-native solutions.

Code Summary

- `torch.distributed.fsdp.fully_shard(module, mesh=..., mp_policy=...)`: Shard a module in place with per-parameter sharding (DTensor)
- `torch.distributed.fsdp.MixedPrecisionPolicy`: Mixed precision configuration for FSDP2
- `torch.distributed.device_mesh.init_device_mesh("cuda", (world_size,))`: Create a device mesh for sharding
- `torch.distributed.checkpoint`: Distributed Checkpoint (DCP) API for saving/loading sharded state dicts
- `torch.distributed.fsdp.FullyShardedDataParallel(module, ...)`: Wrapper class for sharding with FlatParameter
- `torch.distributed.fsdp.wrap()`: Wrap submodules with FSDP1
- `torch.distributed.fsdp.MixedPrecision`: Mixed precision configuration for FSDP1
- `torch.distributed.fsdp.set_state_dict_type()`: Configure state dict type for checkpointing
- `torch.distributed.fsdp.StateDictConfig` / `OptimStateDictConfig`: State dict configuration

Useful links

PyTorch FSDP documentation

- PyTorch FSDP Documentation: `https://pytorch.org/docs/stable/fsdp.html`
- PyTorch FSDP Tutorial: `https://docs.pytorch.org/tutorials/intermediate/FSDP_tutorial.html`
- Per-Parameter-Sharding FSDP RFC: `https://github.com/pytorch/pytorch/issues/114299`
- TorchTitan FSDP Guide: `https://github.com/pytorch/torchtitan/blob/main/docs/fsdp.md`
- PyTorch XLA SPMD: `https://docs.pytorch.org/xla/master/spmd.html`

Tutorials and guides

- UvA Deep Learning - Data Parallel FSDP (JAX): `https://uvadlc-notebooks.readthedocs.io/en/latest/tutorial_notebooks/scaling/JAX/data_parallel_fsdp.html`
- Hugging Face - FSDP and DeepSpeed: `https://huggingface.co/docs/accelerate/concept_guides/fsdp_and_deepspeed`
- Hugging Face - FSDP1 vs FSDP2: `https://huggingface.co/docs/accelerate/en/concept_guides/fsdp1_vs_fsdp2`
- Introduction to Parallelism: `https://ggrigorev.me/posts/introduction-to-parallelism/`

Research

- PyTorch FSDP: Experiences on Scaling Fully Sharded Data Parallel (2023): `https://arxiv.org/abs/2304.11277`
- Distributed Training Optimization (2024): `https://arxiv.org/abs/2411.00284`

Projects

- Wan2.2 (FSDP + DeepSpeed Ulysses for multi-GPU inference): `https://github.com/Wan-Video/Wan2.2`

Notes and references

1. `https://github.com/Wan-Video/Wan2.2`
2. Rajbhandari et al., "ZeRO: Memory Optimizations Toward Training Trillion Parameter Models," SC 2020. `https://arxiv.org/abs/1910.02054`
3. `https://github.com/pytorch/pytorch/issues/114299`
4. **T5** (Text-to-Text Transfer Transformer) is an encoder-decoder model from Google that frames NLP tasks as text-to-text. **FLAN-T5** is the instruction-tuned family of T5 models (e.g. flan-t5-small, flan-t5-xl, flan-t5-xxl), used for tasks like summarization and question answering.
5. `https://docs.pytorch.org/xla/master/spmd.html`

Exercises

Implement manual parameter sharding

Implement a simplified version of FSDP's parameter sharding to understand how it enables training models larger than GPU memory.

Requirements:

- Function signature:

```
def shard_parameters(model: nn.Module, world_size: int, rank: int) -> dict:
    """Shard model parameters across ranks, keeping only local shard."""
    pass

def gather_parameters(sharded_params: dict, world_size: int) -> dict:
    """Gather all parameter shards to reconstruct full parameters."""
    pass
```

- Flatten all parameters into a single tensor
- Divide the flattened tensor into `world_size` equal shards
- Each rank keeps only its shard (1/world_size of total parameters)
- Implement gather to reconstruct full parameters for forward pass

Test your implementation:

```
import torch
import torch.nn as nn
import torch.distributed as dist

model = nn.Sequential(
    nn.Linear(1000, 1000),
    nn.ReLU(),
    nn.Linear(1000, 100)
)

# Shard parameters
sharded = shard_parameters(model, world_size=4, rank=dist.get_rank())
print(f"Rank {dist.get_rank()}: sharded size = {sharded['shard'].numel()}
elements")
```

```
# Gather for forward pass
full_params = gather_parameters(sharded, world_size=4)
print(f"Full params size: {sum(p.numel() for p in full_params.values())}
elements")
```

Compare FSDP sharding strategies

Write a benchmark comparing different FSDP sharding strategies and their memory/performance tradeoffs.

Requirements:

- Test three sharding strategies:
  - `FULL_SHARD`: Shard parameters, gradients, and optimizer states
  - `SHARD_GRAD_OP`: Shard gradients and optimizer states only
  - `NO_SHARD`: No sharding (like DDP)
- Measure for each strategy:
  - Peak GPU memory usage
  - Training throughput (samples/second)
  - Communication volume
- Use a model that doesn't fit in single GPU memory with `NO_SHARD`
- Generate comparison table and plots

Test your implementation:

```
from torch.distributed.fsdp import FullyShardedDataParallel as FSDP
from torch.distributed.fsdp import ShardingStrategy

strategies = [
    ShardingStrategy.FULL_SHARD,
    ShardingStrategy.SHARD_GRAD_OP,
    ShardingStrategy.NO_SHARD,
]

results = {}
for strategy in strategies:
    model = create_large_model()  # e.g., 7B parameter model
    fsdp_model = FSDP(model, sharding_strategy=strategy)

    memory, throughput = benchmark_training(fsdp_model, num_steps=100)
```

```
    results[strategy.name] = {"memory_gb": memory, "throughput": throughput}

# Print comparison table
print("Strategy | Memory (GB) | Throughput (samples/s)")
for name, metrics in results.items():
    print(f"{name:15} | {metrics['memory_gb']:10.1f} | {metrics['throughput']:
10.1f}")
```

Implement custom FSDP wrapping policy

Create a custom auto-wrap policy that wraps transformer layers individually for optimal memory efficiency.

Requirements:

- Class signature:

```
def transformer_auto_wrap_policy(
    module: nn.Module,
    recurse: bool,
    nonwrapped_numel: int,
    min_num_params: int = 1e6
) -> bool:
    """Custom wrap policy for transformer models."""
    pass
```

- Wrap each transformer block (attention + FFN) as a single FSDP unit
- Don't wrap embedding layers (they should be in root FSDP)
- Don't wrap final output projection
- Allow configurable minimum parameter threshold

Test your implementation:

```
from torch.distributed.fsdp import FullyShardedDataParallel as FSDP
from torch.distributed.fsdp.wrap import _module_wrap_policy
from transformers import AutoModelForCausalLM

model = AutoModelForCausalLM.from_pretrained("meta-llama/Llama-3.2-1B")

fsdp_model = FSDP(
    model,
    auto_wrap_policy=functools.partial(
```

```
        transformer_auto_wrap_policy,
        min_num_params=1e6
    )
)

# Verify wrapping
def count_fsdp_units(module, depth=0):
    count = 1 if isinstance(module, FSDP) else 0
    for child in module.children():
        count += count_fsdp_units(child, depth + 1)
    return count

print(f"Number of FSDP units: {count_fsdp_units(fsdp_model)}")
```

Implement mixed precision with FSDP

Configure and benchmark FSDP with different mixed precision policies.

Requirements:

- Test three precision configurations:
  - Full FP32 (baseline)
  - BF16 compute with FP32 parameters
  - BF16 compute with BF16 parameters and gradients
- Measure:
  - Memory savings vs FP32
  - Training loss convergence
  - Throughput improvement
- Handle gradient scaling for FP16 (if applicable)

Test your implementation:

```
from torch.distributed.fsdp import MixedPrecision
import torch

# Define precision policies
fp32_policy = MixedPrecision()

bf16_compute_policy = MixedPrecision(
    param_dtype=torch.float32,
    reduce_dtype=torch.float32,
```

```
    buffer_dtype=torch.float32,
)

bf16_full_policy = MixedPrecision(
    param_dtype=torch.bfloat16,
    reduce_dtype=torch.bfloat16,
    buffer_dtype=torch.bfloat16,
)

policies = {
    "FP32": fp32_policy,
    "BF16 Compute": bf16_compute_policy,
    "BF16 Full": bf16_full_policy,
}

for name, policy in policies.items():
    model = FSDP(create_model(), mixed_precision=policy)
    memory, loss, throughput = train_and_measure(model, num_steps=100)
    print(f"{name}: Memory={memory:.1f}GB, Loss={loss:.4f},
Throughput={throughput:.1f}")
```

Implement FSDP checkpointing

Create a robust checkpointing system for FSDP models with support for resharding.

Requirements:

- Save checkpoints that can be loaded with different world sizes
- Support both full state dict and sharded state dict formats
- Implement checkpoint validation (verify saved == loaded)
- Handle optimizer state saving/loading
- Support resuming training from checkpoint

Test your implementation:

```
from torch.distributed.fsdp import FullyShardedDataParallel as FSDP
from torch.distributed.fsdp import StateDictType, FullStateDictConfig

class FSDPCheckpointer:
    def __init__(self, model: FSDP, optimizer, checkpoint_dir: str):
        self.model = model
        self.optimizer = optimizer
```

```
        self.checkpoint_dir = checkpoint_dir

    def save(self, step: int, full_state: bool = True):
        """Save checkpoint."""
        pass

    def load(self, step: int) -> dict:
        """Load checkpoint and return metadata."""
        pass

    def validate(self, step: int) -> bool:
        """Validate checkpoint integrity."""
        pass

# Test saving and loading
checkpointer = FSDPCheckpointer(fsdp_model, optimizer, "./checkpoints")

# Train for a few steps
train_steps(fsdp_model, optimizer, num_steps=10)

# Save checkpoint
checkpointer.save(step=10)

# Validate
assert checkpointer.validate(step=10), "Checkpoint validation failed!"

# Load and resume
metadata = checkpointer.load(step=10)
print(f"Resumed from step {metadata['step']}")
```

Expected learning outcomes

After completing these exercises, you should be able to:

- Understand how FSDP shards parameters across GPUs
- Compare and choose appropriate sharding strategies for your workload
- Implement custom wrapping policies for transformer models
- Configure mixed precision training with FSDP
- Build robust checkpointing systems for distributed training
- Optimize memory usage while maintaining training throughput

5

Beyond State Sharding with DeepSpeed and Megatron

Extending memory capacity and sharding computation for very large models

> *The future is already here. It's just unevenly distributed.*
>
> *William Gibson, Writer*

Beyond state sharding

In the previous chapter, we explored FSDP—PyTorch's approach to sharding parameters, gradients, and optimizer states across GPUs. FSDP2's full sharding is functionally equivalent to DeepSpeed's ZeRO Stage 3[1]: both eliminate memory redundancy by ensuring each GPU holds only 1/N of the training state.

State sharding solves the memory problem, but it doesn't change *how* computation happens. Every GPU still executes the same operations on the same model architecture—just with different data batches. For the largest models (100B+ parameters), this becomes limiting: individual layers may be too large for efficient single-GPU execution, or the model may be too deep to fit activations in memory even with checkpointing.

This is where **Megatron** comes in[2]. Megatron's tensor parallelism splits large matrix operations across GPUs, and its pipeline parallelism shards the model along the depth dimension. These techniques shard *computation itself,* not just training state. They're essential for training frontier models and remain the backbone of large-scale training infrastructure at NVIDIA, Meta, and elsewhere.

We'll cover DeepSpeed ZeRO first—it's worth understanding the full ZeRO family (stages 1-3, offloading, ZeRO++) since many codebases still use it. But the real focus of this chapter is Megatron-style parallelism: tensor parallelism, pipeline parallelism, and how they combine with state sharding for multi-dimensional parallelism.

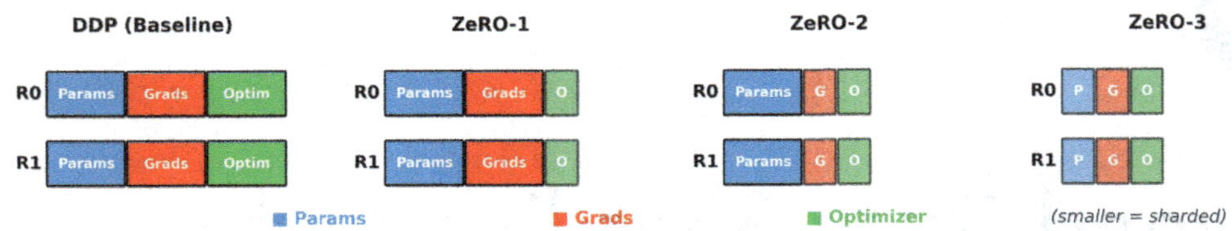

Figure 5.1: ZeRO stages comparison: DDP vs. ZeRO-1/2/3

Figure 5.1 illustrates the memory layout across two ranks (R0–R1) for DDP and each ZeRO stage. Each row represents one GPU, and the three colored blocks show what that GPU stores: P (parameters, blue), G (gradients, red), and O (optimizer states, green). In DDP, all blocks are full-width because every GPU holds complete copies of everything—this is the memory redundancy we want to eliminate. ZeRO-1 keeps parameters and gradients replicated but shards optimizer states (notice the smaller O blocks). ZeRO-2 additionally shards gradients, so both G and O blocks shrink. ZeRO-3 shards all three components—every block becomes half the original size with 2 GPUs. The visual progression from left to right shows how memory per GPU decreases at each stage, with the trade-off being increased communication to reconstruct full tensors when needed.

ZeRO stage 1: optimizer state partitioning

Recall the memory breakdown from the previous chapter: for models using Adam, optimizer states dominate memory usage—each parameter requires storing momentum and variance as two FP32 copies, totaling 8 bytes per parameter. A 7B parameter model needs 56GB just for optimizer states. Mixed-precision training also keeps an FP32 master copy of the weights (another 4 bytes per parameter), so the full optimizer-side footprint is closer to 12 bytes—we use that accounting in the 70B example later in the chapter. In DDP, every GPU holds a complete copy of these states, which is a massive waste.

ZeRO-1's insight is straightforward: since each GPU ultimately updates only its assigned portion of parameters, why store the full optimizer states? With 2 GPUs, each stores only half of the optimizer states. Forward and backward passes proceed normally, and after gradient synchronization, each GPU uses only its local optimizer states to update the corresponding parameter shard. The 56GB of optimizer states get distributed across 2 GPUs, reducing each GPU's burden to 28GB.

Unlike PyTorch's native DDP which requires minimal setup, DeepSpeed uses a configuration dictionary (or JSON file) to control all training settings—optimizer, precision, ZeRO stage, and more. Our examples enable FP16 for portability; on Hopper-and-newer GPUs, BF16 is often the better default (wider dynamic range, no loss scaling). Pass the config to `deepspeed.initialize()`, which returns a wrapped model engine that handles distributed training automatically:

```
import deepspeed

ds_config = {
    "train_batch_size": 32,
    "optimizer": {"type": "Adam", "params": {"lr": 1e-4}},
    "fp16": {"enabled": True},
    "zero_optimization": {"stage": 1}  # Enable ZeRO-1
}

model_engine, optimizer, _, _ = deepspeed.initialize(
    model=model,
    model_parameters=model.parameters(),
    config=ds_config
)

# Training loop uses model_engine instead of model
for batch in dataloader:
    loss = model_engine(batch)
    model_engine.backward(loss)
    model_engine.step()
```

The key difference from DDP: DeepSpeed builds the optimizer from your config, not from a separate `torch.optim.Adam(...)` you may have created earlier—that external optimizer is ignored. The `model_engine` wraps your model and provides `backward()` and `step()` methods.

ZeRO-1 fits scenarios where the model itself fits in GPU memory, but adding optimizer states pushes it over the limit. It requires minimal changes to the training loop and is the easiest to debug, making it a natural first step when migrating from DDP to ZeRO.

To experience the DeepSpeed API, run this minimal example:

```
pip install deepspeed
# Single GPU (for API familiarization)
deepspeed --num_gpus=1 code/zero_minimal.py --zero_stage 1
```

```
# Multiple GPUs (to see actual sharding benefits)
deepspeed --num_gpus=2 code/zero_minimal.py --zero_stage 1
```

You should see output like:

```
ZeRO Stage 1 Demo
Model: 5,248,000 parameters
...
Step 1/10, Loss: 1.0342, Peak Memory: 1.06 GB
...
ZeRO Stage 1 training complete!
Final peak memory: 1.10 GB
```

With a single GPU, sharding has limited effect (there's only one partition). With 2 GPUs, each GPU stores only half of the optimizer states, and you'll observe lower per-GPU memory usage.

ZeRO stage 2: optimizer state and gradient partitioning

ZeRO-1 shards optimizer states, but gradients remain fully replicated. For a 7B model, that's still 14GB of gradients (FP16) sitting on every GPU. ZeRO-2 takes the next step: shard gradients too.

The key insight is that gradients, like optimizer states, are only needed for the parameters each GPU is responsible for updating. During the backward pass, instead of using `all_reduce` (which gives every GPU the full averaged gradient), ZeRO-2 uses `reduce_scatter`—each GPU receives only its assigned slice of the averaged gradient. The rest is discarded immediately, freeing memory as computation proceeds.

With 2 GPUs, each now holds: full parameters + half the gradients + half the optimizer states. For our 7B model, gradient memory drops from 14GB to 7GB per GPU.

The configuration adds bucket size parameters to control how gradients are batched before communication:

```
ds_config = {
    "train_batch_size": 32,
    "optimizer": {"type": "Adam", "params": {"lr": 1e-4}},
    "fp16": {"enabled": True},
    "zero_optimization": {
        "stage": 2,
        "allgather_bucket_size": 5e8,
```

```
            "reduce_bucket_size": 5e8
        }
    }
```

Larger buckets improve communication efficiency by amortizing the overhead of each collective operation, but use more memory. The default of 500M elements works well for most cases.

To compare ZeRO-1 and ZeRO-2:

```
deepspeed --num_gpus=2 code/zero_minimal.py --zero_stage 1
deepspeed --num_gpus=2 code/zero_minimal.py --zero_stage 2
```

ZeRO-2 is a good choice when gradient memory becomes a bottleneck but you still want parameters replicated for fast forward passes.

ZeRO stage 3: full sharding (like FSDP)

ZeRO-2 still keeps parameters replicated on every GPU. For a 7B model, that's 14GB (FP16) of parameters duplicated across all ranks. ZeRO-3 eliminates this last redundancy by sharding parameters too—now every component (parameters, gradients, optimizer states) is distributed.

This is functionally equivalent to PyTorch FSDP. Each GPU holds only 1/N of everything. For a 7B model on 2 GPUs: 7GB parameters + 7GB gradients + 28GB optimizer states = 42GB per GPU, compared to 14GB + 14GB + 56GB = 84GB with DDP.

The trade-off is communication. Since parameters are now sharded, each layer needs an `all_gather` before forward computation to reconstruct the full weights, then the gathered parameters are freed immediately after use. The backward pass does the same, plus a `reduce_scatter` for gradients. This means 3× the model size in communication per iteration (1× forward all-gather, 1× backward all-gather, 1× gradient reduce-scatter).

DeepSpeed mitigates this overhead by overlapping communication with computation—while one layer computes, the next layer's parameters are being gathered in the background. The `overlap_comm` and `stage3_prefetch_bucket_size` parameters control this behavior:

```
ds_config = {
    "train_batch_size": 32,
    "optimizer": {"type": "Adam", "params": {"lr": 1e-4}},
    "fp16": {"enabled": True},
    "zero_optimization": {
```

```
        "stage": 3,
        "overlap_comm": True,
        "contiguous_gradients": True,
        "stage3_prefetch_bucket_size": 5e8,
        "stage3_max_live_parameters": 1e9
    }
}
```

To see the full progression from ZeRO-1 to ZeRO-3:

```
deepspeed --num_gpus=2 code/zero_minimal.py --zero_stage 1
deepspeed --num_gpus=2 code/zero_minimal.py --zero_stage 2
deepspeed --num_gpus=2 code/zero_minimal.py --zero_stage 3
```

ZeRO-3 is the right choice when even replicated parameters don't fit in GPU memory, or when you want maximum memory efficiency and can tolerate some communication overhead. On a single node with NVLink, the performance gap versus ZeRO-2 is often modest (10-20%); across many nodes the all-gather cost grows and the gap widens.

ZeRO-Offload: CPU memory extension

Even with ZeRO-3, you might run out of GPU memory—especially on consumer hardware like an RTX 4090 with 24GB VRAM. ZeRO-Offload addresses this by moving optimizer states (and optionally parameters) to CPU memory, which is typically much larger and cheaper.

The idea is simple: keep forward and backward passes on the GPU where they're fast, but offload the memory-hungry optimizer states to CPU RAM. After gradients are computed, they're transferred to the CPU via PCIe, the optimizer step runs on the CPU, and updated parameters are sent back to the GPU. DeepSpeed overlaps these transfers with computation—while the GPU processes the next batch's forward pass, the CPU is simultaneously running the optimizer step from the previous batch.

The bottleneck is PCIe bandwidth (~32 GB/s for PCIe 4.0, versus ~2 TB/s for GPU HBM). Expect a 20-40% throughput reduction compared to GPU-only training. This isn't a performance optimization—it's a feasibility solution that enables training models that wouldn't otherwise fit.

```
ds_config = {
    "train_batch_size": 32,
    "optimizer": {"type": "Adam", "params": {"lr": 1e-4}},
    "fp16": {"enabled": True},
    "zero_optimization": {
```

```
            "stage": 2,
            "offload_optimizer": {
                "device": "cpu",
                "pin_memory": True
            }
        }
    }
```

The `pin_memory: True` setting uses pinned (page-locked) memory for faster CPU-GPU transfers. To try CPU offloading:

```
deepspeed --num_gpus=1 code/zero_offload_example.py --offload_device cpu
```

You should see output like:

```
Model: 354.3M parameters (0.71 GB in FP16)
Offload device: cpu
...
Step 0, Loss: 11.0607, GPU Memory: 3.41 GB
Step 10, Loss: 11.0829, GPU Memory: 3.52 GB
...
Training complete with CPU offloading!
Peak GPU memory: 3.52 GB
```

Notice how GPU memory stays low (3.5GB) despite the model size—optimizer states live on CPU. ZeRO-Offload is ideal for training on consumer GPUs with limited VRAM but plenty of system RAM.

ZeRO-Infinity: NVMe offload for massive models

ZeRO-Offload moves optimizer states to CPU, but CPU RAM has limits too—typically 256-512GB on a workstation. For truly massive models (hundreds of billions of parameters), even CPU memory isn't enough. ZeRO-Infinity takes offloading one step further by using NVMe SSDs as an additional memory tier.

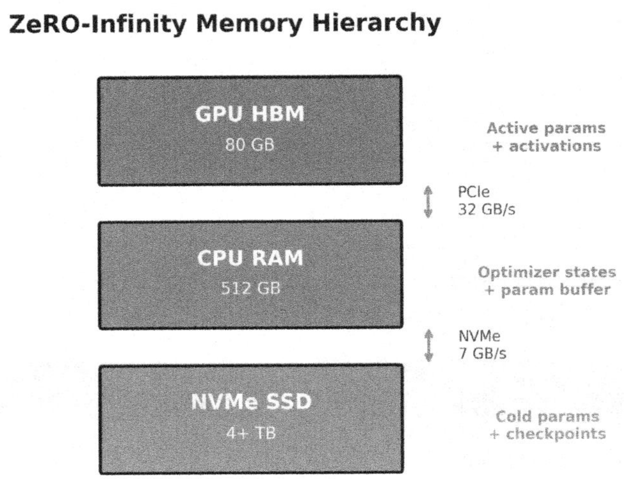

Figure 5.2: ZeRO-Infinity memory hierarchy

Figure 5.2 shows the three-tier hierarchy: GPU HBM (fastest, smallest), CPU RAM (medium), and NVMe (slowest, largest). The Infinity Engine manages data movement across tiers, prefetching parameters from NVMe → CPU → GPU before they're needed and overlapping transfers with computation.

Modern NVMe SSDs offer 5-7 GB/s sequential read speeds (PCIe Gen4), which is slower than CPU memory bandwidth but provides terabytes of capacity at low cost. A typical setup might keep active layer parameters and activations on GPU, optimizer states and parameter buffers on CPU, and cold parameters on NVMe.

The configuration adds NVMe-specific settings:

```
ds_config = {
    "train_batch_size": 32,
    "optimizer": {"type": "Adam", "params": {"lr": 1e-4}},
    "fp16": {"enabled": True},
    "zero_optimization": {
        "stage": 3,
        "offload_optimizer": {"device": "cpu", "pin_memory": True},
        "offload_param": {
            "device": "nvme",
            "nvme_path": "/local_nvme",
            "buffer_count": 5,
            "buffer_size": 1e8
```

```
        }
    },
    "aio": {
        "block_size": 1048576,
        "queue_depth": 16,
        "thread_count": 2
    }
}
```

The aio section configures async I/O for NVMe—queue_depth and thread_count control parallelism for overlapping reads/writes with computation.

To check if you have an NVMe SSD and find where it's mounted:

```
# List NVMe devices and partitions with mount points
lsblk -o NAME,SIZE,MOUNTPOINT | grep nvme
# Example output:
# nvme0n1        1.9T
# └─nvme0n1p7    1.8T /home
```

The nvme_path must be a **directory on a mounted filesystem**, not the raw device path (like /dev/nvme0n1p7). NVMe offloading also requires the libaio library for async I/O:

```
# Install libaio (required for NVMe offloading)
sudo apt install libaio-dev  # Ubuntu/Debian
# or: sudo yum install libaio-devel  # CentOS/RHEL
# Increase open file limit (NVMe offloading opens many file handles)
ulimit -n 65535
# Use a directory path, NOT /dev/nvme*
deepspeed --num_gpus=1 code/zero_offload_example.py \
    --offload_device nvme --nvme_path /home/$USER/nvme_offload
```

Replace /home/$USER/nvme_offload with a directory on your NVMe filesystem. The example trains a 354M parameter model by default—adjust --hidden_size and --num_layers to experiment with larger models. Make sure your chosen path has enough free space (roughly 2-4× the model size for optimizer states and parameter buffers).

NVMe offloading is slower than CPU offloading (expect a 30-50% throughput reduction), which is itself slower than GPU-only training. The value of ZeRO-Infinity isn't performance—it's feasibility. It lets you train models that simply wouldn't fit otherwise.

ZeRO++: Communication-Optimized ZeRO

ZeRO-3 eliminates memory redundancy, but it introduces significant communication overhead[3].

ZeRO++ addresses this with three complementary techniques (the names follow the paper's notation: "q" for quantized, "hp" for hierarchical partitioning, and "Z" for ZeRO). The first, **quantized weights (qwZ)**, reduces all-gather traffic by transmitting parameters in INT8 instead of FP16, then dequantizing after receipt—a 2× reduction in communication volume. INT8 applies only to parameters in transit during all-gather; master weights used for the optimizer step remain in full precision, so rounding error does not carry over between iterations.

The second technique, **hierarchical partitioning (hpZ)**, exploits the fact that intra-node communication (NVLink, ~600 GB/s) is much faster than inter-node (InfiniBand, ~400 GB/s). Instead of sharding uniformly across all GPUs, hpZ replicates parameters within each node and shards only across nodes. This means intra-node all-gathers use fast NVLink, while inter-node traffic is reduced to one representative per node.

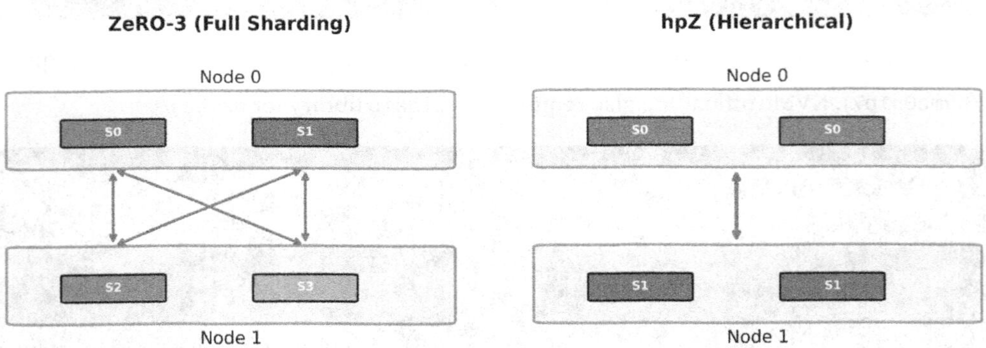

Figure 5.3: hpZ hierarchical partitioning: ZeRO-3 vs hpZ

Figure 5.3 contrasts ZeRO-3 and hpZ for a setup with 2 nodes, 2 GPUs per node (4 GPUs total). In ZeRO-3 (left), each GPU holds a unique shard (S0–S3), so reconstructing full parameters requires all-gather across all 4 GPUs. The red arrows show that every GPU must communicate with every other GPU across the node boundary—S0 and S1 in Node 0 each need to fetch S2 and S3 from Node 1, and vice versa. This cross-node traffic uses the slower InfiniBand interconnect.

In hpZ (right), both GPUs within Node 0 hold the same shard (S0), and both GPUs within Node 1 hold shard S1. The single green arrow represents the simplified communication pattern: only one exchange between nodes is needed to share S0 and S1. Within each node, GPUs already have identical data, so no intra-node communication is required for the replicated portion. This dramatically reduces the amount of slow inter-node traffic.

The third technique, **quantized gradients (qgZ)**, applies the same INT8 quantization to gradients during reduce-scatter.

The configuration enables these optimizations selectively:

```
ds_config = {
    "train_batch_size": 32,
    "optimizer": {"type": "Adam", "params": {"lr": 1e-4}},
    "fp16": {"enabled": True},
    "zero_optimization": {
        "stage": 3,
        "zero_quantized_weights": True,        # qwZ
        "zero_hpz_partition_size": 2,          # hpZ (GPUs per node)
        "zero_quantized_gradients": True       # qgZ
    }
}
```

The `zero_hpz_partition_size` should match the number of GPUs per node in your cluster. To experiment with individual optimizations:

```
deepspeed --num_gpus=2 code/zero_pp_example.py --enable_qwz
deepspeed --num_gpus=2 code/zero_pp_example.py --enable_hpz
```

To enable all three optimizations together:

```
deepspeed --num_gpus=2 code/zero_pp_example.py --enable_qwz --enable_hpz --
enable_qgz
```

You should see output like:

```
Model: 124.0M parameters
World size: 2
ZeRO++ features:
  qwZ (Quantized Weights): True
  hpZ (Hierarchical Partitioning): True
  qgZ (Quantized Gradients): True
...
Using quantizer for weights: CUDAQuantizer
```

```
...
Step 0, Loss: 10.9776
...
ZeRO++ training complete!
Peak GPU memory: 4.00 GB
```

The `CUDAQuantizer` message confirms INT8 quantization is active. Note that ZeRO++ requires FP16 precision—the quantization features dequantize to FP16, so using BF16 will cause dtype mismatches.

ZeRO++ is most valuable for large-scale multi-node training where inter-node communication is the bottleneck. For single-node training or small clusters, the benefits are modest since intra-node communication is already fast.

Megatron: computation parallelism as a second axis

So far, we have focused on **state sharding**—how to distribute parameters, gradients, and optimizer states across GPUs to reduce memory footprint. Techniques such as FSDP2 and DeepSpeed ZeRO fundamentally address a *memory redundancy* problem: eliminating replicated model state so that larger models can fit within the aggregate GPU memory budget.

However, state sharding alone is not sufficient for the largest models. As model sizes continue to grow, a second, orthogonal limitation emerges: **computation itself becomes too large to execute efficiently on a single GPU**, even when memory is fully sharded. This is where Megatron enters the picture.

Megatron-LM emerged from NVIDIA's Applied Deep Learning Research team in 2019, introduced in the paper "Megatron-LM: Training Multi-Billion Parameter Language Models Using Model Parallelism."[4] At the time, GPT-2 with 1.5B parameters was considered large, and the research community was just beginning to explore how to scale beyond what a single GPU could handle. The NVIDIA team recognized that simply adding more GPUs for data parallelism wouldn't solve the fundamental problem: some layers were simply too large to compute on one device. Their solution was to split individual matrix operations across GPUs—what they called *tensor parallelism*. The original Megatron paper demonstrated training of an 8.3B parameter model, unprecedented at the time. Since then, Megatron's techniques have become foundational infrastructure for training models like GPT-3 (175B), Llama (up to 405B), and virtually every frontier model today.

State sharding vs. computation sharding

To understand what Megatron brings to the table, it helps to step back and think about what FSDP and ZeRO actually do. These techniques solve a *storage* problem: they distribute the model's parameters, gradients, and optimizer states across GPUs so that no single device needs to hold everything. When you need to compute a layer, you all-gather its parameters from the other GPUs, perform the forward and backward passes, and then discard the gathered parameters. The key assumption here is that once you have the parameters in hand, the computation itself fits comfortably on one GPU.

This assumption holds remarkably well for models up to tens of billions of parameters. A 7B model's largest layer might have a weight matrix of shape 4096×16384—about 270 million parameters, or roughly 500MB in FP16. That's well within what a modern GPU can handle in a single matrix multiplication.

But what happens when models grow to hundreds of billions of parameters? Consider a hypothetical 175B model where the hidden dimension is 12,288 and the MLP intermediate dimension is 49,152. A single weight matrix in the MLP could be 12,288×49,152—over 600 million parameters, requiring 1.2GB just for that one matrix. The activations scale similarly. At some point, even with perfect state sharding, the computation of a single layer becomes too large: the matrix multiplication itself exceeds what one GPU can efficiently execute or the intermediate activations overflow GPU memory.

This is where state sharding reaches its limit. You can shard the storage as finely as you want, but if the computation itself doesn't fit, no amount of clever memory management will help. Megatron addresses precisely this failure mode by taking the next logical step: instead of just sharding where the model *lives*, it shards how the model *computes*.

Tensor Parallelism: sharding the layer

Megatron's core contribution is **Tensor Parallelism (TP)**—a technique that splits individual matrix operations across multiple GPUs. The key insight is elegant: matrix multiplication is inherently parallelizable along certain dimensions, and we can exploit this to distribute both the computation and the memory footprint.

Consider a simple linear layer $Y = XW$ where X is the input and W is a weight matrix. If W has shape $d \times 4d$ (typical for an MLP's first projection), we can split it column-wise into two halves: $W = [W_0 \mid W_1]$. Now GPU 0 holds W_0 and GPU 1 holds W_1. Given the same input X on both GPUs, each computes its portion: $Y_0 = XW_0$ and $Y_1 = XW_1$. The full output is simply $Y = [Y_0 \mid Y_1]$—no communication needed, just a logical concatenation. This is called **column-parallel linear**.

But what about the next layer? It expects a full input, not a split one. Here's where **row-parallel linear** comes in. If the weight matrix of the second layer is split row-wise as $W' = [W'_0; W'_1]$ (stacked vertically), then each GPU can compute a partial result using its local portion of the input: GPU 0 computes $Y'_0 = Y_0 W'_0$ and GPU 1 computes $Y'_1 = Y_1 W'_1$. The final output is $Y' = Y'_0 + Y'_1$—an all-reduce operation that sums the partial results.

Figure 5.4 illustrates this two-step pattern. The column-parallel linear (top) splits the weight matrix by columns, so each GPU computes a slice of the output with no communication. The row-parallel linear (bottom) splits by rows, and an all-reduce combines the partial results. By pairing these two operations—column-parallel followed by row-parallel—a complete MLP block requires only one all-reduce. This is the key to Megatron's efficiency: communication is minimized to a single synchronization point per layer, rather than at every operation.

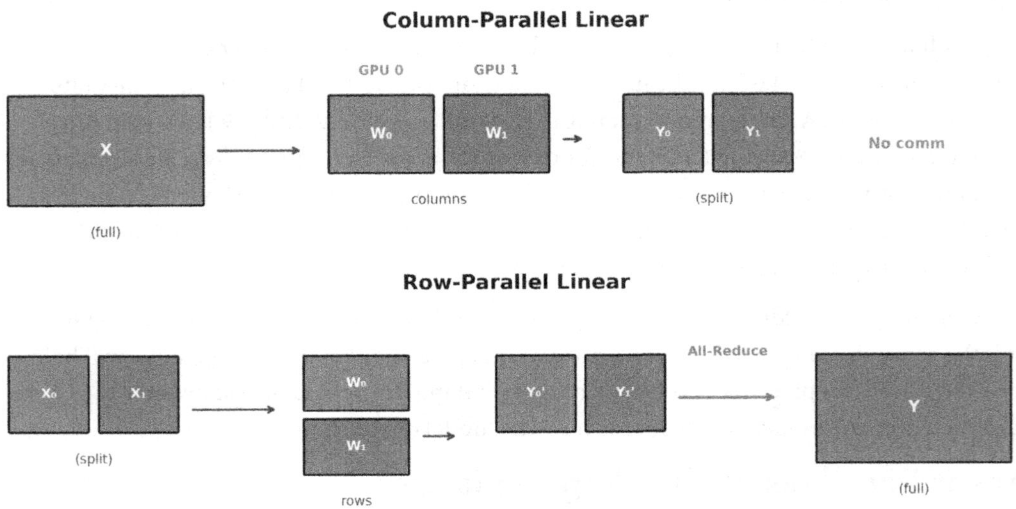

Figure 5.4: Tensor parallelism: column-parallel and row-parallel linear

The same principle applies to self-attention. The Q, K, V projection matrices are split column-wise across GPUs, so each GPU computes attention for a subset of attention heads. Since attention heads are independent, no communication is needed during the attention computation itself. Only the output projection uses row-parallel linear, requiring one all-reduce to combine results.

There's an important subtlety here: tensor parallelism fundamentally changes the communication pattern compared to state sharding. With FSDP or ZeRO, communication happens *between* layers—you all-gather parameters before computing a layer, then move on. With tensor parallelism, communication happens *within* layers—every MLP and attention block requires an all-reduce. This means tensor parallelism is much more sensitive to interconnect bandwidth. In practice, you want TP groups to be within the same node, connected by fast NVLink (~600 GB/s), rather than across nodes over slower InfiniBand (~400 GB/s).

Modern implementations overlap this communication with computation using techniques like `--tp-comm-overlap` in Megatron. While one layer's all-reduce is in flight, the next layer's computation can begin, hiding much of the latency.

When tensor parallelism is enabled, **sequence parallelism** becomes a natural extension. Instead of replicating activations across all TP ranks, sequence parallelism splits activations along the sequence dimension. This reduces activation memory by a factor equal to the TP degree—essential for training with long contexts where activation memory can dominate.

A typical configuration looks like:

```
--tensor-model-parallel-size 2    # 2-way tensor parallelism
--sequence-parallel               # Enable sequence parallelism (recommended with
TP)
--tp-comm-overlap                 # Overlap TP communication with computation
```

To see tensor parallelism in action at a lower level, you can run the pure PyTorch implementation in the code examples:

```
# Tensor parallelism demo with 2 GPUs
torchrun --nproc_per_node=2 code/tensor_parallel_mlp.py
```

This example implements column-parallel and row-parallel linear layers from scratch, showing exactly how weight matrices are split and how the all-reduce combines partial results. Running it helps build intuition for what Megatron does under the hood. An example log is located at `code/tensor_parallel_mlp.log`.

Pipeline Parallelism: sharding the depth

Tensor parallelism splits individual layers across GPUs, but there's another dimension we can exploit: the model's depth. A 32-layer Transformer doesn't need all 32 layers on every GPU—we can assign layers 0–15 to one GPU and layers 16–31 to another. This is **Pipeline Parallelism (PP)**.

The idea is intuitive: data flows through the model like water through a pipe. GPU 0 processes the first half of the layers, then passes the intermediate activations to GPU 1, which processes the second half. But here's the catch—if we naively process one batch at a time, GPU 1 sits idle while GPU 0 is working, and vice versa. This "pipeline bubble" can waste up to 50% of compute.

The solution is to split the batch into smaller **micro-batches** and pipeline them. While GPU 1 is processing micro-batch 1 through layers 16–31, GPU 0 can start processing micro-batch 2 through layers 0–15. With enough micro-batches in flight, we keep all GPUs busy most of the time. This approach is called **1F1B (One Forward One Backward)**: each GPU alternates between forward passes and backward passes, maintaining a steady state where all stages are active.

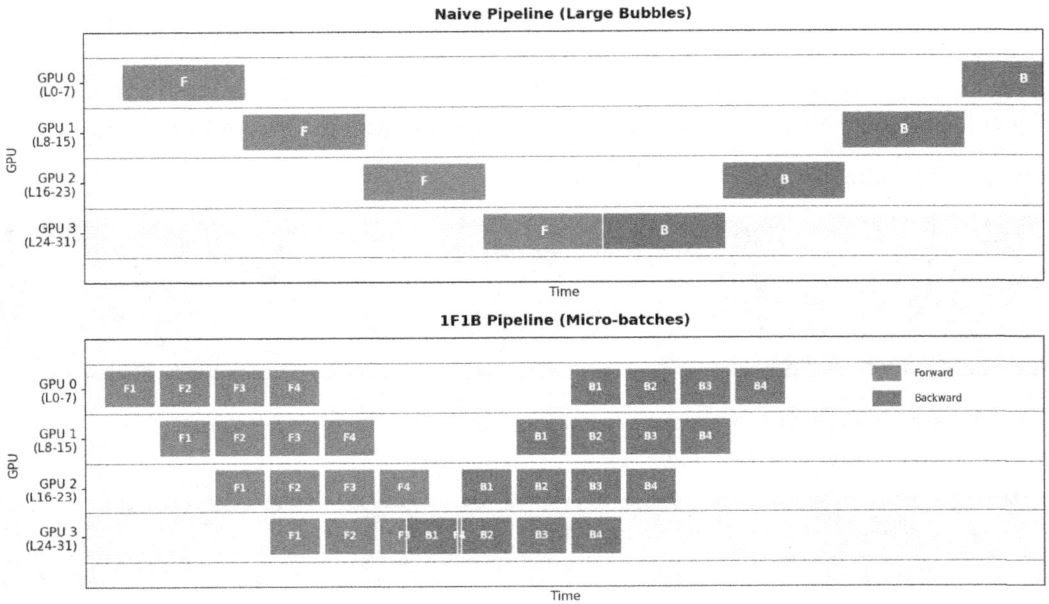

Figure 5.5: Pipeline parallelism: naive vs 1F1B schedule

Figure 5.5 contrasts the naive approach with the 1F1B schedule. In the naive pipeline (top), a single batch flows through all 4 GPUs sequentially—GPU 0 runs forward (F), passes to GPU 1, and so on until GPU 3 completes forward, then backward (B) propagates back. The white space represents idle time (bubbles). In the 1F1B schedule (bottom), we split the batch into 4 micro-batches (F1–F4, B1–B4). Each GPU processes multiple micro-batches in an interleaved fashion, dramatically reducing idle time.

Megatron supports several pipeline schedules. The 1F1B schedule shown above is the most common. The original **GPipe** schedule[6] runs all forward passes first, then all backward passes—simpler but with larger bubbles. **Interleaved pipelines**[5] (also called Virtual Pipeline Parallelism) goes further by assigning multiple non-contiguous chunks of layers to each GPU, reducing bubble size at the cost of more communication.

Virtual Pipeline Parallelism deserves special mention. Instead of assigning layers 0–15 to GPU 0 and 16–31 to GPU 1, we might assign layers 0–7 and 16–23 to GPU 0, and layers 8–15 and 24–31 to GPU 1. Each GPU now runs two "virtual stages." This interleaving reduces the pipeline bubble because micro-batches cycle through stages faster. The trade-off is additional point-to-point communication between stages.

A typical configuration looks like this:

```
--pipeline-model-parallel-size 4           # 4 pipeline stages
--num-layers-per-virtual-pipeline-stage 2 # VPP: 2 layers per virtual stage
```

Pipeline parallelism shines in a specific scenario: **multi-node training**. Within a node, GPUs are connected by fast NVLink (~600 GB/s). Across nodes, you're limited to InfiniBand (~400 GB/s) or worse. Tensor parallelism requires frequent all-reduce operations within each layer—fine over NVLink, painful over InfiniBand. Pipeline parallelism only requires point-to-point communication of activations between stages, which is much more tolerant of slower interconnects.

The practical guideline is: use tensor parallelism within a node (where NVLink keeps communication fast), and pipeline parallelism across nodes (where the communication pattern is more forgiving). This combination—TP within nodes, PP across nodes—is the standard approach for training models at the 100B+ scale.

To see pipeline parallelism in action with a simplified implementation:

```
# Pipeline parallelism demo with 2 stages
torchrun --nproc_per_node=2 code/pipeline_parallel_simple.py
```

This example demonstrates model partitioning, micro-batch scheduling, and forward/backward coordination across pipeline stages.

Sequence parallelism and context parallelism: long contexts

So far we've discussed parallelism strategies that address model size—sharding parameters, gradients, optimizer states, and computation. But there's another dimension that's becoming increasingly important: **sequence length**. Modern models are trained with context windows of 8K, 32K, even 128K tokens. At these lengths, activation memory—the intermediate values stored during the forward pass for use in the backward pass—can exceed the memory needed for the model itself.

Consider a Transformer with hidden dimension 4096 processing a 32K token sequence. Each layer stores activations of shape (batch, 32K, 4096), and with 32 layers, the activation memory can easily reach tens of gigabytes per GPU. This is where **sequence parallelism** and **context parallelism** come in.

Sequence parallelism[7] is the simpler of the two. When tensor parallelism is enabled, certain operations like LayerNorm and Dropout don't participate in the TP communication—they operate on the full hidden dimension locally. Sequence parallelism extends the sharding to these operations by splitting activations along the sequence dimension. If you have TP=4, sequence parallelism means each GPU only stores 1/4 of the sequence's activations for these operations. It's typically enabled alongside tensor parallelism with minimal overhead.

Context parallelism (CP)[8] takes a more aggressive approach. While sequence parallelism only shards the activations of LayerNorm and Dropout, context parallelism partitions *everything* along the sequence dimension—inputs, all intermediate activations, and attention computation itself. With CP=2 on an 8K sequence, each GPU processes only 4K tokens throughout the entire forward and backward pass.

The challenge is attention. In standard self-attention, each token's query must attend to all keys and values in the sequence. If GPU 0 holds tokens 0–3999 and GPU 1 holds tokens 4000–7999, how does a query on GPU 0 attend to keys on GPU 1? Context parallelism solves this using a technique called **ring attention**. The idea is elegant: instead of gathering all KV pairs to every GPU (which would defeat the memory savings), we pass KV chunks around in a ring. GPU 0 computes attention for its queries against its local KV, then sends its KV to GPU 1 and receives GPU 1's KV. Now GPU 0 computes attention against the new KV chunk, accumulating the results. After one full rotation around the ring, every query has seen every key-value pair, but no GPU ever held the full sequence.

The communication pattern is carefully optimized. Modern implementations overlap the KV transfer with attention computation—while computing attention against the current KV chunk, the next chunk is already being transferred. Combined with Grouped-Query Attention (GQA), which shares KV heads across multiple query heads, the communication volume is significantly reduced.

The benefit is substantial. Without CP, training on very long sequences often requires activation checkpointing (recomputing activations during the backward pass), which adds ~30% overhead. With CP, you can eliminate this recompute entirely by simply distributing the activation memory across more GPUs. The trade-off is communication, but for long sequences the compute-to-communication ratio remains favorable.

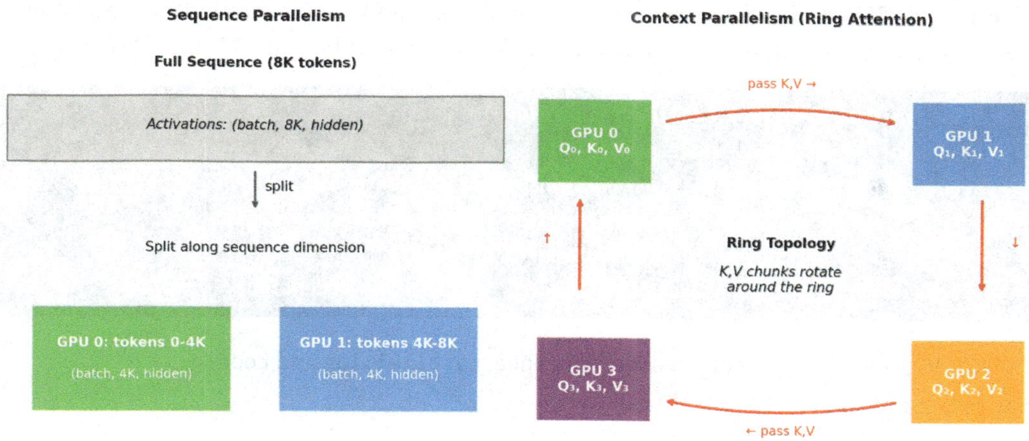

Figure 5.6: Sequence parallelism and context parallelism (ring attention)

Figure 5.6 illustrates both techniques. Sequence parallelism (left) splits activations along the sequence dimension—each GPU stores only its portion of the sequence for LayerNorm and Dropout operations. Context parallelism (right) uses ring attention: each GPU holds local Q, K, V chunks, and K, V pairs rotate around a ring so every query can attend to all keys without any GPU holding the full sequence.

A typical configuration for long-context training:

```
--tensor-model-parallel-size 2
--context-parallel-size 4        # Split 32K sequence across 4 GPUs = 8K per GPU
--sequence-parallel              # Also enable sequence parallelism
```

The rule of thumb: use context parallelism when sequence length exceeds 8K tokens and activation memory is your bottleneck. For shorter sequences, tensor parallelism and sequence parallelism are usually sufficient.

The accompanying `code/sp_demo.py` illustrates these concepts. The `memory` mode calculates activation memory for various sequence lengths—you'll see that a 32K sequence with 32 layers can exceed 40GB, explaining why parallelism is necessary. The `sequence_parallel` mode shows how each GPU holds only a portion of the sequence and applies LayerNorm locally without communication. The `ring_attention` mode demonstrates the core ring attention pattern: each GPU starts with local Q, K, V chunks, then K and V rotate around the ring. After one full rotation, every query has attended to all keys, yet no GPU ever held the full sequence.

```
# Show activation memory scaling (single GPU)
python code/sp_demo.py --mode memory
# Sequence parallelism: split activations along sequence dim (2 GPUs)
torchrun --nproc_per_node=2 code/sp_demo.py --mode sequence_parallel
# Context parallelism via ring attention (2 GPUs)
torchrun --nproc_per_node=2 code/sp_demo.py --mode ring_attention
```

Example logs for these runs are in `code/sequence_parallel.log` and `code/ring_attention.log`.

DeepSpeed-Ulysses: an alternative to ring attention

Ring attention is not the only way to parallelize attention across long sequences. DeepSpeed introduced **DeepSpeed-Ulysses**[9], a different approach that trades communication pattern for simplicity.

The key insight behind Ulysses is straightforward: instead of rotating KV chunks around a ring, why not just gather the full sequence before attention and scatter it back afterward? In ring attention, each GPU computes partial attention scores against different KV chunks and accumulates them—this requires careful bookkeeping of softmax normalization across chunks. Ulysses sidesteps this complexity entirely.

Here's how it works. Before the attention computation, each GPU holds a chunk of the sequence with shape (batch, local_seq, num_heads, head_dim). Ulysses performs an **all-to-all** communication that reorganizes the data: instead of each GPU holding all heads for a portion of the sequence, each GPU now holds all sequence positions for a portion of the heads. After this transpose, the shape becomes (batch, full_seq, local_heads, head_dim). Now each GPU can compute standard self-attention on its subset of heads—no partial scores, no accumulation, just regular attention. After attention, another all-to-all reverses the transformation, returning to the original partitioning.

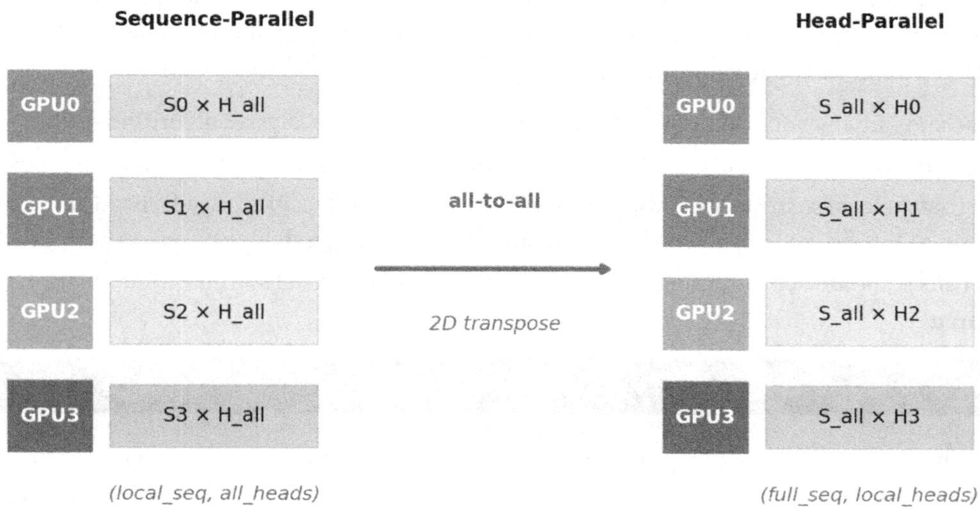

Figure 5.7: DeepSpeed-Ulysses: 2D transpose via all-to-all

Figure 5.7 illustrates this 2D transpose. On the left (sequence-parallel), each GPU holds a local sequence chunk S_i with all heads H_{all}—the tensor shape is (local_seq, all_heads). The all-to-all collectively transposes the data: on the right (head-parallel), each GPU holds the full sequence S_{all} but only its local heads H_i—the shape becomes (full_seq, local_heads). Now each GPU can compute standard self-attention independently on its subset of heads. After attention, another all-to-all reverses the transformation.

The trade-off is communication volume versus communication pattern. Ring attention sends KV chunks P times around a ring of P GPUs, with each transfer overlapped with computation. Ulysses performs two all-to-all collectives (before and after attention), which involve all GPUs simultaneously. For small parallelism degrees (P ≤ 8), Ulysses often wins because all-to-all on modern interconnects like NVLink is highly optimized. For larger P or when interconnect bandwidth is limited, ring attention's overlapped communication can be more efficient.

In practice, DeepSpeed-Ulysses shines in scenarios where you want sequence parallelism without the complexity of ring attention's partial softmax handling. It integrates cleanly with ZeRO and other DeepSpeed optimizations.

The accompanying `code/ulysses_demo.py` implements the core Ulysses algorithm from scratch. It demonstrates the two all-to-all operations: `all_to_all_seq_to_head` transposes from (batch, local_seq, num_heads, head_dim) to (batch, full_seq, local_heads, head_dim), and `all_to_all_head_to_seq` reverses this transformation. Between these two operations, each GPU runs standard self-attention on its subset of heads—no partial softmax accumulation required.

```
torchrun --nproc_per_node=2 code/ulysses_demo.py
```

An example run is in `code/ulysses_demo.log`. When should you choose Ulysses over ring attention? If you're already in the DeepSpeed ecosystem and want straightforward sequence parallelism with moderate parallelism degrees, Ulysses is the easier path. If you're scaling to very long sequences (100K+ tokens) with large parallelism degrees, ring attention's communication overlap may provide better efficiency.

Expert Parallelism: scaling MoE models

Mixture-of-Experts (MoE) models present a unique scaling opportunity: instead of making every layer wider, we add multiple "expert" sub-networks and route each token to only a subset of them. A model like Mixtral 8x7B has 8 experts per MoE layer, but each token only activates 2 of them. This means the model has the capacity of a much larger network while keeping per-token computation manageable. But how do we distribute these experts across GPUs?

This is where **Expert Parallelism (EP)** comes in. The idea is natural: if we have 8 experts and 8 GPUs, put one expert on each GPU. When a token needs to be processed by expert 3, it gets routed to GPU 3, processed, and the result is sent back. The communication pattern is all-to-all: tokens from all GPUs may need to go to any expert, and results flow back to their origin. *Figure 5.8* illustrates this distribution pattern.

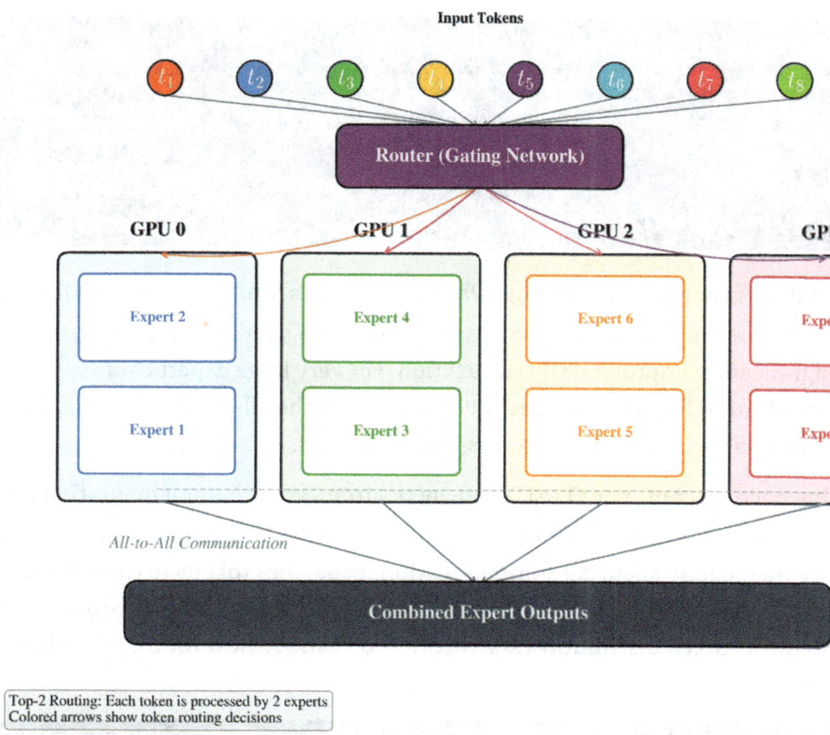

Figure 5.8: Expert parallelism distributes experts across multiple GPUs

The challenge is load balancing. If the router sends 80% of tokens to expert 0 and only 2% to expert 7, GPU 0 is overloaded while GPU 7 sits idle. MoE training typically includes an auxiliary loss that encourages the router to distribute tokens more evenly. Megatron supports several load balancing strategies: auxiliary loss (adds a penalty for imbalanced routing), Sinkhorn (iterative normalization to enforce balance), and aux-loss-free methods that achieve balance through architectural constraints.

Expert parallelism combines naturally with other parallelism dimensions. A typical large-scale MoE training might use EP=8 for the experts, PP=4 for pipeline stages, and DP for data parallelism across nodes. The non-expert layers (attention, LayerNorm) can use tensor parallelism independently. This flexibility is essential for models like DeepSeek-V3 or Qwen-MoE that have hundreds of experts.

A configuration for Mixtral 8x7B training might look like:

```
--num-experts 8
--expert-model-parallel-size 8    # One expert per GPU
--moe-router-topk 2               # Each token activates 2 experts
--moe-router-load-balancing-type aux_loss
--moe-grouped-gemm                # Batch expert computations
--pipeline-model-parallel-size 4
```

The `--moe-grouped-gemm` flag is worth noting: when a GPU hosts multiple experts (EP < num_experts), it batches the computations across experts into a single grouped matrix multiplication, significantly improving GPU utilization. For very large expert counts, specialized communication libraries like DeepEP[10] optimize the all-to-all token dispatching with low-latency GPU kernels and efficient cross-node transfers.

The accompanying `code/expert_parallel_demo.py` is a from-scratch implementation that demonstrates the core EP mechanics without Megatron dependencies. It shows how a router assigns tokens to experts, how all-to-all communication dispatches tokens to their destination GPUs, how each GPU processes tokens with its local expert, and how another all-to-all returns results. The demo prints token distribution statistics so you can see how routing decisions affect load balance.

```
torchrun --nproc_per_node=2 code/expert_parallel_demo.py
```

An example run is in `code/expert_parallel_demo.log`.

Why FSDP2 cannot replace Megatron

A common misconception is that FSDP2 (or ZeRO) and Megatron are interchangeable—that you pick one or the other based on preference. This misunderstands what each system actually does.

FSDP2 and ZeRO shard *state*: parameters, gradients, and optimizer states are distributed across GPUs, then gathered when needed for computation. The key assumption is that each layer's forward and backward pass fits on a single GPU. When GPU 0 needs to compute layer 5, it gathers layer 5's parameters from all GPUs, runs the computation locally, then releases the memory. The computation itself is not distributed—only the storage is.

Megatron shards *computation*: a single layer's matrix multiplication is split across multiple GPUs, with each GPU computing a portion of the result. The communication happens *inside* the layer, not around it. This is fundamentally different from gathering parameters before computation.

Why does this distinction matter? Consider a model where a single attention layer has a 16K × 16K weight matrix. Even if you shard the parameters across 8 GPUs with FSDP2, when it's time to compute, one GPU must gather the full matrix and perform the multiplication. If that matrix doesn't fit in one GPU's memory, or if the computation is too slow on one GPU, FSDP2 cannot help—it only shards storage, not compute.

This is where Megatron becomes necessary. With tensor parallelism, that 16K × 16K matrix is split across 8 GPUs, each holding a 16K × 2K slice. The computation happens in parallel, and only the results are communicated. No single GPU ever needs to hold or compute with the full matrix.

The practical implication: FSDP2 and Megatron are complementary, not competing. You might use Megatron's tensor parallelism to split large layers across GPUs within a node, while using FSDP2-style sharding across nodes for memory efficiency. The choice isn't "which one," but "how to combine them."

Hybrid Parallelism: combining state and computation sharding

Given that FSDP2/ZeRO and Megatron solve different problems, the natural question is: can we use both? The answer is yes, and this is exactly what large-scale training systems do.

Consider training a 70B parameter model on 64 GPUs across 8 nodes. Within each node (8 GPUs connected by NVLink), you use Megatron's tensor parallelism with TP=8 to split the large matrix multiplications. Across nodes (connected by slower InfiniBand), you use ZeRO-3 or FSDP2 to shard the optimizer states and gradients—this reduces memory pressure without requiring the high-bandwidth communication that tensor parallelism demands. If the model is deep, you might add pipeline parallelism to distribute layers across node groups.

This layered approach plays to each technique's strengths. Tensor parallelism needs high bandwidth (hence NVLink within a node), but it enables computation that wouldn't fit on a single GPU. State sharding tolerates higher latency (hence cross-node), but it dramatically reduces per-GPU memory. Pipeline parallelism adds another dimension of scaling with relatively modest communication.

The choice between FSDP2 and ZeRO-3 for the state sharding layer depends on your ecosystem. FSDP2 integrates tightly with PyTorch's compiler stack (torch.compile) and is the native PyTorch solution. ZeRO-3, through DeepSpeed, offers additional features like CPU and NVMe offloading for memory-constrained setups, and has a mature ecosystem of optimizations. Both combine cleanly with Megatron-style computation sharding—they operate on orthogonal axes. If you already run Megatron Core with tensor or pipeline parallelism, Megatron's distributed optimizer or Megatron-FSDP is usually easier to wire up than bolting DeepSpeed ZeRO-3 onto the same job, where process groups must be kept strictly disjoint. Teams that prefer not to assemble Megatron and DeepSpeed manually can also evaluate integrated frameworks such as **Colossal-AI**[11], which bundles hybrid parallelism (DP + TP + PP), ZeRO-style sharding, and **Gemini**[12] heterogeneous memory management (GPU, CPU, and NVMe).

Megatron core: Production-Ready library

Throughout this chapter, we've discussed Megatron's parallelism strategies conceptually. But how do you actually use them in practice? The answer is **Megatron Core**, a library extracted from the original Megatron-LM research codebase and refined for production use.

Megatron Core provides GPU-optimized building blocks: attention layers with tensor parallelism built in, MLP blocks that understand pipeline boundaries, embedding layers that handle vocabulary parallelism. You don't implement the column-parallel and row-parallel patterns yourself—you use `ColumnParallelLinear` and `RowParallelLinear` from the library, and the communication is handled automatically.

Beyond the basic building blocks, Megatron Core includes the infrastructure that large-scale training requires: activation recomputation to trade compute for memory, distributed checkpointing that saves and loads sharded model states efficiently, and FP8 precision support optimized for NVIDIA's latest GPUs (Hopper, Ada, Blackwell). The distributed optimizer shards optimizer states across data-parallel ranks, complementing the computation sharding we've discussed.

Megatron Core requires the Python package pybind11 and the system libraries cuDNN and NCCL. Install them first, then:

```
pip install --no-build-isolation megatron-core[mlm,dev] pybind11

# Or use NVIDIA's container with cuDNN and NCCL pre-installed
docker run --gpus all -it nvcr.io/nvidia/pytorch:25.04-py3
```

The `code/megatron_gpt_pretrain.sh` script in this chapter's code directory demonstrates a production configuration: tensor parallelism across GPUs, distributed optimizer for memory efficiency, flash attention for speed, and the various flags we've discussed throughout this chapter.

Megatron-FSDP: optimized state sharding

We've established that state sharding (FSDP/ZeRO) and computation sharding (Megatron) are complementary. But when you combine them, the implementation details matter. PyTorch's FSDP2 is a general-purpose solution; it doesn't know about Megatron's tensor parallelism or the specific communication patterns involved. This is where **Megatron-FSDP** comes in.

Megatron-FSDP is NVIDIA's implementation of fully sharded data parallelism, designed to work seamlessly with Megatron's other parallelism dimensions. In NVIDIA's published benchmarks, it delivers roughly 15-25% higher throughput and about 23% memory savings versus PyTorch FSDP2.[13] These gains come from optimizations that are only possible when the FSDP implementation understands the surrounding context—better bucketing of parameters, smarter buffer management, and more aggressive overlap of communication with computation.

One technical detail worth noting: Megatron-FSDP uses NCCL's userbuffer feature to reduce GPU Streaming Multiprocessor (SM) consumption during communication. In large-scale training, SMs spent on communication are SMs not available for computation. This optimization keeps more SMs free for the actual matrix multiplications.

Enabling Megatron-FSDP in your training script looks like this:

```
--use-megatron-fsdp
--data-parallel-sharding-strategy optim_grads_params  # Equivalent to ZeRO-3
--overlap-grad-reduce
--overlap-param-gather
```

When should you choose Megatron-FSDP over PyTorch FSDP2? If you're already using Megatron's tensor parallelism, context parallelism, or expert parallelism, Megatron-FSDP integrates naturally and delivers better performance. If you need FP8 training with Transformer Engine, Megatron-FSDP has native support. On the other hand, if you want a pure PyTorch stack with torch.compile support and no external dependencies, PyTorch FSDP2 is the cleaner choice.

Distributed optimizer: Memory-Efficient optimization

Even with tensor parallelism and pipeline parallelism handling the computation, optimizer states remain a significant memory burden. Adam, for example, stores two additional tensors (momentum and variance) for every parameter—that's 8 bytes per parameter on top of the parameters and gradients themselves. For a 70B model, optimizer states alone can consume over 500GB.

Megatron's **distributed optimizer** addresses this by sharding optimizer states across data-parallel ranks, conceptually similar to ZeRO Stage 1. Each GPU only stores the optimizer states for a fraction of the parameters. During the optimizer step, gradients are reduce-scattered (each GPU gets the reduced gradient for its shard), the local optimizer updates its shard, and the updated parameters are all-gathered back.

The memory savings scale with data-parallel size. With 8-way data parallelism using bf16 parameters and fp32 gradients, per-GPU memory drops from 18 bytes per parameter to roughly 7.5 bytes—a 2.4x reduction. The exact formula depends on your precision configuration:

Config	Without distributed	Distributed (d GPUs)
fp16 params, fp16 grads	20 bytes/param	4 + 16/d bytes/param
bf16 params, fp32 grads	18 bytes/param	6 + 12/d bytes/param
fp32 params, fp32 grads	16 bytes/param	8 + 8/d bytes/param

The implementation includes several optimizations beyond basic sharding. Gradients are copied into contiguous buffers as they're computed, enabling efficient reduce-scatter operations. The communication can be overlapped with backward computation (`--overlap-grad-reduce`) and with the next forward pass (`--overlap-param-gather`), hiding much of the latency.

```
--use-distributed-optimizer
--overlap-grad-reduce
--overlap-param-gather
```

FP8 training: Next-Generation precision

The progression from FP32 to FP16/BF16 brought significant speedups and memory savings. NVIDIA's latest GPUs (Hopper, Ada, Blackwell) take this further with native FP8 support—8-bit floating point that halves memory and doubles throughput compared to FP16.

FP8 training isn't as simple as changing a dtype flag. The dynamic range of 8-bit floats is much narrower than 16-bit, so values must be carefully scaled to avoid overflow and underflow. Megatron handles this through Transformer Engine, which tracks the maximum absolute values (amax) of tensors and adjusts scaling factors dynamically. The `--fp8-amax-history-len` parameter controls how many recent amax values to consider when computing scales.

```
--fp8-format hybrid
--fp8-amax-history-len 1024
--fp8-amax-compute-algo max
--fp8-param-gather        # Gather parameters in FP8 to save communication
```

The `hybrid` format uses E4M3 (4 exponent bits, 3 mantissa bits) for the forward pass and E5M2 (5 exponent bits, 2 mantissa bits) for the backward—a balance between range and precision that works well in practice. The `--fp8-param-gather` flag is particularly useful with distributed optimizer: parameters are gathered in FP8 format, reducing all-gather communication volume by half.

FP8 requires hardware support: NVIDIA H100, RTX 4090, or newer GPUs, plus Transformer Engine 1.1 or later. If you have the hardware, the speedup is substantial—often 1.5-2x over BF16 for large matrix multiplications.

When do you need Megatron?

After all this discussion of tensor parallelism, pipeline parallelism, context parallelism, and expert parallelism, a natural question is: when do you actually need any of this? The answer depends on your model and hardware.

If a single Transformer layer fits comfortably on one GPU and computes fast enough, you don't need Megatron. State sharding (FSDP2 or ZeRO) handles memory, and data parallelism handles scaling. Most models under 10B parameters fall into this category on modern GPUs.

Megatron becomes necessary when you hit one of these walls. First, layer size: if your hidden dimension is 16K or larger, a single attention layer's weight matrices may not fit on one GPU, or the computation may be too slow. Tensor parallelism solves this. Second, sequence length: if you're training with 8K+ token contexts, activation memory explodes, and context parallelism or sequence parallelism becomes essential. Third, MoE models: expert parallelism is the natural way to distribute hundreds of experts. Fourth, scale: when you're using hundreds of GPUs, the efficiency gains from Megatron's optimized communication patterns compound significantly.

If none of these apply—your layers fit, your sequences are moderate, you're not using MoE, and you're training on a handful of GPUs—state sharding alone is simpler and sufficient.

Real-World training configurations

Concrete configurations help solidify understanding. The examples below are based on actual Megatron training scripts. The `pretrain_gpt.py` script is part of the Megatron-LM repository:

```
git clone https://github.com/NVIDIA/Megatron-LM.git && cd Megatron-LM
```

The repository contains documentation in `docs/` and example scripts organized by model in `examples/` (e.g., `examples/llama/`, `examples/gpt3/`, `examples/mixtral/`).

LLaMA-3 8B with Long Context (8 × 80GB GPUs):

This configuration trains a LLaMA-3 8B model with 8K context on a single 8-GPU node (A100-80GB, H100, H200, etc.).

```
CUDA_DEVICE_MAX_CONNECTIONS=1 torchrun --nproc_per_node=8 pretrain_gpt.py \
    --use-mcore-models \
    --num-layers 32 \
    --hidden-size 4096 \
    --ffn-hidden-size 14336 \
    --num-attention-heads 32 \
    --group-query-attention \
    --num-query-groups 8 \
    --seq-length 8192 \
    --tensor-model-parallel-size 1 \
    --context-parallel-size 2 \
    --sequence-parallel \
    --fp8-format hybrid \
    --fp8-param-gather \
    --use-distributed-optimizer \
    --overlap-grad-reduce \
    --overlap-param-gather \
    --micro-batch-size 1 \
    --global-batch-size 128 \
    --max-position-embeddings 8192 \
    --mock-data \
    --bf16
```

The model architecture flags define the LLaMA-3 8B structure. `--group-query-attention` with `--num-query-groups 8` enables Grouped-Query Attention, where 32 query heads share 8 KV heads—reducing KV cache memory significantly. For parallelism, we skip tensor parallelism (`--tensor-model-parallel-size 1`) since each layer fits on one GPU, but use context parallelism (`--context-parallel-size 2`) to split the 8K sequence across 2 GPUs. With 8 GPUs total, the effective data-parallel size is 8 / (1 × 1 × 2) = 4—the three factors are tensor, pipeline (both 1 here), and context parallelism. That makes `--global-batch-size 128` work out to 128 / 4 = 32 samples per data-parallel replica, or 32 / `--micro-batch-size 1` = 32 micro-batches per gradient-accumulation cycle. The FP8 flags (`--fp8-format`, `--fp8-param-gather`) provide speedup on Hopper and newer GPUs; remove them for A100s. For 40GB GPUs, reduce model size by lowering `--num-layers`, `--hidden-size`, and `--ffn-hidden-size`.

GPT-3 175B Scale (128 GPUs):

This configuration scales to 175B parameters across 16 nodes (128 GPUs total), requiring both tensor and pipeline parallelism.

```
CUDA_DEVICE_MAX_CONNECTIONS=1 torchrun --nproc_per_node=8 --nnodes=16 \
    pretrain_gpt.py \
    --use-mcore-models \
    --num-layers 96 \
    --hidden-size 12288 \
    --num-attention-heads 96 \
    --seq-length 2048 \
    --tensor-model-parallel-size 8 \
    --pipeline-model-parallel-size 16 \
    --micro-batch-size 1 \
    --global-batch-size 1536 \
    --use-distributed-optimizer \
    --mock-data \
    --bf16
```

At this scale, a single layer with hidden dimension 12288 benefits from tensor parallelism across all 8 GPUs within a node (`--tensor-model-parallel-size 8`). The 96 layers are distributed across 16 pipeline stages (`--pipeline-model-parallel-size 16`), with each stage handling 6 layers. The effective data parallelism is 128 / (8 × 16) = 1, meaning all GPUs are dedicated to model parallelism. The large `--global-batch-size 1536` is achieved through gradient accumulation across many micro-batches.

Mixtral 8x7B MoE (64 GPUs):

This configuration trains a Mixture-of-Experts model with 8 experts distributed across GPUs.

```
CUDA_DEVICE_MAX_CONNECTIONS=1 torchrun --nproc_per_node=8 --nnodes=8 \
    pretrain_gpt.py \
    --use-mcore-models \
    --num-layers 32 \
    --hidden-size 4096 \
    --num-experts 8 \
    --expert-model-parallel-size 8 \
    --tensor-model-parallel-size 1 \
    --pipeline-model-parallel-size 4 \
    --moe-router-topk 2 \
    --moe-grouped-gemm \
    --moe-permute-fusion \
```

```
    --sequence-parallel \
    --use-distributed-optimizer \
    --overlap-grad-reduce \
    --overlap-param-gather \
    --micro-batch-size 1 \
    --global-batch-size 256 \
    --mock-data \
    --bf16
```

The MoE-specific flags define the sparse architecture: `--num-experts 8` creates 8 expert networks per MoE layer, and `--expert-model-parallel-size 8` distributes them one per GPU within the expert-parallel group. `--moe-router-topk 2` means each token is routed to 2 experts. The optimization flags `--moe-grouped-gemm` and `--moe-permute-fusion` batch expert computations and fuse token rearrangement operations for efficiency. Pipeline parallelism (`--pipeline-model-parallel-size 4`) distributes the 32 layers across 4 stages. Tensor parallelism is set to 1 since expert parallelism already distributes the computation.

Complete training example with Megatron

To tie everything together, let's look at how to actually run a Megatron training job. The `code/train_megatron_mcore.py` script in this chapter demonstrates the essential pieces: initializing distributed state, creating a model with `TransformerConfig`, wrapping it with Megatron's `DistributedDataParallel`, and running a training loop with proper gradient synchronization.

Running on a single node with 4 GPUs:

```
CUDA_DEVICE_MAX_CONNECTIONS=1 torchrun --nproc_per_node=4 \
code/train_megatron_mcore.py
```

For multi-node training, specify the cluster topology. On node 0:

```
CUDA_DEVICE_MAX_CONNECTIONS=1 torchrun --nproc_per_node=4 --nnodes=2 \
    --node_rank=0 \
    --master_addr=node0 --master_port=29500 \
    code/train_megatron_mcore.py
```

And on node 1, the same command with `--node_rank=1`. The script uses Megatron Core's `GPTModel`, which has tensor parallelism built in—you don't manually implement the column-parallel and row-parallel patterns. Megatron's DDP wrapper handles gradient synchronization with optimized communication overlap, and the distributed optimizer shards optimizer states automatically.

For models that need both computation sharding and aggressive state sharding, combine Megatron's tensor parallelism with Megatron-FSDP by adding these flags:

```
--use-megatron-fsdp \
--data-parallel-sharding-strategy optim_grads_params \
--tensor-model-parallel-size 4 \
--overlap-grad-reduce \
--overlap-param-gather
```

This combination gives you the best of both worlds: tensor parallelism splits large matrix multiplications across GPUs, while FSDP shards parameters, gradients, and optimizer states across the data-parallel dimension. The overlap flags ensure that communication happens concurrently with computation whenever possible.

A few additional optimizations are worth enabling in production. `--tp-comm-overlap` overlaps tensor parallelism's all-reduce with computation. `--sequence-parallel` reduces activation memory by sharding along the sequence dimension for LayerNorm and Dropout. `--calculate-per-token-loss` optimizes gradient scaling for variable-length sequences.

Beyond these flags, Megatron offers several advanced features. Virtual pipeline parallelism (interleaved scheduling) reduces pipeline bubbles by having each GPU handle multiple non-contiguous stages. Distributed checkpointing saves and loads sharded model states up to 50x faster than naive PyTorch checkpointing, with support for resharding—you can save a checkpoint from a 64-GPU run and load it on 128 GPUs. CUDA graphs capture entire training iterations and replay them with minimal CPU overhead. Activation recomputation lets you selectively recompute activations during the backward pass to trade compute for memory when needed.

Hybrid Parallelism in practice

We've now covered the individual parallelism techniques: ZeRO's state sharding, Megatron's tensor and pipeline parallelism, sequence and context parallelism for long sequences, and expert parallelism for MoE models. But real training systems rarely use just one. A 70B model might use tensor parallelism within nodes, pipeline parallelism across nodes, and FSDP for optimizer state sharding—all simultaneously. How do these pieces fit together?

The Two-Axis view

The key insight is that state sharding and computation sharding operate on orthogonal axes. State sharding (FSDP, ZeRO) addresses memory redundancy: instead of every GPU storing all parameters and optimizer states, each GPU stores a fraction. Computation sharding (tensor parallelism, pipeline parallelism) addresses computational load: instead of one GPU computing an entire layer, multiple GPUs share the work.

These axes are independent. You can have state sharding without computation sharding (a 7B model with ZeRO-3), computation sharding without state sharding (a 70B model with TP=8 and full parameter replication), or both (a 405B model with TP, PP, and FSDP). The choice depends on which bottleneck you're hitting.

Building a hybrid configuration

Let's walk through how you might configure a 70B model training on 64 GPUs across 8 nodes. Each node has 8 GPUs connected by NVLink; nodes are connected by InfiniBand.

Start with tensor parallelism. The model's hidden dimension is 8192, and each attention layer has large weight matrices. We set TP=4, splitting each layer's computation across 4 GPUs within a node. This requires high-bandwidth communication (NVLink), so we keep the TP group within a single node.

Next, consider pipeline parallelism. The model has 80 layers, and even with TP=4, storing all layers' activations is challenging. We set PP=2, splitting the model into two pipeline stages of 40 layers each. Pipeline communication (sending activations between stages) is less frequent than TP communication, so it can tolerate the slower inter-node InfiniBand.

Finally, data parallelism. With TP=4 and PP=2, each "model replica" uses 8 GPUs. We have 64 GPUs total, so DP=8: eight replicas process different micro-batches in parallel. We enable FSDP to shard optimizer states across these 8 replicas, reducing per-GPU memory.

The math: Total GPUs = TP × PP × DP = 4 × 2 × 8 = 64. From a single GPU's perspective, it stores 1/8 of the optimizer states (FSDP), computes 1/4 of each layer (TP), and handles 1/2 of the model's depth (PP).

Why this works

This layered approach succeeds because each technique addresses a different constraint. FSDP eliminates redundant optimizer state storage—critical for Adam's momentum and variance tensors. Tensor parallelism enables matrix multiplications that wouldn't fit or would be too slow on a single GPU. Pipeline parallelism bounds activation memory by limiting how many layers are active simultaneously. Each technique has costs (communication overhead, pipeline bubbles), but when applied to the right bottleneck, the benefits outweigh the costs.

Choosing your configuration

The decision process is incremental. Start simple and add complexity only when needed.

If your model's layers fit on one GPU and compute efficiently, use state sharding alone (FSDP or ZeRO-3). This is the simplest setup and works for most models under 10–15B parameters on modern GPUs.

If layers are too large or too slow on one GPU, add tensor parallelism. Keep TP within a node to leverage NVLink. TP=2, 4, or 8 are common choices depending on layer size.

If the model is very deep or you need to scale across many nodes, add pipeline parallelism. PP introduces bubbles, so use it when necessary rather than by default.

If sequence length is your bottleneck (8K+ tokens), enable sequence parallelism or context parallelism. These reduce activation memory proportionally to the parallelism degree.

If you're training an MoE model, expert parallelism distributes experts naturally. EP often replaces TP for the expert layers since the experts are already separate computations.

Operational realities

Hybrid parallelism adds operational complexity. Tensor parallel groups must be placed on GPUs with fast interconnects—putting a TP group across nodes will cripple performance. Pipeline parallelism requires tuning the number of micro-batches to minimize bubble overhead. Checkpointing becomes more complex: a checkpoint from a TP=4, PP=2 configuration can't be directly loaded into a TP=8, PP=1 setup without resharding.

Debugging also becomes harder. A bug might only manifest with specific parallelism configurations, making reproduction difficult. For these reasons, start with the simplest configuration that meets your needs and add parallelism dimensions incrementally.

Performance optimization best practices

Once you have a working hybrid configuration, there are several optimizations that can significantly improve throughput.

The most impactful is communication overlap. By default, communication and computation happen sequentially—the GPU computes, then communicates, then computes again. With overlap enabled, communication happens in the background while the next computation proceeds. Megatron provides several overlap flags:

```
--overlap-grad-reduce          # Overlap gradient all-reduce with backward
--overlap-param-gather         # Overlap parameter gather with forward
--tp-comm-overlap              # Overlap tensor parallel all-reduce
```

For memory optimization, sequence parallelism reduces activation memory by sharding along the sequence dimension for LayerNorm and Dropout. The distributed optimizer shards optimizer states across data-parallel ranks. Activation recomputation trades compute for memory by recomputing activations during backward instead of storing them.

```
--sequence-parallel
--use-distributed-optimizer
--recompute-activations         # When memory-constrained
```

A few topology guidelines based on communication characteristics: Tensor parallelism and expert parallelism are communication-intensive—keep them within the NVLink domain (same node). Pipeline parallelism tolerates higher latency—it can span nodes. Context parallelism for long sequences works best within a node but can extend across nodes if necessary.

Configuration patterns

A few patterns emerge from production training setups. For dense models under 10B parameters, tensor parallelism is often unnecessary—layers fit on one GPU, so state sharding (FSDP or ZeRO) handles memory while data parallelism handles scaling. For larger dense models (70B+), tensor parallelism becomes essential for the large matrix multiplications, typically TP=4 or TP=8 within a node. Pipeline parallelism adds another scaling dimension when you need more GPUs than fit in a TP group.

MoE models follow a different pattern. Expert parallelism naturally distributes the experts, often replacing tensor parallelism for the expert layers entirely. A Mixtral-style 8x7B model might use EP=8 (one expert per GPU) with no tensor parallelism, plus pipeline parallelism for depth.

Context parallelism appears when sequence length drives memory usage. For 8K+ token sequences, CP=2 or CP=4 can halve or quarter activation memory without the complexity of full model parallelism.

Choosing the right strategy

With so many parallelism techniques available, how do you decide which to use? The answer depends on your specific constraints: model size, layer size, sequence length, available hardware, and whether you're training a dense or MoE model.

A decision framework

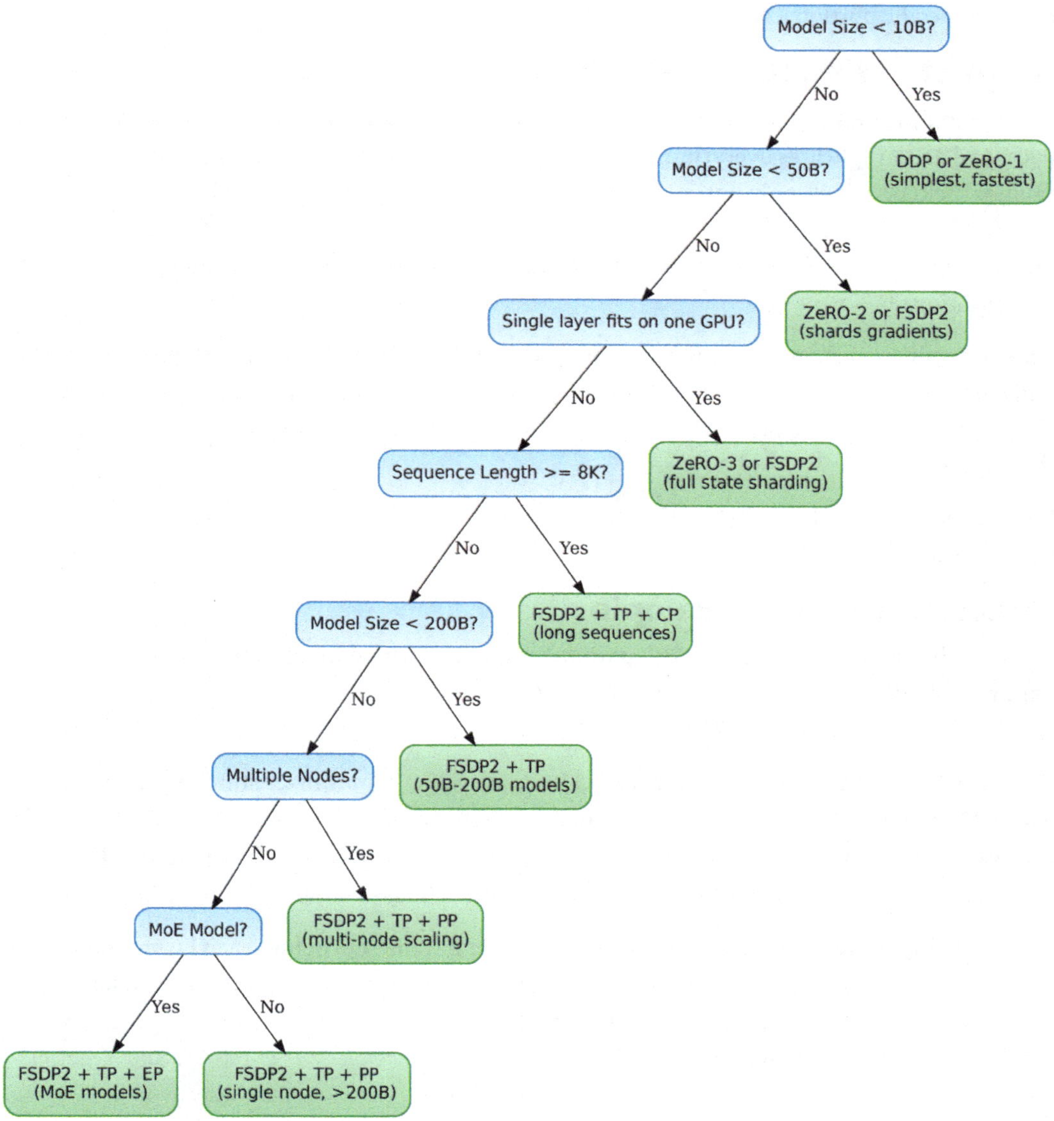

Figure 5.9: Parallelism strategy decision tree

Figure 5.9 provides a visual guide. The decision process starts with the simplest question: does your model fit on one GPU with standard data parallelism? If yes, use DDP—it's the simplest and most efficient. If not, the next question is whether a single layer fits on one GPU. If layers fit but the full model doesn't, state sharding (FSDP2 or ZeRO-3) is your answer. If individual layers are too large, you need computation sharding (tensor parallelism). From there, additional dimensions like pipeline parallelism, context parallelism, and expert parallelism address specific bottlenecks.

Understanding the Trade-Offs

Each technique makes a different trade-off between memory savings and communication overhead. DDP replicates everything—maximum communication efficiency but no memory savings. ZeRO-1 shards only optimizer states, cutting memory roughly in half with minimal overhead. ZeRO-2 adds gradient sharding, and ZeRO-3 shards everything, achieving near-linear memory scaling with GPU count but requiring all-gather operations before each layer's computation.

Tensor parallelism shards computation rather than just storage. It reduces per-GPU memory and compute proportionally to the TP degree, but requires high-bandwidth communication (all-reduce) within each layer. This is why TP works best within a node where NVLink provides the bandwidth.

Pipeline parallelism shards by depth rather than width. It introduces pipeline bubbles (idle time) but tolerates higher-latency communication, making it suitable for cross-node scaling.

Concrete memory example

To make this concrete, consider a 70B parameter model with Adam optimizer. In FP16, parameters take 140GB, gradients another 140GB, and Adam's optimizer states (FP32 master weights, momentum, variance) take 840GB—over 1TB total.

With DDP on 8 GPUs, each GPU stores all 1TB+. With ZeRO-1, optimizer states are sharded: each GPU stores 140GB params + 140GB grads + 105GB optimizer = 385GB. With ZeRO-3, everything is sharded: each GPU stores roughly 140GB total (1/8 of each component). The memory scales linearly with GPU count—add more GPUs, use less memory per GPU.

The catch is communication. ZeRO-3 must all-gather parameters before each layer and reduce-scatter gradients after. For models where layers are small relative to communication latency, this overhead can be significant. For large models with substantial per-layer computation, the overhead is amortized and ZeRO-3 works well.

Summary

This chapter covered two complementary approaches to scaling model training beyond what fits on a single GPU.

State sharding (ZeRO, FSDP2) eliminates memory redundancy by distributing parameters, gradients, and optimizer states across GPUs. ZeRO's progressive stages—from optimizer-only sharding (Stage 1) to full parameter sharding (Stage 3)—let you trade communication overhead for memory savings. Extensions like ZeRO-Offload and ZeRO-Infinity push memory to CPU and NVMe when GPU memory is exhausted, though with throughput penalties. ZeRO++ optimizes multi-node communication through quantization and hierarchical partitioning.

Computation sharding (Megatron) addresses a different problem: when individual layers are too large or too slow for a single GPU. Tensor parallelism splits matrix multiplications across GPUs within a layer. Pipeline parallelism distributes model depth across pipeline stages. Context parallelism and sequence parallelism handle long sequences by sharding activations. Expert parallelism distributes MoE experts naturally.

The key insight is that these approaches are orthogonal. State sharding reduces memory redundancy; computation sharding reduces per-GPU computational load. Modern large-scale training combines both: tensor parallelism within nodes (where NVLink provides bandwidth), pipeline parallelism across nodes (where latency is tolerable), and state sharding for optimizer memory efficiency.

The decision framework is incremental. Start with the simplest approach that works—often just state sharding for models under 30B parameters. Add tensor parallelism when layers become the bottleneck. Add pipeline parallelism for very deep models or multi-node scaling. Add context parallelism for long sequences. Add expert parallelism for MoE models. Each dimension adds complexity, so add them only when needed.

So far, we've focused on distributed training. But training is only half the story. Once you've trained a model, you need to serve it efficiently. The next part of this book shifts to distributed inference: how to run large models at scale, handle high-throughput workloads, and serve models in production.

Code summary

- `deepspeed.initialize()`: Initialize DeepSpeed engine with ZeRO configuration
- `deepspeed.DeepSpeedEngine`: DeepSpeed engine wrapper for model training
- `megatron.core.parallel_state`: Megatron parallel state management
- `megatron.core.tensor_parallel`: Megatron tensor parallelism utilities
- `megatron.core.pipeline_parallel`: Megatron pipeline parallelism utilities
- `deepspeed.zero.Init()`: DeepSpeed ZeRO initialization context manager
- `deepspeed.zero.OffloadOptimizerConfig`: Configuration for ZeRO-Offload
- `deepspeed.zero.OffloadParamConfig`: Configuration for ZeRO-Infinity parameter offload

- `megatron.model.parallel.layers.ColumnParallelLinear`: Column-parallel linear layer for tensor parallelism
- `megatron.model.parallel.layers.RowParallelLinear`: Row-parallel linear layer for tensor parallelism

Useful links

DeepSpeed and ZeRO

- ZeRO: Memory Optimizations Toward Training Trillion Parameter Models (2020): `https://arxiv.org/abs/1910.02054`
- ZeRO-Offload: Democratizing Billion-Scale Model Training (2021): `https://arxiv.org/abs/2101.06840`
- ZeRO-Infinity: Breaking the GPU Memory Wall for Extreme Scale Deep Learning (2021): `https://arxiv.org/abs/2104.07857`
- ZeRO++: Extremely Efficient Collective Communication for Giant Model Training (2023): `https://arxiv.org/abs/2306.10209`
- DeepSpeed Documentation: `https://www.deepspeed.ai/`
- DeepSpeed GitHub: `https://github.com/microsoft/DeepSpeed`

Megatron-LM

- Megatron-LM: Training Multi-Billion Parameter Language Models Using Model Parallelism (2019): `https://arxiv.org/abs/1909.08053`
- Efficient Large-Scale Language Model Training on GPU Clusters Using Megatron-LM (2021): `https://arxiv.org/abs/2104.04473`
- Reducing Activation Recomputation in Large Transformer Models (2023): `https://arxiv.org/abs/2205.05198`
- Megatron-LM GitHub: `https://github.com/NVIDIA/Megatron-LM`
- Megatron Core Documentation: `https://docs.nvidia.com/megatron-core/`

Integrated Frameworks

- Colossal-AI: `https://colossalai.org/`
- NVIDIA NeMo: `https://docs.nvidia.com/nemo-framework/`

Research

- Arctic Long Sequence Training: Scalable Training for Multi-Million Token Sequences (2025): `https://arxiv.org/abs/2507.19845`
- SuperOffload: Large-Scale LLM Training on Superchips (2025): `https://arxiv.org/abs/2502.19811`
- ZenFlow: Stall-Free Offloading Engine (2025): `https://arxiv.org/abs/2502.07846`
- DeepCompile: Compiler Optimization for Distributed Training (2025): `https://arxiv.org/abs/2505.11432`
- Universal Checkpointing for Large-Scale Training (2024): `https://arxiv.org/abs/2503.15758`
- Ring Attention with Blockwise Transformers for Near-Infinite Context (2024): `https://arxiv.org/abs/2310.01889`
- DeepSpeed Ulysses: System Optimizations for Enabling Training of Extreme Long Sequence Transformer Models (2023): `https://arxiv.org/abs/2309.14509`

References

1. Rajbhandari et al., "ZeRO: Memory Optimizations Toward Training Trillion Parameter Models" (2020). `https://arxiv.org/abs/1910.02054`
2. Shoeybi et al., "Megatron-LM: Training Multi-Billion Parameter Language Models Using Model Parallelism" (2019). `https://arxiv.org/abs/1909.08053`
3. Wang et al., "ZeRO++: Extremely Efficient Collective Communication for Giant Model Training" (2023). `https://arxiv.org/abs/2306.10209`. Every forward pass requires an all-gather to reconstruct parameters; every backward pass does the same, plus a reduce-scatter for gradients. For large models on multi-node clusters, this communication can dominate training time.
4. Shoeybi et al., "Megatron-LM: Training Multi-Billion Parameter Language Models Using Model Parallelism," arXiv:1909.08053, 2019. `https://arxiv.org/abs/1909.08053`
5. Narayanan et al., "Efficient Large-Scale Language Model Training on GPU Clusters Using Megatron-LM," SC 2021. `https://arxiv.org/abs/2104.04473`
6. Huang et al., "GPipe: Efficient Training of Giant Neural Networks using Pipeline Parallelism," NeurIPS 2019. `https://arxiv.org/abs/1811.06965`

7. Korthikanti et al., "Reducing Activation Recomputation in Large Transformer Models," MLSys 2023. `https://arxiv.org/abs/2205.05198`
8. Liu et al., "Ring Attention with Blockwise Transformers for Near-Infinite Context," ICLR 2024. `https://arxiv.org/abs/2310.01889`
9. Jacobs et al., "DeepSpeed Ulysses: System Optimizations for Enabling Training of Extreme Long Sequence Transformer Models," arXiv 2023. `https://arxiv.org/abs/2309.14509`
10. DeepEP is DeepSeek's open-source expert-parallel communication library. `https://github.com/deepseek-ai/DeepEP`
11. `Colossal-AI: https://colossalai.org/`
12. Colossal-AI Gemini heterogeneous memory manager (not Google's Gemini): `https://colossalai.org/docs/advanced_tutorials/meet_gemini/`
13. NVIDIA Megatron Core, "Megatron-FSDP." `https://docs.nvidia.com/megatron-core/developer-guide/latest/user-guide/features/megatron_fsdp.html`

Exercises

Compare ZeRO stages

Implement a benchmark comparing DeepSpeed ZeRO stages 1, 2, and 3 on the same model.

Requirements:

- Train a 7B parameter model (or smaller if GPU-limited)
- Test ZeRO Stage 1 (optimizer state partitioning)
- Test ZeRO Stage 2 (+ gradient partitioning)
- Test ZeRO Stage 3 (+ parameter partitioning)
- Measure for each stage:
  - Peak GPU memory per device
  - Training throughput (tokens/second)
  - Communication overhead
- Generate comparison table and memory breakdown

Test your implementation:

```
import deepspeed
import torch
```

```
def benchmark_zero_stage(model, stage: int, num_steps: int = 100):
    """Benchmark a specific ZeRO stage."""
    ds_config = {
        "train_batch_size": 32,
        "zero_optimization": {
            "stage": stage,
            "offload_optimizer": {"device": "none"},
            "offload_param": {"device": "none"},
        },
        "bf16": {"enabled": True},
    }

    model_engine, optimizer, _, _ = deepspeed.initialize(
        model=model,
        config=ds_config,
    )

    # Benchmark training
    memory, throughput = run_training(model_engine, num_steps)
    return memory, throughput

# Compare stages
results = {}
for stage in [1, 2, 3]:
    model = create_model()  # Fresh model for each stage
    memory, throughput = benchmark_zero_stage(model, stage)
    results[f"ZeRO-{stage}"] = {"memory_gb": memory, "throughput": throughput}

print("Stage | Memory (GB) | Throughput (tok/s)")
for name, metrics in results.items():
    print(f"{name} | {metrics['memory_gb']:.1f} | {metrics['throughput']:.1f}")
```

Implement CPU offloading

Configure and benchmark DeepSpeed ZeRO-Offload for training models larger than GPU memory.

Requirements:

- Configure ZeRO Stage 3 with CPU offloading
- Test optimizer state offloading

- Test parameter offloading
- Measure:
    - Maximum trainable model size
    - Training throughput vs GPU-only
    - CPU memory usage
    - PCIe bandwidth utilization

Test your implementation:

```
import deepspeed

# ZeRO-3 with full CPU offload
offload_config = {
    "train_batch_size": 8,
    "zero_optimization": {
        "stage": 3,
        "offload_optimizer": {
            "device": "cpu",
            "pin_memory": True,
        },
        "offload_param": {
            "device": "cpu",
            "pin_memory": True,
        },
        "overlap_comm": True,
        "contiguous_gradients": True,
    },
    "bf16": {"enabled": True},
}

# Test with increasingly large models
model_sizes = ["1B", "3B", "7B", "13B"]
for size in model_sizes:
    try:
        model = create_model(size)
        engine, _, _, _ = deepspeed.initialize(model=model, config=offload_config)

        # Measure memory and throughput
        gpu_mem = torch.cuda.max_memory_allocated() / 1e9
        cpu_mem = get_cpu_memory_usage()
```

```
        throughput = benchmark_throughput(engine, num_steps=10)

        print(f"{size}: GPU={gpu_mem:.1f}GB, CPU={cpu_mem:.1f}GB, {throughput:.
1f} tok/s")
    except RuntimeError as e:
        print(f"{size}: OOM - {e}")
        break
```

Implement Tensor Parallelism

Implement a simplified tensor parallel linear layer to understand Megatron-style parallelism.

Requirements:

- Class signature:

```
class ColumnParallelLinear(nn.Module):
    """Linear layer with column-wise parallelism."""
    def __init__(self, in_features: int, out_features: int, world_size:
int, rank: int):
        pass

    def forward(self, x: torch.Tensor) -> torch.Tensor:
        pass

class RowParallelLinear(nn.Module):
    """Linear layer with row-wise parallelism."""
    def __init__(self, in_features: int, out_features: int, world_size:
int, rank: int):
        pass

    def forward(self, x: torch.Tensor) -> torch.Tensor:
        pass
```

- Column parallel: Split output features across ranks
- Row parallel: Split input features across ranks
- Implement AllReduce for row parallel output
- Verify correctness against standard linear layer

Test your implementation:

```
import torch
import torch.distributed as dist

# Create parallel layers
world_size = dist.get_world_size()
rank = dist.get_rank()

col_linear = ColumnParallelLinear(1024, 4096, world_size, rank).cuda()
row_linear = RowParallelLinear(4096, 1024, world_size, rank).cuda()

# Test forward pass
x = torch.randn(32, 1024).cuda()
y = col_linear(x)  # Shape: (32, 4096 // world_size)
z = row_linear(y)  # Shape: (32, 1024) after AllReduce

print(f"Rank {rank}: input={x.shape}, after col={y.shape}, after row={z.shape}")

# Verify correctness (gather outputs and compare with standard linear)
```

Implement Pipeline Parallelism

Create a simple pipeline parallel training loop with micro-batching.

Requirements:

- Split a model into N pipeline stages
- Implement 1F1B (one forward, one backward) schedule
- Handle micro-batch accumulation
- Measure pipeline bubble overhead
- Compare with data parallel baseline

Test your implementation:

```
class PipelineStage(nn.Module):
    """A single pipeline stage."""
    def __init__(self, layers: nn.ModuleList, stage_id: int):
        super().__init__()
        self.layers = layers
        self.stage_id = stage_id
```

```
    def forward(self, x):
        for layer in self.layers:
            x = layer(x)
        return x

class PipelineParallel:
    def __init__(self, model: nn.Module, num_stages: int, num_microbatches: int):
        self.stages = self.split_model(model, num_stages)
        self.num_microbatches = num_microbatches

    def split_model(self, model, num_stages) -> list:
        """Split model into pipeline stages."""
        pass

    def forward_backward(self, batch):
        """Execute 1F1B schedule."""
        pass

# Test pipeline parallel
model = create_transformer(num_layers=24)
pp = PipelineParallel(model, num_stages=4, num_microbatches=8)

batch = torch.randn(64, 512, 1024).cuda()
loss = pp.forward_backward(batch)
print(f"Pipeline loss: {loss.item():.4f}")
```

Configure Hybrid Parallelism

Set up a training configuration combining data, tensor, and pipeline parallelism.

Requirements:

- Configure 3D parallelism (DP × TP × PP)
- Example: 8 GPUs with DP=2, TP=2, PP=2
- Verify correct process group setup
- Measure scaling efficiency vs single-dimension parallelism
- Document communication patterns for each dimension

Test your implementation:

```
import torch.distributed as dist
```

```
def setup_3d_parallelism(world_size: int, dp: int, tp: int, pp: int):
    """Set up process groups for 3D parallelism."""
    assert dp * tp * pp == world_size, "DP × TP × PP must equal world_size"

    rank = dist.get_rank()

    # Calculate position in 3D grid
    dp_rank = rank // (tp * pp)
    tp_rank = (rank // pp) % tp
    pp_rank = rank % pp

    # Create process groups
    # Data parallel group: same TP and PP position
    # Tensor parallel group: same DP and PP position
    # Pipeline parallel group: same DP and TP position

    return dp_rank, tp_rank, pp_rank, dp_group, tp_group, pp_group

# Test with 8 GPUs: DP=2, TP=2, PP=2
dp_rank, tp_rank, pp_rank, dp_group, tp_group, pp_group = setup_3d_parallelism(
    world_size=8, dp=2, tp=2, pp=2
)

print(f"Rank {dist.get_rank()}: DP={dp_rank}, TP={tp_rank}, PP={pp_rank}")
print(f"DP group size: {dist.get_world_size(dp_group)}")
print(f"TP group size: {dist.get_world_size(tp_group)}")
print(f"PP group size: {dist.get_world_size(pp_group)}")
```

Expected learning outcomes

After completing these exercises, you should be able to:

- Compare and choose appropriate ZeRO stages for your workload
- Configure CPU offloading for training large models on limited GPU memory
- Understand tensor parallelism and implement parallel linear layers
- Implement pipeline parallelism with efficient scheduling
- Configure hybrid 3D parallelism for maximum scaling
- Analyze communication patterns in different parallelism strategies

Get this book's PDF version and more

Scan the QR code (or go to `packtpub.com/unlock`). Search for this book by name, confirm the edition, and then follow the steps on the page.

UNLOCK NOW

Note: Keep your invoice handy. Purchases made directly from Packt don't require an invoice.

6

Distributed Inference and vLLM

Serving large language models at scale with high throughput and low latency

> *Inference is the new web app.*
>
> *Clayton Coleman, Distinguished Engineer at Google*

From training to inference

The previous chapters covered how to train large models across multiple GPUs—state sharding with ZeRO and FSDP, computation sharding with Megatron's tensor and pipeline parallelism. But training is only half the equation. Once you have a trained model, you need to serve it to users, and serving brings an entirely different set of challenges.

Training optimizes for throughput: process as many tokens as possible per second, amortized over long training runs. Inference optimizes for latency and throughput simultaneously: users expect responses in milliseconds, while the system must handle thousands of concurrent requests. Training processes fixed batch sizes; inference must handle variable-length requests arriving at unpredictable times. Training can checkpoint and restart; inference must always be available.

The memory characteristics also differ fundamentally. During training, memory is dominated by optimizer states (momentum, variance) and activation checkpoints. During inference, there are no optimizer states—memory is dominated by model weights and the **KV cache**, the key-value pairs stored from previous tokens to avoid recomputation during autoregressive generation. For long sequences, the KV cache can exceed the model weights in size.

This chapter introduces vLLM, the inference engine that made PagedAttention and continuous batching standard in production LLM serving. We'll explore how PagedAttention revolutionized KV cache management, how continuous batching keeps GPUs busy as requests arrive and finish, and how distributed inference patterns let you serve models that exceed a single GPU's memory.

Introduction to vLLM

When researchers at UC Berkeley set out to build a better LLM serving system in 2023, they faced a fundamental question: why do existing systems waste so much GPU memory? The answer led them to create **vLLM** (virtual Large Language Model), an inference engine that revolutionized how we think about KV cache management.

The key insight was that traditional serving systems treat KV cache like a monolithic block—allocating contiguous memory for each request and hoping for the best. This approach, borrowed from training frameworks, works poorly for inference where requests arrive unpredictably, have wildly different lengths, and finish at different times. vLLM's breakthrough was to apply operating system concepts—specifically, virtual memory and paging—to KV cache management. The result is PagedAttention, which we'll explore in detail later in this chapter.

Today, vLLM has become the de facto standard for LLM serving, powering production deployments at companies ranging from startups to hyperscalers. Its combination of high throughput, memory efficiency, and ease of use makes it an excellent starting point for understanding distributed inference.

Prerequisites

vLLM runs on Linux with Python 3.10 or later. You'll need an NVIDIA GPU with CUDA support —while vLLM also supports AMD GPUs and other accelerators, NVIDIA remains the most common deployment target. Make sure you have a compatible CUDA version installed; vLLM's pip package typically bundles the necessary CUDA runtime, but having a matching driver is essential.

Installation

vLLM can be installed using several methods. **Docker is the quickest way to try vLLM** without installing dependencies locally.

Docker Setup

Docker provides the quickest way to get started with vLLM without installing dependencies locally. Pre-built images are available on the vLLM Docker Hub page

`https://hub.docker.com/r/vllm/vllm-openai.`

vLLM supports a wide range of model architectures. For text generation, you can use base models like `facebook/opt-125m` with the `/v1/completions` endpoint, or instruction-tuned chat models like `Qwen/Qwen2.5-0.5B-Instruct` with the `/v1/chat/completions` endpoint. vLLM also supports embedding models and multimodal models—check the official documentation for the full list of supported architectures.[1]

The vLLM server exposes an OpenAI-compatible API with endpoints for completions, chat completions, embeddings, and more. For a complete list of endpoints with detailed descriptions and usage examples, see the **OpenAI-Compatible API Endpoints** section in the Appendix.

Pull the Latest Image

Pull the latest Docker image. The image requires approximately 8GB of disk space.

```
docker pull vllm/vllm-openai:latest
```

Run the Docker Container

The Docker image runs an OpenAI-compatible server. To serve a base model like `facebook/opt-125m`, run:

```
docker run --runtime nvidia --gpus all \
  -v $HOME/.cache/huggingface:/root/.cache/huggingface --env "HF_TOKEN=$HF_TOKEN"
\
  -p 8000:8000 --ipc=host vllm/vllm-openai:latest \
  facebook/opt-125m
```

Here are some small models suitable for learning purposes:

Model Name in HF	Model Type	Params
`facebook/opt-125m`	Base	125M
`Qwen/Qwen2.5-0.5B-Instruct`	Chat/Instruct	0.5B
`meta-llama/Llama-3.2-1B-Instruct`	Chat/Instruct	1B
`meta-llama/Llama-3.2-1B`	Base	1B
`microsoft/Phi-tiny-MoE-instruct`	MoE/Instruct	~500M (active)

Model Name in HF	Model Type	Params
sentence-transformers/all-MiniLM-L6-v2	Embedding	22M

To use any of these models, replace the model name in the Docker command:

```
... vllm/vllm-openai:latest <MODEL_NAME>
```

For example:

```
... vllm/vllm-openai:latest meta-llama/Llama-3.2-1B-Instruct
```

The `--runtime nvidia --gpus all` flag enables GPU access. To use specific GPUs, replace `--gpus all` with `--gpus '"device=0"'` for a single GPU or `--gpus '"device=0,1"'` for multiple GPUs. You can also set `--env "CUDA_VISIBLE_DEVICES=0,1"` to limit visible GPUs.

The `-v $HOME/.cache/huggingface:/root/.cache/huggingface` volume mount shares your local Hugging Face cache with the container, avoiding repeated model downloads. The container path `/root/.cache/huggingface` assumes the container runs as root. Adjust this path if your container uses a different user or set the `HF_HOME` environment variable to customize the cache location.

The `--ipc=host` flag allows the container to access the host's shared memory, which PyTorch uses for efficient data sharing during tensor parallel inference.

The model name is specified as a positional argument after the image tag. You can append additional vLLM engine arguments after the model name.

Verify the Setup

Once the container is running, you can verify it's working correctly through a series of API calls. The vLLM server exposes an OpenAI-compatible REST API, which means you can use familiar endpoints and request formats. Start by checking that the server is healthy and responsive:

```
curl http://localhost:8000/health
```

You can also list the available models to confirm which model the server is serving:

```
curl http://localhost:8000/v1/models
```

To test actual inference, try a simple text completion request. The `/v1/completions` endpoint accepts a prompt and generates continuation text:

```
curl http://localhost:8000/v1/completions \
  -H "Content-Type: application/json" \
  -d '{"model": "facebook/opt-125m", "prompt": "The result of 1+1 is",
"max_tokens": 3}'
```

For chat-style models (instruction-tuned models designed for conversational interactions), use the `/v1/chat/completions` endpoint instead. This endpoint expects a list of messages with roles (system, user, assistant) rather than a raw prompt:

```
curl http://localhost:8000/v1/chat/completions \
  -H "Content-Type: application/json" \
  -d '{
    "model": "Qwen/Qwen2.5-0.5B-Instruct",
    "messages": [
      {"role": "user", "content": "Hello, how are you?"}
    ]
  }'
```

If you need deterministic output (the same result every time for the same input), set `"temperature": 0` to enable greedy sampling, which always selects the highest probability token:

```
curl http://localhost:8000/v1/chat/completions \
  -H "Content-Type: application/json" \
  -d '{
    "model": "Qwen/Qwen2.5-0.5B-Instruct",
    "messages": [
      {"role": "user", "content": "Hello, how are you?"}
    ],
    "temperature": 0
  }'
```

> **Note**
>
> Setting `temperature=0` enables greedy sampling, but vLLM does not guarantee complete reproducibility by default due to scheduling and batching optimizations. For fully deterministic results, you may need to set `VLLM_ENABLE_V1_MULTIPROCESSING=0` or enable batch invariance (see vLLM's reproducibility documentation).

vLLM also supports embedding models through the `/v1/embeddings` endpoint, which converts text into dense vector representations useful for semantic search and retrieval applications:

```
curl http://localhost:8000/v1/embeddings \
  -H "Content-Type: application/json" \
  -d '{
    "model": "sentence-transformers/all-MiniLM-L6-v2",
    "input": "This is a test sentence"
  }'
```

Install and run from package manager (uv, conda, pip)

If you prefer not to use Docker, you can install vLLM directly into a Python environment. There are several package managers to choose from, each with its own advantages.

Method 1: Using uv (Recommended)

The uv package manager is a modern, fast alternative to pip that handles dependency resolution more efficiently. If you don't have it installed, you can get it with a single command:

```
curl -LsSf https://astral.sh/uv/install.sh | sh
```

Once installed, create a new Python environment and install vLLM:

```
uv venv --python 3.12 --seed
source .venv/bin/activate
uv pip install vllm --torch-backend=auto
```

The `--torch-backend=auto` flag is particularly useful because it automatically detects your CUDA driver version and selects the appropriate PyTorch index. If you need a specific CUDA version, you can specify it explicitly (e.g., `--torch-backend=cu126` for CUDA 12.6). For quick one-off commands without creating a permanent environment, uv run provides a convenient alternative:

```
uv run --with vllm vllm --help
```

Method 2: Using conda

If you're already using conda for environment management, you can create a dedicated environment for vLLM:

```
conda create -n vllm-env python=3.12 -y
conda activate vllm-env
pip install --upgrade uv
uv pip install vllm --torch-backend=auto
```

Note that we still recommend using uv for the actual package installation even within a conda environment, as it handles vLLM's complex dependencies more reliably.

Method 3: Using pip directly

For a traditional Python setup, you can use pip with a standard virtual environment:

```
python3.12 -m venv vllm-env
source vllm-env/bin/activate
pip install vllm
```

> **Note**
>
> When using pip directly, ensure you have the correct PyTorch version installed for your CUDA version. Mismatched versions can cause cryptic runtime errors.

Verifying Installation

Regardless of which installation method you chose, verify that vLLM is correctly installed by checking the version and testing the command-line interface:

```
python -c "import vllm; print(vllm.__version__)"
vllm --help
```

Compile, install, and run from local source

For developers who want to modify vLLM's source code or need the latest unreleased features, building from source is the way to go. Clone the repository and install in editable mode:

```
git clone https://github.com/vllm-project/vllm.git
cd vllm
pip install -e .
```

For a full development setup that includes testing and linting tools, use the `dev` extras:

```
pip install -e ".[dev]"
```

> **Note**
>
> Building from source requires all build dependencies (including the CUDA toolkit and a C++ compiler) and takes significantly longer than package manager installation. This approach is primarily for contributors and advanced users.

Offline inference

With vLLM installed, you can test it with a simple offline inference example. The following script (`code/offline_inference.py`) demonstrates the basic usage pattern: create an `LLM` instance with a model name, configure sampling parameters, and call `generate()` with your prompts:

```
from vllm import LLM, SamplingParams

# Initialize the model
llm = LLM(model="facebook/opt-125m")

# Define prompts and sampling parameters
prompts = ["Hello, my name is", "The capital of France is"]
sampling_params = SamplingParams(temperature=0.8, top_p=0.95)

# Generate outputs
outputs = llm.generate(prompts, sampling_params)

# Print results
for output in outputs:
```

```
    print(f"Prompt: {output.prompt!r}")
    print(f"Generated: {output.outputs[0].text!r}")
```

Run the script with:

```
python code/offline_inference.py
```

Online inference

Start an OpenAI-compatible API server:

```
# Start the server with a chat model
vllm serve Qwen/Qwen2.5-0.5B-Instruct --port 8000
```

In another terminal, test the server:

```
# List available models
curl http://localhost:8000/v1/models

# Test chat completion (for instruction-tuned models)
curl http://localhost:8000/v1/chat/completions \
    -H "Content-Type: application/json" \
    -d '{
        "model": "Qwen/Qwen2.5-0.5B-Instruct",
        "messages": [
            {"role": "user", "content": "Hello, how are you?"}
        ]
    }'

# Test completion (for base models)
curl http://localhost:8000/v1/completions \
    -H "Content-Type: application/json" \
    -d '{
        "model": "facebook/opt-125m",
        "prompt": "The result of 1+1 is",
        "max_tokens": 3
    }'
```

KV cache

In the previous section, we saw how vLLM provides a high-level interface for running inference. But what makes LLM inference fundamentally different from other deep learning workloads? The answer lies in the autoregressive nature of text generation and a critical optimization called the **KV cache**.

When a language model generates text, it doesn't produce the entire output at once. Instead, it generates one token at a time, with each new token depending on all the tokens that came before it. This sequential dependency creates a unique computational challenge: without careful optimization, the model would need to reprocess the entire sequence history for every single token it generates. The KV cache is the solution to this problem—it stores intermediate computations so they can be reused rather than recomputed.

Understanding the KV cache is essential for anyone working with LLM inference at scale. It explains why memory, not compute, often becomes the bottleneck during generation. It's the reason why techniques like PagedAttention (which we'll cover later) can dramatically improve throughput. And it's the foundation for understanding how distributed inference strategies like tensor parallelism affect memory requirements.

Let's start by examining the architecture that makes KV caching both necessary and possible.

Decoder-Only transformer architecture

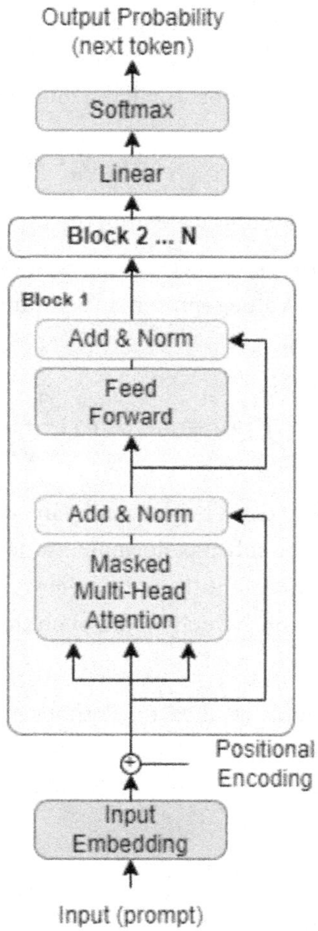

Figure 6.1: Decoder-only transformer

Before diving into KV cache, let's establish a clear picture of the architecture we're working with. Modern large language models—GPT, LLaMA, Qwen, and their variants—all share a common design: the decoder-only transformer. This architecture has proven remarkably effective for autoregressive language modeling, where the goal is to predict the next token given all previous tokens.

A decoder-only transformer consists of a stack of identical layers, typically 32 for a 7B model or 80+ for larger models. Each layer contains two main components: a self-attention sublayer with causal masking, and a feed-forward network (FFN). Residual connections and layer normalization tie everything together, ensuring stable training, and inference.

The self-attention mechanism is where the magic happens—and where KV cache becomes essential. Attention uses three learned linear projections to transform the input: **Query (Q)**, **Key (K)**, and **Value (V)**. For each token at position i, the model computes:

$$Q_i = x_i \times W_Q, K_i = x_i \times W_K, V_i = x_i \times W_V$$

where x_i is the token embedding (or hidden state from the previous layer) and W_Q, W_K, W_V are learned weight matrices. The intuition is that Query represents "what am I looking for?", Key represents "what do I contain?", and Value represents "what information do I provide?" The attention mechanism then computes:

$$Attention(Q, K, V) = softmax(\frac{Q \times K^T}{\sqrt{d_k}}) \times V$$

The $Q \times K^T$ term computes similarity scores between all pairs of tokens—how relevant is each previous token to the current one? The softmax normalizes these scores into a probability distribution, and the result is used to weight the Value vectors. The $\sqrt{d_k}$ scaling factor prevents the dot products from growing too large, which would push the softmax into regions with vanishing gradients.

For autoregressive generation, we apply a causal mask that sets attention scores to $-\infty$ for future positions before the softmax. This ensures that when predicting token i, the model can only attend to tokens 0, 1, ..., i-1—it cannot "peek" at future tokens that don't exist yet during generation.

Figure 6.1 shows a typical decoder-only architecture. Each layer consists of two sub-layers: a masked multi-head self-attention mechanism and a position-wise feed-forward network (FFN). The masked attention ensures that position i can only attend to positions ≤ i, enforcing the autoregressive property. The FFN typically expands the hidden dimension by 4x (or uses SwiGLU with ~2.7x expansion in modern architectures like LLaMA), applies a non-linearity, and projects ack. Residual connections and layer normalization stabilize training. Note that this diagram follows the original Transformer's "Add & Norm" order; modern LLMs like GPT and LLaMA use "Pre-Norm" (normalize before attention/FFN) for better training stability.

Notation

We use the following notation throughout this section:

- B: batch size
- L_1: length of an attending sequence (query);
- l_1: index of a position in this sequence
- L_2: length of a being attended sequence (key/value);
- l_2: index of a position in this sequence
- D: model hidden size (dimension of hidden states/tokens)
- H: number of attention heads
- D_{qk}: dimension of a query/key vector
- D_v: dimension of a value vector, and $D = D_v \times H$
- L: notation used when $L_1 = L_2$

Text generation process: prefill and decode

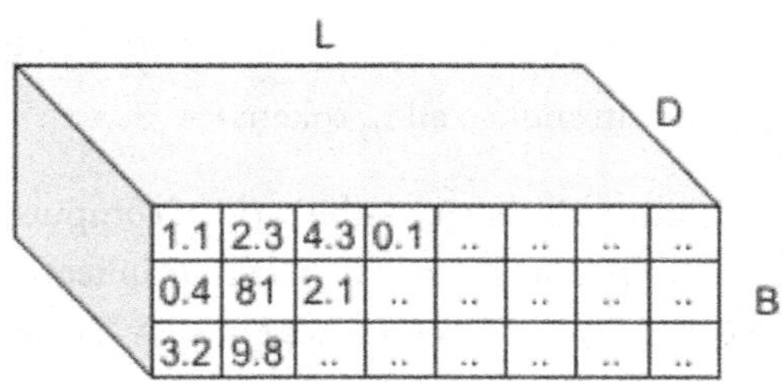

Figure 6.2: Input shape

Figure 6.2 illustrates the input tensor structure. When serving generation requests, we typically batch multiple prompts for higher throughput. The input has shape $B \times L_2 \times D$, where B is the batch size, L_2 is the prompt length (number of tokens), and D is the hidden dimension (e.g., 4096 for LLaMA-7B). Each token is represented as a D-dimensional embedding vector, and the entire prompt becomes a matrix that flows through the transformer layers.

Text generation occurs in two distinct phases, each with fundamentally different computational characteristics. Understanding these phases is essential for optimizing inference performance.

Prefill Phase

The first phase, called **prefill** (also known as the "prompt processing" or "context encoding" phase), processes the entire prompt sequence in parallel. This is where the model "reads" and "understands" the input before generating any output. During prefill, all L_2 prompt tokens are processed simultaneously through every transformer layer.

Figure 6.3 shows the prefill stage in detail. The input X_0 (the embedded prompt tokens with shape $B \times L_2 \times D$) passes through all transformer layers. At each layer, the self-attention mechanism allows every token to attend to all other tokens in the prompt, building up contextual representations. The model produces logits for every position—a tensor of shape $B \times L_2 \times V$ where V is the vocabulary size (e.g., 32,000 for LLaMA). However, we only care about the logits at the last position ($B \times 1 \times V$), as these give us the probability distribution over the vocabulary for the first generated token Y_0.

Crucially, during prefill we also compute and store the Key and Value projections for all prompt tokens at every layer. For a model with N layers, we cache 2N tensors (one K and one V per layer), each of shape $B \times L_2 \times D_{qk}$ (or D_v for values). This **KV cache** will be reused in subsequent decoding steps, avoiding redundant computation of these projections. The prefill stage is compute-bound: we process L_2 tokens in parallel, performing $O(L_2^2)$ attention operations per layer (each token attends to all L_2 tokens).

The prefill stage has high arithmetic intensity—the ratio of compute operations to memory accesses is favorable because we're doing dense matrix multiplications over many tokens. For a batch of long prompts, the GPU's tensor cores are kept busy with large matrix operations, achieving high utilization. This is similar to the forward pass during training, where we also process sequences in parallel.

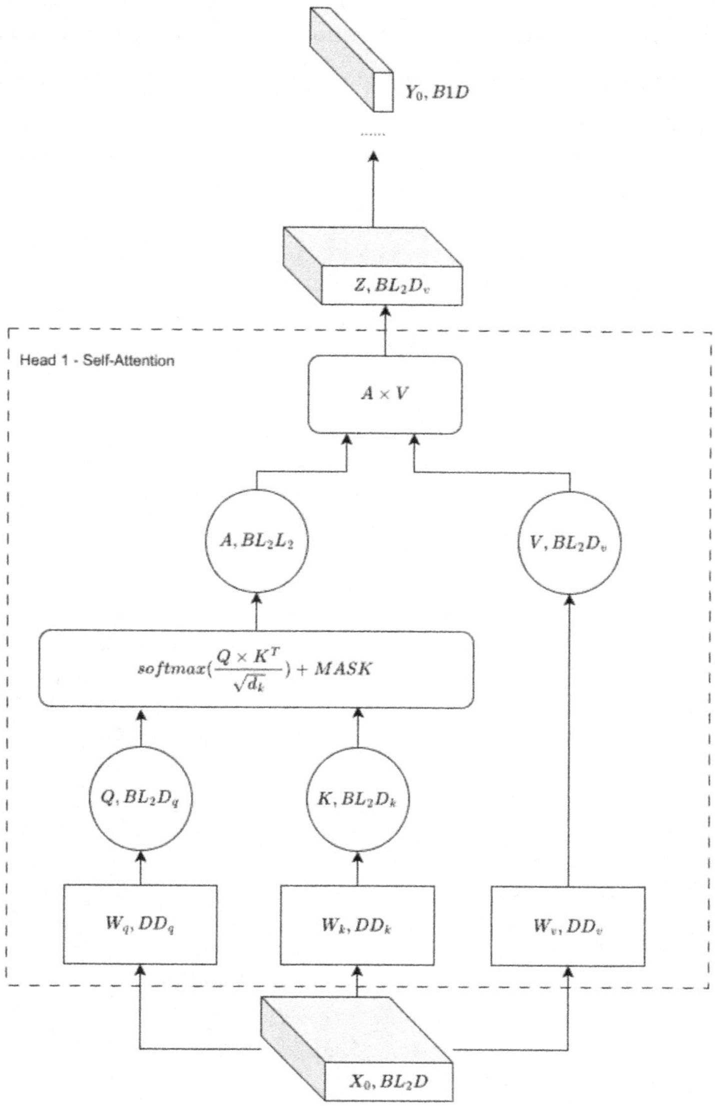

Figure 6.3: Prefill stage

The decode phase and its inefficiencies

After prefill completes, the model enters the **decode** phase. Here, tokens are generated one at a time in an autoregressive loop: generate token Y_0, feed it back as input, generate Y_1, and so on until an end-of-sequence token or maximum length is reached.

Consider generating the first new token after the prompt. The input to the query projection is $X_1 = Y_0$ (the newly generated token), but for attention to work correctly, the Key and Value projections need the full context—the original prompt X_0 concatenated with the new token X_1, resulting in shape $B \times (L_2 + 1) \times D$.

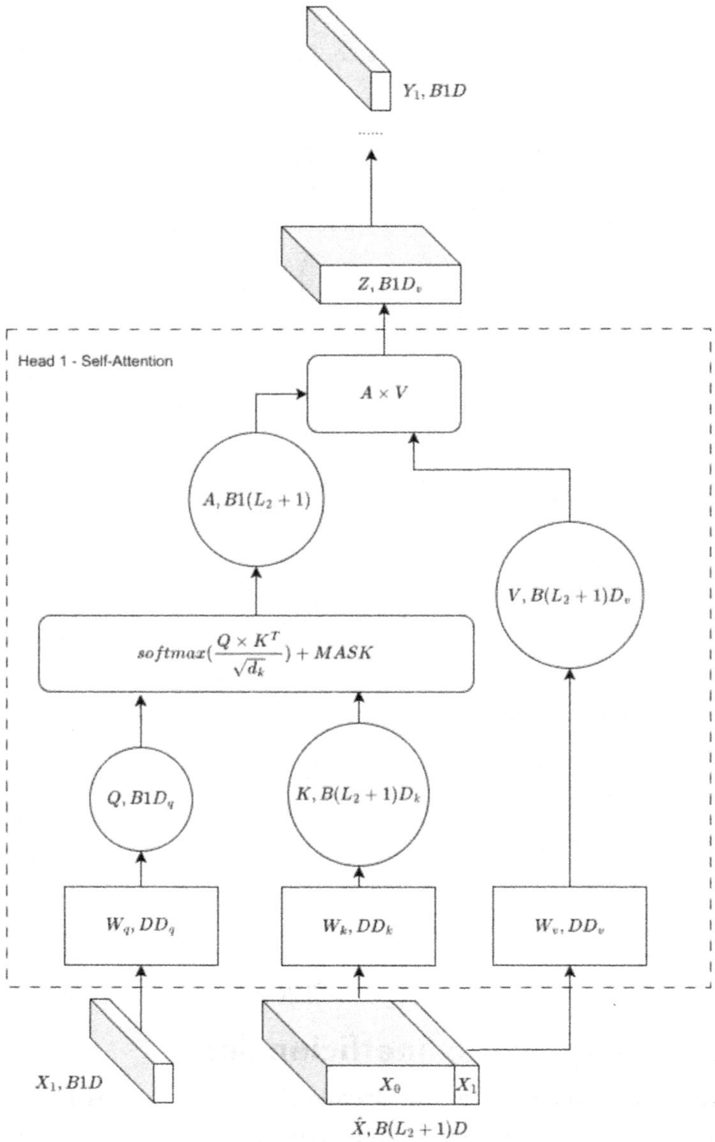

Figure 6.4: Decode without KV cache

Figure 6.4 illustrates this naive approach. The query needs to attend to the entire context so far. For example, if our prompt X_0 is "Time flies" and Y_0 is "like", we use "like" to query the context "Time flies like" and predict the next token, probably "an". Then we use "an" to query "Time flies like an" and get "arrow". This process continues: each newly generated token must attend to all previous tokens (both the original prompt and all previously generated tokens) to maintain context and generate coherent text. However, at each step, we need to recompute the Key and Value vectors for the entire sequence history, even though most of these computations were already performed in previous steps.

From the above figure, we can easily see the inefficiency arises because we need to construct $\hat{X}$ = [X_0 , X_1] and multiply it with WK and WV, even though the X0 part has already been multiplied with these weight matrices during the prefill phase. This duplication occurs at every generation step, requiring recomputation of Key and Value vectors for all previous tokens through the entire transformer stack.

Without caching, this naive approach has time complexity $O(L_{total}^2)$ per step, where L_{total} is the total sequence length $L_2 + L_t$ including prompt and generated tokens. For long sequences, this becomes computationally prohibitive.

KV cache solution

KV cache solves this inefficiency by storing precomputed Key and Value vectors for all previously processed tokens. Instead of concatenating and recomputing, we can simply use X_1 as input for K and V calculation, as long as we cache the previous results. Take Key vector as an example, we only calculate K_{new} which has shape of $B \times 1 \times D_{qk}$ and the time complexity is reduced dramatically.

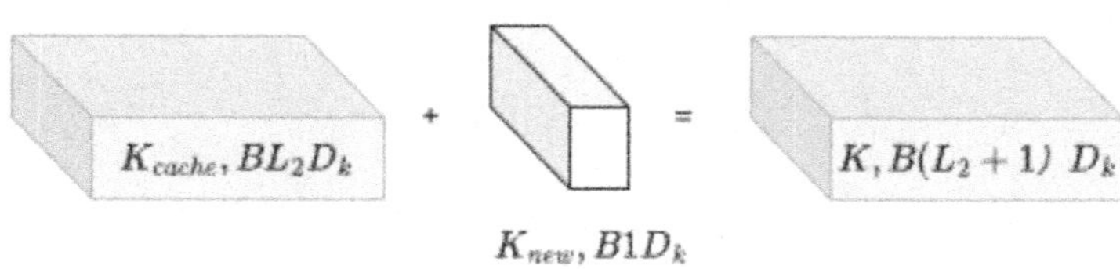

Figure 6.5: KV cache grows with each decode step

Figure 6.5 shows how the KV cache grows with each generated token. With KV cache, the decoding stage becomes much more efficient.

The input shape is $B \times 1 \times D$ and output shape is also $B \times 1 \times D$. The key insight is that only the new token needs attention computation, while all previous tokens reuse their cached K and V vectors.

Time Complexity Analysis:

With KV cache, the computational complexity changes dramatically:

- **Prefill phase**: Processes all L_2 prompt tokens in parallel. The attention computation has complexity $O(L_2^2 \cdot D)$ for the self-attention over the prompt sequence. This is a one-time cost.
- **Decode phase (per token)**:
  - **Without KV cache**: $O(L_{total}^2 \cdot D)$ per step, where $L_{total} = L_2 + L_t$ grows with each generated token. For T generated tokens, total complexity is $O(T \cdot L_{total}^2 \cdot D)$, which becomes $O(T^3 \cdot D)$ when $L_t >> L_2$.
  - **With KV cache**: Only compute K and V for the new token (shape $B \times 1 \times D_{qk}$), then perform attention with cached keys/values. The complexity per step is $O(L_{total} \cdot D)$ for the attention computation, where L_{total} is the current sequence length. For T generated tokens, total complexity is $O(T \cdot L_{total} \cdot D) \approx O(T^2 \cdot D)$ when $L_t >> L_2$.

The key improvement is reducing the quadratic dependency on sequence length in the decode phase to linear, making long-sequence generation feasible. However, this comes at the cost of memory: KV cache requires $O(L_{total} \cdot D)$ memory to store all cached Key and Value vectors.

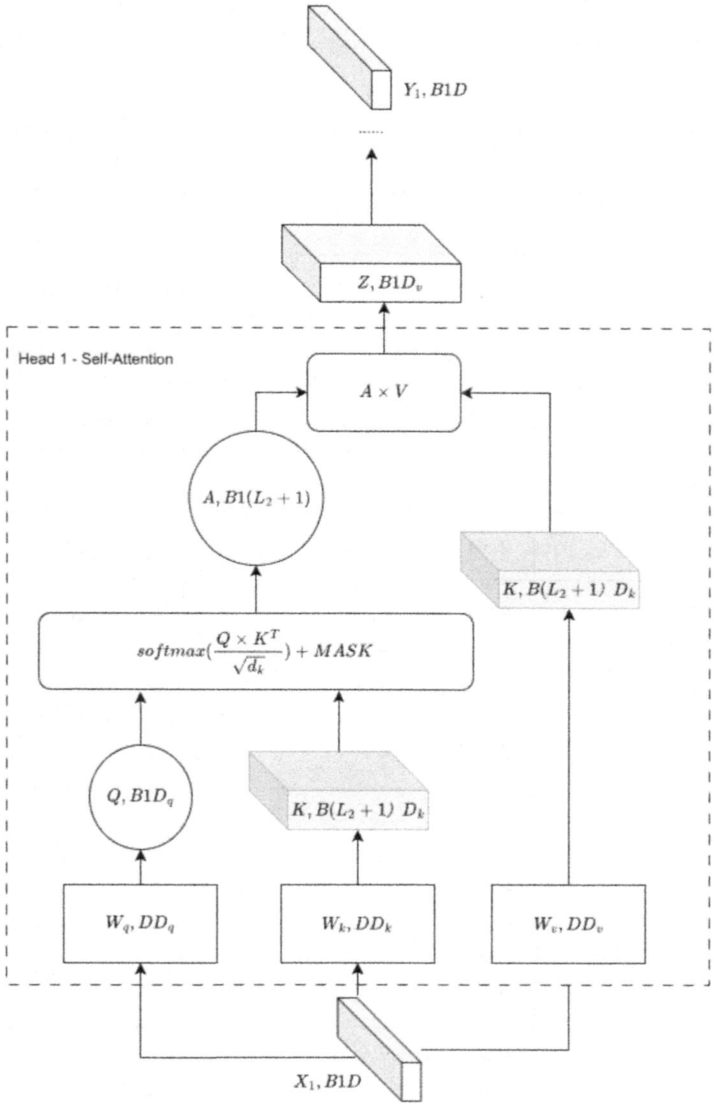

Figure 6.6: Decode with KV cache

Figure 6.6 shows the decode phase with KV cache enabled. The decode phase has a fundamentally different compute profile than prefill. With only one token being processed, the matrix multiplications are essentially matrix-vector operations. The arithmetic intensity is low —we're memory-bound, spending most of the time loading model weights from GPU memory rather than computing. This is why batching multiple decode requests together (continuous batching, covered later) is crucial for efficiency.

Summary of Inference Stages

The following table summarizes the tensor shapes and operations during the prefill and decoding phases:

Stage	Shape	Notes
Prefill Phase		
Input X_{prompt}	$B \times L_2 \times D$	Prompt sequence
Process all tokens	Parallel	Same as training
Cache K, V	$B \times L_2 \times D_{qk/v}$	For reuse
Decoding Phase		
Input x_t	$B \times 1 \times D$	Single new token
$Q_t = x_t W^Q$	$B \times 1 \times D_{qk}$	Query for new token
$K_{textcached}$	$B \times (L_2 + t) \times D_{qk}$	All previous keys
$V_{textcached}$	$B \times (L_2 + t) \times D_v$	All previous values
Attention scores	$B \times 1 \times (L_2 + t)$	New token attends to all previous
Attention A_t	$B \times 1 \times (L_2 + t)$	Upper triangular
Output Z_t	$B \times 1 \times D_v$	
Concat heads	$B \times 1 \times (H \cdot D_v)$	
Final output	$B \times 1 \times D$	Single generated token

PagedAttention: solving KV cache fragmentation

While KV cache dramatically improves computational efficiency, it introduces a critical challenge in production serving systems: **memory fragmentation**. When serving multiple concurrent requests, each with different sequence lengths that grow dynamically, traditional memory allocation strategies lead to significant waste and limit throughput.

vLLM's breakthrough innovation is **PagedAttention**, a memory management algorithm inspired by virtual memory paging in operating systems. PagedAttention is primarily designed to solve KV cache fragmentation in large-scale LLM serving by allocating the cache in fixed-size blocks. A crucial consequence of this block-based design is that attention computation no longer iterates over padded sequence ranges. Instead, it traverses only the blocks that actually exist for each request, thereby eliminating padding-related attention FLOPs.

The KV cache fragmentation problem

In production environments, serving systems must handle multiple concurrent requests simultaneously. Each request maintains its own KV cache that grows dynamically as tokens are generated during autoregressive decoding. Different prompts and generation lengths result in different cache sizes, creating a fundamental allocation challenge.

Traditional systems allocate contiguous memory blocks per request. When sequences finish or have different lengths, this approach leads to wasted space that cannot be efficiently reused.

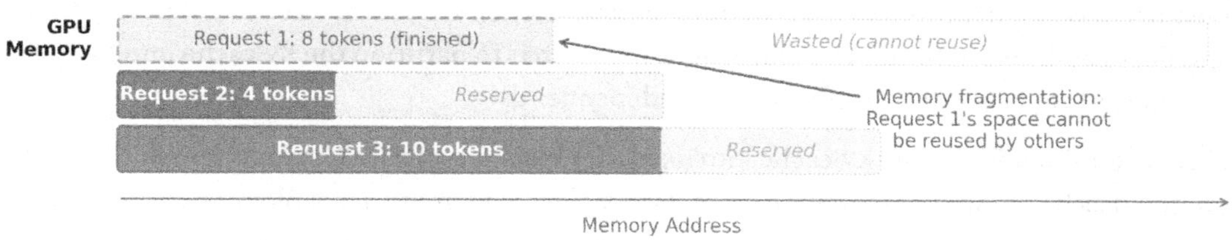

Figure 6.7: KV Cache memory fragmentation

Figure 6.7 illustrates this problem. Request 1 has finished after generating 8 tokens, while Request 2 (4 tokens) and Request 3 (10 tokens) are still active. The memory originally allocated for Request 1 now sits idle—but why can't it be reused? The issue is that Request 2 and Request 3 each require their KV cache to be stored in *contiguous* memory for efficient attention computation. Request 1's freed 8-token block might be too small for a new request that needs 12 tokens, or too large for one that only needs 3 tokens. Even if the size matches, the freed block may not be adjacent to an existing request's cache, so it cannot extend that request's sequence. Meanwhile, Request 2 and Request 3 each reserve space for tokens they may never generate. Freed blocks from finished requests often go unused; active requests hold memory they may never fill. In high-concurrency serving, the combined waste can reach 60-80% of GPU memory—the range reported in the PagedAttention paper.[2]

Beyond memory waste, traditional batching introduces a less obvious but equally critical inefficiency: padding-induced attention computation waste. In batched decoding, different requests typically have different effective context lengths. Let the batch size be B, and let the cached context length for request i be $(L_2^{(i)} + t^{(i)})$. To batch these requests together, conventional attention implementations must pad all sequences to a common maximum length:

$$(L_2 + t)_{max} = max_i (L_2^{(i)} + t^{(i)})$$

As a result, the cached keys and values used in attention have shape $K_{cached}, V_{cached} \in \mathbb{R}^{B \times (L_2+t)max \times Dqk/v}$, and the attention scores for the decode step are computed as:

$$A_t = softmax(Q_t K_{cached}^T + mask), A_t \in \mathbb{R}^{B \times 1 \times (L_2+t)_{max}}$$

Although masking prevents padded positions from influencing the output, the dot products involving padded tokens are still fully computed. Consequently, a large fraction of attention FLOPs is spent on tokens that carry no semantic information, especially when the context lengths within a batch vary widely.

How PagedAttention works

To solve the fragmentation problem, PagedAttention must use fixed-size blocks. Continuous memory allocation inevitably leads to fragmentation when sequences have different lengths and finish at different times. The only viable approach is to partition the KV cache into fixed-size blocks that can be allocated and freed independently.

PagedAttention divides the KV cache into fixed-size blocks, typically 16 tokens per block (denoted as B_{size}), similar to memory pages in OS virtual memory. Each block contains the Key and Value vectors for a contiguous segment of tokens. For request i, the cached KV is represented as $N_i = \lceil (L_2^{(i)} + t^{(i)}) / B_{size} \rceil$ blocks, each block storing keys and values with shape Block $\in \mathbb{R}^{B\_size} \times D_{qk/v}$.

Each request maintains a block table that maps logical sequence positions to physical block addresses, similar to page tables in OS virtual memory. This allows sequences to be logically continuous while physically stored in discrete blocks scattered across GPU memory. Blocks are allocated and freed as sequences grow or complete. When a request finishes, its blocks are immediately returned to a shared block pool. Freed blocks can be immediately reused by new requests, eliminating fragmentation and enabling near-100% memory utilization.

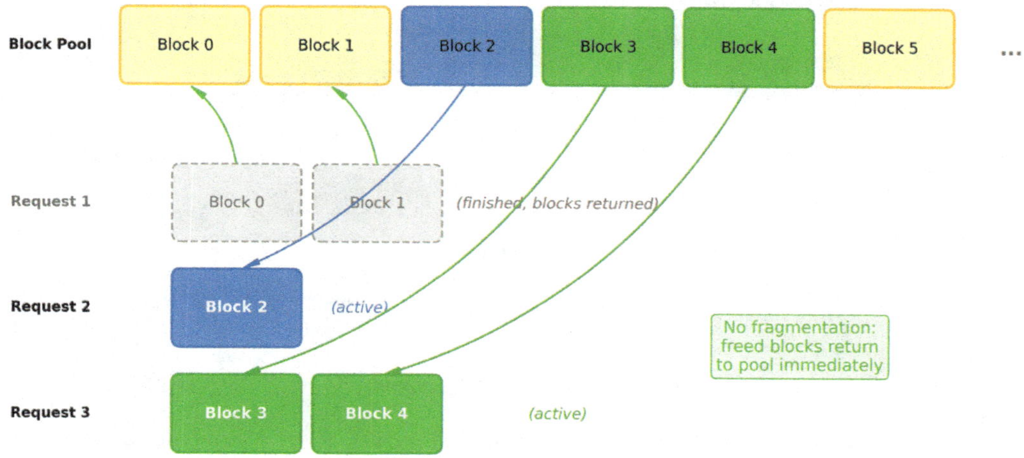

Figure 6.8: PagedAttention block-based memory

Figure 6.8 illustrates this block-based approach. The block pool at the top contains all available blocks. Request 1 has finished and its blocks (Block 0, Block 1) are returned to the pool, shown as free (yellow). Request 2 uses Block 2, and Request 3 uses Blocks 3 and 4. Unlike contiguous allocation, when Request 1 finishes, its blocks immediately become available for any new request—regardless of size. A new request needing 3 blocks can grab Block 0, Block 1, and Block 5 without requiring them to be adjacent.

Eliminating padding FLOPs

Once blocks exist, the iteration semantics of attention computation fundamentally change. This is a crucial consequence of the block-based design, not an additional optimization. With block-based storage, attention computation no longer assumes the KV cache is a continuous sequence from position 1 to $(L_2 + t)_{max}$. Instead, attention iterates over the block table, and tokens that do not exist simply do not have corresponding blocks.

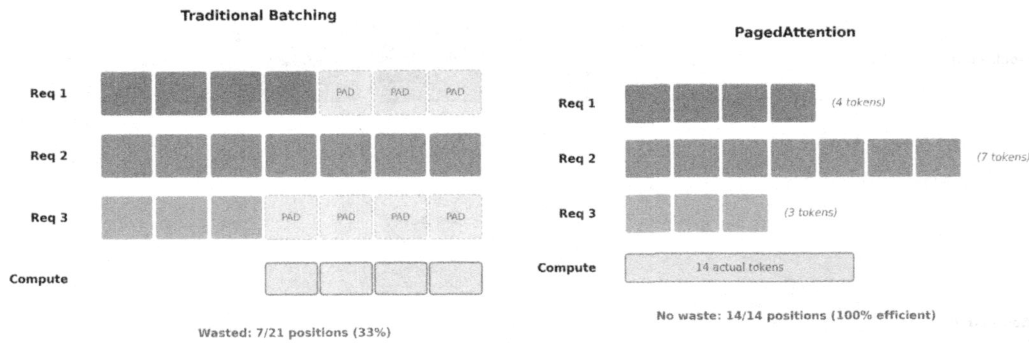

Figure 6.9: Padding vs PagedAttention

Figure 6.9 contrasts the two approaches. In traditional batching (left), three requests with lengths 4, 7, and 3 tokens must all be padded to the maximum length of 7. The attention kernel computes over all 21 positions (7 × 3), but only 14 contain actual tokens—7 positions (33%) are wasted on padding. With PagedAttention (right), each request's attention computation visits only its actual tokens. No padding exists, so all FLOPs contribute to meaningful computation.

During decoding, the attention computation for request i iterates only over the blocks listed in its block table.

$$A_t^{(i)} = softmax(Q_t^{(i)} \cdot \bigcup_{b \in \mathcal{B}_i} K_b^T)$$

where B_i denotes the set of blocks owned by request i. Crucially, this computation depends only on (L_2^{(i)} + t^{(i)}), not on $(L_2 + t)_{max}$. Tokens that do not exist for a given request are never visited by the attention kernel because the corresponding blocks do not exist in the block table.

With PagedAttention, padding tokens are not masked after computation—they are never part of the computation. The attention kernel does not launch dot products for padded positions. As a result, the number of attention FLOPs for each request is proportional to its true context length rather than the maximum context length in the batch. This property eliminates padding-related FLOPs entirely and is a key enabler for efficient continuous batching in large-scale LLM serving systems.

The performance improvement in vLLM comes from both effects working together. Fragmentation reduction allows more concurrent requests to be served simultaneously, while zero padding FLOPs increase the effective compute utilization of decode attention. These are two sides of the same block-based design decision.

Unlike OS page management that focuses on address mapping and access correctness, PagedAttention is optimized for efficient attention computation. Custom CUDA kernels read KV cache from non-contiguous blocks while maintaining coalesced memory access patterns, ensuring high GPU utilization. This attention-aware design means the system understands how attention operations access memory and optimizes accordingly.

The benefits are substantial. Memory efficiency improves dramatically because fragmentation waste from variable-length sequences is eliminated, enabling near-100% memory utilization. Production deployments can serve 2-4x more concurrent requests with the same GPU memory compared to traditional approaches. More importantly, padding overhead is completely eliminated, meaning zero FLOPs are wasted on padding. This dramatically improves throughput in real serving scenarios.

Flexible batching becomes possible because requests with different sequence lengths can be batched efficiently without padding. The system supports dynamic batching where batch composition changes every step, enabling efficient serving of highly variable workloads. Long context support is also enhanced, as the system efficiently handles variable-length contexts without pre-allocating maximum memory. Very long sequences of 100K+ tokens can be served by allocating blocks on demand. The design handles high concurrency naturally, built for high-churn workloads with frequent request arrivals and completions.

Connection to distributed inference

PagedAttention solves memory efficiency within a single GPU, but what happens when even an efficiently-managed single GPU isn't enough? This is where distributed inference becomes essential. When models exceed single GPU memory capacity, when throughput requirements exceed what one GPU can deliver, or when models are simply too large for a single node, we need to spread the workload across multiple devices.

The combination of PagedAttention for memory efficiency and distributed parallelism for scalability is what enables vLLM to serve the largest models in production. PagedAttention ensures we're not wasting memory on fragmentation, while tensor, data, and pipeline parallelism let us scale beyond single-GPU limits.

Motivation: the "out of memory" problem

As language models grow larger, a fundamental constraint emerges: they simply don't fit on a single GPU. DeepSeek R1 has 671 billion parameters. LLaMA 3.1 405B, as the name suggests, has 405 billion parameters. Even with an H100's 80GB of HBM, storing 405B parameters in FP16 (2 bytes per parameter) would require 810GB—ten times what a single GPU provides.

One approach is **quantization**: reducing precision from FP16 to FP8 or even INT4. This helps, but has limits. FP8 halves memory requirements, so our 405B model now needs "only" 405GB

—still five H100s worth of memory. INT4 gets us to ~200GB, but introduces accuracy trade-offs that may not be acceptable for all applications. And we haven't even accounted for KV cache, which for long-context inference can exceed the model weights themselves.

The more scalable solution is to **distribute the model across multiple GPUs**. Rather than compressing the model to fit on one device, we spread it across many devices, each holding a portion of the weights and contributing to the computation. This is the domain of distributed inference, and vLLM provides three fundamental strategies: tensor parallelism, data parallelism, and pipeline parallelism.

Overview of the vLLM architecture

vLLM's architecture centers around a **scheduler-executor-worker** pattern, as shown in *Figure 6.10*. This layered design cleanly separates concerns: request management, distributed coordination, and actual computation.

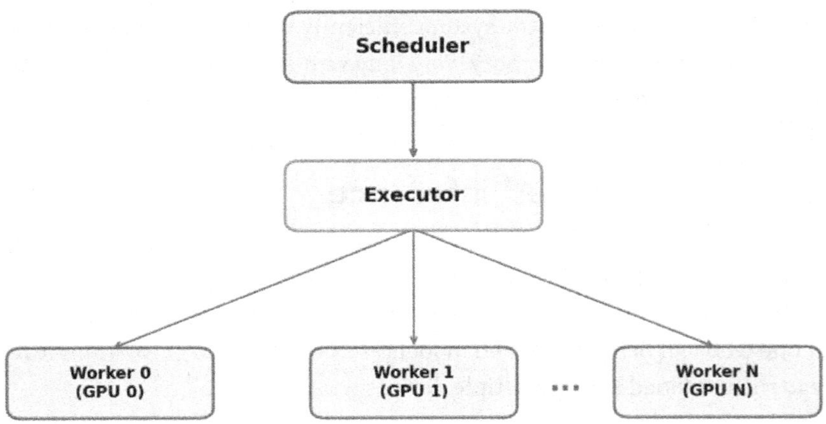

Figure 6.10: vLLM scheduler-executor-worker architecture

The **Scheduler** sits at the top of the hierarchy. It receives incoming requests, groups them into batches based on available memory and scheduling policy, and decides which requests to process in each iteration. The scheduler implements **continuous batching**—the Orca-style pattern of admitting new requests and retiring finished ones within the same batch, rather than waiting for every sequence to complete. This dynamic scheduling maximizes GPU utilization.

The **Executor** acts as the coordination layer between the scheduler and the actual compute resources. It manages the pool of workers and translates high-level scheduling decisions into distributed commands. vLLM supports multiple executor backends depending on the deployment scenario: a simple single-GPU executor for small models, a multi-processing executor for multi-GPU inference on a single node, and a Ray-based executor for distributed inference across multiple nodes. The executor broadcasts commands to all workers and collects their results.

Workers are the compute units, each associated with one GPU (or other accelerator). A worker holds a shard of the model weights, manages its local KV cache, and executes the actual forward passes. In tensor-parallel configurations, workers coordinate through NCCL to perform collective operations like all-reduce. Each worker runs the same model code but operates on different data or model shards depending on the parallelism strategy.

This architecture enables vLLM to scale from a single GPU to hundreds of GPUs across multiple nodes while maintaining the same programming model.

Overview of parallelism strategies in vLLM

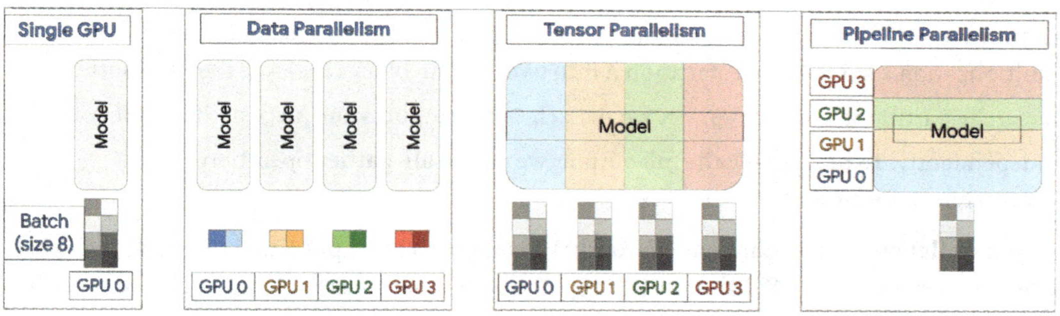

Figure 6.11: Parallelism strategies in vLLM

vLLM provides three fundamental parallelism strategies for distributing computation and memory across multiple GPUs. **Tensor Parallelism (TP)** shards individual layers across multiple GPUs within a node, with each GPU processing a portion of each layer and results synchronized through collective communication. **Data Parallelism (DP)** creates multiple complete replicas of the model, each processing different requests independently to increase throughput. **Pipeline Parallelism (PP)** splits the model's layers across multiple GPUs or nodes, with data flowing through stages sequentially like an assembly line.

Additionally, vLLM provides **Expert Parallelism (EP)** as a special modifier flag for Mixture-of-Experts (MoE) models. EP is not a standalone strategy—it modifies how MoE layers are distributed and must be combined with TP or DP. The `--enable-expert-parallel` flag changes communication patterns and expert distribution for MoE models.

The following sections explore each strategy in detail, then discuss how they can be combined for optimal performance.

Tensor Parallelism (TP)

Tensor Parallelism (TP) shards model weights horizontally across multiple GPUs within a single node, allowing all GPUs to compute concurrently. Unlike pipeline parallelism (which we'll cover later), where GPUs process different layers sequentially, tensor parallelism has every GPU working on the same layer simultaneously—each handling a different slice of the computation. This follows the **SPMD (Single Program, Multiple Data)** paradigm: all GPUs run the same code, but on different portions of the data.

The linear algebra foundations

To understand tensor parallelism, we need to understand how matrix multiplications can be split across devices. There are two fundamental patterns: column parallelism and row parallelism.

Column parallelism splits the weight matrix along its columns. Consider a matrix multiplication $Y = X \times A$. If we partition A into two column blocks $[A_1 \mid A_2]$, then the output naturally partitions as $Y = [X \times A_1 \mid X \times A_2]$. Each GPU computes one piece of the result independently. To reassemble the full output, we use an **all-gather** operation that concatenates the pieces from all GPUs.

Row parallelism takes a different approach. We split both the input X and the weight matrix A along their rows: $X = [X_1; X_2]$ and $A = [A_1; A_2]$. The output becomes $Y = X_1 \times A_1 + X_2 \times A_2$—each GPU computes a partial sum, and we use **all-reduce** to sum these partial results across all GPUs.

The key insight is that these two patterns can be chained cleverly to minimize communication. In a typical transformer MLP (the feed-forward network), we have an "up projection" followed by an activation function and a "down projection". If we apply column parallelism to the up projection, the output is naturally sharded across GPUs. We can then apply the activation function (element-wise, so no communication needed) and feed the sharded result directly into a row-parallel down projection. The only communication required is a single all-reduce at the end—no all-gather in between.

This pattern extends to attention as well. The Q, K, V projections can be column-parallel (each GPU handles a subset of attention heads), and the output projection can be row-parallel. Again, we need only one all-reduce per attention layer.

Benefits of Tensor Parallelism

The most obvious benefit of tensor parallelism is **memory reduction**: each GPU stores only a fraction of the weights. A 140B parameter model that wouldn't fit on a single GPU can be split across two GPUs, with each holding ~70B parameters. But the benefits go deeper than just fitting larger models.

Consider what happens to KV cache capacity. Suppose a 140B model leaves only ~20 GB free on a 141 GB H200 once weights are loaded. With TP=2, each GPU holds half the weights and frees roughly ~70 GB for KV cache—often the real reason to add tensor parallelism, even when the model could technically squeeze onto fewer GPUs.

Tensor parallelism also reduces latency by effectively multiplying memory bandwidth. During inference, especially in the decode phase, we're often memory-bound—waiting for weights to be loaded from HBM rather than waiting for computation. With TP=2, we're loading from two GPUs' worth of HBM simultaneously, doubling effective bandwidth.

The trade-off is communication overhead. Every layer requires an all-reduce operation, transferring data of size `batch_size × sequence_length × hidden_size`. On systems with NVLink (providing 600+ GB/s between GPUs), this overhead is manageable. On PCIe-only systems (32 GB/s), communication can dominate runtime for prefill-heavy workloads—sometimes consuming 60% or more of total time.

One additional constraint to keep in mind: the number of attention heads must be divisible by the tensor parallel size. The same rule applies to KV heads in grouped-query and multi-query models—if the count does not divide evenly, vLLM may replicate KV heads internally. If your model has 32 heads and you want TP=6, you'll need padding or a different TP size. Most modern models are designed with power-of-two head counts specifically to enable flexible TP configurations.

When to use Tensor Parallelism

Tensor parallelism is the right choice when your model doesn't fit on a single GPU and you have good interconnect (NVLink) available. It's particularly effective for latency-sensitive workloads where you want all GPUs contributing to each request. Be cautious with prefill-heavy workloads on PCIe-only systems—profile your specific workload to understand the communication-to-computation ratio before committing to a TP configuration.

Data Parallelism (DP) for throughput scaling

Tensor parallelism splits a single model across GPUs to handle larger models or reduce latency. But what if your model already fits on one GPU (or a small TP group), and your bottleneck is simply serving more concurrent requests? This is where **Data Parallelism (DP)** comes in.

The concept is straightforward: instead of splitting one model across multiple GPUs, we create multiple complete copies of the model, each running independently on its own GPU (or TP group). Each replica handles different requests, and a load balancer distributes incoming traffic across them. There's no communication between replicas during inference—they're completely independent, like running multiple separate vLLM servers.

This independence is both DP's greatest strength and its limitation. Because replicas don't communicate, there's zero communication overhead—throughput scales linearly with the number of replicas. Add four replicas, get four times the throughput. But this also means each replica needs enough memory for a complete model copy, so DP doesn't help when the model itself is too large.

Combining Data Parallelism with other strategies

In practice, DP is often combined with TP. Consider serving a 70B model on a system with 8 GPUs. The model requires TP=2 to fit, leaving us with 4 potential TP groups. We can run DP=4 to create four replicas, each using two GPUs with tensor parallelism. The total GPU count is `DP_size × TP_size = 4 × 2 = 8`.

```
vllm serve $MODEL --data-parallel-size 4 --tensor-parallel-size 2
```

For MoE models, the interaction between DP and expert parallelism is more nuanced. The attention layers can run in pure data-parallel mode (each replica has complete attention weights), while the expert layers use expert parallelism to distribute experts across the DP group. This requires synchronization: even if a DP rank has no requests in a given step, it must participate in the all-to-all communication for expert routing. vLLM handles this automatically, but it's worth understanding that MoE + DP isn't as "independent" as dense model DP.

Deployment modes

vLLM supports two deployment modes for data parallelism:

Internal Load Balancing (Self-Contained)

A single API endpoint with internal load balancing:

```
# Single node: DP=4, TP=2 (8 GPUs total)
vllm serve $MODEL --data-parallel-size 4 --tensor-parallel-size 2
```

Multi-node example:

```
# Node 0 (head node with API server)
vllm serve $MODEL --data-parallel-size 4 --data-parallel-size-local 2 \
                  --data-parallel-address 10.99.48.128 --data-parallel-rpc-port
13345
```

```
# Node 1 (worker node)
vllm serve $MODEL --headless --data-parallel-size 4 --data-parallel-size-local 2 \
                  --data-parallel-start-rank 2 \
                  --data-parallel-address 10.99.48.128 --data-parallel-rpc-port
13345
```

This mode provides a single HTTP endpoint with automatic load balancing based on queue lengths, making deployment simpler. The limitation is that the API server can become a bottleneck at large DP sizes—use `--api-server-count` to scale out API servers if needed.

External Load Balancing

Each DP rank is deployed as a separate vLLM instance with its own endpoint:

```
# Rank 0
CUDA_VISIBLE_DEVICES=0 vllm serve $MODEL --data-parallel-size 2 --data-parallel-
rank 0 --port 8000

# Rank 1
CUDA_VISIBLE_DEVICES=1 vllm serve $MODEL --data-parallel-size 2 --data-parallel-
rank 1 --port 8001
```

An external load balancer (e.g., nginx, HAProxy) routes requests to different ranks based on real-time telemetry (queue lengths, KV cache usage), request characteristics (prefix caching opportunities), and health status. This mode offers better scalability for large DP deployments, more sophisticated KV-cache-aware load balancing, and independent scaling of each rank.

Benefits and Trade-Offs

Data parallelism's appeal lies in its simplicity and effectiveness. Throughput scales linearly—double the replicas, double the throughput. Each replica maintains its own KV cache, so total cache capacity also scales linearly. If one replica fails, the others continue serving, providing natural fault tolerance. And because replicas don't communicate during inference, there's no communication overhead eating into your compute budget.

The trade-offs are equally clear. Memory efficiency suffers because each replica stores a complete copy of model weights. For a 70B model, four DP replicas means storing 280B parameters worth of weights across the system—versus 70B with tensor parallelism. Load balancing becomes important: a naive round-robin approach ignores the fact that different replicas may have different KV cache utilization, leading to suboptimal performance. And for MoE models, the "independence" of DP breaks down because expert routing requires cross-replica communication.

The decision framework is straightforward: use TP/PP first to make the model fit, then add DP to scale throughput. If your model fits on a single GPU and you need more throughput, DP is the simplest solution. If latency is your primary concern, TP (which reduces per-request latency by parallelizing computation) may be better than DP (which doesn't affect single-request latency at all).

Pipeline Parallelism (PP)

When models grow beyond what a single node can hold—think DeepSeek R1 at 671B parameters or LLaMA 405B—we need to distribute layers across multiple machines. This is where **Pipeline Parallelism (PP)** comes in.

While tensor parallelism splits each layer horizontally (all GPUs work on the same layer simultaneously), pipeline parallelism splits the model vertically along layers. GPU 0 might hold layers 0-19, GPU 1 holds layers 20-39, and so on. Data flows through the pipeline sequentially: GPU 0 processes its layers and sends the output to GPU 1, which processes its layers and sends it to GPU 2, and so forth.

The communication pattern is fundamentally different from TP. In tensor parallelism, every layer requires an all-reduce across all GPUs—high frequency, but the data stays within a node where NVLink provides fast interconnect. In pipeline parallelism, communication happens only at stage boundaries—much less frequent, but the data typically crosses node boundaries where network bandwidth is limited. This makes PP well-suited for multi-node deployments where inter-node bandwidth is the bottleneck.

The pipeline bubble problem

The sequential nature of pipeline parallelism creates an efficiency challenge. When GPU 0 is processing a batch, GPUs 1 and 2 sit idle waiting for input. When GPU 2 is processing, GPUs 0 and 1 are idle waiting for the next batch. In a naive implementation, each GPU is active only a fraction of the time—a massive waste of expensive hardware.

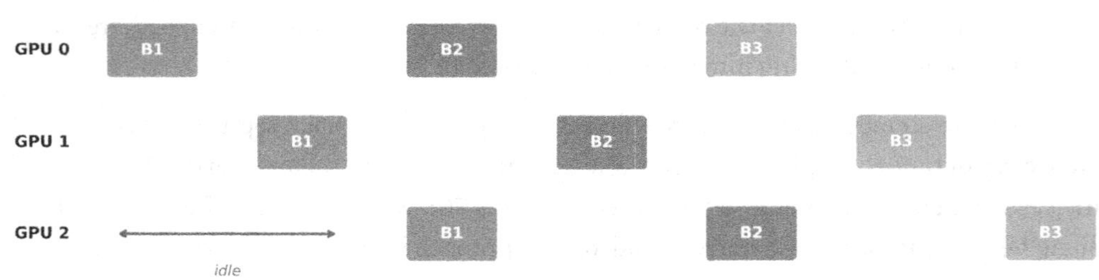

Figure 6.12: Pipeline bubble

Figure 6.12 illustrates this problem. Time flows left to right, and each row represents a GPU in the pipeline. The colored blocks show when each GPU is actively processing a batch—GPU 0 (first stage) processes first, then passes data to GPU 1, which processes and passes to GPU 2. The white gaps between colored blocks are "pipeline bubbles": periods when a GPU sits idle because it's waiting for data from the previous stage or waiting for the next batch to arrive. In a 3-stage pipeline processing a single batch, each GPU is idle 2/3 of the time. With expensive hardware like H100s costing thousands of dollars per hour, this idle time translates directly to wasted money.

vLLM addresses this with **request groups** (also called virtual engines). Instead of processing one batch at a time, the system maintains multiple independent request streams. While GPU 2 is processing Group 1, GPU 1 can be processing Group 2, and GPU 0 can be processing Group 3. The pipeline stays full, and all GPUs stay busy.

The trade-off is that KV cache must be split among request groups. With 4 pipeline stages, each group gets roughly 1/4 of the total KV cache capacity. This limits the maximum batch size per group, which can reduce efficiency for memory-bound decode operations that benefit from larger batches.

Chunked prefill for smoother pipelines

Another source of pipeline bubbles is the mismatch between prefill and decode. Prefill processes many tokens in parallel and is compute-intensive; decode processes one token at a time and is memory-bound. A long prefill can take 10x longer than a decode step, creating bubbles as faster decode operations wait for slower prefills.

Chunked prefill solves this by breaking long prefills into smaller chunks that interleave with decode operations. Instead of processing a 4096-token prompt all at once, the system might process 512 tokens per iteration, spreading the prefill cost across multiple steps. This smooths out the pipeline and prevents any single long prefill from blocking other requests.

Chunked prefill is enabled by default in vLLM v1, but the chunk size may need tuning for your workload. Too large, and you get bubbles; too small, and you add overhead from the extra iterations. Profile your specific prefill-to-decode ratio to find the sweet spot.

Expert Parallelism (EP): A modifier flag for MoE models

Mixture-of-Experts (MoE) models like Mixtral, DeepSeek, and Phi-MoE present a unique parallelism challenge. Unlike dense models where every parameter is used for every token, MoE models route each token to only a subset of "experts"—typically 2 out of 8, 16, or even 256 total experts. This sparse activation pattern means the model has many more parameters than a dense model of equivalent compute cost, but those parameters are distributed across many experts that aren't all active simultaneously.

Expert Parallelism (EP) is vLLM's mechanism for distributing these experts across GPUs. Unlike TP, DP, and PP which are standalone strategies, EP is a modifier flag (`--enable-expert-parallel`) that changes how MoE layers behave when combined with TP or DP. You can't use EP alone—it requires `TP_SIZE × DP_SIZE > 1` to take effect.

To understand why EP matters, we need to first understand how MoE models work. Let's use Phi-tiny-MoE-instruct as a concrete example.

Understanding MoE architecture

In a standard transformer, the feed-forward network (FFN) after attention is a simple two-layer MLP. In an MoE model, this FFN is replaced with multiple expert networks—each expert is itself a complete MLP—plus a routing mechanism that decides which experts process each token.

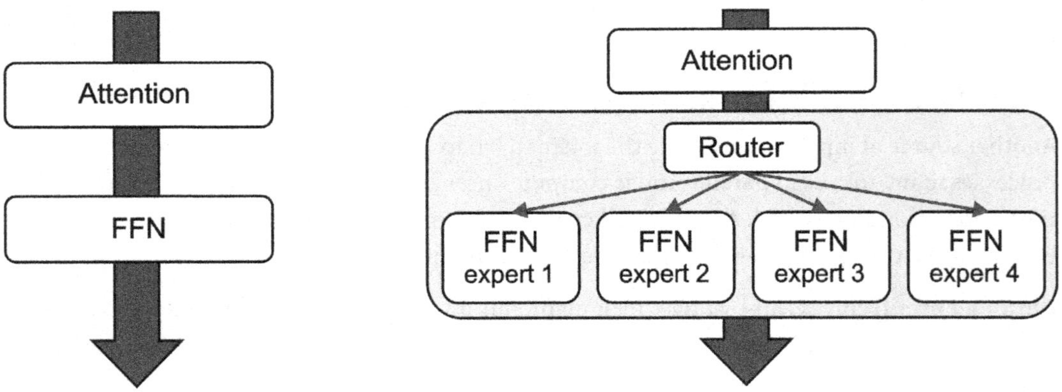

Figure 6.13: MoE architecture

Figure 6.13 contrasts the two architectures. The left side shows a standard dense transformer layer: attention followed by a single FFN. The right side shows an MoE layer: attention followed by a router and multiple FFN experts (4 in this example). The router examines each token and decides which experts should process it—typically selecting the top-k experts (e.g., top-2) based on learned routing weights. Each selected expert processes the token independently, and their outputs are combined. This sparse activation means that even though the model has 4× the FFN parameters, each token only activates a fraction of them, keeping compute cost similar to the dense model while increasing model capacity.

Decoder layer structure

In Phi-tiny, each decoder layer follows the standard Transformer architecture with attention and MoE components:

```
class PhiMoEDecoderLayer(nn.Module):
    def __init__(self, config: PhiMoEConfig, layer_idx: int):
        super().__init__()
        self.self_attn = PHIMOE_ATTENTION_CLASSES[config._attn_implementation]
(config, layer_idx)
        self.block_sparse_moe = PhiMoESparseMoeBlock(config)
        self.input_layernorm = nn.LayerNorm(config.hidden_size,
eps=config.rms_norm_eps)
        self.post_attention_layernorm = nn.LayerNorm(config.hidden_size,
eps=config.rms_norm_eps)

    def forward(self, hidden_states, attention_mask=None, position_ids=None,
                past_key_value=None, output_attentions=False,
                output_router_logits=False, use_cache=False, **kwargs):
        residual = hidden_states
        hidden_states = self.input_layernorm(hidden_states)
        hidden_states, self_attn_weights, present_key_value = self.self_attn(
            hidden_states=hidden_states, attention_mask=attention_mask,
            position_ids=position_ids, past_key_value=past_key_value,
            output_attentions=output_attentions, use_cache=use_cache)
        hidden_states = residual + hidden_states

        residual = hidden_states
        hidden_states = self.post_attention_layernorm(hidden_states)
        hidden_states, router_logits = self.block_sparse_moe(hidden_states)
        hidden_states = residual + hidden_states

        return (hidden_states, self_attn_weights if output_attentions else None,
                present_key_value if use_cache else None, router_logits if
output_router_logits else None)
```

The MoE layer (`block_sparse_moe`) is invoked after the post-attention layer normalization, replacing the standard FFN with a routing mechanism that selects and combines outputs from multiple experts.

Expert structure

Each expert in Phi-tiny is a complete MLP with three linear projections:

```
class PhiMoEBlockSparseTop2MLP(nn.Module):
    def __init__(self, config: PhiMoEConfig):
        super().__init__()
        self.ffn_dim = config.intermediate_size
        self.hidden_dim = config.hidden_size
        self.w1 = nn.Linear(self.hidden_dim, self.ffn_dim, bias=False)
        self.w2 = nn.Linear(self.ffn_dim, self.hidden_dim, bias=False)
        self.w3 = nn.Linear(self.hidden_dim, self.ffn_dim, bias=False)
        self.act_fn = ACT2FN[config.hidden_act]

    def forward(self, hidden_states):
        current_hidden_states = self.act_fn(self.w1(hidden_states)) *
self.w3(hidden_states)
        current_hidden_states = self.w2(current_hidden_states)
        return current_hidden_states
```

The expert uses a gated activation pattern: `w1` projects to the intermediate dimension and is activated, `w3` provides a gating signal, and `w2` projects back to the hidden dimension. This structure is similar to standard Transformer FFNs but with multiple specialized experts.

Routing mechanism

The `PhiMoESparseMoeBlock` implements the routing logic that selects which experts process each token:

```
class PhiMoESparseMoeBlock(nn.Module):
    def __init__(self, config):
        super().__init__()
        self.hidden_dim = config.hidden_size
        self.num_experts = config.num_local_experts
        self.top_k = config.num_experts_per_tok
        self.gate = nn.Linear(self.hidden_dim, self.num_experts, bias=False)
        self.router_jitter_noise = config.router_jitter_noise
        self.experts = nn.ModuleList([
            PhiMoEBlockSparseTop2MLP(config) for _ in range(self.num_experts)
        ])

    def forward(self, hidden_states):
```

```
        batch_size, sequence_length, hidden_dim = hidden_states.shape
        hidden_states = hidden_states.view(-1, hidden_dim)

        router_logits = self.gate(hidden_states)
        routing_weights, selected_experts = sparsemixer(
            router_logits, top_k=2, jitter_eps=self.router_jitter_noise,
            training=self.training)

        final_hidden_states = torch.zeros(
            (batch_size * sequence_length, hidden_dim),
            dtype=hidden_states.dtype, device=hidden_states.device)

        expert_mask = torch.nn.functional.one_hot(
            selected_experts, num_classes=self.num_experts).permute(2, 1, 0)

        for expert_idx in range(self.num_experts):
            expert_layer = self.experts[expert_idx]
            idx, top_x = torch.where(expert_mask[expert_idx])
            if top_x.shape[0] == 0:
                continue

            current_state = hidden_states[None, top_x.tolist()].reshape(-1,
hidden_dim)
            current_hidden_states = expert_layer(current_state) * \
                routing_weights[top_x.tolist(), idx.tolist(), None]
            final_hidden_states.index_add_(0, top_x,
current_hidden_states.to(hidden_states.dtype))

        return final_hidden_states.reshape(batch_size, sequence_length,
hidden_dim), router_logits
```

The routing process has four steps. First, a gate layer computes routing logits for each token over all experts—essentially asking "which experts should handle this token?" Second, the top-k experts (typically k=2) are selected based on these logits, and routing weights are computed to determine how much each expert's output should contribute. Third, each selected expert processes its assigned tokens. Finally, the expert outputs are aggregated, weighted by the routing scores, to produce the final output for each token.

How Expert Parallelism modifies behavior

Without the EP flag, vLLM handles MoE models by sharding each expert's weights across GPUs using tensor parallelism—every GPU has a piece of every expert. With EP enabled, the distribution changes: each GPU holds complete experts, but only a subset of them. The formula is straightforward: `EP_SIZE = TP_SIZE × DP_SIZE`, and each GPU holds `Total_Experts / EP_SIZE` complete experts.

Consider DeepSeek-R1 with its 256 routed experts. With `TP=8, DP=1` and EP enabled, each of the 8 GPUs holds 32 complete experts. With `TP=1, DP=8` and EP enabled, the same distribution occurs—32 experts per GPU—but the communication pattern changes. TP+EP uses all-reduce (same as TP without EP), while DP+EP uses all-to-all communication to route tokens to the GPUs holding their selected experts.

The choice between TP+EP and DP+EP also affects KV cache layout. Under standard multi-head or grouped-query attention, tensor parallelism shards KV cache by head—each TP rank stores only its slice. DP+EP partitions cache by request instead. MLA and MQA models are different: tensor parallelism can replicate the compressed latent cache on every rank, which is why DP+EP is often the better fit for memory-heavy MoE deployments like DeepSeek.

When should you use EP? The flag provides benefits when expert activation density is high enough (>3%) that the all-to-all communication overhead is offset by memory bandwidth gains from distributing experts. For ultra-sparse models (<1% activation), EP may actually hurt performance. The EP flag also requires additional dependencies (DeepEP, pplx-kernels, DeepGEMM) and may not be stable for all model/quantization/hardware combinations—consult the vLLM documentation for your specific setup.

Combining parallelism strategies

Real-world deployments rarely use a single parallelism strategy in isolation. A 405B model might use TP=8 within each node (leveraging NVLink's 600+ GB/s bandwidth) and PP=4 across nodes (where network bandwidth drops to 100-400 Gb/s). An MoE model might combine DP=4 for throughput scaling with EP enabled for efficient expert distribution. Understanding how these strategies interact—and which combinations make sense—is crucial for optimal deployment.

TP + PP: the standard Multi-Node configuration

Tensor parallelism and pipeline parallelism operate along orthogonal axes: TP splits each layer horizontally, while PP splits the model vertically along layers. This orthogonality makes them naturally complementary. The standard pattern is to use TP within nodes and PP across nodes, matching each strategy to the interconnect it works best with.

This combination also reduces inter-node communication. With TP=4 within each node, the data transferred between pipeline stages is only `batch_size × sequence_length ×`

`hidden_size / 4`—each GPU sends only its shard, not the full tensor. For a model with hidden_size=8192, this means transferring 2048 elements per token instead of 8192.

```
--tensor-parallel-size 4 --pipeline-parallel-size 8
```

Expert Parallelism combinations

For MoE models, the choice between TP+EP and DP+EP depends on whether you're optimizing for latency or throughput.

TP+EP distributes experts across TP ranks using all-reduce communication. Every GPU contributes to every request, which suits latency-sensitive workloads at low to moderate concurrency. For MLA/MQA models, the KV-cache tradeoffs above usually favor DP+EP instead.

DP+EP takes a different approach: it enables "DP Attention" where KV cache is partitioned across GPUs rather than duplicated. Each GPU holds cache only for its assigned requests, and experts are distributed across DP ranks using all-to-all communication. This is essential for MLA/MQA models and works well for high-concurrency, throughput-focused workloads.

```
# TP+EP: latency-sensitive, low concurrency
--tensor-parallel-size 8 --enable-expert-parallel

# DP+EP: throughput-focused, high concurrency
--data-parallel-size 8 --enable-expert-parallel
```

One important detail: using `--data-parallel-size` alone (without `--enable-expert-parallel`) for MoE models uses traditional DP with sharded experts, not DP Attention. The EP flag is required to enable the partitioned KV cache behavior.

TP + DP: scaling both ways

When a model needs both sharding (to fit) and replication (for throughput), you can combine TP and DP. Each DP rank contains a complete TP group, so the total GPU count is `DP_size × TP_size`. For example, `--tensor-parallel-size 4 --data-parallel-size 2` uses 8 GPUs: two replicas, each sharded across 4 GPUs.

For MoE models, you can add EP to this combination. The expert parallel size becomes `EP_SIZE = TP_SIZE × DP_SIZE`, and experts are distributed across all GPUs in the combined group. With `--tensor-parallel-size 4 --data-parallel-size 2 --enable-expert-parallel`, experts are distributed across all 8 GPUs.

The EP activation constraint

One subtlety worth understanding: the EP flag only takes effect when `TP_SIZE × DP_SIZE > 1`. If you specify `--enable-expert-parallel` with TP=1 and DP=1, the flag is silently ignored. Additionally, the communication pattern depends on DP size: with DP=1 (TP-only configurations), vLLM uses all-reduce even when EP is enabled; with DP>1, it switches to all-to-all communication to enable the partitioned KV cache behavior.

Hands-On examples

This section provides practical examples for common deployment scenarios. Each example includes the key configuration options and explains when you might use that particular setup.

Basic vLLM setup with Tensor Parallelism

The simplest distributed setup uses tensor parallelism to spread a model across multiple GPUs within a single node. This is the go-to configuration when your model doesn't fit on a single GPU but fits within a single node's GPU memory.

```
# Serve a model with tensor parallelism on 4 GPUs
python -m vllm.entrypoints.api_server \
    --model meta-llama/Llama-2-70b-hf \
    --tensor-parallel-size 4 \
    --port 8000
```

With `--tensor-parallel-size 4`, vLLM shards the model weights across 4 GPUs. Each GPU holds approximately 17.5B parameters (70B / 4), plus its share of the KV cache. The GPUs communicate via all-reduce operations at each layer, so this configuration works best when you have fast interconnect like NVLink between the GPUs.

Multi-Node with TP and PP

For very large models that exceed single-node capacity, combine tensor parallelism within nodes with pipeline parallelism across nodes. This example shows how to serve DeepSeek R1 (671B parameters) across multiple nodes.

```
# Serve DeepSeek R1 with combined parallelism
python -m vllm.entrypoints.api_server \
    --model deepseek-ai/DeepSeek-R1 \
    --tensor-parallel-size 4 \
    --pipeline-parallel-size 8 \
    --enable-chunked-prefill \
```

```
    --max-num-batched-tokens 2048 \
    --port 8000
```

This configuration uses 32 GPUs total (4 TP × 8 PP). Each pipeline stage holds roughly 84B parameters (671B / 8), sharded across 4 GPUs within that stage. Chunked prefill (`--enable-chunked-prefill`) interleaves long prompts with decode work; `--max-num-batched-tokens 2048` caps how many prompt tokens are processed per step—without this, one long prompt can stall the pipeline while other requests wait.

Custom chunked prefill configuration

For offline batch inference or when you need fine-grained control over the engine configuration, use the Python API directly. This example shows how to configure chunked prefill programmatically.

```
# vLLM configuration for optimal chunked prefill
from vllm import LLM, SamplingParams

llm = LLM(
    model="meta-llama/Llama-2-70b-hf",
    tensor_parallel_size=4,
    pipeline_parallel_size=2,
    enable_chunked_prefill=True,
    max_num_seqs=256,  # Adjust based on your KV cache
    max_num_batched_tokens=1024,  # Max tokens per scheduler step; tune for your
prefill/decode mix
)

# Generate text
sampling_params = SamplingParams(temperature=0.8, top_p=0.95)
outputs = llm.generate(["Hello, how are you?"], sampling_params)
```

The `max_num_seqs` parameter limits concurrent sequences, which directly affects KV cache memory usage. With 256 sequences and a 4K context length, you need memory for 256 × 4K × (key_size + value_size) per layer. Setting `max_num_batched_tokens=1024` limits how many prompt tokens the scheduler prefills at once, so long prompts are interleaved with decode steps from other requests.

Profiling with Nsight Systems

Before committing to a parallelism configuration, profile your workload to understand where time is spent. Nsight Systems captures GPU activity, CUDA kernels, and NCCL communication, revealing whether you're compute-bound or communication-bound.

```
# Profile vLLM to understand communication overhead
nsys profile \
    --trace=cuda,nvtx \
    --output=profile.qdrep \
    python -m vllm.entrypoints.api_server \
        --model meta-llama/Llama-2-70b-hf \
        --tensor-parallel-size 4

# Analyze results
nsys-ui profile.qdrep
```

In the Nsight Systems UI, look for NCCL operations (all-reduce, all-gather) and compare their duration to compute kernels. If communication dominates, consider reducing TP size or switching to PP. If compute dominates, you have room to increase TP for lower latency. The profile also reveals pipeline bubbles—gaps where GPUs sit idle—which indicate opportunities to tune chunked prefill or request group sizes.

Best practices

Before deploying, profile your workload with Nsight Systems to understand the communication-to-computation ratio. Tune `max_num_batched_tokens` based on your prefill-to-decode mix: larger values are more efficient for prefill-heavy workloads, while smaller values reduce latency for decode-heavy workloads. Consider your hardware: NVLink makes TP attractive, while PCIe-only systems may benefit from PP even within a single node. Calculate available KV cache space to determine optimal TP size—sometimes more parallelism means more cache capacity, which translates to higher throughput. And remember: what works for one deployment may not work for another. Experiment, measure, and iterate.

Summary

This chapter covered the fundamentals of distributed inference with vLLM, from the memory management innovations that make efficient serving possible to the parallelism strategies that scale beyond single GPUs.

We started with PagedAttention, vLLM's breakthrough contribution to LLM serving. By treating KV cache like virtual memory—allocating fixed-size blocks that can be scattered across GPU memory and reclaimed when requests complete—PagedAttention eliminates the fragmentation that plagued earlier serving systems. The block-based design also eliminates padding FLOPs: attention kernels iterate only over blocks that exist, never wasting compute on padded positions. Together, these innovations enable 2-4x higher throughput compared to traditional approaches.

We then explored the three fundamental parallelism strategies. Tensor parallelism splits each layer horizontally across GPUs, reducing per-GPU memory requirements and latency at the cost of all-reduce communication every layer. Data parallelism replicates the model across GPUs, scaling throughput linearly with zero communication overhead, but requiring each replica to store complete weights. Pipeline parallelism splits the model vertically along layers, enabling multi-node deployments where inter-node bandwidth is limited, but introducing pipeline bubbles that must be mitigated with request groups and chunked prefill.

For MoE models, expert parallelism modifies how experts are distributed and how tokens are routed. Choose TP+EP when you want all GPUs on every request (lower latency); choose DP+EP when you want request-partitioned KV cache and higher throughput—especially for MLA/MQA models.

The decision framework is straightforward: start with the minimum parallelism needed to fit your model (TP first, then PP for multi-node), then add DP to scale throughput. Profile your workload to understand the communication-to-computation ratio, and tune `max_num_batched_tokens` based on your prefill-to-decode mix. Don't set parameters arbitrarily—measure, iterate, and optimize for your specific deployment.

Looking ahead, vLLM continues to evolve with disaggregated prefill/decode (separating the compute-bound prefill from the memory-bound decode onto different hardware), improved EP stability across model/quantization/hardware combinations, and tighter integration with emerging hardware like AMD MI300X and Intel Gaudi.

vLLM's model parallelism approach excels for large models and high-throughput workloads. But what if you need ultra-low latency for interactive applications, or you want to handle thousands of concurrent requests with sophisticated routing and session persistence? The next chapter introduces SGLang, which takes a different approach: rather than focusing on model sharding, SGLang emphasizes request-level routing, prefix caching, and workload disaggregation to achieve different performance characteristics.

Code summary

- `vllm.LLM`: vLLM LLM class for model loading and inference
- `vllm.SamplingParams`: Configuration for text generation sampling

- `vllm.engine.LLMEngine`: Core vLLM inference engine
- `vllm.worker.worker.Worker`: vLLM worker process for distributed inference
- `vllm.engine.arg_utils`: vLLM command-line argument utilities
- `vllm.distributed.parallel_state`: vLLM parallel state management
- `vllm.engine.async_llm_engine.AsyncLLMEngine`: Async inference engine for serving

Useful links

vLLM and PagedAttention

- Efficient Memory Management for Large Language Model Serving with PagedAttention (2023): `https://arxiv.org/abs/2309.06180`
- vLLM Documentation: `https://docs.vllm.ai/`
- vLLM GitHub: `https://github.com/vllm-project/vllm`
- vLLM Roadmap: `https://roadmap.vllm.ai`

Distributed Inference

- vLLM Documentation - Parallelism and Scaling: `https://docs.vllm.ai/en/stable/serving/parallelism_scaling/`
- vLLM Documentation - Data Parallel Deployment: `https://docs.vllm.ai/en/stable/serving/data_parallel_deployment.html`
- vLLM Documentation - Distributed Serving: `https://docs.vllm.ai/en/stable/serving/distributed_serving.html`
- NVIDIA Dynamo KV Cache Manager: `https://docs.nvidia.com/dynamo/archive/0.2.0/architecture/kv_cache_manager.html`

Research

- When to Reason: Semantic Router for vLLM (2025): `https://arxiv.org/abs/2510.08731`
- Distributed Inference with vLLM (Red Hat, 2025): `https://developers.redhat.com/articles/2025/02/06/distributed-inference-with-vllm`

References

1. https://docs.vllm.ai/en/latest/models/supported_models.html
2. Kwon et al., *Efficient Memory Management for Large Language Model Serving with PagedAttention*, 2023.https://arxiv.org/abs/2309.06180

Exercises

Implement KV cache management

Implement a simplified KV cache manager to understand how vLLM manages memory during inference.

Requirements:

- Class signature:

```
class KVCacheManager:
    def __init__(self, num_layers: int, num_heads: int, head_dim: int,
                 block_size: int, num_blocks: int):
        """Initialize KV cache with block-based allocation."""
        pass

    def allocate(self, seq_id: int, num_tokens: int) -> list[int]:
        """Allocate blocks for a sequence. Return block indices."""
        pass

    def free(self, seq_id: int):
        """Free all blocks for a sequence."""
        pass

    def get_cache(self, seq_id: int) -> tuple[torch.Tensor, torch.Tensor]:
        """Get K and V tensors for a sequence."""
        pass
```

- Use block-based allocation (like PagedAttention)
- Track free and allocated blocks
- Support dynamic growth as sequences generate tokens
- Implement defragmentation (optional)

Test your implementation:

```
import torch

# Initialize cache manager
cache_mgr = KVCacheManager(
    num_layers=32,
    num_heads=32,
    head_dim=128,
    block_size=16,
    num_blocks=1000
)

# Allocate for multiple sequences
seq1_blocks = cache_mgr.allocate(seq_id=1, num_tokens=100)
seq2_blocks = cache_mgr.allocate(seq_id=2, num_tokens=50)

print(f"Seq 1: {len(seq1_blocks)} blocks")
print(f"Seq 2: {len(seq2_blocks)} blocks")
print(f"Free blocks: {cache_mgr.num_free_blocks}")

# Free sequence 1
cache_mgr.free(seq_id=1)
print(f"After free: {cache_mgr.num_free_blocks} free blocks")
```

Implement continuous batching

Create a simple continuous batching scheduler that processes requests as they arrive.

Requirements:

- Class signature:

```
class ContinuousBatchingScheduler:
    def __init__(self, max_batch_size: int, max_seq_len: int):
        pass

    def add_request(self, request_id: int, prompt_tokens: list[int]):
        """Add a new request to the queue."""
        pass

    def step(self) -> dict:
```

```
        """Execute one generation step. Return completed requests."""
        pass

    def get_batch(self) -> list[int]:
        """Get current batch of request IDs."""
        pass
```

- Maintain a queue of pending requests
- Add new requests to running batch when space available
- Remove completed requests immediately
- Prioritize prefill for new requests

Test your implementation:

```
scheduler = ContinuousBatchingScheduler(max_batch_size=8, max_seq_len=2048)

# Simulate incoming requests
import time
import random

for i in range(20):
    # Add request with random prompt length
    prompt_len = random.randint(10, 100)
    scheduler.add_request(request_id=i, prompt_tokens=list(range(prompt_len)))

    # Run generation steps
    for _ in range(5):
        completed = scheduler.step()
        if completed:
            print(f"Completed: {completed}")

    print(f"Step {i}: batch size = {len(scheduler.get_batch())}")
```

Benchmark vLLM throughput

Write a comprehensive benchmark for vLLM inference throughput under different configurations.

Requirements:

- Test variables:
    - Batch sizes: 1, 4, 8, 16, 32

  - Input lengths: 128, 512, 1024, 2048
  - Output lengths: 64, 128, 256, 512
  - Tensor parallelism: 1, 2, 4 GPUs
- Measure:
  - Throughput (tokens/second)
  - Time to first token (TTFT)
  - Time per output token (TPOT)
  - GPU memory utilization
- Generate plots and analysis

Test your implementation:

```
from vllm import LLM, SamplingParams

def benchmark_vllm(
    model_name: str,
    batch_size: int,
    input_len: int,
    output_len: int,
    tp_size: int = 1
) -> dict:
    """Benchmark vLLM with specific configuration."""
    llm = LLM(model=model_name, tensor_parallel_size=tp_size)

    # Generate test prompts
    prompts = ["Hello " * (input_len // 2)] * batch_size
    sampling_params = SamplingParams(max_tokens=output_len)

    # Warmup
    _ = llm.generate(prompts[:1], sampling_params)

    # Benchmark
    import time
    start = time.time()
    outputs = llm.generate(prompts, sampling_params)
    elapsed = time.time() - start

    total_tokens = sum(len(o.outputs[0].token_ids) for o in outputs)
    throughput = total_tokens / elapsed
```

```
    return {
        "throughput": throughput,
        "latency": elapsed / batch_size,
        "ttft": outputs[0].metrics.first_token_time,
    }

# Run benchmarks
results = []
for batch_size in [1, 4, 8, 16]:
    for input_len in [128, 512, 1024]:
        metrics = benchmark_vllm(
            "Qwen/Qwen2.5-0.5B-Instruct",
            batch_size, input_len, output_len=128
        )
        results.append({"batch": batch_size, "input": input_len, **metrics})
        print(f"Batch={batch_size}, Input={input_len}: {metrics['throughput']:.
1f} tok/s")
```

Implement speculative decoding

Create a simple speculative decoding implementation to understand the technique.

Requirements:

- Use a small draft model to generate candidate tokens
- Verify candidates with the target model
- Implement rejection sampling for correctness
- Measure speedup vs standard decoding
- Handle variable acceptance rates

Test your implementation:

```
import torch
from transformers import AutoModelForCausalLM, AutoTokenizer

class SpeculativeDecoder:
    def __init__(self, target_model, draft_model, tokenizer, num_speculative: int
= 4):
        self.target = target_model
        self.draft = draft_model
        self.tokenizer = tokenizer
```

```
        self.num_speculative = num_speculative

    def generate(self, prompt: str, max_tokens: int) -> str:
        """Generate with speculative decoding."""
        pass

    def _draft_tokens(self, input_ids: torch.Tensor) -> torch.Tensor:
        """Generate speculative tokens with draft model."""
        pass

    def _verify_tokens(self, input_ids: torch.Tensor,
                       draft_tokens: torch.Tensor) -> tuple[torch.Tensor, int]:
        """Verify draft tokens with target model. Return accepted tokens."""
        pass

# Test speculative decoding
target = AutoModelForCausalLM.from_pretrained("meta-llama/Llama-3.2-1B").cuda()
draft = AutoModelForCausalLM.from_pretrained("Qwen/Qwen2.5-0.5B").cuda()
tokenizer = AutoTokenizer.from_pretrained("meta-llama/Llama-3.2-1B")

decoder = SpeculativeDecoder(target, draft, tokenizer, num_speculative=4)

# Compare with standard decoding
prompt = "The capital of France is"
speculative_output = decoder.generate(prompt, max_tokens=50)
print(f"Speculative: {speculative_output}")
```

Deploy vLLM with OpenAI-Compatible API

Set up a vLLM server with the OpenAI-compatible API and write a client to interact with it.

Requirements:

- Start vLLM server with OpenAI API
- Implement client for chat completions
- Support streaming responses
- Add request timeout and retry logic
- Measure latency distribution

Test your implementation:

```
# Start server (in terminal)
python -m vllm.entrypoints.openai.api_server \
    --model Qwen/Qwen2.5-0.5B-Instruct \
    --port 8000
```

```
import httpx
import asyncio
from typing import AsyncIterator

class VLLMClient:
    def __init__(self, base_url: str = "http://localhost:8000"):
        self.base_url = base_url
        self.client = httpx.AsyncClient(timeout=60.0)

    async def chat(self, messages: list[dict], stream: bool = False) -> str |
AsyncIterator[str]:
        """Send chat completion request."""
        pass

    async def list_models(self) -> list[str]:
        """List available models."""
        pass

async def main():
    client = VLLMClient()

    # List models
    models = await client.list_models()
    print(f"Available models: {models}")

    # Chat completion
    messages = [{"role": "user", "content": "What is machine learning?"}]
    response = await client.chat(messages)
    print(f"Response: {response}")

    # Streaming
    print("Streaming: ", end="")
    async for chunk in await client.chat(messages, stream=True):
        print(chunk, end="", flush=True)
```

```
    print()

asyncio.run(main())
```

Expected learning outcomes

After completing these exercises, you should be able to:

- Understand KV cache management and block-based allocation
- Implement continuous batching for efficient inference
- Benchmark and optimize vLLM throughput
- Understand speculative decoding and its tradeoffs
- Deploy and interact with vLLM's OpenAI-compatible API
- Analyze inference performance bottlenecks

7

Cross-Request Optimization with SGLang

RadixAttention, structured generation, and request-level routing for low-latency inference

The best way to predict the future is to invent it.

Alan Kay, Computer Scientist

A different philosophy for distributed inference

In the previous chapter, we explored vLLM's approach to distributed inference: model parallelism. When a model is too large for a single GPU, vLLM splits the model weights across multiple GPUs using tensor parallelism (TP) or pipeline parallelism (PP). Workers must synchronize—all-reduce operations for TP, pipeline stages for PP—and the system optimizes for throughput by batching as many requests as possible.

SGLang takes a different approach. It supports TP, PP, and Expert Parallelism (EP) just like vLLM, but elevates *cross-request optimization* to a first-class concern. While vLLM primarily focuses on intra-request execution efficiency (how efficiently a single request is processed), SGLang additionally optimizes inter-request execution efficiency (how requests interact and share resources).

The core innovations that enable this are **RadixAttention**[1] and the **zero-overhead scheduler**. RadixAttention organizes KV cache as a radix tree, allowing requests with common prefixes to share cached computations. The scheduler overlaps CPU work with GPU computation, eliminating idle time. These optimizations work at the kernel and scheduler level, forming the foundation of SGLang's performance.

On top of this execution engine, SGLang introduces **request-level routing** as a scaling primitive. Instead of only scaling through model parallelism (splitting weights), SGLang can scale through request routing (distributing requests to independent workers). A router directs traffic based on cache locality, session affinity, and load balancing. This is particularly effective for workloads where models fit on a single GPU or small TP group.

The combination is powerful for specific workloads. For multi-turn conversations with shared system prompts, RadixAttention's prefix caching combined with session affinity can reduce latency by 2-3x on follow-up requests. But this benefit is conditional—it requires prefix reuse, conversational workloads, and non-batch-dominated scenarios. For batch throughput workloads or very large models requiring extensive model parallelism, vLLM's approach may be more appropriate.

SGLang (Structured Generation Language) emerged from the LMSYS team at UC Berkeley—the same group behind the Chatbot Arena leaderboard. While vLLM focused on memory efficiency through PagedAttention, SGLang's creators asked a different question: how can we optimize across requests, enabling them to share computation and benefit from each other?

The answer led to RadixAttention for cross-request KV cache sharing, XGrammar for constrained structured output, and a zero-overhead scheduler that maximizes GPU utilization. Request-level routing emerged later as a production scaling layer that complements these core innovations.

Prerequisites

SGLang runs on Linux with Python 3.10 or later. You'll need an NVIDIA GPU with CUDA support for GPU-accelerated inference. While SGLang also supports other accelerators, NVIDIA remains the most common deployment target.

Installation

SGLang can be installed using several methods. Docker is the quickest way to try SGLang without installing dependencies locally.

Docker Setup

Pre-built Docker images are available on the SGLang Docker Hub page `https://hub.docker.com/r/lmsysorg/sglang`. These images bundle all dependencies, making it easy to get started.

SGLang supports a diverse range of model types, each optimized for different use cases. Base models like `meta-llama/Llama-3.2-1B` are pre-trained language models that use the `/v1/`

`completions` endpoint for text completion. Chat models such as `Qwen/Qwen2.5-0.5B-Instruct` are fine-tuned for conversations and use `/v1/chat/completions`. Embedding models like `Qwen/Qwen3-Embedding-0.6B` generate vector representations through `/v1/embeddings`. For more specialized tasks, SGLang supports diffusion language models for non-autoregressive generation, multimodal models that accept images and videos alongside text, rerank models for search result ordering, and reward models for reinforcement learning applications. SGLang also accelerates diffusion models for image and video generation tasks.

The SGLang server exposes an OpenAI-compatible API, making it a drop-in replacement for applications already using the OpenAI API format. For a complete list of endpoints with detailed descriptions and usage examples, see the **OpenAI-Compatible API Endpoints** section in the Appendix.

Pull the Latest Image

Pull the latest Docker image. The runtime image requires approximately 16GB of disk space.

```
docker pull lmsysorg/sglang:latest-runtime
```

The `latest-runtime` tag provides a production-ready image with minimal dependencies. There's also a `latest` tag that includes development tools and build dependencies, but at around 35GB, it's significantly larger. For most use cases, the runtime image is sufficient.

Run the Docker Container

The Docker image runs an OpenAI-compatible server. To avoid hardcoding the model name, set it as an environment variable:

```
export SGLANG_MODEL="Qwen/Qwen2.5-0.5B-Instruct"
```

Then run the container:

```
docker run --runtime nvidia --gpus all \
  -v $HOME/.cache/huggingface:/root/.cache/huggingface \
  --env "HF_TOKEN=$HF_TOKEN" \
  --env "SGLANG_MODEL=$SGLANG_MODEL" \
  -p 30000:30000 --ipc=host --shm-size 32g \
  lmsysorg/sglang:latest-runtime \
  python3 -m sglang.launch_server \
    --model-path $SGLANG_MODEL \
```

```
    --host 0.0.0.0 \
    --port 30000
```

SGLang supports Llama, Mistral, Qwen, Gemma, Phi, and other HuggingFace architectures; legacy causal LMs such as `facebook/opt-125m` work too, though chat endpoints expect instruct-tuned checkpoints. Some models require `--trust-remote-code`. See the SGLang documentation `https://docs.sglang.io` for the full list.

Here are some small models suitable for learning purposes:

Model Name	Type	Parameter Size
`Qwen/Qwen2.5-0.5B-Instruct`	Chat/Instruct	0.5B
`meta-llama/Llama-3.2-1B-Instruct`	Chat/Instruct	1B
`meta-llama/Llama-3.2-1B`	Base	1B
`microsoft/Phi-tiny-MoE-instruct`	MoE/Instruct	3.8B total, ~1.1B active
`Qwen/Qwen3-Embedding-0.6B`	Embedding	0.6B
`Qwen/Qwen2-VL-2B-Instruct`	VLM/Multimodal	2B
`BAAI/bge-reranker-v2-m3`	Rerank	0.6B
`jason9693/Qwen2.5-1.5B-apeach`	Reward/Classify	1.5B

To use any of these models, replace the model name in the Docker command. For example, to serve `meta-llama/Llama-3.2-1B-Instruct`, change `--model-path $SGLANG_MODEL` to `--model-path meta-llama/Llama-3.2-1B-Instruct`.

The Docker flags deserve explanation. The `--runtime nvidia --gpus all` flag enables GPU access; replace `--gpus all` with `--gpus '"device=0"'` for a single GPU or `--gpus '"device=0,1"'` for specific GPUs. The volume mount `-v $HOME/.cache/huggingface:/root/.cache/huggingface` shares your local Hugging Face cache with the container, avoiding repeated model downloads. The `--ipc=host` flag allows the container to access the host's shared memory, which PyTorch uses for efficient data sharing during tensor parallel inference. Finally, `--shm-size 32g` sets the shared memory size, which is important for SGLang's KV cache management and RadixAttention features.

Verify the Setup

Once the container is running, verify it's working correctly. First, check that the server is responding:

```
curl -w "HTTP Status: %{http_code}\n" http://localhost:30000/health
```

List the available models:

```
curl http://localhost:30000/v1/models
```

Test a base model completion:

```
curl http://localhost:30000/v1/completions \
  -H "Content-Type: application/json" \
  -d '{
    "model": "'"$SGLANG_MODEL"'",
    "prompt": "The result of 1+1 is",
    "max_tokens": 3
  }'
```

Test a chat model:

```
curl http://localhost:30000/v1/chat/completions \
  -H "Content-Type: application/json" \
  -d '{
    "model": "'"$SGLANG_MODEL"'",
    "messages": [
      {"role": "user", "content": "Hello, how are you?"}
    ]
  }'
```

For deterministic output (same result every time), add `"temperature": 0`:

```
curl http://localhost:30000/v1/chat/completions \
  -H "Content-Type: application/json" \
  -d '{
    "model": "'"$SGLANG_MODEL"'",
    "messages": [
      {"role": "user", "content": "Hello, how are you?"}
    ],
    "temperature": 0
  }'
```

For alternative installation methods (pip, uv, or from source), refer to the SGLang installation guide `https://docs.sglang.io/get_started/install.html`. The documentation also covers model-specific requirements and advanced configuration options.

Overview of the SGLang architecture

SGLang's architecture follows a frontend-backend design pattern. The frontend (API Server) handles client requests, while the backend (SGLang Runtime, or SRT) executes inference. This separation allows the system to optimize each layer independently.

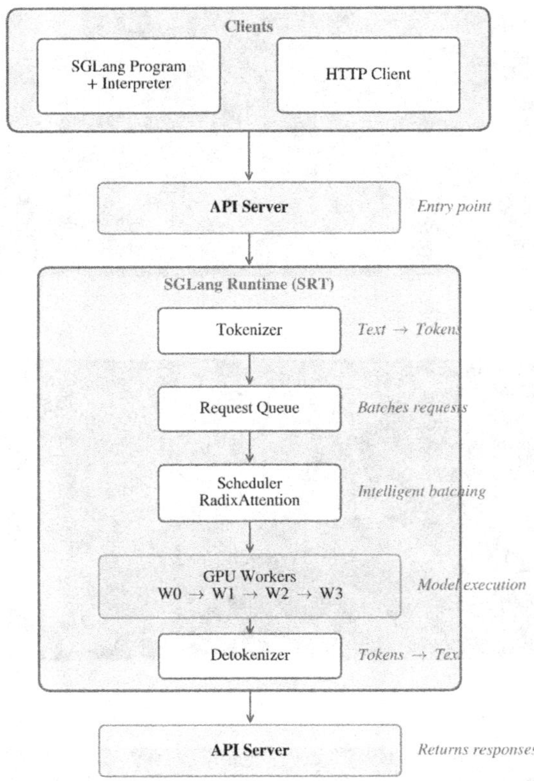

Figure 7.1: SGLang Architecture

Figure 7.1 illustrates the flow of requests through SGLang. Clients (either SGLang programs using the native interpreter or standard HTTP clients) send requests to the API Server, which serves as the entry point. The SGLang Runtime (SRT) then processes these requests through a pipeline of components. The **Tokenizer** converts incoming text into numerical tokens that the model can process. The **Request Queue** buffers these tokenized requests, managing concurrency, and preparing them for batching. The **Scheduler** is where SGLang's intelligence lives—it batches requests intelligently, prioritizes tasks that can benefit from KV cache reuse through RadixAttention, and implements zero-overhead scheduling that overlaps CPU work with GPU computation. The **GPU Workers** execute the actual model inference, and can be organized for tensor parallelism (where workers collaborate on a single request) or as independent workers for data parallelism. Finally, the **Detokenizer** converts generated tokens back into human-readable text, and the response flows back through the API Server to the client.

For distributed deployments, SGLang adds a **Router** (also called Model Gateway) layer above the API Server. The Router distributes requests across multiple SRT instances, maintaining session affinity so that requests from the same conversation go to the same worker (preserving KV cache locality). It includes a control plane for worker management, load monitoring, and health checking, plus a data plane that implements various load balancing policies.

The architectural difference from vLLM lies in optimization focus. vLLM uses a scheduler-executor-worker pattern optimized for intra-request efficiency—PagedAttention for memory management, model parallelism for large models. SGLang's architecture additionally optimizes inter-request efficiency through RadixAttention and cache-aware scheduling. Both systems support TP/PP/EP for model parallelism; SGLang adds request-level routing as a complementary scaling primitive for workloads where models fit on individual workers.

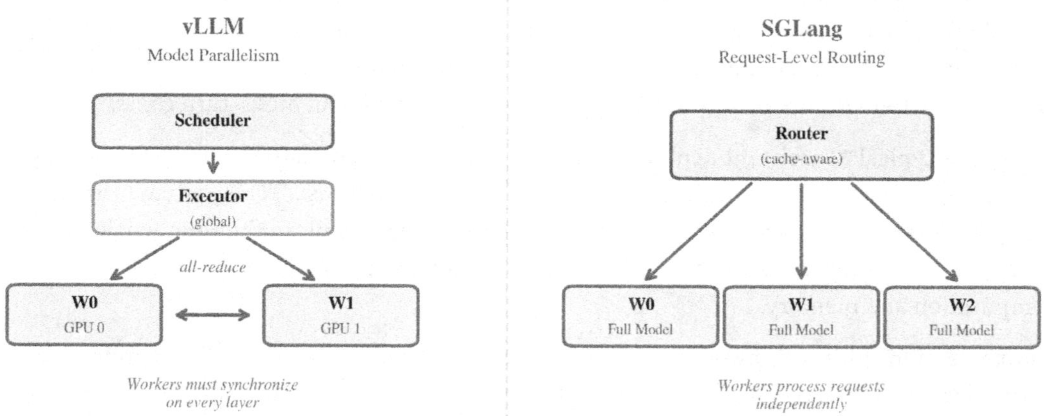

Figure 7.2: vLLM vs SGLang architecture comparison

Figure 7.2 contrasts the two architectural approaches. On the left, vLLM's model parallelism requires workers to synchronize via all-reduce on every layer—necessary for splitting large models, but adding communication overhead. On the right, SGLang's router-based architecture distributes requests to independent workers, each holding a complete model. Workers process requests without inter-worker synchronization, and the router handles load balancing and cache-aware routing. This independence enables horizontal scaling without communication overhead, but requires each worker to hold the full model (or a small TP group).

SGLang core theory

SGLang's performance advantages come primarily from its execution engine innovations. The core technologies are **RadixAttention** for KV cache reuse across requests, a **zero-overhead scheduler** for eliminating CPU/GPU idle time, **XGrammar** for structured output decoding, and **operator fusion** to reduce kernel launch overhead. These kernel-level and scheduler-level optimizations form the foundation, working effectively regardless of deployment topology.

While vLLM focuses on memory efficiency within individual requests (PagedAttention), SGLang emphasizes optimizations that span multiple requests. This makes SGLang particularly effective for workloads where many requests share common patterns—system prompts, few-shot examples, or multi-turn conversations.

RadixAttention: prefix cache reuse

RadixAttention is perhaps SGLang's most distinctive innovation. While vLLM's PagedAttention optimizes memory management within a single request's KV cache, RadixAttention optimizes across multiple requests by sharing KV cache for common prefixes. vLLM's prefix caching (on by default in recent releases) achieves similar reuse by hashing shared token blocks; RadixAttention instead keeps an explicit radix tree and ties prefix lookup directly into batch scheduling. The payoff shows up when many requests share long, identical prefixes—system prompts, few-shot templates, or the early turns of multi-turn chats.

Consider a typical AI assistant deployment. Every request starts with the same system prompt: "You are a helpful assistant. You provide accurate, helpful responses..." This system prompt might be 500 tokens. In a traditional system, if 100 users send requests simultaneously, the system computes KV cache for that 500-token prefix 100 times—a massive waste of computation and memory.

RadixAttention solves this by organizing the KV cache as a radix tree (also called a prefix tree). In this data structure, common prefixes are stored once and shared across all requests that use them. When a new request arrives, the system finds the longest matching prefix in the tree, reuses the existing KV cache for that prefix, and only computes KV cache for the new tokens. As requests complete, shared prefixes remain in the tree for future reuse while unique suffixes are evicted.

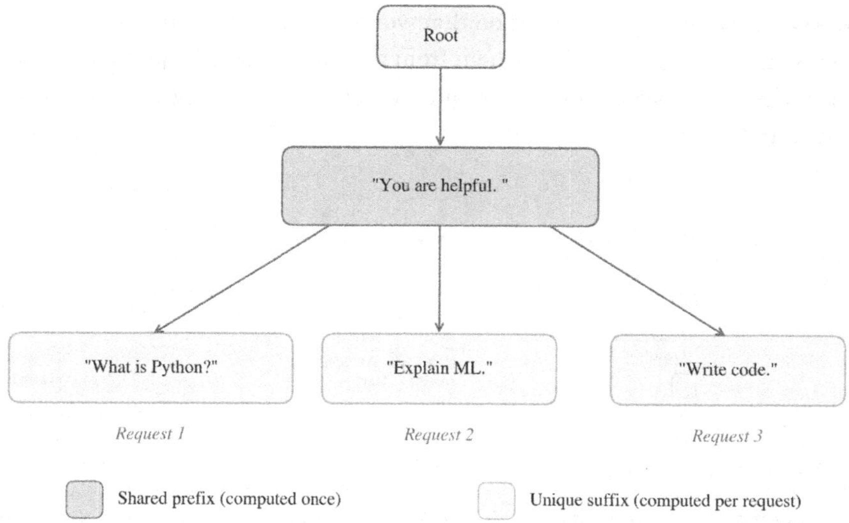

Figure 7.3: RadixAttention prefix sharing

Figure 7.3 illustrates how RadixAttention shares KV cache across requests. Suppose three requests arrive with a common system prompt: "You are helpful. What is Python?", "You are helpful. Explain ML.", and "You are helpful. Write code." The radix tree stores the shared prefix "You are helpful. " once (green node), while each request's unique suffix is stored separately (yellow nodes).

The KV cache for "You are helpful. " is computed once and shared by all three requests. Each unique suffix is computed separately. The savings compound as more requests share the same prefix.

The performance benefits are substantial—but conditional on workload characteristics. For workloads with long shared prefixes (system prompts, few-shot examples, multi-turn conversations), RadixAttention can reduce prefill computation by up to 90%. For workloads without prefix sharing (unique prompts, single-turn interactions), the benefit is minimal. Memory efficiency improves because shared prefixes are stored once rather than per request. Latency drops 2-3x for requests that hit the cache. And throughput increases because reduced per-request memory enables larger batch sizes.

SGLang's scheduler is aware of the radix cache and uses it to optimize batch formation. When selecting the next batch to run, the scheduler sorts requests by their longest matching prefix length and prioritizes requests with longer shared prefixes. This maximizes cache hit rates and GPU utilization.

The cache also integrates with session affinity. When requests from the same session are routed to the same worker, the radix tree on that worker accumulates the conversation history. Follow-up messages in a conversation benefit from the cached KV from previous turns, dramatically reducing latency for multi-turn interactions. But what happens as conversations grow and memory fills up?

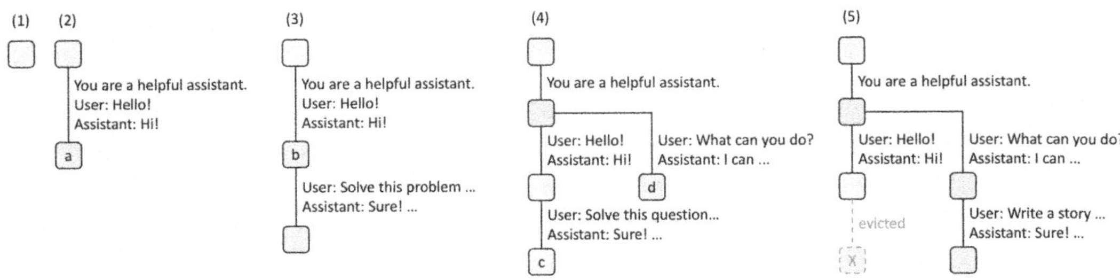

Figure 7.4: RadixAttention tree evolution and LRU eviction-1. Source: Zheng et al., 2023

Figure 7.4, *Figure 7.5*, and *Figure 7.6* trace the lifecycle of a radix tree from birth to maturity. In panel (1), the tree is empty—no requests have arrived yet. Panel (2) shows the first chat session: "You are a helpful assistant. User: Hello! Assistant: Hi!" becomes a single node. When a follow-up message extends this conversation in panel (3), something interesting happens: the tree restructures itself. The original content splits into a shared prefix node and a new branch for the continuation "User: Solve this problem...".

As more users arrive, the tree reveals its true power. Panel (4) shows multiple chat sessions—each starting with "You are a helpful assistant."—branching from a single shared prefix node. One user asks "Hello!", another asks "What can you do?", and a third poses a different question. The system prompt is stored once and shared by all.

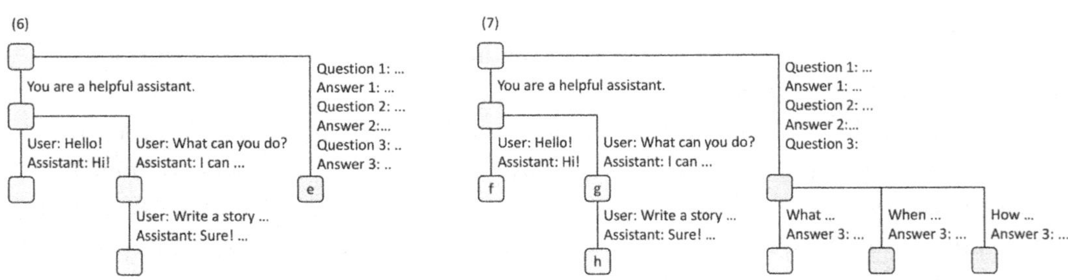

Figure 7.5: RadixAttention tree evolution and LRU eviction-2. Source: Zheng et al., 2023

But memory is finite. Panels (5), (8), and (9) show what happens under pressure. When a new request needs space, SGLang's LRU (Least Recently Used) policy kicks in. In panel (5), node (c) —an older, inactive conversation—gets evicted (marked with an orange dashed box and "X") to make room for "Write a story...".

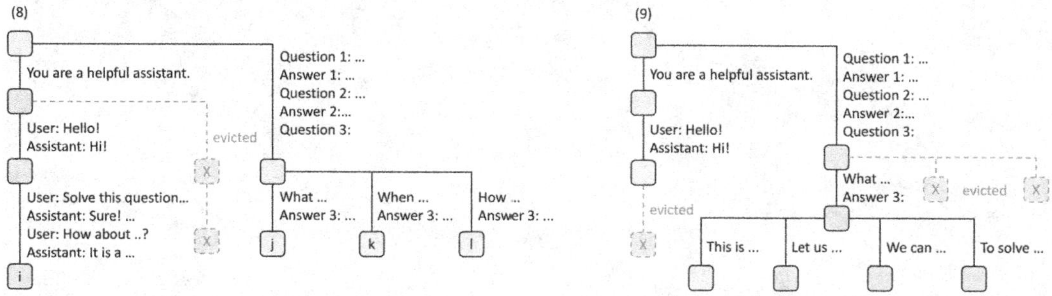

Figure 7.6: RadixAttention tree evolution and LRU eviction-3. Source: Zheng et al., 2023

As pressure mounts in panels (8) and (9), entire conversation branches disappear, but the frequently accessed system prompt and active sessions survive. The tree self-prunes, keeping what matters and discarding what doesn't.

Under the hood, SGLang implements RadixAttention through a two-level memory pool (as of SGLang v0.5). The first level maps each request to its tokens' KV cache indices. The second level stores the actual KV cache data, organized as `[num_layers, max_tokens, num_heads, head_dim]`. The radix tree sits on top of these pools, tracking which prefixes are cached and enabling efficient lookup and sharing.

Structured output decoding with XGrammar

Many applications need LLMs to generate output in specific formats—JSON for API responses, SQL for database queries, or custom schemas for domain-specific tasks. The naive approach to constraint decoding checks each generated token against grammar rules and masks invalid tokens. But with vocabularies of 128K tokens (like Llama-3), checking every token at each step becomes computationally prohibitive.

SGLang routes structured output through **XGrammar** by default, with Outlines and llguidance as alternative grammar backends. XGrammar precompiles valid token sets into finite-state machines for context-free rules—for example, when generating a boolean, only "true" and "false" tokens remain valid. This precompilation covers most tokens in typical JSON or schema constraints. For context-sensitive rules (such as balanced parentheses), it uses pushdown automata with tree-based stack management to avoid expensive stack snapshots.

The result is structured output with guaranteed validity and minimal overhead. Here is the OpenAI-compatible call on a running server:

```
curl http://localhost:30000/v1/chat/completions \
  -H "Content-Type: application/json" \
  -d '{
```

```
    "model": "Qwen/Qwen2.5-0.5B-Instruct",
    "messages": [{"role": "user", "content": "Extract: John is 30 years old, lives
in NYC"}],
    "response_format": {
      "type": "json_schema",
      "json_schema": {
        "name": "person",
        "schema": {
          "type": "object",
          "properties": {
            "name": {"type": "string"},
            "age": {"type": "number"},
            "city": {"type": "string"}
          },
          "required": ["name", "age"]
        }
      }
    }
  }'
```

For offline batch jobs, pass the same schema through `sampling_params` on the Python `Engine`:

```
import json
from sglang import Engine

llm = Engine(model_path="Qwen/Qwen2.5-0.5B-Instruct")
schema = {
    "type": "object",
    "properties": {"name": {"type": "string"}, "age": {"type": "number"}},
    "required": ["name", "age"],
}
outputs = llm.generate(
    ["Extract: John is 30 years old, lives in NYC"],
    {"max_new_tokens": 100, "json_schema": json.dumps(schema)},
)
print(outputs[0]["text"])
```

XGrammar supports context-free grammars broadly—JSON, SQL, domain-specific languages, and other structured formats your application needs.

Operator fusion

Modern GPUs are fast at computation, but each kernel launch carries overhead. Layer normalization, linear projection, and activation as separate kernels mean multiple launches and extra memory traffic. SGLang ships fused CUDA kernels for common transformer patterns —layer norm plus linear plus activation, attention output projections, and MoE routing fused with expert GEMM—so intermediate results stay in registers instead of round-tripping through global memory. For MoE models, specialized kernels combine expert routing with computation to reduce all-to-all overhead.

Zero-overhead scheduler

Traditional inference systems execute scheduling and computation serially: the CPU schedules the next batch, then the GPU computes it, then the CPU processes results and schedules again. The GPU sits idle while the CPU works, and scheduler overhead can consume 50% or more of total time.

SGLang's zero-overhead scheduler eliminates this idle time by overlapping CPU scheduling with GPU computation. The key insight is that while the GPU processes batch N, the CPU can prepare batch N+1 and process results from batch N-1. The GPU never waits for the CPU.

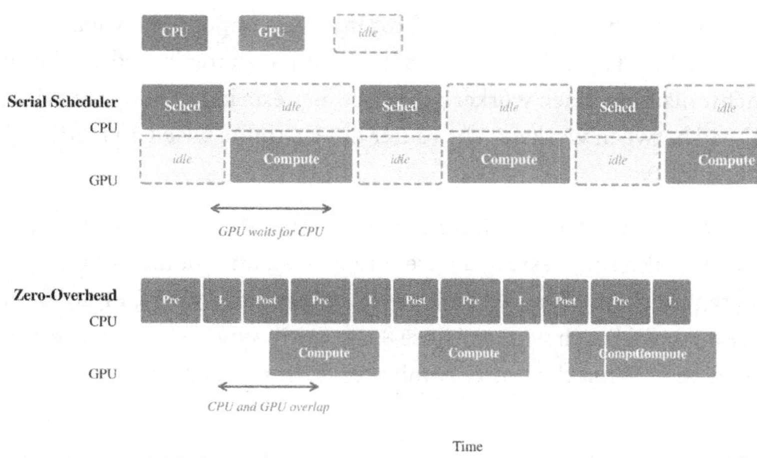

Figure 7.7: Serial vs. zero-overhead scheduler

Figure 7.7 illustrates the difference. In the serial scheduler (top), CPU and GPU alternate: the GPU sits idle during scheduling, and the CPU sits idle during computation. In the zero-overhead scheduler (bottom), CPU work (pre-scheduling, launching, post-processing) overlaps with GPU computation. While the GPU processes one batch, the CPU prepares the next batch and processes results from the previous batch. The GPU never waits.

The scheduler splits CPU work into two logical parts. The "Scheduler CPU" handles pre-scheduling (collecting requests, matching prefixes in the radix tree, allocating memory) and post-scheduling (checking completion conditions, removing finished requests, updating cache). The "Launch CPU" handles kernel launches and result processing. These can overlap because they operate on different batches.

To make this overlap work, SGLang uses a token placeholder mechanism. When the scheduler dispatches a batch to the GPU, it doesn't wait for results. Instead, it allocates placeholder tokens and continues scheduling the next batch. A background thread monitors GPU completion and replaces placeholders with actual tokens when results are ready.

The performance benefits are substantial: up to 2x throughput improvement over serial scheduling, with lower end-to-end latency because the GPU is always busy.

Router-based distributed architecture

Beyond its core execution engine, SGLang introduces request-level routing as a scaling primitive that complements traditional model parallelism. This is not a replacement for TP/PP —SGLang supports those just like vLLM. Rather, routing provides an additional scaling dimension for workloads where models fit on individual workers.

The key distinction: eliminating *intra-layer* synchronization is impossible when using TP/PP—you still need all-reduce for TP, pipeline handoffs for PP. What router-based scaling eliminates is *inter-request* synchronization. Each worker processes requests independently, with no coordination overhead between workers. The router directs traffic based on load, cache locality, and session affinity.

To be precise: router-based architecture eliminates cross-request synchronization (no coordination between workers processing different requests), but not intra-layer collective operations (TP still requires all-reduce, PP still requires pipeline handoffs, EP still requires all-to-all). If you use TP=8 within each worker, those 8 GPUs still synchronize on every layer—the router doesn't change that. What the router eliminates is the need for workers to coordinate with each other.

This is most valuable when models fit on a single GPU or small TP group (2-8 GPUs). For very large models requiring extensive TP/PP across many GPUs, the router adds little value—you're limited by model parallelism anyway. But for smaller models serving high QPS, routing enables horizontal scaling without the communication overhead of traditional data parallelism.

SGLang model gateway architecture

The SGLang Model Gateway (formerly called SGLang Router) is the component that implements request-level routing. It sits in front of multiple SRT instances, directing traffic based on sophisticated policies while providing enterprise-grade reliability features.

The gateway architecture has two main layers: a control plane and a data plane. The control plane manages worker lifecycle—discovering workers, tracking their load, monitoring health, and handling registration/removal. The data plane handles actual request routing across multiple protocols (HTTP, gRPC) with built-in reliability features like retries, circuit breakers, and rate limiting.

The control plane includes several components working together. The Worker Manager discovers worker capabilities and tracks real-time load statistics. The Health Checker continuously probes workers to verify availability, updating circuit breaker state when workers fail. The Load Monitor feeds routing policies with live statistics about pending requests, active sessions, and resource utilization. For Kubernetes deployments, Service Discovery automatically keeps the worker registry aligned with the pod lifecycle.

The data plane implements multiple router types. The HTTP Router handles standard OpenAI-compatible endpoints (`/v1/chat/completions`, `/v1/completions`, `/v1/embeddings`, etc.) with support for streaming and non-streaming modes. The Prefill/Decode Router coordinates disaggregated workloads, merging metadata from prefill and decode phases. The gRPC Router provides higher throughput for performance-critical deployments, with native tokenization and reasoning parser support built in.

For reliability, the gateway implements exponential backoff with jitter for retries, worker-scoped circuit breakers that automatically fail over when workers become unhealthy, and token-bucket rate limiting with queuing. Observability comes through Prometheus metrics (latency, throughput, cache hit rates), OpenTelemetry tracing, and structured logging.

When Router-based architecture excels

Router-based scaling shines in specific scenarios where its strengths align with workload characteristics. High-QPS interactive workloads—chatbot platforms, enterprise multi-tenant deployments, systems handling 100K+ concurrent sessions—benefit most from the router's cache-aware policies that maximize RadixAttention's prefix sharing.

Multi-turn conversations are another sweet spot. Session affinity keeps all turns of a conversation on the same worker, where KV cache from previous messages is already warm. When a user sends "What about Python?" as a follow-up, the worker doesn't need to recompute the system prompt or the previous exchange—it's all cached. Combined with RadixAttention's prefix sharing across users, this can reduce latency by 2-3x for follow-up requests. But this benefit is conditional: it requires conversational workloads with actual prefix reuse. Single-shot prompts won't see these gains.

PD disaggregation lets you scale prefill workers (compute-bound) independently from decode workers (memory-bound). SGLang's router coordinates the two pools and transfers KV cache between them. When a worker fails, the router routes around it—no need to re-shard model weights or restart a distributed group.

That said, router-based architecture isn't universally superior. For batch inference, the router hop adds latency without providing cache locality benefits—you're better off with direct model parallelism. For very large models (70B+) that require extensive TP/PP across many GPUs, the router adds little value since you're constrained by model parallelism anyway. And for throughput-only workloads where latency doesn't matter, vLLM's continuous batching may achieve higher efficiency without the routing overhead.

Prefill/Decode disaggregation

One of SGLang's most powerful distributed patterns is **prefill/decode (PD) disaggregation.** The same split appears across modern serving stacks—DistServe and Mooncake documented the design early; vLLM and NVIDIA Dynamo ship similar modes—but the motivation is universal. Recall from Chapter 6 that prefill processes the entire prompt in parallel (compute-bound), while decode generates tokens one at a time (memory-bound). These phases have fundamentally different resource requirements.

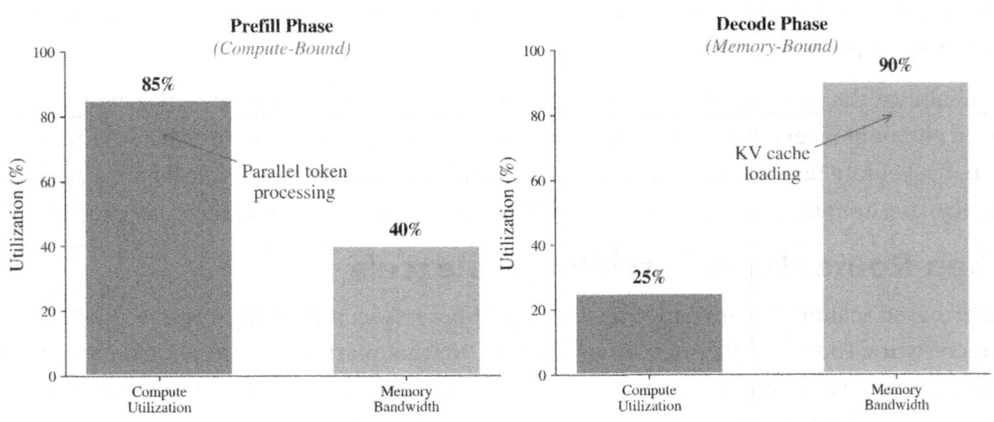

Figure 7.8: Prefill vs. decode resource utilization

Figure 7.8 illustrates why disaggregation makes sense. Prefill processes many tokens in parallel, achieving high compute utilization (85%) but moderate memory bandwidth usage (40%). Decode generates one token at a time, resulting in low compute utilization (25%) but high memory bandwidth usage (90%) as it repeatedly loads KV cache. These opposite resource profiles mean that mixing the phases on the same hardware leads to suboptimal utilization—either compute or memory bandwidth is underutilized at any given time.

In a unified system, prefill and decode compete for the same resources. A long prefill can block decode workers, causing latency spikes for users waiting for tokens. In data-parallel setups, one worker might be doing prefill while another handles decode, leading to inconsistent latency.

PD disaggregation solves this by separating the workloads entirely. Dedicated prefill workers handle initial prompt processing, optimized for compute throughput. Dedicated decode workers handle token generation, optimized for low latency. The router directs new requests to prefill workers, then transfers the KV cache to decode workers for generation.

This is fundamentally different from vLLM's pipeline parallelism (PP), which splits model layers across stages. PP requires strict synchronization between stages—each stage must wait for the previous one. PD disaggregation separates workload types rather than model layers, allowing independent scaling without synchronization overhead.

PD disaggregation architecture

The data flow in PD disaggregation involves both a control plane and a data plane, with the router orchestrating both.

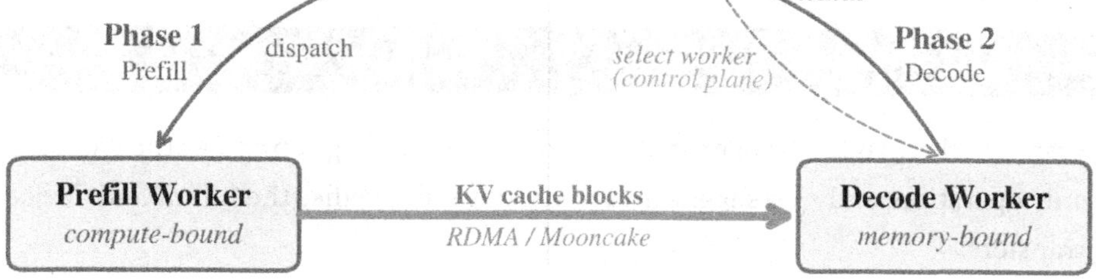

Figure 7.9: PD disaggregation architecture

Figure 7.9 shows the complete flow. A single router handles both ingress and egress. In Phase 1, requests arrive and the router dispatches them to a prefill worker (compute-bound). The router also selects which decode worker will handle generation—this is the control plane (dashed arrow). In Phase 2, the prefill worker transfers KV cache blocks directly to the selected decode worker via RDMA or Mooncake—this is the data plane, a worker-to-worker transfer that bypasses the router. The decode worker (memory-bound) then generates tokens and streams them back through the router to the client. Note that raw prompts never go to decode workers; they only receive KV cache blocks from prefill workers.

The benefits are substantial. You can scale prefill and decode workers independently—add more prefill workers when prompt processing becomes a bottleneck, add more decode workers when generation latency matters. Different hardware can be used for different workloads: high-compute GPUs for prefill, memory-optimized GPUs for decode. Fault isolation improves because failure in prefill workers doesn't affect ongoing decode operations.

Transfer engines

The critical challenge in PD disaggregation is transferring KV cache from prefill workers to decode workers. For long contexts, this cache can be gigabytes of data, so efficient transfer is essential for maintaining low latency.

SGLang supports multiple transfer engines optimized for different network fabrics. **Mooncake** uses RDMA (Remote Direct Memory Access) for direct memory-to-memory transfers without CPU involvement, achieving the lowest latency on InfiniBand networks. **NIXL** provides a UCX-based interface that works across different network fabrics (InfiniBand, Ethernet), offering flexibility at the cost of some performance. **ASCEND** is specialized for Huawei Ascend NPU deployments.

PD disaggregation setup

Setting up PD disaggregation requires starting prefill workers, decode workers, and a router configured to coordinate them. Here's a complete example using the Mooncake transfer engine.

First, install the transfer engine:

```
uv pip install mooncake-transfer-engine
```

Start a prefill worker. The `--disaggregation-mode prefill` flag configures the worker for prefill-only operation, and `--disaggregation-ib-device` specifies the InfiniBand device for RDMA transfers:

```
python -m sglang.launch_server \
    --model-path Qwen/Qwen2.5-0.5B-Instruct \
    --disaggregation-mode prefill \
    --port 30000 \
    --disaggregation-ib-device mlx5_roce0
```

Start a decode worker on a different GPU:

```
python -m sglang.launch_server \
    --model-path Qwen/Qwen2.5-0.5B-Instruct \
    --disaggregation-mode decode \
    --port 30001 \
    --base-gpu-id 1 \
    --disaggregation-ib-device mlx5_roce0
```

Finally, start the router with PD disaggregation enabled:

```
python -m sglang_router.launch_router \
    --pd-disaggregation \
    --prefill http://127.0.0.1:30000 \
    --decode http://127.0.0.1:30001 \
    --host 0.0.0.0 \
    --port 30000
```

For NIXL backend (which works across different network fabrics), replace `--disaggregation-ib-device mlx5_roce0` with `--disaggregation-transfer-backend nixl`.

Distributed inference architecture and parallelism strategies

SGLang's core innovations (RadixAttention, zero-overhead scheduler) work at the execution engine level. For scaling, SGLang supports both traditional parallelism strategies (TP/PP/EP) and router-based request distribution. Understanding when to use each approach—and how they can combine—is crucial for building scalable inference systems.

SGLang supports four parallelism dimensions, which can be combined as needed. **Tensor Parallelism (TP)** splits model weights across GPUs within a node, using all-reduce for synchronization. **Pipeline Parallelism (PP)** splits model layers across GPUs or nodes, using point-to-point communication between stages. **Data Parallelism (DP)** replicates the model across workers, each processing different requests independently. **Expert Parallelism (EP)** distributes MoE experts across devices, using all-to-all communication for token routing.

These dimensions multiply: with TP=8, PP=2, DP=4, and EP=2, you'd use $8 \times 2 \times 4 \times 2 = 128$ GPUs. But the key insight is that SGLang's router-based architecture provides an alternative to traditional DP—instead of replicating models with synchronized training-style data parallelism, you can run independent workers behind a router with no synchronization overhead.

Tensor Parallelism: weight sharding

When a model is too large for a single GPU, tensor parallelism (TP) splits model weights across multiple GPUs. SGLang's TP implementation uses the same Megatron-style algorithm as vLLM —column-parallel and row-parallel linear layers with all-reduce communication—but is tailored to work with SGLang's scheduler and RadixAttention.

The core idea is straightforward: each layer's weights are partitioned across TP ranks, each GPU stores 1/TP of the weights, and all-reduce operations after each layer combine partial results. For attention layers, the QKV projections are split column-wise across ranks. For MLP layers, the up projection uses column parallelism and the down projection uses row parallelism.

The communication overhead is significant: all-reduce operations happen after every attention and MLP layer. This makes TP highly sensitive to network topology—it works best when all GPUs in a TP group are connected via NVLink within a single node. Cross-node TP is possible but requires high-bandwidth interconnects like InfiniBand.

Here's how to configure TP for a single node with 8 GPUs:

```
python -m sglang.launch_server \
    --model-path Qwen/Qwen2.5-0.5B-Instruct \
    --tp 8
```

For multi-node TP (when the model is too large for a single node), you need to specify the distributed initialization address and node ranks:

```
# Node 0
python -m sglang.launch_server \
    --model-path Qwen/Qwen2.5-0.5B-Instruct \
    --tp 16 \
    --dist-init-addr 172.16.4.52:20000 \
    --nnodes 2 \
    --node-rank 0

# Node 1
python -m sglang.launch_server \
    --model-path Qwen/Qwen2.5-0.5B-Instruct \
    --tp 16 \
    --dist-init-addr 172.16.4.52:20000 \
    --nnodes 2 \
    --node-rank 1
```

Pipeline Parallelism: layer sharding

Pipeline parallelism (PP) splits model depth across GPUs or nodes. Unlike TP which splits each layer horizontally, PP assigns contiguous layers to different stages. Stage 0 might handle layers 0-7, Stage 1 handles layers 8-15, and so on.

The communication pattern is simpler than TP: point-to-point transfers between adjacent stages, rather than all-reduce across all ranks. This makes PP more suitable for cross-node deployment where bandwidth is limited.

The challenge with PP is pipeline bubbles—idle time at the start and end of processing when the pipeline isn't full. During startup, later stages wait for earlier stages to produce output. During drain, earlier stages finish before later stages. Various techniques (micro-batching, virtual pipeline parallelism) help minimize these bubbles, but they can't be eliminated entirely.

PP is typically combined with TP: use TP within nodes (where NVLink provides high bandwidth) and PP across nodes (where lower-bandwidth interconnects are acceptable):

```
python -m sglang.launch_server \
    --model-path Qwen/Qwen2.5-0.5B-Instruct \
    --tp 8 \
    --pp 4 \
    --dist-init-addr 172.16.4.52:20000 \
    --nnodes 2 \
    --node-rank 0
```

Data Parallelism: Request-level replication

Data parallelism (DP) replicates the model across multiple workers, with each worker processing different requests. Unlike TP and PP, there's no communication between workers during inference—each operates independently.

This is where SGLang's router-based architecture shines. Traditional DP (as used in training) requires gradient synchronization, but for inference, workers are truly independent. SGLang's router provides intelligent request distribution without any synchronization overhead.

The trade-offs between DP and TP are clear:

Aspect	Data Parallelism	Tensor Parallelism
Memory	Full model per worker	1/TP model per worker
Communication	None (inference)	All-reduce per layer
Latency	Lower (no sync)	Higher (sync overhead)
Throughput	Higher for small batches	Higher for large batches
Scalability	Limited by model size	Scales to very large models

For models that fit on a single GPU, DP with router-based distribution is almost always better than TP. You get lower latency (no synchronization), better fault tolerance (workers are independent), and features like session affinity that TP can't provide.

Here's the simplest DP setup with a router:

```
# Worker 1
python -m sglang.launch_server \
    --model-path Qwen/Qwen2.5-0.5B-Instruct \
    --port 30000

# Worker 2
python -m sglang.launch_server \
    --model-path Qwen/Qwen2.5-0.5B-Instruct \
    --port 30001

# Router
python -m sglang_router.launch_router \
    --worker-urls http://worker1:30000 http://worker2:30001 \
    --policy cache_aware
```

Hybrid Parallelism: combining strategies

Real-world deployments often combine multiple parallelism strategies. The most common pattern is TP within nodes (leveraging NVLink) combined with either PP across nodes or router-based DP.

For large models that require multiple nodes, TP+PP is typical. With 32 GPUs across 4 nodes, you might use TP=8 (within each node) and PP=4 (across nodes). Each pipeline stage has an 8-GPU TP group, and stages communicate via point-to-point transfers.

For high-throughput deployments with models that fit on smaller GPU groups, TP+DP (via router) is often better. With 16 GPUs, you might run 4 independent workers, each using TP=4. The router distributes requests across workers with no synchronization overhead.

For MoE models, expert parallelism (EP) adds another dimension. A large MoE deployment might use TP=4 within nodes, PP=2 across node pairs, and EP=16 to distribute experts. The communication patterns become complex—all-reduce for TP, point-to-point for PP, all-to-all for EP—but the parallelism dimensions are orthogonal and can be configured independently.

Communication patterns

Each parallelism strategy has a characteristic communication pattern. Understanding these patterns helps you choose the right strategy and optimize performance.

Tensor Parallelism uses all-reduce after each layer. Every GPU sends its partial result to every other GPU, and they all compute the sum. The communication volume is O(hidden_size × batch_size) per layer, and it happens frequently—after every attention and MLP layer. This makes TP highly sensitive to interconnect bandwidth.

Pipeline Parallelism uses point-to-point communication between adjacent stages. Only neighboring stages communicate, and they only send activations (not gradients, since this is inference). The communication volume is similar to TP, but the frequency is lower—once per micro-batch rather than per layer.

Expert Parallelism uses all-to-all communication for token routing. Each GPU sends tokens destined for remote experts and receives tokens destined for local experts. The communication pattern is more complex than TP or PP because the routing is data-dependent—different tokens go to different experts.

Router-based DP has no communication during inference. Each worker operates independently, and the router handles request distribution. This is why router-based architecture achieves lower latency for appropriate workloads.

To optimize communication, SGLang supports overlapping communication with computation (enable with `--tp-comm-overlap`), topology-aware placement (keeping TP groups within

NVLink domains), and multiple communication backends (NCCL for general use, DeepEP for MoE, Mooncake for RDMA).

Multi-node SGLang deployment

SGLang supports two fundamentally different approaches to multi-node deployment. For large models that don't fit on a single node, you use tensor parallelism (TP) and/or pipeline parallelism (PP) across nodes—similar to vLLM. For smaller models, you use a router-based architecture with replicated workers on each node—SGLang's distinctive approach.

The choice depends on your model size and workload characteristics. Router-based deployment avoids communication overhead and enables features like session affinity, but requires each node to hold a complete model. TP/PP deployment enables serving models too large for a single node, but adds synchronization overhead.

Multi-node with Tensor Parallelism

For models requiring TP across nodes, you need to configure distributed initialization. The `--dist-init-addr` parameter specifies the master node's address for NCCL initialization. Each node needs a unique `--node-rank` (0 for master; 1, 2, ... for workers), and `--nnodes` specifies the total node count.

Here's an example deploying a model across 2 nodes with TP=16 (8 GPUs per node):

```
# Node 0 (master node)
python3 -m sglang.launch_server \
    --model-path Qwen/Qwen2.5-0.5B-Instruct \
    --tp 16 \
    --dist-init-addr 172.16.4.52:20000 \
    --nnodes 2 \
    --node-rank 0

# Node 1 (worker node)
python3 -m sglang.launch_server \
    --model-path Qwen/Qwen2.5-0.5B-Instruct \
    --tp 16 \
    --dist-init-addr 172.16.4.52:20000 \
    --nnodes 2 \
    --node-rank 1
```

Replace `172.16.4.52:20000` with your master node's IP address and an available port. Both nodes must be able to reach this address for NCCL initialization.

Router-based multi-node deployment

For models that fit on a single node (or small TP group), router-based deployment is usually better. Each node runs an independent worker with a complete model, and the router distributes requests across them.

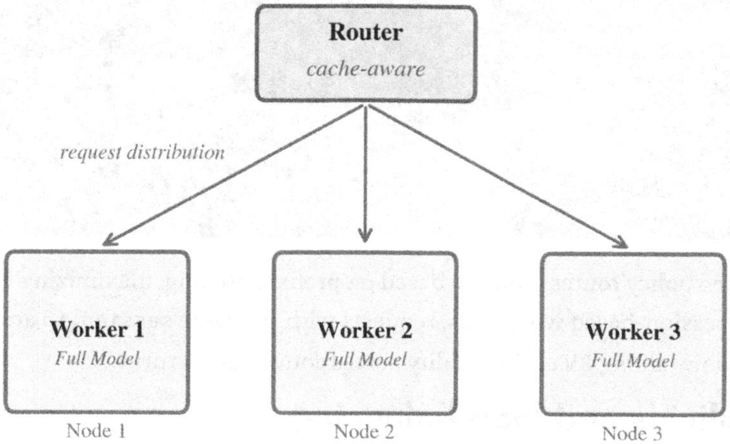

Figure 7.10: Router-based multi-node deployment

Figure 7.10 shows the router-based architecture. The cache-aware router distributes requests across worker nodes, each holding a complete model. Workers process requests independently with no inter-worker synchronization—this is the key advantage over model parallelism, where workers must coordinate on every layer.

The setup is straightforward. Launch a worker on each node:

```
# Node 1
python -m sglang.launch_server \
    --model-path Qwen/Qwen2.5-0.5B-Instruct \
    --port 30000

# Node 2
python -m sglang.launch_server \
    --model-path Qwen/Qwen2.5-0.5B-Instruct \
    --port 30000

# Node 3
python -m sglang.launch_server \
```

```
    --model-path Qwen/Qwen2.5-0.5B-Instruct \
    --port 30000
```

Then configure the router to distribute requests across workers:

```
python -m sglang_router.launch_router \
    --worker-urls \
        http://node1:30000 \
        http://node2:30000 \
        http://node3:30000 \
    --policy cache_aware \
    --port 8080
```

The `cache_aware` policy routes requests based on prefix matching, maximizing RadixAttention cache hits. For session-based workloads, requests with the same `session_id` are routed to the same worker, maintaining KV cache locality across conversation turns.

Router policies and load balancing

The router's policy determines how requests are distributed across workers. SGLang provides several policies optimized for different scenarios.

The **cache-aware policy** is recommended for most workloads. It maintains an approximate radix tree for each worker, tracking which prefixes are likely cached. When a request arrives, the router finds the worker with the best prefix match. If the match exceeds a threshold, the request goes to that worker (cache hit). Otherwise, it falls back to load balancing. This policy maximizes RadixAttention benefits while preventing any single worker from becoming overloaded.

```
python -m sglang_router.launch_router \
    --worker-urls http://node1:30000 http://node2:30000 \
    --policy cache_aware \
    --cache-threshold 0.5 \
    --balance-abs-threshold 10 \
    --balance-rel-threshold 1.5
```

The **round-robin policy** distributes requests evenly across workers without considering cache state. It's simple and predictable, useful when requests don't share prefixes or when you want uniform load distribution.

The **shortest-queue policy** routes to the worker with the fewest pending requests. This adapts to variable request lengths—workers processing long requests naturally receive fewer new requests.

The **power-of-two-choices policy** samples two random workers and picks the less loaded one. This provides good load distribution with lower overhead than checking all workers, a classic technique from load balancing literature.

Session affinity and cache locality

Session affinity is one of SGLang's most powerful features for conversational workloads. The idea is simple: requests from the same conversation should go to the same worker, where the KV cache from previous turns is already warm.

When a request arrives with a `session_id`, the router checks if there's an existing mapping for that session. If so, and the mapped worker is healthy, the request goes to that worker. If not, the router selects a worker using its policy and creates a new mapping.

The latency benefits are dramatic. The first message in a conversation requires full prefill—computing KV cache for the entire prompt. But follow-up messages can reuse the cached KV from previous turns, skipping most of the prefill computation. In practice, this means 2-3x lower latency for follow-up requests in a conversation.

This is something vLLM's model parallelism can't easily provide. In a TP/PP deployment, there's no natural "worker" to route to—the model is distributed across all GPUs. Session state would need to be explicitly managed and potentially transferred between requests. SGLang's router-based architecture makes session affinity a natural consequence of the design.

Fault tolerance

Router-based architecture provides natural fault tolerance. The router continuously monitors worker health through periodic probes to each worker's `/health` endpoint. When a worker fails or becomes unresponsive, the router automatically removes it from the active pool and redistributes traffic to healthy workers.

Circuit breakers prevent cascading failures. If a worker fails repeatedly (typically 5 consecutive failures), the router "opens" the circuit and stops sending requests to that worker for a timeout period. After the timeout, it sends a single probe request—if successful, the worker rejoins the pool; if not, the circuit stays open.

Session migration handles the case where a worker holding active sessions fails. The router remaps affected sessions to healthy workers. The trade-off is that the KV cache must be recomputed on the new worker, so the first request after migration incurs full prefill latency. But subsequent requests benefit from the warm cache on the new worker.

This fault tolerance comes naturally from the architecture. In contrast, TP/PP deployments require all ranks to be available—a single GPU failure can bring down the entire serving group.

Expert for MoE models

We covered the fundamentals of MoE architecture and expert parallelism in Chapters 5 and 6—how tokens are routed to experts, how experts are distributed across GPUs, and the all-to-all communication pattern this requires. Here we focus on SGLang's specific optimizations for MoE inference.

The challenge with MoE inference is that all-to-all communication can dominate runtime, especially at large batch sizes. SGLang addresses this through specialized backends and communication overlap techniques.

For all-to-all communication, SGLang offers multiple backends. DeepEP is optimized for cross-node MoE deployments and is the recommended choice for multi-node setups. Mooncake extends DeepEP with RDMA support for even lower latency on InfiniBand networks. For hybrid EP+TP configurations where you want all-reduce instead of all-to-all, the "none" backend provides that option.

For the actual expert computation (the matrix multiplications inside each expert), SGLang provides DeepGEMM (optimized specifically for MoE patterns), Triton (flexible and portable), and CUTLASS (NVIDIA's high-performance GEMM library). The "auto" setting selects the best option based on your hardware.

A basic MoE deployment looks like this:

```
python -m sglang.launch_server \
    --model-path microsoft/Phi-tiny-MoE-instruct \
    --ep 8 \
    --moe-a2a-backend deepep \
    --moe-runner-backend deep_gemm
```

For larger models like Qwen3-235B, you'll combine EP with other parallelism dimensions:

```
python -m sglang.launch_server \
    --model-path Qwen/Qwen3-235B-A22B \
    --tp 4 --ep 16 --pp 2 \
    --moe-a2a-backend deepep \
    --moe-runner-backend deep_gemm \
    --enable-dp-attention
```

The `--enable-dp-attention` flag is particularly important for models with few KV heads (like those using MLA). It avoids duplicating KV cache across TP ranks, which would otherwise waste memory.

SGLang's most distinctive MoE optimization is communication overlap. Two-Batch Overlap (TBO) splits the batch into micro-batches and pipelines them: while one micro-batch performs all-to-all communication, another runs attention computation. This can nearly double throughput by hiding communication latency behind computation. Single-Batch Overlap (SBO) achieves similar benefits within a single batch using multiple CUDA streams. Enable these with `--enable-two-batch-overlap` or `--enable-single-batch-overlap`.

For best results, keep EP groups within NVLink domains when possible—all-to-all is bandwidth-intensive, and NVLink's 600+ GB/s far exceeds cross-node interconnects.

Speculative Decoding

Speculative decoding is an optimization technique that can significantly accelerate inference. The core idea is to use a smaller, faster "draft" model to predict multiple tokens, then verify them in parallel with the larger "target" model.

Traditional decoding generates one token at a time, with each step requiring a full forward pass through the model. This is memory-bound—the GPU spends most of its time loading model weights rather than computing. Speculative decoding changes this by batching multiple verification steps together.

Here's how it works. The draft model (typically 2-4x smaller than the target) generates N draft tokens quickly. Then the target model verifies all N tokens in a single forward pass. If all draft tokens match what the target would have generated, you get N tokens for the cost of one forward pass—an N-fold speedup. If some tokens don't match, the target model's output is used from the first mismatch point, and the rejected tokens' KV cache is evicted.

In practice, acceptance rates vary based on how well the draft model approximates the target. For well-matched model pairs (same family, same training data), acceptance rates of 70-90% are common, yielding 2-4x speedups.

SGLang supports speculative decoding with configurable draft models:

```
python -m sglang.launch_server \
    --model-path Qwen/Qwen2.5-7B-Instruct \
    --speculative-draft-model-path Qwen/Qwen2.5-0.5B-Instruct \
    --speculative-num-draft-tokens 4
```

The draft and target models should share the same tokenizer and vocabulary. Using models from the same family (like Qwen2.5-0.5B as draft for Qwen2.5-7B) typically gives the best results.

Speculative decoding compounds well with RadixAttention. RadixAttention reduces prefill time by reusing cached KV for shared prefixes, improving time-to-first-token (TTFT). Speculative decoding then accelerates the decode phase by generating multiple tokens per forward pass. Together, they can dramatically reduce end-to-end latency for conversational workloads: RadixAttention handles the prefix, speculative decoding handles the generation.

Data-Parallel attention

Data Parallel Attention (DP Attention) is SGLang's optimization for models with few KV heads, like those using Multi-Head Latent Attention (MLA). The problem it solves is subtle but important.

In traditional tensor parallelism, QKV projections are split across GPUs. But when the number of KV heads is less than the TP size, the KV heads must be replicated across GPUs. For a model with 1 KV head and TP=8, each of the 8 GPUs stores a complete copy of the KV cache—8x memory waste.

DP Attention takes a different approach. Instead of splitting the attention computation with TP, it uses data parallelism: each GPU processes different requests independently, with no KV cache duplication. Before the MLP layer, an all-gather combines the attention outputs from all GPUs. The MLP then runs with tensor parallelism (since MLP doesn't have the KV cache problem), and the outputs are sliced back to each GPU.

The result is up to 1.9x higher decoding throughput for models with few KV heads, because memory isn't wasted on duplicated KV cache. Enable it with:

```
python -m sglang.launch_server \
    --model-path microsoft/Phi-tiny-MoE-instruct \
    --enable-dp-attention \
    --dp-size 8 \
    --tp-size 8
```

DP Attention is most beneficial for large batch sizes where memory efficiency matters. For low-latency, small-batch scenarios, the all-gather overhead may outweigh the benefits.

Production deployment patterns

The right deployment pattern depends primarily on model size. For models under 10B parameters that fit on a single GPU, router-based data parallelism is almost always the best choice—each node runs a complete model, and the router distributes requests with cache-aware routing and session affinity. This configuration typically achieves 50-100 ms TTFT, 1000+ QPS, and 60-80% cache hit rates for conversational workloads.

For models between 10B and 100B parameters requiring 2-8 GPUs, use tensor parallelism within each node and router-based distribution across nodes. Each node runs a TP group, and the router treats each TP group as a single worker. For models over 100B parameters, you'll need TP+PP across nodes, similar to vLLM's approach—the model is too large for router-based replication.

MoE models combine expert parallelism with tensor parallelism. Enable DP Attention if the model has few KV heads, and use TBO/SBO for communication overlap. When prefill and decode have very different characteristics (long prompts with short generations, or vice versa), PD disaggregation lets you scale each phase independently.

A few practical optimizations apply across deployment patterns. For communication, keep tensor parallelism within NVLink domains and configure NCCL appropriately for your network (`NCCL_IB_DISABLE=0`, `NCCL_IB_GID_INDEX=3`, `NCCL_SOCKET_IFNAME=ib0`). For memory efficiency, enable chunked prefill (`--enable-chunked-prefill` with `--max-num-batched-tokens`) for long-context workloads—this breaks long prompts into smaller chunks that interleave with decode operations, avoiding memory spikes, and pipeline bubbles (see Section *Chunked prefill for smoother pipelines* in Chapter 6). Quantization with FP8 or INT4/AWQ reduces memory footprint and can improve throughput. For latency-sensitive workloads, use cache-aware routing and speculative decoding; for throughput-sensitive workloads, scale data parallelism, and enable all overlap options (`--tp-comm-overlap`, `--enable-two-batch-overlap`).

Hands-on examples

With the architectural concepts and optimization strategies in place, let's walk through complete deployment configurations for common scenarios.

Basic multi-node deployment

The simplest SGLang deployment runs workers on multiple nodes with a router for load balancing. This pattern implements the router-based data parallelism architecture described in the *Router-based distributed architecture* section, where each worker holds a complete model and processes requests independently.

```
# Start workers on each node
for i in {1..4}; do
    ssh node$i "python -m sglang.launch_server \
```

```
        --model Qwen/Qwen2.5-0.5B-Instruct \
        --port 30000"
done

# Start router
python -m sglang_router.launch_router \
    --worker-urls http://node1:30000 http://node2:30000 http://node3:30000 http://
node4:30000 \
    --policy cache_aware \
    --port 8080
```

The `--policy cache_aware` flag enables the router's intelligent request distribution based on prefix cache locality. When a request arrives, the router examines its prefix and routes it to the worker most likely to have relevant KV cache entries—this is how RadixAttention's cross-request optimization extends to distributed deployments. Without this flag, the router falls back to round-robin distribution, which still provides load balancing but loses the cache locality benefits.

For production deployments, you'll want to add health checks (`--health-check-interval`), connection timeouts, and potentially TLS termination at the router level. The router exposes Prometheus metrics at `/metrics` for monitoring request latency, cache hit rates, and per-worker load distribution.

PD disaggregation with Mooncake

For workloads with distinct prefill and decode characteristics—such as long prompts with short generations, or RAG applications where context is large but responses are brief—PD disaggregation separates these phases onto specialized workers. This architecture, detailed in the Prefill/Decode Disaggregation section, allows independent scaling of compute-bound prefill and memory-bound decode resources.

```
# Install transfer engine
uv pip install mooncake-transfer-engine

# Prefill worker (compute-optimized)
python -m sglang.launch_server \
    --model-path Qwen/Qwen2.5-0.5B-Instruct \
    --disaggregation-mode prefill \
    --port 30000 \
    --disaggregation-ib-device mlx5_roce0

# Decode worker (memory-optimized)
```

```
python -m sglang.launch_server \
    --model-path Qwen/Qwen2.5-0.5B-Instruct \
    --disaggregation-mode decode \
    --port 30001 \
    --base-gpu-id 1 \
    --disaggregation-ib-device mlx5_roce0

# Router with PD-aware scheduling
python -m sglang_router.launch_router \
    --pd-disaggregation \
    --prefill http://127.0.0.1:30000 \
    --decode http://127.0.0.1:30001 \
    --port 8080
```

The `--disaggregation-ib-device mlx5_roce0` flag specifies the RDMA device for KV cache transfer between prefill and decode workers. This is critical for performance—without RDMA, KV cache blocks must traverse the network stack, adding significant latency. The Mooncake transfer engine handles the zero-copy data movement, as described in the Transfer Engines section.

In production, you'd typically run multiple prefill and decode workers, with the ratio determined by your workload's prefill-to-decode compute ratio. For long-context workloads (prefill-heavy), you might use a 2:1 or 3:1 prefill-to-decode ratio; for chatbot workloads (decode-heavy), a 1:2 ratio may be more appropriate.

Testing session affinity

Session affinity routes consecutive requests from the same conversation to the same worker, maximizing KV cache reuse. This example demonstrates how to use session IDs and measure the resulting speedup—the mechanism is described in the Session Affinity and Cache Locality section.

```
import requests

router_url = "http://router:8080/v1/chat/completions"
session_id = "test-session-123"
model = "Qwen/Qwen2.5-0.5B-Instruct"

# First request creates session and computes KV cache
response1 = requests.post(router_url, json={
    "model": model,
    "messages": [{"role": "user", "content": "Hello!"}],
```

```
    "session_id": session_id
})
print(f"First request: {response1.elapsed.total_seconds()}s")

# Second request reuses KV cache from first request
response2 = requests.post(router_url, json={
    "model": model,
    "messages": [{"role": "user", "content": "What did I say?"}],
    "session_id": session_id
})
print(f"Second request: {response2.elapsed.total_seconds()}s")
print(f"Speedup: {response1.elapsed / response2.elapsed:.2f}x")
```

The speedup you observe depends on the overlap between requests. If the second request's prefix matches the first request's full context (system prompt + conversation history), RadixAttention can skip prefill entirely for the shared portion. In multi-turn conversations with long system prompts, this can reduce TTFT by 50-90%. The router's session affinity ensures these requests land on the same worker where the KV cache resides.

For applications without natural session boundaries (e.g., batch processing), you can still benefit from prefix sharing by sorting requests to group those with common prefixes together, then using the cache-aware routing policy.

MoE model with EP+TP

MoE (Mixture of Experts) models require expert parallelism to distribute experts across GPUs, combined with tensor parallelism for the dense layers. This configuration, detailed in the Expert Parallelism for MoE Models section, demonstrates SGLang's support for hybrid parallelism strategies.

```
python -m sglang.launch_server \
    --model-path microsoft/Phi-tiny-MoE-instruct \
    --tp 8 --ep 16 \
    --moe-a2a-backend deepep \
    --moe-runner-backend deep_gemm \
    --enable-dp-attention \
    --enable-two-batch-overlap
```

The flags break down as follows: `--tp 8` shards dense layers across 8 GPUs using tensor parallelism; `--ep 16` distributes experts across 16 GPUs (with 2 GPUs per expert group in this case). The `--moe-a2a-backend deepep` flag selects the DeepEP backend for all-to-all communication during expert routing—this is optimized for MoE's sparse activation patterns. The `--moe-runner-backend deep_gemm` flag uses fused GEMM kernels for expert computation.

Two additional optimizations are enabled: `--enable-dp-attention` activates Data Parallel Attention (described in the Data Parallel Attention section), which is beneficial for models with few KV heads, like those using MLA or GQA. The `--enable-two-batch-overlap` flag enables Two-Batch Overlap (TBO), which hides all-to-all communication latency by overlapping it with computation from adjacent batches.

Summary

Throughout this chapter, we've explored SGLang's distinctive approach to LLM inference. The key insight is that SGLang doesn't reject model parallelism—it supports TP, PP, and EP just like vLLM. What sets SGLang apart is its elevation of cross-request optimization to a first-class concern. While vLLM focuses primarily on intra-request efficiency (how fast can we process one request?), SGLang additionally asks: how can multiple requests share work and benefit from each other?

The answer to that question led to SGLang's core technical innovations. RadixAttention organizes KV cache as a radix tree, allowing requests with common prefixes to share cached computations. When many users send requests with the same system prompt, that prompt's KV cache is computed once and reused—potentially saving up to 90% of prefill computation for workloads with long shared prefixes. For workloads without prefix sharing, this benefit diminishes, which is why understanding your workload characteristics matters when choosing between systems.

The zero-overhead scheduler addresses a different bottleneck: the traditional serial pattern where GPUs sit idle while CPUs schedule the next batch. By overlapping CPU scheduling with GPU computation—preparing batch N+1 while the GPU processes batch N—SGLang keeps the GPU continuously busy. This is a kernel-level optimization that works regardless of how you deploy the system.

XGrammar tackles structured output generation, a common requirement for applications that need JSON, SQL, or other formatted outputs. Rather than validating each token at runtime—prohibitively expensive with 128K-token vocabularies—it precompiles valid token sets into finite state machines. The result is guaranteed-valid structured output with minimal overhead.

Built on this execution engine, SGLang introduces router-based architecture as a scaling primitive. The router distributes requests across independent workers, each holding a complete model (or small TP group). This eliminates inter-request synchronization—workers don't coordinate with each other, only with the router. Combined with session affinity (routing conversation turns to the same worker) and cache-aware load balancing, this architecture excels for high-QPS interactive workloads where many concurrent sessions share common patterns.

PD disaggregation takes this further by separating prefill (compute-bound) from decode (memory-bound) into specialized workers. The router dispatches new requests to prefill workers, which transfer KV cache blocks directly to decode workers via RDMA. Each worker type can be scaled independently and tuned for its specific resource profile.

When should you choose SGLang over vLLM? The decision isn't about which system is "better"—it's about which optimization focus matches your workload. SGLang shines when cross-request optimization matters: chatbot platforms with shared system prompts, multi-turn conversations where session affinity preserves KV cache, high-QPS deployments where router-based scaling avoids model parallelism overhead, and applications requiring structured output. vLLM excels when you're serving very large models that require extensive TP/PP across many GPUs, when batch throughput matters more than latency, or when single-shot prompts without prefix reuse dominate your traffic.

It's worth noting that vLLM also supports prefix caching and session pinning—the systems aren't mutually exclusive in their capabilities. They represent different design tradeoffs, different answers to the question of what to optimize. Many production deployments use both: vLLM for batch processing and large model serving, SGLang for interactive APIs where RadixAttention and session affinity provide latency benefits. A routing layer directs traffic to the appropriate backend based on workload characteristics.

We've now covered both sides of distributed AI: training systems (DDP, FSDP, DeepSpeed, Megatron) that optimize for throughput and memory efficiency during model development, and inference systems (vLLM, SGLang) that optimize for latency and throughput when serving trained models. The next chapter provides a hands-on guide to running these workloads on HPC clusters using Slurm, the job scheduler that powers most research clusters and cloud GPU providers.

Code summary

- `sglang.Engine`: High-level offline inference API
- `sglang.srt.server.LaunchEngine`: Launch SGLang inference engine
- `sglang.srt.hf_transformers_utils`: HuggingFace transformers integration
- `sglang.srt.engine`: SGLang engine for request processing
- `sglang.srt.server`: SGLang server for distributed serving
- `sglang.srt.model_config`: Model configuration for SGLang
- `sglang.srt.tokenizer`: Tokenizer utilities for SGLang

- `sglang.srt.router`: Request router for distributed SGLang
- `sglang.srt.sampling_params`: Sampling parameters for SGLang generation
- `sglang.srt.server_runner`: Server runner for SGLang deployment

Useful links

SGLang and RadixAttention

- SGLang: Efficient Execution of Structured Language Model Programs (2023): `https://arxiv.org/abs/2312.07104`
- SGLang v0.4: Faster, Longer, and Scalable LLM Serving (2025): `https://arxiv.org/abs/2506.21901`
- SGLang Documentation: `https://docs.sglang.io/`
- SGLang GitHub: `https://github.com/sgl-project/sglang`

Distributed Inference

- SGLang Model Gateway (Router): `https://docs.sglang.io/advanced_features/router.html`
- PD Disaggregation: `https://docs.sglang.io/advanced_features/pd_disaggregation.html`
- Expert Parallelism: `https://docs.sglang.io/advanced_features/expert_parallelism.html`
- Multi-Node Deployment: `https://docs.sglang.io/references/multi_node_deployment/multi_node.html`

Structured Output and Constrained Decoding

- XGrammar: Flexible and Efficient Structured Generation Engine for Large Language Models (2024): `https://arxiv.org/abs/2411.15100`
- Constrained Decoding in SGLang: `https://github.com/zhaochenyang20/Awesome-ML-SYS-Tutorial/tree/main/sglang/constraint-decoding`
- Understanding Constraint Decoding: `https://www.aidancooper.co.uk/constrained-decoding/`

Tutorials and Walkthroughs

- SGLang Code Walk Through: `https://github.com/zhaochenyang20/Awesome-ML-SYS-Tutorial/blob/main/sglang/code-walk-through/readme.md`

- SGLang Scheduler Evolution: `https://github.com/zhaochenyang20/Awesome-ML-SYS-Tutorial/blob/main/sglang/scheduler-evolution/SGLang%20Scheduler%20Evolution.md`
- Why SGLang is a Game-Changer for LLM Workflows (Hugging Face, 2025): `https://huggingface.co/blog/paresh2806/sglang-efficient-llm-workflows`
- Use Cases Favoring vLLM vs SGLang (2025): `https://kanerika.com/blogs/sglang-vs-vllm/`

Reference

1. SGLang: Efficient Execution of Structured Language Model Programs. `https://arxiv.org/abs/2312.07104`

Exercises

Implement RadixAttention cache

Implement a simplified RadixAttention cache to understand SGLang's prefix caching mechanism.

Requirements:

- Class signature:

```
class RadixCache:
    def __init__(self, max_size: int):
        """Initialize radix tree cache."""
        pass

    def insert(self, token_ids: list[int], kv_cache: torch.Tensor) -> int:
        """Insert KV cache for token sequence. Return cache ID."""
        pass

    def lookup(self, token_ids: list[int]) -> tuple[int, torch.Tensor |
None]:
        """Find longest matching prefix. Return (match_length,
kv_cache)."""
        pass

    def evict(self, num_entries: int):
```

```
        """Evict least recently used entries."""
        pass
```

- Use a trie (prefix tree) structure
- Store KV cache at each node
- Implement LRU eviction policy
- Track cache hit rate

Test your implementation:

```
import torch

cache = RadixCache(max_size=1000)

# Insert some sequences
seq1 = [1, 2, 3, 4, 5]
seq2 = [1, 2, 3, 6, 7]
seq3 = [1, 2, 8, 9]

kv1 = torch.randn(5, 32, 128)  # 5 tokens, 32 heads, 128 dim
kv2 = torch.randn(5, 32, 128)
kv3 = torch.randn(4, 32, 128)

cache.insert(seq1, kv1)
cache.insert(seq2, kv2)
cache.insert(seq3, kv3)

# Test lookup
test_seq = [1, 2, 3, 4, 10, 11]
match_len, kv = cache.lookup(test_seq)
print(f"Query: {test_seq}")
print(f"Match length: {match_len}")  # Should be 4 (prefix [1,2,3,4])
print(f"KV cache shape: {kv.shape if kv is not None else None}")
```

Benchmark prefix caching

Compare SGLang's prefix caching performance against vLLM for workloads with shared prefixes.

Requirements:

- Create test workloads with varying prefix sharing:
    - No sharing (random prompts)
    - Moderate sharing (same system prompt)
    - High sharing (few-shot examples)
- Measure:
    - Time to first token (TTFT)
    - Cache hit rate
    - Memory usage
    - Overall throughput
- Generate comparison plots

Test your implementation:

```
import sglang as sgl
from vllm import LLM

def create_shared_prefix_workload(num_requests: int, prefix_len: int, unique_len:
int):
    """Create workload with shared prefix."""
    shared_prefix = "You are a helpful assistant. " * (prefix_len // 30)
    prompts = [
        shared_prefix + f"Question {i}: What is {i}?"
        for i in range(num_requests)
    ]
    return prompts

def benchmark_sglang(prompts: list[str]) -> dict:
    """Benchmark SGLang with prefix caching."""
    # Initialize SGLang runtime
    runtime = sgl.Runtime(model_path="Qwen/Qwen2.5-0.5B-Instruct")

    import time
    start = time.time()

    # Process requests
    for prompt in prompts:
        response = runtime.generate(prompt, max_new_tokens=50)
```

```
    elapsed = time.time() - start

    return {
        "total_time": elapsed,
        "cache_hit_rate": runtime.get_cache_stats()["hit_rate"],
    }

# Compare with different prefix sharing levels
for prefix_len in [0, 100, 500, 1000]:
    prompts = create_shared_prefix_workload(100, prefix_len, unique_len=50)

    sglang_results = benchmark_sglang(prompts)
    print(f"Prefix={prefix_len}: SGLang time={sglang_results['total_time']:.2f}s,
"
          f"hit_rate={sglang_results['cache_hit_rate']:.2%}")
```

Implementing constrained decoding

Create a constrained decoding implementation that enforces JSON schema output.

Requirements:

- Support JSON schema constraints
- Implement grammar-based token filtering
- Handle nested structures (objects, arrays)
- Measure overhead vs. unconstrained decoding

Test your implementation:

```
import sglang as sgl
from pydantic import BaseModel

class Person(BaseModel):
    name: str
    age: int
    occupation: str

@sgl.function
def extract_person(s, text: str):
    s += "Extract person information from: " + text + "\n"
    s += "Output JSON:\n"
```

```
    s += sgl.gen("json_output", max_tokens=200, regex=Person.model_json_schema())

# Test constrained decoding
runtime = sgl.Runtime(model_path="Qwen/Qwen2.5-0.5B-Instruct")

text = "John Smith is a 35-year-old software engineer."
state = extract_person.run(text=text)

print(f"Output: {state['json_output']}")

# Validate output
try:
    person = Person.model_validate_json(state['json_output'])
    print(f"Parsed: name={person.name}, age={person.age},
occupation={person.occupation}")
except Exception as e:
    print(f"Validation failed: {e}")
```

Implement Multi-turn conversation with state

Build a multi-turn conversation system using SGLang's state management.

Requirements:

- Maintain conversation history efficiently
- Reuse KV cache across turns
- Support branching conversations (explore multiple responses)
- Measure memory efficiency vs. naive approach

Test your implementation:

```
import sglang as sgl

@sgl.function
def multi_turn_chat(s, system_prompt: str):
    s += sgl.system(system_prompt)

    # First turn
    s += sgl.user("What is machine learning?")
    s += sgl.assistant(sgl.gen("response1", max_tokens=200))

    # Second turn (reuses KV cache from first turn)
```

```
    s += sgl.user("Can you give me a simple example?")
    s += sgl.assistant(sgl.gen("response2", max_tokens=200))

    # Third turn
    s += sgl.user("How is it different from traditional programming?")
    s += sgl.assistant(sgl.gen("response3", max_tokens=200))

# Run multi-turn conversation
runtime = sgl.Runtime(model_path="Qwen/Qwen2.5-0.5B-Instruct")

state = multi_turn_chat.run(
    system_prompt="You are a helpful AI assistant that explains concepts clearly."
)

print("Turn 1:", state["response1"][:100], "...")
print("Turn 2:", state["response2"][:100], "...")
print("Turn 3:", state["response3"][:100], "...")

# Check cache efficiency
print(f"Cache stats: {runtime.get_cache_stats()}")
```

Implement parallel generation with fork

Use SGLang's fork mechanism to generate multiple responses in parallel.

Requirements:

- Fork conversation state to explore multiple paths
- Generate diverse responses with different parameters
- Implement best-of-N selection
- Measure speedup vs. sequential generation

Test your implementation:

```
import sglang as sgl

@sgl.function
def parallel_generation(s, prompt: str, num_samples: int = 4):
    s += sgl.user(prompt)

    # Fork to generate multiple responses
    forks = s.fork(num_samples)
```

```
    for i, fork in enumerate(forks):
        fork += sgl.assistant(
            sgl.gen(f"response_{i}", max_tokens=200, temperature=0.8)
        )

    # Join forks
    s += sgl.join(forks)

@sgl.function
def best_of_n(s, prompt: str, n: int = 4):
    """Generate N responses and select the best one."""
    s += sgl.user(prompt)

    # Generate N candidates
    forks = s.fork(n)
    responses = []

    for i, fork in enumerate(forks):
        fork += sgl.assistant(sgl.gen(f"candidate_{i}", max_tokens=200))
        responses.append(fork[f"candidate_{i}"])

    # Score and select best (simplified: longest response)
    best_idx = max(range(n), key=lambda i: len(responses[i]))
    s += sgl.select("best", responses[best_idx])

# Test parallel generation
runtime = sgl.Runtime(model_path="Qwen/Qwen2.5-0.5B-Instruct")

import time

# Sequential baseline
start = time.time()
for i in range(4):
    state = runtime.generate("Explain quantum computing", max_new_tokens=200)
sequential_time = time.time() - start

# Parallel with fork
start = time.time()
state = parallel_generation.run(prompt="Explain quantum computing", num_samples=4)
parallel_time = time.time() - start
```

```
print(f"Sequential: {sequential_time:.2f}s")
print(f"Parallel: {parallel_time:.2f}s")
print(f"Speedup: {sequential_time / parallel_time:.2f}x")
```

Expected learning outcomes

After completing these exercises, you should be able to:

- Understand RadixAttention and prefix caching mechanisms
- Benchmark and compare prefix caching performance
- Implement constrained decoding with JSON schemas
- Build efficient multi-turn conversation systems
- Use SGLang's fork mechanism for parallel generation
- Optimize inference workloads with shared prefixes

8

Running Distributed Training with SLURM

Managing GPU resources and coordinating multi-node jobs with SLURM

> *In a room full of top software designers, if two agree on the same thing, that's a majority.*
>
> *Bill Curtis*

Introduction to clusters for HPC and AI training

The previous chapters covered the theory and implementation of distributed training—DDP for gradient synchronization, FSDP for memory efficiency, DeepSpeed for ZeRO optimization, and Megatron for model parallelism. But understanding these frameworks is only half the challenge. The other half is actually running them on real hardware: allocating GPUs across nodes, coordinating processes, managing job queues, and handling the inevitable failures that occur at scale.

Modern AI training happens on clusters—collections of interconnected machines that pool their compute resources. A typical GPU cluster consists of compute nodes (each containing multiple GPUs, CPUs, and memory), a high-speed interconnect (InfiniBand or high-bandwidth Ethernet) linking the nodes, shared storage accessible from all nodes, and a head node that manages job submission and scheduling. The cluster might have dozens to thousands of nodes, representing millions of dollars in hardware that must be shared efficiently among many users and projects.

This shared nature creates a fundamental challenge: how do you allocate resources fairly, ensure jobs don't interfere with each other, and maximize utilization of expensive hardware? In the early days of computing, users would sign up for time slots on a shared machine. Modern clusters use job schedulers—software that accepts job requests, queues them based on priority and resource availability, allocates resources when they become available, monitors running jobs, and cleans up when jobs complete or fail.

Several job schedulers exist in the HPC ecosystem. PBS (Portable Batch System) and its derivatives (Torque, PBS Pro) were dominant in traditional HPC.[1] LSF (Load Sharing Facility) is popular in enterprise environments.[2] HTCondor excels at high-throughput computing workloads where many independent jobs need to be distributed across available machines.[3] Kubernetes has become the standard for cloud-native workloads.[4] But for GPU clusters running AI training workloads, SLURM has emerged as the dominant choice, used by the majority of academic institutions, national labs, and increasingly by cloud providers offering HPC instances.

Why SLURM for AI training?

SLURM (Simple Linux Utility for Resource Management) started as a project at Lawrence Livermore National Laboratory in 2002 and has evolved into a sophisticated resource manager supporting clusters with millions of cores.[5] Several factors make it particularly well-suited for AI training workloads.

First, SLURM has first-class support for GPUs through its Generic Resource (GRES) system. You can request specific GPU types (`--gres=gpu:a100:4`), and SLURM ensures exclusive allocation—no other job can access your GPUs while your job runs. This is critical for training, where GPU memory fragmentation from shared access would cause out-of-memory errors.

Second, SLURM integrates seamlessly with PyTorch's distributed training. When SLURM launches your job across multiple nodes, it automatically sets environment variables that map directly to distributed training concepts: `SLURM_PROCID` becomes the global rank, `SLURM_LOCALID` becomes the local rank within a node, `SLURM_NTASKS` becomes the world size, and `SLURM_JOB_NODELIST` provides the node list needed to establish communication. PyTorch's `torchrun` launcher reads these variables and initializes the process group automatically.

Third, SLURM provides robust job management features essential for long-running training jobs: job arrays for hyperparameter sweeps, job dependencies for multi-stage pipelines, preemption, and checkpointing support for handling time limits, and detailed accounting for tracking resource usage. These features become essential when training runs take days or weeks.

Fourth, SLURM scales efficiently. The same commands and scripts work whether you're running on a 4-node lab cluster or a 10,000-node supercomputer. This portability means skills transfer across institutions and cloud providers.

The integration between SLURM and PyTorch's distributed training is remarkably smooth once you understand the mapping. Your training code doesn't need to know whether it's running on a laptop with 2 GPUs or a cluster with 256—the abstraction handles the details. A job script specifies resource requirements (`--nodes=4 --gres=gpu:8`), SLURM allocates those resources and sets up the environment, and your training script initializes distributed communication using the environment variables SLURM provides.

SLURM architecture: A brief overview

Before diving into usage, it helps to understand SLURM's architecture at a high level. SLURM consists of several daemons that work together to manage the cluster:

- **slurmctld** (controller daemon): The central brain that runs on the head node. It manages the job queue, makes scheduling decisions, allocates resources, and monitors job state. In production clusters, slurmctld typically runs in a high-availability configuration with a backup controller.
- **slurmd** (compute daemon): Runs on each compute node. It receives job allocations from slurmctld, launches and monitors tasks, reports node status back to the controller, and enforces resource limits using Linux cgroups.
- **slurmdbd** (database daemon): Optional but common in production. It stores accounting data (job history, resource usage, user/project allocations) in a MySQL or MariaDB database, enabling fair-share scheduling and usage reporting.

When you submit a job with `sbatch`, the request goes to slurmctld, which queues it and eventually allocates resources based on scheduling policies (priority, fair-share, backfill). Once resources are available, slurmctld notifies the relevant slurmd daemons, which spawn your job's processes and set up the environment variables your training script reads.

SLURM's scheduling algorithms, partition configurations, QOS (Quality of Service) policies, and plugin architecture are rich topics that cluster administrators tune for their specific workloads. This chapter focuses on the **user-facing aspects**—how to submit jobs, request resources, and integrate with distributed training frameworks—rather than cluster administration. For SLURM internals and administration, the official documentation[5] and the SchedMD training materials provide comprehensive coverage.

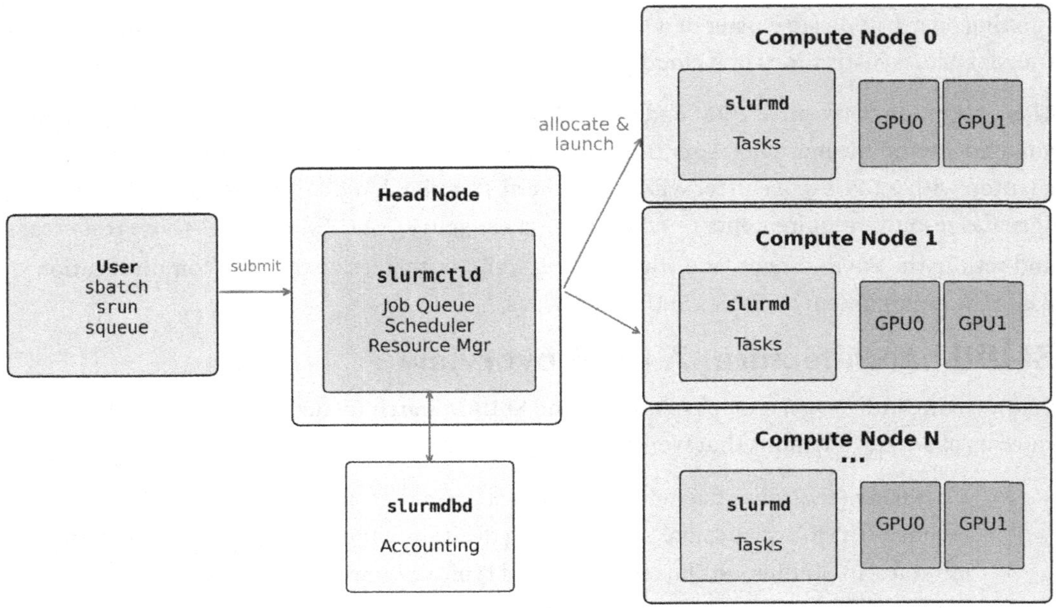

Figure 8.1: SLURM Architecture: slurmctld, slurmd, and slurmdbd daemons

Figure 8.1 illustrates the overall architecture. Users interact with the head node through commands like `sbatch` (submit batch jobs), `srun` (run interactive commands), and `squeue` (query job status). Submitting a new job or starting an interactive allocation goes through slurmctld; once you hold an allocation, `srun` inside it talks directly to the local slurmd daemons on allocated nodes. The controller maintains the job queue, tracks node states, and makes scheduling decisions—when resources become available, it notifies the appropriate slurmd daemons to launch job processes. Each slurmd manages its local node: spawning tasks, enforcing resource limits via cgroups, monitoring process health, and reporting status back to the controller. The optional slurmdbd daemon persists accounting data (job history, resource consumption, user allocations) to a database, enabling fair-share scheduling policies that balance resource usage across users and projects over time.

Setting up SLURM for Multi-GPU training

Most users won't need to install SLURM themselves—cluster administrators handle that. But understanding the configuration helps debug issues when jobs don't behave as expected, and setting up a local test environment is invaluable for developing and debugging distributed training scripts before submitting them to a production cluster.

Simulating a Multi-Node cluster

For development and testing, you can simulate a multi-node cluster on a single physical machine by running multiple SLURM compute daemons (slurmd), each mapped to a different GPU. This lets you test multi-node distributed training code without access to an actual cluster.

The key insight is that SLURM's architecture separates the concept of a "node" from a physical machine. Each slurmd daemon represents one node, and by running multiple daemons on different ports, you can create virtual nodes that SLURM treats as independent machines. The configuration in `slurm.conf` defines these virtual nodes:

```
# Enable multiple slurmd support
# Use $HOSTNAME or $(hostname) to get the actual hostname
NodeName=node6 NodeHostname=$HOSTNAME Port=17016 \
    CPUs=112 RealMemory=240000 Gres=gpu:1 State=UNKNOWN
NodeName=node7 NodeHostname=$HOSTNAME Port=17017 \
    CPUs=112 RealMemory=240000 Gres=gpu:1 State=UNKNOWN
```

Each virtual node listens on a different port (17016, 17017) but shares the same hostname. The `Gres=gpu:1` declaration tells SLURM that each node has one GPU available. The corresponding `gres.conf` file maps these virtual GPUs to physical devices. The paths below (`/dev/nvidiaN`) are NVIDIA-specific; other vendors use different device files—see the SLURM GRES documentation `https://slurm.schedmd.com/gres.html` for your hardware. In this example, we're using an 8-GPU machine and dedicating the last two GPUs (indices 6 and 7) to our virtual cluster:

```
NodeName=node6 Name=gpu File=/dev/nvidia6
NodeName=node7 Name=gpu File=/dev/nvidia7
```

This mapping ensures that when a job requests `--gres=gpu:1` on node6, SLURM sets `CUDA_VISIBLE_DEVICES` to expose only `/dev/nvidia6` to that job. You can adjust the GPU indices to use any available GPUs on your machine—for instance, `/dev/nvidia0` and `/dev/nvidia1` if you want to use the first two GPUs instead. On a real cluster, each physical node would have its own `gres.conf` entry mapping to its local GPUs.

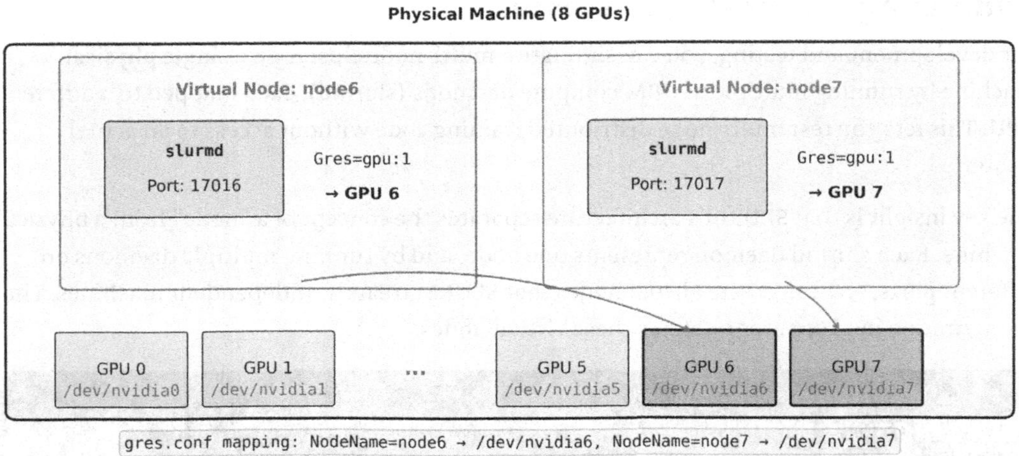

Figure 8.2: Virtual multi-node cluster on a single physical machine

Figure 8.2 shows the virtual node setup. Two slurmd daemons (node6 and node7) run on the same physical machine but listen on different ports. Each virtual node is mapped to a specific GPU through `gres.conf`, allowing you to test multi-node distributed training code locally.

Quick setup and verification

The provided setup script automates the configuration process—creating a SLURM config directory, writing `slurm.conf` and `gres.conf` for the virtual nodes, initializing state directories, and starting `slurmctld` plus one `slurmd` per virtual node:

```
cd code
bash slurm_setup.sh
```

Once the daemons are running, verify the cluster is working correctly. First, add SLURM to your PATH (replace `$SLURM_PREFIX` with your installation prefix, typically `/opt/slurm` or `$HOME/slurm`):

```
export PATH=$SLURM_PREFIX/bin:$PATH
```

The `sinfo` command shows the cluster's partition and node status:

```
sinfo
# Example output:
# PARTITION AVAIL  TIMELIMIT  NODES  STATE NODELIST
# gpu*         up   infinite      2   idle node[6-7]
```

The example output shows a partition named "gpu" (the asterisk indicates it's the default) with 2 idle nodes. For more detailed node information, use `scontrol show nodes`. To verify that jobs can actually run, submit a simple test:

```
srun -N 1 hostname
srun -N 2 hostname
```

The first command runs `hostname` on one node; the second runs it on both nodes simultaneously. If both commands complete successfully and print the expected node names, your SLURM setup is ready for distributed training experiments.

Submitting distributed training jobs

With SLURM configured and verified, the next step is submitting actual training jobs. SLURM provides two primary submission methods: `srun` for interactive execution and `sbatch` for batch submission. Understanding when to use each—and how to structure your job scripts—is essential for productive cluster usage.

Interactive execution with srun

For quick tests and debugging, `srun` executes commands immediately on allocated resources. You specify what you need, and SLURM either runs your command right away (if resources are available) or waits until they become free. The `code/train.py` script is a self-contained example that automatically detects SLURM environment variables, initializes distributed training, and runs a simple 3-layer neural network (`SimpleModel`) on synthetic data (`SimpleDataset`)—useful for verifying your cluster setup:

```
# Two nodes, 1 GPU each
srun -N 2 --gres=gpu:1 --cpus-per-task=4 python code/train.py
```

The flags tell SLURM exactly what resources your job requires: `-N 2` requests two nodes, `--gres=gpu:1` requests one GPU per node, and `--cpus-per-task=4` allocates four CPU cores for data loading and preprocessing—a modest count suited to quick smoke tests. Production batch scripts later in this chapter request more cores (for example 28) when DataLoader workers and preprocessing need the headroom. SLURM finds nodes matching these requirements, sets up the environment, and runs your command across all allocated resources simultaneously.

Interactive execution is convenient for development, but it ties up your terminal and requires you to stay connected. For production training runs that may take hours or days, batch submission is the standard approach.

Batch submission with sbatch

Batch jobs are defined in shell scripts with special `#SBATCH` directives that specify resource requirements. You submit the script to SLURM's queue, and it runs whenever resources become available—even if you've logged off. Here's a typical batch script for distributed training (a runnable version is in `code/train_ddp.sh`):

```
#!/bin/bash
#SBATCH --job-name=ddp-training
#SBATCH --nodes=2
#SBATCH --gres=gpu:1
#SBATCH --ntasks-per-node=1
#SBATCH --cpus-per-task=28
#SBATCH --mem=200G
#SBATCH --time=24:00:00
#SBATCH --output=train_%j.out
#SBATCH --error=train_%j.err

# Get node list and master address
export MASTER_ADDR=$(scontrol show hostnames "$SLURM_JOB_NODELIST" | head -n 1)
export MASTER_PORT=$((29500 + RANDOM % 1000))
export WORLD_SIZE=$SLURM_NTASKS
export RANK=$SLURM_PROCID
export LOCAL_RANK=$SLURM_LOCALID

echo "Master: $MASTER_ADDR:$MASTER_PORT"
echo "World size: $WORLD_SIZE, Rank: $RANK, Local rank: $LOCAL_RANK"

# Run training
srun python code/train_ddp.py
```

The `#SBATCH` directives at the top define the job's resource envelope: 2 nodes, 1 GPU each, 28 CPU cores per task, 200GB memory, and a 24-hour time limit. The `%j` in output filenames expands to the job ID, so each run gets unique log files. These directives are comments to the shell but are parsed by `sbatch` before execution.

The middle section sets up the distributed training environment. The critical piece is `MASTER_ADDR`—the hostname where rank 0 runs and where all other ranks connect to establish the process group. The `scontrol show hostnames` command converts SLURM's compressed node list format (e.g., `node[6-7]`) into individual hostnames, and `head -n 1` extracts the first one as the master. The corresponding Python training script is in `code/train_ddp.py`.

Submit the job with `sbatch`, and SLURM returns a job ID immediately:

```
sbatch code/train_ddp.sh
```

You can then monitor your job's progress through the queue:

```
squeue                          # List all jobs
squeue -u $USER                # List your jobs
scontrol show job <job_id>   # Detailed job info
```

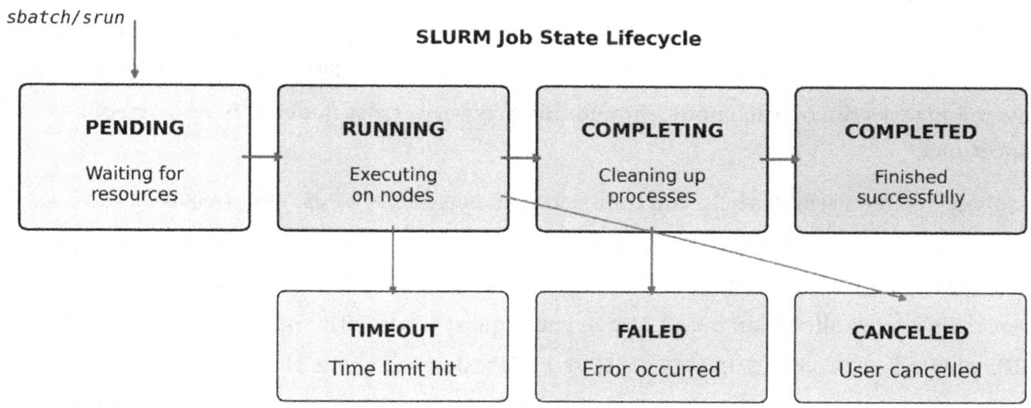

Figure 8.3: SLURM job state lifecycle

Figure 8.3 shows the job state transitions. Jobs start in PENDING while waiting for resources, move to RUNNING when allocated, then COMPLETING during cleanup, and finally COMPLETED on success. Jobs can also transition to FAILED (on error), CANCELLED (user intervention), or TIMEOUT (exceeded time limit). Use `squeue` to see the current state and `sacct` for historical job information.

Understanding SLURM environment variables

When SLURM launches your job, it automatically populates environment variables that your training script can read to configure distributed communication. Understanding these variables is essential for writing portable code that works across different cluster configurations.

At the job level, SLURM provides variables describing the overall allocation. `SLURM_JOB_ID` gives a unique identifier useful for naming log files and checkpoints. `SLURM_JOB_NAME` contains the name you specified with `--job-name` (or defaults to the script name). `SLURM_JOB_NODELIST` lists allocated nodes in compressed format—for example, `node[6-7]` or `gpu-node-[001-004]` —while `SLURM_JOB_NUM_NODES` gives the count. `SLURM_SUBMIT_DIR` records the directory from which you submitted the job, useful for locating config files or data relative to your submission location.

For distributed training, the process-level variables are most critical. Each task launched by SLURM receives `SLURM_PROCID`, a globally unique rank from 0 to NTASKS-1 that identifies this process among all processes in the job. `SLURM_LOCALID` gives the local rank within the current node (0 to tasks-per-node-1), which you typically use for GPU binding—process with `SLURM_LOCALID=0` uses GPU 0 on that node, and so on. `SLURM_NODEID` identifies which node this process runs on (0 to NUM_NODES-1), and `SLURM_NTASKS` provides the total task count, equivalent to world size in distributed training terminology. `SLURM_TASKS_PER_NODE` indicates how many tasks run on each node, though this may vary across nodes in heterogeneous allocations.

Resource-related variables help you tune performance. `SLURM_CPUS_PER_TASK` tells you how many CPU cores are available per task—useful for setting `num_workers` in your DataLoader. `SLURM_GPUS_ON_NODE` reports the GPU count on the current node, and `SLURM_MEM_PER_NODE` gives the memory allocation in MB. When you request GPUs with `--gres=gpu:N`, SLURM's GRES plugin sets `CUDA_VISIBLE_DEVICES` so each task sees only its allocated GPUs—typically remapped to `cuda:0`, `cuda:1`, ... within that task. You usually bind with `LOCAL_RANK` rather than guessing from global rank; this prevents conflicts when multiple jobs share a node.

For establishing network communication, `SLURM_LAUNCH_NODE_IPADDR` provides the IP address of the launching node, and `SLURM_STEP_NODELIST` lists nodes participating in the current job step when using `srun` within an allocation.

The mapping from SLURM to PyTorch distributed training is straightforward: `SLURM_PROCID` becomes `RANK`, `SLURM_LOCALID` becomes `LOCAL_RANK`, and `SLURM_NTASKS` becomes `WORLD_SIZE`. The `MASTER_ADDR`—the address where rank 0 listens for connections—is typically derived from `SLURM_JOB_NODELIST` by extracting the first node's hostname. A typical setup script exports these translations:

```
export MASTER_ADDR=$(scontrol show hostnames "$SLURM_JOB_NODELIST" | head -n 1)
export MASTER_PORT=$((29500 + RANDOM % 1000))
export WORLD_SIZE=$SLURM_NTASKS
export RANK=$SLURM_PROCID
export LOCAL_RANK=$SLURM_LOCALID
```

Once these variables are set, `torchrun` or `torch.distributed.init_process_group(init_method='env://')` reads them and configures the process group automatically. On shared clusters, a fixed port like 29500 can collide with another job and fail with an opaque NCCL error; randomizing `MASTER_PORT` as above avoids most conflicts. This abstraction is powerful: your training code doesn't need to know whether it's running under SLURM, launched by `torchrun` on a single machine, or orchestrated by a cloud provider. The same script works everywhere because it relies on standard environment variables rather than SLURM-specific APIs.

Figure 8.4 illustrates this mapping visually. Your training script can either read SLURM variables directly or use the exported PyTorch-standard variables (`RANK`, `LOCAL_RANK`, `WORLD_SIZE`, `MASTER_ADDR`). The `torchrun` launcher handles this translation automatically when used with SLURM. Note that SLURM provides many additional environment variables for specialized use cases—for a complete reference, consult the `srun` man page or the official SLURM documentation.[5]

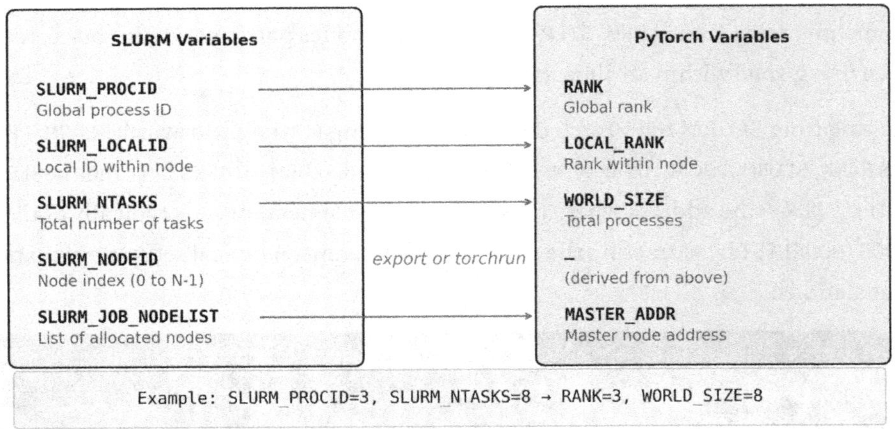

Figure 8.4: SLURM to PyTorch environment variable mapping

Launching distributed training frameworks with SLURM

With the SLURM basics covered, we now turn to the practical question: how do you launch different distributed training frameworks on a SLURM cluster? Each framework has its own launcher and initialization pattern, but they all rely on the same SLURM environment variables we discussed above.

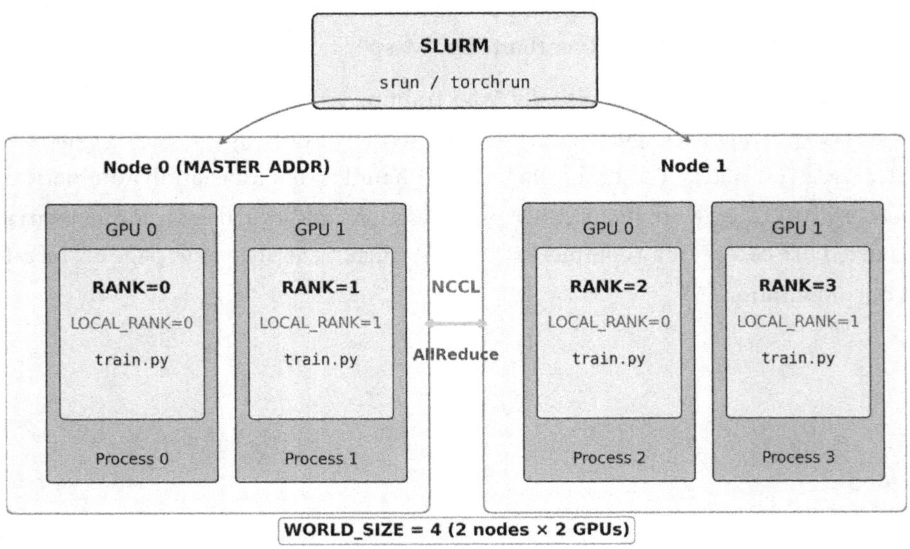

Figure 8.5: Multi-node distributed training with SLURM

Figure 8.5 illustrates the common pattern: SLURM allocates nodes and GPUs, launches processes across the cluster, and sets environment variables that each framework reads to establish distributed communication. The differences lie in how each framework wraps this process.

The table below summarizes the key differences in SLURM integration:

Framework	Launcher	Distributed Init	SLURM Env Handling
DDP	`torchrun` or `srun`	Manual	Export to `RANK`, `WORLD_SIZE`, etc.
FSDP	`torchrun`	Manual	Same as DDP
DeepSpeed	`python`	Automatic	Reads SLURM vars directly
Megatron-LM	`torchrun`	Automatic	Reads SLURM vars directly

"Manual" initialization means you call `dist.init_process_group()` explicitly in your training script and handle environment variable setup in your SLURM batch script. "Automatic" means the framework handles distributed initialization internally—DeepSpeed via `deepspeed.init_distributed()` and Megatron-LM through its own launcher infrastructure—reading SLURM environment variables without requiring explicit setup code.

For detailed explanations of each framework's concepts and internals, refer to the earlier chapters: DDP in *Chapter 3*, FSDP in *Chapter 4*, and DeepSpeed in *Chapter 5*. Here we focus specifically on the SLURM launch patterns and provide complete working examples.

DDP with SLURM

As covered in *Chapter 3*, PyTorch DDP replicates the entire model on each GPU, distributes data across processes, and synchronizes gradients via AllReduce during the backward pass. Because each GPU holds a complete copy of the model, DDP works best when your model fits comfortably in a single GPU's memory. Here we focus on the SLURM-specific launch patterns.

The training script structure is straightforward (full version in `code/train_ddp.py`):

```
import os
import torch
import torch.distributed as dist
```

```
import torch.nn as nn
from torch.nn.parallel import DistributedDataParallel as DDP

def main():
    dist.init_process_group(backend='nccl')
    rank = dist.get_rank()
    local_rank = int(os.environ["LOCAL_RANK"])

    device = torch.device(f'cuda:{local_rank}')
    model = nn.Linear(10, 1).to(device)
    model = DDP(model, device_ids=[local_rank])

    for epoch in range(10):
        # ... training code ...
        if rank == 0:
            print(f"Epoch {epoch} completed")

    dist.destroy_process_group()

if __name__ == '__main__':
    main()
```

The SLURM batch script sets up the environment and launches via `torchrun` (full version in `code/train_ddp.sh`):

```
#!/bin/bash
#SBATCH --nodes=2
#SBATCH --gres=gpu:1
#SBATCH --ntasks-per-node=1

export MASTER_ADDR=$(scontrol show hostnames "$SLURM_JOB_NODELIST" | head -n 1)
export MASTER_PORT=$((29500 + RANDOM % 1000))

srun torchrun \
    --nproc_per_node=1 \
    --nnodes=$SLURM_JOB_NUM_NODES \
    --node_rank=$SLURM_NODEID \
    --master_addr=$MASTER_ADDR \
    --master_port=$MASTER_PORT \
    code/train_ddp.py
```

Alternatively, you can use SLURM's built-in MPI support without `torchrun`:

```
#!/bin/bash
#SBATCH --nodes=2
#SBATCH --gres=gpu:1
#SBATCH --ntasks-per-node=1

export MASTER_ADDR=$(scontrol show hostnames "$SLURM_JOB_NODELIST" | head -n 1)
export MASTER_PORT=$((29500 + RANDOM % 1000))
export WORLD_SIZE=$SLURM_NTASKS
export RANK=$SLURM_PROCID
export LOCAL_RANK=$SLURM_LOCALID

srun python code/train_ddp.py
```

This approach requires your Python code to use `init_method='env://'`, which reads `RANK`, `WORLD_SIZE`, `MASTER_ADDR`, and `MASTER_PORT` from environment variables.

FSDP with SLURM {#sec:slurm-fsdp-example}

As discussed in *Chapter 4*, FSDP shards model parameters, gradients, and optimizer states across GPUs, dramatically reducing per-GPU memory requirements for large models. The SLURM launch pattern is identical to DDP—you use `torchrun` the same way. The difference is in the Python code where you wrap the model with `FullyShardedDataParallel` instead of `DistributedDataParallel`. The example below uses FSDP1's `CPUOffload` helper; on PyTorch 2.4+ with FSDP2, swap in `fully_shard()` and `CPUOffloadPolicy`. As in *Chapter 4*, only the Python wrapper changes, not the SLURM script.

Training script structure (full version in `code/train_fsdp.py`):

```
import torch
import torch.distributed as dist
from torch.distributed.fsdp import FullyShardedDataParallel as FSDP
from torch.distributed.fsdp import CPUOffload
from torch.distributed.fsdp.wrap import size_based_auto_wrap_policy

def main():
    dist.init_process_group(backend='nccl')
    rank = dist.get_rank()

    model = MyLargeModel()
```

```
    model = FSDP(
        model,
        auto_wrap_policy=size_based_auto_wrap_policy,
        cpu_offload=CPUOffload(offload_params=True),
    )

    # Training loop...

if __name__ == '__main__':
    main()
```

SLURM batch script (full version in `code/train_fsdp.sh`):

```
#!/bin/bash
#SBATCH --job-name=fsdp-training
#SBATCH --nodes=2
#SBATCH --gres=gpu:1
#SBATCH --ntasks-per-node=1
#SBATCH --cpus-per-task=28
#SBATCH --mem=200G

export MASTER_ADDR=$(scontrol show hostnames "$SLURM_JOB_NODELIST" | head -n 1)
export MASTER_PORT=$((29500 + RANDOM % 1000))

srun torchrun \
    --nproc_per_node=1 \
    --nnodes=$SLURM_JOB_NUM_NODES \
    --node_rank=$SLURM_NODEID \
    --master_addr=$MASTER_ADDR \
    --master_port=$MASTER_PORT \
    code/train_fsdp.py
```

DeepSpeed with SLURM

As covered in *Chapter 5*, DeepSpeed's ZeRO optimizer provides three stages of memory optimization: ZeRO-1 partitions optimizer states, ZeRO-2 adds gradient partitioning, and ZeRO-3 further partitions model parameters themselves. ZeRO-3 is conceptually similar to FSDP—both shard parameters across GPUs—but DeepSpeed offers additional features like CPU and NVMe offloading that can push the memory boundary even further. The example here uses ZeRO-3 with CPU offloading, but you can easily switch to ZeRO-1 or ZeRO-2 by changing `"stage": 3` to 1 or 2 in the configuration file if you don't need full parameter sharding.

Unlike DDP and FSDP where you explicitly call `dist.init_process_group()` and use `torchrun` as the launcher, DeepSpeed takes a different approach. It handles distributed initialization internally via `deepspeed.init_distributed()`, reading SLURM environment variables directly without requiring a separate launcher. This design simplifies the user experience—you just run `python train.py` with the appropriate environment variables set, and DeepSpeed figures out the distributed topology automatically.

The training script structure reflects this simplicity (full version in `code/deepspeed/train.py`):

```
import torch
import deepspeed
from transformers import AutoModelForCausalLM, AutoTokenizer

def main():
    deepspeed.init_distributed()

    model = AutoModelForCausalLM.from_pretrained("gpt2")
    tokenizer = AutoTokenizer.from_pretrained("gpt2")

    model_engine, optimizer, _, _ = deepspeed.initialize(
        model=model,
        model_parameters=model.parameters(),
        config="ds_zero3_offload.json"
    )

    for epoch in range(10):
        # ... training code ...
        model_engine.backward(loss)
        model_engine.step()

if __name__ == "__main__":
    main()
```

Notice that the script doesn't import `torch.distributed` or call `init_process_group()`—DeepSpeed handles all of that internally. The `deepspeed.initialize()` call returns a `model_engine` that wraps your model with ZeRO optimization, and you use `model_engine.backward()` and `model_engine.step()` instead of the standard PyTorch optimizer methods.

The configuration file controls ZeRO behavior (`code/deepspeed/ds_zero3_offload.json`):

```
{
  "train_batch_size": 2,
  "gradient_accumulation_steps": 1,
  "train_micro_batch_size_per_gpu": 1,
  "fp16": { "enabled": true },
  "zero_optimization": {
    "stage": 3,
    "offload_param": { "device": "cpu", "pin_memory": true },
    "offload_optimizer": { "device": "cpu", "pin_memory": true }
  },
  "optimizer": {
    "type": "AdamW",
    "params": { "lr": 5e-5, "weight_decay": 0.01 }
  }
}
```

The `stage: 3` setting enables full parameter sharding, and the `offload_param` and `offload_optimizer` sections configure CPU offloading when the model exceeds total GPU memory. The `pin_memory: true` option uses pinned (page-locked) CPU memory for faster CPU-GPU transfers. Treat this JSON as a production-scale template—validate NCCL and SLURM wiring with ZeRO stage 1 or 2 first, then enable stage 3 and CPU offload once the job runs cleanly.

The SLURM batch script requires more setup than DDP because we need to manually export the environment variables that DeepSpeed expects (`code/deepspeed/run.slurm`):

```
#!/bin/bash
#SBATCH --job-name=deepspeed-zero3
#SBATCH --nodes=2
#SBATCH --gres=gpu:1
#SBATCH --ntasks-per-node=1
#SBATCH --cpus-per-task=8
#SBATCH --mem=200G

# Replace with your conda path and environment name
source ~/miniconda3/etc/profile.d/conda.sh
conda activate research

export MASTER_ADDR=$(scontrol show hostnames "$SLURM_JOB_NODELIST" | head -n 1)
```

```
export MASTER_PORT=$((29500 + RANDOM % 1000))
export WORLD_SIZE=$SLURM_NTASKS

export NCCL_DEBUG=WARN
export NCCL_SOCKET_IFNAME=^docker,lo
export GLOO_SOCKET_IFNAME=eth0

srun --chdir="$SLURM_SUBMIT_DIR" --label \
    bash -c "
        source ~/miniconda3/etc/profile.d/conda.sh
        conda activate research
        export CUDA_VISIBLE_DEVICES=\$SLURM_LOCALID
        export LOCAL_RANK=\$SLURM_LOCALID
        export RANK=\$SLURM_PROCID
        cd \"$SLURM_SUBMIT_DIR\"
        python train.py --deepspeed --deepspeed_config ds_zero3_offload.json
    "
```

The script sets `MASTER_ADDR`, `MASTER_PORT`, and `WORLD_SIZE` at the job level—derive the master hostname with `scontrol`, not `127.0.0.1`, or each node forms its own one-node process group and gradients never sync across nodes. That failure can stay hidden on the virtual two-node setup earlier in this chapter, where both slurmd daemons share one physical host. `srun` then launches a bash subshell on each node; inside it, we export per-process variables (`CUDA_VISIBLE_DEVICES`, `LOCAL_RANK`, `RANK`) from SLURM's task environment. The `--label` flag prefixes each line of output with the task ID, which helps when debugging multi-node issues.

A few practical considerations when running DeepSpeed on SLURM clusters. DeepSpeed requires the `LOCAL_RANK` environment variable, which you must explicitly export from `SLURM_LOCALID`—unlike `torchrun`, which sets this automatically. If you're using virtual nodes for testing (as described earlier), remember to map node names to GPU indices appropriately—for example, node6 should use GPU 6. IPv6 can cause connection issues on some clusters; setting `NCCL_SOCKET_IFNAME` and `GLOO_SOCKET_IFNAME` to exclude problematic interfaces (like `^docker,lo`) often resolves this. Finally, remember to replace the conda path and environment name in the script with your own setup.

Megatron-LM with SLURM

As introduced in *Chapter 5*, Megatron-LM provides NVIDIA's production-grade framework combining tensor parallelism, pipeline parallelism, sequence/context parallelism, and data parallelism—all composable in a single training run. This multi-dimensional parallelism is essential for training the largest language models where no single parallelism strategy suffices.

Before diving into the SLURM script, there's an important installation consideration (also covered in *Chapter 5*). Unlike PyTorch's built-in DDP and FSDP, Megatron-LM requires installation from source to get the full training infrastructure. The PyPI package `megatron-core` only includes `megatron.core` (the model building blocks), but the training scripts like `pretrain_gpt.py` require `megatron.training`, which is only available when you install from the GitHub repository:

```
conda activate research  # Replace with your environment name
git clone https://github.com/NVIDIA/Megatron-LM.git
cd Megatron-LM
pip install --no-build-isolation '.[mlm,dev]'
```

You'll also need to copy the training scripts (`pretrain_gpt.py`, `gpt_builders.py`, `model_provider.py`) to your working directory, as these aren't installed as part of the package.

With the prerequisites in place, let's look at the SLURM batch script (`code/megatron/run.slurm`):

```
#!/bin/bash
#SBATCH --job-name=megatron-gpt
#SBATCH --nodes=2
#SBATCH --gres=gpu:1
#SBATCH --ntasks-per-node=1
#SBATCH --cpus-per-task=8
#SBATCH --mem=200G
#SBATCH --time=4:00:00
#SBATCH --output=logs/train_%j_%N.out
#SBATCH --error=logs/train_%j_%N.err

# Replace with your conda path and environment name
source ~/miniconda3/etc/profile.d/conda.sh
conda activate research

SCRIPT_DIR="${SLURM_SUBMIT_DIR:-$(dirname "$(readlink -f "$0")")}"
cd "$SCRIPT_DIR"
mkdir -p logs

PRETRAIN_SCRIPT="${SCRIPT_DIR}/pretrain_gpt.py"

export MASTER_ADDR=$(scontrol show hostnames "$SLURM_JOB_NODELIST" | head -n 1)
```

```
export MASTER_PORT=${MASTER_PORT:-6000}
export WORLD_SIZE=$SLURM_NTASKS

export NCCL_DEBUG=WARN
export NCCL_SOCKET_IFNAME=^docker,lo
export NCCL_IB_DISABLE=0
export CUDA_DEVICE_MAX_CONNECTIONS=1
export OMP_NUM_THREADS=$SLURM_CPUS_PER_TASK

# Model and training configuration
NUM_LAYERS=32; HIDDEN_SIZE=4096; NUM_ATTENTION_HEADS=32
TP_SIZE=1; CP_SIZE=1; PP_SIZE=1
MICRO_BATCH_SIZE=1; GLOBAL_BATCH_SIZE=128

srun --chdir="$SCRIPT_DIR" --label \
    bash -c "
        source ~/miniconda3/etc/profile.d/conda.sh
        conda activate research
        export CUDA_VISIBLE_DEVICES=\$SLURM_LOCALID
        export LOCAL_RANK=\$SLURM_LOCALID
        export RANK=\$SLURM_PROCID

        torchrun --nproc_per_node=1 --nnodes=\$SLURM_JOB_NUM_NODES \\
            --node_rank=\$SLURM_NODEID --master_addr=\"$MASTER_ADDR\" \\
            --master_port=\"$MASTER_PORT\" \"$PRETRAIN_SCRIPT\" \\
            --use-mcore-models --num-layers $NUM_LAYERS \\
            --hidden-size $HIDDEN_SIZE --num-attention-heads $NUM_ATTENTION_HEADS 
\\
            --tensor-model-parallel-size $TP_SIZE --pipeline-model-parallel-size 
$PP_SIZE \\
            --micro-batch-size $MICRO_BATCH_SIZE --global-batch-size 
$GLOBAL_BATCH_SIZE \\
            --bf16 --mock-data --tokenizer-type NullTokenizer --vocab-size 128256
    "
```

The script structure follows the same pattern as DeepSpeed: set job-level environment variables, then use `srun` to launch a bash subshell that sets per-process variables and invokes `torchrun`. The model configuration variables (`NUM_LAYERS`, `HIDDEN_SIZE`, etc.) define an 8B parameter GPT model, while the parallelism variables (`TP_SIZE`, `PP_SIZE`, `CP_SIZE`) control how the model is distributed—adjust these based on your hardware and model size. The example uses mock data (`--mock-data`) for demonstration; for real training, you'd provide actual data paths and a proper tokenizer. Remember to replace the conda path and environment name in the script with your own setup before submitting:

```
cd code/megatron
sbatch run.slurm
```

One thing you'll notice when training with Megatron-LM is that checkpoint files can be quite large. For an 8B parameter model, you might see checkpoint directories like this:

```
code/megatron/checkpoints/gpt_8b/iter_0000010/
27G     __0_0.distcp
27G     __0_1.distcp
27G     __1_0.distcp
27G     __1_1.distcp
24K     common.pt
4.0K    metadata.json
```

Why so large? The math is straightforward: model parameters in bf16 consume 8.03B × 2 bytes = 16.06 GB, while Adam optimizer states in fp32 require 8.03B × 8 bytes = 64.24 GB (4 bytes each for momentum and variance). That's already ~80 GB theoretically, and the actual size of ~108 GB includes additional overhead from distributed optimizer sharding, file format metadata, and alignment padding for efficient parallel I/O. Each rank saves its own shard (`__0_0.distcp`, `__0_1.distcp`, etc.) to enable parallel save/load operations across the cluster.

To manage checkpoint storage, consider using `--save-interval` to control how frequently checkpoints are saved, implementing checkpoint rotation to keep only recent checkpoints, and using a distributed filesystem that can handle the I/O load.

Another practical consideration is checkpoint format conversion. Megatron-LM saves checkpoints in a distributed format (`.distcp` files) that requires Megatron-LM to load. If you want to use your trained model with other frameworks like vLLM or SGLang for inference, or simply load it with vanilla PyTorch, you'll need to convert the checkpoint. The provided conversion script (`code/megatron/convert_megatron_checkpoint.py`) handles this:

```
python code/megatron/convert_megatron_checkpoint.py \
    --checkpoint-dir code/megatron/checkpoints/gpt_8b/iter_0000010 \
    --output-dir exported_checkpoint \
    --format pytorch \
    --num-layers 32 --hidden-size 4096 --num-attention-heads 32 \
```

```
    --vocab-size 128256 --max-position-embeddings 2048 \
    --use-mcore-models --bf16
```

The exported checkpoint is completely standalone—no Megatron-LM is required to load it:

```
import torch
checkpoint = torch.load('exported_checkpoint/model.pt', map_location='cpu')
print(checkpoint['model_config'])
state_dict = checkpoint['model_state_dict']
```

The converted checkpoint contains only model weights (no optimizer state), making it significantly smaller and compatible with any PyTorch-based inference framework. For production HuggingFace format conversion with proper layer name mapping and tensor reshaping, consider using Megatron-Bridge `https://github.com/NVIDIA-NeMo/Megatron-Bridge`.

Advanced SLURM features for training

Beyond basic job submission, SLURM offers several advanced features that become invaluable for serious training workflows. This section covers the most useful ones for AI practitioners.

Job arrays for hyperparameter tuning

When you need to run the same training script with different hyperparameters—a common scenario for hyperparameter search—submitting jobs one by one quickly becomes tedious. SLURM's job arrays let you submit a single script that spawns multiple independent jobs, each with a unique task ID that you can use to select different configurations.

The `#SBATCH --array=0-9` directive tells SLURM to create 10 jobs (indices 0 through 9). Each job receives its index in the `SLURM_ARRAY_TASK_ID` environment variable, which you can use to compute hyperparameters. A runnable version is in `code/train_array.sh`:

```
#!/bin/bash
#SBATCH --array=0-9
#SBATCH --nodes=1
#SBATCH --gres=gpu:1

# Each array task gets different hyperparameters
LRS=(0.001 0.0001 0.00001 0.000001)
LR=${LRS[$((SLURM_ARRAY_TASK_ID % 4))]}
BATCH_SIZE=$((32 * (SLURM_ARRAY_TASK_ID / 4 + 1)))
```

```
python code/train.py --lr $LR --batch_size $BATCH_SIZE
```

This example creates a grid search over 4 learning rates and 3 batch sizes (though only 10 of the 12 combinations run). Submit with `sbatch code/train_array.sh`, and SLURM schedules all 10 jobs—they may run in parallel if resources are available or queue up if not.

Interactive jobs with salloc

While `sbatch` is perfect for production training runs, debugging distributed code often requires interactive access. The `salloc` command allocates resources and gives you a shell where you can run commands directly:

```
# Allocate 2 nodes, 1 GPU each, for 1 hour
salloc -N 2 --gres=gpu:1 --time=1:00:00

# Once allocated, run commands interactively
srun hostname
srun nvidia-smi
srun python code/train.py

# Release when done
exit
```

This workflow is invaluable for debugging—you can run your training script, see it fail, fix the code, and immediately retry without waiting in the queue again. Just remember that your allocation has a time limit, and idle time still counts against your quota.

Job dependencies

Real training pipelines often involve multiple stages: data preprocessing, training, evaluation, and checkpoint conversion. Rather than manually monitoring each job and submitting the next, you can chain jobs with dependencies:

```
# Submit first job and capture its ID
JOB1=$(sbatch --parsable train_stage1.sh)

# Submit second job that starts only after first succeeds
sbatch --dependency=afterok:$JOB1 train_stage2.sh
```

The `--dependency=afterok:$JOB1` flag tells SLURM to hold the second job until the first completes successfully. Other dependency types include `afterany` (run regardless of exit status), `afternotok` (run only if the first fails), and `singleton` (run only one job with this name at a time).

Checkpointing and job resumption

Long training runs inevitably encounter interruptions—time limits, node failures, preemption by higher-priority jobs. Robust checkpointing is essential, and SLURM provides a mechanism to gracefully handle time limits.

The `--signal=SIGUSR1@90` directive tells SLURM to send a `SIGUSR1` signal to your job 90 seconds before the time limit expires. Your script can trap this signal and trigger a checkpoint save. That is separate from `SIGTERM`, which SLURM sends on immediate cancelation or preemption (`scancel`, node drain)—handle both in production checkpoint code. A complete example is in `code/train_distributed.sh`:

```
#!/bin/bash
#SBATCH --nodes=2
#SBATCH --gres=gpu:1
#SBATCH --time=24:00:00
#SBATCH --signal=SIGUSR1@90  # Send signal 90 seconds before time limit

# Handle checkpoint signal
trap 'echo "Checkpointing..."; python code/checkpoint.py' SIGUSR1

python code/train.py --resume --checkpoint_dir=/path/to/checkpoints
```

When the signal arrives, the trap handler runs your checkpoint script, giving the training process time to save state before SLURM terminates the job. Combined with the `--resume` flag in your training script, you can seamlessly continue training across multiple job submissions.

Monitoring and debugging

When training jobs run for hours or days across multiple nodes, effective monitoring becomes essential. You need to know whether your job is actually running, how resources are being utilized, and where to look when things go wrong.

Job monitoring

The most basic monitoring starts with `squeue`, which shows the state of jobs in the queue. Wrapping it with `watch` gives you a live dashboard:

```
# Watch job queue, refreshing every second
watch -n 1 squeue -u $USER

# Get detailed information about a specific job
scontrol show job <job_id>

# Watch a specific job's state changes
watch -n 1 scontrol show job <job_id>
```

The `scontrol show job` output includes useful details like the allocated nodes, start time, time limit, and current state. For running jobs, you can check GPU utilization across all allocated nodes:

```
# Check GPU usage across all nodes in your allocation
srun -N 2 nvidia-smi

# For a running batch job, attach to its step instead of SSH
srun --jobid=<job_id> nvidia-smi
```

To monitor job output in real-time, use `tail -f` on the output file. By default, SLURM writes output to `slurm-<job_id>.out` in the submission directory:

```
tail -f slurm-<job_id>.out
```

For long-running jobs, the `sacct` command provides historical information, including resource usage:

```
# Show completed jobs with resource usage
sacct -j <job_id> --format=JobID,JobName,Elapsed,MaxRSS,MaxVMSize,State

# Show all your recent jobs
sacct -u $USER --starttime=2024-01-01
```

Logging and output

SLURM captures stdout and stderr from your job and writes them to files. You can customize the filenames using special format codes:

```
#SBATCH --output=train_%j.out    # %j = job ID
#SBATCH --error=train_%j.err     # Separate file for stderr
#SBATCH --output=train_%j_%N.out # %N = node name (useful for multi-node)
```

One challenge with distributed training is that all ranks write to the same output file by default, making the output interleaved and hard to read. There are several strategies to handle this.

The simplest approach is to use the `--label` flag with `srun`, which prefixes each line with the task ID:

```
srun --label python train.py
```

For more control, implement rank-specific logging in your Python code:

```
import logging
import torch.distributed as dist

def setup_logging():
    rank = dist.get_rank() if dist.is_initialized() else 0

    # Each rank logs to its own file
    logging.basicConfig(
        filename=f'train_rank_{rank}.log',
        level=logging.INFO,
        format=f'[Rank {rank}] %(asctime)s - %(levelname)s - %(message)s'
    )

    # Optionally, only rank 0 logs to console
    if rank == 0:
        console = logging.StreamHandler()
        console.setLevel(logging.INFO)
        logging.getLogger().addHandler(console)
```

This gives you separate log files for each rank, making it much easier to debug rank-specific issues.

Profiling distributed training

When your training is slower than expected, profiling helps identify where time is being spent. PyTorch's built-in profiler integrates seamlessly with SLURM jobs—you just need to be mindful that multiple ranks are running simultaneously.

The basic approach is to wrap a few training steps with the profiler context manager:

```
from torch.profiler import profile, record_function, ProfilerActivity

with profile(
    activities=[ProfilerActivity.CPU, ProfilerActivity.CUDA],
    record_shapes=True,
    profile_memory=True,
    with_stack=True,
) as prof:
    # Profile a few training steps
    for step in range(5):
        with record_function("forward"):
            output = model(input)
        with record_function("backward"):
            loss.backward()
        with record_function("optimizer"):
            optimizer.step()

# Save trace (only on rank 0 to avoid file conflicts)
if dist.get_rank() == 0:
    prof.export_chrome_trace("trace.json")
    print(prof.key_averages().table(sort_by="cuda_time_total", row_limit=10))
```

The `record_function` context managers add named regions to your trace, making it easier to identify which phase of training is the bottleneck. The `with_stack=True` option captures Python call stacks, which helps trace performance issues back to specific lines of code.

The exported trace file can be viewed in Chrome's `chrome://tracing` or in TensorBoard. For distributed training, pay particular attention to communication operations in the trace. If you see `ncclAllReduce` or similar collective operations dominating your profile, you likely have a communication bottleneck. Common remedies include increasing batch size to improve the computation-to-communication ratio, using gradient accumulation to reduce synchronization frequency, or enabling communication-computation overlap if your framework supports it.

When the profiler doesn't give you enough information about communication issues, NCCL provides its own debugging output. Add these environment variables to your SLURM script:

```
export NCCL_DEBUG=INFO        # Detailed NCCL logging
export NCCL_DEBUG_SUBSYS=ALL  # All subsystems
export TORCH_DISTRIBUTED_DEBUG=DETAIL  # PyTorch distributed debugging
```

These produce verbose output showing exactly what NCCL is doing—connection establishment, ring topology, bandwidth measurements, and any errors. This level of detail is invaluable when debugging hangs or unexpected slowdowns, but the output volume makes it impractical for production runs. Enable these flags selectively when investigating specific issues.

Best practices

After working through the examples above, a few patterns emerge that are worth highlighting explicitly.

Resource allocation

One common mistake is relying on cluster defaults for resource allocation. Different clusters have different defaults, and what works on your lab cluster may fail silently on a shared HPC system. Always specify resources explicitly in your batch scripts: `--nodes`, `--gres`, `--cpus-per-task`, `--mem`, and `--time`. This makes your scripts portable and self-documenting.

When you need guaranteed exclusive access to nodes—common for large-scale training where you want to avoid interference from other jobs—use the `--exclusive` flag. This ensures no other jobs share your allocated nodes, even if you're not using all their resources.

Memory allocation deserves special attention. GPU out-of-memory errors are obvious, but CPU memory exhaustion can cause silent failures or mysterious crashes. Request enough memory with `--mem` (per node) or `--mem-per-cpu`, and remember that data loading workers consume CPU memory too.

Checkpointing strategy

For long training runs, checkpointing strategy can make the difference between losing days of work and seamlessly resuming after an interruption. Save checkpoints at regular step intervals rather than just at epoch boundaries—if your epochs are long, an epoch-based strategy means losing significant progress on failure.

When using FSDP, leverage `torch.distributed.checkpoint` for efficient distributed saves that don't require gathering the full model to a single rank. For DeepSpeed and Megatron-LM, use their built-in checkpointing mechanisms, which handle sharded state correctly.

Most importantly, always test your resume logic before starting a long run. Submit a short job, let it checkpoint, cancel it, and verify that resuming produces the same training dynamics. Discovering a bug in your checkpoint loading after losing a week of training is painful.

Handling failures

At scale, failures are inevitable. Nodes crash, network connections drop, and jobs get preempted. Design your training pipeline with this in mind.

Implement health checks that detect hung processes—a common failure mode where one rank crashes but others wait indefinitely at a collective operation. PyTorch's `init_process_group` accepts a `timeout` parameter; set it to something reasonable (e.g., 30 minutes) so hung jobs eventually fail rather than consuming resources indefinitely.

Ensure your data loading is robust to transient filesystem issues. Shared filesystems under heavy load can occasionally return errors; wrapping data loading in retry logic with exponential backoff prevents these transient issues from killing your job.

Finally, consider implementing automatic job resubmission for preemptible queues. Many clusters offer lower-priority queues with shorter wait times but the possibility of preemption. A wrapper script that detects preemption and resubmits the job (with `--dependency=singleton` to prevent duplicates) can dramatically improve your effective throughput on busy clusters.

Troubleshooting common issues

Even with careful setup, things can go wrong. This section covers the most common issues you'll encounter and how to diagnose them.

Nodes not available

Sometimes your job sits in the queue with status `PD` (pending) longer than expected. The first step is checking whether the nodes you're requesting are actually available:

```
sinfo -N -l
```

This shows each node's state. Common states include `idle` (available), `alloc` (in use), `down` (unavailable), and `drain` (administratively disabled). If nodes are down or drained, you'll need to wait for them to come back or adjust your job to use different nodes.

If you're running a local test cluster (as described in the virtual node setup section), you may need to manually resume nodes after a restart:

```
scontrol update NodeName=node[6-7] State=RESUME
```

GPU allocation issues

When jobs fail with GPU-related errors, first verify that SLURM sees the GPUs correctly:

```
scontrol show nodes | grep Gres
```

This shows the generic resources (including GPUs) configured for each node. If GPUs aren't showing up, check the `gres.conf` file in your SLURM configuration directory. You can also test GPU allocation directly:

```
srun -N 1 --gres=gpu:1 nvidia-smi -L
```

If this fails, the issue is likely in SLURM's GPU configuration rather than your training script.

Communication Errors

Distributed training failures often manifest as NCCL errors or timeouts during collective operations. Start by verifying basic network connectivity between nodes:

```
srun -N 2 bash -c 'echo "$(hostname): $(ping -c 1 node6 | grep time=)"'
```

If nodes can't reach each other, check firewall rules, and network configuration. For NCCL-specific issues, enable detailed logging with `NCCL_DEBUG=INFO` to see exactly where communication fails. Common culprits include incorrect network interface selection (fix with `NCCL_SOCKET_IFNAME`), InfiniBand configuration issues (try `NCCL_IB_DISABLE=1` to fall back to Ethernet), and port conflicts (change `MASTER_PORT` if the default is in use).

Job hanging

Perhaps the most frustrating issue is a job that starts but then hangs indefinitely. This typically happens when one rank crashes or gets stuck while others wait at a collective operation.

First, check if all processes are actually running by examining the job's output files and using `squeue -j <job_id>` to see the job state. If the job shows as running but produces no output, try SSHing to the allocated nodes and checking process status with `ps aux | grep python`.

Common causes of hangs include mismatched world sizes (one rank thinks there are more processes than actually launched), data loading issues where one rank can't access a file that others can, and deadlocks from incorrect synchronization in custom code. Setting `TORCH_DISTRIBUTED_DEBUG=DETAIL` and using a reasonable timeout in `init_process_group` helps diagnose these issues—at least the job will fail with an error message rather than hanging forever.

Code summary

- `sbatch`: SLURM command to submit batch jobs
- `srun`: SLURM command to run interactive jobs
- `squeue`: SLURM command to view job queue
- `scancel`: SLURM command to cancel jobs
- `sinfo`: SLURM command to view cluster information
- `sacct`: SLURM command to view job accounting information
- `scontrol`: SLURM command for cluster control and configuration
- `torchrun`: PyTorch launcher compatible with SLURM
- `SLURM_PROCID`: SLURM environment variable for process ID
- `SLURM_NTASKS`: SLURM environment variable for number of tasks

Useful links

SLURM documentation and tools

- SLURM Workload Manager Documentation: https://slurm.schedmd.com/
- SLURM GitHub Repository: `https://github.com/SchedMD/slurm`
- Single-Node SLURM Cluster Docker: `https://github.com/minyang-chen/single-node-slurm-cluster-docker`
- DeepOps (GPU Cluster Deployment): `https://github.com/NVIDIA/deepops`

PyTorch distributed training

- PyTorch Distributed Overview: `https://pytorch.org/tutorials/beginner/dist_overview.html`
- PyTorch FSDP Tutorial: `https://pytorch.org/tutorials/intermediate/FSDP_tutorial.html`
- PyTorch Distributed Checkpoint: `https://pytorch.org/docs/stable/distributed.checkpoint.html`

DeepSpeed and Megatron-LM

- DeepSpeed Documentation: `https://www.deepspeed.ai/`
- DeepSpeed GitHub: `https://github.com/microsoft/DeepSpeed`
- Megatron-LM GitHub: https://github.com/NVIDIA/Megatron-LM
- Megatron-Bridge (Checkpoint Conversion): https://github.com/NVIDIA-NeMo/Megatron-Bridge

Tutorials and guides

- Optimizing Language Model Training with SLURM (Medium, 2024): `https://medium.com/@viktorciroski/optimizing-language-model-training-a-practical-guide-to-slurm-a6621d3c1bf2`
- Deploy an Auto-Scaling HPC Cluster with SLURM on GCP: `https://codelabs.developers.google.com/codelabs/hpc-slurm-on-gcp`

Research

- ZenFlow: Enabling Stall-Free Offloading Training via Asynchronous Updates (2025): `https://arxiv.org/abs/2505.12242`
- Domino: Eliminating Communication in LLM Training via Generic Tensor Slicing and Overlapping (2024): `https://arxiv.org/abs/2409.15241`

References

1. PBS Professional is now maintained by Altair. See `https://www.altair.com/pbs-professional/` for the commercial version, and `https://github.com/openpbs/openpbs` for the open-source OpenPBS.
2. IBM Spectrum LSF is widely used in financial services and life sciences. See `https://www.ibm.com/products/hpc-workload-management`.
3. HTCondor is developed by the Center for High Throughput Computing at UW–Madison. See `https://htcondor.org/` for the official site and `https://www.cs.utexas.edu/facilities/documentation/condor` for an example deployment at UT Austin.
4. Kubernetes can be extended for HPC workloads using projects like Volcano (`https://volcano.sh/`) or the Kubernetes Job API with GPU scheduling plugins.
5. SLURM is maintained by SchedMD. Official documentation and downloads are available at `https://slurm.schedmd.com/`.

Exercises

Write a basic SLURM job script

Create a SLURM job script for distributed PyTorch training with proper resource allocation.

Requirements:

- Request 2 nodes with 4 GPUs each
- Set appropriate time limit and memory
- Configure environment variables for distributed training
- Handle NCCL initialization
- Add logging and error handling

Test your implementation:

```
#!/bin/bash
#SBATCH --job-name=ddp-training
#SBATCH --nodes=2
#SBATCH --ntasks-per-node=4
#SBATCH --gres=gpu:4
#SBATCH --cpus-per-task=8
#SBATCH --mem=128G
#SBATCH --time=04:00:00
#SBATCH --output=logs/%j.out
#SBATCH --error=logs/%j.err

# Your implementation here:
# 1. Load modules (CUDA, Python, etc.)
# 2. Set MASTER_ADDR and MASTER_PORT
# 3. Set NCCL environment variables
# 4. Launch distributed training with srun

# Verify your script:
# sbatch train.slurm
# squeue -u $USER
# cat logs/<job_id>.out
```

Implement automatic checkpointing with SLURM

Create a training script that handles SLURM preemption and time limits gracefully.

Requirements:

- Detect SLURM checkpoint signals: `SIGUSR1` from `#SBATCH --signal=SIGUSR1@90` (grace period before time limit) and `SIGTERM` from `scancel` or preemption
- Save checkpoint before job ends
- Implement automatic job resubmission
- Resume from latest checkpoint
- Track total training time across restarts

Test your implementation:

```
import signal
import os
import torch
import torch.distributed as dist

class SLURMCheckpointer:
    def __init__(self, checkpoint_dir: str, model, optimizer):
        self.checkpoint_dir = checkpoint_dir
        self.model = model
        self.optimizer = optimizer
        self.step = 0
        self.should_stop = False

        # Register signal handlers
        signal.signal(signal.SIGTERM, self._handle_signal)
        signal.signal(signal.SIGUSR1, self._handle_signal)

    def _handle_signal(self, signum, frame):
        """Handle SLURM checkpoint or cancel signals."""
        print(f"Received signal {signum}, saving checkpoint...")
        self.should_stop = True

    def save(self):
        """Save checkpoint (rank 0 only)."""
        pass

    def load(self) -> bool:
        """Load latest checkpoint. Return True if loaded."""
        pass
```

```
    def should_checkpoint(self) -> bool:
        """Check if we should save and exit."""
        return self.should_stop

# Usage in training loop
checkpointer = SLURMCheckpointer("./checkpoints", model, optimizer)
checkpointer.load()  # Resume if checkpoint exists

for step in range(checkpointer.step, max_steps):
    # Training step
    loss = train_step(model, batch)

    if checkpointer.should_checkpoint():
        checkpointer.save()
        # Resubmit job
        if int(os.environ.get("SLURM_PROCID", 0)) == 0:
            os.system("sbatch train.slurm")
        break
```

Configure Multi-Node NCCL communication

Write a diagnostic script that verifies NCCL communication across SLURM nodes.

Requirements:

- Verify all nodes can communicate
- Measure inter-node bandwidth
- Test different NCCL algorithms (Ring, Tree)
- Identify communication bottlenecks
- Generate diagnostic report

Test your implementation:

```
import torch
import torch.distributed as dist
import os
import time

def diagnose_nccl():
    """Diagnose NCCL communication in SLURM environment."""

    # Initialize distributed
```

```
    dist.init_process_group(backend="nccl")
    rank = dist.get_rank()
    world_size = dist.get_world_size()
    local_rank = int(os.environ.get("LOCAL_RANK", 0))

    torch.cuda.set_device(local_rank)

    # Get node information
    node_name = os.environ.get("SLURMD_NODENAME", "unknown")

    print(f"Rank {rank}/{world_size} on {node_name}, GPU {local_rank}")

    # Test AllReduce bandwidth
    sizes_mb = [1, 10, 100, 500]
    results = []

    for size_mb in sizes_mb:
        tensor = torch.randn(int(size_mb * 1e6 / 4)).cuda()

        # Warmup
        for _ in range(3):
            dist.all_reduce(tensor)
        torch.cuda.synchronize()

        # Benchmark
        start = time.time()
        for _ in range(10):
            dist.all_reduce(tensor)
        torch.cuda.synchronize()
        elapsed = time.time() - start

        bandwidth = (size_mb * 2 * 10) / elapsed  # Ring AllReduce ≈ 2× data
moved; NCCL may pick Tree or other algorithms
        results.append((size_mb, bandwidth))

        if rank == 0:
            print(f"Size: {size_mb:4d} MB, Bandwidth: {bandwidth:.1f} GB/s")

    # Test point-to-point (rank 0 to all others)
    if rank == 0:
        print("\nPoint-to-point latency:")
```

```
        for target in range(1, world_size):
            tensor = torch.zeros(1).cuda()

            start = time.time()
            for _ in range(100):
                dist.send(tensor, dst=target)
                dist.recv(tensor, src=target)
            elapsed = time.time() - start

            latency_us = (elapsed / 200) * 1e6
            print(f"  Rank 0 <-> Rank {target}: {latency_us:.1f} us")
    else:
        tensor = torch.zeros(1).cuda()
        for _ in range(100):
            dist.recv(tensor, src=0)
            dist.send(tensor, dst=0)

    dist.destroy_process_group()

if __name__ == "__main__":
    diagnose_nccl()
```

Implement job array for hyperparameter search

Create a SLURM job array for parallel hyperparameter search.

Requirements:

- Define hyperparameter grid
- Map array task ID to hyperparameters
- Run independent training jobs
- Collect and compare results
- Find best hyperparameters

Test your implementation:

```
#!/bin/bash
#SBATCH --job-name=hp-search
#SBATCH --array=0-11
#SBATCH --nodes=1
#SBATCH --gres=gpu:1
#SBATCH --time=01:00:00
```

```
#SBATCH --output=logs/hp_%A_%a.out

# Hyperparameter grid
LEARNING_RATES=(1e-4 3e-4 1e-3 3e-3)
BATCH_SIZES=(16 32 64)

# Calculate indices
NUM_LR=${#LEARNING_RATES[@]}
LR_IDX=$((SLURM_ARRAY_TASK_ID % NUM_LR))
BS_IDX=$((SLURM_ARRAY_TASK_ID / NUM_LR))

LR=${LEARNING_RATES[$LR_IDX]}
BS=${BATCH_SIZES[$BS_IDX]}

echo "Task $SLURM_ARRAY_TASK_ID: LR=$LR, BS=$BS"

python train.py --lr $LR --batch-size $BS --output-dir results/
hp_$SLURM_ARRAY_TASK_ID
```

```
# collect_results.py
import os
import json
import glob

def collect_hp_results(results_dir: str):
    """Collect and compare hyperparameter search results."""
    results = []

    for result_file in glob.glob(f"{results_dir}/hp_*/metrics.json"):
        with open(result_file) as f:
            metrics = json.load(f)
        results.append(metrics)

    # Sort by validation loss
    results.sort(key=lambda x: x["val_loss"])

    print("Top 5 configurations:")
    for i, r in enumerate(results[:5]):
        print(f"{i+1}. LR={r['lr']}, BS={r['batch_size']}, "
              f"Val Loss={r['val_loss']:.4f}")
```

```
    return results[0]  # Best config


best = collect_hp_results("results")
print(f"\nBest: LR={best['lr']}, BS={best['batch_size']}")
```

Monitor and profile SLURM jobs

Create monitoring tools for tracking distributed training jobs on SLURM.

Requirements:

- Monitor GPU utilization across nodes
- Track training progress (loss, throughput)
- Detect stragglers and communication issues
- Generate real-time dashboard
- Alert on anomalies

Test your implementation:

```
import subprocess
import time
import json
from datetime import datetime

class SLURMJobMonitor:
    def __init__(self, job_id: int):
        self.job_id = job_id
        self.metrics_history = []

    def get_node_list(self) -> list[str]:
        """Get list of nodes for this job."""
        result = subprocess.run(
            ["squeue", "-j", str(self.job_id), "-o", "%N", "-h"],
            capture_output=True, text=True
        )
        return self._expand_nodelist(result.stdout.strip())

    def get_gpu_utilization(self, node: str) -> dict:
        """Get GPU utilization on a node via srun (works without SSH access)."""
        result = subprocess.run(
            ["srun", "-w", node, "nvidia-smi",
             "--query-gpu=utilization.gpu,memory.used,memory.total",
```

```
                "--format=csv,noheader,nounits"],
               capture_output=True, text=True
           )
           # Parse output
           lines = result.stdout.strip().split("\n")
           gpus = []
           for line in lines:
               util, mem_used, mem_total = map(float, line.split(", "))
               gpus.append({
                   "utilization": util,
                   "memory_used_gb": mem_used / 1024,
                   "memory_total_gb": mem_total / 1024,
               })
           return gpus

       def collect_metrics(self) -> dict:
           """Collect metrics from all nodes."""
           nodes = self.get_node_list()
           metrics = {
               "timestamp": datetime.now().isoformat(),
               "nodes": {}
           }

           for node in nodes:
               metrics["nodes"][node] = self.get_gpu_utilization(node)

           self.metrics_history.append(metrics)
           return metrics

       def detect_anomalies(self) -> list[str]:
           """Detect potential issues."""
           anomalies = []

           if not self.metrics_history:
               return anomalies

           latest = self.metrics_history[-1]

           for node, gpus in latest["nodes"].items():
               for i, gpu in enumerate(gpus):
                   if gpu["utilization"] < 50:
```

```
                    anomalies.append(f"{node} GPU {i}: Low utilization
({gpu['utilization']:.0f}%)")
                if gpu["memory_used_gb"] / gpu["memory_total_gb"] > 0.95:
                    anomalies.append(f"{node} GPU {i}: High memory usage")

        return anomalies

# Usage
monitor = SLURMJobMonitor(job_id=12345)

while True:
    metrics = monitor.collect_metrics()
    anomalies = monitor.detect_anomalies()

    print(f"\n[{metrics['timestamp']}]")
    for node, gpus in metrics["nodes"].items():
        avg_util = sum(g["utilization"] for g in gpus) / len(gpus)
        print(f"  {node}: {avg_util:.0f}% GPU util")

    if anomalies:
        print("  Anomalies:", anomalies)

    time.sleep(30)
```

Expected learning outcomes

After completing these exercises, you should be able to:

- Write effective SLURM job scripts for distributed training
- Handle job preemption and implement automatic checkpointing
- Diagnose and optimize NCCL communication
- Run hyperparameter searches with SLURM job arrays
- Monitor and profile distributed training jobs
- Troubleshoot common issues in SLURM environments

9

Production LLM Serving Stack

Building end-to-end production systems for reliable LLM serving

> *Everything fails all the time.*
>
> *Werner Vogels, CTO of Amazon*

Anatomy of a production LLM serving system

In the previous chapters, we explored how to train large models at scale using distributed techniques like DDP, FSDP, DeepSpeed, and Megatron-LM. We also examined inference engines like vLLM and SGLang that optimize single-node and multi-node inference. Now it's time to put these pieces together into a complete production system.

AI model serving encompasses a broad spectrum of workloads. Traditional machine learning models—gradient boosted trees, linear models, and small neural networks—are typically served on CPUs with frameworks like TensorFlow Serving or Triton Inference Server. Computer vision models for image classification or object detection can also run efficiently on CPUs using optimized runtimes like ONNX Runtime, which has powered production CV workloads for years; GPUs are only necessary for the larger models or when throughput requirements are higher. These workloads have relatively predictable latency since input sizes are fixed. Diffusion models for image generation (Stable Diffusion, DALL-E) present unique challenges with their iterative denoising process, requiring careful batching strategies and often benefiting from techniques like classifier-free guidance caching.

LLM serving, however, has its own distinct characteristics that set it apart from these other workloads. The autoregressive nature of text generation means that output length is unpredictable—a simple "yes" or "no" question might generate 2 tokens, while a code generation request might produce 2,000. This variability makes batching and resource allocation fundamentally different from fixed-output models. The KV cache grows linearly with sequence length, creating memory pressure that doesn't exist in traditional ML serving. And the streaming nature of chat applications means users expect to see tokens as they're generated, not just a final response.

This chapter focuses specifically on LLM serving, building on the inference engines we covered in Chapters 6 and 7. The architectural patterns we discuss—routing, load balancing, observability—apply broadly to AI serving, but the specific implementations and trade-offs are tailored to the unique demands of large language models.

A production LLM serving system is more than just a model running on a GPU. It's a complex distributed system with multiple components working together to provide reliable, scalable, and cost-effective inference services. Understanding this architecture is essential before diving into specific deployment strategies.

A typical production serving stack includes the following components:

- **API Gateway.** The gateway sits between clients and the backend services, handling request routing, authentication, rate limiting, and load balancing. It's the single entry point that abstracts away the complexity of multiple model runners and routing decisions.
- **Model Runner.** This is the heart of the system: a stateful, GPU-backed inference engine that manages model loading, KV cache, and continuous batching. In production, you'll typically use vLLM or SGLang (covered in Chapters 6 and 7) as the model runner, but the architectural principles apply regardless of which engine you choose.
- **Monitoring and Observability.** Production systems need visibility into what's happening. Rather than a standalone service, observability is typically integrated into each component through instrumentation libraries. This includes metrics collection (typically exported to Prometheus), distributed tracing (OpenTelemetry), and structured logging. Without observability, debugging production issues becomes nearly impossible.
- **Tokenizer Service (optional).** A stateless, lightweight service that handles text tokenization and detokenization. Modern inference engines like vLLM handle tokenization internally, so a separate tokenizer service is less common. It can be useful for counting tokens before inference (for billing or rate limiting), validating input length, or when using custom inference backends.

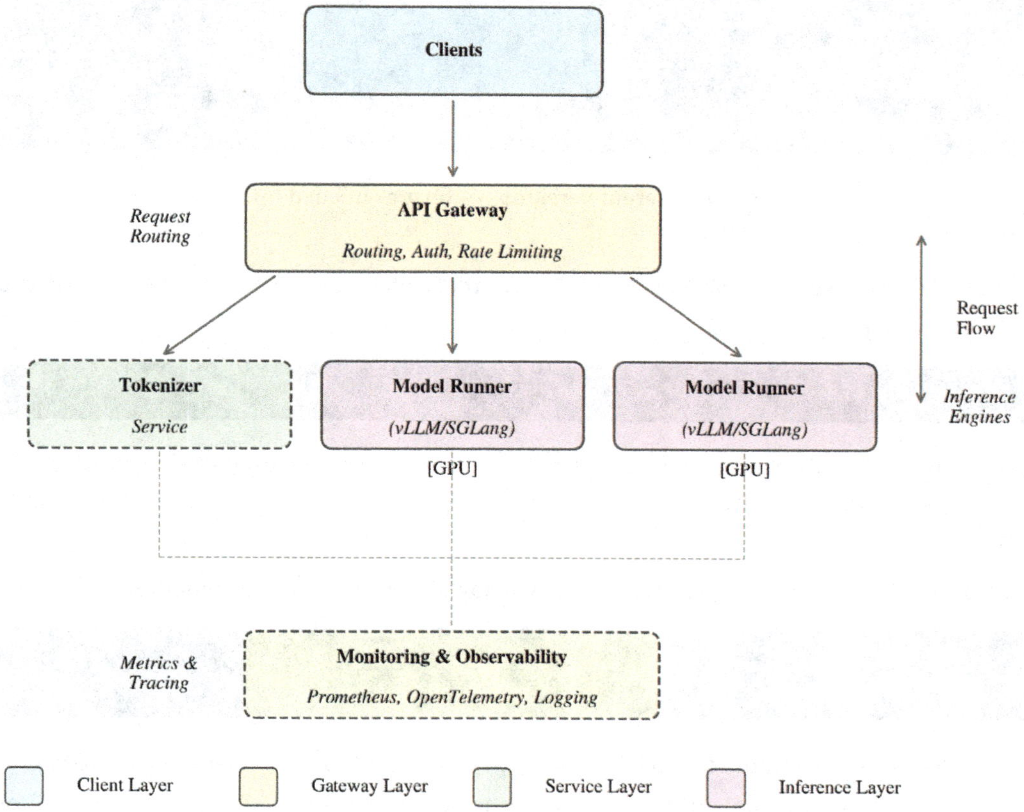

Figure 9.1: Production LLM serving architecture

Figure 9.1 shows how these components fit together. Clients send requests to the API Gateway, which routes them to the appropriate model runner based on the requested model and current load. All components report metrics and traces to the observability stack.

A simplified implementation is available in `code/basic/`. The examples use Qwen2.5-1.5B-Instruct as the default model, which runs comfortably on most GPUs with 8GB+ VRAM. For even smaller footprints, you can substitute Qwen2.5-0.5B-Instruct or TinyLlama-1.1B-Chat by modifying the model name in the code.

To try them out, first install the dependencies. We tested with the following versions in a conda environment:

```
conda create -n usao python=3.12
conda activate usao
pip install fastapi==0.133.1 uvicorn==0.35.0 httpx==0.28.1 \
    pydantic==2.12.5 transformers==4.57.3 vllm==0.15.1
```

Your environment may require different versions—adjust as needed for compatibility with your CUDA and PyTorch setup.

If you encounter a `401 Client Error` or `403 Forbidden` when downloading models, you need to set your Hugging Face token:

```
export HF_TOKEN=your_huggingface_token
```

You can get a token from huggingface.co/settings/tokens https://huggingface.co/settings/tokens. Some models require accepting license agreements on their model page before access is granted.

Start the model runner in one terminal (this will download and load the model):

```
cd code/basic
uvicorn model_runner:app --host 0.0.0.0 --port 8002
```

The model runner (`code/basic/model_runner.py`) is a FastAPI service that wraps vLLM for inference. It loads the model on startup and exposes a `/generate` endpoint. The model loading takes a minute or two on first run as it downloads weights and compiles CUDA graphs.

In another terminal, start the API gateway:

```
uvicorn api_gateway:app --host 0.0.0.0 --port 8000
```

The API gateway (`code/basic/api_gateway.py`) is the public-facing entry point. In this simplified example, it provides rate limiting and routes requests to the model runner. A production gateway would add authentication, load balancing across replicas, and request queuing.

You can then send requests to the gateway:

```
curl -X POST http://localhost:8000/generate \
  -H "Content-Type: application/json" \
  -d '{"prompt": "What is machine learning?", "max_tokens": 100}'
```

The `code/basic/` directory also includes a standalone tokenizer service (`tokenizer_service.py`) that demonstrates how to build a separate tokenization layer. While vLLM handles tokenization internally, a separate service is useful for diffusion models (which need CLIP tokenization), token counting for billing, or custom backends. The service loads two tokenizers on startup: the Qwen2.5-1.5B tokenizer for LLMs and the `openai/clip-vit-large-patch14` tokenizer for diffusion models like Stable Diffusion. To try it, start the service:

```
uvicorn tokenizer_service:app --host 0.0.0.0 --port 8001
```

Tokenizers load vocabulary files on CPU only—no GPU required—so this service can run on any machine. With the service running, you can tokenize text for LLMs:

```
curl -X POST http://localhost:8001/tokenize \
  -H "Content-Type: application/json" \
  -d '{"model": "qwen2.5-1.5b", "text": "Hello world"}'
```

For diffusion models like Stable Diffusion, the text prompt needs CLIP tokenization before the text encoder can process it. The same service handles this with a different model name:

```
curl -X POST http://localhost:8001/tokenize \
  -H "Content-Type: application/json" \
  -d '{"model": "stable-diffusion", "text": "a photo of a cat"}'
```

If you only need the token count—say, for billing or enforcing input length limits—the `/count` endpoint returns just the number without the full token list:

```
curl -X POST http://localhost:8001/count \
  -H "Content-Type: application/json" \
  -d '{"model": "qwen2.5-1.5b", "text": "How many tokens is this?"}'
```

The monitoring layer is not included in this basic example—we'll cover observability patterns in Section *Deploying LLM serving on Kubernetes*.

Request routing and traffic management

In production systems, you often need to serve multiple models simultaneously, route requests intelligently, and balance load across instances. Beyond basic routing, you also need strategies for safely rolling out new model versions and running experiments. This section covers the complete traffic management picture: routing, load balancing, canary deployments, and A/B testing.

Routing strategies

There are three common approaches to routing requests in multi-model deployments:

- **Feature-based routing** examines the request content to determine which model is best suited. For example, code-related prompts might route to Code Llama, while general chat goes to a conversational model. This approach works well when different models have distinct strengths, but requires careful keyword matching or classification logic.
- **A/B traffic splits** use consistent hashing to assign users to model variants. The key insight is using the user ID (or session ID) as the hash input, ensuring the same user always gets the same model. This consistency is crucial for meaningful A/B comparisons—if users bounced between models randomly, you couldn't attribute performance differences to the model itself.
- **Dynamic model selection** considers runtime factors like current load, latency budgets, and cost constraints. A cost-sensitive request might route to a smaller, cheaper model, while a latency-critical request goes to the fastest available option. This approach requires tracking model performance metrics in real-time.

The implementation of all three strategies is available in `code/basic/routing.py`. The `FeatureBasedRouter`, `ABRouter`, and `DynamicRouter` classes demonstrate these patterns.

Load balancing

Once you've decided which model handles a request, you need to choose which instance of that model receives it. The three standard approaches are:

Round-robin distributes requests evenly across instances by cycling through them in order. It's simple and works well when instances have similar capacity and requests have similar cost.

Least connections routes to the instance with the fewest active requests. This naturally handles varying request durations—slow requests don't cause one instance to fall behind while others sit idle.

Weighted balancing assigns different capacities to instances, useful when you have heterogeneous hardware (e.g., some instances on A100s, others on H100s).

All three balancers, plus a health checker that integrates with them, are implemented in `code/basic/load_balancer.py` and `code/basic/health_check.py`.

Canary deployments and A/B testing

Beyond routing to existing models, you need strategies for safely introducing new model versions. Canary deployments allow you to gradually roll out new models while monitoring for issues. A/B testing enables comparing model performance in production. Both techniques are essential for safe, data-driven model updates.

Canary Deployment. The idea behind canary deployment is simple: instead of switching all traffic to a new model at once, you start by sending a small percentage (say, 10%) to the new "canary" model while the rest continues to the stable version. You monitor both versions, comparing error rates, and latency. If the canary performs well, you gradually increase its traffic share. If it performs poorly, you roll back immediately with minimal user impact. The key metrics to track are error rate and latency—a reasonable promotion policy might allow the canary to have up to 10% higher error rate and 20% higher latency than the stable version, with rollback triggered if the canary's error rate exceeds twice the stable version's rate.

Traffic Shifting. This is the mechanism for gradually moving users from stable to canary. A typical progression might be: 10% → 25% → 50% → 75% → 100%. At each step, you wait for enough requests to accumulate (statistical significance) before deciding whether to proceed or roll back.

A/B Testing. A/B testing differs from canary deployment in its goal: canaries are about safe rollouts, while A/B tests are about comparing alternatives to make data-driven decisions. An A/B test might compare two different models, two different prompt templates, or two different inference configurations. The critical requirement is consistent assignment—the same user must always see the same variant, achieved through consistent hashing of the user ID.

A sample implementation lives in `code/basic/canary.py`. The imports below assume your working directory is `code/basic/`:

```
from canary import CanaryDeployment, TrafficShifter, ABTestFramework, ABTestConfig

# Example 1: Canary deployment for a new model version
canary = CanaryDeployment(
    stable_model="llama-2-7b-v1",
    canary_model="llama-2-7b-v2",
    traffic_percent=0.1  # Start with 10% to canary
)

# Route a request
model = canary.route({"prompt": "Hello"})  # Returns stable or canary model
# After getting response, record metrics
```

```
canary.record_metrics(model, latency=0.15, error=False)

# Check if canary should be promoted or rolled back
if canary.should_promote():
    print("Canary performing well, increase traffic")
elif canary.should_rollback():
    print("Canary failing, rolling back")

# Example 2: Gradual traffic shifting
shifter = TrafficShifter("model-v1", "model-v2")
shifter.increase_traffic()  # 0% -> 10%
shifter.increase_traffic()  # 10% -> 25%
# ... continue based on metrics

# Example 3: A/B testing two models
ab = ABTestFramework()
ab.register_test(ABTestConfig(
    test_name="model_comparison",
    variants={"llama-7b": 0.5, "mistral-7b": 0.5},
    metrics=["latency", "quality_score"]
))

# Assign user to variant (consistent across requests)
variant = ab.assign_variant("model_comparison", user_id="user123")
# Record metrics after serving
ab.record_metric("model_comparison", variant, "latency", 0.12)
# Get aggregated results
results = ab.get_results("model_comparison")
```

These patterns integrate with the API gateway—in production, you'd wire the routing logic into your request-handling pipeline.

Operations: observability, reliability, and cost

Beyond traffic management, production systems require operational capabilities: monitoring system health, handling failures gracefully, and optimizing costs. These cross-cutting concerns apply to every component in the serving stack.

Observability

In a distributed LLM serving system, a single request might touch the API gateway, tokenizer service, and model runner—without proper observability, debugging issues becomes nearly impossible. Production LLM serving requires three types of observability:

Distributed tracing with OpenTelemetry tracks requests as they flow through multiple services. Each service creates "spans" that record timing and metadata, linked together by a trace ID that propagates through HTTP headers. When a request is slow, you can see exactly which service contributed the latency.

Metrics collection with Prometheus tracks aggregate statistics: request counts, latency histograms, error rates, and resource utilization. Unlike traces (which are sampled), metrics capture every request, making them essential for alerting and SLO monitoring. Key metrics for LLM serving include requests per second by model, latency percentiles (p50, p95, p99), active request count, and GPU utilization.

Structured logging captures detailed information about individual requests in a machine-parseable format (typically JSON). Unlike traditional logs, structured logs can be queried and aggregated—for example, finding all requests for a specific user that took longer than 5 seconds.

A sample implementation of all three is available in `code/basic/observability.py`.

Reliability and fault tolerance

Cold start mitigation. LLM inference has significant cold start latency—loading a model and warming up the GPU can take 30-60 seconds. Two strategies help: warmup on startup (sending dummy requests through the model immediately after loading) and keep-alive requests (periodic dummy requests to prevent the model from going cold during idle periods).

Autoscaling. Request-based autoscaling adjusts replica count based on traffic. Key parameters include target RPS, scale-up threshold (typically 120% of target), scale-down threshold (typically 50% of target), and cooldown period. For LLM serving, be conservative with scale-down—spinning up a new GPU instance takes minutes, so it's better to have slightly excess capacity than to be caught short.

Backpressure. When traffic exceeds capacity, a bounded request queue provides backpressure—when the queue is full, new requests are rejected immediately with a 503 error rather than timing out after a long wait. This gives clients a clear signal to retry later or route to a different backend.

Cost optimization

GPU instances are expensive, so cost optimization matters. **Spot instances** (or preemptible VMs) cost 60-90% less than on-demand but can be terminated with short notice—a typical strategy uses 50% spot instances for baseline capacity, with on-demand instances absorbing traffic when spot instances are preempted. **Model selection** routes cost-sensitive requests to smaller, cheaper models; a 7B model might cost half as much per token as a 13B model, and for many use cases the quality difference doesn't justify the cost.

A sample implementation of warmup, autoscaling, request queuing, and cost-optimized routing is available in `code/basic/fault_tolerance.py`.

Deploying LLM serving on kubernetes

The concepts we've covered so far—routing, load balancing, canary deployments, observability, and fault tolerance—are platform-agnostic patterns. You could implement them on bare metal servers, with Docker Compose, or on any cloud platform. However, Kubernetes (K8s) has emerged as the dominant platform for production LLM serving.

Kubernetes (Kubernetes official site: `https://kubernetes.io/`) is an open-source container orchestration system originally developed by Google and now maintained by the Cloud Native Computing Foundation (CNCF). At its core, Kubernetes manages containerized workloads across a cluster of machines, handling scheduling, scaling, networking, and storage. You describe your desired state in YAML manifests—how many replicas of a service you want, how much CPU and memory each needs, how they should be exposed to the network—and Kubernetes continuously works to make the actual state match your desired state. This declarative model, combined with self-healing capabilities (automatically restarting failed containers, rescheduling workloads when nodes die), makes Kubernetes well-suited for production systems that need high availability.

For LLM serving specifically, Kubernetes provides native primitives for many of the patterns we've discussed:

Concept	Kubernetes Primitive	In Practice
Load Balancing	Services, Ingress	Model-aware routing via gateway
Autoscaling	HPA (Horizontal Pod Autoscaler: `https://kubernetes.io/docs/tasks/run-application/horizontal-pod-autoscale/`), KEDA (Kubernetes Event-driven Autoscaling: `https://keda.sh/`)	Scale on requests-per-second or queue depth
Health Checks	Liveness/Readiness Probes	`/health`, `/ready` endpoints
Canary Deployments	Ingress traffic splitting	Weighted routing between model versions
Observability	Prometheus, OpenTelemetry	Latency, throughput, GPU metrics
Fault Tolerance	Pod restart (PodDisruptionBudget: `https://kubernetes.io/docs/tasks/run-application/configure-pdb/`)	Graceful shutdown with request draining
GPU Scheduling	Device plugin, requests/limits	`nvidia.com/gpu: 1` in pod spec

Table 9.1: Kubernetes primitives

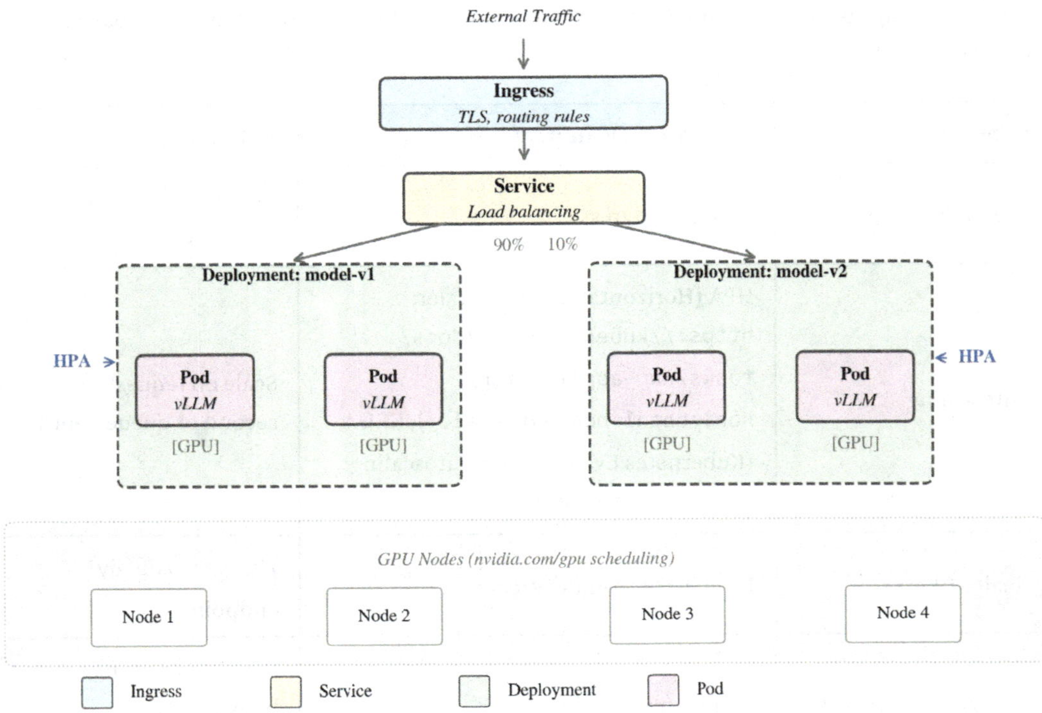

Figure 9.2: Kubernetes primitives for LLM serving

Figure 9.2 illustrates how these primitives fit together in a typical setup. External traffic enters through an Ingress, which routes to a Service that load-balances across Deployments. Each Deployment manages multiple Pods running vLLM, with the Horizontal Pod Autoscaler (HPA) scaling replicas based on demand. The two Deployments (model-v1 and model-v2) enable canary deployments with weighted traffic splitting (90%/10%). At the bottom, GPU nodes schedule workloads using the NVIDIA device plugin.

Rather than implementing these patterns from scratch, Kubernetes lets you declare your desired state and handles the implementation details. This declarative approach—combined with a rich ecosystem of operators and tools—is why production LLM serving stacks like vLLM Production Stack and llm-d are built on Kubernetes.

We'll explore Kubernetes-based LLM serving in two steps. First, we'll set up a local development environment using k3d (to run k3s (Rancher Labs' minimal Kubernetes distribution) in docker: `https://k3d.io/`), a lightweight Kubernetes distribution that runs entirely in Docker. This gives us a safe playground to experiment with configurations before deploying to production. Then, we'll deploy llm-d (Production LLM Serving on Kubernetes: `https://llm-d.ai/`), a production-ready serving stack that implements all the patterns we've discussed—**routing, autoscaling, observability, and fault tolerance**—as Kubernetes-native resources.

Local development with k3d

k3d wraps k3s (Lightweight Kubernetes: `https://k3s.io/`), a lightweight Kubernetes distribution, inside Docker containers, giving you a fully functional Kubernetes cluster in minutes. It's lightweight (no VMs needed), supports GPU passthrough, and produces manifests that work unchanged on production clusters. This makes it ideal for developing and testing LLM serving configurations before deploying to production.

The complete k3d setup scripts are available in `code/k3d/`. The setup involves three main steps: installing prerequisites, building a custom GPU-enabled k3s image, and creating the cluster.

```
cd code/k3d
# Step 1: Install prerequisites (NVIDIA Container Toolkit, k3d)
./install-prerequisites.sh
# Step 2: Build custom k3s-cuda image
./build.sh
# Step 3: Create cluster with GPU support
./create-cluster.sh
```

The `install-prerequisites.sh` script checks for NVIDIA drivers, installs the NVIDIA Container Toolkit, and installs k3d. The `build.sh` script creates a custom k3s image with CUDA and NVIDIA runtime support—necessary because the default k3s image doesn't include GPU support.

The custom image combines k3s with CUDA and the NVIDIA Container Toolkit. The key files are `code/k3d/Dockerfile` and `code/k3d/device-plugin-daemonset.yaml`. The Dockerfile uses a multi-stage build to copy k3s binaries into an NVIDIA CUDA base image, then installs the container toolkit and configures containerd to use the NVIDIA runtime. The device plugin manifest is automatically deployed when the cluster starts, making GPUs visible to Kubernetes as `nvidia.com/gpu` resources.

The `build.sh` script auto-detects your local CUDA version and fetches the latest k3s release, so in most cases you can simply run it without arguments. If you need a specific version, override with environment variables:

```
# Use specific versions (check hub.docker.com/r/rancher/k3s and hub.docker.com/r/
nvidia/cuda)
K3S_TAG=v1.32.0-k3s1 CUDA_TAG=13.0.0-base-ubuntu24.04 ./build.sh
```

The CUDA version must be compatible with your NVIDIA driver. Run `nvidia-smi` to see the maximum CUDA version your driver supports—you can use any version up to that number.

Figure 9.3 shows the architecture of the resulting k3d GPU cluster. The host machine runs Docker Engine, which contains the k3d network with two nodes: a control plane (server-0) running Kubernetes control plane services, and a worker node (agent-0) running application workloads like vLLM pods. Both nodes use the custom k3s-cuda image and have GPU passthrough via `--gpus=all`. The NVIDIA device plugin runs as a DaemonSet, exposing physical GPUs to Kubernetes as `nvidia.com/gpu` resources.

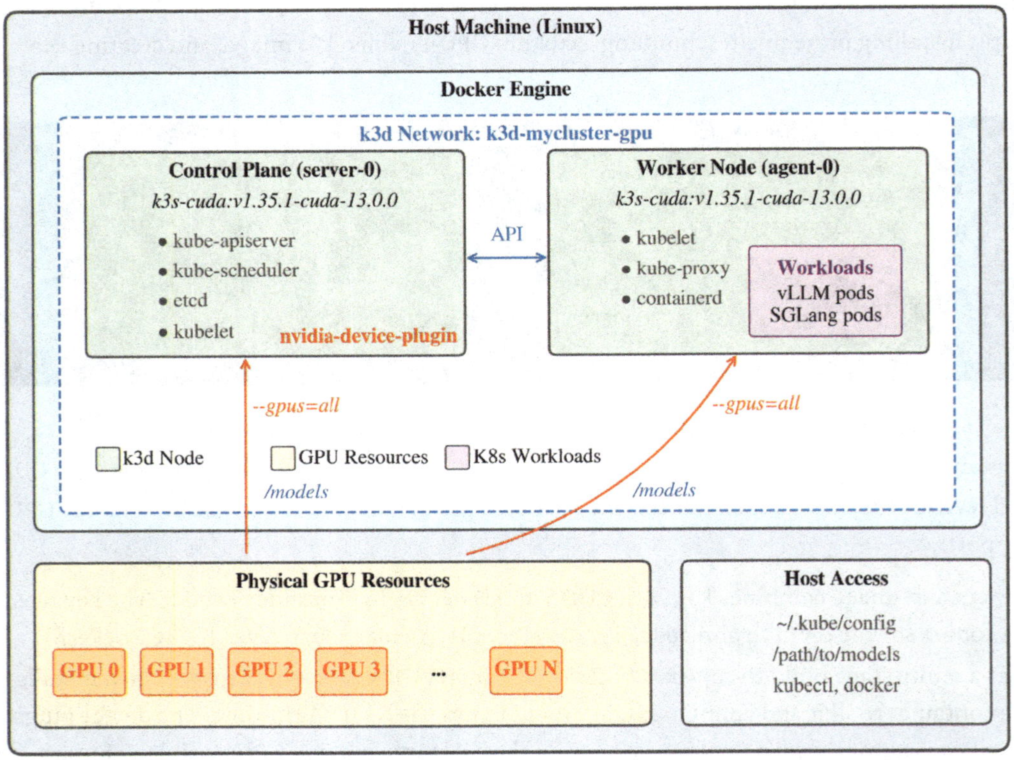

Figure 9.3: k3d GPU cluster architecture

After running the three setup scripts, verify the cluster is working:

```
kubectl get nodes
# NAME                          STATUS   ROLES           AGE   VERSION
# k3d-mycluster-gpu-server-0    Ready    control-plane   41s   v1.35.1+k3s1
# k3d-mycluster-gpu-agent-0     Ready    <none>          37s   v1.35.1+k3s1
```

Then verify that GPUs are accessible to the cluster:

```
kubectl describe nodes | grep nvidia.com/gpu
```

```
kubectl describe node | grep 'nvidia.com/gpu'
  nvidia.com/gpu:     8
  nvidia.com/gpu:     8
  nvidia.com/gpu    0          0
  nvidia.com/gpu:     8
  nvidia.com/gpu:     8
  nvidia.com/gpu    0           0
```

Figure 9.4: kubectl describe nodes

Figure 9.4 shows a sample output from an 8-GPU A100 node (complete output available at `code/k3d/kubectl_describe_node.txt`). In the output, `Capacity` indicates total GPUs detected, `Allocatable` shows how many are available for pod scheduling, and `Allocated` displays current usage as requests/limits (zeros indicate no pods are using GPUs yet). Since k3d passes all host GPUs to each container, every node reports the same GPU count—this is expected behavior for local development.

For cluster customization options such as mounting model directories or selecting specific GPUs, refer to `code/k3d/README.md`.

Deploying vLLM on k3d

With the GPU cluster running, we can now deploy vLLM to serve LLM inference. The `code/k3d/vllm/` directory contains ready-to-use Kubernetes manifests for several models, so you don't need to write YAML from scratch.

Many popular models on Hugging Face are "gated," meaning you need to accept their license terms and authenticate to download them. Llama models fall into this category. If you're deploying a gated model, first create a Kubernetes secret using the `HF_TOKEN` environment variable we set earlier:

```
kubectl create secret generic hf-token-secret --from-literal=token="$HF_TOKEN"
```

Now you can deploy a model. In production, model selection depends on both your available GPU memory and business requirements such as latency, throughput, and output quality. For this demonstration, we use smaller models. Phi-tiny-MoE is a lightweight option that works well for testing on smaller GPUs, while Llama-3.2-1B offers better quality but requires approximately 8GB of GPU memory:

```
cd code/k3d/vllm
kubectl apply -f llama-3.2-1b.yaml
# or ./deploy-phi-tiny-moe.sh for smaller GPUs
```

The deployment manifests handle the details you'd otherwise need to configure manually: GPU resource requests so Kubernetes schedules the pod on a node with available GPUs, health probes with appropriate timeouts for model loading, volume mounts for caching downloaded weights, and Kubernetes services for network access. Watch the deployment progress with:

```
kubectl get pods -l app=vllm -w
# NAME                          READY   STATUS              RESTARTS   AGE
# vllm-llama-32-1b-pod-xxx      0/1     ContainerCreating   0          2m40s
```

The pod will initially show `ContainerCreating` while Kubernetes pulls the vLLM container image. This can take several minutes depending on your network speed. Once the status changes to `Running`, you can view the logs:

```
kubectl logs -l app=vllm --follow
```

```
kubectl logs -l app=vllm --follow
(APIServer pid=1) INFO 02-28 19:03:00 [launcher.py:46] Route: /v1/rerank, Methods: POST
(APIServer pid=1) INFO 02-28 19:03:00 [launcher.py:46] Route: /v2/rerank, Methods: POST
(APIServer pid=1) INFO 02-28 19:03:00 [launcher.py:46] Route: /pooling, Methods: POST
(APIServer pid=1) INFO:     Started server process [1]
(APIServer pid=1) INFO:     Waiting for application startup.
(APIServer pid=1) INFO:     Application startup complete.
(APIServer pid=1) INFO:     10.42.1.1:40220 - "GET /health HTTP/1.1" 200 OK
```

Figure 9.5: vLLM pod logs

Figure 9.5 shows typical log output during model startup. The logs display download progress if the model needs to be fetched from Hugging Face, followed by the model being loaded into GPU memory. Model loading typically takes 2-5 minutes depending on model size and whether the weights are already cached locally. Once the logs indicate "Application startup complete.", the server is ready to accept requests.

To test the API, forward the service port to your local machine and send a request:

```
kubectl port-forward svc/vllm-llama-32-1b-service 8000:8000 &

curl http://localhost:8000/v1/chat/completions \
```

```
  -H "Content-Type: application/json" \
  -d '{
    "model": "meta-llama/Llama-3.2-1B-Instruct",
    "messages": [{"role": "user", "content": "Hello!"}],
    "max_tokens": 50
  }'
```


```
{"id":"chatcmpl-bf0893c1e704049a","object":"chat.completion","created":1
772337841,"model":"meta-llama/Llama-3.2-1B-Instruct","choices":[{"index"
:0,"message":{"role":"assistant","content":"Hello! How can I assist you
today?","refusal":null,"annotations":null,"audio":null,"function_call":n
ull,"tool_calls":[],"reasoning":null,"reasoning_content":null},"logprobs
":null,"finish_reason":"stop","stop_reason":null,"token_ids":null}],"ser
vice_tier":null,"system_fingerprint":null,"usage":{"prompt_tokens":37,"t
otal_tokens":47,"completion_tokens":10,"prompt_tokens_details":null},"pr
ompt_logprobs":null,"prompt_token_ids":null,"kv_transfer_params":null}
```


Figure 9.6: vLLM response from Kubernetes deployment

Figure 9.6 shows a successful response from the vLLM server running in Kubernetes. The JSON response follows the OpenAI chat completions format, including the model name, generated content, and token usage statistics.

Looking at the deployment manifests (`code/k3d/vllm/llama-3.2-1b.yaml` and `code/k3d/vllm/phi-tiny-moe.yaml`), you'll notice several configuration patterns worth understanding. The `--gpu-memory-utilization 0.2` flag tells vLLM to reserve only 20% of GPU memory—well below the default of about 0.85. That conservative setting suits shared-GPU or multi-model clusters; for a single model where you want maximum throughput, use 0.8–0.9 instead.

The health probes deserve special attention. Kubernetes uses liveness and readiness probes to determine if a pod is healthy, but LLM models take significant time to load into GPU memory—often several minutes for larger models. The manifests set `initialDelaySeconds` to 120-180 seconds to give the model time to load; without that delay, Kubernetes restarts the pod in an endless loop. Allow several consecutive failures (`failureThreshold` of 3 or higher) so a single slow probe during GC does not look like a crash.

The volume mount at `/models` persists downloaded model weights across pod restarts. This is important because downloading a 7B-parameter model from Hugging Face takes considerable time and bandwidth. Once cached, subsequent pod restarts load the model directly from disk.

Shared memory at `/dev/shm` is easy to overlook. Docker's default segment is only 64MB, yet tensor-parallel vLLM workers route NCCL and IPC buffers through it—too little space and collectives hang with little diagnostic output. The manifests mount a larger volume (`emptyDir` with `medium: Memory`, or an equivalent `--shm-size` on the container) sized for your tensor-parallel width.

For larger models that don't fit on a single GPU, you can shard the model by setting `--tensor-parallel-size` to the number of GPUs and updating the resource limits accordingly. The `code/k3d/README.md` file provides detailed guidance on multi-GPU configurations and troubleshooting common issues.

Cleanup

When you're done experimenting, clean up the cluster to free resources:

```
k3d cluster delete mycluster-gpu
docker rmi k3s-cuda:<your-tag>  # optional, removes the custom image
```

Multi-Model and Multi-Engine serving

With a single vLLM deployment running successfully, we can now explore more sophisticated serving patterns. Production deployments rarely serve just one model—you might have different models for different tasks (a small model for simple queries, a larger one for complex reasoning), or you might want to A/B test different models or inference engines.

The `code/k3d/` directory provides two management scripts that automate these deployment patterns:

- `manage-cluster-multi-models.sh`: Deploys multiple models (Llama-3.2-1B + Phi-tiny-MoE) using a single engine (vLLM)
- `manage-cluster-multi-engines.sh`: Deploys the same model (Llama-3.2-1B) on multiple engines (vLLM + SGLang)

Multi-Model routing

The key insight is that an API gateway can route requests based on the `model` field in the OpenAI-compatible request body. When a client sends a request specifying `"model": "meta-llama/Llama-3.2-1B-Instruct"`, the gateway looks up which Kubernetes service hosts that model and forwards the request accordingly. This creates a unified endpoint where clients don't need to know which backend server handles which model.

Figure 9.7 illustrates this architecture. Client applications send requests to the API gateway, which parses the `model` field and forwards the request to the appropriate vLLM service. Each model runs in its own pod with a dedicated Kubernetes service.

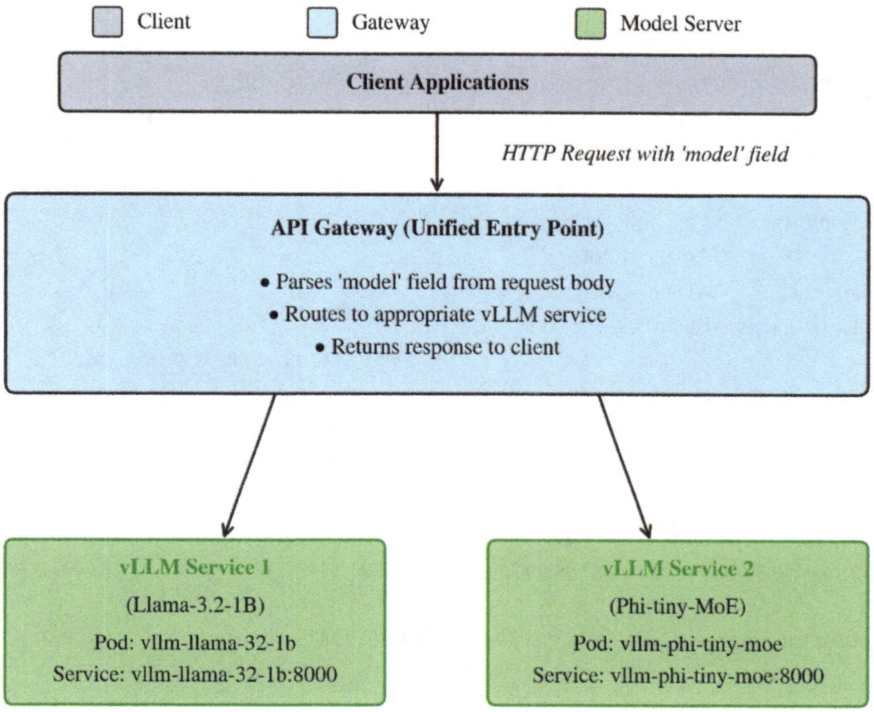

Figure 9.7: Multi-model routing architecture

Let's deploy this architecture. The management script handles all the complexity—creating the namespace, deploying both models, and setting up the gateway:

```
cd code/k3d
./manage-cluster-multi-models.sh start
```

We can check deployment status by:

```
./manage-cluster-multi-models.sh status
```

The status command shows what's running. You should see two vLLM pods (one for each model) and their corresponding services:

```
==========================================
k3d Cluster Status: mycluster-gpu
==========================================
📊 Cluster list:
```

```
NAME              SERVERS   AGENTS   LOADBALANCER
mycluster-gpu     1/1       1/1      true
Switched to context "k3d-mycluster-gpu".
📊 Kubernetes nodes:
NAME                          STATUS   ROLES           AGE     VERSION
k3d-mycluster-gpu-agent-0     Ready    <none>          5h32m   v1.35.1+k3s1
k3d-mycluster-gpu-server-0    Ready    control-plane   5h32m   v1.35.1+k3s1
📊 Namespaces:
NAME                 STATUS   AGE
multi-models         Active   20m
📊 Pods in namespace multi-models:
NAME                                       READY   STATUS    RESTARTS   AGE
vllm-llama-32-1b-pod-76895c5cfb-vkz7w      1/1     Running   0          20m
vllm-phi-tiny-moe-pod-55b8c8c959-nvxjh     1/1     Running   0          2m33s
📊 Services in namespace multi-models:
NAME                         TYPE        CLUSTER-IP      EXTERNAL-IP   PORT(S)
AGE
vllm-llama-32-1b-service     ClusterIP   10.43.178.154   <none>        8000/TCP
20m
vllm-phi-tiny-moe-service    ClusterIP   10.43.55.228    <none>        8000/TCP
20m
```

This script creates a `multi-models` namespace, deploys both vLLM models (Llama-3.2-1B and Phi-tiny-MoE), and sets up the API gateway.

The routing configuration (`gateway/routing-config.yaml`) maps model names to Kubernetes services:

```
routing:
  - model: "meta-llama/Llama-3.2-1B-Instruct"
    service_name: "vllm-llama-32-1b-service.multi-models.svc.cluster.local"
  - model: "microsoft/Phi-tiny-MoE-instruct"
    service_name: "vllm-phi-tiny-moe-service.multi-models.svc.cluster.local"
```

When the gateway receives a request with `"model": "meta-llama/Llama-3.2-1B-Instruct"`, it looks up the service name in this table—here `vllm-llama-32-1b-service.multi-models.svc.cluster.local`, i.e. `<service>.<namespace>.svc.cluster.local`—and forwards the request without exposing backend layout to the client.

Now let's test it. First, set up port forwarding to access the gateway from your local machine:

```
kubectl port-forward svc/vllm-api-gateway 8080:8000 &
```

Then send the request and get the response to LLama:

```
$ curl http://localhost:8080/v1/chat/completions \
  -H "Content-Type: application/json" \
  -d '{"model": "meta-llama/Llama-3.2-1B-Instruct",
       "messages": [{"role": "user", "content": "Hello!"}]}'
{"id":"chatcmpl-8d9100935563642c","object":"chat.completion","created":...,
"model":"meta-llama/Llama-3.2-1B-Instruct","choices":[{"index":0,"message":{
"role":"assistant","content":"Hello! How can I assist you today?"...
prompt_logprobs":null,"prompt_token_ids":null,"kv_transfer_params":null}
```

Now send a request to the Phi model—same endpoint, different `model` field:

```
$ curl http://localhost:8080/v1/chat/completions \
  -H "Content-Type: application/json" \
  -d '{"model": "microsoft/Phi-tiny-MoE-instruct",
       "messages": [{"role": "user", "content": "Hello!"}]}'
{"id":"chatcmpl-a59b963764eb8f41","object":"chat.completion","created":...,
"model":"microsoft/Phi-tiny-MoE-instruct","choices":[{"index":0,"message":
{"role":"assistant","content":" Hello! How can I assist you today?"...
"prompt_logprobs":null,"prompt_token_ids":null,"kv_transfer_params":null}
```

Notice that both requests go to `localhost:8080`, but the gateway routes them to different backends based on the `model` field. This is the power of multi-model routing: clients interact with a single endpoint while the infrastructure handles model placement.

Before moving to multi-engine routing, clean up this deployment to free GPU resources:

```
./manage-cluster-multi-models.sh stop
```

This command stops the port-forward process and removes all resources in the `multi-models` namespace.

Multi-Engine routing

Taking this further, we can deploy the same model on different inference engines (vLLM and SGLang) and route based on an `inference_server` field. This is useful for benchmarking engines or gradually migrating between them.

As shown in *Figure 9.8*, the gateway parses both `model` and `inference_server` fields to determine routing. Use the multi-engine management script:

```
cd code/k3d
./manage-cluster-multi-engines.sh start
```

This creates a `multi-engines` namespace and deploys Llama-3.2-1B on both vLLM and SGLang. We can check the status of the deployment by running:

```
$ ./manage-cluster-multi-engines.sh status
==========================================
k3d Cluster Status: mycluster-gpu
==========================================
📊 Cluster list:
NAME            SERVERS   AGENTS   LOADBALANCER
mycluster-gpu   1/1       1/1      true
Switched to context "k3d-mycluster-gpu".
📊 Kubernetes nodes:
NAME                          STATUS   ROLES           AGE     VERSION
k3d-mycluster-gpu-agent-0     Ready    <none>          6h16m   v1.35.1+k3s1
k3d-mycluster-gpu-server-0    Ready    control-plane   6h16m   v1.35.1+k3s1
📊 Namespaces:
NAME            STATUS   AGE
multi-engines   Active   21m
multi-models    Active   64m
📊 Pods in namespace multi-engines:
NAME                                      READY   STATUS    RESTARTS   AGE
sglang-llama-32-1b-pod-7dc599696d-67f9r   1/1     Running   0          21m
vllm-llama-32-1b-pod-76895c5cfb-m9bbw     1/1     Running   0          21m
📊 Services in namespace multi-engines:
NAME                          TYPE        CLUSTER-IP      EXTERNAL-IP   PORT(S)
AGE
sglang-llama-32-1b-service    ClusterIP   10.43.249.196   <none>        8000/TCP
21m
vllm-llama-32-1b-service      ClusterIP   10.43.89.85     <none>        8000/TCP
21m
```

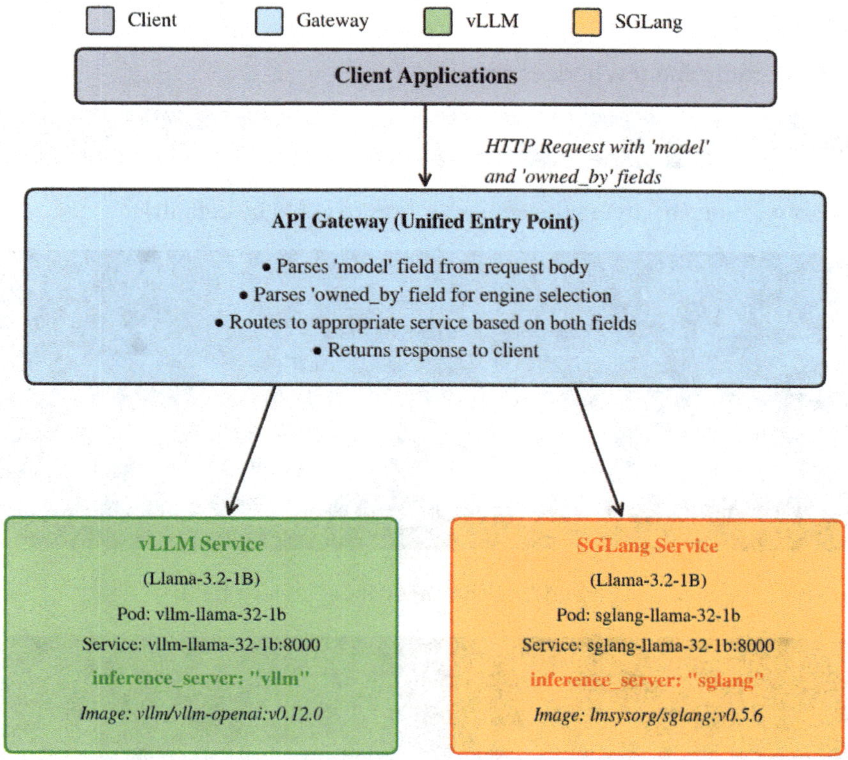

Figure 9.8: Multi-engine routing architecture

The routing configuration (`code/k3d/gateway/routing-config.yaml`) includes engine-specific routes, allowing clients to select their preferred inference engine:

```
routing:
  - model: "meta-llama/Llama-3.2-1B-Instruct"
    inference_server: "vllm"
    service_name: "vllm-llama-32-1b-service.multi-engines.svc.cluster.local"
  - model: "meta-llama/Llama-3.2-1B-Instruct"
    inference_server: "sglang"
    service_name: "sglang-llama-32-1b-service.multi-engines.svc.cluster.local"
  - model: "meta-llama/Llama-3.2-1B-Instruct"
    inference_server: null  # Default to vLLM
    service_name: "vllm-llama-32-1b-service.multi-engines.svc.cluster.local"
```

The third entry with `inference_server: null` acts as a fallback—requests that don't specify an engine go to vLLM by default.

Set up port forwarding and test both engines:

```
kubectl port-forward svc/vllm-api-gateway 8080:8000 &
```

First, a request without specifying the engine (routes to vLLM by default):

```
$ curl http://localhost:8080/v1/chat/completions \
  -H "Content-Type: application/json" \
  -d '{"model": "meta-llama/Llama-3.2-1B-Instruct",
       "messages": [{"role": "user", "content": "Hello!"}]}'
{"id":"chatcmpl-9583dfa06c9b9669","object":"chat.completion","created":...,
"model":"meta-llama/Llama-3.2-1B-Instruct","choices":[{"index":0,"message":{
"role":"assistant","content":"Hello! How can I assist you today?"...
"prompt_logprobs":null,"prompt_token_ids":null,"kv_transfer_params":null}
```

Now explicitly route to SGLang by adding the `inference_server` field:

```
$ curl http://localhost:8080/v1/chat/completions \
  -H "Content-Type: application/json" \
  -d '{"model": "meta-llama/Llama-3.2-1B-Instruct",
       "inference_server": "sglang",
       "messages": [{"role": "user", "content": "Hello!"}]}'
{"id":"e02f545aca204f...3b20","object":"chat.completion","created":...,
"model":"meta-llama/Llama-3.2-1B-Instruct","choices":[{"index":0,"message":{
"role":"assistant","content":"Hello! How can I assist you today?"...
"usage":{"prompt_tokens":37,"total_tokens":47,"completion_tokens":10...}
```

The gateway also aggregates the `/v1/models` endpoint, returning a combined list of all available models across all backends. For production deployments, you'll want to add authentication (API keys or OAuth tokens), rate limiting (per-client request quotas), and observability (request logging, latency metrics, error tracking). The `code/k3d/gateway/api-gateway.py` includes example middleware for these concerns.

Kubernetes deployment with llm-d

In the previous section, we built a local k3d cluster to experiment with vLLM deployments. While this approach offers flexibility and a deep understanding of the underlying components, production deployments at scale often benefit from standardized solutions that handle the operational complexity of distributed inference.

Several Kubernetes-native frameworks exist for LLM serving. **KServe**[1] provides enterprise-grade model serving with traffic governance (canary releases, A/B testing) and multi-model hosting, but requires Istio or Knative as dependencies. **KubeAI**[2] offers a lightweight operator with scale-from-zero and prefix-aware load balancing, requiring no external dependencies—ideal for simpler deployments. **vLLM production-stack**[3] is the official vLLM deployment solution with LMCache integration for KV cache sharing across instances.

This chapter focuses on **llm-d**[4] because it provides a "batteries-included" deployment framework that assembles well-tested components (vLLM, Envoy, NIXL) into a cohesive system, offers production-ready Helm charts with minimal configuration, and supports advanced features like disaggregated prefill/decode and high-speed data transfer over InfiniBand RDMA. The choice between these frameworks depends on your specific requirements: KServe for enterprise traffic governance, KubeAI for lightweight zero-dependency deployments, vLLM production-stack for official vLLM support with KV cache sharing, and llm-d for deployments that need disaggregated inference or high-speed interconnects. A detailed comparison between the manual k3d approach and llm-d is provided in Table 9.2.

What is llm-d?

Think of llm-d as a "batteries-included" deployment framework that assembles best-in-class open-source components into a cohesive system. At its core, llm-d uses vLLM[5] as the model server—the same engine we deployed manually in the k3d section. But llm-d adds several layers of intelligence on top: the Inference Gateway (IGW)[6] acts as a smart request scheduler, Envoy Proxy[7] handles load balancing and routing, and NIXL[8] enables high-speed data transfer over fast interconnects like InfiniBand RDMA or TPU ICI. Kubernetes orchestrates all these components, ensuring they scale and recover gracefully.

Key features

Intelligent Inference Scheduling. One of llm-d's most valuable capabilities is its intelligent request routing. Traditional load balancers distribute requests round-robin or based on simple metrics like connection count. But LLM inference has unique characteristics: a request with a 10,000-token prompt behaves very differently from one with 100 tokens. llm-d's IGW understands this. It can predict request latency and route accordingly, ensuring that long requests don't block short ones. It also implements prefix-cache aware routing—if one vLLM instance already has the KV cache for a particular system prompt, subsequent requests with the same prefix get routed there, dramatically reducing time-to-first-token. For enterprise deployments, SLA-aware scheduling ensures premium customers get priority access to compute resources, while load-aware balancing distributes work based on each instance's current capacity rather than just counting connections.

Prefill/Decode Disaggregation. Perhaps the most innovative feature of llm-d is its support for disaggregated inference. In traditional LLM serving, a single GPU handles both the prefill phase (processing the input prompt) and the decode phase (generating output tokens one by one). These phases have very different computational profiles: prefill is compute-bound and parallelizable, while decode is memory-bandwidth-bound and sequential. By separating them onto different server pools, llm-d can optimize each independently. Prefill servers can use larger batch sizes and higher GPU utilization, while decode servers can be tuned for low latency. The challenge is transferring the KV cache between them—this is where NIXL shines, using RDMA to move gigabytes of cache data in milliseconds. A sidecar container coordinates these transfers, ensuring decode servers receive the KV cache exactly when they need it.

Disaggregated Prefix Caching. Building on vLLM's KVConnector abstraction, llm-d implements a sophisticated caching hierarchy. Independent caching (sometimes called N/S for North/South) offloads KV cache to local memory and NVMe storage, allowing a single instance to serve more concurrent requests than its GPU memory would normally allow. Shared caching (E/W for East/West) enables KV cache transfer between instances, so if one server has computed the cache for a common system prompt, others can retrieve it rather than recomputing. For the most demanding deployments, global indexing provides a cluster-wide view of cached prefixes, enabling optimal routing decisions at the cost of additional coordination overhead.

Variant Autoscaling. Traditional Kubernetes autoscaling (HPA) scales based on CPU or memory utilization, but LLM workloads need smarter scaling. llm-d's variant autoscaler measures the actual capacity of each model server instance—how many tokens per second it can generate given current memory pressure. It then analyzes recent traffic patterns: the mix of request sizes, quality-of-service requirements, and arrival rates. Based on this analysis, it calculates the optimal mix of prefill servers, decode servers, and instances reserved for latency-tolerant batch requests. This enables true SLO-level efficiency, scaling up before latency degrades rather than after.

Hardware Support: One of llm-d's strengths is its broad hardware compatibility. The project directly tests and validates deployments on NVIDIA GPUs (A100, L4, and newer), AMD GPUs (MI250 and newer), Google TPUs (v5e and newer), and Intel Data Center GPU Max series (Ponte Vecchio). This multi-vendor support is increasingly important as organizations seek to avoid lock-in and optimize costs across different cloud providers.

Deployment architecture

Having covered llm-d's key features—intelligent scheduling, prefill/decode disaggregation, distributed caching, and variant autoscaling—let's see how these components fit together in a production deployment.

Figure 9.9 illustrates the complete architecture. To understand how it works, let's trace a request through the system.

Every production API needs a front door—something that handles the messy realities of internet traffic: TLS encryption, authentication, rate limiting, and graceful handling of misbehaving clients. In llm-d, this role falls to Envoy Proxy[7], a high-performance edge proxy widely used in cloud-native deployments. You may already have Envoy in your infrastructure (it powers Istio[9] service mesh and many API gateways); llm-d simply leverages it as the entry point for all inference requests.

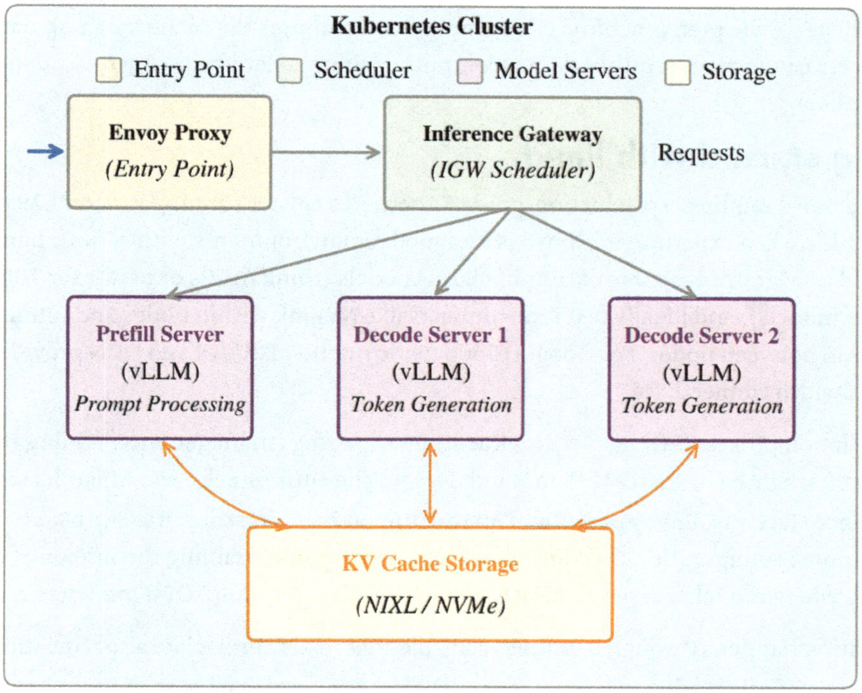

Figure 9.9: llm-d deployment architecture on Kubernetes

From Envoy, requests flow to the Inference Gateway (IGW)[6]—the "brain" of llm-d. While Envoy handles generic HTTP concerns, the IGW understands LLM inference. It examines each request's characteristics: How long is the prompt? Which model is requested? Does any backend already have the relevant prefix cached? Based on this analysis, the IGW routes the request to the optimal model server. This is fundamentally different from traditional load balancers that distribute requests round-robin or based on connection counts—the IGW makes routing decisions based on the actual computational cost of each request.

Behind the IGW sit the model servers that perform inference. In standard mode, each server handles the complete inference pipeline. But llm-d also supports disaggregated mode, where servers specialize: prefill servers process input prompts (compute-intensive, parallelizable), while decode servers generate output tokens (memory-bandwidth-bound, latency-sensitive). When a prefill server finishes processing a prompt, a NIXL[8] sidecar transfers the KV cache to the assigned decode server using RDMA[10], often completing in milliseconds even for large caches. This separation allows each server type to be optimized independently—prefill servers can batch aggressively for throughput, while decode servers tune for minimal latency.

For deployments that serve many requests with shared prefixes (common system prompts, few-shot examples), llm-d can optionally store KV cache on shared NVMe[11] storage. This enables cluster-wide prefix caching: when one server computes the cache for a popular prefix, other servers can retrieve it rather than recomputing, dramatically reducing redundant work across the fleet.

Getting started with llm-d

Deploying llm-d requires a production-grade Kubernetes cluster running version 1.29 or later. Unlike our local k3d experiments, llm-d is designed for environments with serious hardware: you'll need accelerators capable of running large models (think A100s or newer for 70B+ parameter models), and ideally fast interconnects like NVLink within nodes and InfiniBand or RoCE RDMA between nodes. For Google Cloud deployments, TPU ICI and DCN provide similar high-bandwidth connectivity.

The installation process leverages Helm, Kubernetes' package manager. After adding the llm-d repository, a single `helm install` command deploys the entire stack—vLLM model servers, the Inference Gateway, Envoy proxy, and all the supporting infrastructure. The beauty of Helm is that complex configurations become simple key-value pairs: enabling the Inference Gateway, specifying which model to serve, setting tensor parallelism for multi-GPU inference.

Configuration happens through a `values.yaml` file that reads almost like a specification document. You declare what you want—two IGW replicas with cache-aware routing, vLLM serving Llama 3.1 70B across four GPUs at 90% memory utilization, separate prefill and decode server pools with their own replica counts and GPU allocations—and Helm translates this into the dozens of Kubernetes resources needed to make it happen. The autoscaling section is particularly elegant: rather than scaling on CPU utilization (which means little for GPU workloads), you specify target queries per second, and llm-d's variant autoscaler handles the rest.

The accompanying code directory (`code/llmd/`) contains complete, tested deployment configurations. The `llm-d-multi-engine/` subdirectory demonstrates deploying the same model (Qwen2.5-0.5B-Instruct) with both vLLM and SGLang backends, showcasing llm-d's engine-agnostic routing. The `llm-d-multi-model/` subdirectory shows multi-model deployments with different Llama variants. Each directory includes deployment scripts, Helm values files, and troubleshooting guides—everything you need to replicate these setups in your own environment.

Well-Lit paths

The llm-d project uses the term "well-lit paths" to describe deployment patterns that have been thoroughly tested and benchmarked. Rather than leaving users to figure out optimal configurations through trial and error, these paths represent battle-tested recipes for common scenarios.

Intelligent Inference Scheduling is the starting point for most deployments. By placing vLLM behind the Inference Gateway, you immediately gain access to smarter load balancing than round-robin. The IGW predicts request latency based on prompt length and routes accordingly, preventing long requests from blocking short ones. It also tracks which vLLM instances have which prefixes cached, routing repeat requests to instances that can serve them faster. For teams just beginning their production LLM journey, this path offers the best balance of simplicity and performance improvement.

Prefill/Decode Disaggregation becomes valuable when serving large models with long prompts. Consider a 70B parameter model processing a 10,000-token document: the prefill phase (computing attention over all input tokens) is compute-intensive and parallelizable, while the decode phase (generating output tokens one by one) is memory-bandwidth-bound and sequential. By separating these onto different server pools, each can be optimized independently. Prefill servers can batch aggressively for throughput; decode servers can be tuned for minimal latency. The result is reduced time-to-first-token (TTFT) and more predictable time-per-output-token (TPOT). The catch is that KV cache must be transferred between servers, which requires fast interconnects—this path shines with InfiniBand or NVLink, but may not be worth the complexity on slower networks.

Wide Expert-Parallelism targets Mixture-of-Experts (MoE) models like Mixtral or DeepSeek. These models activate only a subset of parameters for each token, making them efficient at inference time but challenging to deploy. Expert parallelism distributes different experts across different GPUs, while data parallelism handles multiple requests simultaneously. llm-d coordinates this complex dance, routing tokens to the right experts while maximizing accelerator utilization. For organizations deploying MoE models at scale, this path can dramatically reduce latency and increase throughput.

Monitoring and observability

Production LLM serving demands visibility into system behavior. llm-d integrates with standard Kubernetes monitoring stacks—Prometheus for metrics collection, Grafana for visualization. Beyond generic metrics like CPU and memory, llm-d exposes LLM-specific telemetry: request latency distributions, tokens-per-second throughput, GPU utilization across the fleet, and crucially, KV cache hit rates. This last metric is particularly telling: high hit rates indicate that the prefix-aware routing is working effectively, while low hit rates suggest you might need cache warming strategies or routing policy adjustments.

Choosing Your Path

For teams new to production LLM serving, the intelligent inference scheduling path offers the gentlest learning curve with immediate benefits. You can deploy it with minimal configuration changes from a basic vLLM setup, yet gain meaningful latency and throughput improvements from smarter routing.

As your deployment matures and you encounter specific bottlenecks, the other paths become relevant. If users complain about slow time-to-first-token on long documents, prefill/decode disaggregation can help—but only if you have the network bandwidth to transfer the KV cache efficiently. If you're deploying MoE models and seeing suboptimal GPU utilization, expert parallelism may be the answer.

The key is to monitor your metrics and let them guide your evolution. Watch KV cache hit rates to assess routing effectiveness. Track TTFT and TPOT separately to understand where latency comes from. Monitor GPU utilization to identify underutilized capacity. And tune autoscaling parameters based on actual traffic patterns rather than theoretical estimates—set minimum replicas high enough to handle baseline load without cold starts, maximum replicas to accommodate peaks, and target QPS based on observed capacity per instance.

Multi-Model serving

Just as we deployed multiple models with k3d, llm-d supports multi-model serving with production-grade infrastructure. The `code/llmd/llm-d-multi-model/` directory contains deployment configurations for serving Llama-3.2-1B and Qwen2.5-0.5B on vLLM.

Figure 9.10 shows llm-d's multi-model architecture. Each model gets its own ModelService, and the InferencePool automatically discovers and routes requests based on the `model` field—no manual service mapping required. This is the key difference from our k3d setup: instead of manually configuring routing rules, llm-d discovers ModelService instances and builds the routing table automatically.

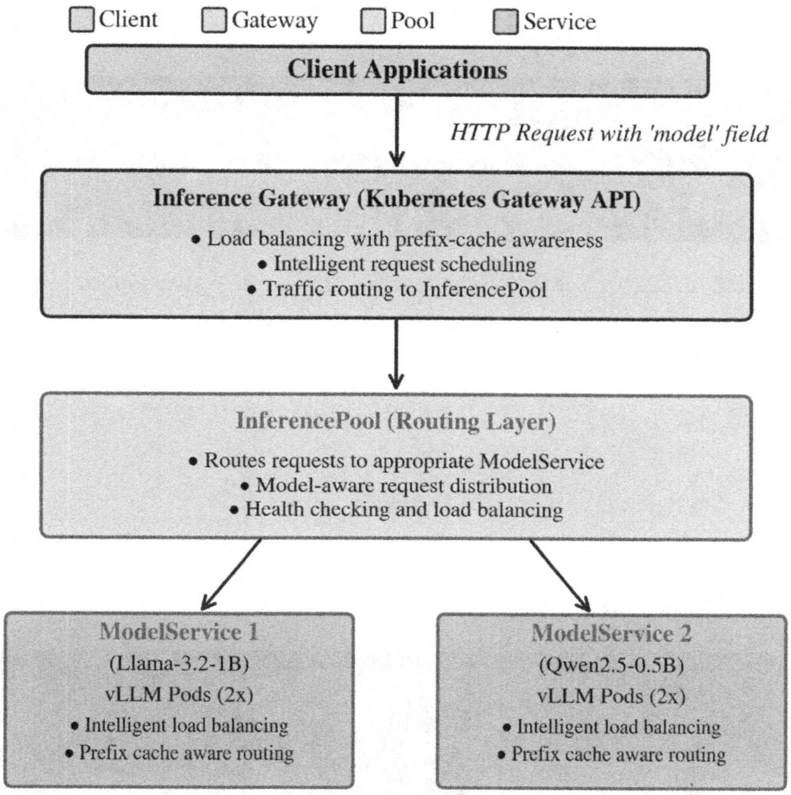

Figure 9.10: llm-d multi-model serving architecture

The `llm-d-multi-model/` directory provides a management script that handles all the complexity. Deploy both models with:

```
cd code/llmd/llm-d-multi-model
./manage-cluster-multi-models.sh start
```

The script pins vLLM v0.14.1 to match llm-d v0.5.0—often a release or two behind the standalone `code/basic/` stack (0.15.1 in the install command above), because llm-d tests against its own image matrix. It also requires a custom k3s-cuda image (the default k3s lacks NVIDIA container toolkit support). Build one for your CUDA version—run `nvidia-smi`, then `cdcode/k3d&&./build.sh.vLLMandllm-dmovequickly;` update image tags in the deployment files as needed (see the README). Check cluster status with `./manage-cluster-multi-models.sh status`.

The script creates the cluster, installs the NVIDIA device plugin, sets up llm-d, and deploys both models. Check deployment status:

```
$ kubectl get pods
NAME                                    READY   STATUS    AGE
vllm-llama-32-1b                        1/1     Running   5m
vllm-qwen2-5-0-5b                       1/1     Running   3m
```

Each model is configured through a Helm values file (`llama-3.2-1b-values.yaml`, `qwen2.5-0.5b-values.yaml`) that specifies the model artifact location, GPU requirements, and replica count. The key configuration is the `modelArtifacts` section that tells llm-d where to fetch the model:

```
modelArtifacts:
  uri: "hf://meta-llama/Llama-3.2-1B-Instruct"
  name: "meta-llama/Llama-3.2-1B-Instruct"
```

Test the deployments by port-forwarding to each service:

```
kubectl port-forward svc/vllm-llama-32-1b 8001:8000 &
kubectl port-forward svc/vllm-qwen2-5-0-5b 8002:8000 &

# Request Llama model
$ curl http://localhost:8001/v1/chat/completions \
  -H "Content-Type: application/json" \
  -d '{"model": "meta-llama/Llama-3.2-1B-Instruct",
       "messages": [{"role": "user", "content": "Hello!"}]}'
{"id":"chatcmpl-...","object":"chat.completion","created":...,
"model":"meta-llama/Llama-3.2-1B-Instruct","choices":[{"index":0,
"message":{"role":"assistant","content":"Hello! How can I help you today?"}...

# Request Qwen model
$ curl http://localhost:8002/v1/chat/completions \
  -H "Content-Type: application/json" \
  -d '{"model": "Qwen/Qwen2.5-0.5B-Instruct",
       "messages": [{"role": "user", "content": "Hello!"}]}'
{"id":"chatcmpl-...","object":"chat.completion","created":...,
"model":"Qwen/Qwen2.5-0.5B-Instruct","choices":[{"index":0,
"message":{"role":"assistant","content":"Hello! How can I assist you?"}...
```

The example above uses the simplest setup—direct service access without the Inference Gateway. This requires separate port-forwards for each model, similar to accessing raw vLLM pods. For production deployments, llm-d provides the Inference Gateway that routes requests to the correct model based on the `model` field in the request body. Let's add it:

```
./manage-cluster-multi-models.sh start --with-gateway
```

This deploys the Gateway API CRDs and an Envoy-based gateway that routes requests based on the `model` field in the request body. Now you can access both models through a single endpoint:

```
$ kubectl port-forward svc/llm-gateway 8000:8000 &
Forwarding from 127.0.0.1:8000 -> 8000

# Request Llama model
$ curl http://localhost:8000/v1/chat/completions \
  -H "Content-Type: application/json" \
  -d '{"model": "meta-llama/Llama-3.2-1B-Instruct",
       "messages": [{"role": "user", "content": "Hello!"}]}'
{"id":"chatcmpl-...","model":"meta-llama/Llama-3.2-1B-Instruct",
"choices":[{"message":{"role":"assistant",
"content":"Hello! How can I assist you today?"}...

# Request Qwen model (same port, different model)
$ curl http://localhost:8000/v1/chat/completions \
  -H "Content-Type: application/json" \
  -d '{"model": "Qwen/Qwen2.5-0.5B-Instruct",
       "messages": [{"role": "user", "content": "Hello!"}]}'
{"id":"chatcmpl-...","model":"Qwen/Qwen2.5-0.5B-Instruct",
"choices":[{"message":{"role":"assistant",
"content":"Hello! How can I assist you today?"}...
```

The gateway extracts the model name from the request body and routes it to the appropriate vLLM service. A complete example log showing the deployment and testing is available in `code/llmd/llm-d-multi-model/example.log`.

Unlike our manual k3d setup where we built a custom API gateway, llm-d's Inference Gateway handles routing automatically using the Kubernetes Gateway API Inference Extension. It also adds intelligence: tracking prefix cache state across instances and routing repeat requests to servers that can serve them faster.

> **Note**
>
> llm-d follows a "vLLM-first" design philosophy. The Inference Gateway's intelligent features—prefix-cache aware routing, NIXL-based KV cache transfer, and the inference scheduler—are tightly integrated with vLLM's internals. SGLang support is under active development (tracked in GitHub issue #403[12]), but as of this writing, llm-d's native routing doesn't support engine selection. For readers interested in multi-engine deployments, the `code/llmd/llm-d-multi-engine/` directory provides a workaround using a custom API gateway layer—see the README for details.

Comparing k3d and llm-d approaches

Table 9.2 summarizes the key differences between our manual k3d setup and llm-d's production stack. The most significant differences are in routing and load balancing: while our k3d setup uses a custom API gateway with basic round-robin distribution, llm-d's Inference Gateway is Kubernetes-native and prefix-cache aware—it routes requests to pods that already have relevant KV cache entries, reducing redundant computation. For multi-model deployments, k3d requires manual service mapping in the gateway configuration, whereas llm-d automatically discovers ModelService instances and builds the routing table. The monitoring story is similar: k3d requires manual Prometheus/Grafana setup, while llm-d includes pre-configured dashboards out of the box.

Feature	k3d (Manual)	llm-d (Production)
Setup	Manual YAML files	Helm charts (automated)
Routing	Custom API Gateway	Inference Gateway (K8s native)
Load Balancing	Basic round-robin	Intelligent (prefix-cache-aware)
Monitoring	Manual setup	Built-in Prometheus/Grafana
Scaling	Manual pod management	HPA-ready, autoscaling support
Multi-Model	Manual service mapping	Automatic discovery
Production Features	Limited	Full production stack

Table 9.2: Comparison of k3d and llm-d deployment approaches

The k3d approach we explored earlier is valuable for learning and local development—you understand exactly what each component does because you built it yourself. But for production deployments serving real traffic, llm-d's battle-tested configurations and intelligent routing provide a more robust foundation. The transition is straightforward: the concepts are identical, only the implementation details change.

Summary

Serving LLMs in production involves far more than loading weights and accepting requests. We explored inference internals—tokenization, attention, KV caching—to understand why frameworks like vLLM and SGLang handle the complex orchestration of batching and memory management for us.

We built a multi-model stack from scratch using k3d, gaining hands-on insight into services, routing, and API gateways. We then contrasted this with llm-d, where the same concepts—InferencePools, model-aware routing, health checks—are packaged into production-ready Helm charts with automatic model discovery.

Production systems demand more than correctness: observability for debugging, canary deployments for safe rollouts, and cost optimization through autoscaling. The journey from laptop to millions of requests is substantial, but the patterns remain consistent: understand your workload, measure everything, and automate what you can.

With serving infrastructure in place, a natural question arises: how well is it performing? The next chapter addresses this directly—benchmarking throughput, latency, and scaling efficiency with tools like genai-bench and PyTorch profiler.

Code summary

- `fastapi.responses.StreamingResponse`: Stream generated tokens to clients over SSE
- `fastapi.FastAPI`: HTTP layer for inference gateways and model runners
- `uvicorn`: ASGI server to launch gateway, model runner, and tokenizer services
- `httpx.AsyncClient`: Async forwarding from API gateway to model runners
- `pydantic.BaseModel`: Validated request and response schemas for inference APIs
- `transformers.AutoTokenizer`: Standalone tokenization for billing, validation, and custom backends
- `prometheus_client`: TTFT, latency percentiles, and throughput metrics
- `opentelemetry.trace`: Distributed tracing spans across serving components
- `kubectl`: Deploy, inspect, and debug vLLM and SGLang workloads on Kubernetes

Useful links

LLM Serving Frameworks

- vLLM GitHub: `https://github.com/vllm-project/vllm`
- vLLM Production Stack: `https://github.com/vllm-project/production-stack`
- SGLang GitHub: `https://github.com/sgl-project/sglang`

Kubernetes and llm-d

- `Llm-d GitHub:` https://github.com/llm-d/llm-d
- `Llm-d Documentation:` https://www.llm-d.ai/
- Inference Gateway: `https://github.com/kserve/inference-gateway`
- k3d (k3s in Docker): `https://k3d.io/`
- NVIDIA Device Plugin for Kubernetes: `https://github.com/NVIDIA/k8s-device-plugin`

Observability and Monitoring

- OpenTelemetry: `https://opentelemetry.io/`
- Prometheus: `https://prometheus.io/`
- Grafana: `https://grafana.com/`

API Gateway and Routing

- Envoy Proxy: `https://www.envoyproxy.io/`
- FastAPI: `https://fastapi.tiangolo.com/`
- Kubernetes Gateway API: `https://gateway-api.sigs.k8s.io/`

Tutorials and Guides

- vLLM Kubernetes Deployment: `https://docs.vllm.ai/en/stable/deployment/k8s/`
- NVIDIA Container Toolkit: `https://docs.nvidia.com/datacenter/cloud-native/container-toolkit/`

References

1. KServe: `https://kserve.github.io/website/`
2. KubeAI: `https://www.kubeai.org/`

3. vLLM production-stack: https://docs.vllm.ai/en/stable/deployment/integrations/production-stack.html
4. llm-d project: https://github.com/llm-d/llm-d
5. vLLM inference engine: https://github.com/vllm-project/vllm
6. Inference Gateway (IGW): https://github.com/kubernetes-sigs/gateway-api-inference-extension
7. Envoy Proxy: https://www.envoyproxy.io/
8. NIXL (NVIDIA Inference Xfer Library): https://github.com/ai-dynamo/nixl
9. Istio service mesh: https://istio.io/
10. Remote Direct Memory Access (RDMA) allows direct memory access between computers without involving the CPU or operating system
11. Non-Volatile Memory Express (NVMe) is a high-speed storage interface protocol designed for SSDs
12. https://github.com/llm-d/llm-d/issues/403

Exercises

Build an API gateway with model routing

Implement an API gateway that routes requests to different model backends based on the `model` field in the request body.

Requirements:

- Function signature:

```
class ModelRouter:
    def __init__(self, model_endpoints: dict[str, str]):
        """Initialize with mapping of model names to backend URLs."""
        pass

    async def route_request(self, request: dict) -> dict:
        """Route request to appropriate backend based on model field."""
        pass
```

- Parse the `model` field from incoming requests
- Forward requests to the correct backend URL
- Handle cases where the requested model is not available (return 404)

- Add basic health checking for backends
- Support both `/v1/chat/completions` and `/v1/completions` endpoints

Test your implementation:

```
import asyncio
import httpx

# Initialize router with model endpoints
router = ModelRouter({
    "llama-3.2-1b": "http://localhost:8001",
    "qwen-0.5b": "http://localhost:8002",
})

# Test routing
request = {
    "model": "llama-3.2-1b",
    "messages": [{"role": "user", "content": "Hello!"}],
    "max_tokens": 50
}

response = asyncio.run(router.route_request(request))
print(f"Response from {request['model']}: {response}")

# Test unknown model
unknown_request = {"model": "unknown-model", "messages": []}
try:
    asyncio.run(router.route_request(unknown_request))
except Exception as e:
    print(f"Expected error: {e}")
```

Implement rate limiting middleware

Create a rate limiting middleware that enforces per-client request quotas.

Requirements:

- Class signature:

```
class RateLimiter:
    def __init__(self, requests_per_minute: int, burst_size: int = 5):
        """Initialize rate limiter with limits."""
        pass
```

```
    async def check_rate_limit(self, client_id: str) -> bool:
        """Return True if request is allowed, False if rate limited."""
        pass

    def get_remaining_requests(self, client_id: str) -> int:
        """Return number of remaining requests for client."""
        pass
```

- Use token bucket algorithm for rate limiting
- Track requests per client (identified by API key or IP)
- Support burst capacity for handling traffic spikes
- Return appropriate headers (`X-RateLimit-Remaining`, `X-RateLimit-Reset`)
- Clean up stale client entries to prevent memory leaks

Test your implementation:

```
import asyncio
import time

limiter = RateLimiter(requests_per_minute=10, burst_size=5)

async def test_rate_limiting():
    client_id = "test-client-123"

    # Should allow burst of requests
    for i in range(5):
        allowed = await limiter.check_rate_limit(client_id)
        remaining = limiter.get_remaining_requests(client_id)
        print(f"Request {i+1}: allowed={allowed}, remaining={remaining}")

    # Should start rate limiting
    for i in range(10):
        allowed = await limiter.check_rate_limit(client_id)
        if not allowed:
            print(f"Rate limited after {i+5} requests")
            break

asyncio.run(test_rate_limiting())
```

Implement canary deployment with automated rollback

Create a canary deployment system that gradually shifts traffic and automatically rolls back on errors.

Requirements:

- Class signature:

```
class CanaryDeployment:
    def __init__(self, stable_endpoint: str, canary_endpoint: str):
        """Initialize with stable and canary endpoints."""
        pass

    def set_canary_percentage(self, percentage: float):
        """Set percentage of traffic to route to canary (0-100)."""
        pass

    @property
    def canary_percentage(self) -> float:
        """Current canary traffic percentage (0-100)."""
        pass

    async def route_request(self, request: dict) -> dict:
        """Route request to stable or canary based on percentage."""
        pass

    def record_result(self, is_canary: bool, success: bool, latency_ms:
float):
        """Record request result for monitoring."""
        pass

    def should_rollback(self, error_threshold: float = 0.05) -> bool:
        """Return True if canary error rate exceeds threshold."""
        pass
```

- Route traffic based on configured percentage
- Track success/failure rates for both stable and canary
- Calculate error rate difference between canary and stable
- Trigger rollback when canary error rate exceeds threshold
- Support gradual traffic increase (10% -> 25% -> 50% -> 100%)

Test your implementation:

```
import asyncio
import random

canary = CanaryDeployment(
    stable_endpoint="http://localhost:8001",
    canary_endpoint="http://localhost:8002"
)

# Start with 10% canary traffic
canary.set_canary_percentage(10)

# Simulate requests
for i in range(100):
    request = {"model": "test", "messages": []}

    # Simulate response (canary has higher error rate)
is_canary=random.random()< 0.1
success=random.random()> (0.1 if is_canary else 0.02)
    latency = random.uniform(50, 200)

    canary.record_result(is_canary, success, latency)

    if canary.should_rollback(error_threshold=0.05):
        print(f"Rollback triggered after {i+1} requests!")
        canary.set_canary_percentage(0)
        break

print(f"Final canary percentage: {canary.canary_percentage}%")
```

Add distributed tracing with OpenTelemetry

Instrument a multi-service LLM serving system with OpenTelemetry for end-to-end request tracing.

Requirements:

- Create spans for each stage of request processing:
    - `gateway.receive`: Request received at gateway
    - `gateway.route`: Routing decision

    - `tokenizer.encode`: Tokenization
    - `model.inference`: Model inference
    - `tokenizer.decode`: Detokenization
    - `gateway.respond`: Response sent
- Add attributes to spans:
    - `model.name`: Name of the model
    - `request.tokens`: Number of input tokens
    - `response.tokens`: Number of output tokens
    - `latency.ttft_ms`: Time to first token
    - `latency.total_ms`: Total latency
- Propagate trace context across service boundaries
- Export traces to console or Jaeger

Test your implementation:

```
from opentelemetry import trace
from opentelemetry.sdk.trace import TracerProvider
from opentelemetry.sdk.trace.export import ConsoleSpanExporter,
SimpleSpanProcessor

# Setup tracing
provider = TracerProvider()
provider.add_span_processor(SimpleSpanProcessor(ConsoleSpanExporter()))
trace.set_tracer_provider(provider)

tracer = trace.get_tracer("llm-serving")

async def process_request(request: dict):
    with tracer.start_as_current_span("gateway.receive") as span:
        span.set_attribute("model.name", request.get("model", "unknown"))

        with tracer.start_as_current_span("tokenizer.encode"):
            tokens = tokenize(request["messages"])
            span.set_attribute("request.tokens", len(tokens))

        with tracer.start_as_current_span("model.inference"):
            output = await model.generate(tokens)
```

```
        with tracer.start_as_current_span("tokenizer.decode"):
            response = detokenize(output)
            span.set_attribute("response.tokens", len(output))

        return response

# Test with sample request
request = {
    "model": "llama-3.2-1b",
    "messages": [{"role": "user", "content": "What is machine learning?"}]
}
response = asyncio.run(process_request(request))
```

Deploy multi-model serving on k3d

Deploy a multi-model LLM serving system on a local k3d cluster with GPU support.

Requirements:

1. Create a k3d cluster with GPU passthrough:

```
k3d cluster create llm-serving \
  --gpus=all \
  --volume /path/to/models:/models \
  --port "8080:80@loadbalancer"
```

2. Deploy two vLLM instances serving different models:
   - Model 1: `Qwen/Qwen2.5-0.5B-Instruct` on port 8001
   - Model 2: `meta-llama/Llama-3.2-1B-Instruct` on port 8002
3. Create an API gateway deployment that routes based on model name
4. Verify the deployment:

```
# List available models
curl http://localhost:8080/v1/models

# Test Model 1
curl http://localhost:8080/v1/chat/completions \
  -H "Content-Type: application/json" \
  -d '{"model": "Qwen/Qwen2.5-0.5B-Instruct", "messages": [{"role": "user",
"content": "Hello!"}]}'
```

```
# Test Model 2
curl http://localhost:8080/v1/chat/completions \
  -H "Content-Type: application/json" \
  -d '{"model": "meta-llama/Llama-3.2-1B-Instruct", "messages": [{"role":
"user", "content": "Hello!"}]}'
```

Deliverables:

- Kubernetes YAML files for vLLM deployments
- API gateway deployment and service YAML
- ConfigMap for model-to-service routing
- Shell script to deploy and test the system

Expected learning outcomes

After completing these exercises, you should be able to:

- Build API gateways that route requests to multiple model backends
- Implement rate limiting to protect services from overload
- Deploy canary releases with automated rollback capabilities
- Instrument distributed systems with OpenTelemetry for observability
- Deploy and manage LLM serving infrastructure on Kubernetes
- Design production-ready serving systems with proper monitoring and fault tolerance

Get this book's PDF version and more

Scan the QR code (or go to `packtpub.com/unlock`). Search for this book by name, confirm the edition, and then follow the steps on the page.

UNLOCK NOW

Note: Keep your invoice handy. Purchases made directly from Packt don't require an invoice.

10

Distributed Benchmarking and Performance Optimization

Measuring and optimizing performance of distributed AI systems

> *If you can't measure it, you can't improve it.*
>
> *Peter Drucker, Management Consultant and Author*

The performance gap in distributed systems

You've built the distributed AI system. DDP synchronizes gradients across your 8-GPU cluster. FSDP shards your 70B parameter model across nodes. vLLM serves inference requests with continuous batching. The production stack from Chapter 9 routes traffic to the right model instances. Everything *works*—but is it working *well*?

This is the question that separates functional systems from optimized ones. A training run that completes is not the same as a training run that efficiently utilizes your $100,000 worth of GPUs. An inference endpoint that returns responses is not the same as one that meets your 200ms P99 latency SLA. The difference between "working" and "working well" can mean days of wasted training time, violated service agreements, and unnecessary cloud costs.

Consider this scenario: your team trains a model on 64 GPUs across 8 nodes. The training completes, the model performs well on benchmarks, and everyone celebrates. But hidden in the logs is a troubling pattern—GPU utilization hovers around 45%, and scaling efficiency from 8 to 64 GPUs is only 52%. You're paying for 64 GPUs but getting the effective compute of 33. Over a two-week run (336 hours per GPU), the idle 48% of that fleet is roughly 31 GPU-equivalents of wasted time—on the order of $50,000 at typical cloud rates of $4–5 per GPU-hour.

This chapter teaches you to find and fix these hidden inefficiencies. We'll cover the complete benchmarking lifecycle: the metrics that actually matter for distributed systems, profiling tools that reveal where time goes, accuracy evaluation to ensure optimizations don't degrade model quality, network diagnostics for communication bottlenecks, and scaling analysis to understand your system's limits. By the end, you'll have the skills to systematically identify performance bottlenecks, make data-driven optimization decisions, and validate that your distributed systems are running at peak efficiency.

Why benchmarking matters

Benchmarking a single-GPU training loop is straightforward: time the forward pass, backward pass, and optimizer step. The numbers are reproducible, the methodology is simple, and the results are actionable. Distributed systems, however, introduce a fundamentally different challenge.

When you scale from one GPU to eight, you're not simply running eight copies of the same workload. Those eight GPUs must synchronize gradients after every backward pass, coordinate memory allocations to avoid fragmentation, and communicate over networks with varying bandwidths and latencies. Each of these coordination points introduces overhead that doesn't exist in single-device training. A 10% inefficiency in gradient synchronization might seem negligible in a single training step, but over a two-week training run, it compounds to days of wasted GPU time.

The challenge is compounded by the fact that distributed system performance depends on factors that are invisible to simple timing measurements. Network topology affects AllReduce performance. Memory fragmentation affects batch size. Data loading throughput affects GPU utilization. Without systematic benchmarking that accounts for these factors, optimization efforts become guesswork.

The consequences of inadequate benchmarking manifest in several ways:

- **Suboptimal technology selection:** A team evaluates vLLM and SGLang using benchmarks with fixed-length prompts. vLLM wins by a small margin. In production, however, request lengths vary dramatically—some prompts are 50 tokens, others are 5,000. SGLang's radix attention provides 40% better throughput for this workload. The benchmark methodology failed to capture production reality.
- **Resource over-provisioning:** Without accurate scaling efficiency measurements, capacity planning relies on conservative estimates. Teams provision twice the

hardware they need "to be safe," doubling infrastructure costs without improving performance.

- **Unidentified bottlenecks:** A training job runs for two weeks on 64 GPUs. Post-hoc analysis reveals that GPU utilization averaged only 45%—data loading was the bottleneck, not compute. A $50 SSD upgrade would have saved 10,000 in wasted GPU time.
- **Production SLA violations:** An inference service passes load testing with synthetic prompts averaging 100 tokens. In production, real user queries include long documents that trigger different code paths. P99 latency spikes to 500ms—2.5x the promised SLA.

This chapter establishes systematic, reproducible measurement practices that address these challenges. We begin with the metrics that matter for distributed systems, then progress through profiling tools, accuracy evaluation, network diagnostics, and scaling analysis.

Benchmarking fundamentals

Before diving into specific tools, let's establish the foundational concepts that apply to all distributed AI benchmarking—whether for training or inference.

Understanding percentile latencies

For any performance measurement, percentile latencies matter more than averages. The P50 (median) represents typical behavior, P95 is often the SLA target, and P99 captures worst-case performance that affects user experience. A system with 80ms average latency but 500ms P99 creates frustrated users—those slow requests matter.

> Note
>
> **Why P99 Matters More Than Average**
>
> Average latency can be misleading. Consider two systems: System A has 100ms average latency with all requests between 90-110ms. System B has 80ms average latency, but 5% of requests take 500ms. System B has better average latency but worse user experience—those 5% of slow requests create frustrated users and potential timeouts. Always report P95 and P99 alongside averages.

Efficiency metrics

Raw performance numbers tell only part of the story. A system that processes 10,000 samples per second sounds impressive—until you learn it requires 64 GPUs to achieve that throughput. Efficiency metrics bridge this gap.

Scaling Efficiency answers a fundamental question: when you double your hardware, do you double your performance? If 8 GPUs deliver only 6.5x throughput instead of 8x, your scaling efficiency is 81.25%—meaning nearly 20% of your additional hardware investment is lost to coordination costs.

Memory Efficiency measures how effectively you utilize GPU memory. Memory fragmentation can leave you with 20GB "free," yet unable to allocate a 10GB tensor because that free space is scattered across non-contiguous regions.

Cost per Token/Sample translates technical metrics into business reality. This metric combines performance measurements with actual infrastructure costs—cloud instance pricing, electricity consumption, cooling requirements—to answer the question that ultimately matters: how much does each unit of useful work cost?

Benchmarking methodology

Rigorous methodology separates meaningful benchmarks from noise. Three critical practices apply to both training and inference:

Warmup before measurement. CUDA operations are lazily compiled—the first execution triggers JIT compilation, memory allocation, and cache population. Run enough warmup iterations that timings stabilize: roughly 5–10 for standard eager PyTorch, or 20–50 when `torch.compile` or CUDA graphs spend early steps on capture and compilation. Start the timer only after warmup, with `torch.cuda.synchronize()` completing before you record the start time.

Measure multiple iterations with statistics. A single measurement tells you almost nothing. Performance varies due to thermal throttling, background processes, memory fragmentation, and network congestion. Run at least 100 iterations and report mean, standard deviation, and percentiles.

Isolate what you're measuring. Pre-load your data, call `torch.cuda.synchronize()` before starting the timer, and call it again before stopping. The synchronization ensures all GPU operations have completed, not just been queued.

See `code/benchmark_warmup.py` for a complete implementation demonstrating proper warmup, synchronization, and statistics reporting.

Training benchmarking

Training a distributed model involves a complex pipeline: data loading, forward pass, backward pass, gradient synchronization, and optimizer updates. Each component contributes to overall training time, and bottlenecks can hide in any of them. Effective training benchmarking requires measuring each phase separately to identify where optimization efforts should focus.

Key training metrics

Samples per Second is your primary training throughput metric—the number of training samples processed per second across all GPUs. This directly determines how long training takes: if you process 1,000 samples/second and have 1 million samples per epoch, each epoch takes ~17 minutes.

GPU Utilization measures what percentage of time GPUs are actively computing versus waiting. Low utilization (below 80%) often indicates bottlenecks elsewhere—data loading too slow, communication blocking computation, or CPU preprocessing creating stalls.

Communication Overhead quantifies the hidden tax of distributed training. Every gradient synchronization consumes time that could otherwise be spent on computation. In well-optimized systems, communication overlaps with backward pass computation, hiding much of this cost. In poorly configured systems, GPUs sit idle waiting for AllReduce operations to complete.

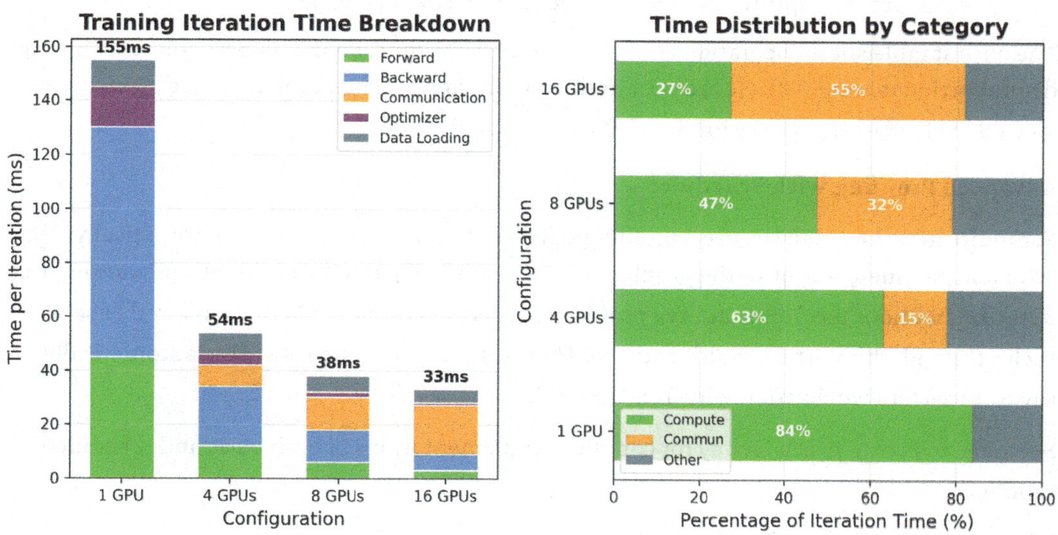

Figure 10.1: Training iteration time breakdown by phase and GPU count

The figure above illustrates a common pattern in distributed training. On the left, absolute iteration time drops as we add GPUs---from 155ms on a single GPU to 33ms on 16 GPUs. But the right panel reveals the hidden cost: communication overhead grows from 0% (a single GPU has nothing to synchronize) to 55% on 16 GPUs. At that point, more than half of each iteration is spent on gradient synchronization rather than actual computation. This is why scaling efficiency decreases---you're paying for 16 GPUs but the communication overhead means you're not getting 16x the throughput. Understanding this breakdown is the first step toward optimization: if communication dominates, you might benefit from gradient compression, larger batch sizes to amortize sync costs, or overlapping communication with computation.

PyTorch profiler

PyTorch's built-in profiler is your first tool for understanding training performance. It captures CPU and CUDA operations, memory allocations, and can export traces for visualization.

Basic Usage:

The PyTorch profiler captures both CPU and CUDA operations, giving you a complete picture of where time is spent. The key is labeling your code regions with `record_function` so you can identify bottlenecks by phase. Key configuration options include:

- `activities`**:** Specify `CPU` and `CUDA` to capture both host and device operations
- `record_shapes`**:** Records tensor shapes, useful for understanding memory patterns
- `profile_memory`**:** Tracks memory allocations and deallocations
- `with_stack`**:** Captures Python call stacks for deeper debugging

The output table shows operations sorted by total CUDA time. Look for operations consuming disproportionate time—these are your optimization targets. The exported `trace.json` can be viewed in `chrome://tracing` for detailed timeline analysis.

Advanced Profiling with Schedule:

For multi-iteration analysis, use a profiling schedule that handles warmup automatically. The schedule parameters control the profiling lifecycle: `wait` skips cold start iterations, `warmup` runs iterations without recording, `active` profiles the specified number of iterations, and `repeat` cycles through this pattern multiple times. The `tensorboard_trace_handler` automatically saves traces for visualization with TensorBoard.

See `code/pytorch_profiler.py` for complete implementations of both basic and scheduled profiling.

NVIDIA Nsight Systems

For deeper analysis—especially of CUDA kernels and NCCL communication—NVIDIA Nsight Systems provides system-level profiling that PyTorch's profiler can't match.

Command Line Usage:

```
# Profile training script
nsys profile --trace=cuda,nvtx,osrt \
    --output=training_profile.nsys-rep \
```

```
    python train.py

# Generate report
nsys stats --report gputrace training_profile.nsys-rep
```

Nsight captures GPU kernel execution time, memory transfer time (H2D, D2H), CUDA API calls, synchronization points, and NCCL communication operations. This level of detail is essential for diagnosing subtle performance issues like kernel launch overhead or suboptimal memory access patterns.

> Note
>
> **When to Use Nsight vs PyTorch Profiler**
>
> Start with PyTorch Profiler for high-level analysis—it's easier to use and integrates with TensorBoard. Move to Nsight Systems when you need to understand CUDA kernel behavior, NCCL communication patterns, or system-level interactions. Nsight is also essential when profiling custom CUDA kernels or debugging performance issues that don't appear in PyTorch's view.

Custom training benchmark

For systematic benchmarking across configurations, a custom benchmark class provides more control than ad-hoc profiling. This class measures each training phase separately—data loading, forward pass, backward pass, and optimizer step—enabling you to pinpoint exactly where time is spent.

Why separate phase timing matters: If your backward pass takes 3x longer than your forward pass, you might have inefficient gradient computation or memory fragmentation. If data loading dominates, you need more DataLoader workers or faster storage. Without phase-level breakdown, you're optimizing blind.

Interpreting the results: The returned `stats` dictionary contains mean, std, and percentiles for each phase. If `data_loading` exceeds 10% of total time, increase DataLoader workers. If `backward` is more than 2x `forward`, check for gradient checkpointing opportunities or memory fragmentation. High variance (large gap between mean and P99) indicates system instability—investigate thermal throttling or competing processes.

See `code/training_benchmark.py` for the complete `TrainingBenchmark` class implementation.

Measuring scaling efficiency

Scaling efficiency quantifies how well your system utilizes additional resources. Perfect linear scaling (100% efficiency) means doubling GPUs doubles throughput, but communication overhead makes this impossible in practice. Measuring scaling efficiency helps you decide when adding more GPUs is cost-effective versus when you've hit diminishing returns.

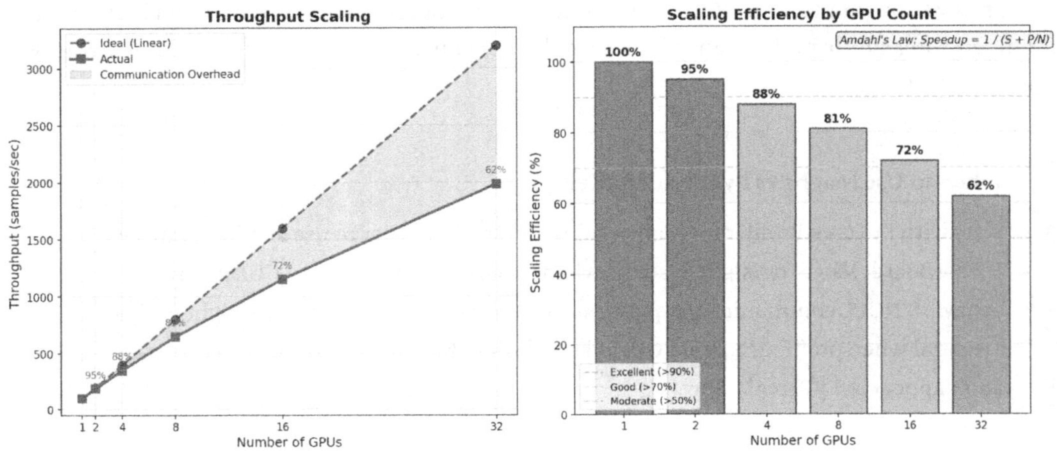

Figure 10.2: Scaling efficiency: ideal vs. actual throughput and efficiency percentages

Interpreting Scaling Efficiency:

- **>90%:** Excellent scaling—your system is well-optimized
- **70-90%:** Good scaling—typical for well-tuned distributed training
- **50-70%:** Moderate scaling—communication overhead is significant, investigate network
- **<50%:** Poor scaling—major bottleneck present, likely communication or data loading

Understanding your scaling efficiency helps with capacity planning. If you have 81% efficiency at 8 GPUs, you can predict that 16 GPUs will provide roughly 13x throughput (not 16x), helping you make informed hardware decisions.

See `code/scaling_efficiency.py` for functions to calculate and benchmark scaling efficiency.

Validating distributed training accuracy

Performance benchmarking measures speed, but accuracy benchmarking measures correctness—and both matter. A critical question for distributed training: does your distributed setup produce the same model quality as single-GPU training?

This isn't a theoretical concern. Bugs in gradient synchronization, different effective batch sizes, or numerical precision issues can cause distributed training to converge to worse solutions. The loss curves might look similar, but downstream task accuracy can be 8% lower. Without systematic accuracy comparison, you'd never know.

The validation approach is straightforward: train the same model with identical hyperparameters on both single-GPU and distributed setups, then compare accuracy on a held-out test set. Use statistical significance tests—a 0.5% accuracy drop with p=0.3 is probably noise, but a 0.5% drop with p=0.001 indicates a real problem that needs investigation.

See `code/accuracy_benchmark.py` for functions to compare centralized vs. distributed training accuracy and test statistical significance.

Network and communication profiling

In distributed training, the network is often the bottleneck. A single slow link between nodes can limit the entire system's performance. Understanding communication patterns and diagnosing network issues is essential for scaling efficiently.

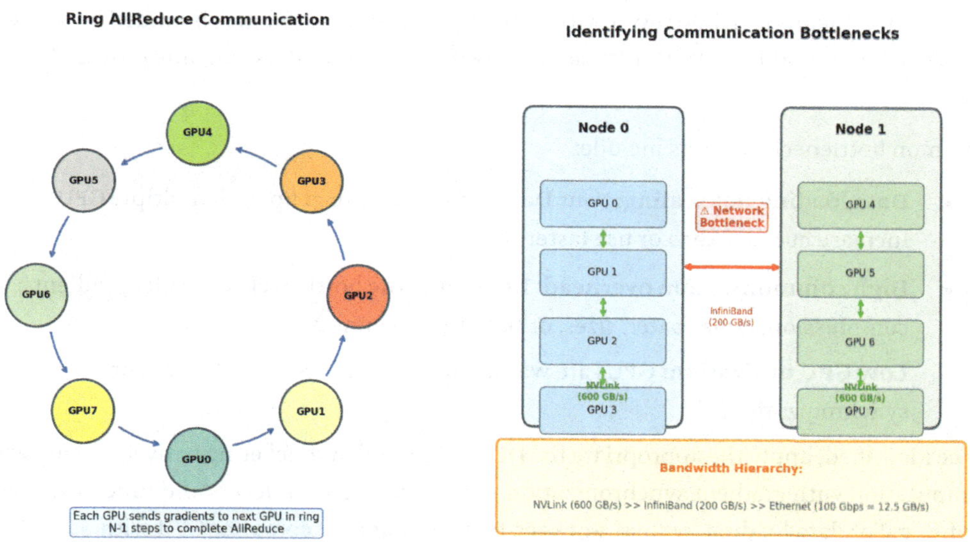

Figure 10.3: Ring AllReduce pattern and multi-node bandwidth hierarchy

The bandwidth hierarchy matters enormously: NVLink between GPUs on the same node provides ~600 GB/s, InfiniBand between nodes provides ~200 GB/s, and Ethernet provides only ~12.5 GB/s (100 Gbps). Communication patterns that cross these boundaries pay significant latency penalties.

Before diving into NCCL-specific profiling, use standard network tools to establish baseline connectivity. `iftop` shows real-time traffic per connection, `nload` displays bandwidth graphs, and `iperf3` measures raw TCP bandwidth between nodes. If iperf3 shows 100 Gbps but your training only achieves 20 Gbps effective bandwidth, the bottleneck is in your communication pattern, not the network hardware.

AllReduce is the dominant communication operation in distributed training—it synchronizes gradients across all GPUs. Testing AllReduce bandwidth separately from training helps isolate network issues from compute issues. Small messages have high overhead (latency-bound), while large messages approach peak bandwidth (bandwidth-bound). If your large-message bandwidth is significantly below hardware specs, check for topology issues or NCCL configuration problems.

See `code/network_diagnostics.py` for AllReduce bandwidth tests and communication overhead analysis functions.

Scaling bottleneck analysis

Once you know your scaling efficiency is poor, the next step is identifying *why*. Amdahl's Law provides the theoretical limit: even with infinite processors, speedup is bounded by the serial portion of your workload. With 10% serial work, even infinite GPUs can only provide 10× speedup.

Common bottleneck patterns include:

- **Data loading not scaling:** Your DataLoader can't keep up with multiple GPUs. Increase `num_workers` or use faster storage.
- **High communication overhead:** Network is the bottleneck. Consider gradient compression, larger batch sizes, or better interconnect.
- **Low GPU utilization:** GPUs are waiting for something—usually data or synchronization.

Once identified, apply the appropriate fix. DDP uses gradient bucketing to overlap backward computation with gradient synchronization—start with 25MB buckets and tune based on profiling. For data loading, set `num_workers` to 2-4x your CPU cores per GPU with `pin_memory=True`. If communication overhead is high, gradient accumulation reduces synchronization frequency by accumulating over multiple micro-batches.

See `code/scaling_bottlenecks.py` for Amdahl's Law calculations, bottleneck analysis functions, and optimization strategy implementations.

> **Note**
>
> **Optimizing Multi-Node Training Clusters**
>
> To improve scaling efficiency (e.g., from 52% to 80%), follow a systematic diagnostic process: (1) profile communication vs compute time, (2) check data loading throughput, (3) measure GPU utilization, (4) test network bandwidth between nodes. Common fixes map to specific bottlenecks: communication bottleneck → enable gradient compression and optimize bucket size; data loading bottleneck → increase `num_workers` and use `pin_memory=True`; compute bottleneck → check for CPU-GPU synchronization points that serialize execution.

Inference benchmarking

Inference benchmarking presents different challenges than training. Request patterns are variable, caching effects matter, and tail latency requirements are strict. A training job that's 10% slower is annoying; an inference endpoint that violates P99 SLA loses customers.

Key inference metrics

LLM inference has its own vocabulary of metrics that capture the unique characteristics of autoregressive generation. Understanding these metrics and their relationships is essential for effective benchmarking.

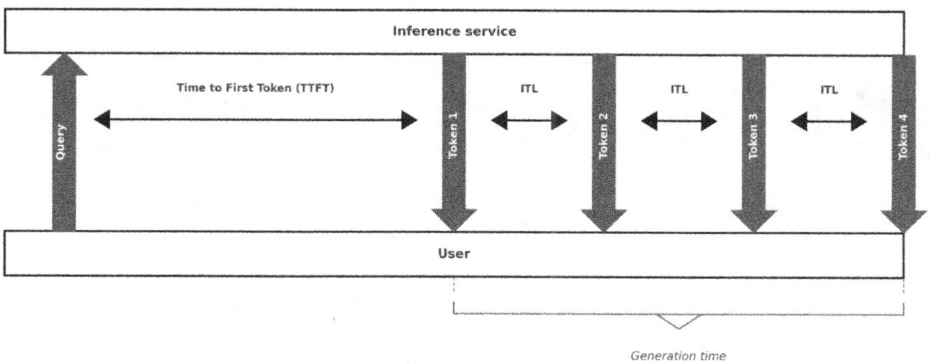

Figure 10.4: Overview of LLM inference performance metrics

Tokens per Second (TPS) measures generation throughput. Total TPS per system accounts for all concurrent requests—as concurrency increases, total TPS increases until GPU compute saturates, then may decrease due to memory pressure.

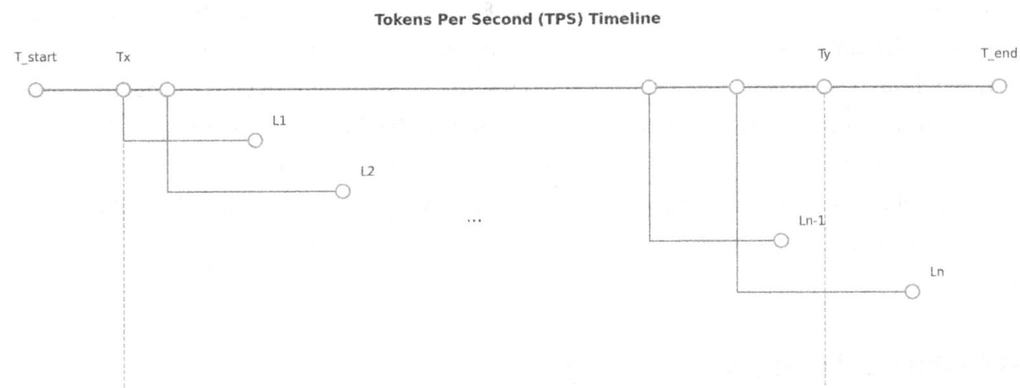

Figure 10.5: TPS timeline showing concurrent request throughput

Requests per Second (RPS) captures the full request lifecycle, including queuing and routing. Unlike TPS, this metric reflects actual API capacity.

End-to-End Request Latency (e2e_latency) is the total time from submitting a query to receiving the complete response, capturing tokenization, prefill, all token generation, and detokenization.

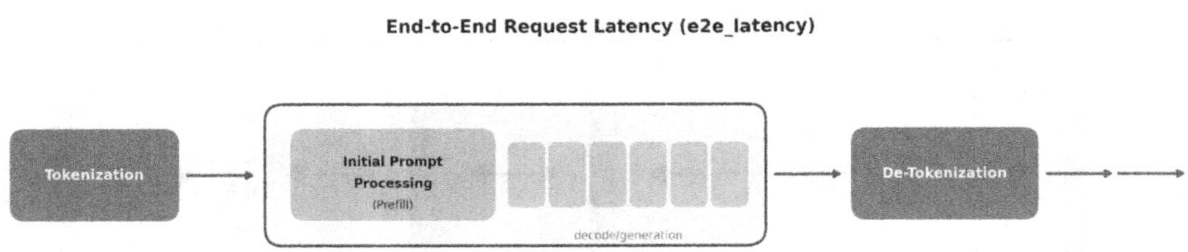

Figure 10.6: End-to-end request latency pipeline

Time to First Token (TTFT) measures how long until the first token appears. Users perceive this as "response time." TTFT includes tokenization, the prefill phase (processing the entire input prompt), generating the first token, and de-tokenization.

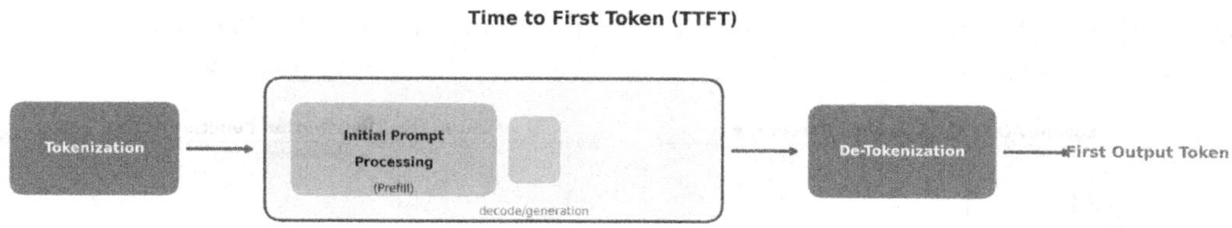

Figure 10.7: TTFT pipeline from input to first output token

Inter-token Latency (ITL), also called Time per Output Token (TPOT), is the average time between consecutive tokens. This determines the perceived "typing speed" of streaming responses:

$$ITL = \frac{e2e\_latency - TTFT}{Total\_output\_tokens - 1}$$

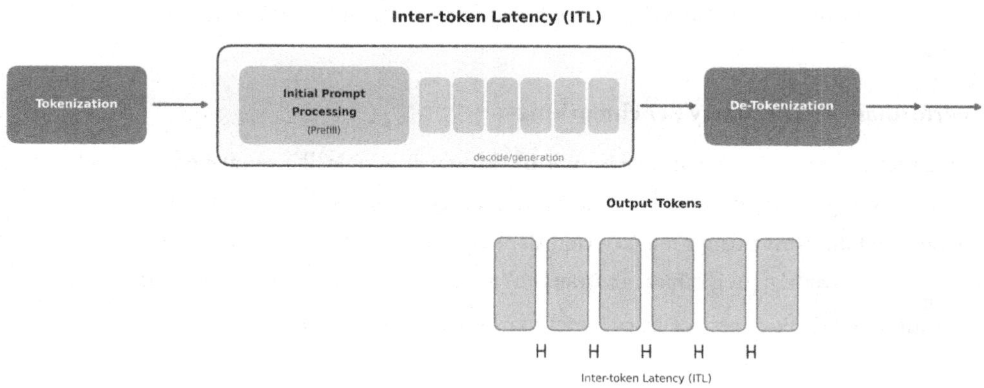

Figure 10.8: ITL pipeline showing output token generation

The relationship between these metrics determines what you should optimize:

e2e_latency = TTFT + (output_tokens - 1) × ITL

For short outputs (10-20 tokens), TTFT dominates—optimizing prefill and KV cache initialization matters most. For long outputs (hundreds of tokens), ITL dominates—memory bandwidth and decode efficiency become critical. For streaming applications, users perceive TTFT as "response time" and ITL as "typing speed," so both require attention.

Understanding the distribution of latencies is essential for setting realistic SLAs. Figure 10.9 shows a typical latency distribution with both a histogram and CDF. The CDF makes it easy to read percentile values directly: P50 where it crosses 50%, P95 at 95%, P99 at 99%.

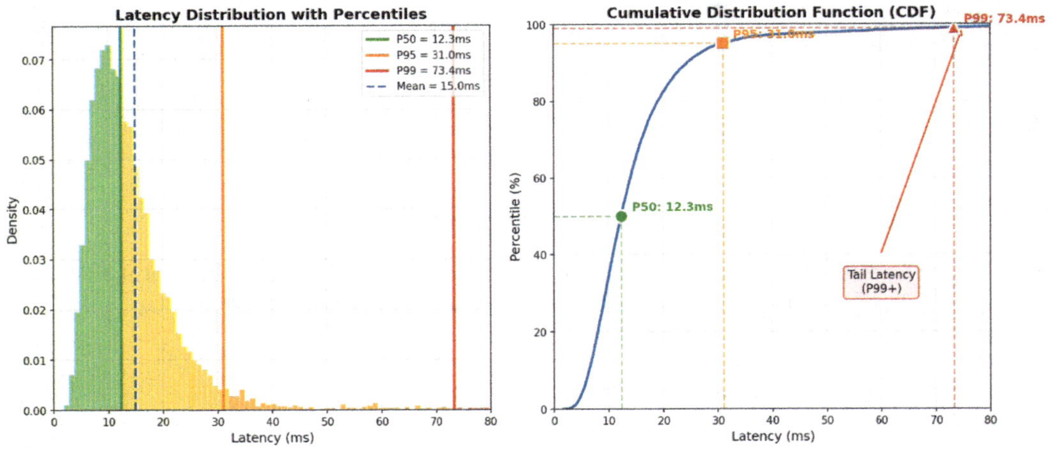

Figure 10.9: Latency distribution histogram and CDF with percentile markers

> **Note**
>
> **Performance vs Accuracy Benchmarking**
>
> This section covers **performance benchmarking** using tools like genai-bench, which measures engineering metrics (throughput, latency, scaling). This is distinct from **accuracy benchmarking** tools like GenAI-Bench for text-to-visual evaluation (`https://linzhiqiu.github.io/papers/genai_bench/`) that measure model output quality. We cover accuracy benchmarking in the next section.

Benchmarking tools: genai-bench

The simplest approach to inference benchmarking—sending identical requests in a loop—misses the complexity of real-world traffic. Production users send prompts ranging from 10 tokens to 10,000 tokens. Load fluctuates from quiet periods with single requests to bursts of hundreds of concurrent users. A benchmark that only tests fixed-length prompts at constant concurrency reveals little about how your system will behave when it matters most.

genai-bench[1] addresses this gap by supporting configurable traffic patterns that mirror production workloads. Rather than sending identical requests, it generates realistic distributions of prompt lengths.

The tool uses traffic scenarios to define request distributions. `D(100,100)` sends deterministic requests with exactly 100 input and 100 output tokens—useful for controlled comparisons. `D(512,512)` tests longer contexts. For realistic benchmarking, you'll want to test a matrix of scenarios: low concurrency with short context establishes baseline latency without batching effects; high concurrency with short context reveals how well your system batches requests; any concurrency with long context exposes memory pressure and KV cache behavior. When latency increases non-linearly as context length grows, you've found a memory bandwidth bottleneck.

Installation is straightforward:

```
pip install genai-bench
```

See `code/genai_bench_example.py` for complete examples of running genai-bench programmatically, including single benchmarks, test matrices, and result analysis.

Custom inference benchmarks

For scenarios where genai-bench doesn't fit—custom models, non-standard APIs, or metrics specific to your application—building a custom benchmark provides the control you need. The key is measuring what matters for your use case while following the same rigorous methodology: warmup, multiple iterations, proper synchronization, and statistical reporting.

Custom benchmarks are particularly valuable for CI/CD integration. You can define performance gates that fail builds when latency regresses or track metrics over time to catch gradual degradation before it affects users.

Cold start vs warm performance

The first request after loading a model behaves very differently from subsequent requests. CUDA kernels must be JIT-compiled, memory must be allocated, and caches must be populated. Cold-start latency is often 3–5× warm decode for small models (1–3B), roughly 16× for mid-size LLMs where kernel compilation and cache fill dominate, and 50× or more for 70B+ checkpoints that take minutes to load from disk.

This matters enormously for autoscaling. If cold starts take 30 seconds but warm requests complete in 100 milliseconds, aggressive scale-down policies create a trap: you save money by terminating idle instances, but when traffic returns, users experience 30-second delays while new instances warm up. The solution is benchmarking both cold and warm performance, then using that data to configure autoscaler minimum instances. Keep enough warm instances running to handle baseline traffic without triggering cold starts.

Reasoning and multi-step models

Traditional benchmarks measure single request-response cycles, but reasoning models—chain-of-thought systems, tool-augmented LLMs, multi-step agents—require a different approach. A single user interaction might involve multiple model calls, external API requests, database queries, and retrieval operations. Measuring only the model inference time misses most of the picture.

Effective benchmarking of reasoning systems requires decomposing latency into its components. Per-step latency (TTFT and ITL for each reasoning step) identifies which steps are slow. End-to-end session latency captures the total user-perceived delay. Most importantly, separating local generation time from external calls reveals where optimization efforts should focus.

In agentic workflows, a surprising pattern often emerges: 60% or more of total latency comes from external calls—tool invocations, API requests, database queries—not from model inference. Optimizing the model provides minimal benefit when users are actually waiting for a slow API response. The benchmark data tell you whether to optimize the model, parallelize tool calls, or cache external results.

See `code/inference_benchmark.py` for complete implementations of custom inference benchmarking, cold start measurement, and reasoning session analysis.

Validating inference accuracy

Speed means nothing if the output is wrong. Inference optimizations—quantization, different serving engines, batching strategies—can subtly degrade output quality in ways that aren't obvious without systematic evaluation.

Consider quantization: INT8 quantization might improve throughput by 2x, but if accuracy on math problems drops 15%, you've made a bad trade. Different serving engines can produce different outputs for the same prompt due to implementation differences in sampling or numerical precision. One might be correct while the other has a bug. Without accuracy benchmarking, these regressions reach production undetected.

The standard approach uses established benchmarks and metrics. For text generation, BLEU and ROUGE measure n-gram overlap with reference text, while BERTScore captures semantic similarity. For task-specific evaluation, use classification accuracy, F1 score, exact match (for QA), or Pass@k (for code generation). Standard benchmarks like GLUE/SuperGLUE, MMLU, HumanEval, and HELM provide consistent evaluation across models and configurations.

When comparing a quantized model to its full-precision baseline, or comparing outputs from different serving engines, statistical significance matters. A 0.5% accuracy drop with $p=0.3$ is probably noise. A 0.5% drop with $p=0.001$ indicates a real regression that needs attention.

See `code/accuracy_benchmark.py` for functions to evaluate quantization impact and test statistical significance.

> **Note**
>
> **Comparing Inference Engines**
>
> When choosing between inference engines (vLLM, SGLang, TensorRT-LLM), define your metrics first: throughput, latency percentiles (P50/P95/P99), and memory usage. Create a realistic workload using production request patterns, run benchmarks with genai-bench for consistency, then analyze tradeoffs. Higher throughput often comes with higher memory usage; lower latency may sacrifice batching efficiency. The "best" engine depends on your specific constraints.

Summary

This chapter has equipped you with the tools and techniques to systematically benchmark and optimize distributed AI systems. The key takeaways are:

1. **Methodology matters:** Proper warmup, multiple runs, and variance analysis separate meaningful benchmarks from noise
2. **Right tools for the job:** PyTorch Profiler and Nsight for training; genai-bench for inference; GLUE, MMLU, and HumanEval for accuracy
3. **Dual benchmarking:** Both performance (speed, throughput) and accuracy (quality, correctness) must be measured—optimizations that degrade accuracy are not optimizations
4. **Network is often the bottleneck:** Communication overhead grows with scale. Profile it, understand it, optimize it.
5. **Scaling has limits:** Amdahl's Law sets theoretical bounds. Measure your scaling efficiency to understand where you stand.
6. **Reproducibility enables progress:** Document everything. Version control benchmark scripts. Fix random seeds.

Skills you've gained:

- Design reproducible benchmark experiments with proper warm-up and measurement
- Profile training workloads using PyTorch Profiler and Nsight Systems
- Benchmark inference systems using genai-bench with realistic traffic patterns
- Evaluate model accuracy using standard benchmarks

- Diagnose network bottlenecks using communication profiling
- Calculate and interpret scaling efficiency

Effective benchmarking is the foundation of performance optimization. Without accurate measurements, optimization efforts are blind guesses. The techniques in this chapter provide the visibility needed to make data-driven decisions about your distributed AI systems.

Throughout this book, we've covered the current state of distributed AI: DDP and FSDP for training, vLLM and SGLang for inference, Slurm for job scheduling, and production serving stacks. But the field is rapidly evolving. The final chapter explores emerging trends and future directions: MoE scaling, hybrid edge-cloud architectures, advanced parallelism strategies, and cost optimization techniques. Understanding where the field is heading will help you position yourself for the next wave of distributed AI innovations.

Code summary

- `torch.profiler`: PyTorch profiler for performance analysis
- `torch.utils.benchmark`: PyTorch benchmarking utilities
- `nvidia-ml-py`: Python library for GPU monitoring
- `psutil`: System and process utilities for resource monitoring
- `mlperf_logging`: MLPerf logging utilities for standardized benchmarks
- `tensorboard`: TensorBoard for visualization of training metrics
- `wandb`: Weights & Biases for experiment tracking
- `py-spy`: Sampling profiler for Python applications
- `nsys`: NVIDIA Nsight Systems for system-level profiling
- `ncu`: NVIDIA Nsight Compute for kernel-level profiling

Useful links

Performance Benchmarking Tools

- genai-bench: `https://github.com/sgl-project/genai-bench`
- PyTorch Profiler: `https://pytorch.org/tutorials/recipes/recipes/profiler_recipe.html`
- NVIDIA Nsight Systems: `https://developer.nvidia.com/nsight-systems`
- NVIDIA GenAI-Perf: `https://docs.nvidia.com/deeplearning/triton-inference-server/user-guide/docs/perf_analyzer/genai-perf/README.html`

- NVIDIA NIM Benchmarking: `https://docs.nvidia.com/nim/benchmarking/llm/latest/index.html`
- IBM FMWork: `https://github.com/IBM/fmwork`

Accuracy Benchmarking

- GLUE Benchmark: `https://gluebenchmark.com/`
- MMLU Benchmark: `https://github.com/hendrycks/test`
- HumanEval (Code Generation): `https://github.com/openai/human-eval`
- HELM (Holistic Evaluation): `https://crfm.stanford.edu/helm/`
- Hugging Face Evaluate: `https://huggingface.co/docs/evaluate/`
- GenAI-Bench (Text-to-Visual): `https://linzhiqiu.github.io/papers/genai_bench/`
- NVIDIA NeMo Evaluator: `https://github.com/NVIDIA-NeMo/Evaluator`

Papers and Standards

- MLPerf Inference Benchmark: `https://arxiv.org/abs/1911.02549`
- LLM-Inference-Bench: `https://arxiv.org/abs/2411.00136`
- MLCommons: `https://mlcommons.org/`

Reference

1. genai-bench: LLM inference benchmark from the SGLang project with configurable input/output length distributions. `https://github.com/sgl-project/genai-bench`

Exercises

Multiple choice questions

1. What is the primary purpose of warmup iterations in benchmarking?

A) To increase the total benchmark runtime B) To eliminate cold-start effects like JIT compilation and cache warming C) To reduce GPU memory usage D) To test error handling code paths

2. When measuring Time to First Token (TTFT), which phases are included?

A) Only the model forward pass B) Tokenization, prefill computation, and first token generation C) All token generation including the final token D) Only network latency

3. A distributed training job shows 85% scaling efficiency at 8 GPUs. What does this mean?

A) 85% of GPU memory is utilized B) The job achieves 85% of ideal linear speedup (6.8x instead of 8x) C) 85% of time is spent on computation D) 15% of gradients are dropped

4. Which metric best captures user-perceived responsiveness in a streaming LLM application?

A) Tokens Per Second (TPS) B) End-to-End Latency (E2E) C) Time to First Token (TTFT) D) GPU Utilization

5. In PyTorch Profiler output, which operations indicate communication overhead?

A) `aten::matmul` and `aten::linear` B) `nccl:all_reduce` and `nccl:all_gather` C) `aten::relu` and `aten::gelu` D) `cuda::memcpy` only

6. What does Amdahl's Law predict about scaling efficiency?

A) Linear scaling is always achievable with more GPUs B) Sequential portions of code limit maximum speedup regardless of parallelization C) Communication overhead decreases with more GPUs D) Memory usage scales linearly with GPU count

7. When benchmarking inference throughput, why is it important to test with varying concurrency levels?

A) To find the maximum batch size B) To identify the saturation point where adding more requests doesn't increase throughput C) To measure cold start latency D) To test model accuracy

8. Which approach correctly measures communication time separately from computation in DDP training?

A) Measure total training time and divide by number of GPUs B) Use `torch.cuda.synchronize()` before and after gradient synchronization C) Count the number of parameters in the model D) Measure only the forward pass time

9. What is the relationship between Inter-token Latency (ITL) and Time Per Output Token (TPOT)?

A) ITL measures the first token, TPOT measures subsequent tokens B) They measure the same thing - the time between consecutive output tokens C) ITL is for training, TPOT is for inference D) TPOT includes network latency, ITL does not

10. When comparing model accuracy between distributed and single-GPU training, what indicates a problem?

A) Identical loss curves B) Statistically significant accuracy degradation beyond expected variance C) Faster convergence with more GPUs D) Lower memory usage per GPU

11. Which percentile metric is most important for SLA compliance in production inference?

A) P50 (median) latency B) P95 or P99 latency C) Average latency D) Minimum latency

12. What is the correct formula for scaling efficiency?

A) `efficiency = throughput_N / throughput_1` B) `efficiency = (throughput_N × N) / throughput_1` C) `efficiency = throughput_N / (throughput_1 × N)` D) `efficiency = N / throughput_N`

13. When profiling network communication, what does `nvidia-smi topo -m` show?

A) GPU memory usage B) GPU interconnect topology (NVLink, PCIe connections) C) Network bandwidth usage D) CUDA kernel execution times

14. Why should benchmarks be run multiple times with statistical analysis?

A) To increase total runtime B) To account for variance and ensure reproducible, statistically significant results C) To warm up the GPU D) To test different model configurations

Short answer questions

1. Explain why communication overhead typically increases as you scale to more GPUs in distributed training.
2. A benchmark shows P50 latency of 50ms and P99 latency of 500ms. What does this distribution suggest about the system's behavior?
3. Describe two ways to reduce communication overhead in distributed training without changing the model architecture.
4. Why might a quantized model (INT8) show different accuracy on different inference engines (vLLM vs SGLang) even with the same weights?
5. What is the difference between "samples per second" in training benchmarks and "tokens per second" in inference benchmarks?

Answer Key

1. B - Warmup eliminates cold-start effects
2. B - TTFT includes tokenization through first token generation
3. B - 85% of ideal linear speedup
4. C - TTFT captures initial responsiveness
5. B - NCCL operations indicate communication
6. B - Sequential code limits maximum speedup

7. B - Find throughput saturation point
8. B - Use synchronization barriers for accurate timing
9. B - Both measure time between consecutive tokens
10. B - Statistically significant accuracy degradation
11. B - P95/P99 for SLA compliance
12. C - `efficiency = throughput_N / (throughput_1 × N)`
13. B - GPU interconnect topology
14. B - Statistical significance and reproducibility

Short Answer Guidelines:

1. More GPUs means more gradient synchronization across more nodes, increasing AllReduce communication volume and potentially crossing slower interconnects (PCIe vs NVLink).
2. High P99/P50 ratio (10x) indicates tail latency issues - most requests are fast but some experience significant delays, possibly due to garbage collection, resource contention, or cold cache effects.
3. Gradient accumulation (fewer sync points), gradient compression (reduced data volume), overlapping communication with computation, using faster interconnects.
4. Different quantization implementations, kernel optimizations, and numerical precision handling can cause slight accuracy variations even with identical weights.
5. Samples/second measures complete training examples processed; tokens/second measures individual token generation rate, which varies with sequence length and batching.

Expected learning outcomes

After completing these exercises, you should be able to:

- Understand key benchmarking concepts and their practical implications
- Interpret benchmark metrics correctly (TTFT, ITL, TPS, scaling efficiency)
- Identify common pitfalls in distributed system benchmarking
- Analyze profiling output to diagnose performance bottlenecks
- Apply statistical thinking to benchmark results

11

The Evolving Landscape of Distributed AI

Exploring emerging technologies and future directions in distributed AI

> *The best way to predict the future is to invent it.*
>
> *Alan Kay, Computer Scientist*

The evolution of distributed AI

Throughout this book, we've explored the foundations of distributed AI: from DDP's gradient synchronization to FSDP's memory optimization, from vLLM's PagedAttention to SGLang's RadixAttention. These technologies have enabled training and serving models that were unimaginable just a few years ago. But the field doesn't stand still—the landscape continues to shift in ways that surprise even seasoned practitioners.

Where we stand today

The numbers tell a remarkable story. Training infrastructure has scaled to over 100,000 GPUs in a single cluster, enabled by new communication frameworks like NCCLX and Torchcomms. SGLang now powers more than 400,000 GPUs worldwide[1], running production workloads for xAI's Grok 3 and Microsoft Azure. Perhaps most striking is the economics: DeepSeek-V3, a 671-billion parameter MoE model with 37 billion active parameters per token, was trained for just $5.5 million on 2,048 H800 GPUs—a cost that would have seemed impossibly low just a few years earlier.

On-device AI has crossed a critical threshold. Models like Gemma 3n run comfortably in 2-3GB of RAM using techniques like Per-Layer Embeddings, making LLMs practical on smartphones. The 4-bit quantization methods that once seemed experimental are now standard practice.

But perhaps the most significant shift is one of priorities. For years, the AI industry focused obsessively on training: building bigger clusters, training larger models, pushing the frontier. That era hasn't ended, but it's no longer the dominant story. Inference workloads now consume over 55% of AI infrastructure spending, and that share continues to grow. Forecasts for the global inference market range from hundreds of billions to well over a trillion dollars in the coming years—the spread reflects whether analysts count silicon, cloud services, or packaged applications.

This shift makes sense when you think about it. Training happens once; inference happens millions of times. As models mature and deployment scales, the economics inevitably favor inference optimization. Infrastructure costs have dropped dramatically over the past few years, making it economically viable to deploy AI in contexts that were previously impractical.

The new bottlenecks

With this growth come new constraints. Interestingly, the primary bottleneck is no longer silicon availability—it's power and cooling. Data centers are being designed around thermal limits rather than rack space. Organizations now factor cooling retrofits into total cost of ownership calculations and negotiate cloud capacity commitments months in advance.

The remaining technical challenges are equally interesting. Scaling beyond 100K GPUs efficiently requires new communication patterns and fault tolerance mechanisms. Balancing latency and throughput in production inference remains an art as much as a science. And cost optimization across hybrid cloud-edge architectures is becoming a discipline unto itself.

Emerging trends at a glance

Before diving into each area, here's a roadmap of what's reshaping distributed AI:

Advanced MoE Architectures: LatentMoE brings hardware-software co-design for optimal accuracy per FLOP, adopted by Nvidia's Nemotron-3. MoSE (Mixture of Slimmable Experts) enables variable-width expert execution for continuous accuracy-compute trade-offs. Elastic MoE scales inference-time expert count to 2-3× training values. ReMoE introduces fully differentiable routing using ReLU instead of TopK+Softmax.

On-Device and Edge AI: Sub-billion parameter models now handle practical tasks effectively. Gemma 3n's Per-Layer Embeddings reduce RAM requirements—5B/8B models run with 2B/4B footprint. Memory bandwidth, not FLOPs, limits edge inference; speculative decoding helps when draft models track the target well.

Next-Generation Communication: Torchcomms, PyTorch's new API, is designed for 100K+ GPU scale with heterogeneous hardware support. NCCLX/RCCLX (Meta's enhanced backends) deliver a 10-50% speedup on AllReduce operations. Async checkpointing is now 6x faster with cached plans and reduced GIL contention.

Inference Engine Evolution: SGLang achieves 16,215 tok/s on H100, with RadixAttention for automatic prefix reuse and pipeline parallelism for million-token contexts. vLLM's PagedAttention reduces KV cache waste from 60-80% to under 4%. Both now support AMD MI355/MI300, Intel Xeon, Google TPUs, and Ascend NPUs.

Mixture of experts: the dominant architecture

We covered MoE fundamentals in Chapter 5 (expert parallelism for training, see Figure 5.8) and Chapter 6 (MoE inference with vLLM). Here we focus on the research frontier pushing MoE capabilities further.

Research continues to push MoE capabilities beyond what we covered in earlier chapters:

LatentMoE[2] uses hardware-software co-design to optimize accuracy per FLOP across different inference scenarios. Adopted by Nvidia's Nemotron-3 models, it demonstrates that the right co-design can significantly improve efficiency without sacrificing capability.

MoSE (Mixture of Slimmable Experts)[3] allows variable-width expert execution. Instead of fixed-size experts, MoSE can dynamically adjust expert width at inference time, enabling continuous accuracy-compute trade-offs. This is particularly valuable for deployment scenarios where latency requirements vary.

Elastic MoE[4] scales the number of active experts beyond training-time values. A model trained with top-2 routing can use top-4 or top-6 at inference time, achieving 2-3x the training-time expert count while improving performance. This decouples training and inference configurations.

ReMoE[5] replaces the non-differentiable TopK+Softmax routing with fully differentiable ReLU-based routing. This enables more efficient dynamic computation allocation and simplifies the training dynamics.

The code in `code/moe_layer.py` provides implementations that extend the concepts from Chapter 5, including load-balanced routing with the auxiliary-loss-free approach.

The Edge-cloud continuum

One of the most profound shifts in distributed AI is the blurring of the boundary between cloud and edge. For years, the assumption was simple: train in the cloud, maybe serve in the cloud, and edge devices are for consumption. That model is breaking down.

Why edge AI matters now

The case for edge AI is compelling. Latency drops from hundreds of milliseconds to single digits when you eliminate network round-trips. Privacy improves dramatically when data never leaves the device. Costs decrease when you're not paying per-token for cloud inference. And offline capability opens entirely new use cases.

What changed to make this practical? Three things converged. First, model architectures got more efficient. Sub-billion parameter models now handle practical tasks that previously required 7B+ models. Second, quantization techniques matured. Going from 16-bit to 4-bit reduces both storage and memory traffic by 4x, with minimal quality loss using methods like GPTQ[6] and AWQ[7]. Third, hardware improved. Mobile NPUs are now capable enough to run these quantized models at acceptable speeds.

But there's a subtlety here that's often missed. The bottleneck on mobile devices isn't compute—it's memory bandwidth. Phones move on the order of 50-90 GB/s; H100-class datacenter GPUs move terabytes per second—a gap of 30-50× in the usual comparison, wider against H200, narrower against older cards like the V100. Quantization matters because it cuts the bytes crossing that bus every forward pass, not just the weights stored on disk.

Practical On-device models

The landscape of edge-capable models has matured rapidly:

Model	Parameters	Memory	Use Cases
Gemma 3n	5B/8B	2–3GB	General assistant
Llama 3.2	1B/3B	1–2GB	Text tasks
Phi-4 mini	3.8B	2GB	Reasoning
Qwen2.5	0.5B-1.5B	<1GB	Lightweight tasks

Google's Gemma 3n uses Per-Layer Embeddings to run 5B and 8B parameter models with the memory footprint of 2B and 4B models respectively—about 2-3GB total. Meta's Llama 3.2 offers 1B and 3B variants specifically designed for edge deployment. Microsoft's Phi-4 mini packs strong reasoning capability into 3.8B parameters. Alibaba's Qwen2.5 ranges from 0.5B to 1.5B for the lightest-weight tasks.

The key insight is that architecture and training quality matter more than raw size at small scales. A well-trained 1B model can outperform a poorly trained 3B model on many tasks.

Edge-cloud coordination

The most interesting systems don't treat edge and cloud as separate worlds—they find ways to make them work together. Remember speculative decoding from Chapter 7? We used it to speed up inference on a single server by having a small draft model propose tokens that a larger model then verifies. The same idea works beautifully across the edge-cloud boundary.

Picture your phone running a tiny but fast model. It generates a sequence of candidate tokens —maybe "The cat sat on the"—and ships them to a powerful cloud model. The cloud doesn't generate anything; it just checks whether each token matches what it would have produced. Verification is cheap: the cloud model can evaluate all five tokens in a single forward pass, whereas generating them one by one would take five passes. When the drafts are mostly correct (and for predictable text, they often are), you get cloud-quality output at edge-like speed. Gains are task-dependent: structured output such as code or JSON often reaches 3-4× end-to-end speedup, while open-ended creative text may improve only 1.2-1.5× because rejections are frequent[8].

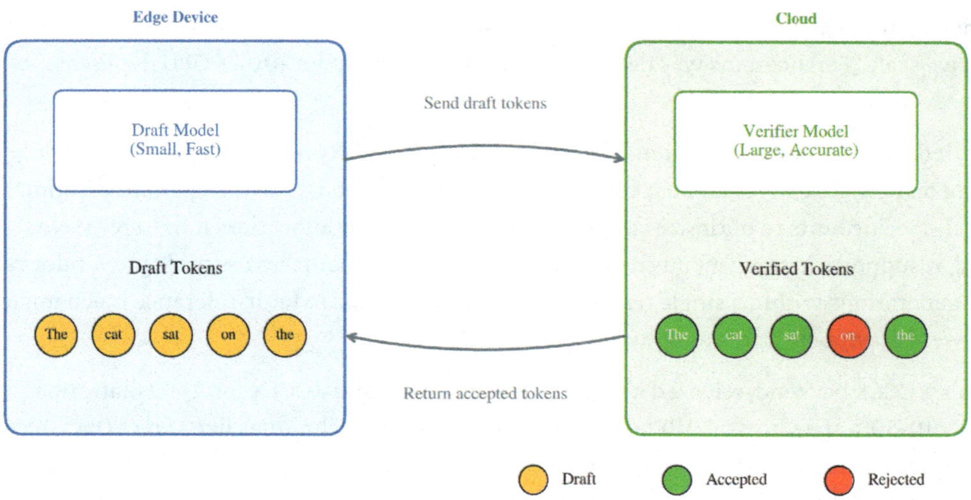

Figure 11.1: Edge-cloud speculative decoding workflow

Figure 11.1 illustrates this dance. The edge device proposes tokens (yellow circles), sends them to the cloud, and the verifier stamps each one as accepted (green) or rejected (red). In this example, "on" gets rejected—perhaps the cloud model prefers a different preposition—so the edge will need to regenerate from that point. But four out of five tokens sailed through, saving significant latency.

Intelligent routing pushes this coordination further. Not every request actually needs the cloud. A well-designed system estimates how hard each request is, checks how confident the edge model feels, glances at network conditions, and decides: handle locally or send to the cloud? Simple queries—"What time is it in Tokyo?"—stay on device. Complex reasoning tasks go to the cloud. The routing logic can even learn from past decisions, getting better at predicting which requests will succeed locally.

The `code/edge_cloud.py` file implements these patterns: `EdgeCloudSpeculativeDecoding` for the draft-verify loop, `IntelligentOffloading` for complexity-based routing, and `AdaptiveRouter` which improves over time.

Parallelism at scale

The parallelism strategies we covered earlier—data parallelism (DDP in Chapter 3, FSDP in Chapter 4), tensor parallelism, and pipeline parallelism (Chapter 5)—remain foundational. But at 100K+ GPU scale, new challenges emerge that require new solutions.

The communication revolution

PyTorch's introduction of Torchcomms marked a significant evolution in distributed training infrastructure. The previous communication stack, while functional, was showing its age at massive scale. Torchcomms was designed from the ground up for 100K+ GPU deployments with several key innovations.

First, it decouples communication primitives from PyTorch's core, allowing researchers to iterate on new collectives and backends independently. Second, it uses eager initialization and model-specific hints to optimize communicator and resource allocation at massive scale. Third, it supports heterogeneous hardware—mixed deployments across multiple vendors and GPU generations within a single training job. Fourth, it builds in fault-tolerance mechanisms that were previously afterthoughts.

Meta's NCCLX backend, released alongside Torchcomms, and RCCLX for AMD platforms, deliver 10-50% speedups on AllReduce operations through techniques like Direct Data Access (DDA). These aren't incremental improvements—they can mean the difference between a training run that's economically viable and one that isn't.

Hierarchical parallelism

At scale, you don't choose one parallelism strategy—you combine them. A typical large training run might use data parallelism across nodes, tensor parallelism within nodes, and pipeline parallelism across model stages. The math is straightforward: if you have `world_size` GPUs, then `dp_size × tp_size × pp_size = world_size`.

The art is in choosing the right combination. Tensor parallelism has low communication overhead within a node (NVLink is fast) but high overhead across nodes. Pipeline parallelism can hide communication latency but introduces bubble overhead. Data parallelism scales well but requires gradient synchronization. The optimal configuration depends on your model architecture, hardware topology, and batch size constraints.

The `HierarchicalParallelism` class in `code/parallelism.py` manages the process group creation for all three dimensions, ensuring that each GPU knows which groups it belongs to for each type of parallelism.

Sequence parallelism for long contexts

As context lengths grow, sequence parallelism becomes essential. The idea is to split the sequence dimension across GPUs. Each GPU computes attention for its local chunk of the sequence, but attention requires seeing the full key and value tensors. This means all-gathering K and V from all sequence-parallel ranks.

SGLang's pipeline parallelism reports strong long-prompt numbers: 3.31× prefill throughput on DeepSeek-V3.1, up to 81% TTFT reduction on million-token contexts, and 82.8% scaling efficiency. Those techniques address memory and latency; retrieval quality is a separate question—many models lose accuracy on long documents well below their advertised context limit.

Ring attention

We introduced ring attention in Chapter 5 as part of context parallelism (see Figure 5.6). Here we revisit it in the context of scaling to million-token sequences.

Ring attention[9] offers a memory-efficient alternative to standard sequence parallelism. Instead of all-gathering the full K and V tensors (which requires O(sequence_length) memory per GPU), ring attention passes K and V chunks around a ring of GPUs, computing partial attention scores at each step. Each GPU starts with its local Q, K, V chunks. In each round, GPUs compute attention between their local Q and the current K, V, then pass K and V to the next GPU. After N−1 rounds, every rank has attended over all keys and values.

This trades communication rounds for memory efficiency—useful when you're memory-constrained but have communication bandwidth to spare. At million-token scale, this trade-off becomes increasingly attractive: the memory savings from avoiding full K, V all-gathers can be the difference between fitting a workload and running out of memory. The `RingAttention` class in `code/parallelism.py` implements this pattern.

When things go wrong: fault tolerance

At 99.9% daily reliability per GPU, a 100,000-GPU cluster should expect on the order of 100 failures every 24 hours. The probability that every device survives the day is $0.999^{100,000} \approx$

3.7×10^{-44}—effectively zero. At this scale, failures are the normal operating condition, not the exception.

The checkpointing challenge

Traditional checkpointing is synchronous: stop training, save state to disk, resume. This was acceptable when checkpoints took seconds and training runs lasted hours. At scale, checkpoints can take minutes, and training runs last weeks. The overhead becomes significant.

PyTorch's Distributed Checkpointing (DCP) introduced several optimizations that achieve roughly 6× faster checkpoint processing:

- **Cached save plans**: Reuse tensor metadata across checkpoints—the shapes and dtypes don't change, so why recompute them?
- **Background saving**: Reduce GIL contention by moving the actual I/O to separate threads
- **Incremental saves**: Only write tensors that have changed since the last checkpoint

The `AsyncCheckpointer` in `code/fault_tolerance.py` implements these ideas. It maintains a background thread that processes save requests from a queue, allowing training to continue while checkpoints are written. It also manages checkpoint retention, automatically cleaning up old checkpoints to save disk space.

Detecting and handling failures

Failure detection sounds simple—just check if workers are responding—but the details matter. How long do you wait before declaring a worker dead? Too short, and you'll have false positives from network hiccups. Too long, and you waste time waiting for a genuinely dead worker.

The `FailureDetector` class uses a heartbeat mechanism. Workers send periodic heartbeats; missing heartbeats trigger failure callbacks. The system can then decide how to respond: continue with remaining workers, restart the failed worker, or checkpoint and abort.

Key design decisions include:

- **Heartbeat interval**: Typically 1-5 seconds, balancing responsiveness with overhead
- **Timeout threshold**: Usually 3-5 missed heartbeats before declaring failure
- **Failure callback**: What action to take—log, alert, checkpoint, or abort

Elastic training

The most sophisticated approach is elastic training, where the system adapts to worker changes without stopping. Workers can join or leave during training. When a worker fails, the system checkpoints, redistributes work among remaining workers, and continues. When a new worker joins, it receives a share of the work.

This requires careful coordination:

- **Gradient averaging** must account for the changing number of workers
- **Data loading** must redistribute shards dynamically
- **Learning rate schedules** may need adjustment for different worker counts
- **Checkpointing** must handle partial states during transitions

The `ElasticTrainer` class in `code/fault_tolerance.py` handles these concerns, providing automatic checkpointing on failure and graceful degradation.

Beyond text: multimodal distributed training

The models capturing the most attention today aren't text-only—they're multimodal. Vision-Language Models (VLMs) that can see and read, models that process video, systems that understand audio alongside text. Distributing these models efficiently requires new patterns.

The Cross-modal challenge

A VLM typically has a vision encoder (often ViT-based) that produces image features, and a language model that processes text while attending to those image features. The cross-modal attention—where text tokens attend to vision features—is where the modalities meet.

This cross-modal attention can be parallelized using tensor parallelism, sharding attention heads across GPUs. But there's a subtlety: the vision encoder and language model may have different optimal parallelism strategies. The vision encoder processes fixed-size images and benefits from different batch sizes than the language model, which handles variable-length text.

The `code/multimodal.py` file provides implementations of these components:

- `VisionEncoder`: ViT-style image encoder with patch embedding and transformer blocks
- `CrossModalAttention`: Text-to-vision attention with tensor parallelism support
- `VisionLanguageModel`: Complete VLM combining vision and language components

Handling multiple modalities

Different modalities have different characteristics:

Modality	Size	Characteristics
Images	Fixed after pre-processing	Batch-friendly, predictable memory
Text	Variable length	Requires padding, dynamic memory
Video	Multiple frames	High memory, temporal structure
Audio	Variable duration	Temporal structure, streaming

`MultimodalDataParallel` handles scattering batches across workers while keeping modalities aligned. This is trickier than it sounds—you need to ensure that the image corresponding to a text prompt ends up on the same worker, even when batch sizes differ across modalities.

Federated learning: an alternative paradigm

Throughout this book, we've assumed that all GPUs can access a shared dataset—or at least shards of it stored in a common data center. But what if the data can't be moved? What if privacy regulations, competitive concerns, or sheer logistics make centralization impossible? This is where federated learning comes in.

The federated paradigm

Federated learning flips the script: instead of bringing data to the model, it brings the model to the data. Each participant—whether a smartphone, a hospital, or a bank—trains on its local data and shares only model updates, never raw data. A central server aggregates these updates to produce a global model. The paradigm has been around since 2016, and it has matured into a practical solution for privacy-sensitive domains.

Figure 11.2 illustrates this architecture. A central server at the top coordinates training and holds the global model. Four clients at the bottom—a hospital with patient records, a bank with transaction data, a mobile app with user behavior, and IoT devices with sensor readings—each train locally on their private data. Blue arrows show the server distributing the current model; green arrows show clients sending back their updates. The crucial point, highlighted at the bottom: data never leaves the client. Only gradients and weights travel across the network.

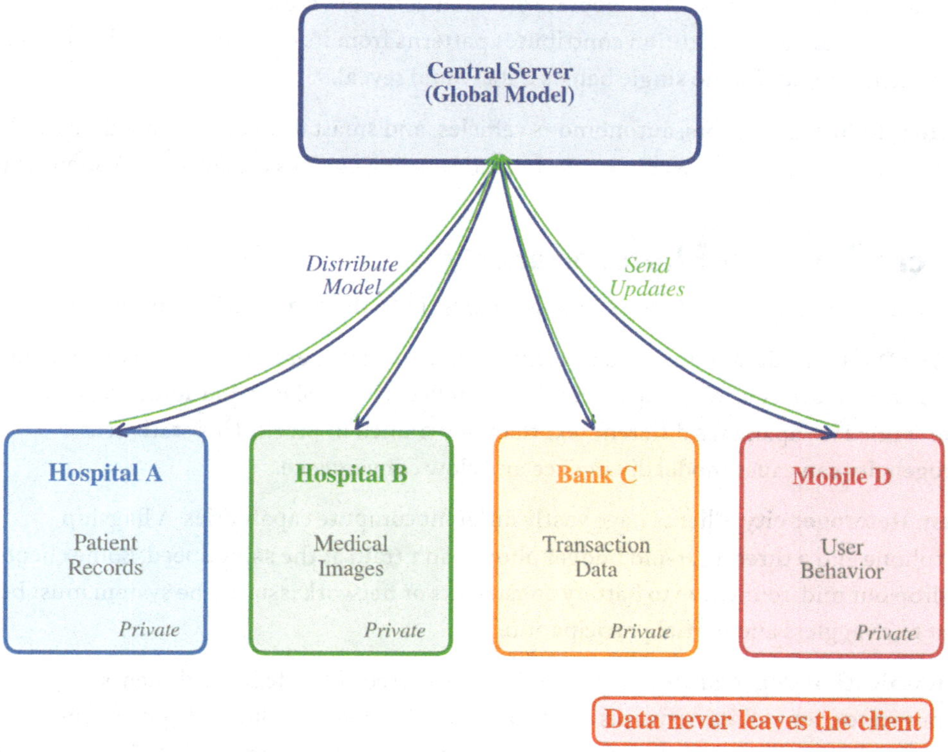

Figure 11.2: Federated learning: data stays on clients

The canonical algorithm is FedAvg[10]. Each round, the server sends the current model to a subset of clients. Clients train locally for several epochs, then send updated weights back. The server averages these weights to produce a new global model. Simple as it sounds, this protocol has proven remarkably effective—and the field has built many refinements on top of it.

Where federated learning thrives

Federated learning has found strong adoption in specific verticals:

Healthcare: Hospitals can collaboratively train diagnostic models without sharing patient records. Projects like NVIDIA FLARE[11] enable multi-institutional medical imaging research while maintaining HIPAA compliance. A model trained across 20 hospitals sees more diverse pathology than any single institution could provide.

Mobile Keyboards: Google's Gboard uses federated learning to improve next-word prediction without uploading what users type. The model learns from millions of devices while keeping text on-device. This was one of the first large-scale production deployments of federated learning.

Financial Services: Banks can collaborate on fraud detection models without sharing transaction data. Each institution contributes patterns from its customer base; the combined model catches fraud that no single bank's data would reveal.

Edge IoT: Industrial sensors, autonomous vehicles, and smart devices generate data that's expensive or impractical to centralize. Federated learning enables model improvement without massive data transfers.

The challenges of heterogeneity

Federated learning faces challenges that don't exist in traditional distributed training:

Non-IID Data: In a data center, you can shuffle data to ensure each GPU sees a representative sample. In federated learning, each client's data reflects its local distribution. A keyboard model trained in Japan sees different text than one trained in Brazil. This statistical heterogeneity can cause model divergence and slow convergence.

System Heterogeneity: Clients have vastly different compute capabilities. A flagship smartphone and a three-year-old budget phone can't train at the same speed. Some clients may drop out mid-round due to battery constraints or network issues. The system must be robust to stragglers and partial participation.

Communication Constraints: Unlike NVLink-connected GPUs, federated clients communicate over mobile networks or the internet. Bandwidth is limited and expensive. Techniques like gradient compression, quantization, and infrequent synchronization become essential—not for performance, but for feasibility.

Modern federated techniques

Research has addressed these challenges with increasingly sophisticated methods:

FedProx[12] adds a proximal term to the local objective, preventing clients from drifting too far from the global model. This stabilizes training when data is highly non-IID.

Scaffold[13] uses control variates to correct for client drift, achieving faster convergence than FedAvg on heterogeneous data.

Differential Privacy can be layered on top of federated learning to provide formal privacy guarantees. By adding calibrated noise to updates, even the aggregated model reveals limited information about any individual's data. This is particularly important in healthcare and finance.

Secure Aggregation[14] ensures the server only sees the sum of client updates, not individual contributions. Even a compromised server can't extract any single client's model update.

Federated learning for LLMs

Applying federated learning to large language models presents unique challenges. A 7B parameter model can't fit on a smartphone, and even fine-tuning requires significant memory. Recent work explores several approaches:

Federated Fine-Tuning with LoRA: Instead of updating all parameters, clients train low-rank adapters. This reduces communication (only adapter weights are exchanged) and memory (adapters are small). FedIT[15] and similar approaches make federated LLM fine-tuning practical.

Split Learning: The model is split between client and server. Clients run early layers on their data and send activations (not raw data) to the server, which completes the forward pass. This enables training large models without requiring clients to hold the full model.

On-Device Personalization: Rather than training a single global model, each device maintains a personalized version. The global model provides a starting point; local fine-tuning adapts to individual users. This is particularly relevant for assistants that should reflect user preferences.

The flower framework

Flower[16] has emerged as the leading open-source federated learning framework. It provides:

- A simple API for defining federated training loops
- Support for various aggregation strategies (FedAvg, FedProx, etc.)
- Integration with PyTorch, TensorFlow, and JAX
- Simulation capabilities for development and research
- Production deployment tools

The framework abstracts away much of the complexity, letting researchers focus on algorithms rather than infrastructure. A basic federated training setup requires just a few dozen lines of code.

When to consider federated learning

Federated learning isn't a replacement for traditional distributed training—it's a tool for specific situations:

Consider federated learning when	Stick with traditional training when
Data can't leave its source (privacy, regulation)	Data can be centralized
Data is naturally distributed (mobile, edge)	You control the infrastructure
Participants don't trust each other	Single-organization training
Communication is expensive	High-bandwidth interconnect available

The overhead of federated learning—slower convergence, communication constraints, heterogeneity challenges—means it's not the right choice when you can simply centralize data. But when privacy or logistics make centralization impossible, federated learning enables collaboration that wouldn't otherwise happen.

Agentic AI: the next frontier

Perhaps the most exciting recent development is the rise of agentic AI—systems that don't just respond to prompts but plan, use tools, and take actions. These systems push distributed inference in new directions.

Why agents need distribution

Consider what happens when an agent decides to call a tool. The tool might be a code interpreter, a web browser, a database query, or an API call. Each tool has different resource requirements and latency characteristics. Some tools are stateful and need to run on specific workers. Some are embarrassingly parallel; others are sequential bottlenecks.

Multi-agent systems add another layer. Multiple agents might collaborate on a task, each with different capabilities. They need to communicate, coordinate, and sometimes disagree. This communication can happen within a single node or across a distributed system.

Long reasoning chains—the kind that models like o1 and DeepSeek-R1[17] produce—require sustained inference over many steps. Each step might involve tool calls, memory lookups, or coordination with other agents. The inference isn't a single forward pass; it's an extended computation that might run for minutes.

Multi-agent patterns

How do you orchestrate multiple agents working together? Three patterns have emerged as the workhorses of multi-agent systems, each suited to different problem structures.

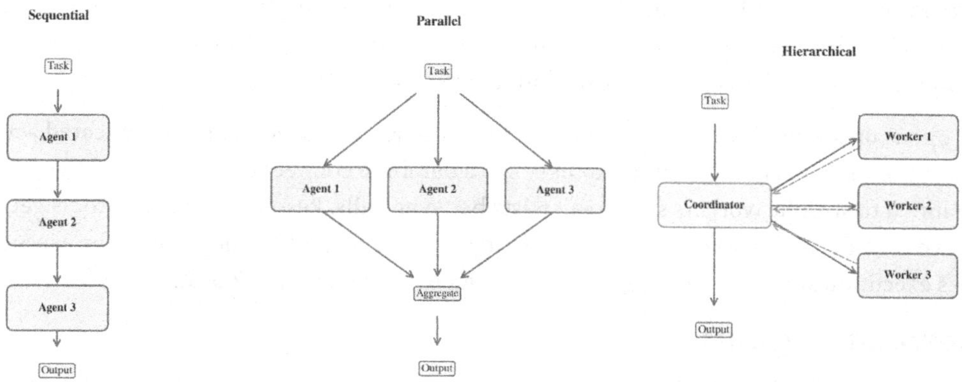

Figure 11.3: Three common multi-agent coordination patterns

Figure 11.3 illustrates these patterns. In **sequential processing**, agents form a pipeline: one extracts information, the next reasons about it, the third formats the response. Each agent's output becomes the next agent's input. This works well when the task naturally decomposes into stages with clear handoffs.

Parallel processing takes a different approach—multiple agents tackle the same task simultaneously. Perhaps you want diverse perspectives: one agent might find a creative solution while another finds a safe one. Or you're racing strategies, taking whichever finishes first. Results flow to an aggregator that combines or selects among them.

Hierarchical processing mirrors how human teams often work. A coordinator receives the task, breaks it into subtasks, and delegates to specialized workers. The workers report back (green dashed arrows in the figure), and the coordinator synthesizes their results into a final output. This shines for complex tasks that decompose naturally—the coordinator handles strategy while workers handle tactics.

The `code/agentic_inference.py` file implements all three patterns, along with the routing logic to choose among them based on task characteristics.

Distributed tool execution

When an agent decides to call a tool, where does that tool actually run? Not all tools are created equal. A code interpreter needs a sandboxed environment with proper security isolation—you can't just run arbitrary code anywhere. A web browser might need GPU acceleration for rendering. A simple calculator, on the other hand, can run on any worker with spare cycles.

The `DistributedToolExecutor` in `code/agentic_inference.py` handles this routing. Tools register themselves with optional worker constraints: "I need sandboxing," "I require GPU," or "I'm stateless, run me anywhere." When an agent requests a tool, the executor finds an appropriate worker, dispatches the call, and returns the result.

This opens up sophisticated placement strategies. Frequently-used tools get replicated across workers for load balancing. Stateful tools—like a database connection or a browser session—get pinned to specific workers so state persists between calls. Resource-intensive tools get isolated to dedicated workers, preventing them from starving other operations. The executor tracks execution statistics, learning over time which placements work best.

Reasoning agents

The most sophisticated agents don't just respond—they think. Given a complex problem, they break it down, try approaches, observe results, and adjust. This is the territory of reasoning agents like o1 and DeepSeek-R1, where inference isn't a single forward pass but an extended deliberation that might span dozens of steps.

The `ReasoningAgent` in `code/agentic_inference.py` captures this pattern. It maintains a reasoning trace—a running record of thoughts, tool calls, and observations. At each step, the agent faces a choice: think more deeply about the current state, call a tool to gather information, or commit to a final answer. When it calls a tool, the result becomes a new observation that feeds into the next thought. The loop continues until the agent is confident enough to answer or hits a step limit.

This is a simplified version of what production reasoning systems do, but it captures the essential dynamic: the interplay between thinking and acting, between internal deliberation and external observation, that enables agents to solve problems too complex for a single inference pass.

The economics of scale

As distributed AI matures, economic considerations become increasingly important. The days of "just throw more GPUs at it" are ending; efficiency and cost optimization are now first-class concerns.

Workload distribution

Enterprise workload distribution shows no single dominant category:

Workload type	Share
Inference at scale	34.6%
Foundation model training	24.9%
Domain-specific training	23.3%
Fine-tuning	17.2%

This diversity means that infrastructure must be flexible—optimized for one workload type, it won't serve the full range of needs.

Organizations are adopting hybrid strategies:

- **Public cloud**: Handles elastic and variable workloads where demand is unpredictable
- **On-premises**: Serves high-volume production inference where predictable costs matter
- **Near-edge data centers**: Handle latency-sensitive, user-facing AI services

Resource management

Dynamic resource allocation is essential when workloads vary. The `AdaptiveGPUAllocator` in `code/resource_management.py` estimates GPU requirements based on:

- Model size (memory requirement)
- Batch size (throughput requirement)
- Job priority (business importance)

It maintains a queue for jobs that can't be immediately scheduled and processes the queue as resources become available.

Multi-tenant GPU sharing

`MultiTenantGPUScheduler` implements time-sliced GPU sharing:

- Priority-weighted round-robin scheduling
- Fair distribution across tenants
- Queue management for pending work
- Preemption for high-priority jobs

This allows multiple teams or services to share GPU resources fairly, with priorities reflecting business importance.

Gradient compression

At scale, communication overhead can dominate computation time. `GradientCompression` in `code/resource_management.py` reduces this overhead:

Top-k Sparsification[18]: Keep only the k largest gradient values. With k=1% of gradients, you achieve 100x compression. Error feedback—accumulating dropped gradients for the next iteration—preserves convergence.

Quantization: Reduce precision to 8-bit. This achieves 4x compression with minimal impact on training dynamics. Can be combined with sparsification for even higher compression.

The key insight is that gradients are highly compressible. Most gradient values are small and contribute little to learning. By focusing communication on the largest values and accumulating the rest, you can dramatically reduce bandwidth requirements without sacrificing convergence.

Preparing for the future

Skills to develop

MoE and Sparse Architectures: Understanding expert routing strategies (TopK, ReLU-based), load balancing mechanisms, and elastic expert scaling at inference time is increasingly essential as MoE becomes the default architecture.

Edge-Cloud Coordination: Speculative decoding implementation, memory bandwidth optimization for mobile, and quantization techniques (GPTQ, AWQ) open new deployment options that weren't practical until recently.

Large-Scale Communication: Torchcomms API and NCCLX/RCCLX backends, async checkpointing strategies, and heterogeneous hardware deployments enable bigger training runs and more efficient infrastructure utilization.

Inference Optimization: RadixAttention and PagedAttention internals, pipeline parallelism for long contexts, and multi-tenant GPU scheduling improve serving efficiency and reduce costs.

Agentic Systems: Multi-agent orchestration patterns, distributed tool execution, and reasoning chain optimization represent the next application frontier where distributed AI meets complex problem-solving.

Staying current

The field moves fast—techniques that seem cutting-edge today may be standard practice in six months. Staying current requires building habits around a few key information sources.

For day-to-day learning, arXiv is indispensable. New papers in cs.DC and cs.LG drop daily, and the best work often appears here months before conference publication. Set up alerts for keywords like "distributed training," "inference optimization," and "mixture of experts." Open-source projects are equally important: vLLM, SGLang, DeepSpeed, and Megatron-LM are where theory meets practice. Watch their release notes and GitHub discussions—that's where you'll learn what actually works at scale. Industry blogs from teams at xAI, Anthropic, Google, and Meta regularly publish technical deep-dives that reveal practical insights never found in papers. And don't overlook communities: Hugging Face forums, PyTorch Discuss, and the SGLang Discord are where practitioners share war stories and debug tricky issues together.

For deeper dives, conferences remain essential. Research venues like NeurIPS, ICML, and ICLR are where new algorithms and architectures debut—pay special attention to workshops on efficient ML and large-scale systems. Systems conferences like MLSys, OSDI, and SOSP focus on infrastructure, communication optimization, and production deployment; if you care about making things fast, these are essential reading. Industry events like GTC and PyTorch Conference are where vendors announce new hardware and frameworks, giving you a preview of what's coming in the next 12–18 months.

The References section at the end of this chapter provides URLs for the key papers and projects mentioned throughout.

Summary

This chapter has explored the current state of distributed AI and the trends shaping its future:

1. **The great shift to inference**: Inference workloads now consume over 55% of AI infrastructure spending, with training becoming a smaller fraction of total compute. This reshapes infrastructure priorities and optimization targets.
2. **MoE dominance**: Architectures like DeepSeek-V3 demonstrate that 671B parameter models can be trained for $5.5M with only 37B active parameters per token. Understanding expert routing, load balancing, and parallelism is essential.
3. **On-device AI is practical**: Sub-billion parameter models, 4-bit quantization, and techniques like Per-Layer Embeddings enable LLMs on mobile devices. Memory bandwidth, not compute, is the bottleneck.

4. **100K+ GPU scale**: New communication APIs (Torchcomms, NCCLX/RCCLX) and async checkpointing enable training at unprecedented scale. Heterogeneous hardware support is increasingly important.
5. **Fault tolerance is essential**: At scale, failures are expected—roughly 100 per day in a 100K GPU cluster. Elastic training and async checkpointing are mandatory, not optional.
6. **Multimodal and agentic**: VLMs and multi-agent systems require new distributed patterns for cross-modal attention and tool execution. These represent the next application frontier.
7. **Federated learning as alternative paradigm**: When data can't be centralized due to privacy or regulatory constraints, federated learning offers a mature alternative. Techniques like FedProx and secure aggregation address the unique challenges of non-IID data and untrusted participants.
8. **Inference engine evolution**: SGLang achieves 16,215 tok/s with RadixAttention; vLLM's PagedAttention reduces KV cache waste to under 4%. Both support diverse hardware platforms.

The technologies covered in this book—DDP, FSDP, DeepSpeed, Megatron-LM, vLLM, SGLang—remain foundational, but the landscape continues to evolve rapidly. Power and cooling constraints, not silicon availability, are now the primary bottleneck.

If you read straight through from Chapter 1, you began where most practitioners do: a model that outgrew one GPU, and a growing set of questions about hardware, parallelism, training frameworks, inference engines, and production deployment. This chapter situates those pieces in what comes next—MoE at scale, on-device inference, fault tolerance, and a world where inference, not training, drives most infrastructure spend. The tools will keep changing; the systems mindset you built along the way does not.

The future of distributed AI is being written now, by researchers pushing boundaries and practitioners deploying at scale. Having worked through this book, you are better equipped to follow that work—and to help invent it.

Code summary

- `torch.distributed.checkpoint.save`: Async distributed checkpointing with DCP
- `torch.distributed.checkpoint.load`: Load sharded checkpoints across ranks
- `torch.distributed.elastic.multiprocessing`: Elastic training with fault tolerance
- `torch.ao.quantization.quantize_dynamic`: Dynamic quantization for model compression

- `flwr.client.NumPyClient`: Flower federated learning client interface
- `flwr.server.strategy.FedAvg`: Federated averaging aggregation strategy
- `megatron.core.transformer.moe.router.TopKRouter`: Megatron MoE top-k routing
- `vllm.LLM`: vLLM inference engine with PagedAttention
- `sglang.Engine`: SGLang runtime with RadixAttention

Useful links

MoE Architectures

- DeepSeek-V3 Technical Report: `https://arxiv.org/abs/2412.19437`
- LatentMoE: Toward Optimal Accuracy per FLOP: `https://arxiv.org/abs/2601.18089`
- MoSE: Mixture of Slimmable Experts: `https://arxiv.org/abs/2602.06154`
- Elastic MoE: Inference-Time Expert Scaling: `https://arxiv.org/abs/2501.03140`
- ReMoE: Fully Differentiable MoE with ReLU Routing: `https://arxiv.org/abs/2412.14711`

Communication and Scale

- NVIDIA NCCL: `https://developer.nvidia.com/nccl`
- Torchcomms API: `https://pytorch.org/blog/torchcomms/`
- RCCLX for AMD Platforms: `https://engineering.fb.com/2026/02/24/data-center-engineering/rrcclx-innovating-gpu-communications-amd-platforms-meta/`
- PyTorch Distributed Checkpoint: `https://pytorch.org/docs/stable/distributed.checkpoint.html`
- Async Checkpointing Improvements: `https://pytorch.org/blog/6x-faster-async-checkpointing/`
- Deep Gradient Compression: `https://arxiv.org/abs/1712.01887`

Inference Engines

- SGLang (RadixAttention): `https://arxiv.org/abs/2312.07104`
- SGLang Pipeline Parallelism: `https://lmsys.org/blog/2026-01-15-chunked-pipeline/`
- SGLang Documentation: `https://sgl-project.github.io/`
- vLLM (PagedAttention): `https://arxiv.org/abs/2309.06180`

- vLLM Documentation: `https://docs.vllm.ai/`
- Speculative Decoding: `https://arxiv.org/abs/2211.17192`

Memory-Efficient Attention

- Multi-head Latent Attention (DeepSeek-V2): `https://arxiv.org/abs/2405.04434`
- Ring Attention: `https://arxiv.org/abs/2310.01889`
- FlashAttention-2: `https://arxiv.org/abs/2307.08691`

On-Device AI and Quantization

- GPTQ: Post-Training Quantization: `https://arxiv.org/abs/2210.17323`
- AWQ: Activation-aware Weight Quantization: `https://arxiv.org/abs/2306.00978`
- KV Cache Compression: `https://arxiv.org/abs/2405.12981`
- Google LiteRT: `https://ai.google.dev/edge/litert`
- Gemma 3n: `https://ai.google.dev/gemma/docs/gemma-3n`

Reasoning and Agentic AI

- DeepSeek-R1: `https://arxiv.org/abs/2501.12948`
- ReAct: Reasoning and Acting in Language Models: `https://arxiv.org/abs/2210.03629`

Fault Tolerance and Elastic Training

- PyTorch Elastic: `https://pytorch.org/docs/stable/elastic/run.html`
- TorchSnapshot: `https://pytorch.org/torchsnapshot/`

Federated Learning

- FedAvg: Communication-Efficient Learning from Decentralized Data: `https://arxiv.org/abs/1602.05629`
- FedProx: Federated Optimization in Heterogeneous Networks: `https://arxiv.org/abs/1812.06127`
- SCAFFOLD: Stochastic Controlled Averaging: `https://arxiv.org/abs/1910.06378`
- Secure Aggregation for Privacy-Preserving ML: `https://eprint.iacr.org/2017/281`
- Flower Framework: `https://flower.ai/`
- NVIDIA FLARE: `https://github.com/NVIDIA/NVFlare`
- FedIT: Federated Instruction Tuning of LLMs: `https://arxiv.org/abs/2409.12568`

References

1. LMSYS/SGLang project updates. https://github.com/sgl-project/sglang, https://lmsys.org/blog/
2. LatentMoE: Toward Optimal Accuracy per FLOP. https://arxiv.org/abs/2601.18089
3. MoSE: Mixture of Slimmable Experts. https://arxiv.org/abs/2602.06154
4. Elastic MoE: Inference-Time Expert Scaling. https://arxiv.org/abs/2501.03140
5. ReMoE: Fully Differentiable Mixture-of-Experts with ReLU Routing. https://arxiv.org/abs/2412.14711
6. GPTQ: Accurate Post-Training Quantization for Generative Pre-trained Transformers. https://arxiv.org/abs/2210.17323
7. AWQ: Activation-aware Weight Quantization for LLM Compression and Acceleration. https://arxiv.org/abs/2306.00978
8. Fast Inference from Transformers via Speculative Decoding. https://arxiv.org/abs/2211.17192
9. Ring Attention with Blockwise Transformers for Near-Infinite Context. https://arxiv.org/abs/2310.01889
10. Communication-Efficient Learning of Deep Networks from Decentralized Data. https://arxiv.org/abs/1602.05629
11. NVIDIA FLARE: Federated Learning Application Runtime Environment. https://github.com/NVIDIA/NVFlare
12. Federated Optimization in Heterogeneous Networks. https://arxiv.org/abs/1812.06127
13. SCAFFOLD: Stochastic Controlled Averaging for Federated Learning. https://arxiv.org/abs/1910.06378
14. Practical Secure Aggregation for Privacy-Preserving Machine Learning. https://eprint.iacr.org/2017/281
15. Federated Instruction Tuning of LLMs with Domain Coverage Augmentation. https://arxiv.org/abs/2409.12568
16. Flower: A Friendly Federated Learning Framework. https://flower.ai/

17. DeepSeek-R1: Incentivizing Reasoning Capability in LLMs via Reinforcement Learning. `https://arxiv.org/abs/2501.12948`

18. Deep Gradient Compression: Reducing the Communication Bandwidth for Distributed Training. `https://arxiv.org/abs/1712.01887`

Exercises

Multiple choice questions

1. What is the primary advantage of MoE (Mixture of Experts) architectures?
   a) Faster training convergence b) Scales model capacity without proportional compute increase c) Eliminates the need for distributed training d) Reduces model size

2. In a typical MoE layer with 64 experts and top-2 routing, how many experts process each token?
   a) 1 b) 2 c) 32 d) 64

3. What is the main bottleneck for on-device LLM inference on mobile devices?
   a) CPU compute b) Storage space c) Memory bandwidth d) Battery capacity

4. What does speculative decoding achieve in edge-cloud scenarios?
   a) Reduces model size b) Uses a small draft model to propose tokens verified by a larger model c) Eliminates network latency d) Compresses gradients

5. At 100K GPU scale with 99.9% per-GPU reliability, approximately how many failures occur per day?
   a) 1 b) 10 c) 100 d) 1000

6. What is the purpose of load balancing loss in MoE training?
   a) Reduce memory usage b) Encourage uniform expert utilization c) Speed up inference d) Compress model weights

7. Which communication pattern is most expensive in expert parallelism?
   a) Broadcast b) Reduce c) All-to-all d) Gather

8. What does Ring Attention trade for reduced memory usage?
   a) Accuracy b) More communication rounds c) Larger batch sizes d) Fewer experts

Short answer questions

1. Explain why inference workloads now consume over 55% of AI infrastructure spending, while training was dominant just a few years ago.

2. Describe the key difference between synchronous and asynchronous checkpointing, and why async checkpointing matters at scale.

3. A VLM (Vision-Language Model) uses cross-modal attention. Explain what this means and one challenge in distributing it.
4. Compare top-k gradient sparsification with quantization for gradient compression. What are the trade-offs?

Hands-on exercise

Implement basic MoE routing

Create a simple MoE router that:

- Takes input tokens and routes them to top-k experts
- Computes load balancing loss
- Returns weighted expert outputs

Reference `code/moe_layer.py` for guidance. Test with 4 experts, top-2 routing, and measure expert utilization across a batch of inputs.

12

Unlock Your Exclusive Benefits

Your copy of this book includes the following exclusive benefits:

Follow the guide below to unlock them. The process takes only a few minutes and needs to be completed once.

Unlock this Book's Free Benefits in 3 Easy Steps

Step 1

Keep your purchase invoice ready for *Step 3*. If you have a physical copy, scan it using your phone and save it as a PDF, JPG, or PNG.

For more help on finding your invoice, visit `https://www.packtpub.com/en-us/unlock?step=1`.

> **Note**
>
> If you bought this book directly from Packt, no invoice is required. After *Step 2*, you can access your exclusive content right away.

Step 2

Scan the QR code or go to `packtpub.com/unlock`.

On the page that opens (similar to *Figure 12.1* on desktop), search for this book by name and select the correct edition.

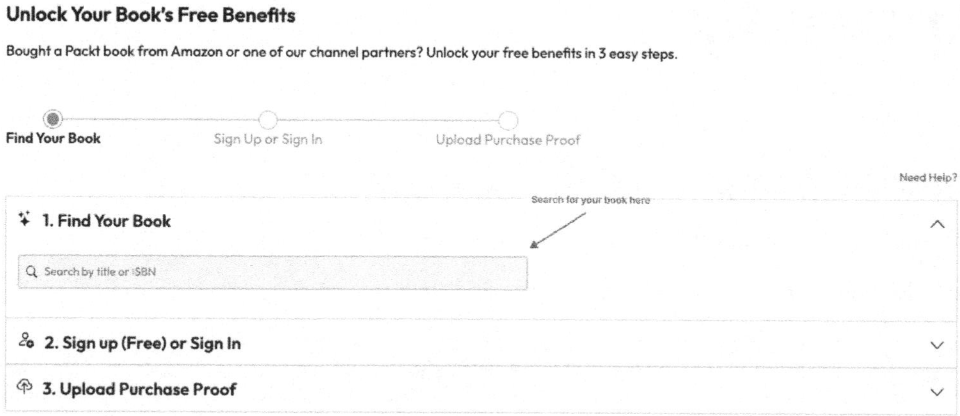

Figure 12.1: Packt unlock landing page on desktop

Step 3

After selecting your book, sign in to your Packt account or create one for free. Then upload your invoice (PDF, PNG, or JPG, up to 10 MB). Follow the on-screen instructions to finish the process.

Need Help

If you get stuck and need help, visit `https://www.packtpub.com/unlock-benefits/help` for a detailed FAQ on how to find your invoices and more. This QR code will take you to the help page.

> **Note**
>
> If you are still facing issues, reach out to `customercare@packt.com`.

Appendix

OpenAI-Compatible API Endpoints

Both vLLM and SGLang expose OpenAI-compatible APIs.

The following table lists common endpoints and their usage:

Endpoint	Method	Description	Usage
`/v1/models`	GET	List available models	`curl http://localhost:8000/v1/models`
`/v1/completions`	POST	Text completion for base models	Use with `prompt` parameter for base models
`/v1/chat/completions`	POST	Chat completion for instruction-tuned models	Use with `messages` parameter for chat models
`/v1/embeddings`	POST	Generate embeddings from text	Use with `input` parameter for embedding models
`/v1/rerank`	POST	Rerank documents by relevance to a query	Use with `query` and `documents` parameters (SGLang only)
`/v1/classify`	POST	Classify text inputs	Use with `input` parameter for classification models
`/generate`	POST	Generate text using diffusion models	Use with `text` parameter for diffusion language models (SGLang only)

Endpoint	Method	Description	Usage
`/health`	GET	Health check endpoint	`curl http://localhost:8000/health`
`/metrics`	GET	Prometheus metrics	`curl http://localhost:8000/metrics`
`/docs`	GET	API documentation (Swagger UI)	Open in browser: `http://localhost:8000/docs`

Note: The default port is 8000 for vLLM and 30000 for SGLang. Adjust the port in the examples above accordingly. For detailed API documentation and model-specific requirements, refer to the respective documentation:

- vLLM API Reference
- SGLang Documentation

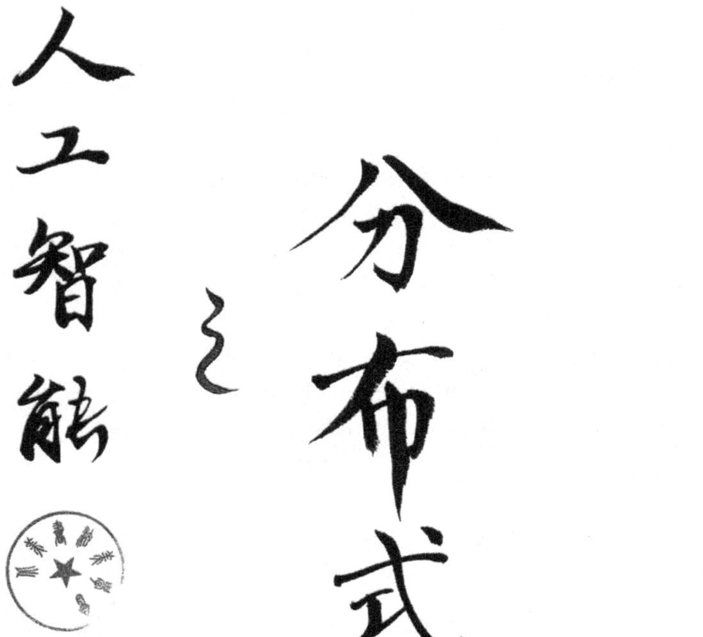

2026

packtpub.com

Subscribe to our online digital library for full access to over 7,000 books and videos, as well as industry leading tools to help you plan your personal development and advance your career. For more information, please visit our website.

Why subscribe?

- Spend less time learning and more time coding with practical eBooks and Videos from over 4,000 industry professionals
- Improve your learning with Skill Plans built especially for you
- Get a free eBook or video every month
- Fully searchable for easy access to vital information
- Copy and paste, print, and bookmark content

At www.packtpub.com, you can also read a collection of free technical articles, sign up for a range of free newsletters, and receive exclusive discounts and offers on Packt books and eBooks.

Other Books You May Enjoy

If you enjoyed this book, you may be interested in these other books by Packt:

GPU Programming with C++ and CUDA

Paulo Motta

ISBN: 9781805124542

- Manage GPU devices and accelerate your applications
- Apply parallelism effectively using CUDA and C++
- Choose between existing libraries and custom GPU solutions
- Package GPU code into libraries for use with Python
- Explore advanced topics such as CUDA streams
- Implement optimization strategies for resource-efficient execution

Hands-On Software Engineering with Python

Brian Allbee

ISBN: 9781835888018

- Distinguish software engineering from general programming
- Break down and apply each phase of the SDLC to Python systems
- Create system models to plan architecture before writing code
- Apply Agile, Scrum, and other modern development methodologies
- Use dataclasses, pydantic, and schemas for robust data modeling
- Set up CI/CD pipelines with GitHub Actions and cloud build tools
- Write and structure unit, integration, and end-to-end tests
- Evaluate and integrate tools like Poetry, pytest, and Docker

Python Illustrated

Maaike van Putten, Imke van Putten

ISBN: 9781836646334

- Set up Python and write your first program
- Understand variables, data types, and conditional statements
- Use loops, lists, dictionaries, and tuples to handle data efficiently
- Write and use functions to create reusable code
- Manage files and understand object-oriented programming and inheritance
- Debug your Python code to ensure it works flawlessly
- Discover how you can keep learning and building beyond this book

Packt is searching for authors like you

If you're interested in becoming an author for Packt, please visit `authors.packt.com` and apply today. We have worked with thousands of developers and tech professionals, just like you, to help them share their insight with the global tech community. You can make a general application, apply for a specific hot topic that we are recruiting an author for, or submit your own idea.

Share your thoughts

Now you've finished *Distributed AI Systems*, we'd love to hear your thoughts! Scan the QR code below to go straight to the Amazon review page for this book and share your feedback or leave a review on the site that you purchased it from.

`https://packt.link/r/1807301710`

Your review is important to us and the tech community and will help us make sure we're delivering excellent quality content.

Subscribe to Deep Engineering

Join thousands of developers and architects who want to understand how software is changing, deepen their expertise, and build systems that last.

Deep Engineering is a weekly expert-led newsletter for experienced practitioners, featuring original analysis, technical interviews, and curated insights on architecture, system design, and modern programming practice.

Scan the QR or visit the link to subscribe for free.

`https://packt.link/deep-engineering-newsletter`

Index

Symbols

1F1B (One Forward One Backward) **232**
2D torus **73**
3D torus **73, 74**

A

A/B testing **413**
A/B traffic splits **412**
AI Cores **76**
AI clusters **60**
  inference requirements 60
  metrics 61 – 63
  training requirements 60
AMD GPUs **85**
ASCEND **336**
AWS Trainium **76**
AllGather **37, 38, 86**
AllReduce **36, 37, 85, 115, 116, 460**
AlltoAll **46, 47**
Ascend SuperPoD **79**
accuracy benchmarking **464**
activation checkpointing **193**
  using 193, 194
activation memory
  optimizing 197
activation output **8 – 13**
activation table
  conventions 11
advanced DDP features
  communication hooks 156, 157
  gradient hooks 156
  uneven inputs, handling with join() 157, 158
advanced SLURM features
  checkpointing 389
  job arrays, for hyperparameter tuning 387, 388
  job dependencies 388
  job resumption 389
  salloc, for interactive jobs 388
agentic AI **486**
  distributed tool execution 487
  reasoning agents 488
agents
  need for distribution 486
aggregate sequential read **66**
algorithm bandwidth **101**
all-gather **172, 173, 294**
all-reduce **294**
all-to-all communication **236**
atomic checkpointing **155**
autoscaling **415**
availability **63, 71**

B

B200 **71**
BF16 throughout **15**
Blackwell (2024) **69**
Broadcast **39**
backpressure **415**
backward prefetching **192**
bandwidth testing **97**
bandwidth-optimal **116**
benchmarking **452 – 454**
  consequences, of inadequate benchmarking 452
  efficiency 453
  inference benchmarking 461
  percentile latencies 453
  training benchmarking 454
block **82**
buffers **117**

bus bandwidth **101**

C

CPU cores **66**
CPU offloading **194, 195**
CPU-GPU interaction **65**
CUDA
- memory hierarchy 84
- thread indexing 83
- using 84, 85

Cambricon MLU **77**
Central Processing Unit (CPU) **64**
- architecture 64
- NUMA topology 65
- requirements, for distributed training 66

Colossal-AI **242**
Context Parallelism **89, 95, 233, 234**
c10d backend **161**
cache-aware policy **344**
canary deployments **413**
checkpointing
- best practices 155
- challenge 480

checkpoints
- loading 153
- saving 153

chip programming systems **81**
chunked prefill **299**
cluster throughput **62**
clusters **59, 60**
- for HPC and AI training 365

cold start mitigation **415**
collective operations **36**
- AllGather 37, 38
- AllReduce 36, 37
- AlltoAll 46, 47
- Broadcast 39
- Gather 42
- Reduce 40, 41
- ReduceScatter 45
- Scatter 43
- selecting 48

column parallelism **294**
column-parallel linear **229**
communication
- optimizing 196

communication efficiency **62**
communication hooks **156, 157**
communication latency **63**
computation sharding
- versus state sharding 228, 229

computational power **57, 58**
continuous batching **292**
cost optimization **416**
cost per token/sample **454**
cross-modal **481**

D

DCP API **187**
DDP performance
- bucket sizes, tuning 151
- communication overlap optimization 150
- computation-communication overlap, analyzing 145, 146
- gradient accumulation 149
- mixed precision training 148, 149
- optimizing 148
- profiling 141
- static graph optimization 152
- torch.profiler.profile, using 141 – 143
- unused parameters, finding 151

DDP training
- debugging and troubleshooting 133 – 141

DGX (Deep GPU Xceleration) **70**
Data Parallel (DP)
- versus Distributed Data Parallel (DDP) 113

Data Parallel Attention (DP Attention) **348**
Data Parallelism **339, 340**
Data Parallelism (DP) **85, 113, 295, 337**
- benefits 297
- combining, with other strategies 296

Replicated Data Parallelism (DDP) 89
Sharded Data Parallelism (FSDP/ZeRO) 89
trade-offs 297

DataLoader
single-process, versus multi-process 124

Decoder-only transformer architecture **277, 278**

DeepSpeed **218**
with SLURM 380 – 383

DeepSpeed-Ulysses **236 - 238**

Detokenizer **325**

Differential Privacy **484**

DistributedDataParallel (DDP) **48, 49, 202**
AllReduce operation 115, 116
best practices 158, 159
buffer synchronization 117
common patterns 158, 159
communication-computation overlap 114, 115
computation-communication overlap implementation 118
device selection, best practices 125
forward pass implementation 117
gradient bucketing 114
gradient scaling 116
internal working 111, 112
mixed precision 116
single node example 126 – 128
with SLURM 377 – 379
with transformer 162

DistributedDataParallel (DDP) workflow
backward pass 112
forward pass 112
gradient synchronization 112
parameter update 113

DistributedSampler **49, 125**
using 121 – 123

decision tree **22**

distributed AI
bottlenecks 474
current situation 473
emerging trends 474
evolution 473

distributed AI stack **31 - 33**

distributed communication **85, 86**

distributed inference **319**

distributed jobs
launching 50

distributed optimizer **243**

distributed systems **1**
performance gap 451

distributed tracing **415**

distributed training
environment setup 24, 25
extended training 28, 29
multi-GPU distributed training 26
single-GPU baseline 25
throughput scaling 30

distributed training frameworks
with SLURM 376

dynamic model selection **412**

E

Edge TPU **77 - 79**

Elastic MoE **475**

End-to-End Request Latency (e2e_latency) **462**

Ethernet **80**

Executor **292**

Expert Parallelism (EP) **90 - 92, 95, 238 - 240, 293, 299, 337, 341**
behavior, modifying 303

edge AI **476**

edge-capable models **476**

edge-cloud **477**

efficiency **453**

elastic **160**

elastic agent **161**

elastic data parallelism **160**

elastic training **480**
launching 161
using 162
working 160

energy efficiency 63
environment variables 121
etcd backend 161
etcd-v2 backend 161
execution models 81

F

FLOPS per Watt 63
FP8 training 244
FSDP issues
  deadlocked 201
  debugging 201
  incorrect results 202
  Out of Memory (OOM) 201
  slow training 201
FSDP training
  profiling 195, 196
FSDP via SPMD 172
FSDP1 171, 176, 182
  policies 184
  versus FSDP2 174, 175
  wrapper 184
FSDP2 172, 175 - 177, 182, 203, 240
  compiler integration 205
  device mesh 178
  hierarchical sharding 181
  mixed precision policy 185
  other integrations 205
  parameters 179, 180
FashionMNIST 26
FedProx 484
Fully Sharded Data Parallel (FSDP) 171
  data loading 204
  debugging tools 202
  gradient clipping 204
  initialization best practices 204
  mixed precision 204
  practical tips 203
  progressive optimization 204
  via SPMD for TPU/XLA 205
  with SLURM 379, 380
  working 173
failure detection 480
fault tolerance 415
fault-tolerant 160
feature-based routing 412
federated learning 482, 483, 486
  for LLMs 485
federated techniques 484
fine-grained multithreading (FGMT) 83
flat-parameter design 174
floating-point operations per second (FLOPS) 57, 58
flower framework 485
forward prefetching 191
foundation models 18
full state dict 190

G

GCP/Google channels 75
GPU Workers 325
GPU hardware
  inspecting 97, 98
GPU utilization 62
GPUDirect RDMA 80
GPipe schedule 232
Gather 42
Gemini 242
GenAI-Bench 464
Graphics Processing Unit (GPU) 66
  architecture features 71, 72
  architecture milestones 69
  compute architecture 66 – 68
  distributed training, considerations 69
  memory architecture 66 – 68
  product families 70
  selecting 71
  versus Neural Processing Unit (NPU) 78
  versus Tensor Processing Unit (TPU) 74, 75
gradient accumulation 16
gradient bucketing 114
gradient compression 490
gradient hooks 156
gradient scaling 116

grid 82

H

H100 71
H200 71
HGX (Hyperscale GPU eXchange) 70
Hopper (2022) 69
Huawei Ascend 76
Hybrid Parallelism 241, 249, 341
- configuration patterns 252
- configuration, selecting 250, 251
- hybrid configuration, building 250
- operational realities 251
- performance optimization best practices 251
- two-axis view 249, 250

hardware inspection 97
hardware topology
- inspecting 98

heterogeneity
- challenges 484

hierarchical parallelism 478
hierarchical partitioning (hpZ) 226
high-speed interconnects 79 - 81
hybrid sharding (HSDP) 205
hyperscaler stacks 79

I

InfiniBand 80, 198
Intelligent Inference Scheduling 431, 435
Inter-node (InfiniBand) 63
Inter-token Latency (ITL) 463
Intra-node (NVLink) 63
inference 20, 267
inference NPUs
- versus training NPUs 77

inference benchmarking 461
- cold start, versus warm performance 465
- custom inference benchmarks 465
- inference accuracy, validating 466, 467
- key inference metrics 461 – 464
- multi-step models 466
- reasoning 466
- tools 464

inference strategy decision tree 94, 95
- considerations 96

inter-GPU communication
- benchmarking 100 – 102

interleaved pipelines 232

J

JAX 73

K

KServe 431
KV cache 267, 276
- solution 283 – 285

KV cache fragmentation problem 287, 288
KubeAI 431
Kubernetes 416
- LLM serving, deploying 417, 418
- URL 416

k3d 419
- for local development 419 – 421
- URL 419
- versus llm-d 440, 441
- vLLM, deploying on 421 – 423

L

LLM serving
- deploying, on Kubernetes 417, 418

LatentMoE 475
learning phase 20
least connections 412
linear scaling 61
llm-d 431, 434
- deployment architecture 433, 434
- Disaggregated Prefix Caching 432
- Hardware Support 432

Intelligent Inference Scheduling 431
monitoring and observability 436
Multi-Model serving 436 – 439
path selection 436
Prefill/Decode Disaggregation 432, 435
Variant Autoscaling 432
versus k3d 440, 441
well-lit paths 435
Wide Expert-Parallelism 435

load balancing **412**
least connections 412
round-robin 412
weighted balancing 412

M

MIG (Multi-Instance GPU) **72**

MTBF (Mean Time Between Failures) **63**

MTTR (Mean Time To Recovery) **63**

MXFP8 **5**

Matrix Multiply Unit (MXU) **73**

Megatron **217, 228**
complete training example 248
context parallelism 234
distributed optimizer 243
Pipeline Parallelism 231, 232
real-world training configurations 245 – 248
sequence parallelism 233
Tensor Parallelism (TP 229, 230

Megatron Core **242**

Megatron-FSDP **242**

Megatron-LM
with SLURM 383 – 387

MoE architecture **300**
decoder layer structure 301
expert structure 302
routing mechanism 302, 303

MoSE (Mixture of Slimmable Experts) **475**

Model FLOPS Utilization (MFU) **61**

Mooncake **336**
PD disaggregation 350, 351

Multi-Engine routing **427 – 430**

Multi-Model routing **424 – 427**

Multi-Node FSDP
checkpointing 199
network configuration 198
scaling considerations 200
setting up 198
SLURM integration 199, 200

manual sharded checkpointing **188, 189**

memory **66**

memory efficiency **454**

memory fragmentation **286**

memory profiling **197**

metrics collection **415**

micro-batches **231**

mixed precision **15, 116, 184**

mixture of experts **475**

modalities **482**

model parallelism **85, 89, 113**
Context Parallelism 89
Expert Parallelism (EP) 90
Pipeline Parallelism (PP) 90
Sequence Parallelism 89
Tensor Parallelism (TP) 89

model resource requirements
estimating 5
GPU 17
inference 16, 17
memory 6 – 16
real-world considerations 17

model selection **416**

modern AI
distribution 2
scale challenge 4

modern AI model lifecycle **19, 20**
inference 20
serving 21
training 20

multi-agent patterns **487**
hierarchical processing 487
parallel processing 487
sequential processing 487

multi-node DDP **128**
- architecture 129
- environment variables 132
- example 132
- network configuration 131
- profiling 146 – 148
- SLURM, using 130
- training 129, 130

multi-node SGLang deployment **342**
- cache locality 345
- fault tolerance 345
- load balancing 344
- router policies 344
- router-based multi-node deployment 343, 344
- session affinity 345
- with tensor parallelism 342

multi-node training **233**

multi-process data loading
- working 125

multi-tenant GPU sharing **489**

N

NCCL **85**

NIXL **336**

NVFP4 **5**

NVIDIA Nsight Systems **456**

NVLink **79**

NVLink-C2C **72**

NVMe storage **66**

NVSwitch **80**

Neural Processing Unit (NPU) **76**
- architecture 77
- inference 77
- interconnects 78
- landscape 79
- scaling 78
- significance 76
- software stack 78
- training 77
- versus Graphics Processing Unit (GPU) 78

O

observability **415**
- distributed tracing 415
- metrics collection 415
- structured logging 415

opaque XLA compilation errors **75**

operator fusion **326, 331**

optical circuit switching (OCS) **73, 74**

optimizer state **6, 7**

original FSDP **175**

out of memory problem **291**

P

P99 latency **63**

PCIe **79**

PCIe lanes **66**

PUE (Power Usage Effectiveness) **63**

PagedAttention **287**
- connection, to distributed inference 291
- padding FLOPs, eliminating 289 – 291
- working 288, 289

Pipeline Parallelism (PP) **90 - 92, 95, 231, 232, 293, 298, 337 - 341**

PyTorch profiler **456**

parallelism **86, 478**
- communication revolution 478
- composition patterns 90, 91
- data parallelism 89
- determination 88
- hierarchical parallelism 478
- model parallelism 89
- right strategy, selecting 252 – 254
- ring attention 479
- sequence parallelism 479
- strategies, combining 90, 304 – 306
- taxonomy table 87

per-GPU throughput **62**

per-parameter sharding **175**

percentile latencies **453**

performance benchmarking 464
pipeline bubble problem 298
policy 184
power-of-two-choices policy 345
prediction/generation phase 20
prefetching 191, 192
 backward prefetching 192
 forward prefetching 191
prefill/decode (PD) disaggregation 334, 335
 architecture 335
 setup 336
 transfer engines 336
process group 34
 initializing 34, 35
production LLM serving system
 anatomy 407 – 411
production deployment patterns 348
production serving stack
 API gateway 408
 Model Runner 408
 monitoring and observability 408
 Tokenizer Service (optional) 408
production system 21
programming models 81

Q

quantization 291, 490
quantized gradients (qgZ) 227
quantized weights (qwZ) 226

R

RDMA (Remote Direct Memory Access) 80
RNG state
 saving 154
ROCm 85
RadixAttention 319, 326 – 328
ReMoE 475
Reduce 40, 41
ReduceScatter 45, 85
Replicated Data Parallelism (DDP) 89 – 91
Request Queue 324
Requests per Second (RPS) 462
ResNet18 26
RoCE (RDMA over Converged Ethernet) 80
Router 325
ranks 34
reduce-scatter 172, 173
reliability metrics 63, 415
rendezvous 160
rendezvous backend 161
request-level parallelism 94
request-level routing 320
resource management 489
resource utilization 62
ring AllReduce 115
ring attention 234, 479
ring topology 115
round-robin 344, 412
router-based DP 341
routing
 A/B traffic splits 412
 dynamic model selection 412
 feature-based routing 412
row parallelism 294
row-parallel linear 229

S

SGLang 319, 320
 architecture 324, 325
 basic multi-node deployment 349
 Data Parallel Attention (DP Attention) 348
 Data Parallelism 339, 340
 Docker setup 320 – 323
 expert for MoE models 346, 347
 Hybrid Parallelism 341
 installation 320
 MoE model, with EP+TP 352

operator fusion 331
parallelism strategies 337
PD disaggregation, with Mooncake 350, 351
Pipeline Parallelism 339
prefill/decode (PD) disaggregation 334, 335
prerequisites 320
RadixAttention 326 – 328
router-based distributed architecture 332, 333
session affinity, testing 351, 352
speculative decoding 347
Tensor Parallelism 338
XGrammar 329, 330
zero-overhead scheduler 331, 332

SGLang Runtime (SRT) **324**

SGLang model gateway
architecture 333

SIMD execution units **85**

SIMT (Single Instruction, Multiple Thread **82**

SIMT, over SIMD
branch divergence 83
data alignment 83
dynamic grouping 83
programming model 83

SLURM
architecture 367
common issues, troubleshooting 394, 395
distributed training, profiling 392, 393
environment variables 373 – 375
for AI training 366
job monitoring 390
logging and output 391
multi-node cluster, simulating 369
setting up, for multi-GPU training 368
setup and verification 370
useful links 396
with DDP 377 – 379
with DeepSpeed 380 – 383
with FSDP 379, 380
with Megatron-LM 383 – 387

SLURM, best practices
checkpointing strategy 393
failures, handling 394
resource allocation 393

SPMD (Single Program, Multiple Data) **81, 82, 294**
in distributed training 85

Scaffold **484**

Scatter **43**

Scheduler **292, 325**

Sequence Parallelism **89, 92, 231 – 233, 479**

Sharded Data Parallelism (FSDP/ZeRO) **89 – 91**

Sparse Core **73 – 75**

SuperPOD **70, 76**

salloc command **388**

sbatch
for batch submission 372, 373

scale compute **59**

scale memory **59**

scale storage **59**

scaling efficiency **454**

scheduler-executor-worker pattern **292**

sequence length **233**

serving **21**

shortest-queue policy **345**

single-GPU baseline **182**

single-GPU memory bandwidth
measuring 99, 100

single-node DDP
setting up 118

slurmctld **367**

slurmd **367**

slurmdbd **367**

speculative decoding **347**

spot instances **416**

squeue **390**

srun
for interactive execution 371, 372

state sharding **217, 228**
versus computation sharding 228, 229

structured logging **415**

systolic arrays **73**

T

T5 (FLAN-T5) 182
TPU 8t workloads 75
TPU 8t/8i 73
TPU Pod
  architecture 73
TPU7x/Ironwood 73
Tensor Cores 71
Tensor Parallelism (TP) 89, 92, 95, 228 – 230, 293, 294, 337, 338, 341
  benefits 294
  usage 295
Tensor Processing Unit (TPU) 72
  architecture 73
  generations 73
  programming model 75
  significance 72
  Sparse Core 75
  versus Graphics Processing Unit (GPU) 74, 75
TensorFlow through XLA 73
Through Pascal (2016) 69
Time to First Token (TTFT) 462
Tokenizer 324
Tokens per Second (TPS) 462
Torch Distributed Elastic (TDE) 160
Torchcomms 478
Trainium 79
Trainium2 76
Transformer Engine 71
Trillium 73
text generation process 279
  decode 281 – 283
  prefill 280
thread 82
throughput 62
top-k sparsification 490
torch.profiler.profile
  using, for DDP analysis 141 – 143
torchrun 126
  using 118 – 120
traffic shifting 413
training 20, 267
training NPUs
  versus inference NPUs 77
training benchmarking 454
  bottleneck analysis, scaling 460
  custom training benchmark 457
  distributed training accuracy, validating 458, 459
  key training metrics 455
  network and communication profiling 459, 460
  scaling efficiency, measuring 458
training stage 13 – 16
training strategy decision tree 91, 92
  considerations 94
tree AllReduce 115, 116

V

Volta and Ampere (2017-2020) 69
v5e/v5p 73
vLLM 268
  architecture 292, 293
  basic setup, with Tensor Parallelism 306
  conda, used for installation 273
  custom chunked prefill configuration 307
  deploying, on k3d 421 – 423
  deployment modes, for data parallelism 296, 297
  Docker setup 268 – 272
  installation 268
  multi-node, with TP and PP 306
  offline inference 274
  online inference 275
  parallelism strategies 293
  pip, used for installation 273
  prerequisites 268
  profiling, with Nsight Systems 308
  uv, used for installation 272
vLLM production-stack 431

von Neumann architecture 64

W

Wan2.2 176
warp 82
warp execution 82
weighted balancing 412
well-lit paths 435
workers 293
workload distribution 489
wrap policy 184

X

XGrammar 326, 329
structured output decoding 329, 330
XLA (Accelerated Linear Algebra) 75

Z

ZeRO 202
ZeRO++ 226 - 228
ZeRO-1 218 - 220
ZeRO-2 220, 221
ZeRO-3 221
ZeRO-Infinity 223 - 225
ZeRO-Offload 222
zero-overhead scheduler 319, 326, 331

Made in the USA
Monee, IL
13 September 2026

63137520R00306